Comparative Politics

Comparative Politics

Political Economy, Political Culture, and Political Interdependence

Second Edition

Monte Palmer

American University of Beirut

F. E. Peacock Publishers, Inc.
Itasca, Illinois

Cover image: © Stone/Ralph Mercer

Library of Congress Catalog Card No. 99-75113
ISBN 0-87581-427-1

Printed in the United States of America
10 9 8 7 6 5 4 3 2 1
06 05 04 03 02 01

Brief Contents

Contents

Part Two   Politics in Advanced Industrial Democracies

Part Three   The Decline of Communism:
Transitions to Democracy and Capitalism

Preface

The field of comparative politics is witnessing an ongoing debate over the relative importance of economic, cultural, and international factors in the shaping of political events. Some of the current comparative government texts embrace one perspective to the detriment of the others, while other texts ignore the debate altogether. The present text starts from the premise that each of the above approaches offers important insights into comparative political analysis but that none, of itself, adequately conveys the richness of the political process. The text also integrates the insights provided by culture, economics, and international interdependence with the traditional comparative emphasis on institutions, elites, parties, groups, and mass behavior.

The vision of comparative politics presented in this text also integrates the "political development" and "advanced industrial society" perspective of comparative politics and stresses the defining issues of the coming decade: democracy, human rights, economic reform, social equity, and environmental degradation.

The second edition of *Comparative Politics* also reflects changes that have occurred in the world community since the publication of the first edition. Major shifts to the left have occurred in Britain, France, and Germany. Economic liberalization has gained momentum in the Third World, albeit with inconsistent results. Democracy has made gains in countries such as Nigeria and Mexico, but has lost ground in others. Changes in the second edition also reflect thoughtful assessments of the first edition, leading to simplification of the theoretical materials and replacement of the chapter on Brazil with a chapter on Mexico.

I would again like to thank the many people listed in the preface to the first edition, most of whom were also of tremendous help in preparing the second edition: J. A. Allan, Gawdat Bahgat, Leslie Calman, Jung Chang, Scott Flanagan, Lawrence P. Frank, David B. Goetze, Selwa Goma, Ronald J. Hrebanar, Roger Kangas, Leslie Kitching, Marcelo T. Lopez, Dianjun Ma, Lee Metcalf, Neil Mitchell, Mary O'Shea, R. M. Punnett, James L. Ray, Sam C. Sarkesian, Dillon David Sessions, Sheryl Shirley, Donley T. Studlar, John Vanderoef, Juergen Wanke, and Koichi Yoshimine.

Editorial support from F. E. (Ted) Peacock, Dick Welna, and Janet Tilden continued to be exemplary. Special thanks are due to Stephen D. Morris for his willingness to contribute the chapter on Mexico. I must also say with candor that this edition would not have been possible without the guidance and critical judgment of my wife, Dr. Princess Palmer. Again, errors of fact and judgment are mine alone.

A few words from the editor concerning boldface type and abbreviations: Terms that are defined in the glossary are printed in boldface type the first time they appear in each chapter. Thus, the same term may appear in boldface in more than one chapter. The names of frequently cited periodicals are given in an abbreviated form when they are cited in the text: *NYT* stands for *New York Times*; *CSM* represents *Christian Science Monitor*; and *SCMPI* refers to *South China Morning Post International*.

Part One

An Introduction to Comparative Politics

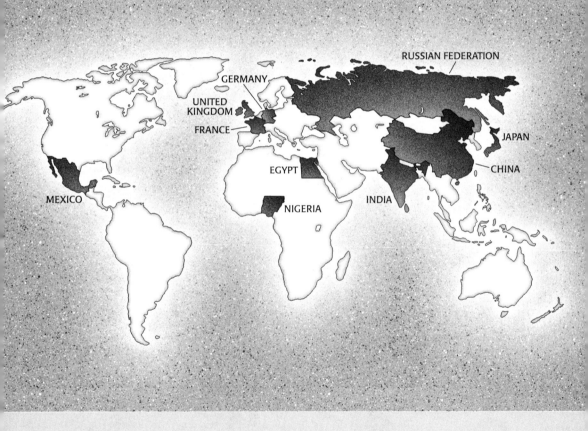

1

An Introduction to Comparative Politics

As the world community enters the twenty-first century, it is embarking on an era of unprecedented change. Tomorrow's world will bear little resemblance to the world community as we know it today. The countries of Western Europe, for example, are evolving into a European supra-state that may soon rival the economic and military power of the United States. China and India, two countries that collectively possess more than 30 percent of the world's population, are also primed to become major actors on the world stage. Both are nuclear powers, and both possess almost unlimited economic potential. While that potential has yet to be realized, the era of Asia may not be long in coming. Japan is now the world's second largest economy, and China may not be far behind. Fears of a major power confrontation between the US and Russia—fears that dominated the politics of the post–World War II era—have all but disappeared.

The past decade has also witnessed a global revolution in democracy and human rights. The world now has a greater number of democratic political systems than at any time in recent history. Some scholars believe that this democratic revolution is irreversible and that dictators will find it increasingly difficult to remain in power (Huntington 1991). Although such predictions may be unduly optimistic, authoritarianism is clearly on the defensive.

Global increases in democracy have been paralleled by dramatic increases in capitalism. Socialist or "command" economies in which the state manages most economic activity are giving way to capitalist economies in which most economic activity is determined by the free enterprise of individuals and firms, with minimal interference from the government. Even Russia and China, once the world's foremost advocates of socialism, are struggling to develop capitalist economies in which the give and take of economic activity is determined by the marketplace rather than the government.

Inhabitants of the rich and powerful countries of the world, often referred to as the First World, predict that the spread of democracy and capitalism will lead to an era of unprecedented freedom and prosperity. They note that democracy—a *political* system—increases the individual's ability to shape his or her environment, while capitalism—an *economic* system—stimulates economic growth by rewarding individual effort. They also point out that democracies seldom make war on other democracies (Ray 1995). If this is the case, increases in democracy should herald an era of world peace. The skeptics, however, are many.

One might note, for example, that the rich and powerful countries of the First World represent only a small portion of the world's population, while the poorer states of Asia, Africa, and Latin America, often referred to as the Third World, possess little in the way of either freedom or prosperity. It is also important to realize that more than two-thirds of the world's population subsist on an annual income of less than $500 per person. A similar percentage of the world's population enjoys neither democracy nor a reasonable standard of human rights. While some states of the Third World are approaching economic parity with the United States and its wealthy allies, many others are sinking deeper into debt and despair.

The world community is changing in other ways as well. The independence and sovereignty of all countries is being challenged by a variety of supranational institutions, such as the World Bank, the International Monetary Fund, the European Community, and the World Trade Organization (organizations that will be discussed later in this chapter). Many multinational corporations—businesses with operations in a variety of countries—also possess greater financial resources than most countries of the world. Indeed, the financial resources of many multinational corporations have become so vast that these corporations are difficult for any single country to regulate. If the costs of labor or environmental regulation are too stringent in one country, the corporation merely shifts its operations to another location.

In the chapters that follow, we will survey the politics of ten of the world's most important countries: Great Britain, France, Germany, Japan, Russia, China, India, Mexico, Egypt, and Nigeria. Chapter 1 provides a framework for the country studies by outlining the major components of **comparative political analysis.** These components include institutions, elites, political parties, pressure groups, and public opinion. They also include the country's cultural, economic, and international environment.

Conflict and Cooperation: The Two Faces of Politics

Two definitions of **politics** have found wide acceptance among political scientists. The first suggests that *politics is the process of deciding "who gets what, when, and how"* (Lasswell 1958). The second definition is similar, suggesting that *politics is the authoritative allocation of scarce values* (Easton 1953). Both definitions address the main source of conflict in human societies: a shortage of the things that people value most. While different people value different things, most place a heavy emphasis on money, power, prestige, and security—values that are always in short supply (Maslow 1954). This is as true of tribal societies as it is of modern states and the international community. All societies must cope with conflict over scarce values.

Politics involves conflict over scarce values, but it also involves cooperation. Because human beings are social animals, their survival and development depend upon their ability to maintain effective social organizations (Parsons 1977). The more a society succeeds in generating cooperation among its members, the more developed and prosperous it is likely to become. Tribal and village societies evolved into countries in order to achieve greater security, wealth, prestige, and power (Herz 1959). The same process is evident in the unification of Western Europe. Most

> ## Questions to Consider
>
> ■ Why are some countries moving toward greater unity while others are disintegrating?
>
> ■ What has triggered the upsurge in democracy, and can this trend be maintained?
>
> ■ Why is socialism giving way to capitalism, and what has been the role of politics in this process?
>
> ■ What is the relationship between democracy and capitalism?
>
> ■ Why have some countries developed economically while others have not, and what has been the role of politics in this process?
>
> ■ Why have some countries become protective of the environment while others pillage the environment with little concern for their citizens, their neighbors, or their future?

European leaders believe that a unified Western Europe will enjoy greater wealth, power, prestige, and security than a Europe divided against itself. This topic will be discussed shortly.

Conflict is the enemy of social organization. If unchecked, it fragments societies into warring factions and squanders valuable resources. This, unfortunately, is the scenario currently being played out in many areas of the Third World.

Politics, then, has two faces: conflict and cooperation. Wars, revolutions, terrorism, intimidation, assassinations, and ethnic conflict are all part of the political process. Politics, however, also involves **conflict management** and the establishment of stable societies in which individuals are able to cooperate for their common good. If conflict is to be managed, some mechanism must exist for allocating scarce resources in an authoritative and orderly manner. **Governments** are that mechanism. They are the authoritative element in the political process. It is they who make and enforce the laws concerning "who gets what, when, and how."

Governments are created to manage conflict, but they are also the focal point of that conflict. The act of establishing governments invariably creates winners and losers; the winners seek to consolidate their position, and the losers press for change. By controlling the government, the winners in a political conflict acquire three means of conflict management: coercion, persuasion, and economic rewards. In a few societies, the winners rule mainly by coercion, using their control over the police and the army to impose their authority on a reluctant population. Regimes that rule by force alone, however, are often short-lived and unstable. Violence begets violence.

All governments use coercion, persuasion, and economic rewards as techniques for managing conflict, but the extent to which they use each of these techniques varies from country to country. Governments that have been most effective in achieving democracy, stability, and other goals of good government (a topic to be discussed shortly), place persuasion and economic rewards above coercion. A mark of their success is the fact that they use coercion only sparingly.

Conflict can be managed, but it cannot be eliminated. Continuing tension between the winners and losers is the essence of politics. Some governments manage conflict better than others, but all political systems are in a state of flux as diverse groups in the society attempt to protect or extend their share of society's resources.

American history, for example, is a pageant of change produced by constant tension between the rulers and the ruled. In the early years of independence, American politics was dominated by a quasi-aristocracy of wealthy landowners (Beard 1913). Over time, the winner's circle was expanded to include all white males and eventually white females, black Americans, and other groups, but the process of assuring equal opportunities for all citizens remains incomplete.

Controlled conflict can be a positive force in the development of societies. Without conflict, there would be little incentive for change and societies would remain stagnant (Olson 1982). Thomas Jefferson even suggested that revolutions "from time to time" were not necessarily a bad thing. The challenge of government is to manage conflict in a manner that promotes the development of society rather than its destruction.

Governments that have endured over long periods of time usually are those in which the winners have been able to persuade their fellow citizens that the rules are **legitimate**—*that they are in the best interests of all citizens and should be followed voluntarily*. Some governments attempt to persuade people of their legitimacy on religious grounds, claiming that the established order has been decreed by God. This is certainly the case in Iran, a country governed by religious leaders. Communist leaders in the USSR and the People's Republic of China attempted to gain legitimacy by socializing (indoctrinating) their citizens to view Marxism as the path to a just society. Western democracies base their legitimacy on an electoral process that allows citizens a more or less equal voice in the selection of leaders.

Establishing legitimacy, however, involves far more than socialization or indoctrination. It is also a matter of economic self-interest. Western democracies also receive the support of their citizens because the majority of those citizens have an acceptable standard of living. Economics is only one of several factors influencing political behavior, but it is an important one (Lewis-Beck 1990).

Four Worlds of Development

In the early 1950s, two French journalists were so distraught by the poverty that they found in Asia, Africa, and Latin America that they described these regions as belonging to an entirely different world from that of Western Europe and North America. Thus they initiated the concept of three "worlds" of development.[1] The **First World** consisted of *the advanced industrial societies and the West,* while the **Third World** was made up of *countries more in poverty and despair.* The Soviet Union and other communist countries were considered to be a **Second World** *somewhere between the First and Third Worlds.* Although the Second World was less prosperous than the First World, many people of the era believed that the totalitarian nature of communist governments would soon enable them to outproduce the West. In their view, countries that controlled the totality of an individual's life, including the information they received and the groups they joined, would surely be more effective in promoting economic growth than countries that left their citizens to make their own social, economic, and political choices. The growing military strength of the Soviet Union supported this illusion.

With the collapse of the Soviet Union in 1991 and the crumbling of communism in China, it became obvious that communism had failed to fulfill its promise of rapid economic development. By and large, Russia and other members of the Communist Bloc had simply merged with that broad mass of countries we refer to as the Third World. There is no longer a Second World, but the terms First World and Third World have established themselves as part of the political science vocabulary.

Differences between the First and Third Worlds can be described in terms of six areas established by the Charter of the United Nations (UN) and related international documents as the standards of good government to which all nations should aspire. Good governments, according to the United Nations and its related agencies, are stable, democratic, concerned with the rights of their citizens, capable of sustained economic

[1]*Le Monde, cossiers et documents,* 1989.

Six UN Standards of Good Government
1. Democracy
2. Quality of life
3. Human rights
4. Stability
5. Equality of opportunity
6. Concern for environment

growth, equal in the distribution of opportunities, and protective of the environment (World Bank 1992a, 1992b).

The United Nations Charter affirms "faith in fundamental human rights, in the dignity and worth of the human person, in the equal rights of men and women." It also calls upon the nations of the world community to "promote social progress and better standards of life in larger freedom." These six standards of good government have subsequently been reaffirmed at a variety of international summits attended by most leaders of the world community.

Almost without exception, the countries of the First World have been more democratic, stable, prosperous, egalitarian, and concerned with human rights and the environment than the countries of the Third World. The countries of the First World monopolize most of the earth's wealth and consume most of its energy. They also guide the activities of the United Nations, the World Bank, the International Monetary Fund (IMF), and the World Trade Organization. The World Bank and the IMF guide the flow of international economic assistance to the countries of the Third World, while the World Trade Organization regulates the terms of trade between nations. The influence of these bodies on the domestic politics of the Third World is profound.

If the First World represents the elite of the world community, the Third World includes the broad mass of countries that lag behind the countries of the First World in terms of the UN indicators of development. Even here, however, wide variations exist. Some countries of the Third World rival the First World in terms of economic productivity but are weak in the areas of democracy, human rights, and concern for the environment. This is the case for South Korea, Taiwan, Singapore, and Brazil, which are sometimes referred to as newly industrialized countries, or NICs. India, in contrast, is the most enduring democracy in the Third World but remains desperately poor. Other Third World countries have provided citizens with full employment and a broad range of health and human services without achieving either prosperity or democracy. This is the case in China and many other communist and former communist societies.

The least fortunate of the world's countries are sometimes referred to as the **Fourth World.** Enmeshed in poverty, dictatorship, and despair, they are unable to provide their citizens with a minimally acceptable quality of life. Most, such as Angola and Rwanda, are racked with tribal conflict, if not open civil war. Human rights are ignored, and inequality is endemic in all areas of political, economic, and social life. Environmental protection is minimal at best.

The Countries Examined in This Text

The ten countries examined in Chapters 2 through 11 can be classified into the four worlds of development as shown in Table 1.1. The arrows indicate movement of the

Table 1.1
The Four Worlds of the Countries in This Text

First World	Postcommunist World (Second)	Third World	Fourth World
United Kingdom	Russia ⟶	India	
France	China ⟶	Mexico	
Germany		Egypt	
Japan		Nigeria ⟶	

Russia and China, once Second World countries, are now considered Third World countries. Nigeria, once considered a Third World country, could well become a Fourth World country if present trends continue.

former Second World countries to the Third World and of one Third World country to the Fourth World.

Based upon the UN standards of good government, the classic countries of the First World are the United States, Japan, Canada, Australia, New Zealand, the United Kingdom (Great Britain), France, Germany, Italy, the Scandinavian states, the Benelux states (Belgium, the Netherlands, Luxembourg), Finland, and Switzerland.

The United Kingdom, France, and Germany are charter members of the First World, but each represents a radically different political tradition. Japan, the country that most recently gained entry into the First World, is also the only non-Western country to have done so. The Japanese path to political and economic success has varied substantially from the Western model, and many Japanese believe that their way is superior.

Russia and China represent the two dominant countries of the postcommunist or Second World. While sharing most of the characteristics of Third World countries, both remain imposing military and economic powers. Indeed, China, with approximately one-fifth of the world's population, may soon become the world's dominant economy in terms of its gross national product. How Russia and China resolve "who gets what" domestically will greatly influence the shape of the world during the coming decade.

Each of the Third World nations discussed in this text—India, Mexico, Egypt, and Nigeria—represents a different configuration of political and economic problems. Each also reflects the problems faced by its regional neighbors. India is the world's largest democracy and the only large country in the world to have maintained a viable democracy in an environment of crushing poverty and religious strife. Mexico exemplifies both the promise and the political stress experienced by most newly industrialized countries. Unrestrained economic development has transformed it into one of the dominant economic powers in the Latin world, but it has also created a social and environmental nightmare of staggering proportions. Mexico is struggling to achieve a balance between concerns for democracy, human rights, and equality on the one hand, and economic growth on the other. Whether this task can be accomplished is still open to question.

In terms of regional influence, Egypt is the dominant country in the Arab world. The direction of Egyptian politics will greatly influence the future stability of the Middle East, a region that possesses most of the world's oil and that has been in the forefront of world conflict for more than half a century. Egypt has made progress toward both democracy and economic development but has yet to achieve either objective.

Our analysis of Nigerian politics is subtitled "The Politics of Hope and Despair." Hope springs from Nigeria's position as one of the largest and richest countries of sub-Saharan Africa as well as its return to democratic rule. Despair flows from a history of ethnic conflict and political chaos that has seldom been

No country is exempt from environmental problems. Here, most of the presidents and prime ministers of the industrialized world meet at an Earth Summit to discuss environmental policy.

rivaled in the modern world. Nigeria stands as a tragic illustration of how the lack of effective government can rob a country of its natural wealth and preclude it from developing economically. If past trends continue, Nigeria could well become a member of the Fourth World.

Defining Political Development: Democracy, Growth, and More

The United Nations defines **political development** (or good government) as the achievement of a stable democracy that promotes the economic well-being of its citizens in an equitable, humane, and environmentally conscientious manner. There are several advantages to using this definition.

1. *It acknowledges the full range of human needs.* Governments must do more than rule; they must also provide for the economic and social well-being of their citizens. It is important, for example, that governments pursue policies that stimulate economic growth. Beyond this, however, it is also the responsibility of governments to provide all of their citizens with a reasonable quality of life. Among other things, that quality of life should include equal access to education, health services, and employment, as well as reasonable distribution of society's resources. These and other indicators of quality of life are summarized in the United Nations Quality of Life Index.

2. *It provides a uniform standard for comparing existing countries on the basis of reasonably stable criteria.* Striking differences exist between the countries of the First World and those of the Third and Fourth Worlds. It is important to understand why such differences exist and how they can be overcome.

3. *It raises important questions about the relationship between politics and the broader cultural and economic context in which politics occurs.* Is it possible to have stability, democracy, human rights, and concern for the environment in the midst of abject poverty? Can democracy and human rights be achieved in societies that are torn by ethnic conflict or have long traditions of authoritarian rule? These and related questions are examined throughout this text.

Defining political development in terms of the UN's indicators of good government also has severe disadvantages. *The definition is ethnocentric, implying the superiority of values that have evolved from Western philosophical traditions.* Western culture, for example, is individualistic, often placing the rights of individuals above the rights of the group. Most Eastern cultures, by contrast, are collectivist, placing the rights of society above the rights of the individual. As a result of this differing view of the rights of the individual, Eastern and Western cultures have differing concepts of democracy and human rights. Many states of the Third and Fourth Worlds find the Western emphasis on democracy, human rights, equality of income, and environmental protection to be hypocritical. The plight of the Third and Fourth Worlds, in their view, is the result of exploitation by the West. How are they to meet the standards of good government when states of the First World interfere in their internal affairs and when the conditions of world trade work to their disadvantage?

The precise nature of democracy, in turn, has long been a topic of debate among political scientists (Gillespie 1987; World Audit, Dec. 10, 1999, www). Many scholars see its essence as the ability of the masses to hold their leaders accountable (Bollen 1979; Sartori 1965). As Joseph Schumpeter warned almost fifty years ago, "Democracy does not and cannot mean that people actually rule.... Democracy means that people have the opportunity of accepting or refusing the men who rule them" (Schumpeter 1950, 284–85).

Some scholars have focused on the procedural requirements that enable citizens of a state to make their leaders accountable to them (Lipset 1960). Five of these requirements have been specified by Robert Dahl (1971, 1985) as being particularly important.

1. Leaders must be elected in free and fair elections open to all citizens, regardless of race, creed, color, gender, educational level, or economic status.
2. The elections must be held at regularly scheduled intervals. (One-time elections are not enough.)
3. The electorate must have the opportunity to choose from among a meaningful slate of candidates.
4. The electorate must possess sufficient information to evaluate the choices before it. (Forcing people to vote in an informational vacuum makes a mockery of the very concept of democracy.)
5. Those elected must be allowed to rule. (Many countries in the world, including some examined in the present text maintain the fiction of democracy while the military rules from behind the scenes. Democratically elected leaders take office, but they do not rule.)

In addition to Dahl's narrow procedural requirements, modern democracies are also strengthened by a number of factors (Diamond, Linz, and Lipset 1990). Of these, the most important are political parties, pressure groups, and an active and free mass media. Democracy is also facilitated by the presence of political elites who believe in the democratic process as well as by the existence of established political institutions that meet the needs of citizens. Democracy also works better in some environments than others. It is difficult, for example, to achieve democracy in an environment of illiteracy and poverty because citizens have little opportunity to become informed about candidates and issues (Lerner 1958). Democracy also works best in a cultural climate of tolerance and openness in which individuals identify with their political institutions and understand their responsibilities as citizens.

Another difficulty with using the UN criteria for good government as a definition of political development is that it implies that the countries of the First World have arrived at some mythical end point of political development. This clearly is not the case. All countries of the First World continue to face problems in the areas of democracy, stability, human rights, economic growth, quality of life, and environmental concern. The countries of the First World merely do better, on average, than the countries of the Third World. Indeed, one reason human rights are discussed separately from democracy is the fact that many countries have been able to meet the procedural requirements for democracy while simultaneously continuing to violate the human rights of minorities.

It could also be argued that countries are losing their utility as political units. The fragmentation of the world community into hundreds of mini-states and territories does little more than generate conflict and waste resources. The apex of political development, from an evolutionary perspective, would be the creation of a world government with the power to provide for all of the world's people regardless of race, sex, religion, or place of origin. In this grand view of historical evolution, countries merely mark a point between tribal governments and world government (Herz 1959). This view, of course, is not universally accepted. Some fear that a world government would merely become a stifling bureaucracy. In their view, bigger is not necessarily better (Schumacher 1973). Others believe that smaller territories can help keep governments close to the people and preserve cultural diversity.

Whatever its philosophical merits, a definition of political development that integrates democracy, stability, human rights, economic growth, quality of life, and environmental concern is the one that the United States and other states of the First World are attempting to impose upon the rest of the world. For Third World states, the UN model has become a political reality (Epstein, Grahm, and Nembhard 1993). Countries that conform to the UN model receive needed economic assistance and favorable terms of trade. Others, for the most part, do not.

Comparative Analysis

Political scientists attempt to understand why political events unfold as they do and, on this basis, to predict how they are likely to unfold in the future. Political scientists who specialize in comparative politics believe that the objectives of explanation and prediction are most fruitfully achieved by examining and comparing the political process in a broad range of political, economic, and socio-cultural environments (Dogan and Pelassy 1990). *By placing the study of democracy in comparative perspective, for example, we are better able to understand what makes democracy work and why democracy succeeds in some countries and fails in others.* By the same token, comparing the experience of different countries may help us to understand the dynamics of such critical issues as poverty, violence, and environmental decay.

The study of democracy, for example, can be approached by conducting case studies that examine how democracy has succeeded or failed in specific states. Democracy can also be studied by attempting to identify those factors that distinguish democracies from other political systems, comparing countries on a global or regional basis. The same principle applies to all other issues of interest to political scientists.

A second practical benefit of comparative political studies is that they provide a vast laboratory of political experience that may be transferable from one country to another. Many of the proposals for national health legislation in the United States, for example, have drawn heavily upon the experience of long-established health programs in Europe and Canada. While the European and Canadian programs are not without their drawbacks, they do provide important insights into the challenges involved in providing affordable health care. The experience of other countries is also relevant in areas such as crime and social welfare. The murder rate for the United States, for example, is more than twenty times greater than the murder rate in the states of Western Europe. Perhaps the United States has something to learn from the criminal justice programs of its peers. Similarly, Germany has been able to provide its citizens with a shorter work week and more social welfare benefits than any other industrialized state of the First World, yet it has suffered no loss in productivity. Could similar policies be introduced in the United States and elsewhere? The possibilities are certainly worth considering.

Components of Comparative Political Analysis

Three basic components of comparative political analysis are studied throughout this text:

1. The political institutions through which the government of a country allocates resources.
2. The actors who give life to these institutions and carry out the work of governments.
3. The environmental contexts in which the political process takes place.

The study of formal **political institutions** is an important aspect of comparative analysis because these governmental structures represent the arena of political conflict. It is the executives, legislatures, courts, bureaucracies, and other agencies of government that authoritatively allocate the scarce resources of the state.

Politics, however, encompasses much more than the formal institutions of government. It also includes the **actors** who give life to those institutions. Many political scientists find elites to be the critical element in the political process because elites run the political institutions and decide who gets what, when, and how. Other political scientists find the essence of the political process to be the interplay of political parties and pressure groups. Elites, they point out, do not exist in a vacuum. It is the support of political parties and pressure groups that makes them effective. Still other experts focus on the masses or public, recognizing that governments and elites must gain public support if they are to endure.

In addition to institutions and actors, many comparative political analysts have also found it useful to study the broader cultural, economic, and international contexts in which politics occurs. Advocates of a cultural approach to politics believe that the way people behave politically is profoundly influenced by the culture in which they have been raised. The more one understands the culture of a society, they argue, the easier it will be to predict the pattern of its politics. Political economists, in turn, find politics to be indivisible from economics. In their view, it is difficult to find any form of political activity that is not influenced in one way or another by economics. Finally, a growing number of comparative political scientists find domestic politics to be profoundly influenced by broader international pressures. The countries of the world are becoming increasingly interdependent, and all must adjust to the demands of the international community.

States, Governments, and Political Systems

All societies create rules, laws, and other organizational mechanisms for determining how the scarce resources of society will be allocated. Such institutions, commonly referred to as governments, are the grand prize of politics. The winners in the political contest use their control of governmental institutions to give expression to their values and to achieve their goals. They also use those institutions to manage conflict within society. Many people also refer to the political institutions of a society as its political system or method of doing politics.

In primitive societies, the mechanism for enforcing the rules—the government or the political system—consisted of little more than a tribal chief and a council of elders. As societies became more complex, informal rules were codified into law and casual meetings of tribal leaders evolved into the complex governmental institutions that we know today. A few tribal societies remain, but most eventually gave way to a more common comprehensive entity we know as the state.

According to international law, a **state** is *a well-defined geographic area in which the population and resources are controlled by a government* (Brierly 1963). States are also said to have sovereignty, a tricky term that implies that a state, or more precisely its leaders, can do as they wish within the state's territory (Nordlinger 1981; Evans, Rueschemeyer, and Skoupol 1985). As described in the report of an international commission convened after World War II,

> A sovereign state at the present time claims the power to judge its own controversies, to enforce its own conception of its rights, to increase its armaments without limits, to treat its own nationals as it sees fit, and to regulate its economic life without regard to the effect of such regulations upon its neighbours. These attributes of sovereignty must be limited.[2]

Knowing the type of political system (government) that a country possesses provides important clues about how it does politics. In this regard, political scientists have found it useful to classify the countries of the world into three basic categories based upon their political systems: democratic political systems, authoritarian political systems, and quasi-democratic or mixed political systems. Each of these main categories, in turn, possesses numerous variants, the most obvious of which are outlined in Figure 1.1.

Each type of political system is presumed to have both strengths and weaknesses (Caporaso 1989). Understanding these strengths and weaknesses helps comparative political analysts to predict and explain the goals that each type of political system can best achieve.

Democratic Political Systems

Democratic political systems are said to be reconciliation systems because they attempt to reconcile the interests of as many groups and individuals as possible. The strength of democratic political systems lies in their ability to maximize public expression, political freedom, and human rights. The ability of democracies to make rapid decisions, however, is often questionable. Democratic regimes are reluctant to make decisions that are unpopular with the electorate. A broad range of groups must be brought into the fold before policy can move ahead. In many states of the Third World, moreover, group conflict is so intense that it is not easily reconciled. In our discussion of Indian and Nigerian politics we will examine this problem in great detail.

---

[2]Stubbs (1941), cited in Brierly (1963, 47) from the *International Conciliation Pamphlet,* 1941.

While the above comments apply to democratic regimes in general, they are more applicable to some democracies than others. Political power in the United States is more severely fragmented than it is in countries such as Mexico or Brazil, whose legislatures are intimidated by very strong presidents. Parliamentary democracies, in contrast to presidential democracies, do not fragment power between the executive and the legislature (Lijphart 1992). Rather, the voters elect the legislature and the legislature elects the executive. If a single party dominates the legislature, its leader becomes the prime minister. In such a system, conflict between the executive and the legislature is minimal as long as the dominant party has the votes to implement its program. The will of the majority party cannot be derailed by a powerful committee chairman or minority blocs. This model is referred to as the British or Westminster model of parliamentary democracy. The Parliament is elected democratically, but the party in power has wide latitude to do as it wishes. The Westminster model of parliamentary democracy is far more efficient at making decisions than are most presidential democracies. It is also inclined to ignore the views of minorities. Indeed, opposition parties often complain of the tyranny of the majority. These and related themes will find extensive elaboration in the discussion of British politics (Chapter 2).

The efficiency of the Westminster model in Britain is made possible by the existence of two dominant political parties, one or the other of which possesses a majority of the seats in the Parliament. Many parliamentary democracies, however, do not possess a two-party system. Rather, the seats in the Parliament are fragmented among several political parties, none of which can claim a majority. The election of a prime minister, accordingly, requires a coalition of political parties. **Coalition governments** are notoriously unstable, for the prime minister can rule only as long as he or she retains the support of all members of the coalition. If one party leaves the coalition, the prime minister is usually forced to resign. Japan is currently suffering through a series of unstable coalitions, a topic discussed in Chapter 5. France has attempted to combine the presidential and parliamentary models of democracy in the hopes of achieving the best of both systems. It is not clear that this has happened, but it has made for interesting politics. Russia is now attempting to implement the French model.

Authoritarian Political Systems

Authoritarian regimes are *characterized by the concentration of power in the hands of a single dictator or a small group of powerful individuals.* The advantage of dictatorial regimes lies in the ability of their leaders to pursue a narrow set of goals with ruthless efficiency. Mass emotions and the reconciliation of group interests are of less concern to dictators than they are to democratic politicians who must face the electorate on a regular basis. If the goal of the ruling elite is rapid economic development, all of the resources of the country can be focused on that goal. The economic development of South Korea, Brazil, Singapore, Taiwan, and other countries of the Third World that are now approaching economic parity with the First World was led by dictatorial regimes. Without strong governments, moreover, many countries of the Third World would either fragment into mini-states of questionable viability or dissolve into civil war. This tragic situation is discussed in Chapter 11, "Nigeria: The Politics of Hope and Despair." Economic growth, however, does not guarantee equality.

The disadvantage of authoritarian regimes is that the public has little to say about either the goals pursued by the regime or the manner in which those goals are implemented. The assumption that authoritarian regimes can promote economic development more efficiently than democratic regimes, moreover, is clearly open to challenge (Weede 1983, 1984). While authoritarian regimes have facilitated economic

Figure 1.1
Types of Political Systems and Variants

1. Democratic Political Systems
   a. Presidential
      (1) Two-party (United States)
      (2) Multiparty (Brazil)
      (3) Single-party dominant (Singapore)
   b. Parliamentary
      (1) Westminster model (Britain, Germany)
      (2) Coalition model (Japan)
      (3) Single-party dominant (India)
   c. Mixed presidential/parliamentary system (France, Russia)
2. Authoritarian Political Systems
   a. Totalitarian (Nazi Germany, Soviet Union)
   b. Dictatorships
      (1) Military (Sudan)
      (2) Civilian (People's Republic of China)
   c. Monarchies (Saudi Arabia)
   d. Theocracies (Iran)
3. Quasi-Democratic Political Systems
   a. Some democracy, military dominant (Egypt)
   b. Some democracy, one-party dominant (Mexico)*
   c. Some democracy, monarchy dominant (Jordan)

---

*Mexico illustrates the problem of assigning states to specific categories. Mexicans vote in regularly scheduled elections and share most attributes of a democracy. The PRI, the dominant party in Mexico, has not lost a presidential election since its founding in 1929. Most of its victories have been tainted by fraud. Does this make Mexico a democracy or a quasi-democracy?

development in a handful of states, they have failed miserably in others. The collapse of the USSR revealed how profoundly inefficient authoritarian regimes could be. The picture in China is much the same. The goals of many authoritarian regimes, moreover, have little to do with either economic development or the advancement of the population. Many dictators seize power with the best of intentions but lose sight of their developmental goals once they have become entrenched in office. Unlike democracies, authoritarian regimes have no built-in corrective mechanisms to put them back on track.

As in the case of democracies, authoritarian states come in numerous varieties. Traditional monarchies were generally content to dominate the political system, leaving economic activity to the business community and culture to the church. The same is true of most dictatorships. **Totalitarian societies** such as Nazi Germany and the Soviet Union, by contrast, *placed all political, economic, and cultural activity under the direct control of the state* (Friedrich and Brzezinski 1956). The topic of totalitarianism is a controversial one, and it is examined at greater length in the discussion of Russian politics (Chapter 6).

Theocracies, which are *ruled by religious leaders,* use the full power of the state to assure mass compliance with a particular set of religious doctrines. Iran is currently the world's only pure theocracy, but an increasing umber of countries are strengthening the links between their political and religious institutions. Many states of the Third World have *political systems that blend democratic and authoritarian tendencies* into **quasi-democratic** political systems. Most possess democratic legislatures, but real power lies with a dictator of one form or another. By and large, a dictatorship is justified by its leaders on the grounds that both economic development and political stability require a strong central government. This topic will be explored in our discussions of Mexico and Egyptian politics (Chapters 9 and 10).

The Structures of Government

Governments consist of three basic elements: legal and organizational structures, decision makers (elites), and administrative officials or (bureaucrats). All are critical to the political process. Laws, procedures, and organizational arrangements are inanimate structures. Much like an automobile, political structures such as laws, constitutions, and organizational charts are devices that help people get from one point to another. They have no life of their own. The analysis of political structures helps us to predict and explain political events in a variety of ways (Fried 1966).

First, political structures such as laws, regulations, voting procedures, and organizations, favor some groups over others (Lijphart 1990). Some political arrangements concentrate wealth and power in the hands of a narrow elite, while others fragment power and wealth among a broad range of groups. The more equitably political structures distribute the resources of a society, the more likely they are to be supported by a broad cross section of the population.

Second, organizational complexity of political structures influences the type of activities a government can successfully pursue (Alexander and Colmy 1990). Simple machines are designed to perform simple tasks; complex machines perform complex tasks. The same is true of political structures. In the few primitive and tribal governments that remain, for example, the tribal chiefs perform the full range of governmental functions. One individual or a small group of individuals makes and implements decisions and resolves disputes among members of the tribe. The chief also assesses the concerns of the population and assures that support for the clan or tribe is not lagging. The division of political labor is minimal.

Modern political structures, by contrast, are very complex. One institution is assigned responsibility for making decisions, while other institutions are charged with implementation of those decisions and adjudication of disputes. Still other specialized institutions exist to assess the demands of the population and to build support for the system. The greater division of labor of modern political structures enables their leaders to better mobilize the state's human and material resources in support of their objectives. Nowhere is this difference between primitive and modern governments clearer than in the area of warfare. Modern wars employ weapons of mass destruction and are fought by armies numbering in the millions. Primitive wars are fought with arrows and spears by tribal warriors.

Third, the flexibility of structural arrangements influences the capacity of a political system to adapt to changing circumstances. Democratic political arrangements tend to be flexible and adaptive. As circumstances change, disadvantaged groups can alter the rules of the game by participating in elections and open debate. For the most part, violence is avoided. Dictatorial regimes, in contrast, tend to be rigid. When circumstances change, few provisions exist for redressing the balance between the winners and the losers. Virtually all of the countries experiencing extreme political violence in the world today possess non-democratic political systems. Flexible political structures, then, are more likely to change by evolution, while rigid political structures are likely to change only by violence or revolution.

Fourth, many people believe that political structures can be used to change or control undesirable aspects of human nature. The framers of the American Constitution, for example, believed that people naturally craved power. Elected leaders, in their view, would be tempted to transform themselves into kings. To combat this presumed defect in human nature, power was divided between the executive and the legislature. The ambition of one branch would check that of the other (Mendelson

> ### Three Basic Elements of Governments
>
> 1. Legal and organizational structures
> 2. Decision makers (elites)
> 3. Administrative officials (bureaucrats)

1980). The Mexican and Brazilian constitutions attempt to control their leaders by limiting presidents to a single term.

In one way or another, most modern political structures attempt to control power and corruption by forcing politicians to work within a maze of laws and procedures. Decisions require ratification by a variety of groups, and all are open to legal challenge. Each year the number of hoops through which politicians must jump seems to increase. Legal and organizational constraints may limit abuses of power but, as we are constantly reminded, do not eliminate them. Excessive rules and regulations, moreover, often choke the political process by fragmenting power among too many institutions or actors. The logical outcome of too many checks and balances is no movement at all.

The Human Dimension of Political Institutions

While structural arrangements influence the performance of governmental institutions such as parliaments and administrative agencies, those institutions are far more than lifeless structures. Institutional performance is also a function of the decision makers and bureaucrats who control and manage the political structures. Much as the driver of an automobile determines its destination and chooses the route to be followed, the drivers of governmental institutions determine the goals that those institutions will pursue and the speed and ruthlessness with which they will be pursued. Much also depends upon the skills of political leaders and bureaucrats. Some individuals can get more out of their machinery than others.

It is the human element in governmental institutions that seemingly provides them with a life of their own. Institutions outlive the individuals who created them because they develop an organizational or institutional culture that is passed on from one generation to another. A new member of the British Parliament, for example, is immediately confronted with traditions and practices that have evolved over the centuries. To violate these traditions is to be ostracized by other members of Parliament and to lose the support of constituents who believe in the parliamentary system and who expect their representatives to play by the rules. Things change in Britain, but they change very slowly.

Political institutions that evolve slowly over time, earning a respected place in the society, are said to be **institutionalized** (Huntington 1991; Bollen and Jackman 1985). Samuel Huntington (1968, 12) defines **institutionalization** as *"the process by which organizations and procedures acquire value and stability."*

Most political institutions in the First World are well institutionalized, and one can predict with reasonable confidence that established patterns of operation will persist over time. By contrast, most institutions in the Third World are poorly institutionalized and change frequently. Together, the countries of Latin America have had more than 200 constitutions in the same time period in which the United States has had one. Because constitutions in Latin America and other countries of the Third World change so frequently, they are often viewed with cynicism by the populations affected, as discussed in Part Four.

Actors in the Political Arena

The individuals and groups that give direction to the political process are often referred to as **political actors.** Elites and bureaucrats are political actors, as are individual citizens attempting, by one means or another, to influence their governments. Political parties and pressure groups are also considered actors, for both represent individual citizens who are taking collective action to achieve their political objectives.

Elites: The Movers and the Shakers of the Political Arena

Inequality is a fact of political and economic life. Some individuals simply have more influence over the political process than others. *Those individuals who dominate the policy-making process* are referred to as **political elites.** As expressed by Bill and Hardgrave, elites are *"the people who create institutions and write constitutions; personalities who plan, plot, dictate, and decide"* (Bill and Hardgrave 1981, 161).

Most of these decision makers occupy senior positions in the government. Others may exert political influence by virtue of their extraordinary financial resources, their status in society, or their ability to speak for the members of a large group such as a labor union or religious community. In many states of the Third World, the military dominates the elite structure. Even when the generals are not in office, they cast a long shadow over the political process. Elites play a predominant role in setting the policy agenda, and they usually have the final voice in determining who gets what, when, and how. In most instances, *they* "get most of what there is to get" (Lasswell 1958).

Types of Elites: Unitary and Pluralistic. Many societies possess a single **unitary elite** in which *decision-making authority is concentrated in the hands of a small group of individuals. A government with a unitary elite* is often referred to as an **oligarchy.** Unitary elites are common in dictatorships but can also occur in democracies when a single group of elected officials enjoys extraordinary power. In the British political system, for example, enormous power is concentrated in the hands of the prime minister and the Cabinet. Various groups may offer their opinions, but it is Britain's unitary elite that usually makes the final decision.

In other societies, *political power is distributed among a broad range of decision makers.* Some may dominate the shaping of economic policy, while others dominate policy making in the areas of education or health. Such elites are often referred to as **pluralistic elites** (Dahl 1961). The United States is a prime example of a country with a pluralistic elite structure. Even a subcommittee of the US Congress can block national policy until its demands have been met.

Which is better, governments dominated by unitary elites or governments dominated by pluralistic elites? This question does not have a simple answer. Democracy is generally enhanced by a system of pluralistic elites. The more elites fight among themselves, the more inclined they are to seek support among the masses. Advocates of law and order, by contrast, are often distressed by political institutions that find it difficult to make firm decisions. Such institutions, they feel, foster social disorganization and chaos.

In one of the classic works of comparative politics, *The Iron Law of Oligarchy* (1915/1959), Robert Michels argues that all political organizations tend to become oligarchies. Once individuals are in positions of authority, Michels explains, they consolidate their power by manipulating organizational procedures, placing supporters in high positions, and managing the information

---

Advantages and Disadvantages of Unitary Elites

- A major advantage of unitary elites is their ability to take decisive action without endless delay and compromise.

- A disadvantage of unitary elites is their tendency to take extreme positions without concern for the diverse opinions of their citizens. A change of unitary elites can also lead to dramatic changes in policy, as happened with the collapse of the Soviet Union.

Advantages and Disadvantages of Pluralistic Elites

- A major advantage of pluralistic elites is their responsiveness to diverse groups and interests. Most segments of society can make their voices heard, and governmental decisions tend to emphasize compromise and reconciliation.

- A disadvantage of pluralistic elites is their lack of decisive action. Coherent and farsighted programs are often watered down by the need for compromise because too many groups are involved in the decision-making process.

---

they make available to the general public. If Michels's view is correct (and many political theorists believe it is), rule by oligarchies, or small groups of individuals, is inevitable, regardless of how democratic the governmental structure may be (Dye 1976).

Elites and Political Analysis. The politics of a state is also influenced by the openness or flexibility of its elites. Absolute monarchies represent a closed elite in which the recruitment of new members is restricted to the royal family or a narrow group of aristocrats. Unless the elite group is willing to relinquish its authority, violence is the only path to political change. The British monarchy gradually gave up its political authority and has survived as an institution; the French monarchy did not give way to popular demands for change and was crushed. The more open the process of elite recruitment, the more peaceful the process of political change is likely to be.

In sum, the role of political elites in the political process is extremely important. Political elites have more to say about the allocation of a society's scarce resources than any other individuals in a society. Many people also believe that they receive a disproportionate share of those resources. Whatever the case, the values, perceptions, and skills of the ruling elite greatly influence the course of politics in a society.

Bureaucrats: The Functionaries of Government

Elites play a dominant role in deciding who gets what in a society, but their decisions are not self-enforcing. The **bureaucrats** (administrators) are responsible for *seeing that decisions are implemented.* This is particularly the case in today's world, a world in which governments are faced with the need to make informed decisions on topics as complex and diverse as nuclear waste, crime prevention, the ozone layer, international trade, health care, drugs, and a crumbling natural environment, to mention but a few. Decisions in such complex areas cannot be implemented by a handful of cronies or a council of tribal elders. Rather, each area of decision making requires its own specialized agency.

As decision making grows more complex, the influence of bureaucrats increases proportionally (Blau and Meyer 1987). In many instances, it is they, not the elites, who determine which policies the government will pursue and how

---

Elite Analysis

Understanding the values and predispositions of a country's leaders often provides important insights into the policies they are likely to pursue.

If the values of Hitler and Stalin had been better understood by Western democracies, the world might have been spared infinite suffering. In much the same manner, elite values have much to say about the practice of democratic principles. The commitment of India's leaders to these principles has helped to sustain that country's democracy through more than four decades of economic and social adversity. The commitment of Russia's leaders to democracy, by contrast, is an unknown factor. Can former communists become converted democrats, or is the West deluding itself in thinking so?

---

those policies will be implemented (Aberbach 1981). The behavior of bureaucrats influences policy decisions in a variety of ways, the following of which are among the most important.

1. *Political leaders are generalists, while bureaucrats possess the specialized technical information that political elites need to make informed policies.* The more complex the issue, the more heavily a political elite must rely on the expertise of its support staff.

2. *Bureaucrats decide how quickly and efficiently elite decisions will be executed.* Elites, by definition, are few in number. They simply lack the time and energy to keep tabs on everything. Two or three programs can be highlighted for special attention, but seldom more. Bureaucrats, by contrast, number in the tens if not hundreds of thousands. They know how to manipulate the complexities of the administrative apparatus. Programs that have the approval of functionaries are executed with dispatch, while others tend to lag—waiting, perhaps, for a change of regime.

3. *Bureaucrats constitute an important pressure group.* Bureaucrats occupy a privileged position in most societies, receiving generous salaries and, barring extraordinarily poor behavior, a guaranteed job for life. In the view of many, it is the bureaucrats who receive most of what there is to be gotten. While efforts to curb the costs of bureaucracy are frequent, successes are few.

4. *The capacity of a bureaucracy to execute elite decisions depends upon the skills of its members.* Japanese bureaucrats are generally credited with orchestrating Japan's phenomenal economic growth, and the cold efficiency of German bureaucrats is legendary. The bureaucrats of many newly independent countries, by contrast, lack the skill and experience to implement programs in a timely and efficient manner. However farsighted the decisions of the elites may be, their decisions are not being implemented effectively.

5. *Public attitudes toward the government are directly influenced by the behavior of bureaucrats.* Few people come in contact with their leaders, but virtually everyone comes in contact with bureaucrats. When public officials are honest, service-oriented, and impartial, they help to build a strong bond of legitimacy between government and citizens. Bureaucratic behavior characterized by indifference, favoritism, and corruption, by contrast, breeds mass hostility. Changing dysfunctional bureaucratic behavior, unfortunately, is a slow process at best. Once in place, a bureaucratic culture tends to perpetuate itself as new officials acquire the attitudes of the old.

In an ideal world, bureaucrats would be responsive to the policy directives of elected leaders, efficient in the performance of services, creative in finding solutions for society's problems, courteous and helpful in their dealings with the public,

---

How the Masses Shape the Political Process

■ *First, mass discontent often is the source of the tension and conflict that permeate all political processes.* While the masses may display remarkable patience with their political leaders, the tolerance of even the most docile population has its limits. In the present era of instant communications, moreover, the masses have been made acutely aware of the gap between their lives and those of the upper classes.

■ *Second, the mobilization of the masses is essential for the growth and development of any society.* It is the common people who do most of what gets done in a country. In times of war, for example, the elites give the orders, the bureaucrats mobilize the masses, and the masses do the fighting. The same arrangement also is found in peacetime; that is, the elites set the goals for the nation, the bureaucrats work out the details, and the masses do the work. The masses staff the factories, farms, offices, and mines that generate a society's wealth; and the masses pay most of the taxes. Political institutions can endure without the support of the masses, but they cannot prosper.

---

objective in offering advice to political leaders, sparing in the expenditure of public funds, and unobtrusive and restrained as a pressure group. The more the bureaucracy of a country approaches this model, the better positioned the country will be to achieve the goals of good government. As the country chapters in this book will illustrate, this scenario is rare indeed.

Masses, Classes, and Politics

While elites and bureaucrats are key actors in the making and implementation of political decisions, the politics of a country also depends on the opinions and support of its population—the **masses,** as *the public* may be referred to by political theorists.

The analysis of mass political behavior offers two powerful tools for comparative political analysis. The first focuses on the intensity of mass **demands** for a reallocation of society's scarce resources. If mass demands are moderate, the pace of political change is likely to be moderate and evolutionary. As the intensity of mass demands increases, the probability of political violence also increases (Feierabend, Feierabend, and Nesvold 1967). The second tool focuses on the extent of mass **support** for political institutions. The more individuals support their political institutions, the stronger those institutions will be. Support for the political system is expressed in a variety of ways. It is shown by obeying the laws of the land, paying taxes, serving in the military, cooperating with government agencies, and participating in elections. Political support also encompasses loyalty, discipline, and hard work. Anything that strengthens the ability of the political system to function effectively is supportive.

The masses, then, have a major impact on the political process. Many decisions made by elites are, in reality, forced by mass pressures. It is often the level of mass support that determines what the government can and cannot accomplish. It is hard to fight wars if the soldiers are demoralized, just as it is difficult to feed the people of a state if its workers are sluggish.

For all of their impact on the political process, the influence of the masses is seldom direct. As a unit, the masses are simply too big, too diverse, too unstructured, and too beset by internal contradictions to focus on more than a handful of issues. Even then, mass opinion is often the product of information provided by the elites or by the diverse political parties and groups to which most people belong.

Collective Action: Groups and Interests

While individual citizens play an important role in the political process, their influence is far stronger when they come together as a group. Indeed, most political activity is group activity. *Groups that form for the express purpose of influencing governmental policies* are often referred to as **pressure groups.**

As governments grew larger and more complex, the need for collective action became imperative and pressure groups began to play an integral part in the political process. It is now impossible to envision politics in the United States or any other modern society without pressure groups. The strategies of pressure groups differ markedly from country to country, but the fundamental principle remains the same: collective action is more effective in bringing about changes in governmental policy than action by individuals working alone.

In addition to being one of the basic units of political action, pressure groups also play an important role in the **linkage** of the elites and masses. Pressure groups, for example, *provide an important channel of communication between political leaders and key segments of the population.* Group members are provided with the opportunity to articulate interests, while political leaders are given the opportunity to build support among group members.

Pressure groups also simplify mass–elite relationships by aggregating the demands of their members. Rather than having to cope with the random demands of millions of disorganized workers, political leaders can focus on the precise demands of labor union leaders. If union leaders agree on a contract, the rank and file usually go along and sustained conflict is avoided. By satisfying a limited number of group demands, then, political leaders are often able to control and mobilize many of the best-organized groups in society (Kornhauser 1959).

Other functions of pressure groups are to advise their members on issues and shape their attitudes toward the government and its leaders. If the major groups in society support the existing order, its stability is largely assured. The opposite is equally true. Rare, indeed, is a government that can survive the sustained opposition of the dominant groups in society.

Groups and Political Analysis. Group analysis can be a very powerful tool in comparative politics. Indeed, some scholars believe that group analysis is more effective in predicting and explaining political events than either elite analysis or mass analysis (Truman 1951). Most elites, after all, do not get to be elites without the support of a strong group. They must be careful not to alienate group members. In much the same

---

Purposes of Pressure Groups

1. *To protect their members from capricious acts of the government by means of collective action.* During the early years of the industrial revolution, the exploitation of workers was openly condoned by the governments of the day. Individual workers, by themselves, had little recourse against the system. It was only after the establishment of labor unions that rampant exploitation subsided.

2. *To promote the special interests of their members.* Often, this has meant securing a larger share of society's resources for members of the group. Workers wanted higher wages and better working conditions. Employers wanted fewer taxes and protection from foreign competition.

3. *To impose a particular view of social morality on society as a whole.* Pressure groups have been responsible for the enactment of a broad range of social legislation, including child labor laws, Prohibition, and environmental legislation.

Cross-Cutting Cleavages

In many instances the solidarity of groups is undermined by the diverse interests of their members. A successful businessperson from working-class origins, for example, may be torn between the demands of the business community and sympathy for the rights of workers. He or she may resolve this internal conflict simply by not taking sides. *Groups whose members are divided by conflicting religious, ethnic, economic, political, or other loyalties* are said to have **cross-cutting cleavages.** Because the interests of their members are contradictory or cross-cut, these groups find it more difficult to take concerted political action than those whose members share common political values (Lipset and Rokkan 1967).

manner, it is the group that gives structure and direction to the masses. Without structure, these scholars say, the masses are a herd, a mob. It is the act of organization that transforms the masses into a political force.

Several dimensions of group analysis are particularly useful in predicting and explaining political events. Government policies generally reflect the views of the most powerful groups in society. The greater one's ability to chart the group map of a society, the easier it will be to chart the direction of its leaders. In this regard, the influence of groups often results from several factors including organizational structure, the dedication of group members, cohesion, adequate finances, access to the centers of power, the ability to threaten the dominant elites, and the extent to which group goals are embraced by the general population (Truman 1951).

Some of these factors are more important than others in determining a group's strength. Leaders rarely disregard the views of groups that keep them in power. They also attempt to accommodate those groups that are in the strongest position to challenge their authority. Many governments in the Middle East, for example, now find themselves challenged by religious fundamentalists demanding an Islamic (Muslim) government. While attempting to crush the militants, these governments have also brought their policies more in line with Islamic principles, a topic discussed at length in our examination of Egyptian politics (Chapter 10). A small but cohesive group of dedicated members will often have more influence on policy than a larger group whose members are apathetic or divided among themselves. Groups that vote as a solid bloc get the attention of politicians.

Political Parties and Party Systems

Pressure groups attempt to achieve their objectives by exerting pressure on the government. Political parties, by contrast, attempt to achieve their objectives by controlling the government. A **political party** is generally defined as *a group of individuals working together to achieve common goals by controlling all or part of the government* (Epstein 1967; Lawson 1976; Robertson 1976; Sartori 1976). Often the ruling party determines who will run the institutions of government and how the resources of society will be allocated.

Major Types of Political Parties. Political parties take a variety of forms depending upon their primary objectives.

Catch-All Parties. The primary objective of the Republican and Democratic parties in the United States is to win elections. Each has a basic program that it would like to pursue, but it will readily sacrifice that program to achieve its goal of winning elections. Much the same is true of the major political parties in the United Kingdom and Germany. Such parties are often referred to as **catch-all parties** because *they are willing to relax ideological concerns in order to appeal to a broad spectrum of the voting public* (Kirchheimer 1966).

Catch-all parties thrive by capturing the center of the political spectrum and generally avoiding extremist positions that would alienate a large group of voters. They ask little of their supporters and tend to have loose organizational structures. While some people formally join catch-all parties, most of their adherents do not. Meetings and conventions are attended only by the party faithful, and most party affairs are managed by a small cadre of leaders who speak in the name of the party.

Mass-Membership or Devotee Parties. At the opposite end of the party hierarchy from catch-all parties one finds mass-membership or devotee parties. **Devotee parties** *have well-defined ideological goals and expect members to devote their lives to the achievement of those goals* (Duverger 1954). While strategic alliances might be made for the sake of achieving power, ideology is more important than votes. Devotee parties have tight organizational structures, with party leaders serving in the role of high priests. Party members are expected to belong to a variety of party study groups and social organizations and to spend most of their free time in organizational work. The integration of members' lives within the party framework provides them with a sense of belonging and reinforces their ideological commitment by enabling them to feed upon the zeal of the group. The early communist parties of Russia and China are perhaps the best examples of devotee parties. Party members were dedicated to Marx's vision of a communist utopia in which individuals would give according to their abilities and take according to their needs. The orders of party leaders were absolute and executed with discipline. Indeed, it was the dedication and discipline of party members that enabled relatively small parties to seize control of two of the largest countries in the world. Once in office, both communist parties lost much of their revolutionary zeal, a phenomenon that is examined in Chapters 6 and 7.

Social Democrats: From Mass Membership to Catch-All Parties. Between the extremes represented by the catch-all and devotee parties lies a bewildering array of party arrangements (Janda 1980). Many of the early Social Democratic parties of Europe, for example, attempted to create mass-membership parties dedicated to both socialism and democracy (Neumann 1956, 395–42). The government was to manage economic activity for the mutual benefit of all citizens, but the country itself would remain a democracy. Much like the devotee parties, the early Social Democratic parties attempted to integrate all aspects of their members' lives within the party community. In addition to attending regularly scheduled branch meetings, party members were encouraged to join socialist labor unions, to participate in socialist study groups, and to spend their free time in party recreational activities. The party also furnished members with health care and other social services that were seldom provided by employers. Unlike the devotee parties, the organizational procedures of Social Democratic parties were democratic in nature and allowed greater scope for ideological dialogue. In practice, however, political control generally resided in a narrow oligarchy (Michels 1915/1959). In recent years, many Social Democratic parties have taken on the characteristics of large catch-all parties. While reference to socialism has been retained in the party name, they no longer advocate the nationalization of industry. Rather, they now argue the state's responsibility is to provide its citizens with health care, education, and related social services. This more moderate position has increased the voting base of Social Democratic parties by broadening their appeal beyond the working class. It has also weakened their organizational structure by diluting the ideological fervor of their members.

Still other political parties *focus on a narrow range of issues.* The Green parties of Europe, for example, are concerned primarily with environmental and related social issues. As such, they are often referred to as **single-** or **limited-issue parties**. While Green parties have been too narrowly focused to gain power, they have been extremely effective in publicizing the serious environmental and social problems facing Europe.

Political Parties and Political Analysis. The bewildering array of political parties found throughout the world makes them difficult to classify (Gross and Sigelman 1984; Sartori 1976). Classification is made more complicated by the constant evolution of political parties. Mass-membership parties are evolving into catch-all parties, and the large single parties are splintering into a multitude of minor parties. Even the former communist parties are taking on democratic trappings.

Ideological Classifications: Left, Right, and Center. For practical purposes, most comparative political analysts find it useful to classify political parties on the basis of their ideology, a practice that evolved in revolutionary France.[3] The French parliament of the era took the shape of a large semicircle in which supporters of the church and monarchy sat on the far right, while advocates of direct popular democracy sat on the far left. Over time, it became customary to refer to *monarchists, supporters of the church, and extreme nationalists* as the **far right.** The **moderate or democratic right** consisted of a broad range of *parties favoring private property, free enterprise, low taxation, and law and order.* The **far left** consisted of the *communists, anarchists, and other parties advocating a mass revolution by violent means.* The **moderate left** was the preserve of the Social Democrats, while the political **center** was dominated by *largely middle-class parties that advocated a reasonable balance between capitalism and social welfare.*[4]

As the middle class has grown, so have the parties of the center. Definitions of right and left have also shifted with time. With rare exception, monarchist parties have become a footnote in history, as have the anarchists. Christian Democratic parties now dominate the center right of many European countries, advocating programs that support private enterprise and champion moral responsibility. Social Democratic parties are inching ever closer to the political center, downplaying their socialist origins. Communist parties continue to dominate the far left but have fallen out of favor. The center is where the voters are.

Political systems in which the dominant parties cluster near the political center generally are more stable, more moderate, and more democratic than those in which the parties are polarized at the extreme left and right. It is relatively easy for moderate parties to compromise their differences, but extremist parties find it far more difficult to do so.[5] How, for instance, can the views of an anti-religious communist party calling for total state ownership of the means of production be reconciled with

---

[3]Strong support for classifying parties on the basis of ideology is provided by Kim and Fording (1994) and by Budge, Robertson, and Hearl (1987). Kim and Fording combine party ideology with voting returns to facilitate cross-national comparisons.

[4]Connotations of left and right in the United States are less well defined than they are in most European states.

[5]Extremist parties often form temporary alliances to strengthen their opposition to democratic parties of the political center, but that cooperation tends to be short-lived.

Political Parties: Right, Left, and Center

Far Left	Center Left	Center	Center Right	Far Right
Communist parties	Social Democratic parties	Middle-class parties	Conservative, business-oriented parties	Monarchist parties
			Christian Democratic parties	Parties advocating a religious or quasi-religious government
				Parties advocating extreme nationalism

---

those of an ultra-nationalist party advocating the fusion of church and state and a revival of laissez-faire capitalism? This is one of the many challenges facing Russia and the other newly independent states created by the collapse of the Soviet Union. Similar patterns of extreme polarization exist throughout the Third World.

Numerical Classifications of Party Systems. In addition to classifying political parties on the basis of organizational structure or ideology, comparative political analysts have also found it useful to classify party systems on the basis of the number of political parties that have a reasonable chance of controlling the government (Sartori 1976; Blondel 1968). The governments of the United States, Great Britain, and Germany, for example, are referred to as **two-party systems.** While more than two parties exist, *the government is always dominated by one of the country's two major parties.* Many countries have **multiparty systems** in which *several parties compete for voter support, and no party is able to gain a majority of the vote in any election.* In a recent Polish election, for example, more than 100 political parties vied for power. Not all of these parties gained seats in the Polish parliament, but many did.

Democracies that are overwhelmingly dominated by a single political party are called **single-party-dominant** systems. Mexico, a country in which the PRI has dominated the political system for more than fifty years, is a prime example of a single-party-dominant system. Communist states are said to have **single-party-authoritarian** systems because *the ruling party totally controls all political activity.*[6] Finally, some countries do not have any political parties. Such **no-party** states are *authoritarian regimes in which kings or dictators are afraid to allow their subjects even the pretense of representation.* Libya and Saudi Arabia are both examples of no-party states. Unfortunately, not all party systems fit neatly into these categories, forcing a proliferation of terms such as party-and-one-half systems and two-and-one-half-party systems.[7]

The analysis of political parties provides a powerful tool for explaining and predicting political events. As a general principle, states with catch-all parties will be more moderate and more plodding in their policy making than countries dominated

---

[6]Some scholars distinguish between authoritarian parties whose only objective is to maintain political power and totalitarian parties whose objective is to transform society totally by controlling all dimensions of social, economic, and political life (Friedrich and Brzezinski 1964). This topic is discussed at length in Chapter 6.

[7]Also problematic is diversity in the cohesion or solidarity of political parties. Parties that are cohesive or that possess a solid center of gravity tend to be far more effective in achieving their goals than parties that lack internal cohesion or are hamstrung by severe ideological polarization. Some analysts, accordingly, argue that parties should also be classified in terms of organizational cohesiveness (Gross and Sigelman 1984).

Numerical Classifications of Party Systems

Classification	Definition	Examples
Two-party	The government is always dominated by one of the country's two major parties.	US, Great Britain, Germany
Multiparty	Several parties compete for voter support, and no party is able to gain a majority of the vote in any election.	Russia, Poland, France
Single-party dominant	The government is dominated by a single party.	Mexico, Egypt
Single-party-authoritarian	Communist states in which the ruling party totally controls all political activity.	Cuba, China
No party	Authoritarian regimes in which kings or dictators totally control all political activity.	Saudi Arabia, Libya

by large mass-membership parties. They have to be moderate in order to attract the largest number of votes.

Two-party systems tend to be more stable than multiparty systems, inasmuch as one party or the other is firmly in control of the government. This is much less the case in multiparty systems. Between the end of World War II and the year 2000, for example, the average life of an Italian cabinet was less than a year. No sooner was one cabinet confirmed than shifting party alliances undermined its authority.[8]

Countries in which the dominant political parties cluster around the political center are almost always more moderate in their actions than countries characterized by extreme polarization of the electorate. The politics of countries with polarized political parties also tend to be far more violent than those of their centrist counterparts. All of these points will be elaborated in later analysis.

The Environment of Politics: Economics, Culture, and International Interdependence

Although political institutions and political actors occupy center stage in the political process, that process is profoundly influenced by the broader economic, cultural, and international context in which it occurs. Indeed, some comparative analysts believe that the behavior of any country is largely a reflection of its cultural and economic systems, together with its position in the global community. Whether or not one accepts this point of view, efforts to predict or explain the politics of any country in the modern world would be incomplete without a close look at these three factors.

Economic Systems and Comparative Politics

Advocates of a **political economy** approach to comparative political analysis find *most areas of political life to be shaped by economic relationships* (Clark 1991).

---

[8]Italy revised its electoral system in 1994 to create a more stable party system.

The more one understands the link between economics and politics, in their view, the easier it will be to explain and predict political events.

Although political economists are unified in their belief that economic factors underlie most forms of political activity, they disagree violently over the best strategy for achieving a prosperous and equitable society (Staniland 1985; Gilpin 1987). The dominant schools of political economy are Marxism, free-market (neoclassical) capitalism, and state capitalism. Marxists argue that prosperity and equality are best assured by a socialist economic system in which the government owns the factories, farms, and other means of production. Neoclassical or free-market economists, by contrast, argue that only the free market can assure prosperity and equality. It is the free flow of economic activity unencumbered by the government, in their view, that leads to a society of plenty. While socialists argue that growth and prosperity require government control, free-market capitalists see the government as the enemy of equality and prosperity. State capitalists, in turn, argue that prosperity and equality require both capitalism and a strong dose of government planning.

The United States and many of its allies favor free-market capitalism. Japan and many of the newly industrialized countries of Asia are advocates of state capitalism. Until the 1990s, Russia and China adhered to socialist economic principles. The countries of the Third World have experimented with various combinations of socialism (Marxism), free-market capitalism, and state capitalism. As we will see in subsequent chapters, adherence to differing economic philosophies has led to dramatic differences in how countries do politics. Indeed, it is difficult to understand the political process in the world today without some awareness of the basic components of Marxism, free-market (neoclassical) capitalism, and state capitalism. Accordingly, we will explore these topics next.

Marxism. The world's most famous political economist was Karl Marx (Coker 1934). A philosopher of the mid-nineteenth century, Karl Marx witnessed both the rewards and the abuses of industrialization in Europe. For the first time in human history, industrialization had made it possible for society to provide an advanced quality of life for all of its citizens. The problem, from Marx's perspective, was that the fruits of industrialization were monopolized by a *narrow class of industrialists and merchants* he referred to as the **bourgeoisie.** While the bourgeoisie reaped huge profits, the majority of *the working class*—the **proletariat**—lived in poverty and squalor. Industrialization had made it possible for human society to attain new heights of prosperity and intellectual development, but that goal had been subverted by the greed of the capitalist bourgeoisie.

How, then, Marx asked, could the fruits of industrialization be used for the development of mankind? The task would not be easy, for the political process was controlled by the rich and powerful. Governments, in Marx's words, were merely a "committee of the rich" charged with keeping the masses in servitude. The masses, moreover, were distracted from their true economic interests by myths of religion and nationalism. Indeed, Marx went so far as to refer to religion as the "opiate" of the masses. The solution, Marx reasoned, was for the masses to come together as a class and seize power from the rich. This accomplished, the masses would use their control of the means of production to assure that everyone received an equitable share of society's wealth.

Fundamental to this argument was Marx's belief that human nature was basically good. With ample resources at their disposal, the working class would be more than willing to "give according to their abilities and take according to their needs." *Everything would be owned in common,* hence the reference to a Marxist society as a **communist** or communal society.

Marx's theory of class conflict may have stemmed in part from his knowledge of London's slums. Dudley Street, shown here in a woodcut by Doré, was close to Dean Street, where Marx once lived with his family. Both of Marx's sons and his daughter died from illnesses related to undernourishment and poor living conditions.

Friedrich Engels, an early colleague of Marx, believed that the state would simply "wither away" once communism had been achieved. The Marxist utopia would be a worker's paradise. It would also be free of religious and national conflict, for religions and nations would cease to exist.

Marx believed that his theory of class conflict underscored the scientific and inevitable unfolding of history. The historical role of capitalism was to industrialize society, and the role of the proletariat was to seize power from the bourgeoisie and use the fruits of industrialization to establish a truly humanistic state. This process was inevitable and could not be reversed. While Marx believed that he had discovered a scientific principle of social evolution, his philosophy was also highly moralistic. In his view, it was the moral obligation of the proletariat to seize the means of production and to use its profits to create a just society.

Communism, as practiced in the states of the former Soviet Union and in the People's Republic of China, proved to be profoundly inefficient. Although important gains were made in the areas of education, health care, and social services, productivity was sluggish and the quality of workmanship was poor. The failure of **Marxism** in the Soviet Union and China will be discussed at length in Chapters 6 and 7, respectively.

Free-Market Capitalism.   The capitalist version of political economy is as simple and as beguiling as that of the Marxists. Capitalist political economy finds its origins in the works of Adam Smith (1776) and other "classical" economists of the eighteenth and nineteenth centuries. Individuals, in the view of Adam Smith, were rational economic actors. Each was primarily concerned with maximizing his or her economic self-interest. Industrialists and merchants wanted to sell their goods at the highest possible price, just as workers wanted to receive the highest possible wages for their labor.

Ultimately, the price of goods and labor was determined by the law of supply and demand. Adam Smith described this principle as an "unseen hand" regulating the marketplace.

Adam Smith believed the free market provided the key to social and economic development. Technological development was assured because individuals would always seek to increase their wealth by inventing new goods and services. The production of new goods and services, in turn, would provide jobs for the masses. Indeed, as the number of factories increased, there would not be enough workers to go around, and wages would be driven up by the law of supply and demand. Increased wages would enable workers to buy more goods, thereby stimulating ever-faster economic development. Finally, competition among producers would assure that goods were reasonably priced. By the very nature of the free market, successful products would be overwhelmed by lower-priced imitators. Adam Smith's world, then, would be an abundant world. By attempting to increase his or her personal wealth, each individual would assure that there was enough for all. Some people would be richer than others, but that determination would be made by the market.

Adam Smith's idyllic version of an abundant society required an undistorted free market. In the real world, unfortunately, distortions in the free market lurk around every corner (Edwards 1985). The most influential of these are monopolies and governments. In Adam Smith's ideal world, the pursuit of wealth would lead to greater innovation and productivity. In the real world, it often leads to monopolies and price fixing. How can the law of supply and demand work effectively if manufacturers agree among themselves to charge a common price for their goods and to pay a common wage to their workers? It cannot. In much the same manner, it is difficult for the free market to work effectively in an environment of excessive regulation and taxation. Taxes reduce innovation and productivity by reducing rewards. Why should people work hard and innovate if the fruits of their labor are merely absorbed by the government? Regulations also cripple productivity by distorting the law of supply and demand. It is not the market that determines the type, cost, and quality of goods, but the government.

The modern advocates of free-market economics are referred to as **neoclassical economists** (Friedman and Friedman 1980). They have taken the classical economic theories of Adam Smith and other capitalist philosophers and adapted them to fit the needs of the present era. *Neoclassical economists, accordingly, argue for a world in which monopolistic practices are prohibited and in which the economic role of governments is reduced to facilitating free-market competition.* Currencies are to be strong, taxes low, and regulations few. International trade, also, is to be free of tariffs and monopolistic practices, allowing each state to seek the highest price for its goods and labor. If Mexican labor is willing to work for less than US labor, so be it.

The neoclassical vision of a capitalist world is of far more than theoretical interest, for it has become the guiding vision of the International Monetary Fund, the World Bank, and other international economic agencies. It is that vision that the states of the First World are attempting to establish throughout the Third World, including Russia (Walters and Blake 1992).

In reality, of course, Adam Smith's abundant society is as much a utopian vision as Karl Marx's ideal society whose inhabitants give according to their abilities and take according to their needs. Most states of the First World maintain enough of a **free-market economy** to benefit from the energy of human initiative. Most forms of economic activity, however, are regulated by the state in one way or another. In reality, the political process in most countries of the West represents a continuing effort to strike a balance between the raw energy of free-market competition and the need to regulate the excesses of that competition. Canada, Britain, and most other "free-market states" also provide a broad array of welfare services, most of which are managed by the state.

State Capitalism. A third version of political economy is referred to as state capitalism (Edwards 1985). **State capitalism** *accepts the proposition that capitalist competition is the most effective way to generate economic growth, but it rejects the principle that the free market is the most efficient way to regulate the economy.* From the point of view of the state capitalists, the economy is simply too important to be left to the "unseen hand" of the marketplace. Individual capitalists, in their view, are too concerned with immediate profits to recognize either their own long-term interests or those of the country as a whole.

The basic formula of state capitalism, accordingly, calls for most economic activity to be in the hands of individual capitalists. The desire for wealth is a powerful motivator that must not be destroyed. Political leaders, however, determine those industries that are best suited to the needs of the country. The government then uses its power and resources to support private-sector firms that invest in these areas. Priority firms receive special financing, pay lower taxes, and are protected from foreign competitors during their formative years. The principle of competition, however, is retained. Several national firms compete in each area, thereby assuring that market forces will produce quality products at a reasonable price. Japan and the **tigers of Asia**—*Taiwan, South Korea, and Singapore—are the world's foremost advocates of state capitalism* (Wang 1994). Germany also inclines toward state capitalism.

State capitalism has produced many variations, depending upon the circumstances of the country. The *ideal version of state capitalism* is often referred to as **growth with equity** (Todaro 1997). *Under the doctrine of growth with equity, the government uses the power of the state both to develop the economy and to assure that all members of society share in the benefits of that development.* Japan and Germany have an enviable record of achieving both growth and equity. Many of the newly industrialized states of Asia and Latin America, by contrast, have stressed growth at the expense of equity. The power of the state has been used to assure that mass protests do not stand in the way of economic development.

The world's most recent convert to state capitalism has been the People's Republic of China. While the communist regime remains firmly in control, communism, as an economic system, is becoming a thing of the past. This topic is discussed in Chapter 6.

Political Economy and Comparative Political Analysis. Despite their philosophical differences, most political economists share the following propositions which illustrate the major focus of political economy research in the study of comparative politics.

1. *Political conflict is largely economic conflict.* As a general principle, political conflict will usually be more intense in societies with declining economic resources than it is in societies with increasing economic resources (Davies 1963). By the same token, one can usually predict that political violence will reflect the distribution of wealth within a society. The greater the disparities of wealth, the greater the potential for political violence. One sees this today in the growing political turmoil in Asia and Russia.

2. *Economic prosperity reduces conflict.* Support for political institutions and political leaders is based upon their ability to meet the needs of their citizens. The most legitimate political systems in the world are also among the most prosperous. The abundant distribution of wealth increases tolerance among competing groups, as all share a common interest in assuring that the system survives.

3.   *The goals that a regime can pursue are limited by its financial resources.* Rich states have a broader range of options than poorer states, but all states have finite resources. The better a state's economic situation is understood, the easier it is to predict what policies political leaders can or cannot pursue, as well as the consequences of those choices.

4.   *All things being equal, wealthier individuals and groups will have more political influence than poorer individuals and groups.* Political leaders generally pursue policies that are favored by their financial supporters. This proposition has withstood the test of time so consistently that it requires little elaboration.

5.   *Most political parties and pressure groups evolve to promote the economic interests of their members.* While the fit is far from perfect, the parties to the right of center are favored by the prosperous segments of society, while the parties to the left are favored by the working class.

6.   *As a general principle, the political activities of individuals will mirror their economic interests.* This approach to political economy is often referred to as public choice analysis. The basic premise of public choice analysis is that individuals are "egotistic, rational, utility maximizers" (Mueller 1979, 1). Greed is the great political motivator. In some instances, the link between economic logic and political behavior is direct, with individuals supporting the candidate or position that is most likely to provide an immediate economic payoff such as lower taxes or increased welfare payments. More often than not, however, individuals vote according to their general assessments of how well the country is doing. If the country is viewed as prospering, the incumbents are supported. If the country is perceived to be in an economic decline, the ruling party or coalition is frequently turned out of office (Lewis-Beck 1988). This is not always the case, but such patterns occur with sufficient frequency to establish economics as one of the primary predictors of mass voting behavior.

Most of the principles of political economy also apply to politics at the international level. As with domestic politics, international politics is underscored by conflict over scarce resources. Conflict management at the international level often involves economic payoffs. Rich states usually enjoy greater influence in the international arena than poor states. Much like individuals, states may be predicted to act as rational utility maximizers in pursuing their economic interests. The more one examines the economic dimensions of international politics, political economists argue, the greater will be one's ability to explain and predict international political events (Frieden and Lake 1987).

Culture and Comparative Politics

Economics is an important aspect of comparative political analysis, yet it is but one part of a very complex puzzle. As Karl Marx himself would note, people often have a difficult time understanding their own economic self-interest. Rather than behaving as rational economic actors, observed Marx, people often allow themselves to be swayed by the emotions that accompany religion and nationalism. Economics is important, but so are security, freedom, power, pride, religiosity, love, belonging, nationalism, and a list of other values too long to mention (Maslow 1970; Kroeber and Kluckhohn 1963).

What Karl Marx was referring to, of course, was the influence of culture on politics.

The Two Faces of Culture.   Because culture is such a broad and complex phenomenon, it may be helpful to view culture as having two faces: an external face and an internal

---

What Is Culture?

The way people respond to their political leaders and political institutions depends upon what they consider to be important. It is **culture** that tells people what they should consider important, that defines standards of good and bad and right and wrong, and that provides individuals with an identity. It tells individuals who they are and what they are. Culture also defines the roles that an individual is to play in life and explains how those roles are to be played (Douglas and Wildavsky 1982). It tells individuals what is expected of them and how to get along with other people (Gross and Rayner 1985). Beyond that, culture provides individuals with religions and ideologies that explain how their society came to exist, why it is the best of all possible worlds, and why some individuals should have more of the good things of life than others.

---

face. The **external face of culture** consists of *national myths, ideologies, religions, and other belief systems that a society uses to socialize or "program" its citizens.* **Socialization** is *the process of indoctrinating people into their culture.* The socialization process begins with the parents and continues through a wide variety of religious, social, and political institutions. The schools play a major role in the socialization process, as does the mass media. The more effective a society is at socializing its citizens, the more likely it is that those citizens will absorb a common set of political, economic, and social values.

The second face of culture is **internal**. *It is based on the psychology of the individual and consists of the cultural beliefs that have actually been absorbed by the citizens of a society.* It is important to recognize the differences between the two faces of culture. External culture is the content of socialization; it is what a society would like its people to believe. Internal culture, by contrast, is what people actually believe. It consists of the predispositions, values, and attitudes that shape the way in which they view their world.[9] The more individuals buy into their culture, the more cohesive society is likely to be.

Political socialization in most First World societies is very effective. Parents, peers, schools, churches, and the media all convey more or less the same message: "The political system is fair, and it must be supported. It may not be perfect, but all things considered, it is the best one for us."

Many less-developed countries are experiencing a great deal of cultural turmoil. The government has one vision of what society should look like, while religious, ethnic, regional, and political groups have other ideas. Individuals in such societies tend to be poorly socialized. The message presented by the government in the media and in the schools conflicts with that being presented by parents and by religious or ethnic associations. Who is to be believed: the state, the church, or the family? Should ethnic and religious loyalties be set aside for the sake of the unity of the country, or should each ethnic group fight to create its own independent country?

Diversity in Culture. *The cultural values and predispositions that individuals absorb from the socialization process* provide them with a **cultural map** for making choices about politics, economics, and almost everything else of importance in their lives. Individuals are bombarded with so many pieces of information on a daily basis that they cannot possibly worry about them all. Their cultural map helps them sort things out. If communism is bad, everything related to communism is bad. If democracy is good, everything related to democracy must also be good. As a practical matter, most

---

[9]It is important to note that values and attitudes do not always determine behavior. For example, people often have a strong emotional feeling for one party but vote for another one for economic reasons. The converse is equally true.

Cultures often change gradually, as a result of outside influences. Here, two Chinese women are shown conversing outside a McDonald's restaruant in northeastern Beijing.

attitudes and opinions come prepackaged in the cultural map. The more an individual's cultural map is understood, accordingly, the easier it will be to predict and explain his or her political behavior.

As most individuals are socialized to accept the culture of their society, it is reasonable to assume some degree of cultural uniformity among the citizens of that society. Not all Americans share the same cultural map, but the cultural map internalized by most Americans tends to be distinct from the cultural map internalized by most Russians or most Chinese.

While it is reasonable to say that certain values or attitudes are very prevalent in German or Russian society, it would be profoundly inaccurate to suggest that all Germans or all Russians possess the same cultural map. If they did, predicting German or Russian politics would be remarkably simple. Quite obviously, this is not the case. While most Germans share some values in common, the variations within German society remain infinite. Most Germans, as will be elaborated in Chapter 4, possess a strong commitment to democratic principles. A minority, however, continue to manifest the fascist views of an earlier era. Culture, moreover, is forever changing. The authoritarian virtues of an earlier era are being replaced by more liberal and egalitarian values of the present era. The ebb and flow of change occurs within all cultures.

Political Culture. Culture not only possess an external face and an internal face, but it also comes in several varieties. It is now common to speak of political culture, economic culture, and artistic culture, among others. **Political culture** is *that aspect of culture that seems to have the greatest influence in shaping the way people behave politically* (Almond 1956). From the **external** perspective, political culture consists of *ideologies, myths, and religions that individuals are socialized to believe*. It is the content of political socialization. From the **internal** or individual perspective, political culture focuses on *people's orientations to politics: their attitudes and opinions about political leaders, political movements, political events, and political institutions*. It encompasses their feelings of legitimacy and alienation, their sense of national identity, and the political groups with which they identify.

Unfortunately, it is not always easy to draw a clear line between what is political and what is not (Inglehart and Abramson 1994). The **economic culture** of a society, *or the value that it places on hard work and innovation*, plays a critical role in determining both the quality of life that its citizens will enjoy and the resource base that will be available to its politicians. **Artistic culture** is also intensely political. *Politics lives on symbols, and it is the arts that give expression to those symbols*. As such, they are part and parcel of the processes of political control and political mobilization. While it is useful to speak of a political culture, it is important that the line between political culture and other specialized cultures not be drawn too precisely. It is difficult to find any dimension of culture without political relevance.

Culture and Comparative Political Analysis. Culture has become such an important dimension of comparative politics that its uses as an analytical tool are not easily summarized. The following points, however, are among the most important.

First, the type of culture that a society possesses often influences the type of political system that it can sustain (Mueller and Seligson 1994). Democratic political systems seem to work best in cultures that emphasize tolerance, individual freedom, trust, civic responsibility, and the belief that individuals can play a major role in shaping their own destinies (Almond and Verba 1963).[10] Cultures that preach racial or religious purity provide a difficult environment for democracy, as do cultures that stress the values of obedience, conformity, and power. Following the end of World War II, many people openly questioned whether the cultures of Germany and Japan could sustain democratic regimes. They survived, but they also underwent changes. The same questions are now being asked in regard to the countries of the former Soviet Union, a region profoundly lacking in democratic traditions.

Second, cultural problems also challenge the internal cohesion of many countries in the Third World, some of which remain mosaics of diverse ethnic, tribal, and religious groups united by little more than a common colonial history (Diamond 1994). Cultural attachments to ethnic or religious groups remain stronger than cultural attachments to the state, and interactions among members of different ethnic and religious groups are marked by suspicion and distrust. The tragic results of this state of affairs in Nigeria are examined at length in Chapter 11.

Third, culture influences the ability of political leaders to control their populations and to mobilize those populations in support of their policy objectives. During the Second World War, the fascist regimes in Germany and Japan used nationalistic symbols to wring extraordinary sacrifices from their populations, as did the British and the

---

[10]Recent research suggests that this may be less the case than originally assumed, but the debate on the issue will not be resolved for some time (Mueller and Seligson 1994).

Americans. Such sacrifices were made possible by the intense sense of national identity among the populations involved. The collapse of the USSR in 1991, by contrast, was underscored by a lack of cultural support among its citizens. Slogans and other symbols calling for increased sacrifice and productivity fell on deaf ears. The Soviet state was strong enough to control its citizens by force, but it lacked the cultural symbols necessary to mobilize the Soviet population in support of its goals.

Finally, cultural analysis helps us to predict the future course that the politics of a country is likely to take. Cultures are always changing and evolving. German and Japanese cultures, for example, have become increasingly democratic over the course of the past five decades. Most students of Germany and Japan feel confident that the democracies of both countries now rest on a firm bedrock of democratic culture. Authoritarianism, in their view, has become a thing of the past.

Some cultural analysts find the countries of the First World to be developing a post-material culture (Inglehart 1990). The culture of hard work and productivity that created their prosperity and world dominance now shows signs of eroding as concern for leisure time and the environment outpace the drive for wealth. Not all cultural analysts, however, are convinced that this situation is permanent, arguing that economic values will reassert their influence during periods of scarcity (Flanagan 1987).

International Interdependence and the New World Order

The collapse of the Soviet Union in 1991 marked a dramatic turning point in world affairs. The Cold War that had maintained the world on the brink of a nuclear holocaust for more than four decades had come to an end. The United States and its allies in the First World proclaimed the existence of a "new world order" based upon international cooperation and interdependence. The goals of the new world order were to build an international community that was democratic, stable, prosperous, humane, equitable in the distribution of life's opportunities, and protective of the environment. Capitalism would lead to economic prosperity.

Whatever the fanfare accompanying the proclamation of a new world order, the growing interdependence of the world community was already becoming an accomplished fact (Keohane and Nye 1989; Parry 1994). Reflecting this interdependence, many scholars now find it useful to speak of a **world political system** and a **world (capitalist) economic system** (Rogowski 1994). Such concepts are difficult to pin down with precision. The concept of a world (international) political system derives from the observation that relations between nations seem to follow certain regularized patterns (Kaplan 1957). Prior to the Second World War, the international system was characterized by a balance of power. If one state became too aggressive, the other major powers of the world would unite to cut it down to size. Following World War II, the international system was dominated by "Cold War" conflict between two superpowers, the United States and the Soviet Union. After the Soviet Union collapsed, the system evolved into a new world order dominated by the US and its allies. As yet, however, there is no international body to enforce the standards of the new world order.

The concept of a world economic system is based upon the observation that economic activity in the world today is dominated by the world's capitalist superpowers and by an expanding list of multinational corporations that rival individual countries in their power and influence (Wallerstein 1984).

The international economic system finds tangible expression in a variety of organizations (Walters and Blake 1992).

G-7: The world's seven major capitalist powers: the United States, Canada, Japan, the United Kingdom, France, Germany, Italy.

> ## Limited Powers of the UN
>
> The United Nations aspires to enforced the standards of the new world order but lacks the authority to implement its lofty ideals. Its powers are limited to those granted it by the United States and other major powers on a temporary and ad hoc basis. When the major powers agree on policy, the UN is effective in executing that policy. When they do not, it is ineffective.

International Monetary Fund (IMF) and the World Bank: These two organizations were established at the end of World War II to facilitate the reconstruction of a war-torn Europe and to reestablish order within the world economy. Once the reconstruction of Europe was complete, the IMF and the World Bank became the major economic agencies charged with stimulating economic development in the poorer states of the Third World. World Bank and IMF loans are designed to facilitate the economic development of the states of the Third World and to assist them in paying their debts to their creditors, most of whom reside in the First World. The World Bank makes long-term loans, and the IMF specializes in short-term loans.* The World Bank has also placed increased emphasis on stimulating democracy in the states that it assists. Both organizations are controlled by member countries with voting power reflecting the size of a state's financial contribution.† Countries that follow the "rules" of the international system receive loans, and those who break them do not. As most Third World states are hopelessly in debt, the IMF and the World Bank exert enormous influence over their domestic politics.

The World Trade Organization (WTO): The WTO is designed to regulate the level of tariffs that countries can place on the exports of their competitors. As in the case of the international political system, the international economic system works best when the major powers are in agreement. Nothing can be imposed on a major power against its will.

The tremendous wealth and economic power of multinational corporations enables them to evade the control of individual countries and to shape the economic policies of their host governments. Perhaps more problematic is the conflict of interests between individual countries and multinational corporations. The policies of most multinational corporations reflect the interests of shareholders rather than those of individual countries and their leaders. The political leaders of the United States, for example, would prefer that US-based corporations create jobs in the United States rather than in Europe, Asia, or Latin America. Such decisions, however, are made on the basis of corporate interests rather than the immediate interests of the United States. Indeed, a situation now exists in which globalization of economic affairs has far surpassed the globalization of political affairs. Multinational corporations are international in scope, but there is no corresponding international political authority to keep them in check. The international system is presumed to work to the advantage of the world's stronger economies. States with weaker economies survive by following the rules established by the "system." Those who choose not to play by the rules find themselves ostracized from the system and suffer accordingly.

---

*The World Bank operates as a bank, while the IMF operates as a large, international credit union. Member states pay into the IMF and have the right to borrow up to 20 percent of the contribution without restriction. Larger loans must be approved by the governing board of the IMF (Bird 1995).
†This arrangement provides the rich states of the First World with a determining voice in both organizations.

Interdependence or Dependence? Some political observers believe that *the powerful countries of the First World use their dominant economic power to keep Third World countries in a permanent state of dependence or poverty.* This view is referred to as **dependency theory** (Cardoso 1972; Frank 1984; Chilcote 1981). The central theme of dependency theory is strikingly simple. The international society, like all societies, suffers from a shortage of scarce resources. If some states are to be rich, others must be poor. Much as in colonial days, the large industrial countries of the West increase their wealth by using the Third World as a cheap source of raw materials. They also use the poor countries of the Third World as a dumping ground for industrial products they can't sell elsewhere. In the eyes of the dependency theorists, nothing has really changed. Old-fashioned military colonialism has merely been replaced by more insidious forms of economic and cultural colonialism. While the countries of the Third World are nominally independent, the First World continues to dictate the pace of their economic, political, and social development.

In seeming contradiction to dependency theory, many countries in the Third World have experienced dramatic economic development in recent decades. This has been particularly true in South Korea, Singapore, and Taiwan, the tigers of Asia. It has also been true of Brazil, Chile, and Mexico. Indeed, most of the traditional industrial powers of the First World are now seeing their industrial base eroded as multinational corporations shift their production to the countries of the Third World in search of cheaper labor and relaxed environmental standards.

Some countries of the Third World are experiencing economic miracles, yet most remain desperately poor. Indeed, many dependency theorists believe that the countries of the First World have allowed a few countries of the Third World to develop in order to better dominate the majority. According to this argument, the tigers of Asia were allowed to develop because the countries of the First World needed a counterweight to the power of Communist China in the Far East.

In dependency jargon, the countries of the First World represent the core of the international system, while the poor countries of the Third World represent the periphery. States of the Third World that have been allowed to develop are referred to as semi-periphery (Wallerstein 1984).

Most of the countries that have been allowed to develop, moreover, have experienced uneven development in which the rich have gotten richer, but the poor remain locked in poverty. This is particularly the case in Brazil and Mexico. Regardless of whether the dependency point of view is correct, most people in the poorer countries of the Third World believe that it is. Why else would they be poor? Dependency theory will be examined at greater length in the chapters on Indian, Mexican, Egyptian, and Nigerian politics.

In reality, the realignments forced by the new interdependence have placed stress on all countries of the world community, rich as well as poor. As tariffs and other obstacles of free trade have fallen by the wayside, an increasing number of industries have relocated to countries and regions that enjoy a comparative advantage in terms of costs and efficiency (Chenery and Moshe 1975). According to the doctrine of **comparative advantage**, *a truly free world market will allow each country to specialize in what it does best.* Countries with cheap labor will become the focal point of labor-intensive industries, while countries with a highly skilled work force, such as the United States, Japan, and Germany, will specialize in high-tech industries. One illustration of this phenomenon can be found in the European coal industry. Abundant coal resources were the backbone of the industrial revolution in Western Europe, but European coal mines are now too deep and too expensive to operate in comparison with mines located in the less-industrialized areas of the world. Many Western European mines, accordingly, are now in the process of being closed.

As one would expect, those domestic forces that stand to prosper from increased global interdependence have been using their political and economic influence to pave the way for ever-greater cooperation within the world community. The prospective losers—and there are many—are marshalling their political resources to restrict further erosion of their political, economic, and cultural positions. This battle is currently being fought in almost every country in the world.

The Emergence of Supra-States: The Case of the European Union. For more than three centuries, the state has represented the world's dominant form of political organization. International organizations existed, but sovereignty resided with the state. Increasingly, however, states have found that the coordination of their affairs requires the transfer of at least some sovereignty to supranational organizations. The **European Union (EU)** represents by far the most advanced stage in this process, with its *fifteen member countries having transferred broad areas of their economic sovereignty to a supranational government located in Brussels.* (See Figure 1.1.) The member countries of the EU have also signed a treaty that may eventually lead to the formation of a United States of Europe. While it is premature to speak of a European supra-state, the process of regional integration has reached the point at which it is no longer possible to discuss the politics of Britain, France, Germany, or other Western European countries without reference to the European Union.

The influence of the EU, moreover, extends far beyond the confines of its member countries. Eastern European and Middle Eastern countries aspiring to join the EU are now attempting to bring themselves in line with its political and economic standards. Among other things, this has encouraged the establishment of free-market economies and the strengthening of democratic institutions. Even countries far removed from the EU have had to adjust to the presence of a competitor far more formidable than any one of the fifteen Western European countries standing alone. Clearly, the evolution of a European supra-state has been a major force in stimulating the greater economic integration of both North America and the Far East.

The Evolution of the European Union. The first major step leading to the integration of Western Europe was the creation of the European Coal and Steel Community in 1951, an agreement that transferred the regulation of coal and steel production to a supranational body established by the member states. In 1957, the Treaty of Rome created the European Economic Community (EEC), thereby establishing the framework for a European common market. In 1965, the governing bodies of the Coal and Steel Community and the EEC were merged into a single European Community, as were the governing bodies of related organizations such as the European Atomic Energy Commission and the European Economic and Social Council.[11]

Although the integration of Europe began as a largely economic venture, the 1960s also saw the creation of a symbolic **European Parliament**,[12] the first direct

---

[11]France, Germany, Belgium, The Netherlands, Italy, and Luxembourg were the initial signatories to the agreement creating the Coal and Steel Community, thus establishing themselves as the core of the unification effort, Britain, long a skeptic, was admitted to the EEC in 1971, and by the mid-1990s, membership in the European Union had expanded to include Spain, Portugal, Ireland, Greece, Sweden, Denmark, Austria, and Finland, bringing the total membership to fifteen.

[12]The European Parliament was referred to as the European Assembly until 1986.

Figure 1.1
The fifteen members of the European Union (shaded countries).

elections to which were held in 1979. While representatives to the European Parliament currently have little power, elections to the European Parliament are used as a test of strength by all the major political parties in Europe and are hotly contested. A seat on the European Parliament is also a mark of considerable prestige, and there is no shortage of qualified candidates. If the present pace of integration can be maintained, the power of the European Parliament will eventually rival that of national parliaments.

The next step in the evolution of a European supra-state was the signing of the **Maastricht Treaty,** the terms of which entered into force on January 1, 1993. *The Maastricht Treaty transformed the European Community into the European Union (EU) and provided the framework for the eventual political unification of its member countries.* Within a transition period of approximately ten years, according to the Maastricht Treaty, the government of the European Union would create one common European currency **(the euro)** to replace all national currencies and assume broad authority in the areas of foreign affairs, trade, and environmental policy. Wealth would also be equalized among the member states, and a common

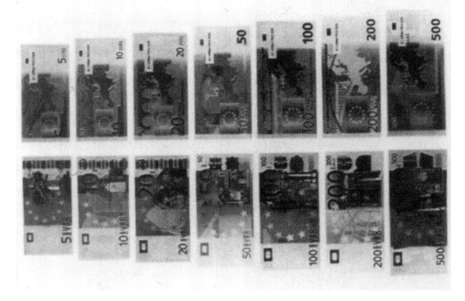

Many, but not all, of the countries in the European Union have adopted the "euro" as their common currency. A euro from any participating EU country can be used to purchase goods or services within any other participating EU country.

European citizenship would enable citizens of the EU to work and vote in the region of their choice. Particularly sensitive were negotiations for a "social chapter" that called for uniform standards of health insurance, social security, unemployment benefits, gender equality, and labor relations.[13]

Despite initial skepticism, the turn of the century has seen important progress being made toward achieving the goals of Maastricht. Commerce now flows with minimal restraint among the member countries of the EU much as it flows among the fifty states of the US. Eleven members of the EU adopted the "Euro" as a common currency on January 1, 1999. This represents a major delegation of national sovereignty, as the participating states can no longer use their currency as a tool of national policy. Some countries, for example, borrow heavily or print generous amounts of money as a means of paying their bills, a process that weakens the value of their currency and leads to inflation. People in debt prefer limited inflation, because it makes it easier to pay off their loans. Other countries regulate their currencies with great rigor in order to assure that inflation will not undermine the value of investments and destroy the value of people's savings. These decisions are now being made by a Central European Bank with powers similar to those of the Federal Reserve Bank in the US. Most, but not all, countries have accepted the "social chapter" of the Maastricht Treaty, a process that has led to common labor and welfare laws throughout much of Europe.

The Future of Europe. While dramatic progress has been made toward the unification of Europe, many problems have yet to be resolved. The common currency is used only in some of the core states, with other states being either reluctant to give up a

---

[13]The Maastricht Treaty is an incredibly complex document, only parts of which were signed by all states. Many of the provisions took the form of special annexes or were the product of complex bilateral negotiations.

Table 1.2
Power Sharing in the EU

EU Member	% of EU Population	Votes in Council of Ministers	Seats in EU Parliament	No. of EU Commissioners
Germany	22.0	10	99	2
Britain	15.7	10	87	2
France	15.6	10	87	2
Italy	15.4	10	87	2
Spain	10.5	8	64	2
Netherlands	4.1	5	31	1
Greece	2.8	5	25	1
Belgium	2.7	5	25	1
Portugal	2.7	5	25	1
Sweden	2.4	4	22	1
Austria	2.2	4	21	1
Denmark	1.4	3	16	1
Finland	1.4	3	16	1
Ireland	1.0	3	15	1
Luxembourg	0.1	2	6	1

Source: The Economist, February 1, 1997, 54.

major slice of their national sovereignty (Britain) or failing to qualify for the rigorous standards set for membership in the currency union.

Britain and Denmark have refused to accept the social chapter of the Maastricht Treaty, and both Germany and Britain believe that they are paying more than their fair share of EU expenses. Both, accordingly, are unlikely to favor larger transfer payments to the poorer members of the EU.

Other problems abound as well. Proponents of greater unity enjoy only a slight majority in most countries. Presumably, they could opt out with a major swing in public opinion, although that is most unlikely. The member states also disagree on the pace of future unification. Germany and France appear anxious to move toward total federation, while Britain and Scandinavian states are reluctant to expand beyond present levels of economic integration. Indeed, the British prefer a broad menu of unification possibilities, with each state being able to pick and choose those options most compatible with its national interests. The Germans and French, by contrast, reject what they refer to as an "à la carte" approach to nation building, proposing instead that an "inner core" within the European Union move rapidly toward full integration, leaving the remainder to catch up as they see fit.

Fault lines exist between the rich states and the poor states. As indicated in Table 1.2, all EU institutions are biased in favor of the smaller states. Tiny Luxembourg with only .1 percent of the EU's population possesses two votes on the Council of Ministers, while Germany with 22 percent of the EU's population has but ten. The ratio is even worse on the European Commission, with Germany having two commissioners to Luxembourg's one.

Also problematic are differing economic philosophies, with Britain and Germany advocating laissez-faire economic policies, while France and Spain favor

Governing Institutions of the EU
(Arranged from Most Powerful to the Least Powerful)

Institution	Composition	Role
European Council	A periodic "summit meeting" of the prime ministers of the fifteen member states in the European Union.	Sets the broad guidelines of the EU policy. All decisions must be unanimous if they are to become EU policy. In effect, this means that any country, however small, can block major policy initiatives.
Council of Ministers	Consists of a cabinet-level minister from each country assisted by a number of "permanent representatives" depending on the size of the country. As indicated in Table 1.2, the larger states have 10 votes on the Council, while the smallest have 2. All representatives on the Council of Ministers are selected by their national government and vote as a unit.	Representatives of the Council of Ministers are selected by their national governments and vote as a unit. Some issues on the Council of Ministers are decided by a plurality of 70 percent. Most issues involving education, the environment, transportation, and health fall in this category. Issues of defense, security, and foreign affairs require unanimity, as do issues of great sensitivity in all areas.
European Commission	The European Commission consists of a "college" of twenty members nominated by the member countries of the European Union with the implied accord of the other member countries and the president of the Commission. The president of the Commission is selected by the member countries with the agreement of the European Parliament. Commissioners serve four-year terms and supervise the bureaucracy of the European Union. They are expected to act in the best interests of the EU and not to receive instructions from their home countries. Each of the twenty members of the Commission, including the president, has one vote.	At least for the moment, the role of the European Commission is to execute the decisions taken by the Council of Ministers within the general guidelines established by the European Council Supporters of greater integration hope that the European Commission will evolve into a government of Europe guided by the European Parliament. This is not currently the case, but the officials of the European Commission execute the powers available to them with great vigor—too much vigor for the taste of some member countries.

(continued on next page)

strong doses of government intervention. Fears also persist over continued German domination of the EU. Germany possesses the strongest economy in the EU, as well as the largest population. Its geographic location would also make it the core of an expanded union that included the more prosperous states of Eastern Europe.

Finally, it should be noted that the members of the EU are finding the prospect of political unity to be far more daunting than that of economic unity. In forging an economic union, the circle of potential winners within each country was larger than the circle of potential losers. The situation is far less clear and far more emotional with regard to political unity. While proponents of closer federalism argue that true economic integration requires closer political integration, nationalism and the myth of national sovereignty continue to be powerful emotional forces throughout Western Europe.

Governing Institutions of the EU
(Arranged from Most Powerful to the Least Powerful)

European Parliament	Consists of some 626 deputies chosen in direct election by the populations of the member states. Seats in the Parliament are allocated roughly in proportion to the population of the member states.	The Parliament meets in Strasbourg and must approve the EU budget, can veto some legislation, and must approve the appointment of the Commission President. These are minor powers when compared to those of the Council of Ministers, but they will increase as the member states move, however hesitantly toward greater political unity.
European Court of Justice	The court currently consists of fifteen judges selected by the mutual agreement of the member states.	Located in Luxembourg, the European Court of Justice adjudicates disputes arising from EU treaties and laws. Its decisions are binding upon member states as long as they remain with the scope of the treaties in force.
Central European Bank	Made up of countries that are members of the European Monetary Union (countries that use the euro as a common currency). The Bank began operation in 1999.	Located in Frankfurt, the Central European Bank serves as the central regulatory bank for countries that are members of the European Monetary Union.

Despite all of the obstacles that stand in the way of a federated Europe, the European Union has emerged as a powerful supranational entity that has a profound impact upon the policies of its member countries. The full integration of Western Europe now appears to be inevitable, the only question being one of time. Eleven other countries are also expected to join the EU in the next few years, an expansion that will allow it to surpass the US in population and economic clout.

Political Interdependence and Comparative Political Analysis

The growing interdependence of the international community has a profound influence on the politics of its member countries, the most important dimensions of which are listed below.

1. *Economic interdependence strengthens political interdependence.* The more countries create integrated economic zones such as the European Union or the North American Free Trade Area, the more policy making will shift from national governments to international agencies. This process is in its infancy in North America but has become a reality in Western Europe.

2. *Countries are increasingly being forced to pursue policies that enhance their international competitiveness.* Those that are less competitive in the world market will find it difficult to survive. The increasing globalization of the world economy is thus forcing a reorientation in domestic labor relations throughout the industrialized world. The classic struggle between business and labor is giving way to a struggle between industries that prosper from international competition and those that do not. The more the economy becomes globalized, the more this trend will continue.

3.   *Most countries of the Third World lack the capacity to compete with the countries of the First World in the production of "clean," technologically sophisticated products.* Their comparative advantage, accordingly, lies in cheap labor and in their willingness to accept dirty industries cast off by the West. It also lies in the export of minerals and other primary products. This forces the citizens of the Third World to work in low-paying, labor-intensive jobs that often pose a risk to their health. It also increases unemployment in the countries of the First World as multinational corporations move factories to the countries of the Third World in search of higher profits. The countries of the First World may soon find that the price of retaining their traditional heavy industries is a reduction in wages and environmental standards. Such possibilities are the topic of heated debate throughout the countries of the First World, with the outcome still uncertain.

4.   *Citizens of poor countries will seek employment in rich states* (Weiner 1995). Immigrant populations are blamed for unemployment problems in the countries of the First World. They are also blamed for increases in crime and social unrest. Whether or not this is the case, immigration will continue for as long as the states of the Third World remain locked in poverty.

5.   *Countries that are dependent upon foreign assistance are increasingly being forced to institute capitalist economic systems and democratic political systems.* They are also being pressured to display greater concern for human rights and the environment. Such pressures, however, are tentative, and the donor community has been fearful of pushing too hard in the area of democracy and human rights for fear of offending member countries.[14]

Global problems require global solutions. Pollution, war, terrorism, immigration, and other threats to the life style of the First World are increasingly rooted in the poverty and social instability of the Third and Fourth Worlds. They will not come to an end until that poverty and social instability also comes to an end.

Putting the Parts Together: Analyzing Total Systems

Each of the diverse components of comparative political analysis reviewed in this chapter offers important insights into the ways in which societies decide who gets what, when, and how. Politics, however, is more than the sum of its parts. It is a total process that involves the continuous interaction or meshing of those parts. All of the components of the political process are influenced to some extent by the others.

Efforts to predict or explain politics that focus on a single factor, such as economics, elites, or culture, often produce results that, while persuasive, are one-sided and incomplete. In this regard, one is reminded of the parable of the three blind men and the elephant.

> The first blind man seized the elephant's trunk and pronounced him to be long and tubular, much like a giant snake. The second encountered the elephant's ear and found him to be thin, flat, and supple. The third came to his tail, declaring him to be much like a whip.

The more political analysis can integrate all of the various dimensions of the political process, the more accurate it is likely to be.

---

[14]The author has been a consultant for several aid-granting agencies.

Using This Text

In the chapters that follow, we use the perspectives of comparative political analysis outlined in Chapter 1 to examine the politics of the United Kingdom, France, Germany, Japan, Russia, the People's Republic of China, India, Mexico, Egypt, and Nigeria. Each chapter begins with an examination of the *history* of the country in question. This historical survey is followed by review of the country's *political institutions* and a discussion of the *elites, political parties, pressure groups, and masses* that give life to those institutions. This accomplished, we turn next to the broader *cultural, economic, and international context* underlying the political process in each country. Finally, we conclude each country study by examining the challenges that the country faces in the areas of *democracy, stability, human rights, economic growth, quality of life, and concern for the environment,* which are the criteria established by the United Nations and its related agencies as the standards of good government.

References

Aberbach, J. 1981. *Bureaucrats and Politicians.* Cambridge, MA: Harvard University Press.

Alexander, Jeffrey C., and Paul Colmy, eds. 1990. *Differentiation Theory and Social Change.* New York: Columbia University Press.

Almond, Gabriel A. 1956. "Comparative Political Systems." *Journal of Politics* 18: 391–409.

Almond, Gabriel, and Sidney Verba. 1963. *The Civic Culture.* Princeton, NJ: Princeton University Press.

Beard, Charles A. 1913. *An Economic Interpretation of the Constitution of the United States.* New York: Macmillan.

Bill, James A., and Robert L. Hardgrave, Jr. 1981. *Comparative Politics: The Quest for Theory.* Lanham, MD: University Press of America. (Originally published in 1973.)

Bird, Graham. 1995. *IMF Lending to Developing Countries: Issues and Evidence.* London: Routledge.

Blau, Peter, and M. Meyer, eds. 1987. *Bureaucracy in Modern Society.* 3rd ed. New York: Random House.

Blondel, Jean. 1968. "Party Systems and Patterns of Government in Western Democracies." *Canadian Journal of Political Science* 1(2): 180–203.

Bollen, Kenneth. 1979. "Issues in the Comparative Measurement of Political Democracy." *American Sociological Review* 44: 572–87.

Bollen, Kenneth, and Robert Jackman. 1985. "Political Democracy and the Size Distribution of Income." *American Sociological Review* 50: 438–57.

Brierly, J. L. 1963. *The Law of Nations: An Introduction to the International Law of Peace.* New York: Oxford University Press.

Budge, Ian, David Robertson, and Derek Hearl, eds. 1987. *Ideology, Strategy and Party Change.* Cambridge: Cambridge University Press.

Caporaso, James A., ed. 1989. *The Elusive State: International and Comparative Perspectives.* Newbury Park, CA: Sage.

Cardoso, Fernando H. 1972 (July–Aug.). "Dependency and Development in Latin America." *New Left Review* 74: 83–95.

Chenery, Hollis, and Syraquin Moshe. 1975. *Patterns of Development, 1950–1970.* New York: Oxford University Press for World Book.

Chilcote, Ronald H. 1981. *Theories of Comparative Politics: The Search for a Paradigm.* Boulder, CO: Westview.

Clark, Barry S. 1991. *Political Economy: A Comparative Approach.* New York: Praeger.

Coker, Francis. 1934. *Recent Political Thought.* New York: Appleton-Century-Crofts.

Dahl, Robert A. 1961. *Who Governs.* New Haven, CT: Yale University Press.

Dahl, Robert. 1971. *Polyarchy: Participation and Opposition.* New Haven, CT: Yale University Press.

Dahl, Robert. 1985. *A Preface to Economic Democracy.* Berkeley, CA: University of California Press.

Davies, James. 1963. *Human Nature and Politics.* New York: Wiley.

Diamond, Larry, ed. 1994. *Political Culture and Democracy in Developing Countries.* Boulder, CO: Lynne Rienner.

Diamond, Larry, Juan L. Linz, and Seymour Lipset. 1990. *Politics in Developing Countries: Comparing Experiences with Democracies.* Boulder, CO: Lynne Rienner.

Dogan, Mattei, and Dominique Pelassy. 1990. *How to Compare Nations: Strategies in Comparative Politics.* Chatham, NJ: Chatham House.

Douglas, Mary, and Aaron Wildavsky. 1982. *Risk and Culture.* Berkeley: University of California Press.

Duverger, Maurice. 1954. *Political Parties: Their Organization and Activity in the Modern State.* New York: Wiley.

Dye, Thomas R. 1976. *Who's Running America?* Englewood Cliffs, NJ: Prentice-Hall.

Easton, David. 1953. *The Political System: An Inquiry into the State of Political Science.* New York: Knopf.

Edwards, Chris. 1985. *The Fragmented World: Competing Perspectives on Trade, Money, and Crisis.* New York: Methuen.

Epstein, Gerald, Julie Grahm, and Jessica Nembhard, eds. 1993. *Creating a New World Economy: Forces of Change and Plans for Action.* Philadelphia: Temple University Press.

Epstein, Leon D. 1967. *Political Parties in Western Democracies.* New York: Praeger.

Evans, Peter, Dietrich Rueschemeyer, and Thelda Skoupol. 1985. *Bringing the State Back In.* Cambridge: Cambridge University Press.

Feierabend, I. K., R. L. Feierabend, and B. A. Nesvold. 1967. "Social Change and Political Violence: Cross-National Patterns." In *Violence in America: Historical and Comparative Perspectives,* ed. G. D. Graham and T. R. Gurr. New York: Bantam Books.

Flanagan, Scott. 1987. "Value Change in Industrial Societies." *American Poltical Science Review.* 81(4): 1303–19.

Frank, Andre. 1984. *Critique and Anti-Critique: Essays on Dependence and Reformism.* New York: Praeger.

Fried, Robert C. 1966. *Comparative Political Institutions.* New York: Macmillan.

Frieden, Jeffry A., and David A. Lake. 1987. *International Political Economy: Perspectives on Global Power and Wealth.* New York: St. Martin's.

Friedman, Milton, and Rose Friedman. 1980. *Freeedom to Choose.* New York: Harcourt Brace Jovanovich.

Friedrich, Carl, and Zbigniew K. Brzezinski. 1956. *Totalitarian Dictatorship and Autocracy.* New York: Praeger.

Friedrich, Carl, and Zbigniew K. Brzezinski. 1964. *Totalitarian Dictatorship and Autocracy.* New York: Praeger.

Gillespie, Charles G. 1987. "From Authoritarian Crisis to Democratic Transition." *Latin American Research Review* 22: 165–85.

Gilpin, Robert. 1987. *The Political Economy of International Relations.* Princeton, NJ: Princeton University Press.

Gross, Donald A., and Lee Sigelman. 1984. "Comparing Party Systems: A Multi-Dimensional Approach." *Comparative Politics* 2: 463–79.

Gross, Jonathan, and Steve Rayner. 1985. *Measuring Culture.* New York: Columbia University Press.

Herz, John H. 1959. *International Politics in the Atomic Age.* New York: Columbia University Press.

Huntington, Samuel P. 1968. *Political Order in Changing Societies.* New Haven, CT: Yale University Press.

Huntington, Samuel P. 1991. *The Third Wave.* Norman, OK: University of Oklahoma Press.

Inglehart, Ronald. 1990. *Culture Shift in Advanced Industrial Society.* Princeton, NJ: Princeton University Press.

Inglehart, Ronald, and Paul R. Abramson. 1994 (June). "Economic Security and Value Change." *American Political Science Review* 88(2): 336–54.

Janda, Kenneth. 1980. *Political Parties. A Cross-National Survey.* New York: Free Press.

Kaplan, Morton A. 1957. *Systems and Processes in International Relations.* New York: Wiley.

Keohane, Robert O., and Joseph S. Nye. 1989. *Power and Interdependence.* 2nd ed. Glenview, IL: Scott, Foresman.

Kim, HeeMin, and Richard Fording. 1994. "Measuring Voter Ideology: A Cross-National Analysis of Western Democracies, 1949–1982." Paper presented at the APSA Convention, New York.

Kirchheimer, Otto. 1966. "The Transformation of the Western European Party Systems." In *Political Parties and Political Development,* ed. Joseph La Palombara and Myron Weiner. Princeton, NJ: Princeton University Press.

Kornhauser, William. 1959. *The Politics of Mass Society.* Glencoe, IL: Free Press.

Kroeber, A. L., and CLyde Kluckhohn. 1963. *Culture: A Critical Review of Concepts and Definitions.* New York: Vintage.

Lasswell, Harold D. 1958. *Politics: Who Gets What, When, How.* New York: World Publishing Co.

Lawson, Kay. 1976. *The Comparative Study of Political Parties.* New York: St. Martin's.

Lerner, Daniel. 1958. *The Passing of Traditional Society.* Glencoe, IL: Free Press.

Lewis-Beck, Michael S. 1988. *Economics and Elections.* Ann Arbor, MI: University of Michigan Press.

Lewis-Beck, Michael S. 1990. *Economics and Elections: The Major Western Democracies.* Ann Arbor, MI: University of Michigan Press.

Lijphart, Arend. 1990 (June). "The Political Consequences of Electoral Laws, 1945–1985." *American Political Science Review* 84(2): 481–96.

Lijphart, Arend, ed. 1992. *Parliamentary Versus Presidential Government.* New York: Oxford University Press.

Lipset, Seymour M. 1960. *Political Man.* Garden City, NY: Doubleday.

Lipset, Seymour M., and Stein Rokkan, eds. 1967. *Party Systems and Voter Alignments: Cross-National Perspectives.* Glencoe, IL: Free Press.

Maslow, Abraham H. 1954. *Motivation and Personality.* New York: Harper & Row.

Maslow, Abraham H. 1970. *Motivation and Personality.* 2nd ed. New York: Harper & Row.

Mendelson, Wallace. 1980. *The American Constitution and the Judicial Process.* Homewood, IL: Dorsey Press.

Michels, Robert. 1959. *Political Parties,* transl. Edan and Cedar Paul. New York: Dover. (Originally published by Free Press, Glencoe, IL, in 1915.)

Mueller, Dennis. 1979. *Public Choice.* New York: Cambridge University Press.

Mueller, Edward N., and Mitchell A. Seligson. 1994 (Sept.). "Civic Culture and Democracy: The Question of Causal Relationships." *American Political Science Review* 88(3): 635–52.

Neumann, Sigmund. 1956. *Modern Political Parties.* Chicago: University of Chicago Press.

Nordlinger, Eric A. 1981. *On the Autonomy of the Democratic State.* Cambridge, MA: Harvard University Press.

Olson, Mancur. 1982. *The Rise and Decline of Nations: Economic Growth, Stagflation and Social Rigidities.* New Haven, CT: Yale University Press.

Parry, Geraint, ed. 1994. *Politics in an Interdependent World: Essays Presented to Ghita Ionescu.* Brookfield, VT: Edward Elgar.

Parsons, Talcott. 1977. *Social Systems and the Evolution of Action Theory.* Glencoe, IL: Free Press.

Putnam, Robert D. 1976. *The Comparative Study of Political Elites.* Englewood Cliffs, NJ: Prentice-Hall.

Ray, James Lee. 1995. *Democracy and International Conflict: An Evaluation of the Democratic Peace Proposition.* Columbia, SC: University of South Carolina Press.

Robertson, David B. 1976. *Theory of Party Competition.* New York: Wiley.

Rogowski, Ronald, ed. 1994. *Comparative Politics in the International Political Economy.* Brookfield, VT: Edward Elgar.

Sartori, Giovanni. 1965. *Democratic Theory.* New York: Cambridge University Press.

Sartori, Giovanni. 1976. *Parties and Party Systems.* London: Cambridge University Press.

Schumacher, Ernest F. 1973. *Small Is Beautiful: Economics as if People Mattered.* New York: Harper & Row.

Schumpeter, Joseph A. 1950. *Capitalism, Socialism, and Democracy.* New York: Harper & Row.

Smith, Adam. 1776. *The Wealth of Nations.* New York: Random House. Republished 1937.

Staniland, Martin. 1985. *What Is Political Economy?* New Haven, CT: Yale University Press.

Todaro, Michael P. 1997. *Economic Development.* 6th ed. New York: Addison-Wesley.

Truman, David B. 1951. *The Governmental Process.* New York: Knopf.

Wallerstein, Immanuel. 1984. *The Politics of the World-Economy.* New York: Cambridge University Press.

Walters, Robert S., and David H. Blake. 1992. *The Politics of Global Economic Relations.* 4th ed. Englewood Cliffs, NJ: Prentice-Hall.

Wang, James C. F. 1994. *Comparative Asian Politics.* Englewood Cliffs, NJ: Prentice-Hall.

Weede, Erich. 1983. "The Impact of Democracy on Economic Growth: Some Evidence for Cross-National Analysis." *Kylos* 36: 21–39

Weede, Erich. 1984. "Political Democracy, State Strength, and Economic Growth in LDCs: A Cross-National Analysis." *Review of International Affairs* 10: 297–312.

Weiner, Myron. 1995. *The Global Migration Crisis: Challenge to States and to Human Rights.* New York: HarperCollins.

The World Bank. 1992a. *World Development Report, 1992: Development and Environment.* New York: Oxford University Press.

The World Bank. 1992b. "Governance and Development." Washington, DC: The World Bank.

Zeigler, Harmon. 1993. *Political Parties in Industrial Democracies.* Itasca, IL: Peacock.

Part Two

Politics in Advanced Industrial Democracies

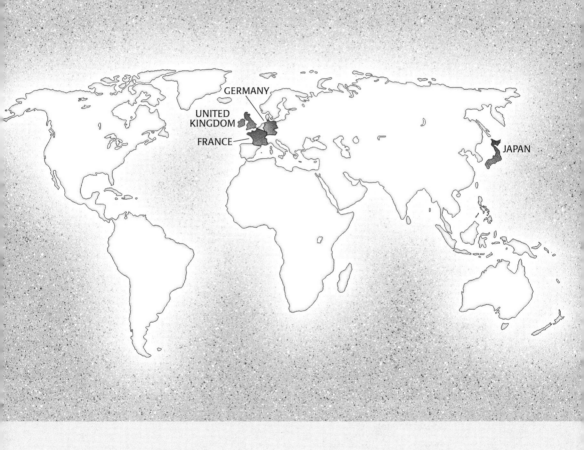

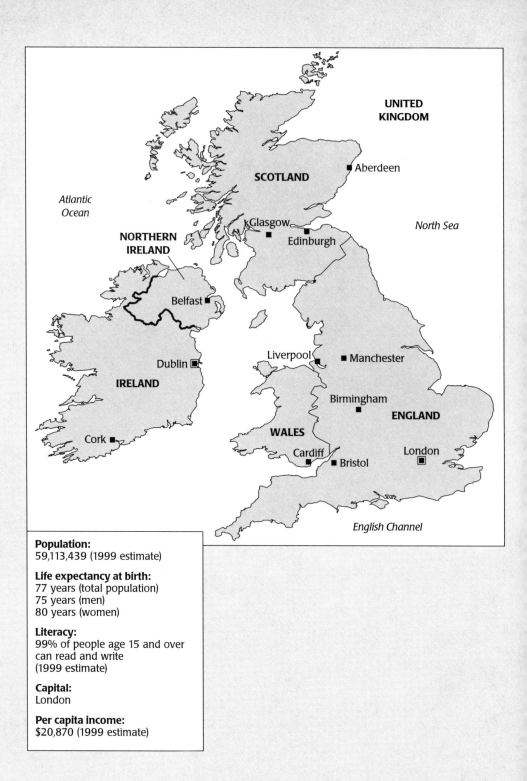

Population:
59,113,439 (1999 estimate)

Life expectancy at birth:
77 years (total population)
75 years (men)
80 years (women)

Literacy:
99% of people age 15 and over
can read and write
(1999 estimate)

Capital:
London

Per capita income:
$20,870 (1999 estimate)

2

The United Kingdom of Great Britain and Northern Ireland
The Origins of Parliamentary Government

> This royal throne of kings, this scepter'd isle,
> This earth of majesty, this seat of Mars,
> This other Eden, demi-paradise,
> This fortress built by Nature for herself
> Against infection and the hand of war,
> This happy breed of men, this little world,
> This precious stone set in the silver sea,
> Which serves it in the office of a wall,
> Or as a moat defensive to a house,
> Against the envy of less happier lands,
> This blessed plot, this earth, this realm, this England.
>
> *Shakespeare, Richard II*

Parliamentary democracy originated in the British Isles. It was exported by the British (albeit without enthusiasm) to their colonies in North America, Australia, and New Zealand. In time, these colonies would form the core of what Winston Churchill would refer to as "the English-Speaking Peoples." Great Britain, the United States, Canada, Australia, and New Zealand, in Churchill's view, represented a unique and superior political tradition (Churchill 1956). All were democratic, all were stable, all were pragmatic in their approach to political affairs, and all were prosperous.

One studies British politics for a variety of reasons.

1. *All democratic political systems in the world today are patterned after either the British parliamentary system or the presidential system of the United States. Most are a blend of both.* It is difficult to understand the differences between the parliamentary and presidential systems, or the blending thereof, without at least a rudimentary understanding of British politics. It should also be noted that parliamentary democracy is the world's most widely practiced form of democratic government.

2. *Britain is one of a small number of First World states that shape the political and economic order of today's world.* Britain is a permanent member of the United Nations Security Council, a charter member of the G-7 club that controls the world economy, the United State's most reliable partner in world affairs, and a key member of the European Union. It is Britain, along with France and Germany, that will determine the future of that Union.

3. *Britain has produced a political system that is among the most tolerant, orderly, and nonviolent in the world.* Perhaps the lessons of British political development are transferable to the emerging nations of Asia, Africa, Latin America, and Eastern Europe. Particularly interesting is the fact that the British do not possess a written constitution. Aside from a few historical documents such as the Magna Carta, the British Constitution is a set of informal traditions that represent a popular consensus concerning the manner in which reasonable people conduct the affairs of state. The British Constitution, moreover, is far more binding than most of the written constitutions in the world today. This suggests that the way people behave is of far more importance to the political process than the words they put on paper.

Our analysis of British politics begins with a brief review of British political history. Next, we study the formal institutions of the British government; then we review the elites, political parties, pressure groups, and citizens who give life to these institutions. Our next focus of discussion is the broader cultural, economic, and international context of British politics. We conclude by considering the challenges that Britain faces in the decade to come.

In the course of analyzing the British political process, we will place special emphasis upon those elements that underscore the remarkable stability of British democracy. We will also examine the problems that Britain has experienced in adjusting to the evolution of a European supra-state of which it must inevitably be a part.

Britain in Historical Perspective: England, Great Britain, and the United Kingdom

Geographically, the British Isles consist of two main islands: Great Britain and Ireland. Great Britain, the larger of the main islands, historically consisted of three countries: England, Wales, and Scotland. The kingdoms of England and Scotland were merged in 1707, but Wales, being considerably smaller than Scotland, had been more or less absorbed by England during an earlier period (Judge 1993). A strong undercurrent of nationalist sentiment remains in both Scotland and Wales, and both have now received increased autonomy from London, including their own parliaments. Alarmed by this trend, a few authors have begun to speak of the unraveling of Britain. While it is doubtful that the United Kingdom is unraveling, there can be no doubt that its informal constitution is being transformed (Keating 1998). The populations of England, Scotland, and Wales are 50 million, 5 million, and 3 million people, respectively.

The Irish component of the United Kingdom is less easy to summarize. The English occupied Ireland in the sixteenth century and ruled the island until the Irish Civil War of

Officials from Northern Ireland and the Irish Republic sign an agreement establishing a new all-Ireland Council and cross-border implementation bodies—an important step in the peace process.

1921.[1] The Civil War of 1921 resulted in the independence of all of Ireland with the exception of Ulster, a region in the north of Ireland dominated by Protestants of largely Scottish origin. Ulster was incorporated into Britain at the end of the war, and the formal title of the British state became the United Kingdom of Great Britain and Northern Ireland. The population of Northern Ireland is slightly less than 2 million people.

The granting of Irish independence, however, failed to solve the "Irish Problem." Although Ulster was ruled by its Protestant majority, a large portion of the population remained Catholic. The incorporation of Northern Ireland into the United Kingdom protected the privileged position of the Protestant majority, but it did little to help a Catholic community suffering from poverty and unemployment. In 1969, the lethal mix of religious, economic, and nationalistic emotions erupted into a war of terror and repression that has claimed more than 3,000 victims over more than a quarter of a century. The Irish Republican Army, moreover, would take its battle for Irish independence to the streets of London, planting bombs in pubs, shopping centers, subway stations, and airports. A tentative agreement between the two sides shows signs of bringing the long conflict to an end. Optimism also stems from the fact that the Catholic middle class is approaching parity with its Protestant counterpart. Poverty and unemployment, however, continue to afflict the lower classes of both religious groups, threatening to make class rather than religion the main source of friction in the politics of the region.

England, then, is the largest single component of the United Kingdom of Great Britain and Northern Ireland. Britain, however, is far more than just England, and it is inaccurate to refer to citizens of Scotland or Wales as English. The word "British"

[1]Events leading to the war began as early as 1916. Home rule was granted in 1922.

refers to all citizens of the United Kingdom of Great Britain and Northern Ireland but not to the citizens of the Republic of Ireland.

The Evolution of British Democracy

England was unified for the first time with the Norman Conquest of 1066. William the Conqueror, the leader of the Norman (French) armies, rewarded his officers with large grants of land and various aristocratic titles such as Duke, Earl, and Viscount. Collectively, the *landed aristocracy* formed a **baronage.**

The baronage, in turn, formed the backbone of a political, economic, and social order known as **feudalism.** The function of the barons was to maintain order in their domains, to provide the king with knights and foot soldiers in times of war, and to contribute generously to the royal household. The peasants formed the bottom of the social pyramid, living in near-servitude (Woodward 1962). As described by the noted British historian E. L. Woodward: "Over most of England, the average peasant had to stay where he was, do as he was told, and work for others as well as for himself" (Woodward 1962, 24).

Over time, the feudal system became more complex as the wealthier barons followed the kingly practice of giving grants of land in return for service and soldiers. A knight—originally any man with armor and a horse—enjoyed far greater social status than a peasant, but he still was not a member of the aristocracy.

The relative stability provided by the feudal system led to the growth of towns and thereby to the emergence of a vigorous merchant class. Merchants, like knights, enjoyed far greater status than the peasants. They also possessed considerable wealth. Collectively, the knights and the merchants (burgesses) formed the core of the **commons.** Feudal England, then, can be thought of as possessing three basic estates: the monarchy, the aristocracy, and the commons (Judge 1993). The higher clergy also received large grants of land from the king and constituted part of the aristocracy. Even today, senior bishops of the Church of England continue to sit in the House of Lords, and the Church retains massive landholdings that rival those of the royal family.

The Birth of Parliament

The origins of Parliament, in the broadest sense of the term, can be traced to the Great Councils convened by the Norman kings to keep in touch with their barons. The Great Councils discussed the grand issues of war and peace, as well as the king's insatiable need for money. Over time, the barons used the king's need for money as a vehicle for extending their influence over the affairs of the state (Punnett 1988). The link between democracy and economics has a long history, indeed.

While several Great Councils played a dominant role in shaping the British Constitution, two were of particular importance: The Great Council of 1215, which led to the issuance of the Magna Carta, and the Great Council of 1295, commonly referred to as the Model Parliament. The Magna Carta established the principle that kings did not hold absolute power and that they would henceforth rule "according to ancient customs of which public opinion approved" (Woodward 1962, 33). Public opinion, in this instance, referred to the opinions of the aristocracy.

The Great Council or Model Parliament of 1295, in turn, marked the successful entry of the Commons into the political fray. In desperate need of money, Edward I summoned barons, clergy, knights, and burgesses to meet in Council. The king was provided with the money that he demanded, but only on the principle that

Fifteenth-century depiction of the British House of Lords under Edward I, king of England from 1239 to 1307. The growth of parliamentary liberties in England sprang from the signing of the Magna Carta in 1215.

"what touches all should be approved by all" (Punnett 1988, 182). Translated into American parlance, this means "no taxation without representation."

The Great Councils were not parliaments. Rather, they were councils in which both the Lords and the Commons could have their grievances addressed by the king in exchange for their financial support. The limits on the king's authority were "outer limits," the violation of which would threaten the king with rebellion. The concept of outer limits was crucial, for it established the principle that the king had to operate within the circle of acceptable traditions and opinions. Over the course of the next several centuries, that circle of traditions and opinions—the British Constitution—would become tighter, clearer, and far more binding. In the process, Great Councils would evolve into a bicameral parliament in which power would be shared between the monarch, the House of Lords, and the House of Commons. The House of Lords was the preserve of the aristocracy, while the House of Commons gave expression to the concerns of the masses. Prior to the nineteenth century, it should be noted, the House of Commons was not very common, as suffrage was restricted to male property owners, a group that constituted some 5 percent of the population.

The Industrial Revolution

This evolutionary process of constitutional development, while remarkable for a society yet emerging from feudalism, would be severely challenged by the Industrial Revolution. Originating with the invention of the steam engine in the mid-eighteenth century, the Industrial Revolution would transform Britain from an agrarian society into an industrial state. Cities mushroomed as peasants were lured from the farm to the factory in search of higher wages and a better quality of life. For the most part, they found neither. The squalor of the early factory towns defied description, and wages provided little more than bare subsistence. As late as 1902, approximately 43 percent of the workers in York, a major industrial center, lived below the poverty level (Woodward 1962). Figures for London were in the 30 percent range (Woodward 1962). The magnitude of their misery forced the workers of the era to invent a new unit of political action: the labor union. For the first time in history, workers formed organizations to advance their collective interests.

The industrial revolution, then, added two new elements to the British political equation: the industrial **bourgeoisie,** or *capitalist class,* and the **proletariat,** or *industrial working class.* They would soon become the dominant elements in that equation. The enfranchisement of the working class began with the Reform Acts of 1867 and 1884, acts that extended the right to vote to approximately 28 percent of the British population, all of it male.[2]

In 1918, the right to vote was extended to females over the age of 30, with the proviso that their husbands meet certain minimal property requirements. Finally, the Representation of the People Act of 1928 removed all property restrictions on voting, thereby providing **universal suffrage** to all citizens of the United Kingdom. It was not until 1949, however, that the principle of "one person, one vote" was enacted into law. Prior to this time, business owners and university graduates received two votes apiece: one for their residence and one for their business or university affiliation.

The expansion of the electorate produced two fundamental transformations in British politics. First, with each expansion of the franchise, the power of the House of Lords, a non-elected body, decreased. Nevertheless, the two houses of the British Parliament retained their relative equality until 1911.

The second major change in British politics was the emergence of political parties. By the advent of the seventeenth century, it had become customary for members of Parliament sharing similar views to meet on an informal basis for the purpose of coordinating their strategies. The two main parties of the era were the **Tories** and the **Whigs**.[3] (See box on p. 57 for details.)

There was no need to organize the masses, because the masses could not vote. With the expansion of the electorate, however, the masses took on political relevance, and the two major parliamentary parties of the time—the Conservatives and the Liberals—began to organize local electoral districts in the hope of electing candidates compatible with their views. The Labour Party would emerge in the early 1900s, replacing the Liberals as Britain's second major party.

Over the course of the ensuing years, power would alternate between the Conservative and Labour Parties. The former championed capitalism and the interests of the business class, while the latter attempted to transform Britain into a socialist democracy. The political system, according to the Labour Party, would be democratic, but the government would run the larger firms and provide its citizens

---

[2]The Reform Act of 1832 had increased the electorate from 5 percent of the population to approximately 7.5 percent.

[3]"Whig" is an abbreviation of Wiggammores, a band of Scottish rebels (Punnett 1988).

First Political Parties

Tories were the "royalists" who supported the Crown, the rights of the landed aristocracy, and the dominant position of the Church of England. The Tories adopted the Conservative label in the nineteenth century following a campaign speech in which a Tory leader declared that the goal of his party was to "conserve all that was good in existing institutions" (Punnett 1988, 74). The popular press continues to refer to the Conservatives as "Tories."

Whigs were the prosperous members of the middle class who advocated less restrictive economic laws and a reduced role for the Crown and the Church of England in the affairs of the country. The Whigs would later evolve into the Liberal Party.

---

with a broad range of welfare services. Because neither side could dominate the other, the two parties informally agreed to maintain England as a mixed socialist-capitalist economy. Labour curtailed its welfare demands, while the Conservatives resisted efforts to denationalize Britain's heavy industry (Childs 1992). Once the world's leading exponent of free trade, Britain had turned inward.

The Thatcher Revolution

The tacit compromise between Labour and the Conservatives was shattered by the election of Margaret Thatcher in 1979 (Thatcher 1993). During her eleven years as prime minister, Thatcher slashed welfare benefits, denationalized British industries, and did everything within her power to force British firms to become more competitive on a global scale. The Thatcher revolution, while ostensibly economic, also represented a dramatic change in the way the British did politics:

> Most observers, whether supporters or detractors, agreed that "Thatcher's revolution" involved four main changes. The first was in the way Britain was governed. Direction and leadership replaced negotiation and compromise; government by conviction replaced government by consensus. Thatcher reasserted the authority of the core executive over organized interests and the public sector, and within the executive she stamped her personal authority over the cabinet and the civil service. The second change was in the economy. A broadly corporatist economy was turned into a broadly market economy: Most state-owned industries and services were privatized; subsidies to private industry ceased; economic planning was scrapped; and large swathes of economic activity, notably finance, were deregulated. A third change was social and communal. More people than before, especially in the South and the Midlands, owned their own homes, bought shares, and acquired consumer luxuries; but more people than before, especially in the North and Scotland, were unemployed and in poverty. The fourth change was cultural. Not only in the media but among ordinary people the old values of class loyalty, national planning, and welfare seemed out of tune with the times; the new accent was on the individual, choice, and "getting on" (King et al., 1993, 1).

Margaret Thatcher was replaced as prime minister by John Major, a less controversial figure who was successful in leading the Conservatives to an upset victory over the Labour Party in the 1992 general elections (Sked and Cook 1993). Major's reign as prime minister was scarred by deep conflict within the Conservative Party, much of it revolving around his efforts to strengthen Britain's participation in the European Union. A hard core of Conservative legislators bitterly opposed closer British ties with the European Union, and their hostility toward Major threw the Conservative leadership into disarray. As the 1997 elections approached, the British press was virtually unanimous in predicting the defeat of a Conservative Party that had ruled the country for eighteen consecutive years. They were not to be proven wrong.

Anthony Charles Lynton Blair (Tony Blair, Prime Minister)

Tony Blair (born in 1953) was first elected to Britain's House of Commons in 1983, where he served on various shadow cabinets of the Labour Party for the next decade. In July 1994, he assumed leadership of the Labour Party. "New Labour, New Britain" was his slogan, encapsulating Blair's ambition to restructure Britain's then-minority party into an appealing centrist organization capable of winning general elections. He proposed a tough but liberal crime policy, readiness for a free-market economy, anti-inflationary tactics, and full support of Britain's induction into the European Union. (*Source:* www.geocities.com/journo/blair4.html.)

On May 2, 1997, Labour swept to a crushing victory, capturing 418 of the 659 seats in the House of Commons (Watkins 1998). John Major moved out of 10 Downing Street, the official residence of the prime minister, on the following day to be replaced by Tony Blair, the leader of the Labour Party (Butler and Kavanagh 1998). In a brief speech following a formal meeting with the queen in which he was asked to form a Government, Blair, the first Labour prime minister in eighteen years and the youngest prime minister in more than a century, announced that Labour had campaigned as New Labour and would rule as New Labour, a stern warning to those who expected a return to Labour's socialist orientation of old.

Changes were equally sweeping throughout the Government as Tory (Conservative) ministers were replaced by their counterparts on Labour's "**shadow cabinet**" (leadership of the opposing party). In sharp contrast to the American experience of forming a new administration, a process that often takes months and usually involves rancorous bickering between the White House and the Senate, the members of the shadow cabinet had been in place long before the election and had received regular briefings from Britain's senior civil servants.

In years past, a victory for Labour might have signaled a radical change in British politics. Ironically, one of the keys to Labour's victory may have been its promise not to change the programs that the Conservatives had put in place. Gone were the slogans of socialism, welfare, and nationalization of industry. Labour, at least as portrayed by Tony Blair, had become a party of the Center. Many British commentators, accordingly, referred to the transformation of Labour as a victory for Thatcherism (Kennedy 1998). Not only had Thatcher transformed the British economy, but the success of her reforms had forced Labour to disassociate itself from its socialist past and break its subservience to the unions.

The evolutionary pattern of British democracy demonstrates that social and economic change can be accomplished peacefully. Nevertheless, the evolutionary nature of political change in Britain has perpetuated the existence of two non-democratic political institutions, the Crown and the House of Lords. The Crown and the Lords have very little power, but they are part of the political process. The evolutionary pattern of British politics has also resulted in a society that is far more class-conscious than other modern industrial societies. The existence of a monarchy and the House of Lords, at least from the perspective of some members of the Labour Party, perpetuates this sense of class consciousness. In much the same manner, the evolutionary nature of British politics has perpetuated an elitist educational system that provides the upper classes with a superb education while locking the lower classes in mediocrity.

The victory of Labour in the 1997 elections would trigger yet another shift in the evolution of British politics as the hereditary lords—those members of the House of Lords who inherited their seats from their aristocratic forebears—were stripped of their voting power and Scotland and Wales have been given substantial autonomy from London. There is even talk of altering the British voting

Tony Blair, Britain's youngest prime minister in more than a century, used the campaign slogan "New Labour, New Britain" to lead the Labour Party to victory over the Conservatives.

system. In the best British traditions, however, these changes to the British constitution are being carried out in a peaceful manner.

The Political Institutions of Britain

The formal institutions of the British government consist of the Crown (king or queen), the House of Lords, and the House of Commons. Collectively, the Lords and the Commons constitute the Parliament.[4] The Crown and the House of Lords give symbolic expression to Britain's aristocratic past but have little influence in shaping public policy.

The House of Commons, by contrast, is the core of British democracy. Bills passed by the House of Commons are the law of the land, and they cannot be vetoed by any other branch of the British government. The authority of the Commons, moreover, is total. There are no inalienable rights reserved for minorities or individuals, nor can a bill passed by the Commons be overturned by the British courts. Indeed, the only restraints on the power of the House of Commons are the informal constitutional restraints of tradition and reasonableness.[5]

Members of the House of Commons are chosen by the British population in elections that are held at least once every five years. The leader of the majority party in the Commons is then requested by the Crown to form a Government. A Government consists of the prime minister, the Cabinet, and other senior political officials who assist the prime minister and the Cabinet in the formulation and execution of policy.

[4]Historically, the Crown was considered part of the Parliament (Punnett 1988).
[5]The one exception to this rule is that elections must be held at least once every five years.

As used herein, **Government** (with a capital G) refers to the prime minister, Cabinet, and other relevant positions selected by the prime minister.

The prime minister is the dominant member of the Government, followed in turn by senior members of the Cabinet, most of whom head a major administrative department. Of these, the Ministers of Foreign Affairs, Defense, and the Treasury (The Chancellor of the Exchequer) wield exceptional power. Some Cabinet positions are also reserved for senior party officials whose responsibilities are purely political[6] (Punnett 1988).

Governments rule for as long as they enjoy the confidence of a majority of the members of the Commons or until the five-year term of the Commons expires. Should a majority of the members of the Commons vote to "bring down" the Government—a vote of no confidence—the entire Government must resign, thereby paving the way for new elections.[7] As long as a single party enjoys a majority in Commons, however, a successful vote of no confidence is an unlikely event.

Executive Power in Britain: Prime Ministers and Governments

A British prime minister supported by a strong majority in the House of Commons is more powerful than the American president (Rose 1989). The powers of the prime minister stem from a variety of sources, four of which are of particular importance. *First, the prime minister possesses the prestige of holding the highest political office in the land.* As described by James:

> He is not just leader of the party; he is head of the government. Ministers are not only his colleagues but his subordinates. A few may be rivals; some may dislike him; some will clash with him on policy; but all must accord him the respect due to his office. This attitude is reinforced by civil servants, who have a great respect for No. 10 and its utterances:[8] they may not agree with what the Prime Minister says, but they have a keen nose for where power lies (James 1992, 93–94).

Second, the prime minister is the leader of his or her party. It is the prime minister who has the major voice in determining the legislative program that the ruling party will implement during its term in office. As the leader of the party, moreover, the prime minister selects the members of the Government. Powerful leaders in the party must be accommodated, but prime ministers also use their appointment powers as a means of rewarding friends and punishing enemies. **Members of Parliament (MPs)** who hope to move up the ranks of the party hierarchy can defy the prime minister only at grave risk to their political careers (Rose 1989; *New Statesman* 1996, 1998).

In much the same manner, the prime minister has the final word in shaping the electoral strategy of the ruling party. Particularly important, in this regard, is the timing of elections. By way of background, it should be noted that it is within the power of the prime minister to call a general election at any time within the

---

[6]Cabinet members without specific departmental responsibilities are often allocated one of the grand historical titles which, being obsolete, continue to make the nomenclature of British politics impenetrable to outsiders. Foremost among such honorific titles are the Lord President of the Council and the Lord Privy Seal. The Lord Privy Seal is the Government's political manager in the House of Commons, while the Lord President of the Council chairs important cabinet committees in lieu of the prime minister. Both are important political positions (Rose 1989).

[7]In less-stable parliamentary systems, new elections are often avoided by asking the leader of the opposition to form a Government.

[8]"No. 10" refers to the prime minister's residence at 10 Downing Street, and thus to the prime minister, just as "the White House" often refers to the president of the United States.

Powers of the British Prime Minister

To understand the powers of the British prime minister, four points must be noted.

1. The power of the House of Commons is absolute and cannot be overridden by any other political institution.
2. The power of the majority party in the Commons is absolute and cannot be blocked by the opposition.
3. The power of the Government is absolute because members of the ruling party vote as a cohesive bloc.
4. The prime minister is the dominant figure in the Government. John Smith, the former leader of the Labour Party, used to lament, "We have an elective dictatorship" (*Economist,* April 18, 1998, 7).

---

statutory five-year term of a Parliament. (The prime minister sets the stage for new elections by requesting the monarch to dissolve the Parliament.) Few Parliaments run their full five-year course, for the governing party is anxious to "go to the people" at a time when it has the best chance of winning a new term in office. Timing can be everything. The best time for calling an election, however, is often a matter of considerable debate within the ruling party, and it is the prime minister who resolves the issue (Punnett 1988).

Third, prime ministers derive considerable power from their organizational position as the chairperson of the Cabinet. Cabinets face such a wide range of issues that they can accomplish their tasks only by dividing into committees, often as many as 160 (Hennessy 1991). Prime ministers set the agenda of the Cabinet by determining both the issues to be addressed and the amount of time to be spent on each issue. They also decide the membership of the various cabinet committees and chair the committees of their choosing. The organizational powers of the prime minister are strengthened, moreover, by the existence of a personal staff or "Private Office" designed to keep the prime minister in touch with the diverse issues before him or her (Barber 1991).

In addition to the organizational advantages discussed above, it is the prime minister who speaks for the Government. The Cabinet seldom votes on issues, it being the prime minister who "sums up" the discussion and who conveys the "sense" of the Government's decision to Parliament (Punnett 1988). As anyone who has participated in a small-group discussion well knows, a chairperson's interpretation of what transpired may differ markedly from the interpretations of the group's members.

Finally, the power of the prime minister derives from the growing personalization of British politics that has accompanied the advent of television. The prime minister is the focal point of media coverage, and no politician, regardless of party, can compete with a popular and dynamic prime minister (Barber 1991). Popularity, however, is fleeting, and a prime minister lagging in the polls may find the members of his or her cabinet becoming increasingly aggressive (Conley 1990).

An important point to be noted in the above discussion is that the powers of the prime minister are largely informal. The British Constitution is an unwritten set of traditions, and there are no formally enumerated powers of the prime minister. Much, accordingly, depends upon the skills and the personality of the individuals involved. A skillful and determined prime minister will be far more powerful than a less-experienced prime minister or a prime minister inclined to share large areas of responsibility with his or her peers. Margaret Thatcher's popular label as the "Iron Lady" conveyed a grudging respect for her skill and determination. It was she who dominated the Cabinet. The reign of John Major, by contrast, witnessed a reassertion of ministerial influence. In the words of a senior minister, "John sums up at the end of the meeting rather than the beginning" (Heseltine, cited in Sampson 1992, 22).

While the powers of the prime minister are formidable, they are far from absolute (James 1992). The senior members of the Cabinet each represent powerful wings within the ruling party and, more often than not, their position on the Cabinet is recognition of that power. Prime ministers theoretically are free to choose their Cabinet ministers, but the practical requirements of party cohesion demand that all major wings of the party find adequate representation within the Cabinet. Ideological divisions are a constant source of tension within the Government, as are personality conflicts. Many senior Cabinet ministers also view themselves as potential prime ministers and are not averse to using their Cabinet positions to achieve that end. During 1999, for example, Tony Blair was forced to forego the usual summer Cabinet reshuffle because of pressure from within the Party (*Daily Telegraph,* July 29, 1999, p. 1).

Cabinet Government or Government by the Prime Minister? Because of the substantial power wielded by senior ministers, the nature of the division of power between the prime minister and the senior members of the Cabinet has always remained something of a mystery. Traditional wisdom had long maintained that the prime minister was the first among equals. More recently, however, students of British government have expressed the fear that the British system has been transformed from a "Cabinet Government" based on collective decision making into a "Prime Ministerial Government," or even a "Presidential Government" in which the Cabinet is subservient to the prime minister (Punnett 1988, 243). As expressed by Tony Benn, a senior official in the Labour Party:

> The wide range of powers at present exercised by a British Prime Minister, both in that capacity, and as Party Leader, are now so great as to encroach upon the legitimate rights of the electorate, undermine the essential role of Parliament, usurp some of the functions of collective cabinet decision making, and neutralise much of the influence deriving from the internal democracy of the Party (Benn 1979, as cited in Barber 1991, 124).

Why British Governments Are Cohesive and Stable. The essence of British politics is the ability of a single political party to sustain a Government in the House of Commons over the life of its appointed term. As long as the members of the majority party in the Commons vote as a unified bloc, there is nothing the opposition can do to block the Government's program. There are no checks and balances in the British system, nor are there any inalienable rights reserved for the minority. The winner takes all.

The power and stability of British Governments rest upon two pillars: strong party discipline that forces members of Parliament to support their party's leadership, and an electoral system that facilitates one-party rule. The elements of party cohesion will be examined in this section, while the mechanics of the British electoral system will be analyzed in the next section.

The members of a political party in the House of Commons are referred to as its **parliamentary party**. Following an election, the leader of the majority parliamentary party becomes the prime minister, while the leader of the defeated parliamentary party becomes the leader of the opposition. Parliamentary parties are highly organized, and their members are expected to vote as instructed by the leadership of the parliamentary party. In British parlance, members of the parliamentary party are expected to accept the "whip" (Brand 1992).

The **whips** are senior members in each parliamentary party charged with assuring that the party's MPs understand the leadership's position and vote accordingly. As Anthony Sampson points out, they are the "party policemen":

> The whips, the party policemen who press members to vote for the government, have a much longer history, and members exchange horror stories of rough treatment by former chief whips. They hold the keys to promotion and favours, ranging from free trips to knighthoods or jobs in the government. And as fewer members have independent means or jobs, still fewer can resist the lures of office. The Tory whips became more dreaded and effective under Thatcher: they could compel members of parliament with their three-line whips to stay up late at night, to prevent the opposition laying an ambush to deprive the government of a majority… "It wasn't until I joined government," said one just-retired minister, "that I realised just how irrelevant parliament was" (Sampson 1992, 12).

The term *whip* is also applied to the formal instructions sent to party MPs by the party whips prior to votes in parliament. Each whip is underscored with one to three lines, indicating its degree of urgency. A one-line whip urges members to try and make the vote if they can, while a two-line whip indicates a vote of major importance to the party and its leadership. Barring compelling personal reasons, MPs are expected to conform to two-line whips. Three-line whips are reserved for issues that threaten the life of the Government and its program. In extreme cases, three-line whips have resulted in MPs being literally carried to the Parliament from their deathbeds. Violation of a three-line whip constitutes nothing less than a challenge to the party leadership and is treated as such.

The willingness of MPs to accept their party's whip and vote as a solid bloc is not difficult to understand. If the members of the ruling party do not vote as a bloc, the Government will fall and all members of the Commons will be faced with new elections. By the same token, if the members of the opposition do not vote as a bloc, they lose any hope of challenging the Government.

Back benchers *are MPs not in the Government or shadow cabinet.* They sit on the back benches of the House of Commons. While the pressures for party cohesion are formidable, it would be a mistake to suggest that back benchers are a docile lot who display mindless obedience to the party leadership. This is not the case. Indeed, one of the major roles of the party whips is to head off potential confrontations between the leadership and the back benchers by discussing pending issues with the latter prior to party meetings. The Government may compromise far less than the back benchers, but it does compromise.

Elections and Politics in Britain: Stability Versus Democracy. The stability of British Governments is reinforced by the British electoral system (Blackburn 1995). Each of the 659 members of the House of Commons is elected in a **single-member, simple-plurality district**. Each electoral district elects one member of the House of Commons, and the candidate who receives *the most votes,* a **plurality**, wins the seat. A majority is not necessary, merely the most votes. Assume, for example, that a London district has candidates representing the Labour Party, the Conservative Party, and the Liberal Democratic Party. Assume also that the Labour Party receives 34 percent of the vote and that the Conservatives and the Liberal Democrats each receive 33 percent of the vote. In this instance, the Labour Party candidate with 34 percent of the vote—a simple plurality—wins the seat in Commons.

What are the consequences of this situation? *The first consequence is that a party is not required to win a majority of the popular vote in order to win a majority in Commons.* All that is required is that a party win a majority of the 659 constituency elections on the basis of simple pluralities (Jeffery 1998). More often than not, the majority party in Commons receives around 40 percent of the popular vote. In the 1997 election, for example, the Labour Party won 63 percent of the seats in Commons on the basis of some 44 percent of the popular vote The Liberal Democrats[9] garnered 17 percent of the popular vote but received 7 percent of the seats in Commons. If candidates for the Commons were required to win their seats by an absolute majority (50 percent plus 1), it would be difficult for any single party to form a Government.

The ability of a single party to win a majority of the seats in the Commons with less than a majority of the popular vote promotes stability in British politics by avoiding the need for coalition Governments in which two or more political parties share power. Coalition Governments have been rare in Britain, but the history of coalition Governments in Europe and elsewhere has been a pageant of conflict and instability as each partner in the coalition has sought to pursue its policies to the detriment of the others. On average, coalition Governments in Italy have lasted less than a year. Britain has avoided this instability.

The second consequence of the British electoral system is that it squeezes out small parties (Conley 1990). As only one candidate can win in each district, most British citizens vote for either the Labour or the Conservative Parties, believing that it would make little sense to vote for a party that couldn't win. Even if a small party such as the Scottish Nationalist Party wins a few districts, it has no hope of forming a Government. The big loser in the British electoral system has been the Liberal Democrats, a party that receives a large number of votes in many districts but seldom enough to win a plurality.

A third consequence of the British electoral system is that votes are wasted. Returning to the above example, it will be recalled that the Labour candidate won our hypothetical district with 34 percent of the vote. This means, in effect, that 66 percent of the votes in the district were wasted and that the MP for the district did not represent the views of a majority of its voters. In the electoral system based on proportional representation, by contrast, parties are awarded seats in Parliament in proportion to their popular vote. If a party wins 30 percent of the popular vote, it wins 30 percent of the seats in Parliament. Many people feel that proportional representation is more democratic than single-member, simple-plurality districts because every vote counts. Under proportional representation, to return to the 1997 example, the Liberal Democrats, having won 17 percent of the popular vote, would have won 17 percent of the seats in the House of Commons. The Liberal Democrats, needless to say, would like to see a change in the British electoral system.

As the British experience demonstrates, no electoral system is neutral or without its consequences. The single-member, simple-plurality electoral districts employed by the British facilitate two-party government and the political stability inherent therein. Single-member, simple-plurality districts, however, are less democratic than proportional-representation systems because voters have fewer parties from which to choose and because so many votes are wasted.

Interestingly enough, the 1999 elections for the European Parliament were conducted on the basis of proportional representation. This procedure has been met with an uproar of criticism, but could well pave the way for electoral reform in the future (MacShane 1998).

---

[9]During the 1987 elections, the party that was to become the Liberal Democrats ran under the Alliance label.

Changing of the Guard. A change in British Governments may occur in two ways. Most commonly, *Governments come to an end when the prime minister requests the monarch to dissolve Parliament.* A request to dissolve Parliament (Commons) must be made within five years of the previous general election, but it can be made at any time within that period. The ruling party prefers to time elections to its maximum advantage: moving for early elections if it senses victory, and delaying elections as long as possible if it senses defeat. New elections for the House of Commons are held three weeks following the dissolution of Parliament, the British having avoided the American practice of perpetual campaigns.

    Governments also "fall" when they lose a "vote of no confidence" in the House of Commons. Originally, Governments fell if they failed to receive a majority vote on any major piece of legislation. More recent practice, however, requires a specific vote of no confidence to bring down a Government (Punnett 1988). When a Government falls, the outgoing party generally requests the monarch to call new elections in the hope of gaining a new mandate.

    The last British Government to fall as a result of a vote of no confidence was the Labour Government of James Callaghan in 1979. Callaghan began his term with a slim majority but saw it wither as deaths and resignations depleted the Party's ranks in the Commons. Subsequent **by-elections** (elections held to replace MPs who have resigned or died) were lost by the Labour Party, strengthening the position of the opposition.

    The majority party in Commons may also change prime ministers simply by electing a new party leader, a procedure that led to the replacement of Margaret Thatcher by John Major. This was a purely internal matter within the majority party. The Government had not fallen, and the new leader merely replaced the old as the prime minister. Almost invariably, a successful challenge to the power of the prime minister by the members of his or her own party results in the selection of a safe candidate deemed capable of rebuilding party unity.

Legislative Power in Britain: The Parliament

Britain possesses a bicameral parliament consisting of two houses: the **House of Commons** and the **House of Lords.** The power of the House of Lords is largely symbolic, while the House of Commons is the heart of British democracy.

The House of Commons. The House of Commons consists of 659 members elected by universal suffrage for a maximum term of five years. If a member of Commons dies or resigns, the vacant seat is filled in a special by-election in the relevant constituency.

    The formal powers of the House of Commons are virtually unlimited. The Commons can pass legislation in any area of its choosing by a simple majority vote. Indeed, the only constraint on the power of the Commons is the ability of the Lords to delay some bills passed by the Commons for a period of up to one year. By and large, however, the majority party in Commons merely ratifies the program of the Government. It is the Government, and the prime minister in particular, that is the power center of British politics (Riddell 1998).

    Bills presented in the House of Commons undergo three readings. *The first reading involves little more than a simple announcement of the bill's title.* This accomplished, the bill is allocated a spot on the legislative calendar for a second reading.

Three Categories of Bills Introduced to Parliament

1. Public Bills: Bills of general concern that are usually introduced by a minister or other member of Government.

2. Private Bills: Bills of local interest that are introduced by individual members of Parliament on behalf of their constituents.

3. Hybrid Bills: Bills that fall between the two extremes of public and private bills.

The second reading provides the members of Parliament with the opportunity to debate the major principles addressed by the bill. A bill dealing with the construction of public housing, for example, would almost certainly trigger a verbal confrontation between the Conservative and Labour Parties over the relative merits of public housing and the proper role of the government in meeting the housing needs of its citizens. Nothing would be resolved by this debate, but each party would have been given the opportunity to voice its opinion on a key ideological issue. The details of the bill are not addressed at this stage, nor is it common for a vote to be taken. Rather, bills are accepted in principle and sent to a **standing committee** for further consideration.

Following consideration by a standing committee, a bill advances to its *third and final reading, which gives the opposition one final opportunity to attack a bill with spirited if futile debate.* The passage of a Government bill is largely assured by the discipline of the majority party. If the opposition had possessed the power to kill the bill, it would have done so long before.

Once a bill passes the chamber in which it has been introduced, it is sent to the other chamber, where the process repeats itself. Should differences arise between the bills of the House of Commons and those of the House of Lords, they are resolved by consultation (Punnett 1988). The contest, however, is an unequal one, for the opposition of the Lords is easily overridden by the Commons. The bill is then given royal assent—an automatic process—and becomes law. The legislative process described above has focused on the House of Commons, but the procedures of the House of Lords are similar.

Given the nature of things, bills introduced by the Government almost always become law because the Government possesses the votes to impose its will (Maor 1998). Amendments are made to bills, but they are few and of a largely technical nature. Be this as it may, the amendment process consumes inordinate amounts of legislative time and is a source of considerable frustration for many MPs. As described by Andrew Adonis,

> The passage of the Water Bill took up almost 300 hours of parliamentary time spread over more than seven months. Yet for all that, not one amendment of any substance was made by either House. The sole change of any consequence—a Lords amendment which would have obliged the privatised water companies to achieve levels of drinking water quality specified by the European Community by 1993—was reversed by the Government's majority in the Commons and not insisted upon by the peers. It is fair to ask, therefore: is parliamentary scrutiny of government legislation anything more than "sound and fury signifying nothing"? (Adonis 1990, 72).

Bills lacking the support of the Government, by contrast, seldom see the light of day. In some instances, private bills are introduced largely to publicize a specific issue, such as the preservation of an endangered species or gay rights.

The Question Period. As things stand today, the most visible means of Parliamentary control over the actions of the Government is the **Question Period**. Four days a

---

Standing Committees

Although their deliberations are a lengthy part of the legislative process, Britain's standing committees share none of the power of their counterparts in the United States. Indeed, as the following example suggests, they often have little power at all:

...it was the Water Bill which showed the standing committees at their most absurd. Twenty-seven hours were spent discussing the bill's first clause, and after a total of seventy-five hours of debate the committee had reached only clause 9—out of the bill's 180.... In all, therefore, the bill took more than 150 hours to pass through committee, virtually all of it spent debating amendments which ministers never had any intention of meeting with other than a blank refusal. Ritual run riot? (Punnett 1988, 103–4).

---

week, Monday through Thursday, *one hour is set aside for members of the Commons to question members of the Government about any issue of concern.* Some questions focus on major policy issues, while others dwell on the latest scandal.

The Prime Minister speaks only in parliamentary debates that focus upon major foreign or economic issues or questions of confidence in the government. Twice a week the Prime Minister appears in the House of Commons at question time, engaging in rapid-fire repartee with a highly partisan audience. Unprotected by a speechwriter's script or by television's possibility for recording and editing statements, the Prime Minister must show that she or he is a good advocate of the government's actions, or face the demoralization of parliamentary party supporters. The Prime Minister's question time is intended to test how well the nation's leader can respond to debating points (more than one-third of questions are not for information but designed to trap the Prime Minister in embarrassing responses) or handle major issues (one quarter of questions concern economic matters) (Rose 1989, 72).

Opposition parties use the Question Period to needle Government ministers and to highlight the shortcomings of Government policy. In some instances, fear of harsh questioning may force the Government to address sensitive issues far more quickly than would otherwise be the case (Punnett 1988). Members of the majority party, by contrast, often "stage" questions to allow a minister to address a point of interest or to highlight a Government success.

Beyond their legislative and watchdog roles, members of Parliament are also expected to look after the interests of their constituents (Adonis 1990). Most of the private members' bills introduced into the Commons, for example, focus on the special needs of a district or its constituents. Many of the questions addressed to the Government during the Question Period are also of a local nature. Unlike the American experience, however, party discipline takes precedence over the needs of the district (Adonis 1990).

The House of Lords. Members of the House of Lords are referred to as "Peers." The House of Lords contained 1,144 members until 1999, nearly two-thirds of whom were hereditary peerages. The remainder were life peerages awarded in honor of outstanding service to the state.[10] In 1999, 666 hereditary peers lost their "sitting" and "voting" rights in the first stage of the Government's reform package. Ninety-two hereditary peers remain, at least for the moment (BBC, Nov. 26, 1999, www). Only about 300 Peers attend the sessions of the House of Lords on any given day, but the number may vary with the importance of the issue at hand (Punnett 1988).

---

[10]Life peers are appointed by the monarch upon the recommendation of the prime minister.

Members of both Houses of Parliament listen to a speech given by a visiting dignitary at the Royal Gallery of the House of Lords.

The Lords, while no longer in a position to challenge the Commons, are not without influence. Members of the House of Lords can and do serve as members of the Cabinet, although it is no longer likely that a Peer would serve as prime minister. Lords can also introduce and amend legislation, although most Government Bills originate in the House of Commons. All fiscal or money bills must originate in the Commons and cannot be amended by the Lords (Punnett 1988).

The main power of the House of Lords lies in its ability to delay acts of the Commons for a period of up to one year[11] (Adonis 1990). Following this period, the Commons can override the Lords' veto by a simple majority vote. While the delaying power of the Lords may seem a trifling matter, this is not always the case. A bill delayed during the last year of a Parliament will have to face a whole new Commons if it is to become law. A year's delay, moreover, gives opponents of a bill time to marshal public opinion in support of their cause. The House of Lords does not use its power to delay often, but it does use it. Indeed, in 1998 it threatened to become a thorn in the side of a Labour Government openly hostile to its existence. The Government prevailed and the House of Lords was reformed.

Finally, the Government may use the Lords' opposition to a bill as a means of burying all or parts of poorly designed legislation that was passed for reasons of political expediency (Edward Heath, CSPAN, Nov. 28, 1994).

In the less formal sense, the Lords also derive some power from their ability to debate and publicize important issues. Debates in the House of Lords generally attract less attention than those of the Commons, but they often cover issues that the House of Commons has neglected. The House of Lords also contains many highly

---

[11]The House of Lords does retain absolute veto power in one area: the requirement that elections for the House of Commons be held at least once every five years. This power is largely theoretical, for elections have been postponed only during periods of war, and then with the agreement of all major parties.

honored specialists, and their views on technical matters carry a great deal of weight (Edward Heath, CSPAN, Nov. 28, 1994).

The most interesting facet of the House of Lords is not its minimal authority, but its very existence. Not only is the House of Lords an undemocratic institution, but it is also an institution that possesses a strong conservative bias.

All of this, however, changed radically in the fall of 1998 when the Blair government announced that one of the cornerstones of its 1999 legislative program would be a bill designed to strip hereditary peers of their voting rights (*Times,* Nov. 25, 1998). The bill was passed in 1999, thereby limiting voting rights to "life peers."

The House of Lords has thus been transformed into a meritocracy in which those voting, while not democratically elected, represent the most distinguished segment of British society. This, in itself, should raise the stature of the House of Lords. The balance of power in the Lords would also be adjusted, for Labour has nearly as many "life peers" as the Conservatives and could create more at will.

It is far from clear, however, that the Blair Government will take the next logical step and transform the House of Lords into an elected chamber much like the US senate. As discussed by Richards,

> In other words, a more democratic second chamber would have the right to stifle the will of the Commons. But it is precisely that prospect which has killed off Lords reform in the past, and many Labour MPs are still opposed to any changes which challenges their legitimacy. As Lord Richard, the former leader of the Lords, observed in the NS interview in July, "Whatever you do to the Lords is going to make the second chamber more troublesome for the Commons. There's no getting away from that and I know a lot of MPs on both sides who are worried" (Richards 1998, 7).

The Crown: The Crisis of Commonness

The monarch is Britain's head of state. In theory, the Government is the monarch's Government, and its ministers are the monarch's ministers. The monarch must also give an assent before acts of Parliament can become law. If a Government either falls or resigns, it is the monarch who dissolves the House of Commons, thereby setting the stage for new elections. In practice, of course, all of these acts are performed by the Government acting in the name of the monarch, whose main role is to symbolize the continuity of the British Constitution (Hanson and Walles 1990). The leader of the majority party in Commons is automatically asked to form a Government, and a ruling monarch has not vetoed an act of Parliament since 1703. As the titular head of state, however, the monarch does receive visiting heads of state, a task that would otherwise absorb the time of the prime minister.

While the Crown continues to enjoy the support of the British electorate, that support rests on an aura of "uncommonness." The royal family embodies the myth of England's past, a myth of chivalry and grandeur that stands in sharp contrast to the dull realities of modern Britain. In return for its storied life style, the royal family is expected to perpetuate that myth (Nairn 1994). It is their share of the bargain. Anthony Sampson describes one of the Queen's ritual duties in the following passage:

> In the summer of 1992 the Queen was spending her customary week in Edinburgh, as part of the unchanging ritual of bringing the monarchy to Scotland. The royal household moved into the seventeenth-century Palace of Holyrood on the edge of the old city, at the end of the Royal Mile, below the open hillside of Arthur's Seat. The Queen presided over the usual garden parties and receptions, in this make-believe setting: guests were escorted up the wide staircase flanked by constables in bright blue uniforms with funny hats, holding batons over their shoulders—who looked suspiciously like Edinburgh businessmen—and assembled in clusters in the Throne Room to await the Queen.

Tradition or elitism? Today, as in the past, few British judges are nonwhite or female.

The ritual was all the more reassuring in a fragmented world, when the United Kingdom itself seemed less united, and the Queen seemed to sail above it. But nobody asked the question which was on all their minds, which had suddenly erupted in the Press a month before. Did the monarchy have a future when the heir to the throne was at odds with his wife, when over half of the family was divorced, and when there was open talk of republicanism? (Sampson 1992, 57–58).

The problem of "commonness," however, transcends divorce. Half-nude photos of Princess Diana became commonplace in the British tabloids during the 1990s, and taped telephone conversations between the Crown Prince and his mistress were made available on the British equivalent of a 900 number. The royalty, it seems, are very real people. Perhaps more damning, the cover of a recent issue of *The Economist,* a conservative news magazine inclined to support the monarchy, referred to it as "an idea whose time has passed" (Oct. 22, 1994).

Law and Politics in Britain

The British legal system is based upon a concept of **common law** that traces its origins to the time of the Norman invasion of 1066. The judges of that era adjudicated disputes on the basis of tradition and custom, and the law was said to be "common" because it emanated from the people. Over time, precedents based upon those customs and traditions evolved into a code of laws, a process that continues today.

British scholars generally consider their judicial system to be nonpolitical, and many textbooks on British politics ignore the topic altogether (Norton 1994). Several factors would seem to explain this view of the British legal system. British judges are selected on a nonpartisan basis and have established an enviable record of impartiality. The structure of British politics, moreover, allows minimal scope for political intervention by the judiciary. Acts of Parliament, for example, are supreme and cannot be overturned by litigation. The British Constitution, moreover, is not subject to judicial interpretation in the manner of the United States Constitution. If the British Constitution requires formal interpretation, that interpretation will be made by the Parliament. The role of British judges is also narrower and more formal than the role of American judges. While American courts are often used to "force" political issues, British judges are disinclined to make "creative" interpretations of the law that might invite political controversy (Atkins 1988–89, 1990).

British judges strive to be impartial, but it is difficult for anyone in high office, whether elected or appointed, to be totally neutral. Approximately 93 percent of England's[12] senior (appellate) judges possess Oxbridge[13] degrees, an elitist background that introduces a systematic conservative bias into the legal system. By the very nature of their upper-class background, many Oxbridge-trained judges are inclined to support the status quo. This conservative bias, although unintentional, restricts the ability of the lower classes and the minorities to challenge the political establishment by means of the legal system (Atkins 1988–89, 1990). Indeed, as late as 1993, only three British judges were nonwhite, and only 6 percent were women (*NYT,* July 8, 1993, 3).

Government and Bureaucracy in Britain

The powers of the British civil service are less visible than those of the Parliament, but they are very real. Indeed, it is difficult to find any area of political and economic life in Britain that is not touched by the bureaucracy.

The British civil service consists of two distinct groups: a narrow group of senior civil servants who run Britain's large bureaucratic agencies and a broader group of lesser officials whose duties are confined to the execution of policy. The senior service is recruited on the basis of an exhaustive process that begins with two full days of written examinations. Candidates who successfully complete the first stage of the examination process are then subjected to an additional two days of written and oral examinations. The second series of exams places strong emphasis on "social" skills. Successful candidates are then placed on the fast track to bureaucratic power and have the opportunity to become part of Britain's bureaucratic elite. Ordinary civil servants are recruited on the basis of less exacting requirements, but most are now university graduates (Punnett 1988).

The relationship between ministers and higher civil servants is a complex one. Ministers, as elected officials, have the final say in all policy decisions, and civil servants are expected to accept those decisions. As a practical matter, ministers come and go, while civil servants do not. By exercising judicious restraint in the execution of those policies that they oppose, senior bureaucrats can often out-wait ministers, the average tenure of whom is approximately three years. It is the senior bureaucrats, moreover, who control the information that ministers require

---

[12]The Scottish legal system is distinct from that of Britain.
[13]"Oxbridge" is a combined reference to Oxford and Cambridge, Britain's most prestigious universities.

Attributes of the Senior Service

Two attributes of the senior civil service are particularly noteworthy.

First, the members of the Higher Civil Service are permanent and continue from one regime to the next.* The insulation of the senior service from the stress of political combat provides administrative continuity from one regime to the next. Unfortunately, it also reduces the responsiveness of the bureaucracy to the demands of elected officials.

Second, British civil servants are assumed to be politically neutral. In line with this assumption, senior civil servants are precluded from running for public office, and they are expected to serve all Governments efficiently and without political bias. While this standard is generally adhered to, the Higher Civil Service does possess a class bias. Oxford and Cambridge graduates, for example, represent 20 percent of the applicants for the senior service, yet garner more than 60 percent of the available positions. Coming from elite backgrounds, they possess the "social" skills that play such a critical role in the examination process (Punnett 1988). Questions of political neutrality aside, senior officials steeped in Oxbridge traditions naturally see things differently from elected officials from working class origins. They come from different worlds. Perhaps this is the reason that the British bureaucracy is characterized as being cautious, slow, and formal (Nagler 1979).

*The prime minister must approve appointments to the senior service but cannot remove its members.

---

to make sound decisions, and it is they who know how to get things done. As described by James:

> One factor…is the amateurism of ministers as opposed to the professionalism of civil servants. Another, linked to this, is the culture difference between the two. A Whitehall department is an elaborate pyramid of career civil servants, groomed in a tradition of discreet and apolitical administration. Onto this structure ministers—ambitious, publicity-seeking and above all, political—are grafted like rough plants into refined soil. The two do not live in permanent conflict: usually a civilized working relationship develops fairly quickly. Yet it is important that each remains rooted in its own culture. Ministers are meant to be agents of change, questioners, challengers, occasionally irritants. Officials safeguard good administration by keeping the machine running, proposing changes to ministers when needed and querying political ideas when these seem unpractical or flawed (James 1992, 31).

The Actors in British Politics:
Elites, Parties, Groups, and Citizens

Political institutions are the arena of politics, but it is the actors in the political process who give life to those institutions. In this section, we shall examine four main categories of political actors in Britain: elites, political parties, groups, and citizens. As we shall see, each of these groups plays a critical role in determining who gets what, when, and how in Britain.

Elites and Politics in Britain

Until the mid-1800s, political power, wealth, and social status were all concentrated in the hands of a landed aristocracy (Scott 1991). As Britain became an industrial empire, power and wealth shifted to the leaders of commerce and industry. Social status continued to cling to the heirs of noble titles, but few aristocrats currently enjoy either great wealth or political power.

The most important figure in Britain's political elite is the prime minister. Other members of the political elite include Cabinet ministers, the higher ranks of civil servants, senior judges, the chief executive officers of Britain's largest companies, and very senior military officers (Scott 1991). It is this group, particularly the prime minister and the inner circle of the Cabinet, that determines how the scarce resources of the British state are to be allocated.

The dominant role of the prime minister and other senior officials is seldom debated, being, for the most part, self-evident. What is debated is the openness of Britain's political elite. Is political power the preserve of a self-perpetuating ruling class, or is it available to all British citizens regardless of their origins? The answer to this question has much to say about the quality of British democracy.

British scholars are sharply divided on the issue. In the view of some, class rule is a thing of the past (Sampson 1982; Guttsman 1963). The Labour Governments of the post–World War II era, in this view, forced a redistribution of the nation's wealth and shifted political power to the middle class. Indeed, both Margaret Thatcher and John Major, the most recent Conservative prime ministers, shared middle-class origins. Major, in fact, was a high school dropout.

Other scholars suggest that the role of Labour in redistributing wealth and power was ephemeral (Scott 1991). Real power, in this view, resides in the hard core of higher civil servants and corporate directors who rule from behind the scenes. Most were educated in Britain's elitist "public" (private) schools[14] and received their university degrees from Oxford or Cambridge. The elite can perpetuate its rule because it has received an education far superior to that of the general population, because it has forged a network of political connections based upon "old school ties," and because it possesses the wealth to implement its agenda (Scott 1991). With the Thatcher revolution in 1979, moreover, the capitalist elite reasserted its power and rolled back many of the egalitarian programs that Labour had enacted during an earlier era (*Sunday Times*, Mar. 26, 2000, www).

The debate over the role of class in British politics is unlikely to be resolved in the near future, as each side in the argument emphasizes a different dimension of British political reality. On one hand, the most powerful positions in Britain are held by elected officials drawn largely from the middle class. On the other hand, elitist schools play a far greater role in filling positions of authority in Britain than they do in the United States and most other First World countries, with the possible exception of Japan (Scott 1991). It remains to be seen if this will change under the Blair Government.

Parties and Politics in Britain

Since the end of World War II, only the Labour Party and the Conservative Party have possessed sufficient strength in Commons to form a Government (Rose 1989). A third party, The Liberal Democratic Party, consistently garners some 10 to 20 percent of the popular vote but seldom possess enough votes in any one district to win a seat in the Commons.[15] The strength of the Liberal Democrats, however, appears to be increasing, and in the 1997 elections, the party won 17 percent of the popular vote.

In addition to its three national parties, Britain also possesses a large number of fringe parties, most of which are of a regional nature. Foremost among these are the Scottish Nationalist Party and the smaller Plaid Cymru, the nationalist party of Wales. A variety of small parties also exist in Northern Ireland, a region largely neglected by the major parties. All in all, the fringe parties account for about 3 percent of the seats in Commons (Punnett 1988).

---

[14]"Public" schools in Britain are equivalent to private schools in the United States.
[15]Based upon the record of Liberal, Alliance, and Liberal Democratic Parties.

Britain's three major parties are **catch-all** political parties: *coalitions of diverse groups held together by the desire to form a Government compatible with their views.* Ideology is important, but it is less important than winning elections. Much as in the United States, most voters identify with a political party without actually joining it.

Britain's major parties are reasonably well organized and operate at three distinct levels: the parliamentary level, the national level, and the local or constituency level. The MPs of each party in the Commons constitute its parliamentary party (Brand 1992). Parliamentary parties meet regularly to discuss strategy, and their members are expected to vote as a bloc. When a party possesses a majority in the Commons, its leaders form the Government.

Each of Britain's three major parties also maintains a national party organization and a vast network of constituency organizations. The national party organization is responsible for fundraising, campaigning, and coordinating local party organizations. Constituency organizations, in turn, nominate candidates from a list of names compiled in cooperation with the national party organization. Should the constituency organization reject its suggestions, the national party organization has the option of withholding its label from the candidate. This has yet to occur in the Conservative Party but does happen from time to time within the ranks of Labour. In such cases, the local candidate may run on a label such as the "true Labour candidate." The national parties attempt to avoid conflict with their constituency organizations, the most probable outcome of which would be an election loss.

The Conservative Party. The Conservative Party, as its name suggests, occupies the center right of the political spectrum. It is the party of big business, small government, and lower taxes. Its detractors would say that it is also the party of privilege and inequality.

The business and middle- to upper-class orientation of the Conservative Party is also reflected in the "public school," Oxbridge background of many of its candidates. Approximately one-third of the Conservative candidates during the 1980s had attended either Oxford or Cambridge, a figure that jumps to 50 percent among Cabinet ministers and to 66 percent among senior Cabinet ministers.[16] The business community is strongly represented in Conservative Governments, as are lawyers. The business community also provides most of the Party activists at the constituency level (Punnett 1988). In spite of its upper- and middle-class orientation, the Conservative Party often receives between 30 and 40 percent of the working-class vote, most of it coming from the prosperous constituencies of southern England.

The leader of the Conservative Party traditionally has been elected by Conservative members of Parliament. The leader of the Conservative Parliamentary Party, in turn, appoints other senior party officials, including the Chairman of the Party, the Chief Whip, and the Deputy Whip. When the Party is in power, the dominant members of the Parliamentary Party—the front benchers—form the Government. When the Party is not in power, the leader appoints a "shadow cabinet," the members of which lead the Party's attack on the Government. The Conservative back benchers, for their part, meet as the "Committee of 1922," a group from which ministers are excluded.[17] Issues are discussed under informal rules, and votes are not taken. Signs of unrest within the Committee of 1922, however, often signal changes in the leadership structure.

---

[16]Based upon Dod's Parliamentary Companion.
[17]The Committee of 1922 takes its name from the year in which Conservative back benchers came together as an organized group (Hanson and Walles 1990, 60).

The strength of the Conservative Party outside of Parliament is its large network of local party organizations, officially referred to as Conservative Constituency Associations.[18] The functions of the local party organizations are to nominate candidates, to support the party's electoral efforts, and to keep the party in touch with local opinion. It is the Conservative Parliamentary Party, however, that makes policy.

The Conservative Party Conference (Convention) meets annually for a period of two or three days and debates a variety of policy issues. Everyone associated with the Party and its various constituency, regional, and professional associations is entitled to attend, but only about half of the 6,000 eligible participants actually do so. By and large, the Conservative Conference is a passive gathering, the affairs of which are orchestrated by the Parliamentary leadership.

With the overwhelming victory of Labour in the 1997 elections, the Conservatives now find themselves a divided and fragmented party (*IHT,* Oct. 4, 1999, www). While the debate over closer British participation in the European Union is at the heart of Conservative woes, the Party is also rife with personality conflicts and the lethargy that comes from having been in power for more than eighteen years. The Thatcher revolution, moreover, has run its course, and the Party now lacks a clear sense of direction (Whiteley, Seyd, and Richardson 1994). Adding to these problems is a declining and aging membership and a growing public image of the Conservatives as "sleazy and selfish" (Willetts 1998, 6; Garnett and Gilmour 1998).

In a desperate effort to rekindle popular support, the Conservative Party has embarked upon a bold program to double the Party's membership by providing members with previously unavailable opportunities to participate in Party decision making. This will be done by a series of periodic ballots distributed to Party members. The leadership has promised a ballot on the Party's next electoral platform, a radical departure from past practice in which things were controlled by the Parliamentary leadership of the Party. The leadership has also promised that the selection of the next Party leader will be made on the basis of a primary election by Party members, an even more radical departure from the past. The "new" Conservative Party, the leadership promised, would be open to all, not merely the rich. It would also be a party that listened to Britain and dispelled the image of selfishness and sleaze so effectively implanted in voters' minds by Tony Blair and the Labour Party (Willetts 1998; Gamble and Wright 1998).

As gloomy as its immediate outlook may seem, the Conservative Party has demonstrated its resiliency for well over two centuries, and that it is unlikely to change (Charmley 1998). The Tories did very well in the 1999 European elections, much to the dismay of Labour (*Sunday Times,* June 13, 1999, www). Nevertheless, recent polls continue to place the Conservatives well behind Labour (MORI Polls, 1979–1999, www).

---

[18]The local party organizations come together in a National Conservative Association headed by a president and an Executive Committee consisting of some 150 members, including the party leader and senior cabinet ministers. The Executive Committee meets every two months to oversee the administrative affairs of the party. It also coordinates the work of special committees dealing with finance, policy, publicity, and affiliate groups such as the Young Conservatives. The National Conservative Association also sponsors twelve Regional Councils in order to better keep in touch with regional issue (Punnett 1988).

The National Conservative Association is joined at the national level by the Conservative Central Office. The Conservative Central Office is headed by a Party Chairman appointed by the Party Leader. The Chairman is a senior member of the Parliamentary Party and often sits in the Cabinet. The primary function of the Central Office is to keep the Constituency Associations in touch with the policies of the Parliamentary leadership. The local agents of the Central Office "suggest" suitable candidates to the Constituency Association (Punnett 1988).

The Labour Party. The Labour Party was formed in the early 1900s as an alliance between the labor unions and various socialist groups of the era. Of the latter, the most important were the Fabian Society, the Social Democratic Federation, and the Cooperative Movement. The Social Democratic Federation was a radical Marxist organization that advocated the overthrow of the monarchy and the establishment of a workers' republic. The Fabians, by contrast, were socially concerned intellectuals, not the least of whom was playwright George Bernard Shaw (Piachaud 1993). The Cooperative Movement was a "hands-on" organization that provided low-cost food and clothing via a network of cooperative (worker-managed) shops. All remain within the Labour Party today, but the role of the labor unions is dominant.

The Labour Party was created to force a fundamental change in the allocation of Britain's wealth. Wages were to be increased, jobs made secure, and work rules improved. If this required socialism, so be it.

The financial and organizational power of the unions soon enabled the Labour Party to overtake the Liberal Party as the main challenger to the Conservatives, a feat that was accomplished shortly after the end of World War I. Henceforth, British citizens would have a choice between two fundamentally different views of the world. The Conservatives argued that the primary responsibility of government was to promote the growth of business and industry. The larger the size of the economic cake, from the Conservative perspective, the easier it would be for the government to meet the needs of all its citizens. Labour, by contrast, argued that the primary responsibility of government was to assure an equitable distribution of the nation's wealth and to protect the health and welfare of its citizens. When British citizens cast a ballot for a Conservative or a Labour MP, accordingly, they have a very clear picture of what they are voting for. This is not always the case in the United States.

The leader of the Labour Party is selected at the annual Labour Conference by an electoral college in which one-third of the delegates are chosen by the Labour members of Parliament, including Labour MPs in the European Parliament; one-third by a ballot of the 4.5 million members of Britain's trade unions; and one-third by some 250,000 full members of the Party's constituency associations[19] (*NYT,* May 16, 1994, A3; *Economist,* July 23, 1994, 51). Policies adopted by the 5,000 eligible delegates to the annual conference are binding upon the Labour Party leadership in Parliament "as far as may be practicable." This escape clause in the Party constitution provides the Labour leadership in the Commons with ample room for maneuverability, as does the vague wording of many Conference resolutions. Only about half of the union delegates attend the annual conference, giving the more radical activists sway to launch scathing, if ineffective, attacks on a party leadership dominated by the unions[20] (Punnett 1992).

The social background of the Labour Party, as one would expect, is quite different from that of the Conservative Party. The majority of Labour voters either have working-class origins or belong to a managerial middle class consisting of bureaucrats, teachers, and people in various other white-collar occupations. The middle class dominates both the constituency associations and the Parliamentary

---

[19]Tony Blair was the first Labour leader to be elected by these rules. Under earlier rules, 40 percent of the votes are allocated to the Trades Union Congress and 30 percent each to the constituency associations and the Labour Parliamentary Party. The new rules reduce the influence of the TUC in the selection of the Labour leadership.

[20]Constituency and regional associations are capped by a National Executive Committee (NEC) that meets on a monthly basis. The NEC is elected annually by a complex process that includes representation from the unions, the constituency associations, and the various other socialist parties. Representation is also provided for youth (The Young Socialists) and women. As always, the labor unions represent the largest bloc of votes on the Council. A majority of members of the Council are also members of Parliament, thereby providing a policy link between the Parliamentary Labour Party and the Labour Party outside of Parliament.

Party. While Labour boasts some 6.25 million members, approximately 6 million of these are affiliate members who belong to the Labour Party by virtue of their union membership. Labour Party dues are automatically deducted from the union dues of British workers unless they specifically opt out. The remainder of the Labour Party membership consists of individuals who have joined Labour constituency organizations or who belong to the socialist and cooperative organizations that originally participated in the formation of the Labour Party. Most union affiliate members of the Labour Party are passive, thereby allowing the members of the constituency associations to play a more vigorous role than their numbers would warrant.

Reflecting its working-class orientation, the Labour Party has traditionally found its strongest support in Britain's industrial centers, particularly the industrial and mining regions of Northern England and Scotland. This has become even more the case since the Thatcher revolution. Labour has also found disproportionately more support among males, younger voters, and non-Anglicans. (Anglicans are members of the Church of England.)

After competing with the Conservatives on an equal basis during the 1950s, 1960s, and 1970s, Labour fell from grace during the 1980s as the Conservatives dominated British politics for eighteen consecutive years. Labour, in the eyes of British voters, particularly the middle class, was too closely tied to Britain's labor unions to adequately address Britain's mounting economic problems. The 1997 general election, then, was to pose a critical test for Labour. If Labour could win the election, it would reestablish itself as one of Britain's two dominant parties. A Labour loss, however, would have excluded Labour from power for another five-year period and called into question Labour's role as a serious challenge to the Conservatives. The Liberal Democrats played upon this theme, suggesting that they, not Labour, were the party of the future.

The stakes of the 1997 election, then, were high indeed. Above all, Labour had to present an electoral manifesto (platform) that would enable it to recapture a large share of the middle-class vote. Indeed, so anxious was Labour to attract the middle-class vote in its 1997 campaign that journalists began referring to the Labour program as "designer socialism."

In the meantime, Labour had undertaken a major reorganization of its own affairs in order to convince the public that it was not the docile tool of the labor unions. An important step in this direction was the 1994 election of Tony Blair as the new leader of the Labour Party. Among other things, Blair pledged to scrap clause four of the Labour Party's constitution, a clause that committed the Party to the "nationalization of the means of production, distribution, and exchange" (McIlroy, 1998). Blair has also called for the transformation of Britain into a meritocracy in which hard work and achievement would be rewarded. While such views hardly pleased the unions, they were applauded by a middle class increasingly disenchanted by conservative rule (Whiteley, Seyd, and Richardson 1994).

Blair skillfully coined the term "New Labour" and boldly declared that "Nobody seriously believes in this day and age that the business of the Labour Party is to be the political arm of the trade union movement" (*Observer Review,* Sept. 10, 1995). Beyond this, Blair pronounced Labour to be "business friendly," and quietly accepted the main tenets of the Thatcher Revolution including the privatization of state-owned enterprises, the deregulation of industry, and legislation designed to reduce the militancy of the trade unions (Kennedy, 1998).

The strategy was successful, and Labour scored a dazzling victory in the 1997 elections, the results of which are summarized in Table 2.1. Blair became the prime minister, and much as he had tamed the unions, he began to tame the Labour Party. Accused of being a "control freak," Blair responded by saying that if "control freakery" means "wanting [Labour] to be a modern, disciplined party with a strong

Table 2.1
The 1997 British Elections

Party	Seats in Commons	Gains/Losses	Percent of Seats	Percent of Votes
Labour	418	+146	63.4	43
Conservatives	165	- 178	25.0	31
Liberal Democrats	46	+ 30	7.0	17
Other Parties	30	+ 5	4.6	9
	659*		100%	100%

*Including the speaker.
Source: Compiled from various newspapers.

center," then he was guilty. He went on to add that "Our party won't return to the factionalism, navel-gazing or feuding of the '70s or '80s, no matter how much a few people long for those heady days of electoral disaster" (*Time International,* Nov. 30, 1998, 25).

The Liberal Democrats. The origins of the Liberal Party parallel those of the Conservative Party. The Conservatives were the heirs of the Tories, while the Liberals were the heirs of the Whigs. The image portrayed by the early Liberals was one of reform, change, and opposition to the Church of England. The Liberals, however, were very much a middle-class party, and conflict between the Liberals and the Conservatives was essentially a conflict within the same social class.

The emergence of the Labour Party in the early 1900s pre-empted the Liberals' position as the party of change and reform, relegating the Liberals to the status of a third party falling somewhere between the more clearly defined positions of the Conservatives and Labour.

The Liberals managed to survive as a third party largely on the strength of a large network of constituency organizations created during their days of glory. Times, however, were difficult, and by 1970, the Liberal representation in the House of Commons had dropped to a low of six (Crewe 1993). Equally problematic were matters of finance. People may have been willing to vote for a losing cause, but they were not willing to pay for it. This was particularly the case among the large pressure groups whose ability to influence policy depended upon access to the Government (Rose 1989). As discussed earlier, parties that do not form Governments have little influence in the British scheme of things.

Liberal fortunes were to increase dramatically with the decline of the Labour Party in the 1980s. In 1981, four moderate leaders of the Labour Party broke ranks and formed a new center-left Social Democratic Party. The Social Democrats and the Liberals soon worked out a common electoral strategy, running a joint campaign under the Alliance label. Following a strong showing in 1987, the two parties merged to form the Liberal Democratic Party. The organizational structure of the Liberal Democrats builds upon the strong constituency network inherited from the Liberals and is capped with an annual conference that is far more open and democratic than that of either Labour or the Conservatives.

Despite an optimistic outlook for the future, the Liberal Democrats continue to be stymied by Britain's single-member, simple-plurality election system. Although they garnered some 17 percent of the vote in the 1997 election, the

---

The Functions of British Political Parties

Political parties represent the very essence of British politics. They organize the affairs of Commons; they assure that the Government in power is kept under constant scrutiny; they recruit and train new generations of political leaders; they organize, socialize, and mobilize the British electorate; and they keep the party leadership in touch with grassroots opinion. In this latter function, British political parties provide an important communication link between the Government and the masses. The competition among British parties, moreover, defines the major issues of the day and provides the electorate with a choice between ideological alternatives.

The above functions are common to political parties in most democratic political systems. The genius of the British party system, however, has been its ability to promote political moderation. As only one of the two major parties is in a position to form a Government, all major groups within society are forced to join one party or the other. Competing interests must compromise their differences for the sake of attaining at least a limited degree of political influence. The highly disciplined nature of Britain's major parties also facilitates both political stability and political responsibility by enabling Governments to stay the course of their constitutional term of office. The victorious party has the power to implement its campaign promises, and voters expect it to do so (Hofferbert and Budge 1992).

Liberal Democrats received less than 7 percent of the seats in Commons. Both Labour and the Conservatives also possess far more "safe" districts in which they are more or less assured of victory than do the Liberal Democrats, a fact that provides the two larger parties with a critical mass that the Liberal Democrats do not possess.

The best hope for the emergence of the Liberal Democrats as a major force in British politics would be a change in Britain's election laws from single-member, simple-plurality districts to proportional representation. Based upon the 1997 results, for example, proportional representation would have given the Liberal Democrats approximately 112 seats in Commons, a far cry from the 46 seats they actually received. No single party would have been able to form a Government, and the Liberal Democrats would almost certainly have been part of a ruling coalition Government. Proportional representation would also have assured the public that a vote for the Liberal Democrats was no longer a wasted vote. This, however, was not to be, and Labour scored an overwhelming victory in the 1997 elections. Needless to say, the Liberal Democrats paid close attention to Tony Blair's experiment with proportional representation in the 1999 elections for the European Parliament. It was their best hope for the future.

Pressure Groups and Politics in Britain

As in all modern industrial democracies, Britain possesses thousands of pressure groups. Of these, the most powerful are the large economic **peak associations** (or umbrella organizations) that aggregate a variety of smaller organizations (Coxall 1992). Most of Britain's 100-plus labor unions, for example, come together in the Trades Union Congress, and industrial groups find representation in the Confederation of British Industry (McIlroy 1998). Other peak business organizations include the Retail Consortium, the British Bankers Association, the Association of British Chambers of Commerce, and the National Federation of Building Trades Employers. Approximately 90 percent of British farmers find representation in the National Farmers Union. Other dominant groups include the British Medical Association, the Society of Civil Servants, and the Police Federation.

Not all of Britain's major pressure groups are economic in nature. The Royal Society for the Protection of Birds, the largest of some 1,000 environmental groups in Britain, has more card-carrying members than the three major British political parties combined (*Economist*, Aug. 13, 1994, 49). The membership of the far more radical Greenpeace has passed the 350,000 mark (ibid.). The environmentalists, in turn, are joined by more than seventy animal rights groups and at least forty groups attempting to alleviate the plight of the poor. In the human rights area, Amnesty International enjoys a membership surpassing 100,000 (ibid.).

Most members of the social and environmental groups are college-educated individuals from middle-class backgrounds, a voting category of vital interest to British politicians. Indeed, many British citizens now find pressure groups to be more effective in representing their views than political parties (*Economist,* Aug. 13, 1994, 49).

The goal of British pressure groups is similar to that of pressure groups everywhere: to protect and promote the special interests of their members. Most of Britain's larger peak associations work through either the Labour Party or the Conservative Party in the hope of gaining direct access to the Government. When the Labour Party is in power, the ability of the Trades Unions Congress to achieve its objectives is formidable. It was the Labour Governments of the 1950s and 1960s, for example, that nationalized key British industries and legislated sweeping social welfare programs. The influence of the labor union has now weakened considerably as the Labour Party has moved to the center of the political stage. As McIlroy points out, the interests of the union and the Labour Party do not coincide, but they do intersect (1998, 537; *Times,* Sept. 15, 1999). British business groups, in turn, find strong representation in the Conservative Party. It was the strong Conservative Governments of the 1980s that denationalized Britain's key industries, lowered taxes, and scaled back the welfare system.

Not all British pressure groups choose to work through a political party, a process that renders them hostage to the uncertainties of a national election. The British Medical Association and the Society of Civil Servants, for example, remain unaffiliated, allowing the major parties to vie for their support.

In addition to their electoral strategies, politically important groups such as the police, the Medical Association, and the Farmers Union work closely with the Government in designing legislation relevant to their respective professions. In many instances, they also have a major say in the regulation of their professions.

Pressure groups unable to reach the ear of a Cabinet minister often use individual MPs to press their cause in the Question Period or to introduce supportive legislation via a private member's bill. Such bills seldom see the light of day but may make their point by stimulating debate on a particular social issue.

A. H. Hanson and Malcolm Walles (1990) cite a particularly bitter commentary on interest politics by James Callaghan, a former minister of the Exchequer (Finance):

> When I look at some Member discussing the Finance Bill I do not think of them as the Hon. Member for X, Y or Z. I look at them and say "investment trusts," "capital speculators," or "that is the fellow who is the Stock Exchange man who makes a profit on gilt-edged." I have almost forgotten their constituencies, but I shall never forget their interests. I wonder sometimes whom they represent, the constituents', or their own or their friends' particular interests (Hanson and Walles 1990, 187).

Hanson and Walles go on to note that the power of individual MPs to influence policy is limited by the requirements of party discipline.

Citizens and Politics in Britain

The British population expresses its political views by means of elections, public opinion polls, civic action movements, and a vigorous press. Of the above, the general

---

British Opinion Polls

Public opinion polls are a regular part of British life, and rare indeed is the topic that has not been probed by one poll or another. During the early 1990s, for example, opinion polls indicated that the British population was largely concerned with issues of law and order, unemployment, and health care, the same basic concerns that dominated opinion polls in United States (*Times,* July 1, 1993, 4). The concerns of people in both countries remain much the same today (MORI Polls, "Political Attitudes in Great Britain for July 1999," *Times,* July 29, 1999, www).

---

elections are the ultimate expression of public opinion and portray a population that is increasingly centrist in its political views (Nadeau, Niemi, and Amato 1994). By-elections (replacement elections) and local elections also provide an important sounding board for public opinion, and a rebuff to the ruling party sends a clear signal of public disaffection with the affairs of state. By-elections in the run-up to the 1997 elections, it is interesting to note, revealed a precipitous decline in popular support for John Major and his Conservative Government.

Protests, demonstrations, and other forms of civic action are also a regular part of British life and tend to focus on social issues such as AIDS, gay rights, nuclear power, and environmental protection. By and large, their influence on policy is minimal, although the environmentalists have been successful in blocking road-building projects that threaten forests and other "green spaces."

The more politically aware members of British society find superb political coverage in newspapers such as *The Guardian, The Times, The Independent, The Telegraph,* and *The Financial Times,* papers that are read by British policy makers. All but *The Guardian* incline toward the Conservative Party, but even the more conservative papers criticize the Conservative leadership in Parliament. The popular press, by contrast, thrives upon sex and scandal, providing a sedative for the less intellectually inclined. The United States has fewer high-quality newspapers than Britain, but American newspapers seldom sink to the level of Britain's popular press. The British press is highly centralized; all major papers are published in London. The press in the United States is highly decentralized, with only *The New York Times, The Wall Street Journal,* and *The Washington Post* providing in-depth coverage of a broad range of national and international issues (Rose 1989, 202–3).

Not all citizens, of course, express their views with equal vigor. Most vote in national elections, but only a small minority belong to political parties.

How much, then, do the opinions of the British population actually influence public policy? There is no easy answer to this question. All British parties are sensitive to shifts in public opinion, but never more so than at the time of elections. British politicians are also particularly sensitive to issues of widespread concern. For the most part, however, the influence of public opinion is of a temporary nature (Conley 1990).

The Context of British Politics: Culture, Economics, and International Interdependence

It is relatively easy to describe the general features of the British political system, but it is a much more difficult task to explain why it works the way it does. How have the British managed to achieve such an exemplary blend of democracy, stability, human rights, and economic prosperity? For many observers, the answer to this question lies in the existence of a uniquely British political culture that has evolved over the course of several centuries (Almond and Verba 1965).

The Culture of British Politics

Britain's unique political culture is shaped by several factors. First, there is a strong sense of British identity or "we feeling." The British are very proud of being "British" (Rose 1989; McCrone, Kiely, and Bechhofer 1998). Second, the British population believes in the effectiveness of its political institutions. Their legitimacy is beyond question. Third, British political culture reflects a broad popular consensus concerning the unwritten rules of politics. Central to this consensus is a strong sense of fair play, tolerance, and patience. It is this consensus on the proper way to do politics that provides the essence of Britain's unwritten Constitution. Fourth, British society places a high value on orderliness and self-control. Few manifestations of British culture are more visible to the foreign observer than the British penchant for standing in line. People who willingly stand in long lines must surely be easier to govern than those who do not. Finally, the British population abhors violence (Rose 1989). Ordinary police, or "bobbies," for example, carry nightsticks rather than guns. When people have been properly socialized, guns are unnecessary.

British political culture, it should be stressed, is merely one facet of a more generalized British culture that sets the overall tone of British politics. British culture, for example, has traditionally stressed hard work, innovation, and endurance. It was these cultural characteristics that fueled the industrial revolution and enabled Britain to maintain its vast colonial empire. Prosperity does not just occur; it happens because people work hard and take the risks necessary to make it happen.

To say that Britain possesses a unique culture is not to suggest that all members of the British population share in this common culture or that all citizens of the United Kingdom are equally enamored of their political institutions. Northern Ireland's Catholic population has long been at odds with London, and small but important separatist parties also exist in Scotland and Wales. Both now have their own parliaments. For the most part, however, the overwhelming majority of the British population does manifest a strong sense of national identity, does believe in the legitimacy of its political institutions, and does share a common set of expectations about how reasonable people should conduct their political affairs. This high level of consensus on the political rules of the game has led some scholars to classify Britain as a homogeneous political culture (Almond and Verba 1965).

The existence of a culture that stresses moderation, fair play, tolerance, and order, then, goes a long way toward explaining why the British political system works the way it does. It is the strength of British culture, for example, that checks the inordinate powers of a British Government and guarantees the civil rights of British citizens. The British Constitution is a cultural constitution rather than a legal constitution, but it is just as binding. Indeed, a written constitution unsupported by a cultural constitution is largely meaningless.

Political culture has continuity, but it is also in a constant state of evolution. Each new generation is **socialized** into its political culture, yet each generation must adjust established cultural norms to meet the needs of its own circumstances. It was not until the early twentieth century, it will be recalled, that British culture deemed women fit to vote.

Historically, it was the British family that passed cultural values from one generation to the next. In the modern era, however, schools and the mass media have played an increasingly important role in the socialization process, as have political organizations and professional associations. Particularly important in the evolving nature of British culture has been the rapid expansion of comprehensive schools based upon the American pattern. The political values transmitted in a system of mass education must inevitably differ from those conveyed by

---

British Woes Tied to Cultural Attachments to the Past

The Economist, a British news journal, finds Britain's woes to be rooted in a deep cultural attachment to the past:

> The transformation of Japan from an incinerated ruin to a gleaming economic superpower shows what a scrap-and-build approach to investment can achieve in just 40 years. Come to Britain and one is confronted with a preoccupation with the past—an obsession with patching up jerry-built Victorian slums rather than bulldozing them away, the self-satisfied acceptance of genteel (read shabby) decay, the endless repeats of period dramas on television. Why are there no skyscrapers in Birmingham, Manchester, Glasgow, Liverpool, or Leeds? Why do Londoners put up with such a dirty and dilapidated underground? Why are prices so high and services so poor? (*Economist,* "Down But Not Out: A Survey of Britain," Oct. 24, 1992, 12–13).

---

an elitist system of "public" (private) schools that minister to some 7 percent of the British population (Rose 1989).

In the aftermath of the Second World War, British political culture was forced to adjust to Britain's declining role as a world power. It must now adjust to a dramatic restructuring of Britain's economic base as the heavy industries that fueled Britain's rise as an industrial power give way to high-tech and service industries. Over time, Britain has also become a multiracial society; today some 5 percent of the British population are of foreign origin.

Some observers suggest that these and other changes in Britain's socioeconomic environment have eroded the homogeneity of British culture (Punnett 1988). The Thatcher revolution, in particular, is seen as having pitted the rich against the poor, undermining traditional sensitivities toward the needs of the community as a whole. Similarly, it has been suggested that Britain is becoming a post-materialist society in which the traditional British values of innovation, hard work, and sacrifice have given way to a pervasive concern for comfort and environmental harmony.

Political Economy and Politics in Britain

While some observers find the key to British politics in its political culture, others find British politics to be an expression of its political economy. British parliamentary democracy itself, they note, evolved from economic conflict between the Crown and the Barons. It was the Industrial Revolution, moreover, that gave rise to both the bourgeoisie and the working class, each turning to politics as an avenue for advancing its economic interests.

The competing interests of the bourgeoisie and the working class continue to be the defining parameters of political conflict in Britain today. The Conservatives seek to stimulate economic growth by freeing the business community from excessive regulations, while Labour demands that the powers of government be used to achieve a more equitable distribution of the nation's wealth. The Liberal Democrats, in turn, are attempting to forge a middle ground between the two extremes.

British voting behavior over the course of the past several decades also reflects a pervasive sensitivity to economic issues. The swing to Labour during the 1950s and 1960s reflected a widespread belief that a Labour Government would be able to achieve both economic growth and social equity. The move toward socialism, however, proved to be a disappointment as taxes increased and the economy stagnated. The British voters turned away from Labour in 1979, hoping that a Conservative victory would revive Britain's faltering economy. More recently, disenchantment with Conservative economic policies was a strong factor leading to the Labour victory in the 1997 elections.

It is also interesting to observe that the battle lines between the Conservative and Labour Parties correspond closely to an economic map of Britain. Labour remains dominant in the depressed areas of Britain, particularly Scotland and the north of England. The Conservatives reign supreme in the high-tech and prosperous south.

International political economists, in turn, suggest that British domestic politics is increasingly being shaped by foreign economic pressure. Intense competition from the Germans and the Japanese, in their view, leaves the British government little choice but to increase the competitiveness of British industry regardless of the social costs entailed therein. An economy that relies on foreign trade for its survival has no other option.

International Interdependence and British Politics

Throughout most of its history, Britain was able to forge an international environment that was much to its liking. A vast colonial empire provided British industries with secure markets and a cheap source of raw materials, while a powerful navy protected commercial routes and kept European tyrants at bay. Foreign pressures influenced domestic politics, but they were not determinant.

The end of World War II, however, would find Britain reduced to the status of a secondary power, its colonies in revolt, and its navy powerless to stem the threat of nuclear missiles. British industry, moreover, had been crippled by German bombardments and was patched up to carry on as best it could. The industrial infrastructures of Germany and Japan, by contrast, had been destroyed by the war and were rebuilt using advanced technology. Britain's competitive edge, accordingly, was dulled.

During the period following World War II, the world was dividing into two hostile camps: *a democratic capitalist camp under the hegemony of the United States and an authoritarian socialist camp dominated by the Soviet Union.* No longer able to depend upon its navy for protection from foreign adversaries, Britain sought security under the nuclear shield of the United States. British forces were also integrated into those of the **North Atlantic Treaty Organization (NATO)**, the commander of which was also an American. British policy makers, while uncomfortable with their dependence upon the United States, had little choice in the matter. Not to accept American dominance was to risk the Soviet occupation of Germany and, inevitably, the continent as a whole. British policy, accordingly, focused on creating a "special relationship" with the United States. The United States was sensitive to British interests, and Britain supported US foreign policy initiatives regardless of how ill-advised they found those initiatives to be.

Britain's special relationship with the United States is now giving way to a far greater concern with Europe. Opinion polls conducted in 1969, for example, found relations with the United States to be of far greater importance to the British public than relations with the continent. By contrast, some 54 percent of British adults polled during the early 1990s placed concerns for Europe above concerns for the United States (*Economist,* Sept. 26, 1992, 59). As *The Economist* comments, however, "Britain is still pulled both ways" (*Economist,* Sept. 26, 1992, 60). Be this as it may, Britain will soon be forced to choose between Europe and the United States as the interests of the European Union are increasingly at odds with those of the United States.

In the economic sphere, the post–World War II era found Britain moving in the direction of a mixed socialist-capitalist economy as labor and industry forged a political compromise that provided job security for workers in outmoded industries while simultaneously offering the private sector protection from foreign competition. This compromise increased the cost of British goods and reduced the ability of Britain to compete with aggressive German, Japanese, and American companies on the world market. Tax revenues fell, as did the funding for Britain's welfare state.

By the mid-1970s, Britain came face-to-face with the hard realities of the world economic system. Countries that wish to remain competitive in the modern world must adopt the practices of their most productive competitors, whatever the costs of those practices may be in terms of domestic politics. This is particularly the case for countries such as Britain that must depend upon exports for their survival. Britain could either reassert its capitalist traditions or see its economic base continue to crumble. In many ways, then, the impetus for the Thatcher revolution came from Britain's international competitors.

The vulnerability to external pressures experienced by Britain in the aftermath of World War II pales in comparison to the challenges to British sovereignty posed by the European Union. Britain reluctantly joined the Economic Community in 1971, shifting the locus of key economic decisions from London to Brussels. The Europeanization of the British economy increased dramatically in 1992 with the creation of the European Union, a broad framework for the eventual unification of Western Europe. (See Chapter 1.) If these efforts are successful, Britain will be relegated to the status of one province of a larger European state, not necessarily the dominant one. Britain has resisted this process—it did not adopt the common European currency in 1999—and some influential British leaders argue that Britain should join the North American Free Trade Agreement (NAFTA) rather than European Union, although this seems unlikely. The economic benefits, according to this argument, would be equivalent and Britain would retain its sovereignty. The "special relationship" with the US would also be retained. This is not the dominant view in Britain, but the point of view does have its adherents (*CSM*, Aug. 12, 1998, 7). The economic integration of Britain into the European Union is becoming an accomplished fact. In economic and environmental matters, British administrators are guided by European rules almost as much as they are by acts of Parliament. Civil rights activists also use the European "Bill of Rights" to plead their cases in British courts (Oliver 1991). Be this as it may, British reluctance to adopt the euro may relegate it to "second-rank" status in European policy councils (*Independent*, July 26, 1999, 1).

Although external pressures play an ever-larger role in determining British policy, it would be a mistake to assume that Britain has ceased to be a major actor on the world scene. This is not the case. Britain is a permanent member of the United Nations Security Council, a charter member of the G-7 economic club that determines world economic policy, and one of three main pillars of the European Union. Indeed, the British position will have much to say about both the ultimate shape of the EU and the pace of its evolution. When British colonies demanded independence, moreover, Britain skillfully fashioned the British Commonwealth, an association of former British colonies that continues to serve Britain's economic interests.

Challenges of the Present and Prospects for the Future

In Chapter 1, we outlined six characteristics generally associated with "good government": democracy, human rights, stability, quality of life, equality of opportunity, and concern for the environment. How well does Britain score on these six measures of good government? The answer depends upon one's standard of comparison. Judged within the world community as a whole, Britain scores exceptionally well, possessing

Nicknamed the "Chunnel," a tunnel beneath the English Channel speeds travel between England and France, facilitating England's economic integration with Europe.

one of the most democratic, stable, humane, and environmentally conscious political systems in the world. It also has a political system that provides most of its citizens with a superior quality of life. When Britain is judged in comparison with other states of the First World, however, the picture is less comforting (Studlar 1996). Britain is clearly a member of the First World, but it is no longer at the top of that most privileged grouping.

Democracy and Stability

Britain is one of the world's oldest and most stable democracies, its lone civil war having occurred in the mid-1600s. The British, however, have begun to question the way in which they practice democracy. The prime minister and Government, in the view of many, are too powerful. Others note that there is too little opportunity for citizen input between elections (Oliver 1991; Brazier 1991). The winner-take-all nature of British politics is also criticized for creating dramatic shifts in policy whenever one party replaces another (Jeffery 1998). Labour, for example, nationalized key industries during the 1950s only to see the Conservatives denationalize them a few years later. In each case, the minority party was helpless to intervene. Dramatic shifts in social and economic policy, moreover, are carried out by Governments that have received well under 50 percent of the popular vote—hardly a popular mandate. Other criticisms of British democracy focus on the House of Lords and on the lack of formal minority rights.

Are political reforms likely to be implemented in the near future? The answer to this question rests largely with the British electorate. The Hereditary Lords have been stripped of their voting rights and the Blair Government has experimented with proportional representation voting schemes in the elections for the European Parliament. More radical changes may be difficult to come by,

---

Advocates of Political Reform

Charter 88, a civic action group devoted to political reform, advocates the establishment of a written constitution complete with a Supreme Court and an American-style Bill of Rights. Charter 88 would also transform the House of Lords into a popularly elected "second chamber," designed to curb the tyranny of the majority. The Liberal Democrats, as discussed earlier, advocate a shift to proportional representation, a reform that would end the problem of wasted votes and give equal representation to minorities.

---

as most British citizens seem reluctant to change a system that has worked so well for so long.

Human Rights

Britain does not have a Bill of Rights, but few countries in the world can match Britain's record in the area of social justice. Critics, however, worry that Britain's tradition of tolerance may be showing signs of erosion. Four areas of particular concern include anti-terrorist measures designed to curb the attacks of the Irish Republican Army (IRA) and the Islamic Fundamentalists, reduced procedural guarantees for suspects in criminal cases, increased incidents involving racism, and abuses of the Official Secrets Act.

Until very recently, Northern Ireland was a war zone. British troops openly patrolled the streets, and human rights abuses had become commonplace. As the IRA carried its battle to the streets of London, moreover, British security forces came under intense pressure to curb IRA terrorism. The threat of the IRA had hardly declined before Britain found itself the center of Islamic Fundamentalist networks attempting to destabilize friendly countries in the Middle East. The Government responded by rushing out a new set of anti-terrorist laws (*Times,* Jan. 13, 1999). This pressure led to growing disregard for the rights of suspects and, in extreme cases, to false arrest and imprisonment.

The picture is much the same in regard to the fight against crime. Britain has witnessed a dramatic increase in crime over the past decade, and law and order have become a major concern of the British public[21] (*Times,* July 1, 1993, 4). Responding to the magnitude of the crime problem, a Royal Commission established to examine the British system of criminal justice went so far as to suggest that jury trials, a British invention, be suspended in certain cases (*NYT,* July 18, 1993). While this recommendation is unlikely to be enacted, it illustrates the tremendous pressure to which traditional rights are being subjected.

Human rights have also been strained by the growing multiracial character of British society. Approximately 5 percent of the British population is "nonwhite" today, compared to approximately 2 percent in the mid-1960s. Britain's black minority, approximately 500,000 in number, complains bitterly of racial discrimination in employment, housing, education, and health care. They also complain bitterly of police brutality (*Sunday Times,* Dec. 17, 1995, 15). Britain's 2 million Muslim citizens fare better than the blacks, but also find themselves subjected to prejudice in a predominantly white, Anglo-Saxon society (*CSM,** Jan. 8, 1992, 3).

---

[21]MORI poll for *The Times.* (MORI is a polling agency.)
*CSM stands for the *Christian Science Monitor.*

The increased multiracial character of British society has also spawned racist movements among lower-class whites, with some 7,000 attacks on racial minorities being recorded in 1992, up 76 percent from 1988 (*NYT*, Sept. 19, 1993, 8). While the situation is far less pronounced in Britain than in France or Germany, racist candidates have also begun to capture seats on local government councils. Acknowledging this reality, Britain passed a Race Relations Act to fight racism among civil servants (*Times*, Feb. 25, 1999, www).

Critics of Britain's human rights record also express concern over the Government's excessive use of the Official Secrets Act. Under the Official Secrets Act, the Government can suppress any information that it believes to be harmful to the interests of the nation (Oliver 1991; *Sunday Times*, Apr. 30, 2000, www). The Government alone makes this decision, and legal recourse is nil. The same sense of secrecy pervades the bureaucracy and judiciary (*NYT*, July 8, 1993, 3). As summed up by Margaret Thatcher's press secretary, "The game is the security of the state, not the public's right to know" (Lloyd in Rose 1989, 210). As if to underscore this view, the British secret service (MI5) is building a new communication center that will enable it to monitor e-mails (*Sunday Times*, Apr. 30, 2000, www).

Economic Growth and Quality of Life

Britain has traditionally been one of the wealthiest countries in the world. Labour Governments during the early post–World War II era, moreover, enacted sweeping welfare legislation assuring that all of Britain's citizens, not merely the upper classes, would share in the nation's prosperity. Among other things, the Labour legislation guaranteed all citizens free health care, unemployment insurance, retirement benefits, adequate housing, and free education at newly established comprehensive schools. Wealthier citizens retained the right to send their children to exclusive "public" (private) schools and to consult private doctors.

The Thatcher revolution of the 1980s struck back against a culture of dependency and attempted to create a Britain that was "lean and mean" by cutting back on welfare. Productivity increased, but only in certain sectors. Mining and heavy industry could not compete without state subsidies, and most of Britain's older coal mines and steel mills were forced to close, thereby swelling unemployment rolls. British comprehensive schools also continued to turn out graduates and near-graduates possessing few technical skills, a problem that is equally serious in the United States. Indeed, British public schools entered the millennium faced with a shortage of 10,000 teachers and no end in sight to a worsening crisis (*Sunday Times*, Jan. 3, 1999.) The picture was much the same in regard to health care, with the National Health Service "falling apart," according to representatives of the British Medical Association. Blair himself has made secret trips to government hospitals in an effort to get a better grip on the situation (*Times*, Jan. 14, 1999).

Britain, then, is rapidly becoming a **dual society**: *a society of managers and skilled workers who prosper in the more productive environment of the post-Thatcher era, and a society of minimally skilled and unemployed workers who are locked in a culture of poverty* (*NYT*, Oct. 5, 1999, www). The minorities are particularly disadvantaged, with unemployment among blacks and Muslims being two and three times the national average, respectively. Unemployment among youth, particularly minority and working-class youth, is particularly severe (*Economist*, Feb. 20, 1993, 55).

Flaws in Britain's Welfare System

Britain's welfare system had two basic flaws. First, it was too expensive. The Government lacked the resources to provide a consistently high level of health and educational services to all of Britain's citizens. As the British economy declined, the quality of service declined accordingly. The children of the wealthy parents, meanwhile, received a superior private education and the British elite system continued to perpetuate itself.

Second, the welfare system created a culture of dependence and mediocrity that would see the competitiveness of British industry fall below that of most other states of the First World (*Economist,* June 26, 1993, 111). Particularly devastating was an educational system that downplayed technical training and saw two out of every three students leave school before the age of 18 (*Economist,* "Down But Not Out: A Survey of Britain," Oct. 24, 1992, 12–13). Faced with a declining economy, many of the school dropouts could not find adequate employment and went on public assistance.

The Environment

Britain is one of the world's more environmentally concerned states, but less so than most other states of the First World. Japan, Germany, France, the United States, and Canada all have stronger environmental regulations than does Britain (Weale 1992). Britain's nuclear record has been a particular cause for concern (*NYT*, Apr. 19, 2000, www).

The reasons for Britain's slower response to its environmental challenges are largely economic in nature. Britain's industrial plant is older than that of most other advanced industrial states, making its cleanup costs proportionally greater. Excessive environmental regulations would also cripple the industrial centers of Northern England and Scotland, areas already suffering from chronic unemployment. The choice between protecting the environment and preserving jobs is difficult.

Britain's membership in the European Union has brought with it a growing body of European environmental legislation, much of it far more rigorous than that implemented by Parliament (Mathews 1991). It is the European legislation that will shape the future course of environmental legislation in Britain.

Prospects for the Future

The challenges facing Britain today are manageable. Britain's commitment to democracy is beyond question, and the political debate over constitutional reform merely aspires to make one of the world's oldest democracies even more responsive to the demands of its citizens. The recent uproar over human rights violations, while justified, does not alter the fact that Britain remains one of the most tolerant societies in the world.

Britain's inability to provide a high quality of life for all of its citizens is a more daunting problem. The growing emergence of a dual society, one rich and one poor, is deeply rooted in the structure of British society and does not submit to easy solution.

Ironically, Britain's reluctant entry to the European Union could prove to be its economic salvation. Free access to the European market has stimulated the growth of Britain's more productive industries. American and Japanese firms, moreover, have chosen Britain as the preferred point of entry to the EU market. Roughly 40 percent of both American and Japanese corporate investment, for example, is now in England, and approximately one-fourth of all British manufacturing is now in foreign hands. Foreign investors create new jobs and new prosperity, even though they inevitably transform the British way of doing things. Further progress, however, may depend on Britain's acceptance of the euro as the common currency of the European Union.

References

Adonis, Andrew. 1990. *Parliament Today*. Manchester, UK: Manchester University Press.

Almond, Gabriel A., and Sidney Verba. 1965. *The Civic Culture: Political Attitudes and Democracy in Five Nations*. Boston: Little, Brown.

Atkins, Burton. 1988–89. "Judicial Selection in Context: The American and English Experience." *Kentucky Law Journal* 77(3): 577–618.

Atkins, Burton. 1990. "Interventions and Power in Judicial Hierarchies: Appellate Courts in England and the United States." *Law and Society Review* 24(1): 71–103.

Barber, James. 1991. *The Prime Minister Since 1945*. Oxford, UK: Blackwell.

Benn, A. 1979. *The Case for a Constitutional Premiership*. Institute for Workers' Control. (No city listed, London presumed.)

Blackburn, Robert. 1995. *The Electoral System in Britain*. New York: St. Martin's.

Brand, Jack. 1992. *British Parliamentary Parties: Policy and Power*. Oxford, UK: Clarendon Press.

Brazier, Rodney. 1991. *Constitutional Reform: Re-Shaping the British Political System*. Oxford, UK: Clarendon Press.

Butler, David, and Dennis Kavanagh. 1998. *The British General Election of 1997*. New York: St. Martin's Press.

Charmley, John. 1998 (April–June). "The Conservative Defeat: An Historical Perspective." *Political Quarterly* 69(2): 118–125.

Childs, David. 1992. *Britain Since 1945: A Political History*. 3rd ed. London: Routledge.

Churchill, Winston. 1956. *A History of the English-Speaking Peoples*. New York: Dodd-Mead.

Conley, Frank. 1990. *General Elections Today*. Manchester, UK: Manchester University Press.

Coxall, W. N. 1992. *Political Realities: Parties and Pressure Groups*. London: Longman.

Crewe, Ivor. 1993. "Parties and Electors." In *The Developing British Political System in the 1990s*, 3rd ed. (pp. 83–111), ed. Ian Budge and David McKay. London: Longman.

Gamble, Andrew, and Tony Wright. 1998 (April–June). "The Conservative Predicament." *Political Quarterly* 69(2): 107–9.

Garnett, Mark, and Ian Gilmour. 1998 (April–June). "The Lessons of Defeat." *Political Quarterly* 69(2): 126–27.

Guttsman, William L. 1963. *The British Political Elite*. London: MacGivvon and Kee.

Hanson, A. H., and Malcolm Walles. 1990. *Governing Britain: A Guidebook to Political Institutions*. 5th ed. London: Fontana Press.

Hennessy, P., cited in James Barber. 1991. *The Prime Minister Since 1945*. Oxford: Blackwell, p. 77.

Hofferbert, Richard I., and Ian Budge. 1992 (Apr.). "The Party Mandate and the Westminster Model: Election Programs and Government Spending in Britain: 1948–1955." *British Journal of Political Science* 22(2): 151–83.

James, Simon. 1992. *British Cabinet Government*. London: Routledge.

Jeffery, Charlie. 1998 (July–September). "Electoral Reform: Learning from Germany." *Political Quarterly* 69(3): 241–251.

Judge, David. 1993. *The Parliamentary State*. London: Sage Publications.

Keating, Michael. 1998 (Winter). "Reforging the Union: Devolution and Constitutional Change in the United Kingdom." *Publius* 28(1): 217.

Kennedy, Simon. 1998 (February). "New Labour and the Reorganization of British Politics." *Monthly Review* 49(9): 14–26.

King, Anthony B., Ivor Crewe, David Denver, Kenneth Newton, Philip Norton, David Sanders, and Patrick Seyd, eds. 1993. *Britain at the Polls: 1992*. Chatham, NJ: Chatham House.

MacShane, Denis. 1998 (November). "Open Lists Will Give Us Closed Minds." *New Statesman (1996)* 127(4413): 30.

Maor, Moshe. 1998 (July). "The Relationship between Government and Opposition in the Bundestag and House of Commons in the Run-up to the Maastricht Treaty." *West European Politics* 21(3): 187–207.

Mathews, Jessica Tuchman, ed. 1991. *Preserving the Global Environment: The Challenge of Shared Leadership*. New York: W. W. Norton.

McCrone, Robert Steward, Richard Kiely, and Frank Bechhofer. 1998 (November). "Who Are We? Problematising National Identity." *The Sociological Review*, p. 629.

McIlroy, John. 1998 (December). "The Enduring Alliance? Trade Unions and the Making of New Labour, 1994–1997." *British Journal of Industrial Relations* 36(4): 537.

Nadeau, Richard, Richard Niemi, and Timothy Amato. 1994 (June). "Expectations and Preferences in British General Elections." *American Political Science Review* 88(3): 371–83.

Nagler, N. 1979. "The Image of the Civil Service in Britain." *Public Administration* 127–42.

Nairn, Tom. 1994. *The Enchanted Glass: Britain and Its Monarchy*. London: Vintage.

Norton, Philip. 1994. *The British Polity*. 3rd ed. New York: Longman.

Oliver, Dawn. 1991. *Government in the United Kingdom*. Philadelphia: Open University Press.

Piachaud, David. 1993 (June). "What's Wrong with Fabianism?" *Fabian Society Pamphlet* 558.

Punnett, R. M. 1988. *British Government and Politics.* 5th ed. Prospect Heights, IL: Waveland Press.

Punnett, R. M. 1992. *Selecting the Party Leader: Britain in Comparative Perspective.* New York: Harvester/Wheatsheaf.

Richards, Steve. 1998 (November). "The Wars of the Lords Will Go On and On." *New Statesman (1996)* 127(4413): 6.

Riddell, Peter. 1998. *Parliament Under Pressure.* London: Victor Gollancz.

Rose, Richard. 1989. *Politics in England: Change and Persistence.* 5th ed. London: Macmillan.

Sampson, Anthony. 1982. *The Changing Anatomy of Britain: Democracy in Crisis.* London: Hodder and Stoughton.

Sampson, Anthony. 1992. *The Essential Anatomy of Britain: Democracy in Crisis.* London: Hodder and Stoughton.

Scott, John. 1991. *Who Rules Britain?* Cambridge: Polity Press.

Sked, Alan, and Chris Cook. 1993. *Post-War Britain: A Political History.* London: Penguin Books.

Studlar, Donley. 1996. *Great Britain: Decline or Renewal?* Boulder, CO: Westview Press.

Thatcher, Margaret. 1993. *The Downing Street Years.* New York: HarperCollins.

Watkins, Alan. 1998. *The Road to Number 10: From Bonar Law to Tony Blair.* London: Duckworth.

Weale, Albert. 1992. *The New Politics of Pollution.* Manchester, UK: Manchester University Press.

Whiteley, Paul, Patrick Seyd, and Jeremy Richardson. 1994. *True Blues: The Politics of Conservative Party Membership.* Oxford: Oxford University Press.

Willetts, David. 1998 (April–June). "Conservative Renewal." *Political Quarterly* 69(2): 110–117.

Woodward, E. L. 1962. *History of England: From Roman Times to the End of World War I.* New York: Harper & Row.

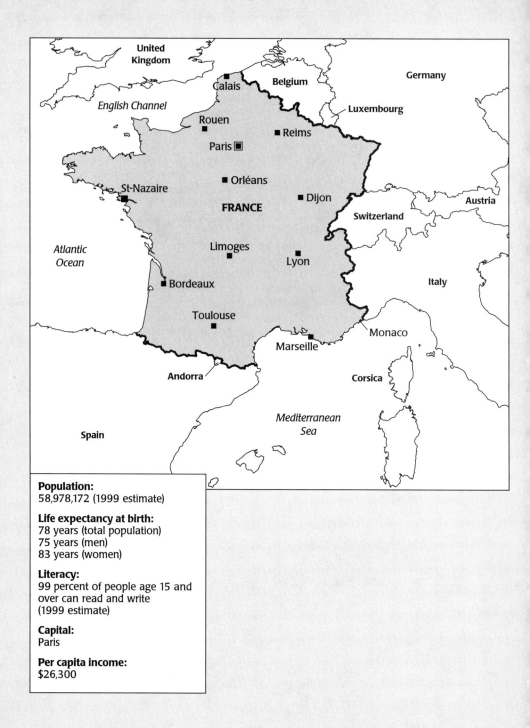

Population:
58,978,172 (1999 estimate)

Life expectancy at birth:
78 years (total population)
75 years (men)
83 years (women)

Literacy:
99 percent of people age 15 and
over can read and write
(1999 estimate)

Capital:
Paris

Per capita income:
$26,300

3

France
Politics in the Fifth Republic

Two nations, more than any others, have shaped the political traditions of the Western world: Britain and France. French culture was the preferred culture of the European aristocracy, and the French language long reigned as the international language of culture, commerce, and diplomacy. The French empire spanned the globe, bringing French civilization to broad areas of Asia, Africa, and the Americas, while France's Napoleonic Codes provide the foundation of most legal systems in the world today (Singer and Langdon, 1998).

France, moreover, is one of the small handful of states that dictate world economic and social policy. France is a nuclear power and a key member of both the UN Security Council and the G-7 club of industrial powers. France is also one of the core states in the European Union and has been a driving force in efforts to create a European supra-state. Little happens in the world arena without the participation of the French.

To study France simply because it is a major power, however, would be short-sighted. One studies France because it possesses one of the most innovative political systems of recent history. While the British have remained wedded to the past, the French have treated their political institutions with a disdain that other countries find disconcerting. Even today, France is far more willing than most of its neighbors to merge its political institutions with those of a politically unified Europe.

Beyond politics, one studies France for its art, its music, its language, its cuisine, its philosophy, its science, and above all, for the quality of French life. It is doubtful that the citizens of any other nation squeeze more personal enjoyment out of life than do the French (Zeldin 1982).

The opening of Euro Disney, an American-style theme park in Paris, met with mixed responses from French citizens. To critics, it was seen as another example of foreign encroachment on French culture.

Despite their country's power and exceptional quality of life, the French find themselves in something of a malaise. Once the most powerful nation in Europe, France now is overshadowed by the United States, Japan, and Germany. France remains a major power, but not a power of the first rank. French culture, moreover, is under siege. English has replaced French as the international language of culture, commerce, and diplomacy, and France's leading scientific research is now published in English as well as French. Even the French cinema, long Europe's most innovative, is struggling to survive in a pop culture dominated by Hollywood.

In the ensuing discussion of French politics, we will trace the evolution of French political traditions and describe the institutions that give expression to those traditions today. Next, we will examine the elites, political parties, pressure groups, and citizens who give life to French politics, as well as the cultural, economic, and international context in which those politics take place. Special emphasis will be placed on the evolution of democracy in France, an evolution that has been far more conflictive than that of Britain (described in the preceding chapter). While British political traditions have stressed tolerance and compromise, those of France have been characterized by revolution and violence.

France in Historical Perspective

France possesses two contradictory political traditions: an authoritarian tradition and a democratic tradition, with the latter sometimes bordering on anarchy (Brubaker

1992; Hazareesingh 1994). Efforts to reconcile these conflicting political traditions have not been easy for the French, but they have made for interesting politics.

France's emergence as an independent power is generally traced to the rise of Charlemagne, King of the Franks, in approximately 800 AD. Britain would not be unified for another two centuries and the German states would remain divided among themselves well into the nineteenth century.

The evolution of the French state, like that of the British state, began with efforts by feudal kings to extract ever-greater financial sacrifices from their subjects. In Britain, the monarch's need for money led to power sharing, first with the Lords and eventually with the Commons. In France, the need for money led to authoritarianism and to the establishment of a centralized bureaucracy that would tax the masses with ruthless efficiency.

French kings ruled with the support of the Catholic Church and the landed aristocracy, the latter having received huge land grants in return for their service to the crown. The Church legitimized the monarchy by preaching the divine right of kings. In return, it received absolute control of religious life in France. The aristocracy, for its part, subsidized the monarchy and maintained order in the countryside, its sons staffing the ever-expanding bureaucracy. The Church, too, provided the state with skilled administrators, the most illustrious of whom was Cardinal Richelieu (1624) (Wright 1987). Richelieu modernized the state apparatus and laid the groundwork for a modern standing army.

Over time, a "haute bourgeoisie" (big businessmen) of rich commoners replaced France's self-indulgent aristocracy in the upper echelons of the political structure and used its wealth to buy hereditary titles[1] (Popkin 1994). Unlike their British counterparts, however, the French bourgeoisie did not serve as a counterweight to the monarch. Rather, they chose to glorify their association with royalty. Supporting this grand edifice of royalty, aristocracy, church, and bourgeoisie were the French masses. By the end of the eighteenth century, the masses had been reduced to famine and had nothing more to give. The state, for its part, was bankrupt.

On May 5, 1789, King Louis XVI convened the "Estates General" in a desperate attempt to raise new taxes for his faltering regime. The Estates General was an irregular parliamentary body that had evolved to give expression to the three estates of the nation: the nobility (First Estate), the clergy (Second Estate), and the commoners (Third Estate). The king, standing above the three estates, considered himself the embodiment of the nation. The nobility were represented in the Estates General by 330 deputies, the clergy by 326 deputies, and the common people by 661 deputies. Voting was to be by estate or order, a procedure that made the voice of the nobility and the clergy equal to that of the masses. The deputies of the Third Estate protested, demanding that voting be "by head" rather than by order. The king refused, and on July 14, 1789, Paris erupted in revolution.[2]

A newly proclaimed Assembly declared France to be a democratic republic, issuing the *Declaration of the Rights of Man and Citizen,* a document that stands beside the American *Declaration of Independence* as one of the world's fundamental statements of human liberty (Popkin 1994). France's revolutionaries, however, had little experience with either democracy or human rights, and the Assembly soon fell under the sway of extremists demanding vengeance for centuries of aristocratic oppression. In a wave of mass hysteria, churches were sacked and aristocrats were hunted as animals.[3] Having destroyed the monarchy,

---

[1] Hereditary titles are referred to as *noblesse de robe.*
[2] The king, disguised as a servant, was seized in flight two years after the revolution.
[3] The Cathedral of Paris was seized and renamed the Temple of Reason.

In this depiction of the plight of the French peasant, an old farmer is bowed down by the weight of the privileged aristocracy and clergy. Meanwhile, birds and rabbits, protected by unfair game laws, nibble away at his crops.

the revolution then turned upon itself, finding traitors in every shadow. Tens of thousands of French citizens were hung, shot, or guillotined before Robespierre and other leaders of the "terror" were themselves executed during the summer of 1794 (Wright 1987).

Not all of France's citizens accepted the revolution's ideals with equal fervor. The excesses of the terror had raised serious questions concerning the ability of the French masses to govern themselves, and many French citizens recoiled from the radical anti-clericalism of the revolution. France, for all of its revolutionary rhetoric, remained a profoundly Catholic country. The revolution, accordingly, created a deep and fundamental division in French politics, one that pitted monarchy and religion against a populist republicanism that was virulently anti-clerical. Between the two extremes dwelt a great many individuals who distrusted both extremes. Remnants of this polarization remain today.

The First Empire: Napoleon I

General Napoleon Bonaparte seized power in November 1799, bringing ten years of revolutionary carnage to an end. The revolution established the principle that all citizens were equal before the law. It also established the principle that power resided with the people and their elected representatives, and that the church and state were to be separate, each within its own domain. The Napoleonic Codes, in turn, created a legal system that would be emulated by much of the world. The French bureaucracy was opened to all citizens on the basis of merit, and a series of Grandes Ecoles (elite colleges) was created to provide the French state with an impartial meritocracy dedicated to the revolutionary principles of reason and logic[4] (Antoine 1968). French revolutionaries, interestingly enough, did not question the centralization of the state. The issue was not the power of the state, but who would direct that power.

The Second Republic and the Second Empire

French history for the next two hundred years was to witness variations on the themes of republicanism and authoritarianism. The main events of this period are outlined in Table 3.1. The defeat of Napoleon at Waterloo in 1815 spelled the end of the First Empire, and the monarchy was restored (Popkin 1994). It was as if, in the words of one commentator, the revolution had not occurred (Besson 1988). In 1830, however, the Parisians again took to the streets, forcing the establishment of a British-style constitutional monarchy. The Revolution of 1830, in turn, was followed by the Revolution of 1848 and the birth of the Second Republic. The Second Republic established the principle of **universal manhood suffrage** (*allowing all competent adult males to vote*) but was less than three years old when its elected president, Louis Napoleon Bonaparte (nephew of Napoleon I), asked the citizens of France to make him an absolute dictator. The issue was put to the electorate in the form of a *plebiscite* in 1851 in which France's citizens could vote either yes or no. A **plebiscite** is *an election in which voters indicate their approval or disapproval* of a proposal put forth by the government. The authority was granted, with Louis Napoleon Bonaparte duly proclaiming himself Napoleon III, Emperor of France. The Second Empire had begun (Wright 1987). In spite of its authoritarian nature, the Second Empire retained the Parliament, a body consisting of a Senate appointed by the emperor and an Assembly elected by universal manhood suffrage. The emperor, however, remained the only source of effective power.

The political turmoil of the mid-1800s was a reflection of the deeper economic and social turmoil besetting French society (Wright 1987). The Industrial Revolution had taken root in France, its business leaders becoming among the most affluent in Europe. The workers and peasants, however, benefited little from the new prosperity, often being forced to work in conditions of near-servitude. Indeed, it was the plight of French workers that inspired Marx's Communist Manifesto (Sabine 1961).

The Third Republic

The Second Empire collapsed in the Franco-Prussian War of 1870, a war initiated by France in the hope of forestalling the unification of Germany. With the empire discredited, the deputies of the Assembly had little choice but to piece together a government capable of prosecuting the war.

No sooner had the Third Republic been established, however, than Paris again erupted in violence, with the rioters establishing a Commune to rule in the name of the people[5] (Popkin 1994). For a brief period, it appeared that the revolutionary visions of Marx would carry the day, but such was not to be. The Paris Commune was crushed by the leaders of the Third Republic, and the birth of a communist state would have to await the Russian Revolution of 1917.

---

[4]While the Grands Ecoles were not to attain their promise until the end of the Second Empire, it was Napoleon who established the principles of rule by an elitist technocracy that stood above the political fray.
[5]The Paris Commune was headed by a committee of radical leaders who spoke in its name.

Table 3.1
Napoleon and After: Chronology of French Politics

1799	General Napoleon Bonaparte seizes power in a coup d'état (sudden, forceful overthrow of the government).
1804	Napoleon Bonaparte is proclaimed Emperor for life in a national plebiscite. The vote was 3,572,000 for and 2,579 against. The First Empire begins.
1814	Napoleon abdicates power following a series of military defeats, and the monarchy is restored.
1815	Napoleon again seizes power and rules for 100 days before being defeated by the British at Waterloo. Louis XVIII is restored as the absolute monarch of France.
1830	A popular rebellion forces the establishment of a constitutional monarchy.
1842	A new law stimulating the development of railroads initiates the Industrial Revolution in France. The bourgeoisie grow wealthy, while the peasants, who represent more than 75 percent of the French population, remain locked in poverty.
1848	A popular rebellion establishes the Second Republic. Universal suffrage is proclaimed. Louis Napoleon Bonaparte is elected President of France.
1851	Louis Napoleon Bonaparte is elected emperor and granted dictatorial powers in a plebiscite. France is rapidly becoming an industrial power, as its cities more than double in size.
1852	The Second Empire is proclaimed as Louis Napoleon Bonaparte assumes the title of Napoleon III.
1870–71	The Second Empire collapses in the face of the Prussian invasion, and power is seized by a provisional regime that sues for peace. Following another popular uprising in Paris, the framework of the Third Republic takes shape.
1940	The Third Republic collapses following the occupation of Paris by German forces. Unoccupied areas of France are ruled by a pro-German government established in Vichy.
1944	General de Gaulle heads a provisional government following the Allied liberation of Paris and is charged with drafting a new constitution.
1945	De Gaulle resigns following rejection of his demands for the creation of a strong presidency. The new constitution extends the vote to women.
1946	The Fourth Republic is established.
1958	French generals attempting to crush the rebellion in Algeria defy the orders of the Government and establish a Committee for Public Safety in Algiers. De Gaulle is asked to head a new Government as a means of avoiding civil war. He agrees to do so on the condition that his constitution be accepted, without modification, by a plebiscite. De Gaulle's constitution is accepted by the voters of France.
1959	The Fifth Republic begins.
1968	Riots erupt in Paris as French citizens demand sweeping social and educational reforms. De Gaulle's proposals are rejected in a national plebiscite. He withdraws from politics.
1969	Georges Pompidou is elected president.
1974	Valery Giscard d'Estaing is elected president.
1981	François Mitterrand is elected president.
1988	François Mitterrand is reelected president.
1995	Jacques Chirac is elected president.

The Third Republic was beset by conflict from the moment of its origin. Reflecting the fundamental dualism of France's political traditions, the **political right** was dominated by *monarchists, clerics, and supporters of the church,* while the **political left** was fragmented among *communists, socialists, anarchists, and other diverse groups claiming to be the heirs of the Revolution.* The two positions were irreconcilable.

By the end of the 1930s, French politics had also begun to mirror the broader ideological conflict of a world preparing for total war. The Communist Party echoed the views of the Soviet Union, while the French right found much to praise in the policies of Adolf Hitler.

The intense fragmentation of the French political spectrum made it difficult for any bloc, left or right, to form a stable Government. The picture was further complicated by a rampant "opportunism" that saw deputies vote Governments out of office simply in the hope of gaining a seat on a newly formed cabinet (Safran 1991). The average life of a Government during the Third Republic was approximately eight months.

Despite its inherent instability, the Third Republic endured far longer than its predecessors, collapsing only with the Nazi invasion of 1940. One explanation for the survival of the Third Republic can be found in the professionalism of France's elitist bureaucratic technocracy. While the politicians squabbled, the technocrats ran the country.

German Occupation: Vichy, France

The humiliating collapse of the French military in World War II was to deepen the ideological fragmentation of French society and create scars that would take decades to overcome. Scarcely six weeks into the war, France was forced to sue for peace. German forces occupied Paris and the areas adjoining the German border, while the remainder of France was ruled by means of a puppet regime headquartered in the provincial village of Vichy (Wright 1987). The Vichy regime, "unoccupied France," was legitimized by the presidency of Marshal Philippe Petain, the aging military hero of World War I. The French right openly collaborated with the Nazis, their ranks being swollen by opportunists who believed that Germany would soon dominate the world. Many French citizens of moderate political views also supported the Vichy regime, not the least of whom was François Mitterrand, later to become the first socialist president of France (*Economist,* Sept. 10, 1994, 2).

Collaboration with the Nazis found its counterpart in the intensity and the sacrifice of the French resistance. External resistance to the Germans centered on the person of Charles de Gaulle, the charismatic leader of the Free French forces in Britain (Cook 1983). Establishing himself as the personal embodiment of French glory, de Gaulle proclaimed that France would be liberated by the French. A new "man on horseback" had arrived.

Domestically, the picture was far more complex. French resistance to the Nazis was organized by a variety of groups, the most important of which were the Communist Party, the Catholic Church, and the Gaullists.[6] Coordination between the resistance forces was tenuous, with each group positioning itself to emerge from the war as the dominant force in French politics.

---

[6]Gaullists were supporters of Charles de Gaulle.

The Fourth Republic

With the liberation of France by the Allied forces, General de Gaulle was proclaimed the head of a provisional government and charged with the task of providing France with a new constitution. De Gaulle argued for the creation of a strong executive capable of rebuilding the devastated nation, but his views were rejected. The French population, perhaps in response to the brutal authoritarianism of the occupation, chose instead to concentrate power in the hands of a popularly elected Assembly. The presidency remained largely symbolic.[7] Matters were further complicated by the establishment of a voting system based on proportional representation. If a party received 5 percent of the vote, it received 5 percent of the seats in the Assembly. Given the fragmentation of the French electorate, the Fourth Republic was doomed to be as unstable as its predecessor.

Declaring the new constitution unworkable, de Gaulle retired from politics, vowing to return only when his demands for a powerful executive had been met (Furniss 1960). Nevertheless, his supporters, remained active, launching a *Gaullist movement* called the **Rally of the French People (RPF)**. The platform of the RPF would become the cornerstone of the French right, but de Gaulle's popularity transcended class lines, and he also enjoyed broad support among France's middle and working classes. This was particularly the case among practicing Catholics.

The Fourth Republic was inherently unstable because its proportional-representation electoral system assured that each nuance of the political spectrum would find representation in the Assembly. No single party was able to form a Government, or, for that matter, a stable coalition. The Communist Party controlled a quarter of the seats in the Assembly and threatened to bring down any Government that opposed either its views or those of the USSR. The Gaullist RPF, for its part, could be counted on to oppose all leftist legislation and made little secret of its hostility to the Fourth Republic as a whole (Hoffman 1963).[8]

Unable to provide firm leadership, the Fourth Republic soon found itself embattled on all fronts. Strikes paralyzed the French economy, the Cold War threatened an armed confrontation with the USSR, and France's colonial empire was in open revolt. No issue, however, was more divisive than the revolutionary war in Algeria. Algeria was more than a colony; it was a department (province) of France and the home of some 2,000,000 French settlers (Brace and Brace 1965; Williams 1968). The political right supported the war, demanding that Algeria remain French whatever the war's costs in terms of human suffering and economic sacrifice. The left, led by the communists, demanded immediate independence for Algeria and a complete dismantling of France's colonial empire.

By 1958, the war had raged for eight years, dividing France against itself and bankrupting the French economy. With victory no longer in sight, the Government lost its will to prosecute the war and sought a political solution to the conflict. Accusing the Government of treason, the French commanders in Algeria defied orders from Paris to scale back the war and established a provisional government in Algeria. Gaullist supporters soon took control of the "Committee for Public Safety," as the rebellious generals termed their breakaway government, demanding that Charles de Gaulle be made the leader of France (Wright 1987). Leftists filled the streets of Paris in support of the Fourth Republic, but to no avail. The political system had become immobilized.

---

[7]The strong Senate of the Third Republic was replaced by a weakened Council of the Republic, the powers of which were poorly defined (Safran 1991). Executive power would reside with a prime minister responsible before the Assembly.

[8]The replacement of proportional representation with single-member districts did little to improve the situation, as deputies in the Fourth Republic continued the earlier practice of bringing down Governments in the hope of gaining a cabinet position in the next reshuffle (Safran 1991).

Arms upraised, General Charles de Gaulle addresses a crowd of 100,000 in the Place de la Republique in Paris.

The Fifth Republic

The president of the Fourth Republic capitulated to the demands of the rebellious generals, inviting Charles de Gaulle to form a Government. De Gaulle did so under the condition that a new constitution of his personal design be submitted to the French people for ratification by a plebiscite. They could either accept or reject it, but there were to be no amendments. If the voters accepted the new constitution, de Gaulle would serve. If they rejected it, he would leave France to its fate (Rioux, 1998).

The constitution was accepted, giving birth to the Fifth Republic. Much to the dismay of the military, one of de Gaulle's first acts was to grant Algeria its independence. Other colonies were offered the option of total independence or attachment to France via the French Union, a loose association similar to the British Commonwealth. Colonialism, in de Gaulle's view, was an anachronism incompatible with the forging of a new France.

De Gaulle would serve his purpose. France would be spared civil war and its economy would be revived. French prestige would also be restored, at least to some degree. France's citizens, however, soon became restive under de Gaulle's authoritarian rule, and in 1968, one decade after the promulgation of the Fifth Republic, Paris again erupted in anger. Students poured into the streets, burning cars and erecting barricades. Radical workers seized factories, proclaiming the era of capitalist exploitation to be at an end. Once again, or so it seemed at the moment, France was teetering on the brink of civil war (Ardagh 1990).

De Gaulle crushed the riots and drafted a new program of social and economic reforms designed to alleviate their causes. The reforms were duly presented to the French population in a plebiscite. As in earlier plebiscites and referenda, de Gaulle's propositions could either be accepted or rejected, but they could not be modified. The referendum was rejected, and de Gaulle withdrew from French politics.

If historical patterns were to hold true, the events of 1968 should have triggered a return to "popular rule" in which weak coalition Governments were dominated by a strong Assembly. It did not. De Gaulle withdrew from politics, but his party and his constitution remained in power. In retrospect, the events of 1968 were but one dimension of a "new" French revolution that had been taking place since the end of World War II. As described by Mendras and Cole (1991, 1–2):

> The last thirty-five years have witnessed a new French Revolution. Although peaceful, this has been just as profound as that of 1789 because it has totally overhauled the moral foundations and social equilibrium of French society. This judgment must not be impaired by the fact that violence had no part within this second French Revolution, except for the limited violence of May 1968.

France, the country of political extremes, was becoming a country of the political center. Although vigorous protests remained a part of French politics, violence became ephemeral, with some observers suggesting (perhaps regretfully) that the French were becoming as staid as the British (Ardagh 1990). This was far from the truth.

Following the resignation of de Gaulle, France would have four additional presidents: Georges Pompidou (1969–1974), Valery Giscard d'Estaing (1974–1981), François Mitterrand (1981–1995), and Jacques Chirac (1995–present). Each would play an important role in consolidating the political institutions created by de Gaulle and transforming them into the foundation of a new French political system that would have little in common with the political systems of France's tumultuous past (Derbyshire 1990).

In the pages that follow, we will examine many of the factors that transformed France from a country divided against itself into one of the most stable, productive, and democratic countries in the world. Some of these factors are cultural in nature, while others are rooted in economics or in a changing world system. All play a part in explaining what must be considered one of the most remarkable political and social transformations in world history (Mendras and Cole 1991).

The Political Institutions of France

The Constitution presented to the French voters in the summer of 1958 was a complex document that called for a strong president, a prime minister of uncertain powers, a popularly elected Assembly, an indirectly elected Senate, a constitutional Council (Supreme Court), a Social and Economic Council designed to accommodate France's major interest groups, and a Council of State charged with coordinating relations between the Government and the bureaucracy. Civil rights were protected by an extensive Bill of Rights, but the new Constitution also provided the president with sweeping emergency powers to use in times of crisis (Maus 1998). As one observer of the era would comment, "after having tried out over a century and a half all possible systems, we have adopted a Constitution pregnant with almost every system" (Duhamel 1986).

Elections and Politics in France

French presidents are elected by direct popular vote once every seven years. An absolute majority of the popular vote, at least 50 percent plus 1, is required for victory.[9] If no candidate receives an absolute majority during the first round of balloting, a second

[9]Direct election of the president was introduced by constitutional amendment in 1962.

Table 3.2
The 1995 Presidential Election

First Round	
Party/Candidates	**Percentage of Vote**
Extreme Left	
Laguiller	5.30
Communist	
Hue	8.64
Socialist	
Jospin	23.30
Green	
Voynet	3.32
RPR	
Chirac	20.84
Balladur	18.58
Nationalist	
De Villiers	4.74
National Front	
Le Pen	15.00
Others	
Cheminade	0.28

Second Round	
Party/Candidates	**Percentage of Vote**
RPR	
Jacques Chirac	52.63
Socialist	
Lionel Jospin	47.37

Source: Adapted from *L'Election presidentielle: 23 avril–7 mai, 1995.* Paris: Numero special, Dossiers et documents du *Monde,* pp. 36, 62.

election is held between the two dominant candidates. All of France's major political parties field candidates in the first stage of the presidential election, as do different wings of the same party. The sheer number of candidates in the first round of presidential elections virtually assures a second-round election between the two main contenders. A list of the first- and second-round candidates and their party affiliations in the most recent presidential election (1995) is provided in Table 3.2. It is interesting to note that Jacques Chirac, the reigning president, received only 20.8 percent of the popular vote in the first round of the presidential elections, not a great deal more than Edouard Balladur, a competing candidate from his own party.

Confident that the "real" election will take place a few weeks hence, French voters often use the first-round election to vent their frustration with France's mainline politicians. The most striking result of the first round of the 1995 elections, for example, was the fact that approximately 15 percent of the vote was garnered by Jean-Marie le Pen, leader of the far-right National Front, a political movement advocating the expulsion of all foreign workers from France, along with other extremist measures.

Elections for the Assembly follow a similar pattern, albeit a pattern played out in each of France's 577 electoral districts (Suzzarini 1986). Many candidates contend for the primary round of the elections, with the two dominant candidates entering the runoffs. This procedure, in which the *winning candidate must receive a majority of the popular vote,* is referred to as a **single-member, simple-majority voting system**.

The single-member, simple-majority format of French elections has encouraged French political parties to coalesce into two reasonably well-defined blocs—the left and the right. As there can be only one winner, like-minded parties must come together if an ideologically acceptable candidate is to have any hope of victory. Nevertheless, the single-member, simple-majority format of French elections also allows France's diverse political factions to retain their identity during the first round of the electoral process. Only when the relative strength of the various parties and factions has been determined does the bargaining process begin in earnest. Thus, France's single-member, simple-majority electoral system forces fragmented political groups into grand coalitions, or "party families," but it does not force them into cohesive political parties on the pattern of the British Conservative or Labor Parties[10] (Rae 1967; Schlesinger and Schlesinger, 1998).

Executive Power in France: The President and the Prime Minister

The de Gaulle Constitution presented to the French voters in the summer of 1958 was designed to provide France with an executive capable of taking decisive and sustained action. The president, not the parliament, was to become the centerpiece of the new political system (Quermonne 1993; Massot 1993).

Although he created a strong presidency, de Gaulle was reluctant to transform France into a presidential system on the American pattern. Rather, he chose to create a hybrid political system in which France would possess both a president and a prime minister. The president would establish the broad parameters of public policy; and the prime minister, who had been nominated by the president, would guide the president's program through the parliament (Elgie 1993).

The President. The president is by far the most powerful player in French politics. Some of the president's powers are enumerated in the Constitution, while others have been "implied" from a generous interpretation of its articles. Still other presidential powers have been established by precedent or have resulted from the broader informal context of French politics.

The enumerated powers of the French president are sweeping, but they are not without limits. The president names the prime minister and Cabinet and can, presumably, change both at will (Stevens 1992). The National Assembly can force a prime minister to resign by means of a vote of no confidence, but the president is not forced to honor that resignation.[11] Should the prime minister and the Assembly

---

[10]British voting laws provide for single-member, simple-plurality districts. Like-minded groups must come together before the one-shot election, for there is no grace period between first- and second-round elections in which to work things out. Two-party systems are characteristic of single-member, simple-plurality voting procedures, while large but shifting "party families" are characteristic of single-member, simple-majority electoral procedures. Multiparty systems are characteristic of proportional representation voting procedures. How the rules are structured *does* make a difference.

[11]As a practical matter, the president has little to gain by retaining a prime minister who lacks the confidence of the Assembly, the latter merely destroying the program of the former.

Presidential Powers in France and the United States

The enumerated powers of the French president exceed those of the American president. The framers of the American Constitution were intent on avoiding the tyranny of the executive, while de Gaulle crafted his constitution to counter the tyranny (and immobilization) of the legislature. Indeed, de Gaulle would write to his son that he viewed the president as being a "popular monarch" (Hayward 1993).

---

become deadlocked, the president has the option of dissolving the Assembly and calling for new elections.[12]

The president is also the commander-in-chief of the armed forces and may negotiate and ratify treaties. These provisions have provided French presidents with total dominance in the areas of defense and foreign policy[13] (Howorth 1993). Beyond this, Article 5 of the Constitution calls upon the president to "see that the Constitution is respected" and to "ensure by his arbitration, the regular functioning of the governmental authorities." While the exact meaning of this article has been subject to considerable debate, it is certainly sweeping in its potential implications.

The Constitution of the Fifth Republic goes on to state that it is the president who shall make appointments to the civil and military posts of the state. This clause, in itself, assures that the president will be the state's primary distributor of patronage. The term of the presidency, moreover, is seven years, thereby providing French presidents with sufficient time to pursue long-range policies that might otherwise be avoided by politicians required to go to the electorate on a more frequent basis. Finally, de Gaulle provided the president with the power to rule by decree during states of emergency. The emergency powers of the president were very much on de Gaulle's mind in drafting the constitution, for as noted above, he was brought to power by the threat of civil war. These emergency powers were used to quell the revolt of the generals in Algeria but have not been used since.

The presidential powers explicitly enumerated in the Constitution are not open to serious challenge. This is less the case in regard to the president's implied powers and the presidential powers derived from precedents established by de Gaulle during the formative years of the Fifth Republic (Massot 1993).

In this regard, it should be noted that the French Constitution is a particularly vague document that invites interpretation. As mentioned previously, Article 5 calls upon the president to "ensure by his arbitration, the regular functioning of the governmental authorities," a passage that continues to stir heated debate among French jurists.

In point of fact, de Gaulle interpreted all of the clauses of the constitution in an imperial fashion. De Gaulle, for example, left little doubt that the decision to dissolve both Governments and Assemblies rested squarely with the president. De Gaulle also forced his prime ministers to "resign in advance," thereby establishing the precedent that it was within the president's power to change Governments at will (Massot 1993).

Many of the powers of the president are "shared" between the president and the prime minister, the naming of the Cabinet ministers and the nomination of senior administrative officials being cases in point. In these and other instances, de Gaulle considered the countersignature of the prime minister to be little more than a formality and acted accordingly (Massot 1993).

---

[12]The president cannot veto legislation but can force the National Assembly to reconsider legislation. This, given the divisiveness of the Assembly, is often enough to kill legislation that that the president opposes.
[13]Treaties calling for the expenditure of funds must be ratified by Parliament.

De Gaulle established the tradition of an imperial presidency, a tradition maintained by his successors (Duhamel 1991). As a frustrated leader of the opposition, François Mitterrand, would complain of then-President Valery Giscard d'Estaing:

> [The] president of the republic can do anything, the president of the republic does everything, the president of the republic substitutes for the government, the government for the parliament, thus the president of the republic substitutes himself for parliament. The president of the republic takes care of everything, even the gardens along the Seine (Tiersky 1994, 53).

President Mitterrand would later comment, however, that "the institutions were not of my intention, but they serve me well" (Massot 1993, 38).

The formal and implied powers of the French president are further augmented by a variety of informal powers. If the party of the president controls the National Assembly, it is the president and not the prime minister who determines the legislative program. The prime minister will undoubtedly be an important member of the president's party or coalition, but his or her position will be secondary to that of the president. This means, in effect, that a president supported by a majority in the Parliament controls both of the major branches of government, the legislative and the executive. *It is only when the president does not have the support of a majority of the deputies in the Assembly that a clear division of power between the president and prime minister exists.* This occurred for the first time in the two-year period between 1986 and 1988, a period known as the **cohabitation**. It occurred again during the years from 1993 to 1995, again in 1997, and could potentially become a regular feature of French politics. During a period of cohabitation, the powers of the prime minister equal those of the president, a topic to be discussed shortly.

The president's informal powers include the ability to mold French public opinion (Perry 1998). The president is the centerpiece of French media coverage, and French presidents have used their domination of the media to cultivate an image of paternal aloofness that places them above the petty squabbles of ordinary politicians (Stevens 1992). De Gaulle's imperial grandeur gave birth to this style, but it was refined, if not extended, by his successors (Giesbert 1990).

The Prime Minister and Cabinet: The Council of Ministers. What powers, then, accrue to the prime minister? This is not an easy question to answer. In contrast to its lengthy elaboration of presidential powers, the Constitution of the Fifth Republic merely stipulates that "the Government shall determine and direct the policy of the nation" (Article 20) and "the prime minister shall direct the operation of the Government" (Article 21). Clearly, the role of the prime minister did not weigh heavily on the mind of Charles de Gaulle. Be this as it may, the power to "determine and direct the policy of the nation" would seem to rival the powers of the presidency itself (Wright 1993). As noted above, moreover, the appointment of Cabinet ministers and senior officials also requires the approval of the prime minister.

In constitutional terms, then, the division of powers between the president and the prime minister is characterized by considerable ambiguity. As a practical matter, the balance of power between the two executives depends upon which coalition of political parties controls the National Assembly. If the president's coalition controls the National Assembly, the role of the prime minister is that of "floor manager" for the president. The president selects most of the members of a "friendly" Government (Council of Ministers) and presides over their meetings. Indeed, Mitterrand selected his first Cabinet upon being elected the president of France before naming the prime minister who was to head that Cabinet (Giesbert 1990). Senior ministers, moreover, have direct access to the president and often bypass the prime minister entirely. The picture is much the same in regard to public opinion and the media. Not only do the media focus primarily on the president, but much of the media attention that does accrue to the prime minister is negative. When things go well, presidents assume credit for their programs. When things go poorly, presidents change prime ministers.

Cohabitation: Who Rules France? The first two decades of the Fifth Republic were characterized by strong presidents supported by clear majorities in the National Assembly. Prime ministers were secondary figures, changed at will by the president. This precedent was shattered with the initiation of the first period of cohabitation in 1986. President Mitterrand, a socialist, was confronted with an Assembly overwhelmingly dominated by the parties of the political right. The strongest of these was the Gaullist RPR led by Jacques Chirac (the current president of France). It was within Mitterrand's power to name a prime minister from within the ranks of the socialists, but little was to be gained by the appointment of a socialist Government that lacked the votes required to implement its program (Stevens 1992). The people, moreover, had spoken.

Chirac, supported by a majority coalition in the National Assembly, wasted little time in fulfilling his constitutional charge to "determine and direct the policy of the nation." The cornerstone of Chirac's program was the liberalization of the French economy, including the privatization of key government-owned industries. Chirac also rolled back several of the welfare programs that the socialists had put in place upon assuming power in 1981. Mitterrand continued to dominate the areas of foreign policy and defense, but not without some pressure from Chirac in these areas as well.

Unable to block Chirac's program, Mitterrand stressed his role as France's paternal elder statesman, using his dominance of the media to focus attention on Chirac's errors and to publicize the social hardships resulting from Chirac's attacks on the welfare system. Mitterrand, however, did not attack Chirac's program of privatization and other measures designed to stimulate the French economy. Hard-core socialism had become passé, and Mitterrand, the consummate politician, was positioning himself for the coming elections.

For Chirac, time was of the essence. Serving at the pleasure of a president whose policies he was seeking to reverse, he had only two years in which to position himself for the forthcoming 1988 presidential election (Giesbert 1990). A dynamic and successful prime ministership could well have made Chirac the next president of France. Chirac, however, did not exploit the opportunity to the fullest, and Mitterrand captured the presidency for a second seven-year term. The socialist coalition also regained control of the National Assembly, allowing Mitterrand to reestablish the imperial presidency. As Chirac would later lament, he had been lulled into a false sense of security by Mitterrand's friendly demeanor:

> I believed that he allowed me to implement my program because it was the voters' will. Naturally, he would mention that I had made a mistake here or there, but it was always with a smile (Giesbert 1990, 336, translated by Monte Palmer).

In spite of its brevity, the initial period of "cohabitation" demonstrated the extent to which de Gaulle's imperial presidency depended upon the ability of the president to maintain a majority in the Assembly. Mitterrand was the first president of the Fifth Republic to face a hostile majority in the Assembly, and he responded by allowing the opposition to form a Government. More importantly, he allowed a hostile Government to implement its programs. In setting these precedents, Mitterrand enabled the Constitution of the Fifth Republic to evolve into an instrument that promoted both democracy and stability (Ardagh 1990). Not to have done so would, in all probability, have spelled the end of the Fifth Republic.

Problems with Dual Executives

In addition to redefining the powers of the prime minister, the first period of cohabitation also illustrated the problems inherent in having dual executives of equal authority. As described by Tiersky:

At a meeting of heads of government, would Mitterrand or Chirac represent France? When heads of government and foreign ministers met, would Chirac sit with his foreign minister, Jean-Bernard Raimond, or would Mitterrand? At the first G-7 meeting to face the French cohabitation regime, an additional chair was found. But another time Chirac gave way to the president, and yet another time the foreign minister, Raimond, was made to give up his place to the prime minister, so that Chirac could sit at the table alongside Mitterrand. Throughout these humiliating shenanigans, Mitterrand and Chirac both repeated solemnly and unconvincingly to the international press that "France speaks with a single voice" (Tiersky 1994, 57).

The second experiment in cohabitation was to occur between 1993 and 1995, a period that coincided with the final years of the Mitterrand presidency. As in the earlier case, Mitterrand allowed the leaders of the right to form a Government while he returned to a position of critical aloofness. Unlike Chirac, Mr. Balladur, the new rightist prime minister, went out of his way to work in cooperation with the socialist president and, while harmony would be too strong a word to describe France's second experiment in cohabitation, the easy relationship between the two leaders demonstrated that cohabitation could work effectively (*Financial Times,* June 24, 1993, 3). Balladur, in retrospect, was also preparing for the 1995 presidential elections and spared no effort to demonstrate his centrist credentials. The strategy was not successful, however, and Balladur finished behind Jacques Chirac, a member of his own party, in the first-round elections.

Having crushed the left in the 1993 Assembly elections, the right, led by Jacques Chirac, captured the presidency in 1995. Chirac would thus have three years to reestablish the imperial presidency and implement the program of the right before the next round of mandatory legislative elections in 1998. Chirac, however, dissolved the Assembly in April of 1997, hoping to retain his legislative majority for an additional five years. This proved to be a disastrous gamble, for the left swept to a dazzling victory in the 1997 elections, crippling the program of the right, and forcing Chirac to share power with a socialist prime minister, Lionel Jospin (Szarka, 1997). To add insult to injury, Chirac also saw control of his own party pass to one of his main adversaries.

Stunned by the magnitude of the disaster that he had brought upon himself and his party, Chirac seemed to go into retreat while the socialist prime minister tackled the affairs of state (Lawday 1998). Indeed, it was not until 1999, midway through his term, that Chirac began to counterattack and reassert his authority, a move that the French newspaper, *Le Monde,* interpreted as Chirac's attempt to lay the groundwork for the 2002 presidential election (*Le Monde,* Jan. 2, 1999, 2).

In sum, then, the balance of power between the president and prime minister during periods of cohabitation is still evolving. In many ways, it is as if France has two political systems: one system when the same party family controls both the presidency and the Assembly, and another when power is split between the left and right. While others find this arrangement confusing, the French, always skeptical of politicians, seem to relish their discomfort (Duhamel and Mechet 1998). Be this as it may, many French political analysts have increasingly blamed cohabitation for immobilizing the French political process. To paraphrase *Le Monde,* "Everything demonstrates that cohabitation is a deceptive system that accentuates the risks of blockage, paralyzes the (popular) will, and stifles initiative (*Le Monde, les dossiers en ligue,* 1998). The tensions between the prime minister and the president, moreover, show no signs of easing (*Le Monde,* Feb. 27, 2000, www).

The Constitutions of the Fifth Republic and the United States

The Constitution of the Fifth Republic and the Constitution of the United States provide an interesting study in contrasts. The Constitution of United States delineates in great detail what the American executive can and cannot do. The French Constitution, by contrast, stipulates in great detail what the French Parliament can and cannot do. The French Constitution, for example, stipulates that all "laws" must be passed by Parliament. Having said this, the Constitution goes on to establish a clear distinction between "laws" and "regulations." Regulations do not require parliamentary approval.

The Parliament Versus the President. De Gaulle had little respect for legislatures, the members of which, in his view, placed self-interest before the greater interests of France. In framing the Constitution of the Fifth Republic, he sought to assure that the Parliament would not be in a position to jeopardize the effective functioning of the state. As discussed by Professor Claude Emeri of the Sorbonne:

> The fathers of the Constitution of 1958 had never disguised their intention: clean up French Parliamentarianism which, rightly or wrongly, is generally imputed to be responsible for the paralysis of the "system" of the Fourth Republic…. One of the first readers of the proposed constitution placed his view in the context of an elementary syllogism: the political parties are incapable of governing, the National Assembly is the locus of their power, the Government of France must escape the National Assembly (Chagnollaud 1992, 82, translated by Monte Palmer).

Parliamentary approval is required for legislation in the areas of civil rights, criminal and civil law, finance, taxation, nationalization of private property, employment, health, education, welfare, the organization of local government, and the declaration of war (Article 34, Title 5). In areas not specifically designated as "law," the executive has established the precedent of ruling by decrees that carry the full weight of the law (Safran 1991). The areas of defense and foreign policy, while often debated by Parliament, have been the almost exclusive domain of presidential decree (Safran 1991). Should the Parliament fail to reach a decision on a finance bill within seventy days, moreover, "the provisions of the bill may be enforced by ordinance" (Constitution, 5-47).

Parliament has been weakened in other ways as well. Issues on which Parliament is unwilling to act can be taken directly to the people in the form of a referendum (Brechon 1993). If approved by the majority of the electorate, they become law. It is the Government, moreover, that sets the agenda of Parliament. Unlike the United States Congress, the French Parliament cannot avoid an issue simply by ignoring it. The Government can also force the Parliament to accept "blocked" legislation, in which Government bills must be accepted or rejected without modification. A critical dimension of "blocked bills" is the requirement that the prime minister submit his or her resignation to the president if the legislation fails. Placing the fate of a Government on the line raises the stakes of political debate, for the collapse of a Government could well lead to the dissolution of the Assembly and new elections. This prospect is relished by few deputies, and most blocked bills do succeed (Emeri 1993).

The weakness of Parliament is also evident in the fact that it is the president, not the Assembly, who names the prime minister.[14] The National Assembly may bring down a Government by forcing a vote of no confidence (census in French parlance), but the President is not forced to honor that vote.

---

[14]Members of the Parliament, moreover, may not serve in the Government. To do so, they must resign their seats in Parliament.

Chambers of the French Parliament

National Assembly	Senate
■ 577 members	■ 321 members
■ Maximum five-year terms	■ Nine-year terms
■ Elected by universal suffrage	■ Elected by electoral college
■ Determines final version of legislation	■ Formal powers—to delay and obstruct legislation
■ Dominant chamber of Parliament	

The National Assembly and the Senate. The French Parliament consists of two chambers, the National Assembly and the Senate. The 577 members of the Assembly are elected by universal suffrage for terms not to exceed five years. The president of the Republic has broad latitude in dissolving the Assembly, but its dissolution must be followed within three weeks by the election of a new Assembly. The 321 members of the Senate are elected for nine-year terms by an electoral college that consists of the vast majority of France's elected politicians, including the members of the National Assembly, some 3,000 members of Departmental (provincial) Councils, and more than 100,000 members of City Councils. The dominance of Departmental and City Councils in the selection of senators provides the Senate with a strong provincial orientation. French citizens residing in France's overseas territories also find representation in the Senate. The Senate cannot be dissolved by the president.

All bills are considered by both chambers. If both approve a bill, it is sent to the president for signature. Should the Assembly and Senate pass conflicting versions of a bill, three procedures are used to reconcile their differences: (1) a period of shuttle diplomacy (*navette*) may take place in which informal efforts are made to work out the differences between the two versions of the bill; (2) the Government may request that a formal conference committee be convened to work out a compromise bill; or (3) the Government may request each chamber to reconsider the legislation. Of these procedures, the conference committee is the most common (Safran 1991). If it proves impossible to reconcile the differences between the Assembly and the Senate, it is the Assembly, upon the request of the Government, that determines the final version of the legislation. In this instance, the passage of a bill requires an absolute majority of all members of the Assembly, not merely those members present and voting (Constitution, 5-44).

The National Assembly, then, is the dominant chamber of Parliament, with the formal powers of the Senate being those of delay and obstruction. By and large, the obstructive power of the Senate is inversely proportional to the size and cohesion of the dominant coalition in the Assembly. The less cohesive the Assembly, the stronger the voice of the Senate.

How a Bill Becomes a Law. Both the Government and individual legislators have the right to introduce legislation. The former are referred to as Government bills (projects), the latter as private-member bills (propositions). As might be expected, Government bills fare much better in the legislative process than private-member bills. Among other things, it is the Government that determines the order in which legislation is considered. Once a Government bill is introduced into the Assembly, it is sent to the Council of State for an advisory opinion on its legality.[15] The bill may also be sent to the Economic and Social Council for its opinion. The Economic and

---

[15]This step is not required of private-member bills.

Representatives in the National Assembly are elected for terms of up to five years. The National Assembly is the dominant chamber of Parliament, with the Senate's powers consisting mainly of delay and obstruction.

Social Council provides French pressure groups with a formal mechanism for expressing their views on pending legislation.

Bills are then assigned to the appropriate committee. The committee studies the bill to examine its compatibility with existing legislation, often making minor amendments. Such amendments tend to be of a technical nature and often have the prior approval of the Government. Unlike American practice, committees cannot change the intent of the bill.[16] The bill is then scheduled for debate by the full Assembly. That debate will be vigorous, but its influence in shaping the final version of the bill will depend largely upon the strength of the Government's coalition in Parliament. The stronger the ruling coalition, the fewer amendments will be tolerated (Prost and Jacout 1993). In the case of a "blocked bill," no amendments are permitted and the Assembly must either accept or reject the Government bill as it stands. Once a bill passes in the Assembly, it is sent to the Senate and the process repeats itself. If the Senate version of the bill differs from that of the Assembly, the two versions of the bill are reconciled by the techniques discussed above. Once passed in the Assembly and the Senate, a bill is sent to the Government for the necessary signatures and then to the president for his or her signature.[17]

If a president disapproves of the legislation—a likely circumstance during periods of cohabitation—three options are available.

---

[16]Committees in the Third and Fourth Republics had often amended Government bills until they were beyond recognition, but de Gaulle's rules assured that this would not be the case in the Fifth Republic.
[17]In some instances, both the signatures of the prime minister and the minister responsible for the legislation are required.

1. *First, the legislation can be returned to the Parliament for reconsideration.* This may be an effective strategy in killing bills that lack a firm majority, but it can do little to alter the will of a determined Parliament.
2. *Second, the president can refuse to sign the legislation.* This does not stop the legislation from becoming law, but it does disassociate the president from the legislation. Mitterrand, for example, did not sign the legislation denationalizing many of France's major industries. By withholding his signature, he reaffirmed his socialist credentials and distanced himself from a process that caused many workers to lose their jobs.
3. *Finally, the president can challenge the constitutionality of the legislation in the Constitutional Council* (Massot 1993). As will be discussed in the ensuing section, the Constitutional Council has become a major actor in the legislative process.

Parliament as a Watchdog. The Parliament is also expected to keep a watchful eye on the activities of ministers and bureaucrats. Special committees are formed from time to time to investigate the improprieties of a particular minister, but such committees are partisan in nature and are reluctant to embarrass the Government (Emeri 1993).

Members of Parliament also have the right to question the Government on a wide range of issues of concern to their party or their constituents. Questions may be presented either orally or in writing, but the presentation of oral questions is organized by the Conference of Presidents, which goes out of its way to spare the Government undue embarrassment (Emeri 1993).

The weakness of the National Assembly in relation to the executive has created a sense of futility among many deputies, and absenteeism has become a problem of critical proportions. Traditionally, less than 60 of the 577 members of the National Assembly were present for all but the most pressing debates, with those in attendance voting on behalf of their absent colleagues (Prost and Jacout 1993, 17). This process, referred to as the "dance of the crabs," has now been outlawed (Jarreau 1993). Absenteeism is also increased by the tendency of many deputies to serve as mayors or to occupy other political positions. The low salaries of French legislators often leave them little choice but to seek a second position. Staff support is also minimal. For all of the above reasons, French legislators are less effective than their counterparts in the United States, Britain, and Germany (Tiersky 1994).

Law and Politics in France: The Constitutional Council and the Council of State

One of the most innovative dimensions of de Gaulle's Constitution was the establishment of a Constitutional Council or Supreme Court. Unlike most other provisions of the Constitution, virtually all of which found precedence in one or another of France's political traditions, the concept of a Supreme Court was alien to France. French courts had traditionally been prevented from interference in the legislative process, it being unthinkable that a small group of appointed judges would have the power to set aside the laws passed by the elected representatives of the people (Rosseau 1993). Equally problematic was the transitory nature of French constitutions. In sharp contrast to the American experience, the French did not view constitutions as divine law. Rather, constitutions were practical documents that embodied the prevailing consensus on the best way to decide "who gets what, when, and how." They certainly were not inviolable, a sentiment that de Gaulle expressed with great clarity:

Three things count in constitutional matters. First, the higher interest of the country…and of that I alone am the judge. Second, far behind, are the political circumstances, arrangements, tactics.… Third, much further behind, there is legalism.… I have accomplished nothing in my life except by putting the welfare of the country first and by refusing to be entrapped by legalisms (Stone 1989, 30).

It is probable that de Gaulle included a Supreme Court in his Constitution as yet one more device for curbing what he considered to be the legislative tyranny of the Third and Fourth Republics (Rosseau 1993). As indicated by the comments cited above, he did not, himself, intend to be bound by its dictates.

The Constitutional Council consists of nine judges, with three of its members being appointed by the president, three by the president of the National Assembly, and three by the president of the Senate (Constitution, VII-56). Terms are staggered, with the composition of the Council changing at three-year intervals. The president of the Constitutional Council is appointed by the president of the republic and votes only in the case of ties. In sharp contrast to the practice of the Supreme Court of the United States, the Constitutional Council rules on the constitutionality of laws prior to their promulgation by the president.[18]

In addition to declaring proposed legislation unconstitutional, the Constitutional Council has the option of declaring only one part of the proposed bill unconstitutional. In this instance, it may either kill the entire bill because of the "centrality" of its unconstitutional elements or allow passage of the bill devoid of its offending elements. In this situation, the Constitutional Court is exercising a line-item veto, keeping what it likes and rejecting the rest— a powerful role, indeed.

As originally instituted, the Constitutional Council could only rule on the constitutionality of legislation brought to it by the president or the prime minister. As such, the Council was just one more weapon in the arsenal of the executive (Rosseau 1993). Ordinary citizens did not have access to the Council, nor did members of Parliament. This was to change in 1974, when a joint session of Parliament amended the Constitution to read that a petition signed by sixty deputies or sixty senators could also force the Council to review pending legislation. By allowing sixty members of either the Assembly or the Senate to test the constitutionality of pending legislation, this amendment allowed a small minority in Parliament to obstruct the will of the majority by sending a bill to the Constitutional Council for review. A new hurdle had thus been added to the legislative process, and not a hurdle of minor import. Approximately 25 percent of the laws submitted to the Council between 1975 and 1981 were declared at least partially unconstitutional. By 1990, that figure would jump to 50 percent (Stone 1989; Emeri 1993). By and large, the increased use of the Constitutional Council reflects its utility as a means of blocking Government legislation. Council rulings, for example, were used by the parties of the political right during the early 1980s to slow Mitterrand's efforts to transform France into a welfare state. They have subsequently been used by the political left to slow the dismantling of the welfare state (Tiersky 1994).

In sum, then, the legalisms so abhorred by de Gaulle have now become a central element in the French political process (Chagnollaud 1993). To make matters worse, pressures are now building to allow individual citizens to contest the constitutionality of laws (Rosseau 1993).

---

[18]"A provision declared unconstitutional may not be promulgated or implemented. The decisions of the Constitutional Council may not be appealed to any jurisdiction whatsoever. They must be recognized by the governmental authorities and by all administrative and judicial authorities" (Constitution, VII-62).

The Council of State is the Government's official legal advisor. Government bills introduced into the Parliament are sent first to the Council of State for an opinion on both the bill's constitutionality and its "goodness of fit" with existing laws and projects. The Council's opinions are advisory and may be ignored by the Government, but there is little to be gained by pushing through Parliament a bill that is destined to be declared unconstitutional (Stone 1989).

The Council of State also heads France's system of administrative courts, playing an important role in resolving disputes between various administrative departments and agencies (Safran 1991). The Council may also initiate studies of pressing social and administrative problems, making appropriate recommendations to the Government (Safran 1991).

Bureaucracy and Politics in France

The bureaucratization of France paralleled the concentration of power by French kings. The greater the centralization of the state, the greater the need for bureaucrats. Napoleon rationalized the structure of the bureaucracy, his Grandes Ecoles drawing France's best and brightest into the service of the state. France, in Napoleon's design, was to be "managed" by a dedicated technocracy that placed the interest of the state above the petty squabbles of its politicians (Stevens 1992; Armstrong 1973).

The power of the bureaucratic elite expanded during the Third and Fourth Republics as fragmented Parliaments granted the bureaucracy sweeping powers to make policy, only the bare outlines of which had been approved by Parliament[19] (Safran 1991). It was the competence and dedication of the senior bureaucracy that kept the affairs of state on an even keel while the elected politicians of the era devoted more energy to destroying Governments than they did to running the country. In time, both the Parliament and the population grew accustomed to rule by administrative decree (Quermonne and Rouban 1986; Sardan 1993).

The elitist nature of the senior bureaucracy was further increased with the establishment of the Ecole Nationale d'Administration, or ENA (National School of Administration), in 1946. The ENA was a new "Grande Ecole" created to provide senior administrators with advanced training in economics, planning, and public administration. As described by Pierre Birnbaum,

> These senior bureaucrats, utterly different from the professional politicians, cut off in every way from the deputies—office workers, teachers, doctors, and lawyers—and ministers of similar background, were by this time all trained by a single school, the ENA, which imparted a uniform view of the world, superb competence, and an acute awareness of their own effectiveness, which they looked upon as something politically neutral…these officials lived in a world apart and were distrustful of the political process, which they often regarded as reflecting the power of special interests (Birnbaum 1982, 40, 41).

As noted previously, French parliaments have traditionally delegated broad and sweeping powers to the bureaucracy, a practice that continues today. Senior bureaucrats also shape policy by controlling the information that ministers require to make informed decisions. This is not a minor consideration, for members of the Government are heavily dependent upon the bureaucracy for technical expertise. Finally, the bureaucratic elite often uses its control of the administrative process to determine when and how policies will be executed. Those programs that it supports are facilitated, those that it opposes find an endless series of obstacles in their path. Ministers have the power to force the issue but are usually too busy to do so.

---

[19]The sweeping bureaucratic powers are referred to as *lois cadres.*

> ## Organization of the French Bureaucracy
>
> In terms of organizational structure, the French bureaucracy is divided into four broad classes: administrative, executive, clerical, and custodial. Of these categories, some 10,000 senior members of the administrative class are considered to be an elite service that stands above the ordinary civil service. Heavily weighted in favor of *graduates of the ENA*, or "**enarques,**" it is they who control the bureaucratic apparatus. Of these, a very small group, the "**grands fonctionnaires,**" is preeminent. Its members possess inordinate power and represent a key element in the French political elite.

The strong policy-making role played by France's enarques has called into question precisely who it is that rules France. Is it France's elected representatives or its bureaucratic elite? This question becomes all the more pertinent when one realizes that fifteen of the Fifth Republic's sixteen prime ministers have been civil servants, as have 249 members of the National Assembly elected in 1997 (Banks 1998).

The Actors in French Politics: Elites, Parties, Groups, and Citizens

As noted throughout this text, political institutions represent the arena of politics, but the actors in the political process play a critical role in deciding who gets what, when, and how. In this section, we will look at four broad categories of political actors in France—elites, parties, groups, and citizens.

Elites and Politics in France

Despite its revolutionary traditions, France is a profoundly elitist society (Rioux 1991). The core of France's elitism is its system of Grandes Ecoles, the graduates of which monopolize senior positions in both government and business. Entrance to the Grandes Ecoles, while open to all French citizens on the basis of competitive examinations, is heavily weighted in favor of the upper classes. Indeed, only 5 percent of the "enarques," the ENA graduates who dominate the government, come from "modest means" (Denni 1993, 419). French universities educate the masses, but they are inferior to the "Grandes Ecoles." Mitterrand sought to reverse this trend by infusing both the Cabinet and bureaucracy with leftist academicians, but the elitist orientation of the government remains pronounced. Elitism also exists at the local and regional levels, with political families tending to pass mayorships and other senior positions from one generation to the next (Denni 1993).

The focal point of France's political elite, needless to say, is the presidency. Presidents wield enormous power, and they wield that power for a seven-year term. The more an individual has direct access to the president, the more influential that person is likely to be.

Prime ministers and senior Cabinet ministers also rank high in the elite hierarchy, as do top business leaders, senior members of the president's office (personal staff), generals, and labor leaders. All have a voice in shaping how the scarce resources of the French state will be allocated.

In many ways, France possesses two distinct political elites: an elected elite that sets the direction of public policy and an administrative-business elite that determines how policies will be executed. Until the Mitterrand presidency, both elites shared a common vision of a strong French state guided by a partnership between business and government. The enarques served both, often *beginning their careers in government service and then jumping to the private sector,* a process the French refer to as **pantoflage**. Indeed, the heads of almost half of France's major companies are graduates of the ENA or one or another of the Grandes Ecoles (*Economist,* May 6, 1995, 70).

It would be a mistake, however, to draw too sharp a line between the elected elite and the administrative elite. As Denni points out, all of the presidents of the Fifth Republic, with the exception of Mitterrand, were career public servants. That trend has now been continued with the election of Chirac; both he and Lionel Jospin, the defeated Socialist Party candidate in the second-round elections, and a recent prime minister, are graduates of the ENA.

Parties and Politics in France

The fluidity of France's political institutions has been paralleled by the fluidity of its political parties. Much like a kaleidoscope, French political parties emerge on the political scene only to splinter and reconstitute themselves in differing forms (Borella 1993).

The Concept of Party Families. Given the fluidity and complexity of French politics, no attempt will be made to trace the historical antecedents of today's parties—a daunting task for even the most ardent student of French politics. Rather, our discussion will focus on the two major tendencies in French politics: the political left and the political right. While far from unified, the left and the right constitute *party families,* the members of which cooperate with each other on most occasions. The concept of **party families** is an important one, for most French parties tend to be *composed of several wings, as well as a variety of "clubs" and various personality groupings, any one of which could splinter into a separate political party or join forces with an opposing party* (Wilson 1989).

In order to appreciate the bitterness of conflict within party families, it is necessary to understand that a French president, once elected, does little consulting with party leaders other than those of his own party. In point of fact, consultation is thin even within the president's party. Being a partner in the winning coalition, accordingly, does not provide party leaders outside of the president's inner circle with a great deal of influence. It merely assures them that the reigning president is closer to their point of view than to the point of view of the opposition. For most politicians, that is not enough.

The Center Right: The Rally for the Republic (RPR) and the Union for French Democracy (UDF). The decade of economic and colonial turmoil following France's liberation by the Allied forces in 1944 culminated in the intense polarization of French society. The political right sought salvation in the return of Charles de Gaulle, the proverbial man on horseback, while the left coalesced around the Communist Party and its socialist allies.

As originally constituted, the Gaullists were a melange of business, military, Catholic, and related groups unified by the charisma of de Gaulle and a fear of communism. They also drew upon a deeply embedded sense of French nationalism, reflecting justifiable pride in France's historical, cultural, and scientific accomplishments[20] (Baudouin 1993).

---

[20]Georges Pompidou, de Gaulle's successor as president, consolidated the Gaullist position by creating a well-organized network of local party organizations, but control of the party machine, in the best Gaullist traditions, remained with the party leader (Wilson 1989).

By the mid-1970s, however, the party's future was in doubt. Its problems were many: de Gaulle was gone, fears of a communist takeover had diminished, personality conflicts were sapping the party's strength from within, and big businesses and small businesses were finding it difficult to work within the confines of the same party. More fundamentally, the party was losing its identity. Was it a party of the center or a party of the far right?

Divided among themselves, the Gaullists would split into two separate parties: a new party of the center right named the **Union for French Democracy** or *l'Union pour la democratie français* (UDF) and the **Rally for the Republic** or *Rassemblement pour la republique* (RPR).

The restructuring of the French right would find the Gaullist RPR championing the interests of *small merchants, artisans, farmers, retirees,* and other members of France's **petite bourgeoisie** (Charlot 1993). Its goals would be those of the traditional French right: law and order, morality, low taxes, and high tariffs. The RPR also had reservations about moving too rapidly toward the integration of Europe, fearing that many of France's older industries would find it difficult to compete on a European scale.

The UDF, by contrast, attempted to build a centrist coalition that would unite the interests of big business with those of France's large white-collar class (Ysmal 1993). Ideologically, the UDF would become the party of economic liberalism and European unity. The sooner the free market was allowed to weed out the weaker segments of the French economy, from the UDF's perspective, the better off France would be. Workers losing jobs by the closure of inefficient plants, according to the UDF, would soon find work via expanded production in those industries that were competitive on a world scale.

The UDF's economic liberalism was matched by a strong emphasis on individual freedom. It was not the responsibility of the government, from the UDF's perspective, to legislate morals (Ysmal 1993). The UDF's emphasis on personal freedom was designed to appeal to a salaried middle class that had been pushed to the left by the moral inflexibility of the right. The ideological differences between the two parties, while significant, were not beyond compromise. Personality differences between the leaders of the RPR and the UDF have proven more difficult to overcome and, in all probability, led to the defeat of the "right" in the 1988 presidential elections. By 1995, reason prevailed and a union of the two parties captured the presidency. The alliances fell apart during the debacle of the 1997 elections, but were cobbled together again in 1998 (Duhamel and Mechet 1998).

The Far Right: The National Front. The history of the Fifth Republic has witnessed the transformation of France from a country of political extremes to a country in which the political center of gravity resides firmly in the middle. Nevertheless, extremist parties continue to receive some 20 percent of the first-round popular vote on a consistent basis. The *dominant extremist party of the left* is the **Communist Party,** while the *dominant extremist party of the far right* is the **National Front** (Birenbaum 1992). The Communists are declining in influence, but support for the National Front has stabilized and may be increasing.

By the early 1900s, the National Front could claim 3 councilors general, 33 mayors, 239 regional councilors, 1,666 municipal councilors, and 10 deputies in the European parliament (Birenbaum 1992). The National Front also polled some 15 percent of the first-round ballots in both the 1988 and and 1995 presidential elections, a percentage retained in the 1997 legislative elections. Although the National Front has done well in the first-round elections, its extreme positions have precluded it from achieving any second-round victories. As with most

French political parties, it is prone to fragmentation and internal conflicts (*Le Monde,* Apr. 30, 2000, www). Nevertheless, more than 3,000,000 French citizens typically voted for the National Front during the first-round elections, a figure that has not gone unnoticed by the other parties of the political right.

The platform of the National Front is strikingly simple. France, according to the National Front, suffers from record unemployment, exorbitant taxes, escalating crime, and an epidemic of drug use. All could be solved, according to the National Front, by reducing France's large immigrant community, most of which comes from North Africa. The Party has also benefited from the charisma of its leader as well as from a strong organizational structure (Birenbaum 1992).

Both the UDF and the RPR have disavowed any ties with the National Front, with Chirac publicly denouncing the National Front as "a racist and xenophobic" party that is "unworthy and dangerous" (*Economist,* Mar. 28, 1998, 46).

Be this as it may, some 25 percent of the people who voted for Chirac in 1995 favor closer cooperation with the National Front (Duhamel and Mechet 1998). There have even been calls for a new party of the right that would incorporate the National Front, although this is unlikely to occur (*IHT,* Apr. 25, 1998, 2). Clearly the French right has an identity crisis. Is its center of gravity on the center right or the far right? Until it resolves this issue, unity will be difficult to achieve.

The Political Left: The French Communist Party and the Socialist Party. The French Communist Party (PCF) emerged from the Second World War as one of the strongest political parties in France, having been in the vanguard of the resistance forces (Baudouin 1993). Communist doctrine, moreover, found broad appeal in a society characterized by low wages, inferior working conditions, and a widening gap between rich and poor. Many French citizens also voted communist to indicate their displeasure with a political system seemingly bent on self-destruction (Wright 1987; Wilson 1993). Finally, the Communist Party benefited from a strong party organization that included control of France's largest labor union, the CGT. All in all, support for the PCF would peak at 28.2 percent of the vote in the 1946 elections, a figure that would remain stable throughout the Fourth Republic (Becker 1988; Furniss 1960). The size of the communist vote destabilized the Fourth Republic, raising very real fears that the Communists would "vote" themselves into power.

The Socialist Party, by contrast, was a much smaller party which, while advocating the nationalization of French industry and greater social equality, was less radical than the Communists. It was the Communists, however, that set the tone for the French left.

The rise of de Gaulle marked a slow but unrelenting decline in communist fortunes (Jensen 1991). Unemployment decreased in the wake of economic reforms, and Gaullist social legislation eliminated the worst inequities of French society (Baudouin 1993). The Constitution of the Fifth Republic also weakened the Communist Party by shifting political power from the legislature to a popularly elected presidency. The Communist Party was guaranteed representation in the Assembly by virtue of its strong support in working-class districts, but its programs were too radical to enable it to compete effectively for the presidency (Wilson 1989).

The Communist Party was thus faced with a choice between popularity and ideological purity. Broader electoral appeal could be achieved by championing the doctrine of **Euro-communism,** *a democratic version of communism that presented social welfare and the socialist economic policies as desirable alternatives to the inequities of capitalism* (Antonian 1987; Schwab 1978).

The French Communist Party, however, was dominated by resistance leaders who chose to maintain its ideological purity (Gaffney 1989; Hazareesingh 1991). Electoral support, according to the communist leaders of the era, was to be achieved by using the smaller Socialist Party as a front. The Socialists could steal the electoral limelight, but the Communists would remain the power behind the throne (Godt 1989). This strategy was formalized in a 1971 "Common Program" worked out between the Communist Party and the newly reconstituted Socialist Party of François Mitterrand. In retrospect, this was a mistake. The center of gravity of the French left, buoyed by an improving economic environment, shifted from the Communists to the Socialists. The shift was sealed by Mitterrand's election to the presidency in 1981, an election that saw the Communists capture a meager 7 percent of the vote in the first-round elections. The Communists continue to poll between 5 percent and 7 percent of the first-round vote in French elections. Belatedly, 1999 would see the Communist Party drop the hammer and sickle from the masthead of its ninety-five-year-old paper, *l'Humanité* (*IHT,* March 19, 1999, www). They have also been beset by internal conflict (*Le Monde*, Apr. 23, 2000, www).

The 1988 elections saw Mitterrand transform the Socialist Party from a Marxist party into a broad-based Social Democratic Party advocating a mild form of socialism that amounted to little more than capitalism with a conscience. He was rewarded with a second seven-year term of office. Ideological purity, once the hallmark of French socialism, had given way to the expediency of winning elections. Indeed, many Socialists now find the extremism of the Communists to be something of an embarrassment. The Communists screamed betrayal but had little choice but to support the Socialists.

The 1990s, however, were unkind to the Socialists. Again, the problems are many. French voters had swung to the right, yet many of the Party's most ardent supporters remained loyal to their Marxist traditions (Wilson 1989; Safran 1991; Gaffney 1998). It is they who were the workhorses of the Party, and it was difficult for the Party to prosper without their support.

The Socialists, moreover, had experienced severe financial problems. The Socialist Party maintained a large network of constituency organizations but lacked the funds to exploit them to maximum benefit. The position of the Socialist Party was also weakened by the absence of a direct link with France's highly fragmented labor movement. In France, unlike many other European countries, union support for the Socialists cannot be taken for granted (Portelli 1993). The unions, moreover, were themselves losing membership, a trend that bodes ill for the left in general.

Despite all of its problems and despite its defeat in the 1995 presidential elections, the Socialists rebounded in 1997 with an overwhelming victory in the Assembly elections of that year. The victory of the Socialists in 1997 reflected a new pragmatism that saw the program of the Socialists closer than ever to the political center. The days of radical socialism were over (Krause 1997). As noted earlier, the Socialist victory also owed a great deal to the ineptitude of Chirac and the political right.

The Greens. Over the course of the past three decades, the Greens have emerged as an important force on the center left of the French political spectrum, capturing some 10 percent of the first-round vote in the 1993 legislative elections. They are particularly strong at the local levels, having polled almost 15 percent of the vote in the 1992 regional elections. This trend continued in the 1997 elections with the Greens capturing eight seats in the National Assembly, and participating in the Government for the first time. The Greens now believe that they can replace the communists as the second party of the left in a few years (*Le Monde*, Sept. 13, 1998, 6). However, the Greens remain largely a first-round party, being too small to challenge the larger parties of the left and right in the more important second-round elections (Deleage and Saul 1997).

This situation is unlikely to change in the near future, as the Greens are a loosely knit organization that is divided into two competing branches. One branch of the party identifies strongly with the Socialists and advocates a broad range of social welfare issues. The other, in contrast, prefers to focus strictly on environmental issues, thereby allowing the Greens to enlist support from environmentally concerned citizens of all persuasions (Boy 1993). The party has also been fragmented by personality conflicts and constrained in its operations by a lack of resources (*Le Monde,* Apr. 27, 2000, and Apr. 16, 2000, www).

As environmentalism has become popular, France's major parties, especially the Socialists, have attempted to capture the Green vote by appearing to be environmentally concerned. Mainline candidates masquerading as environmentalists—"false Greens"— siphoned off much of the Green vote in the 1993 legislative elections (Boy 1993), and the Socialists picked up 35 percent of Green voters in the first round of the 1995 presidential elections (*Le Monde, L'Election presidentielle: 23 avril–7 mai, 1995*).

As in most European countries, the Greens find their major support among young professionals, as well as among teachers, social workers, and students (Boy 1993). This base, while articulate, is too narrow to challenge France's larger parties in the second-round elections.

The French Party System: An Assessment. For all of its diverse parties and factions, it seems quite probable that the French party system will continue to solidify around two broad coalitions: a right-of-center coalition centering on the RPR and UDF, and a left-of-center coalition dominated by the Socialists (Schlesinger and Schlesinger 1990).

The increasing stability of party families has allowed the French party system to sustain Governments over the life of their term, something that was largely impossible during the Third and Fourth Republics. It has also eliminated much of the post-election horse trading that characterized the Third and Fourth Republics. The French electorate is now confident that the Assembly will either be dominated by a moderate party of the center left or a moderate party of the center right. While the range of electoral options has been reduced, the consequence of electoral choices has been clarified. French parties, accordingly, are also becoming increasingly responsible; that is, the French electorate can reasonably expect them to carry out their campaign promises.

While the evolution of two large party families has contributed to the growing stability and moderation of French politics, French parties do not serve as an effective check on the powers of the executive. Elected leaders are minimally constrained by their party organizations, and personalities dominate parties, not the contrary (Schain 1989).

Pressure Groups and Politics in France

Pressure groups play such an active role in French politics that the distinction between party factions and pressure groups is often difficult to discern. The Constitution of the Fifth Republic established a special Economic and Social Council that provides France's major pressure groups with the opportunity to comment on relevant legislation before it is passed into law. More specialized consultative councils also exist in most administrative departments. Groups, then, are vitally important to the political process in France.

The Economic and Social Council consists of some 230 members, slightly more than half of whom are appointed by the Government. The remainder are elected by the members of France's diverse labor unions, trade associations, and professional groups. Labor unions receive the largest representation on the Council (sixty-nine members), followed in turn by business associations (twenty-seven members) and agricultural associations (twenty-five members). Other interests represented on the Council are cooperatives, mutual societies, renters' and savers' associations, public enterprises, artisans, and various professions including doctors and lawyers (Mouriaux 1993).

The influence of the Economic and Social Council on the legislative process is a matter of some debate. With so many interests represented, it is not easy for the members of the Council to speak with a common voice; even then, their voice is merely advisory. Be this as it may, those groups represented on the Council *enjoy direct and formalized entry to the legislative process.*[21] *In return, they are expected to be moderate in their demands and to work in harmony with government agencies.* This arrangement is referred to as **neocorporatism.** Not all groups in French society, it is important to note, find representation on the Economic and Social Council, the most glaring exceptions being immigrants and women.

Labor. Labor is represented by at least six major unions, each reflecting a different ideological position. Of these, the most important are the General Confederation of Labor[22] (CGT), a labor union closely linked to the Communist Party; the French Confederation of Christian Workers[23] (CFTC), a labor union linked to the Catholic Church; and the Work Force[24] (FO), a moderate labor union that inclines toward the Socialist Party.

Labor is well aware of the problems caused by its disunity, but attempts to unify the movement succeed for the moment, only to collapse in the face of disputes over strategy, ideology, or personality (*Le Monde*, Apr. 29, 2000, www). All in all, the power of the French unions peaked with the general strike of 1968 and has declined since that time (Mouriaux 1993). Even the election of a socialist president in 1981 did not bring unity to the unions or revive their influence (Mouriaux 1993). The situation remains much the same today.

The declining position of French labor has also paralleled the decline of France's "rust belt" industries. The economy of France, like that of the rest of the First World, is becoming a high-tech and service-oriented system. The pool of industrial workers, the core of the French union movement, has simply shrunk. A persistent unemployment rate of more than 10 percent has also made workers fearful that joining a union will jeopardize their employability. The same logic has depressed their willingness to engage in "industrial action." Although strikes by truckers, civil servants, and transportation workers continue to be part of the French political scene, most are short lived (Singer 1997).

Business. Business in France is better organized than labor but is also divided among itself. The National Council of French Employers (CNPF) serves as the

---

[21]Most of France's major professional groups find representation in specialized consultative councils such as the Conseil supérieur d'éducation, Assemblée permanente des chambres d'agriculture, Assemblée permanente des chambres de commerce, and the Assemblée permanente des chambres de métiers (craftsmen). These councils are quasi-official in nature and were created by the government to give professionals a role in drafting legislation relevant to their professions (Stevens 1992). The councils also play an important regulatory role within their professions. Representation on the various consultative assemblies is determined within each profession and is often the source of intense competition between groups and factions. The network of consultative councils is capped by the Economic and Social Council.
[22]Confederation general du travail.
[23]Confederation française des travailleurs chretien.
[24]Force ouvrière.

peak association for several hundred specialized business associations and more than 900,000 individual firms. The CNPF is dominated by France's larger corporations and has a pronounced "big business" orientation. As such, it often finds itself in conflict with the General Confederation of Small and Medium Enterprises (CGPME), many members of which are threatened by the expansionist tendency of France's larger firms.[25] The spread of supermarkets is of particular concern to the CGPME, for small food shops have traditionally been the mainstay of France's petite bourgeoisie (Ardagh 1990).

The conflict between the two organizations also finds political expression, with the CNPF supporting the moderate UDC while CGPME inclines toward the Gaullist RPR (Jones 1993). The CGPME also criticizes the CNPF for its "cozy" relationship with the bureaucracy and unions[26] (Jones 1993).

The Catholic Church. The Catholic Church, once the bastion of conservativism and conformity, has also seen its power eroded by factionalization and public disinterest. As described by John Ardagh:

> The Church, from being a central pillar of society, has come more to resemble a loose network of semi-autonomous groups, militants in the midst of a largely irreligious nation, and priests and laity alike are splintered into highly varied tendencies. While some priests flirt with Marxism, others return to the purest dogmas of integrism, insisting on the Mass in Latin. While some preach and even practice sexual freedom, others fiercely denounce the abortion reforms (Ardagh 1990, 430).

Be this as it may, France remains a profoundly Catholic country in which 90 percent of the population is statistically classified as Catholic and 80 percent of the population identifies itself as Catholic (Tiersky 1994). While only 10 percent of the population admits to being "practicing" Catholics, most French citizens are not hostile to the Church (*NYT,* June 18, 1994, 5). Indeed, a 1984 bill placing greater restrictions on public assistance to Catholic schools was withdrawn by Mitterrand in the face of the largest public outcry since the protests of 1968 (Tiersky 1994). At least in some areas, then, the Church retains a significant political voice. As indicated in Table 3.3, Catholics voted for Chirac more heavily than did members of other religions (Protestants, Jews, Muslims), with the figure for practicing Catholics reaching 74 percent.

Students and Intellectuals. Students and intellectuals, long the revolutionary vanguard of French politics, are heavily oriented toward the political left. France's two largest student organizations are the Marxist *Solidarité étudiante,* or student solidarity, and the more socialist-oriented *Independent democratique.* Students continue to protest Government policies, but their influence on policy making is minimal. As Tiersky laments,

> Young people in France, like industrial workers and nostalgia, are also not what they used to be politically and culturally. Whereas a French student of the 1950s or '60s could be found or at least easily imagined arguing politics and philosophy in a cafe, today students at a *fac* (a public university), a *lycée* or a *collège* (a lower secondary school) want to be tied into international fads more than existentialists and trendsetters of political engagement.
>
> Urban, upwardly mobile French youth are no longer even sure to know the difference between political "right" and "left," or worse still, to think that it matters much (Tiersky 1994, 30).

---

[25]The relationship between the CGME and the CNPF is complex, the former being a component of the latter.

[26]The peak association for agriculture is the Federation nationale des syndicats exploitants agricoles (FNSFA), and the peak association for education is the Federation d'éducation nationale (FEN).

Table 3.3
Religion and Party Preference in the 1995 Presidential Elections

Religion	Jospin (Left) %	Chirac (Right) %
Practicing Catholics	26	74
Nonpracticing Catholics	41	59
Other religion	56	44
No religion	69	31

Source: Adapted from *L'Election presidentielle: 23 avril–7 mai, 1995.* Paris: Numero special, Dossiers et documents du *Monde,* p. 72.

Table 3.4
The Concerns (Values) of French Youth

Elements	Very Important/Indispensable
A successful family life	91%
An interesting job	91%
To be among good friends	84%
To be of service to others	57%
To make a lot of money	41%
To have a long life	36%
To have a spiritual life	24%

Source: Based upon data presented in Olivier Duhamel and Philippe Mechet. *L'Etat de l'opinion* (pp. 238–239) by SOFRES © Editions du Seuil, 1998. Reprinted with permission. Data adapted from a poll presented by *Pelerin* magazine, July 15, 1997. N=40, Youth between the ages of 15 and 25.

Nevertheless, student protests in the spring of 1994 forced the Government to abandon its proposal to exclude "youth" from France's minimum wage law (*NYT,* Mar. 29, 1994, 1). So shaken was the Government by the protest, estimated to involve 200,000 students, that it sent a questionnaire to all French youth between the ages of 15 and 25 asking their views on topics ranging from school to social welfare (*NYT,* June 18, 1994, 5; *Le Monde,* Oct. 20, 1998). Among other things, the results suggested that the majority of French youth have little confidence in the future and believe their educations will be of little utility in helping them find jobs. Such responses are hardly surprising, given the fact that unemployment confronts one-fourth of France's citizens between the ages of 18 and 25 (*NYT,* Oct. 6, 1994, A7). As indicated in Table 3.4, French youth also remain family oriented.

More than 500,000 Lycée students also poured into the streets of some 350 French cities during 1998 protesting the degeneration of French education marked by a shortage of teachers, inadequate facilities, overstuffed classrooms, and excessive course loads (*Le Monde,* Oct. 17, 1998, 1). The protests were poorly organized, amounting to what *Le Monde* referred to as "joyous anarchy" (*Le Monde,* Oct. 15, 1998). It was not, however, a joyous event for socialist Prime Minister Lionel Jospin, who was desperately struggling to match his promises of social reform with the realities of the French budget (*Le Monde,* Nov. 3, 1998). French youth may have lost their interest in the grand ideological debates of the past, but they do expect their political leaders to provide them with jobs. The prospects for reduced unemployment among youth, however, are not bright (*Le Monde*, Apr. 21, 2000).

The same decline in ideological debate and political activism has become increasingly apparent among France's teachers and professors, with membership in the FEN dropping off sharply in recent years.

Over the course of the Fifth Republic, then, the violent group confrontations of an earlier era have given way to a responsible pluralism that provides a strong foundation for French democracy. Particularly interesting, in this regard, has been the evolution of civic action groups or "new social movements" designed to give expression to the rights of those lacking a voice in the traditional channels of French politics. In February of 1997, for example, more than 100,000 people filled the streets of Paris to protest planned legislation designed to impose further restrictions on illegal immigration. Other movements have arisen to protest the fascist tendencies of the extreme right, to champion the rights of women, and to urge support for victims of AIDS (Waters 1998).

Citizens and Politics in France

The power of the bureaucratic elite in shaping public policy raises serious questions about the role of elections and public opinion in the French political equation. Just how important is citizen politics in France? The answer to this question is straightforward. French citizens have little to say about the day-to-day affairs of their government, but they play a profound role in shaping the long-term direction of public policy (Hoffman 1963). Mass protest, it will be recalled, signaled the end of the Fourth Republic, just as the mini-revolution of 1968 spelled the end of the de Gaulle regime. The French electorate also brought the Socialists to power in 1981, only to temper socialist rule with right-of-center Governments in 1986 and 1993, a trend consolidated by the election of a right-of-center president in 1995. By 1997, however, the public mood had again shifted, and the Socialists recaptured the Assembly. It is the growing moderation of the French electorate, moreover, that has forced French parties to move to the center of the political spectrum. Conversely, public concern over unemployment and crime has forced the Government to take a hard line on immigration.

The responsiveness of France's elites to public opinion depends upon a variety of factors. All democratic leaders, French or otherwise, find it difficult to resist views that are shared by a broad cross section of the public. They also find it difficult to resist opinions of great intensity held by an articulate segment of that public. Hostility toward foreign immigrants currently falls in both categories. Much, of course, also depends on the nearness of elections.

French public opinion is expressed largely in three ways: elections, public opinion polls, and demonstrations. The second round of presidential and legislative elections are taken very seriously by French voters, while first-round elections are often used as a protest vote to express dissatisfaction with current policies (Grunberg 1993). Both the Greens and the National Front, for example, have done very well in the first-round elections but have found it difficult to elect members to the National Assembly. Their large first-round vote, however, has not gone unnoticed by France's larger parties. The Socialists have become increasingly Green, while the RPR has moved to capture the National Front vote by sponsoring stringent anti-immigration laws. The trend toward protest voting continued during the 1995 presidential elections, with extremist parties receiving more than 34 percent of the first-round vote. Such figures do not place French democracy in jeopardy, but they do suggest a strong sense of frustration among the French electorate. (See Table 3.2.) The figures presented in Table 3.5 (next section) portray a French public that is also increasingly skeptical of its political leaders.

> **Public Opinion Polls in France**
>
> Public opinion polls captured the imagination of the French electorate in 1965 by accurately predicting that Charles de Gaulle would be forced into a second-round runoff in the presidential elections of that year. Since that time, the French have become among the most polled individuals on earth. Unemployment and taxes have been the preeminent concerns of the French public throughout the 1990s, followed in turn by foreign immigration problems and security (Charlot 1993; Duhamel and Mechet 1998).

Public opinion polls take on added importance in France as a 1990 law prohibited paid advertising three months before elections. This has forced politicians to place heavy reliance on opinion polls in shaping their electoral strategy (Maarek 1997).

Protests and demonstrations continue to be a viable expression of French public opinion, although their numbers have decreased markedly in recent years. Aside from the students, the most visible demonstrators have been truckers, farmers, and fishermen protesting increased foreign competition. Strikes occur, but they tend to be of short duration. Taken collectively, the three avenues of French public opinion portray a society that is increasingly centrist in orientation, that places issues above ideology, and that is primarily concerned about economic issues.

The Context of French Politics: Culture, Economics, and International Interdependence

In addition to the influence of institutions and actors, the political process in France is also shaped by the broader context in which it occurs. Accordingly, in this section we will examine how French politics is influenced by its political culture, its political economy, and its interactions with the rest of the world.

The Culture of French Politics

Historically, France possessed a heterogeneous or fragmented political culture (Almond and Verba 1963). While some French citizens embraced a revolutionary or populist political culture, others internalized an ideology of authoritarianism and state dominance (Gaffney and Kolinsky 1991; Gemie 1998; Parry 1998). Traditional French culture was also characterized by high levels of interpersonal distrust, each family being an island unto itself and each looking to the state to protect it from its neighbors (Wright 1987; Crozier 1964). Groups and parties formed, but they seldom endured.

The political **immobilisme** of the Third and Fourth Republics was, from the culturalist perspective, the result of a nation fragmented by conflicting political values. If French politicians seemed to do little but bicker, it was because the gulf separating the political left and the political right was too vast to be bridged. There was nothing else they could do but bicker (Hoffman 1963).

The France of today is more unified than at any time in the past, a fact reflected in the growing centrism of French voters (Tiersky 1994). This growing centrism, from the culturalist perspective, is the result of changes in French society. Culture changes slowly, but it does change. The deep scars of the Second World War and the de Gaulle era are far less relevant to new generations of French citizens than they are to their parents. The younger generation of French citizens, moreover, has

---

Four Decades of Change in France

France, has undergone profound changes in the past four decades. As described by Gordon Wright:

Looking back from the 1980s over the past four decades, it would seem that change has been the dominant leitmotif. France has become an urban nation: more than half of all Frenchmen now live in communities of over 10,000 population—12 million of them in the swollen conurbation of Paris alone. French values, habits, and life styles have been extensively modified. The bonds of family, the domination of the younger by their elders, have been relaxed (though by no means broken)...Frenchmen and Frenchwomen have changed their tastes; they spend proportionately less on food and more on health, housing, travel, vacations, and education.... Living the good life seems to have replaced politics as the Frenchman's favorite off-the-job avocation. And the good life is plainly better, and more widely shared, than was the case in France a generation ago (Wright 1987, 454).

---

matured in an environment of stability and prosperity. They are also the product of MTV and the popularization of international youth culture (Tiersky 1994). In line with the general trend toward post-industrial values throughout the First World, French citizens are more concerned with quality of life and environmental issues than they are with the fine points of ideology (Inglehart 1990). Be this as it may, the French retain a healthy skepticism of politics and politicians, a fact amply demonstrated by the data in Table 3.5.

Political Economy and Politics in France

Virtually all major events in French history, from a political economic perspective, are economic in character. Feudalism was as much an economic system as it was a political system, and the French Revolution, whatever its romantic overtones, was a confrontation between wealth and poverty. The same confrontation between wealth and poverty, from the political economic perspective, continues to define the basic parameters of political conflict in France today. The French left draws a preponderance of its support from the working class, while the center of gravity on the right is found in the bourgeoisie. Even the divisions within party families are economic in nature. The communists are more hard-core working class than the socialists, and the RPR inclines toward the petite bourgeoisie while the UDF gives expression to the interests of big business.

As in most countries, then, France's major political parties are essentially coalitions of economic interests. Particularly vivid is the correlation between unemployment and support for the neo-fascist National Front. While much of the growing French middle class is moving toward the political center, the economically disadvantaged are moving toward the extremes of the political spectrum, particularly the far right. The most economically disadvantaged members of France's large Islamic community are also the primary supporters of Islamic extremism in France (*L'Eventment du jeudi*, Sept. 1994, 19–39; Duhamel and Mechet 1998).

For most of its modern history, France has pursued a mild version of state capitalism referred to as *dirigisme* (Cerny 1989). Under the rules of **dirigisme,** *state planners set the goals for the French economy and then used the financial resources of the state to encourage private-sector compliance with those goals.*

Many of France's larger businesses were also owned, at least in part, by the government. France's complex network of consultative councils, moreover, made both business and labor part of the dirigsme arrangement by providing them with a voice in the planning process. While parts of the French economy prospered under state guidance, dirigisme also saw the state subsidize many of France's less-

Table 3.5
Skepticism Toward Politicians and the Political System

Year	Percent of Respondents Who Believe That Democracy Does Not Function Well in France (Poorly or Not at All)	Percent of Respondents Who Find Politics to Be a Less Than Honorable or a Dishonorable Profession
1985	42%	26%
1990	45%	41%
1991	61%	44%
1992	52%	49%
1993	49%	33%
1994	44%	42%
1995	48%	35%
1996	54%	32%
1997	45%	35%

Source: Based upon data presented in Olivier Duhamel and Philippe Mechet. *L'Etat de l'opinion* (pp. 244–246) by SOFRES © Editions du Seuil, 1998. Reprinted with permission.

productive industries in the belief that it was in the country's national interest to maintain a balanced and self-sustaining economy.

With the advent of cohabitation in 1986, dirigisme came under attack from a political right enamored of neoclassical economic philosophy (Cerny 1989). Many government-owned firms were denationalized, taxes were reduced, and France's regulatory superstructure was at least partially dismantled. The attack on dirigisme continued with a victory of the right in 1993 and 1995. Nevertheless, one job in four continues to be in the public sector (Banks 1998).

Quite logically, each school of political economy attempts to interpret French politics in a manner that justifies its own philosophical position. This point is well illustrated by the diverse political-economic explanations of the decline of French socialism. From the perspective of the radical political economists, the shift away from socialism was the result of the intense pressure that was placed on France by the world capitalist system. The power of the German economy, in particular, was seen as forcing a socialist president to abdicate the principles of a lifetime and embrace a Europe unified by free-market economics. From the perspective of neoclassical economists, the shift to the center was the result of rational economic voting by the French electorate. French voters, in the neoclassical view, had become convinced that a free-market economy was their best guarantee of economic prosperity. Mitterrand could either modify his socialist views or see his party defeated. He chose the former course of action.

Whatever the case, there can be little question that the shift from state interventionism to free-market economics has presaged the unraveling of France's "social contract" that had been put in place under de Gaulle (Bonoli 1997). The highly respected newspaper, *Le Monde,* warned that an inegalitarian order is quietly being put in place that will divide France into two groups: the winners and the losers. While the winners will predominate, the losers will number in the millions and become a continuing source of political instability in French society (*Le Monde, L'Election presidentielle: 23 avril–7 mai, 1995*).

Indeed, the two main issues in the 1995 presidential campaign were unemployment and the "excluded." The excluded, as defined by William Pfaff, are "unskilled immigrants, people whose unemployment protection has run out, and the large number of young people who have never found a job" (*IHT,* Apr. 20, 1995, 8). It was concern for the maintenance of their social contract that helped the Socialists recapture the Assembly in 1997.

International Interdependence and the Politics of France

French politics has been so absorbed by the resolution of its conflicting historical traditions that one might assume international considerations were of minor import. This would be a mistake, for few states have been more intricately involved with their international environment than France.

France, as noted in the introduction to this chapter, has always been one of the dominant powers of Europe. Napoleon's empire spanned the entirety of continental Europe, stopping only at the gates of Moscow. France's colonial empire was surpassed only by that of Britain. The twentieth century, however, would not be kind to France, making it the battleground of two world wars and stripping it of its colonial empire. Military threats to French security faded with the stabilization of Europe, only to be replaced by the challenges of German and Japanese economic power. Battered by the Germans on the continent and the Japanese in the Third World, French heavy industry declined and its auto industry was placed in peril. French leaders, accordingly, had little choice but to bring France's economic system in line with those of its competitors by stressing greater efficiency. The same trend continues today as international pressures are forcing France to privatize many of its state-controlled industries and scale back state welfare programs[27] (Moisi, 1998). The process has not been as rapid as that of Britain and many other countries of Western Europe, but it appears irreversible.

The most direct international influence on French politics, of course, is the growing integration of the European Union (Garaud and Seguin 1992; Smith 1997). With the signing of the Maastricht Treaty in 1992, it is difficult to find any area of the French economy that is not at least partially influenced by EU regulations (*Economist,* "Survey of France," 1991). Protests by French farmers, truckers, and fishermen, for example, all have their origins in European legislation eliminating restrictions on foreign (EU) goods and services. France has also signed the social chapter of the Maastricht Treaty, thereby making its labor and social policies subordinate to those of the EU. Much the same is true in terms of environmental legislation.

French leaders have been in the forefront of the drive to create a politically federated Europe. Together with Germany, they have called for the creation of an inner core of the EU that will, in broad outline, resemble other federated countries such as the United States or Canada. Britain and other countries that oppose the closer integration of the EU will continue to participate in the EU as presently constituted, but they will not be allowed to obstruct the greater unity of its core states.

France's enthusiasm for an integrated Europe, while having waned somewhat, is not difficult to understand. As one of the four "big" members of the European Union, France is a major force in shaping European affairs. Without an integrated Europe, by contrast, France would almost certainly see its economic position slip farther behind that of a reunified Germany that is rapidly establishing its economic dominance over most of Eastern Europe. Rather than being an equal partner in EU policy making, France would find itself attempting to adjust to a German economic colossus over which it had little control. Unlike the insular British, the French do

---

[27]The Germans and Japanese also practice state capitalism but are less inclined to protect inefficient firms than the French. This topic is discussed in Chapters 4 and 5, respectively.

Protesting EU cuts of farm subsidies, farmers hurled potatoes at police in Quimper, Brittany. Farmers, truckers, and fishermen have objected to EU legislation eliminating restrictions on foreign goods and services.

not have a "special relationship" with the US and cannot pretend that they are not part of Europe.

While lacking superpower status, France remains among the most powerful nations on earth. France possesses a nuclear arsenal independent of the United States, is a permanent member of the Security Council, and is a charter member of the G-7 economic club that dictates world economic policy. France, along with Germany and Britain, will also determine the pace and scope of European unity.

The French take great pride in their role as a world leader but are now finding that the costs of world power are difficult to justify in the post–Cold War era. Maintaining the expense of an independent nuclear arsenal, for example, serves little strategic purpose since the collapse of the USSR. Its utility is also called into question by the growing integration of the European Union. Be this as it may, France continues to resent "America's grand design to 'gendarmer' (police) the planet" (*Le Monde, L'Election presidentielle: 23 avril–7 mai, 1995*) and has pursued a foreign policy independent of Washington. France, for example, was the first major state to break the US/UN-imposed embargo on Saddam Hussein's Iraq and has defied the US oil embargo on Iran (*NYT,* Jan. 7, 1995, 3; *IHT,* March 2, 1999, www).

Challenges of the Present and Prospects for the Future

In Chapter 1 we looked at six goals that have come to symbolize good government among the states of the First World: democracy, stability, human rights, advanced quality of life, economic growth, and concern for the environment. France is among the world's leaders in each of the six areas, but problems remain.

Democracy and Stability

France's first experiment with democracy began with the French Revolution of 1789. The leaders of the revolution seized power in the name of the people and proclaimed France to be a republic governed by the principles of liberty, equality, and fraternity. Democracy, however, would not come easily for the French, as each assertion of popular rule collapsed in acrimony and dictatorship. In spite of its tortured political history and fragmented political culture, the Fifth Republic would evolve into a political system that is as democratic and as stable as any political system in the First World today.

How did this miraculous transformation come about? This question is of more than theoretical interest, for perhaps the same formula could be used to strengthen democracy in the states of Eastern Europe, Africa, Asia, and Latin America. As might be expected, the explanations of France's democratic miracle are complex. Five points, however, are of particular importance.

First, the leaders of the post–de Gaulle era have been committed to democracy and, unlike de Gaulle, have adhered to the Constitution. Particularly important, in this regard, was Mitterrand's willingness to let the prime minister play a role equal to that of the president during periods of cohabitation. The parties of the right had won a majority of seats in the National Assembly by democratic means, and they were allowed to rule. Any other choice would, in all probability, have spelled the end of the Fifth Republic. Chirac has continued Mitterand's tradition.

Second, the Constitution established single-member, simple-majority election procedures. Those procedures worked to the disadvantage of extremist groups by forcing France's political factions to come together into coherent party families capable of electing a president and forming stable majorities in the Parliament. Single-member, simple-majority electoral systems cannot guarantee moderation, but they help.

Third, French democracy reflects an evolving political culture that finds French voters discarding old prejudices and becoming increasingly moderate in their views. With the electorate moving toward the political center, politicians and political parties have had little option but to follow suit. It would be unrealistic to say that ideological extremism is totally a thing of the past, with some 20 percent of the French electorate continuing to vote for extremist parties. The center of gravity of French public opinion, however, now lies firmly in the center of the political spectrum.

Fourth, the past thirty years have been years of growing prosperity for the average French citizen. Prosperity, as political economists point out, reinforces democracy by giving a broad cross section of the population an economic stake in its political institutions.

Finally, French democracy has benefited from a conducive international environment. The American presence in Europe shielded France from the threat of foreign invasion and promoted both democracy and economic stability throughout the region. As the American role in Europe has declined, regional stability has been provided by an increasingly vigorous European Union.

Human Rights

Few documents in world history speak more eloquently of human rights than the *Declaration of the Rights of Man and Citizen* produced by the French Revolution. Much as in the case of French democracy, however, the fragmentation and intolerance of French political life would slow the establishment of a just and humane society until the post–de Gaulle era. Even now, French attitudes toward human rights differ from those of many Americans. Most American citizens, for example, would be

---

Women's Emancipation Proceeds Slowly

French women have been slow to receive the legal rights of men. In the words of John Ardagh:

> One silent revolution of the France of the past thirty years has been the progress of women towards fuller emancipation—legal, professional, and sexual. It has happened later than in most advanced countries. Only in the 1970s did women begin to make an impact in politics or was abortion made legal and female contraception at last widely practiced....And until the 1964 Matrimonial Act, a wife still had to obtain her husband's permission to open a bank account, run a shop or get a passport, while much joint property was legally the husband's and the divorce courts were obliged to regard a wife's infidelity as more serious than a man's (Ardagh 1990, 330–31).

---

shocked by the latitude given to the French police in investigating criminal cases. The French, for their part, find the American penal system to be unduly permissive. The rights of society, in the view of many French citizens, must take precedence over the rights of individuals.

By far the biggest threat to human rights in France today takes the form of racism toward immigrants from the Middle East, Africa, and Asia. Public opinion polls suggest that hostility toward foreigners by native French citizens remains a major concern (Duhamel and Mechet 1998). More than 4,000,000 foreign nationals, about 6 percent of the French population, now reside in France. Most are Muslim, making Islam France's second religion (*Le Monde,* Sept. 16, 1998). One quarter of the French population, moreover, consists of either naturalized French citizens or their children. Although most immigration from the Third World is now banned, some 100,000 illegal immigrants continue to enter France each year (*Economist,* June 12, 1993).

Racism toward foreign immigrants focuses on three overlapping issues: unemployment, crime, and cultural diversity (Cesari 1998). France has an unemployment rate of more than 10 percent, and rightly or wrongly, unemployed French citizens blame their woes on the abundance of foreign immigrants willing to work for low wages under relaxed safety standards. Immigrants are also blamed for France's epidemic of drugs and crime, much of which emanates from immigrant ghettoes (*NYT,* Dec. 5, 1993, 1). Finally, French citizens resent the growing unwillingness of immigrants from the Middle East and other areas of the Third World to become "French." Muslim immigrants, in particular, have persisted in religious and cultural traditions that clash with France's social heritage, a process symbolized by the tendency of Muslim girls to wear long dresses and head scarves to school. A sign of piety among Muslims, religious dress is viewed as a rejection of French culture by their hosts.

Responses to the foreign presence in France have taken three forms: legal restrictions on immigrant activity, protest voting for racist parties, and community efforts to force immigrants to abandon their indigenous culture. The National Assembly, for example, has given police sweeping powers to check the identity papers of immigrants without warning, thereby opening the door, in the view of the immigrants, to unrestrained police harassment. Other proposed legislation seeks to deport suspected troublemakers with minimal due process and to make French citizenship more difficult to obtain. Racism also finds expression in the growing vote for the National Front, a party that openly advocates deporting all immigrants who do not possess French citizenship. French school authorities, moreover, have launched a frontal attack on multiculturalism, with girls wearing Islamic dress being sent home from school. The only values recognized in French schools are French values (*NYT,* Dec. 5, 1993, 1). On the positive side, France has avoided much of the anti-immigrant violence that has plagued Germany. Steps are even being taken to initiate an "affirmative action" program for minority youth (*Le Monde,* Aug. 26, 1998, 8).

Economic Growth and Quality of Life

France is a prosperous country with a per capita income of $26,300 (*CIA Factbook,* 1999). A cradle-to-grave welfare system, while now being scaled back, has also assured a reasonably fair distribution of wealth throughout French society.

Despite this social safety net, critics complain that the gap between rich and poor is larger in France than it is in most other European states. These problems, however, are significant only within the context of a prosperous First World state in which the vast majority of the citizens do have an economic stake in preserving the system. This was not the case thirty years ago.

The ability of France to maintain its generous welfare system is, however, now being called into question. As in most other countries, the costs of health care, education, and related services have escalated while their quality has declined (Hirsch 1993; Bonoli 1997). Everybody understands the problem, but few politicians are willing to increase taxes that already exceed those of Japan, the United States, or Britain. The right-wing Governments of the 1990s promised to trim welfare and scale back the burden of French taxes, a fact that led to a social-ist victory in the Assembly elections of 1997. Most French citizens are reluctant to see their social safety net dismantled.

Environment

French concern for environmental protection was minimal during the 1960s but has increased in vigor since that period. The Socialists have been particularly conscious of environmental concerns, hoping to incorporate the Green vote into the ranks of a center-left coalition. All things considered, France's environmental legislation is on a par with that of most of its European neighbors, all of whom are increasingly bound by the stringent environmental standards of the European Union. Much remains to be done, however, and air pollution in France is among the worst in Europe. Moreover, France remains committed to both the development and exportation of nuclear generating facilities, and it also continues to retain its arsenal of nuclear weapons. Nevertheless, the presence of the Greens in the Government and growing environmental awareness has led to proposals for an environmental super agency (*Le Monde*, Apr. 24, 2000, www).

Prospects for the Future

France is one of the more fortunate states of the world community. For the most part, its citizens can look forward to a future that is stable, democratic, humane, prosperous, equitable, and environmentally concerned. Not all French citizens, however, will share in this rosy outlook. The French safety net is slowly being dismantled, and there is little optimism that unemployment will fall much below 10 percent in the near future. Most of the losers in this picture will be immigrants and people who find their livelihood adversely affected by the growing integration of the European economy. The former are blamed for the plight of the latter, and immigrants' civil rights have suffered accordingly. These and related tensions have fueled support for the National Front and other extremist movements, but there is little indication that extremism poses a serious threat to a mature democracy that has become increasing centrist in its political outlook.

References

Almond, Gabriel, and Sidney Verba. 1963. *The Civic Culture*. Boston: Little, Brown.

Antoine, Rector. 1968. "Les Etudiants et la nouvelle université." *Realités* 274: 70–81.

Antonian, Armen. 1987. *Toward a Theory of Eurocommunism: The Relationship of Eurocommunism to Eurosocialism*. New York: Greenwood Press.

Ardagh, John. 1990. *France Today*. London: Penguin.

Armstrong, John A. 1973. *The European Administrative Elite*. Princeton, NJ: Princeton University Press.

Banks, Howard. 1998. "A Giant Kick in the Pants." *Forbes* 161, 11: 80–81.

Baudouin, Jean. 1993. "Le parti communist français." In *La Vie politique en France* (pp. 292–307), ed. Dominique Chagnollaud. Paris: Editions du Seuil.

Becker, Jean-Jacques. 1988. *Histoire politique de la France depuis 1945*. Paris: Armand Colin Editeur.

Besson, Jean-Louis. 1988. *Le Livre de l'histoire de France*. Paris: Gallimard.

Birenbaum, Guy. 1992. *Le Front National en politique*. Paris: Editions Balland.

Birnbaum, Pierre, trans. 1982. *The Heights of Power*, by Arthur Goldhammer. Chicago: University of Chicago Press.

Bonoli, Giuliano. 1997 (Oct.). "Pension Politics in France: Patterns of Co-operation and Conflict in Two Recent Reforms." *West European Politics* 20(4): 111–114.

Borella, François. 1993. "Le system des partis." In *La Vie politique en France* (pp. 223–42), ed. Dominique Chagnollaud. Paris: Editions du Seuil.

Boy, Daniel. 1993. "Les ecologists." In *La Vie politique en France* (pp. 310–27), ed. Dominique Chagnollaud. Paris: Editions du Seuil.

Brace, Richard, and Joan Brace. 1965. *Algerian Voices*. Princeton, NJ: D. Van Nostrand.

Brechon, Pierre. 1993. "Elections et referendums." In *La Vie politique en France* (pp. 367–84), ed. Dominique Chagnollaud. Paris: Editions du Seuil.

Brubaker, Rogers. 1992. *Citizenship and Nationhood in France and Germany*. Cambridge, MA: Harvard University Press.

Cerny, Philip G. 1989. "From Dirigisme to Deregulation? The Case of Financial Markets." In *Policy-Making in France: From de Gaulle to Mitterrand* (pp. 142–64), ed. Paul Godt. New York: Pinter.

Cesari, Jocelyne, Ed. 1998. *Musulmans et republicains: Les jeunes, l'islam et la France*. Paris: Complexe, Les Dieux dans la cité.

Chagnollaud, Dominique, ed. 1992. *Etat politique de la France*. Paris: Quai Voltaire.

Chagnollaud, Dominique. 1993. "Droit et politique sous Cinquième Republique." In *La Vie politique en France* (pp. 11–23), ed. Dominique Chagnollaud. Paris: Editions du Seuil.

Charlot, Jean. 1993. "Le Rassemblement pour le Republique." In *La Vie politique en France* (pp. 243–54), ed. Dominique Chagnollaud. Paris: Editions du Seuil.

CIA Factbook. 1994.

Cook, Don. 1983. *Charles de Gaulle: A Biography*. New York: G. P. Putnam's Sons.

Crozier, Michel. 1964. *The Bureaucratic Phenomenon*. Chicago: University of Chicago Press.

Deleage, Jean-Paul and Mahir Saul. 1997 (Winter). "The Fragile Victory of French Ecologists." *Environmental Politics* 6(4): 159–165.

Denni, Bernard. 1993. "Les elites en France." In *La Vie politique en France* (pp. 418–31), ed. Dominique Chagnollaud. Paris: Editions du Seuil.

Derbyshire, Ian. 1990. *Politics in France: From Giscard to Mitterrand*. Paris: Chambers.

Duhamel, Alain. 1991. *De Gaulle–Mitterrand: La Marque et la trace*. Paris: Flammarion.

Duhamel, Olivier. 1986. "L'hypothese de la contradiction des majorites en France." In *Les Regimes semi-presidentielles* (p. 271), ed. Maurice Duverger. Cited in *De Gaulle to Mitterrand: Presidential Power in France*, ed. Jack Hayward. London: Hurst and Company.

Duhamel, Olivier, and Philippe Mechet. 1998. *L'état de l'opinion: 1998*. Paris: Seuil.

Elgie, Robert. 1993. *The Role of the Prime Minister in France: 1981–91*. New York: St. Martin's.

Emeri, Claude. 1993. "Le Parlement." In *La Vie politique en France* (pp. 53–82), ed. Dominique Chagnollaud. Paris: Editions du Seuil.

Furniss, Edgar S. 1960. *France: Troubled Ally: De Gaulle's Heritage and Prospects*. New York: Praeger.

Gaffney, John. 1989. *The French Left and the Fifth Republic*. London: Macmillan.

Gaffney, John. 1998. "Socialism in France: An Appraisal." *West European Politics* 21(3): 208–213.

Gaffney, John, and Eva Kolinsky, eds. 1991. *Political Culture in France and West Germany: A Comparative Perspective*. London: Routledge.

Garaud, Marie-France, and Philippe Seguin. 1992. *De l'Europe en general et de la France en particulier.* Paris: Le Pre Aux Clercs.

Gemie, Sharif. 1998 (April). "Octave Mirbeau and the Changing Nature of Right-Wing Political Culture: France, 1870–1914." *International Review of Social History* 43(1): 111–135.

Giesbert, Franz-Olivier. 1990 *Le president.* Paris: Editions du Seuil.

Godt, Paul, ed. 1989. *Policy-Making in France: From de Gaulle to Mitterrand.* New York: Pinter.

Grunberg, Gerard. 1993. "Le comportment electoral des français." In *La vie politique en France* (pp. 385–401), ed. Dominique Chagnollaud. Paris: Editions du Seuil.

Hayward, Jack. 1993. "The President and the Constitution: Its Spirit, Articles, and Practice." In *De Gaulle to Mitterrand: Presidential Power in France* (pp. 36–75), ed. Jack Hayward. London: Hurst and Company.

Hazareesingh, Sudhir. 1991. *Intellectuals and the French Communist Party: Disillusion and Decline.* Oxford: Clarendon Press.

Hazareesingh, Sudhir. 1994. *Political Traditions in France.* New York: Oxford University Press.

Hirsch, Martin. 1993. "La protection social." In *La Vie politique en France* (pp. 176–85), ed. Dominique Chagnollaud. Paris: Editions du Seuil.

Hoffman, Stanley. 1963. "Paradoxes of the French Political Community." In *In Search of France* (pp. 1–117), ed. Stanley Hoffman. Cambridge, MA: Harvard University Press.

Howorth, Jolyon. 1993. "The Presidents, the Parties, and Parliament." In *De Gaulle to Mitterrand: Presidential Power in France* (pp. 150–89), ed. Jack Hayward. London: Hurst and Company.

Inglehart, Ronald. 1990. *Culture Shift in Advanced Industrial Society.* Princeton, NJ: Princeton University Press.

Jarreau, Patrick. 1993. "Elections legislatives." *Le Monde,* 21 mars–28 mars 1993, pp. 5–7.

Jensen, Jane. 1991. "The French Left: A Tale of Three Beginnings." In *Searching for the New France* (pp. 85–112), ed. James F. Hollifield and George Ross. New York: Routledge.

Jones, H. S. 1993. *The French State in Question: Public Law and Political Argument in the Third Republic.* Cambridge: Cambridge University Press.

Krause, Axel. 1997 (July–Aug.). "Jospin's Socialist Team: Lean, Feminine, and Pro-Europe." *Europe* 368: 16.

Lawday, David. 1998. "Chirac Shrinks the Presidency." *New Statesman* 127(4394): 20–21.

Maarek, Philippe J. 1997 (July). "New Trends in French Political Communication: The 1995 Presidential Elections." *Media, Culture & Society* 19(3): 357–368.

Massot, Jean. 1993. "Le president de la Republique et le premier ministre." In *La Vie politique en France* (pp. 53–83), ed. Dominique Chagnollaud. Paris: Editions du Seuil.

Maus, Didier. 1998. *Les Grands Textes de la practique constitutionnelle de la V Republique.* Paris: La Documentation française.

Mendras, Henri, and Alistair Cole. 1991. *Social Change in Modern France: Towards a Cultural Anthropology of the Fifth Republic.* Cambridge: Cambridge University Press.

Moisi, Dominque. 1998. "The Trouble with France." *Foreign Affairs* 77(3): 94–104.

Le Monde. 1995. L'election presidentielle: 23 avril–7 mai, 1995. Paris: Numero special, Dossiers et documents.

Mouriaux, Rene. 1993. "Les Syndicats sous la Cinquième Republique." In *La vie politique en France* (pp. 344–63), ed. Dominique Chagnollaud. Paris: Editions du Seuil.

Parry, D. L. L. 1998 (March). "Political Culture, Political Class, and Political Community." *The Historical Journal* 41(1): 311–315.

Perry, Sheila. 1998 (June). "Thirty Years of French Political Television." *Historical Journal of Film, Radio and Television.* 18(2): 213–229.

Popkin, Jeremy D. 1994. *A History of Modern France.* Englewood Cliffs, NJ: Prentice-Hall.

Portelli, Hughes. 1993. "Le Parti Socialist." In *La Vie politique en France* (pp. 272–91), ed. Dominique Chagnollaud. Paris: Editions du Seuil.

Prost, Dominique, and Pierre Jacout. 1993. *Un Deputé ca sert à quoi.* Lony: Editions Prost.

Quermonne, Jean-Louis. 1993. "Genèse et évolution du régime." In *La Vie politique en France* (pp. 24–52), ed. Dominique Chagnollaud. Paris: Editions du Seuil.

Quermonne, Jean-Louis, and Luc Rouban. 1986. "French Public Administration and Policy Evaluation: The Quest for Accountability." *Public Administration Review* 46(5): 397–406.

Rae, Douglas. 1967. *The Political Consequences of Electoral Laws.* New Haven: Yale University Press.

Rioux, Jean-Pierre. 1991 (Sept.). "Ces Elites qui nous gouvernent." *L'histoire* 147: 48–57.

Rioux, Jean-Pierre. 1998 (Sept. 27–28). "La Vie Republique Plebiscitée." *Le Monde,* 12.

Rosseau, Dominique. 1993. "Le conseil constitutional." In *La Vie politique en France* (pp. 109–32), ed. Dominique Chagnollaud. Paris: Editions du Seuil.

Sabine, George H. 1961. *A History of Political Theory.* 3rd ed. New York: Holt, Rinehart and Winston.

Safran, William. 1991. *The French Polity.* 3rd ed. New York: Longman.

Sardan, Pierre. 1993. "L'administration." In *La Vie politique en France* (pp. 148–67), ed. Dominique Chagnollaud. Paris: Editions du Seuil.

Schain, Martin A. 1989. "Politics at the Margins: The French Communist Party and the National Front." In *Policy-Making in France: From de Gaulle to Mitterrand* (pp. 73–90), ed. Paul Godt. New York: Pinter.

Schlesinger, Joseph, and Mildred Schlesinger. 1990 (Dec.). "The Reaffirmation of a Multiparty System in France." *American Political Science Review* 8(4): 1077–102.

Schlesinger, Joseph and Mildred S. Schlesinger. 1998 (Feb.). "Dual-ballot Elections and Political Parties: The French Presidential Election of 1995." *Comparative Political Studies* 31(1): 72–97.

Schwab, George, ed. 1978. *Eurocommunism: The Ideological and Political-Theoretical Foundations.* Westport, CT: Greenwood Press.

Singer, Barnett, and John Langdon. 1998 (May). "France's Imperial Legacy." *Contemporary Review* 272 (1588): 231–237.

Singer, Daniel. 1997 (July–Aug.). "The French Winter of Discontent." *Monthly Review* 49(3): 130–139.

Smith, Andy, 1997 (Winter). "Studying Multi-Level Governance. Examples from French Translations of the Structural Funds." *Public Administration* 75(4): 712–230.

Stevens, Anne. 1992. *The Government and Politics of France.* London: Macmillan.

Stone, Alec. 1989. "Legal Constraints to Policy-Making: The Constitutional Council and the Council of State." In *Policy-Making in France: From de Gaulle to Mitterrand* (pp. 28–41), ed. Paul Godt. New York: Pinter.

Suzzarini, M. F. 1986. *L'état c'est vous!* Alleur, Belgium: Marabout.

Szarka, Joseph. 1997 (Oct.). "Snatching Defeat from the Jaws of Victory: The French Parliamentary Elections of 25 May and 1 June 1997." *West European Politics* 20(4): 192–199.

Tiersky, Ronald. 1994. *France in the New Europe: Changing Yet Steadfast.* Belmont, CA: Wadsworth.

Waters, Sarah. 1998 (July). "New Social Movement Politics in France: The Rise of Civic Forms of Mobilisation." *Western European Politics* 21(3): 170–186.

Williams, Ann. 1968. *Britain and France in the Middle East and North Africa, 1914–1967.* London: Macmillan.

Wilson, Frank L. 1989. "Evolution of the French Party System." In *Policy-Making in France: From de Gaulle to Mitterrand* (pp. 57–72), ed. Paul Godt. New York: Pinter.

Wilson, Frank L. 1993. *The Failure of West European Communism: Implications for the Future.* New York: Paragon House.

Wright, Gordon. 1987. *France in Modern Times.* 4th ed. New York: W. W. Norton.

Wright, Vincent. 1993. "The President and the Prime Minister: Subordination, Conflict, Symbiosis or Reciprocal Parasitism?" In *De Gaulle to Mitterrand: Presidential Power in France* (pp. 101–19), ed. Jack Hayward. London: Hurst and Company.

Ysmal, Colette. 1993. "Centristes et liberaux." In *La Vie politique en France* (pp. 257–71), ed. Dominique Chagnollaud. Paris: Editions du Seuil.

Zeldin, Theodore. 1982. *The French.* New York: Pantheon.

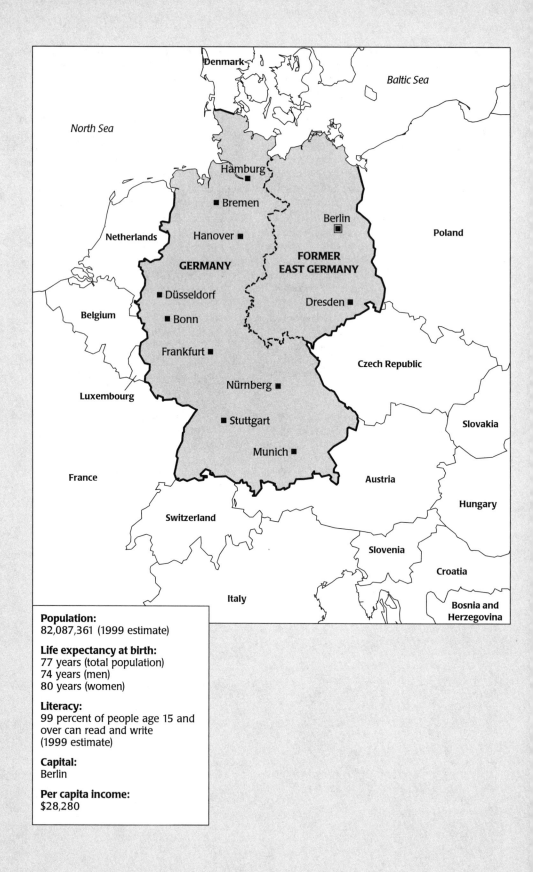

Denmark

Baltic Sea

North Sea

Hamburg ■

■ Bremen

Netherlands

Hanover ■

Berlin ◻

Poland

GERMANY

**FORMER
EAST GERMANY**

Belgium

■ Düsseldorf

■ Bonn

Dresden ■

Luxembourg

Frankfurt ■

Czech Republic

Nürnberg ■

Slovakia

■ Stuttgart

Munich ■

France

Austria

Hungary

Switzerland

Slovenia

Croatia

Italy

Bosnia and
Herzegovina

Population:
82,087,361 (1999 estimate)

Life expectancy at birth:
77 years (total population)
74 years (men)
80 years (women)

Literacy:
99 percent of people age 15 and
over can read and write
(1999 estimate)

Capital:
Berlin

Per capita income:
$28,280

4

Germany

The Dominant Power in Europe

Germany is the dominant economic power of Europe. This was true before the unification of East and West Germany in the fall of 1990, and it will be the case for the foreseeable future.

Germany's mounting economic power has given rise to fears of a German military revival (Geipel 1993). Such fears are not easily discounted, for German aggression produced two world wars during the twentieth century, the second of which resulted in the systematic killing of more than 6,000,000 Jews. The Second World War also destroyed much of Europe, with the Soviet Union, alone, suffering 27,000,000 deaths as a result of the German invasion (Nove 1992).

Could it happen again? Most scholars say no. Conradt bluntly states that "Germany and the Germans have changed" and chides Americans for watching too many old war movies on television (Conradt 1986, xviix). Edinger similarly states that the "haunted have departed" (Edinger 1977). Their views are supported by the resounding success of German democracy over the course of the past five decades. Few states in the world today are as democratic as Germany.

Nevertheless, doubts remain. In 1990, Nicholas Ridley, a member of the British Cabinet, created a crisis in Anglo-German relations by proclaiming that Germans were "authoritarian and expansionist by nature," a recurring theme in the political science literature of the 1950s and 1960s (Almond and Verba 1965). The Minister duly resigned, but his views are shared by many Europeans.

For those who question the depth of Germany's commitment to peace and democracy, the revival of a small neo-Nazi movement during the 1990s served as a reminder of things past. Fueled by a permanent unemployment rate of more than 10 percent, the neo-Nazis launched violent attacks against immigrant workers, often bombing the apartment complexes in which they resided. By the end of 1993, then-Chancellor Helmut Kohl was forced to admit that neo-Nazis posed a "serious problem." The neo-Nazi movement is embryonic in form and remains smaller than similar movements in France and most other European nations. It is Germany's past that makes it seem so frightening.

Despite lingering fears concerning a revival of German authoritarianism, most political observers find the German population to be fully committed to the principles of liberal democracy. While not unmindful of the past, they view the new Germany as an integral member of an evolving European state (Edinger and Nacos, 1998).

In the pages that follow, we will examine how the German population decides "who gets what, when, and how." Special focus will be placed on Germany's successful transition from an authoritarian dictatorship into a liberal democracy. Perhaps the lessons of the German experience will benefit Russia and other states that are making similar transitions.

Germany in Historical Perspective

The First Reich (936–1870)

The emergence of Germany as a historical entity is frequently traced to the breakup of Charlemagne's empire in approximately 843 AD, an event that saw Otto the Great (936–973) establish his domain over many of the German-speaking areas of Central Europe. Otto's empire was subsequently referred to as the Holy Roman Empire, a misleading title honoring the defeat of Rome by German tribes. Placed in historical perspective, the Holy Roman Empire represents the first German **Reich,** or *empire.*

The Holy Roman Empire was not a state in the modern sense of the word, representing little more than a loose confederation of tribes and principalities, the cohesion of which varied with the power of the emperor. By the end of the thirteenth century, the Empire existed in name only, having been fragmented into hundreds of principalities and free cities (Detweiler 1976).

Germany was to remain fragmented well into the eighteenth century. While Britain and France used their growing industrial might to forge powerful empires, the Germans, divided by petty squabbles, remained largely pastoral. By British and French standards, Germany possessed all of the characteristics of a "developing area." It was not industrial, it had yet to evolve a large and politically conscious middle class, and it lacked "national" political institutions.

Napoleon invaded Germany in 1806, forcing the smaller German states to merge with their larger neighbors. Full unification, however, would not be achieved until 1871, a date marking the defeat of France by a confederation of German states under the leadership of Otto Von Bismarck, Chancellor of Prussia. With the war's end, Prussian dominance left its allies little choice but to accept Bismarck's demands for the creation of a unified German state, a process that was already well underway (Hucko 1987). The Second Reich was born.

The Second Reich (1871–1918)

Economically, the Second Reich represented a period of accelerated industrialization that would place Germany on a par with England and France. Industrialization, in turn, sparked the urbanization of German society and led to a rapid expansion of both the middle and working classes. Unlike the British and French experiences,

Proclamation of the German Empire, Second Reich, at Versailles in 1871 (based on a painting done by Anton von Werner in 1885).

however, Germany's industrial revolution was not matched by a political revolution. Rather, German politics under the Second Reich was dominated by an aristocratic coalition of industrialists, landed nobility, and generals (Schonhardt-Bailey 1998). The middle class, content with its growing wealth, was largely swept along by the tide of German nationalism, as was much of the working class[1] (Grunberger 1971).

The Second Reich dissolved in the ashes of World War I. The war, launched by Kaiser Wilhelm II to establish German primacy in Europe, was to have been the crowning demonstration of German military genius (Scheele 1946). The Kaiser's dreams, however, evaporated in the trenches of France. As the military found itself checked on the ground and punished by an Allied naval blockade, popular support for the war began to erode. With victory beyond hope, the Kaiser abdicated his throne, proclaiming Germany to be a republic. A republic, he reasoned, would be in a stronger position to negotiate a "just peace" with the Allied Powers than a discredited monarchy (Tuchman 1962).

Hopes for a "just peace" were to remain unfulfilled. Indeed, it has been argued that the origins of the Second World War are to be found in the harsh conditions imposed upon the defeated German state by the Allied Powers at the termination of World War I.

The French provinces of Alsace and Lorraine, which had been seized by Germany in the Franco-Prussian war of 1871, were returned to France, thereby depriving Germany of 15 percent of its arable land and 10 percent of its population. Germany was also stripped of all of its foreign colonies, as well as much of its merchant navy and railway stock. The Allied Powers, moreover, demanded billions of dollars in reparations for the damage wrought by the German armies.[2]

The bitterness of defeat found direct expression in fragmentation of the German population. The military condemned liberal politicians for deserting the

---

[1]A brief democratic revolution occurred in Frankfurt in 1848.
[2]The reparations were largely financed by American bank loans on which Germany later defaulted.

war effort, insinuating that they had "stabbed the military in the back" (Hucko 1987, 60). Liberals, in turn, derided the conservative alliance of industrialists, generals, and landed aristocracy for its misplaced dreams of national grandeur. Communist movements, fueled by the harsh working conditions that had accompanied Germany's belated industrialization, mushroomed throughout the country, temporarily seizing power in the German province of Bavaria (Grunberger 1971).

The Weimar Republic (1919–1933)

It was in this environment that a constitutional assembly was convened in 1919 to draft a new Constitution for the German republic. Meeting in the town of Weimar, the delegates to the assembly attempted to design a Constitution so democratic that it would forever preclude a return to power by Germany's military-industrial elite. Toward this end, the new Germany was provided with both a popularly elected president and a prime minister elected by the lower house of the parliament (Reichstag), each possessing the power to check the other. Germany was to have a bicameral parliament, with the Reichstag (lower house) elected by direct universal manhood suffrage and the Bundesrat (upper house) by the Lander (states). Representation in the Reichstag, moreover, was to be on the basis of proportional representation. If a party received 2 percent of the popular vote, it would receive 2 percent of the seats in the Reichstag. No political group in Weimar Germany, accordingly, would be without a voice in parliament.

By attempting to preclude a return to authoritarianism, the framers of the Weimar Constitution had created a political system that was unable to take decisive action in times of crisis. Unfortunately, the Weimar Republic was to have no shortage of crises. Politically fragmented by its defeat in the war and crippled by punitive reparations, the German state would soon find itself in the throes of a world economic depression. By 1932, Germany had become a country without hope as roughly one-half of its population was touched in one way or another by unemployment.

Fueled by despair, extremist parties proliferated. An attempted military coup or "putsch" was put down in 1920, only to be followed by an abortive communist coup in the state of Saxony (1923) and an abortive Nazi coup in Munich (1923). The system of proportional representation, moreover, assured that extremist groups of all varieties would find representation in the Reichstag, including a powerful Communist Party that advocated class warfare and world revolution. The communists had seized power in Russia in 1917, and many observers felt that it was only a matter of time before they seized power in Germany as well.

By 1932, the Nazis had become the largest party in the Reichstag, their major opponents being the Communists. The Social Democratic, Liberal, and Catholic parties, the core of German democracy, controlled only 30 percent of the seats in the Reichstag, less than half of their representation in 1919. With parliamentary government having become impossible, the German president—the aging General Von Hindenburg—invoked the Constitution's emergency provisions and ruled by decree (Grunberger 1971). The government, however, was becoming irrelevant as pitched battles between opposing Nazi and Communist militias pushed Germany to the brink of civil war.

The history of the Weimar Republic testifies to the fact that structural arrangements alone cannot guarantee either democracy or human rights. Constitutions and other structural arrangements can facilitate the exercise of democracy, but they cannot compensate for the absence of a population dedicated to democratic principles. The history of the Weimar Republic also raises interesting questions concerning the fragmentation of political power. It is dangerous to concentrate excessive power in the hands of a narrow oligarchy, but it is equally dangerous to deprive the government of the capacity to rule.

Hitler and the Third Reich (1933–1945)

Hitler's meteoric rise to power has been recounted so many times that it requires little retelling.[3] Formed in Munich in 1919, Hitler's **Nazi Party** was one of a multitude of fringe parties that appealed to the marginal elements in German society. Under normal circumstances, the Nazi Party would probably have remained a fringe party of little consequence. Circumstances, however, were far from normal. By 1930, German society was in a state of collapse, and the government was losing its capacity to rule. Germany's social and economic institutions were also disintegrating, creating a condition that sociologists refer to as **anomie**, or *normlessness*. A German population long noted for its disciplined adherence to rules found itself with few rules to follow.

When the rules of society collapse, observed the German sociologist Max Weber, the masses will seek a charismatic leader to lead them to salvation.

The term **charisma**, according to Weber, can be applied to *"a certain quality of an individual's personality by virtue of which he is set apart from ordinary men and treated as endowed with supernatural, superhuman, or at least specifically exceptional powers or qualities*. These as such are not accessible to the ordinary person, but are regarded as of divine origin or as exemplary, and on the basis of them the individual concerned is treated as a leader. In primitive circumstances this peculiar kind of deference is paid to prophets, to people with a reputation for therapeutic or legal wisdom, to leaders in the hunt, and heroes in war. Charisma is often regarded as resting on magical powers" (Weber 1947, 328).

The Hitler of 1920 bore little resemblance to Weber's superhuman prophet, his virulent message of anti-Semitism and Aryan superiority appealing largely to a handful of misfits living on the margins of society. As the economic and political structure of German society collapsed, however, virtually all segments of German society had become marginalized (Anheir, Neidhardt, and Vortkamp 1998). The size of Hitler's following increased apace, a process described by Hans Gerth (1940, 526–27):

> Persons whose career expectations are frustrated or who suffer losses in status or income in the intensive vocational competition of modern capitalism should be especially likely to accept the belief in the charismatic leader. Those placed on the disadvantaged side of life always tend to be interested in some sort of salvation which breaks through the routines associated with their deprivation. Such "unsuccessful" persons were to be found in every stratum of German society. Princes without thrones, indebted and subsidizedlandlords, indebted farmers, virtually bankrupt industrialists, impoverished shopkeepers and artisans, doctors without patients, lawyers without clients, writers without readers, unemployed teachers, and unemployed manual and white collar workers joined the movement. National Socialism as a salvationary movement exercised an especially strong attraction on the "old" and "new" middle classes, especially in those strata where substantive rationality is least developed and will be most highly represented among those seeking salvation by quasi-miraculous means—or at least by methods which break through the routines which account for their deprivation.

Nazism was also embraced by Germans who feared a communist revolution or who dreaded the prospect of civil war (Brustein 1998). This included members of

[3]See William Shirer's *The Rise and Fall of the Third Reich* (published by Simon & Schuster in 1990) for a detailed analysis of Hitler's rise to power.

the middle class and the conservative aristocracy of landowners, generals, and industrialists that had long dominated German politics (Grunberger 1971; Lipset 1960). Hitler, in their view, was a tool to be used for the moment and discarded when the crisis had passed. As it turned out, it was they who were to be discarded.

The 1933 elections saw Hitler and his allies gain 51 percent of the popular vote, and Hitler was duly proclaimed chancellor (Grunberger 1971; Flint 1998). The communists were crushed and the Third Reich was born. Hitler's authoritarian methods would transform Germany from a bankrupt nation on the brink of civil war into a military and industrial power that came within a hairsbreadth of world domination. It would also establish the doctrine of fascism as one of the dominant political philosophies or "isms" of the modern era.

Fascism. Fascism, as preached by Hitler and the Nazi Party, was a *fanatical blend of racism, extreme nationalism, and paranoia.* The Germans, according to Hitler, were a **master race**, historically destined to rule the world. The German state was the logical expression of German racial superiority, its role being to fulfill Germany's historical mission of world conquest.

In Hitler's demented mind, the Jews were the source of both Germany's socio-economic decline and the organizers of an international conspiracy designed to deny Germany its rightful place in the world (Smith 1998). Germany could not achieve its historical mission, according to Hitler, until the Jews had been exterminated. Fascists also preached **Social Darwinism,** or the *survival of the fittest.* There was no room for the handicapped in Nazi Germany; the purity of the Aryan race was not to be diluted (Sargent 1987, 161–77; Reich 1990, 6–19).

While declining as a major force in Western Europe, fascist parties remain part of the political landscape in most areas of the world in which democratically elected governments have found it difficult to cope with mounting social and economic problems. Nationalistic calls for ethnic purity, for example, have increased throughout Eastern Europe, as have attacks on minorities and Jews. Particularly disquieting are the growing manifestations of fascism surfacing in Russia, a topic examined at length in Chapter 6.

The Two Germanys (1945–1989)

With the unconditional surrender of Nazi Germany in May 1945, the victorious Allied Powers divided German territory into American, British, French, and Soviet occupation sectors, coordination among which was to be achieved by a Supreme Allied Command located in Berlin.

The unity of the wartime allies collapsed shortly after the German surrender, and in 1948, defeated Germany was divided into two independent countries: the German Democratic Republic (East Germany) and the Federal Republic of Germany, or West Germany. The Cold War had begun in earnest.

A constitutional convention was convened shortly after the merging of the American, French, and British zones into West Germany. Delegates to the constitutional assembly, however, displayed little enthusiasm for drafting a Constitution that would give permanent expression to the division of their country into two separate entities. It was decided, accordingly, that they would draft a "**Basic Law**" to serve in place of a Constitution.

The Basic Law was not imposed by force, but the occupying powers left little doubt that the Federal Republic of Germany was to be a democratic and demilitarized state in which former Nazis would have no voice. As if to underscore the

During World War II, Hitler's Nazi forces systematically slaughtered millions of Jews and other "non-Aryans" in concentration camps. In this photo taken shortly after the war, General Dwight D. Eisenhower walks around a cluster of corpses while viewing a former concentration camp in Gotha.

differences between the new Germany and its predecessors, the capital of the Federal Republic was located in Bonn, a sleepy college town that possessed neither the imposing elegance of Berlin nor its symbols of imperial grandeur (Bertram, 1998).

For the next four decades, each of the two Germanys would go its own way (Ardagh 1991). West Germany pursued a path of democracy and capitalism, becoming one of the wealthiest states in the world. East Germany, by contrast, had merely traded one form of totalitarianism for another and languished in socialist mediocrity.

While East Germany and West Germany had become independent countries, the Allied Powers continued to maintain their occupation zone in Berlin, a city that was totally encircled by East Germany. East Germans soon found this Western enclave in the middle of their country to be a convenient avenue for defecting to the West. In 1961, accordingly, the communist authorities encircled West Berlin with a fortified prison wall (the **Berlin Wall**), shooting defectors on sight.

As the Soviet Union began to crumble in the late 1980s, its puppet regime in East Germany found it increasingly difficult to prevent its citizens from defecting tothe West (Wallach and Francisco 1992). On November 9, 1989, the citizens of East Berlin took matters into their own hands, smashing the wall that had imprisoned them for some forty years. The East German regime had collapsed.

Both the West and the USSR were stunned by the speed with which the East German regime had fallen. For the USSR, it signaled the end of communism in Eastern Europe, if not the Soviet Union itself. The West rejoiced, but its euphoria was soon tempered by the realization that the reunification of the two Germanys was inevitable. Indeed, the reunification agreement was formally signed on October 3, 1990, less than twelve months after the breach of the Berlin Wall. By and large,

Rebuilding Germany after the war was a massive undertaking. This photo was taken in the city of Dresden, located in what would become East Germany, shortly after the city was bombed by Allied forces.

The Cultural Impact of the Berlin Wall

The wall separating East and West Germany was more than physical. It was also cultural. New generations of West Germans were socialized to believe in democracy and capitalism, while new generations of East Germans were socialized to accept authoritarianism and socialism. Many East Germans also succumbed to a socialist work culture that stifled initiative and placed dependence on the State above self-reliance (Fuller 1998). What was the advantage of working hard when promotions were based on seniority rather than merit?

East Germany was simply absorbed by West Germany, agreeing to accept the Basic Law as well as all West German social and economic legislation.[4]

While allowing the unification of Germany, Western countries remained apprehensive about the status of a reunified Germany in the world community. Would the new German state continue on its path of democracy, or would it revert to its former authoritarian traditions? World War II had ended more than four decades earlier, but its scars ran deep.

The Incomplete Reunification (1990–   )

The reunification of the two Germanys occurred in a rush of euphoria and optimism. West Germans understood that economic sacrifices would have to be made, but most assumed that the period of adjustment would be relatively short. East Germany had been the most productive area of the communist bloc and Germans, after all, were Germans.

---

[4]Some provisions of the West German law were to be phased in over time.

Meeting with little resistance from authorities, East Germans made history in November 1989 with the destruction of the Berlin Wall.

The optimism that preceded the reunification of the two Germanys was soon to be shattered, for few West Germans had understood precisely how much the East German economy had deteriorated.[5] As described by Smyser,

> The East German economy, 40 years after the founding of the German Democratic Republic (GDR) and almost 30 years after the building of the Wall, presented a shabby picture at the time of the merger. Few firms could compete internationally. Consumer goods were of such low quality that many persons refused to buy them even when they were available. The infrastructure was in disrepair. Building walls and plumbing were in decay. Environmental damage was so great that children throughout the Southern GDR suffered massively from bronchial disorders and the water throughout much of the region was unsafe to drink (Smyser 1992, 150).

As the costs of reunification continued to mount, West Germans began to question the enormous subsidies that were being paid to East Germans in an effort to ease the pain of the transition from socialism to capitalism (Pond 1993; Pickel 1997). East Germans, in the West German view, were not pulling their weight. Matters were made all the more difficult by the onset of a broader European economic recession that would find West Germans suffering economic hardships unknown since the end of the Second World War.

Bitterness, however, was not reserved for the West Germans. East Germans faced the brunt of the reunification process as former state-run factories were either closed by the German government or streamlined by their new owners. By 1993,

---

[5]East Germany's land mass was approximately 40 percent the size of West Germany, with about 25 percent of its population. Its economic production, however, was less than 15 percent of West Germany's.

hundreds of thousands of East German jobs were lost. Some of the displaced workers found new jobs, but others did not, and unemployment figures for the unified state soon exceeded the 10 percent level, with unemployment figures for the area of the former East Germany exceeding 16 percent, a figure that continues to haunt the region today.

The frustrations generated by the unification process found expression in a resurgence of neo-fascist parties, the venom of which was directed at Germany's large population of guest workers from Turkey and Eastern Europe, many of whom had resided in Germany since the 1960s. This outbreak of right-wing extremism posed little threat to German democracy, but memories of the past had clearly been revived. Perhaps German democracy was less secure than its neighbors had believed.

There can be little doubt that the problems of reunification will be worked out with time and that the new Germany will be more powerful than the old (Conradt 1993). It is unlikely, however, that full integration will be achieved for at least another decade (*IHT*, Oct. 4, 1999, www).

The Political Institutions of Germany

As we have seen in the preceding chapters, a country's political institutions provide the arena for its political process. In this section, we will look at the formal structure of German government, as provided in Germany's Basic Law.

The Basic Law (Constitutional Document) of Germany

The framers of Germany's Basic Law attempted to design political institutions that would be strong enough to provide effective leadership yet remain responsive to the will of the masses. They distrusted a strong executive but feared that a weak and divided government would be unable to solve the massive problems confronting the war-torn nation. Weak governments, as the experience of the Weimar Republic had well demonstrated, were an invitation to tyranny.

It was thus determined that the Federal Republic would be governed as a parliamentary democracy in which executive power would be vested in a chancellor responsible before a popularly elected **Bundestag** (*lower house of Parliament*). Germany would also have a largely symbolic president who played a role similar to that of the monarch of England. The chancellor would serve at the pleasure of the members of the Bundestag and could be removed at their will. To further guard against the resurgence of an authoritarian regime, Germany was to become a federal state. Laws affecting the states, or **Lander**, were to require the approval of the **Bundesrat**, or *upper house of Parliament,* the members of which were selected by the Lander. Laws affecting the Lander would also be administered by the Lander, thereby assuring a maximum of "home rule." Finally, as one last impediment to the return of an authoritarian regime, the acts of the federal government were subject to the review of an independent judiciary headed by a "Supreme" Constitutional Court. Merely issuing rules, of course, offers no guarantee that the "players" will abide by those rules. Nevertheless, the framers of the Basic Law clearly attempted to compensate for the structural problems of the past.

Elections and Politics in Germany

In an electoral system that is among the most complex in the world today, German voters cast two ballots. The first ballot is for a member of the Bundestag to be elected on the basis of single-member, simple-plurality districts.[6] The candidate who receives the most votes in a district wins the seat in the Bundestag. The second ballot designates the voter's political party of choice. It is this second, or party, ballot that determines the actual number of seats that a party will receive in the Bundestag.[7] If the Christian Democratic Union wins 50 percent of the party vote, for example, it is assured 50 percent of the seats in the Bundestag. The occupants of CDU's seats in the Bundestag will be determined first by the results of the district elections and secondly by the "party list." In this instance, the CDU's 50 percent of the popular vote now entitles it to 336 (or one-half) of the 672 seats in the Bundestag. Assume also that CDU candidates won 290 seats in the district elections. To reconcile the results of the two elections, the 290 seats won in the district election would be subtracted from the CDU's allocated total of 336 seats. The remaining 46 seats would be filled in numerical order from the names on the party list. The CDU's representation or "fraction" in the Bundestag, accordingly, would consist of the 290 party candidates victorious in the district elections, as well as the top 46 names on the CDU's electoral list.

This system of voting is sometimes referred to as a personalized proportional representation system.[8] It is a proportional voting system because a party is guaranteed a number of seats in the Bundestag equivalent to the percentage of its popular vote. It is a personalized system because the German voters are provided with the opportunity to select most of their representatives in district elections.

The only proviso to this system is that a party must receive at least 5 percent of the popular vote. Barring this, its votes are wasted. The 5 percent provision was a reaction to the experience of the Weimar Republic and was designed to prevent the legislative process from being obstructed by an excess of minor parties, most of which were little more than narrow pressure groups. It was also designed to keep small radical groups from using the Parliament as a political forum.

The order of names on a party's election list is determined by the party leadership. Party leaders are thus assured a seat in the Bundestag in the unlikely event they should lose their district elections. The list system also provides the party leadership with the ability to "discipline" its members by removing them from the party list.

The German electoral system, then, represents an attempt by the framers of the Basic Law to gain the benefits of both single-member districts and proportional representation. As we saw in the discussion of British politics, single-member, simple-plurality districts promote stability by limiting the number of viable political parties. As the party with the most votes wins the single seat available, like-minded groups must combine their efforts if they are to have any hope of victory. The disadvantage of single-member, simple-plurality systems is that votes are wasted. The losers, often a majority, have no influence on policy. The advantages and disadvantages of proportional representation, by contrast, are exactly the opposite. Allocating seats in Parliament in proportion to the popular vote provides an accurate reflection of the popular will but often leads to political instability by creating too many parties in the legislature, none of which has the capacity to lead.

The framers of the Basic Law were vitally concerned with assuring the stability of the new state, but they also wanted to create a political system that would be

---

[6]The nomination of candidates in the single-member districts is made either by a secret ballot of the party members in the district or by a nomination committee elected by a secret ballot of the party members therein (Conradt 1986).

[7]The seats allocated by list are adjusted for the size of the Land, with the larger Lander receiving more seats than the smaller Lander (Paterson and Southern 1991, 182).

[8]Some scholars reserve the term "personalized proportional representation" for states such as Ireland and Finland, in which the voter can select a candidate of choice from the party list.

as democratic as possible. By combining single-member districts and proportional representation, they hoped to achieve both objectives (Jeffery 1998).

Executive Power in Germany: Chancellors, Governments, and Presidents

Germany possesses both a chancellor and a president. The **chancellor** is Germany's *chief executive,* his role being parallel to that of the British prime minister. The German **president** is the symbolic head of state and plays a role similar to that of the British monarch.

The Chancellor and Cabinet (Government). Executive authority in Germany is vested in a chancellor (prime minister) elected by the Bundestag from among its members. In practice, the chancellor is usually the head of the dominant party or dominant coalition of parties in the Bundestag. The chancellor, in turn, selects the members of the Cabinet. Collectively, *the chancellor and the Cabinet* are referred to as the "**Government.**" The Government is responsible before the Bundestag and can be forced to resign by a "positive" vote of no confidence, a topic to be discussed shortly. The Government, however, stands and falls as a whole, and the Bundestag cannot remove individual ministers.

Technically speaking, chancellors possess the authority to appoint and remove Cabinet ministers as they see fit. In reality, however, most Cabinet positions are filled by powerful politicians who represent important wings of the chancellor's party. Their removal, if not threatening the collapse of the Government itself, would surely trigger a crisis within the dominant party.

The chancellor is precluded by law from intervening in the day-to-day affairs of the respective ministries. Each minister is a powerful policy maker who is supreme in his or her domain. The exact line between the independent responsibility of the ministers and the chancellor's power to set "the general guidelines for governmental policy" remains imperfectly defined, with much depending on the relative power of the individuals involved (*NYT,* Mar. 22, 1999).

It would be a mistake, however, to overstate the power of individual ministers, as the chancellor possesses the constitutional authority to override ministerial decisions that are contrary to his or her general policy guidelines. Individual Cabinet ministers, moreover, are precluded from making major policy statements without the prior clearance of the chancellor, and they must also keep the chancellor informed of the activities of their ministries. Overall, German ministers are somewhat less powerful than their British counterparts (Conradt 1986).

Also falling in the realm of executive authority is the Chancellor's Office. Consisting of more than 400 individuals, the Chancellor's Office represents his personal staff and is organized into departments paralleling the various Cabinet ministries. Each is headed by a senior official possessing the expertise to "keep tabs" on the activities of his or her ministerial counterpart. The "head" of the Chancellor's Office is a member of the Cabinet without portfolio; that is, he doesn't head a major administrative agency (Conradt 1986).

The formal powers of the German chancellor are also strengthened by a variety of informal powers. The chancellor is usually the head of his or her political party and, as such, will have much to say about how names will be ordered on the party electorate lists. The chancellor is also the focal point of the German mass media, a position that facilitates the manipulation of public opinion. While others respond to policy, it is the chancellor who sets the policy agenda.

The President. The German president is the symbolic head of Germany. The president must sign all bills passed by the Parliament, and it is also the president who dissolves the Bundestag prior to new elections. These roles, much like those of the monarch of England, are pro forma—the real power lies with the chancellor. Nevertheless, presidents have often played forceful moral roles in German society by speaking out against racism (*NYT,* Sept. 1, 1993, A5). The German president is elected for a five-year term by an electoral college consisting of all parliamentary representatives at the federal and Land level, some 1,338 in all. German presidents are limited to two terms in office, and candidates for the office are respected political figures. Johannes Rau, a very prominent Social Democrat, became Germany's eighth postwar president in 1999.

Legislative Power in Germany: The Bundestag and the Bundesrat

Legislative authority in the Federal Republic of Germany is divided between the Bundestag and the Bundesrat. The Bundestag is the popularly elected lower house of the German Parliament, while the Bundesrat (or upper house) represents the Lander (states).

The Bundestag. The heart of German politics is the Bundestag, consisting of 672 members elected by the German population. They are the only individuals at the national level elected directly by the population. The deputies of the Bundestag, in turn, elect the chancellor (prime minister). Elections to the Bundestag must be held within a four-year period, the exact timing of the elections being determined by the chancellor and the dominant members of his coalition. By and large, most elections in Germany run their full four-year cycle.

As in most parliamentary systems, the Bundestag can bring down the Government by a vote of no confidence. It must, however, be a "positive" vote[9] of no confidence in which the fall of the old Government is contingent upon the election of a new Government within fourteen days. Again, the requirement for a positive vote of no confidence was designed to avoid the instability that had undermined the Weimar Republic. There have been only two successful votes of no confidence in the history of the FGR, both in the mid-1970s.

The Bundestag also keeps in touch with the Government by means of a "Question Hour" and a "Current Hour." Adopted from the British practice, the **Question Hour** allows members of the Bundestag to question the Government on issues ranging from matters of national policy to the personal grievances of constituents. The Question Hour, being alien to German practice, was used less than 400 times during the four-year period of the first Bundestag. The practice was soon to catch on, however, and by the seventh Bundestag (1972–1976), the Government found itself compelled to answer some 19,000 queries, a figure that has remained steady through the 1990s (Conradt 1986; Dalton 1993). The Current Hour was added in 1965, and it allows deputies to force a question period on issues of particular importance.[10]

---

[9]The word *positive* means that in Germany, unlike most parliamentary systems, the country cannot be left without a majority government for a long period of time.

[10]Deputies also possess the right to submit petitions to the Government requesting answers to specific questions. A petition signed by twenty-five deputies constitutes a "small inquiry" and commands a formal response from the Government. A petition of thirty signatures constitutes a "large inquiry" and commands both a formal response from the Government and a full debate on the Government's response. Large inquiries were particularly common during the formative years of the Bonn Republic but have been employed less frequently as the Republic has matured (Conradt 1986).

In addition to helping the Bundestag keep tabs on the Government, the Question Hour provides opposition parties with an active forum for criticizing Government policy. In the final analysis, the effectiveness of the Question Hour as a political forum for the opposition probably outweighs its utility as a mechanism for controlling the activities of the Government.

The Bundestag also possesses the power to investigate Government officials, but the process is a cumbersome one and is seldom used.[11] The Bundestag's investigative capacity is also limited by its inadequate staff support, not to mention the reluctance of the majority party to investigate its own leaders.

The primary function of the Bundestag is legislation (Maor 1998). All bills must receive a majority vote in the Bundestag before they can become law. While individual members of the Bundestag possess the right to introduce legislation, most legislation originates with the Government.

As in most parliamentary systems, Government bills fare much better than private bills. Indeed, the strong cohesion of German political parties makes the passage of Government bills a near certainty. Those bills, moreover, are unlikely to be amended by committee deliberations or by subsequent debate within the Bundestag. Amendments do occur, but they are of a technical nature and usually have the support of the Government.

The dominant position of the Government in the legislative process rests upon the cohesion of *German parliamentary parties* or **Fraktionen**.[12] If the members of the majority party or coalition do not vote as a cohesive unit, they will lose their majority and the Government will fall. This, in most cases, would result in the formation of an opposition Government or in a call for new elections, neither of which would serve the interests of the dominant party.

The German electorate, moreover, expects the majority party or coalition to carry out its platform. The dominant vote in German elections, it will be recalled, is a party vote. Deputies are expected to represent local interests, but they are also expected to support the Government.

Finally, the leaders of Germany's political parties use their control of party finances to impose party discipline (Paterson and Southern 1991). German elections are very expensive and far exceed the resources available to the average candidate for state or national office.

The German government subsidizes the electoral process by allocating funds to the parties in rough proportion to their success at the polls (Kloss 1991, 49–50), but this money is also allocated by the party leadership. This is not a minor consideration, for by the mid-1980s, these subsidies amounted to approximately one dollar per vote (Conradt 1986). Pressure groups also contribute generously to Germany's major parties, but again it is the party leadership that largely determines how those funds will be allocated.

At the broader level, the chancellor's dominance of the Bundestag is also a function of information. The meager staff support provided to the members of the Bundestag is no match for a Government supported by both the federal bureaucracy and the chancellor's personal staff.

The tradition of a strong chancellor, moreover, possesses deep roots within German culture. While Germany's commitment to democratic government is not in doubt, public opinion polls suggest little desire for a weak executive.

---

[11] Initiation of an investigation requires the approval of one-fourth of its members.
[12] A Fraktionen consists of all of a party's deputies in the Bundestag, with the leader of the majority Fraktionen becoming the chancellor.

German Parliament

Bundestag (Lower House)	Bundesrat (Upper House)

Bundestag (Lower House)

- 672 members
- Elected by German population
- Up to four-year terms
- Members elect chancellor
- Power of vote of no confidence

Bundesrat (Upper House)

- 69 members
- Selected by Land governments
- Provides German Lander with active voice in federal policy
- Majority vote required for passage of legislation
- Considers most federal legislation not directly related to foreign policy and national defense

---

The Bundesrat and German Federalism. The Bundesrat, or upper house of the German parliament, was expressly designed to provide the German Lander with an active voice in federal policy making. It consists of sixty-nine members selected by the Land governments. A majority vote in the Bundesrat is required for all legislation of direct relevance to the rights and responsibilities of the Lander, the nature of which are either specified or implied by the Basic Law. Education, the police, local finance, most transportation issues, land use, and boundary disputes between the Lander all fall within the purview of the Bundesrat, as do national emergencies and amendments to the Basic Law. Bills that do not receive the approval of the Bundesrat in these areas are effectively vetoed and cannot become law. On all other bills, the opposition of the Bundesrat can be overridden by either an absolute majority or a two-thirds majority in the Bundestag, depending upon the circumstances.

As in the United States, the precise line between the powers of the federal government and the powers retained by the German Lander remains fluid and subject to judicial interpretation. In sharp contrast to the American experience, however, the power of the German Lander has increased rather than decreased over the course of the past four decades. According to some estimates, the framers of the Basic Law assumed that the Bundesrat would possess "veto power" over about 10 percent of the legislation considered by the Bundestag. In current practice, however, approximately 60 percent of federal legislation requires the approval of the Bundesrat (Conradt 1996).

In large part, the expanded power of the Bundesrat is the result of a liberal interpretation of the *Doctrine of Co-Responsibility* by the Constitutional Court. This doctrine makes the Lander responsible for the administration of federal laws. In additional to their own primacy in the areas of education, internal security, and justice, moreover, the state bureaucracies also collect federal taxes and share "joint responsibility" with the federal government in the areas of higher education, regional planning, and agrarian reform. In one way or another, then, the Bundesrat has asserted its right to consider most federal legislation not directly related to questions of foreign policy and national defense.

The sixty-nine members of the Bundesrat are apportioned among Germany's sixteen Lander on the basis of population.[13] The most populous Lander receive six seats in the Bundesrat, while the others receive between three and five seats each, depending on their size. The delegates to the Bundesrat are instructed by their Land governments on the policies to be pursued and on the votes to be cast.

---

[13]The German Lander today differ from the German Lander of the pre–World War II era.

Many members of the Bundesrat are ministers in Land governments and, as such, have a major voice in determining the policies of their own Land. Their role in the Bundesrat enhances their ability to see that the policies of their Land are implemented and also enables them to play an effective role in coordinating the affairs of the national and Land governments (Dalton 1993).

In keeping with the general tenor of German government, relations between the Bundesrat and the Bundestag tend to be more cooperative than conflictual. Nevertheless, some conflict is inevitable when the Bundesrat is controlled by the parties of the opposition. The 1994 elections, for example, gave parties of the opposition a two-thirds majority in the Bundesrat, thereby providing them with the power to veto most legislation proposed by the Government. The Social Democrats captured the Bundestag in the 1998 elections, but they faced a Bundesrat that was evenly balanced (*IHT,* Feb. 8, 1999). While Government legislation is sometimes rejected by the Bundesrat, it is far more common for the Government to work informally with members of the Bundesrat's leadership to shape legislation that will be acceptable to the parliament as a whole. Bundesrat rejection of Government legislation does not constitute a vote of no confidence, but it is a source of considerable embarrassment.

Law and Politics in Germany: The Federal Constitutional Court and the Judicial System

The Federal Constitutional Court is similar in function to the Supreme Court of the United States. It reviews the constitutionality of both federal and state (Land) legislation, interprets the various articles of the Basic Law, settles disputes between Land governments, adjudicates conflicts between the Land governments and the Federal Government, and serves as the final guarantor of those civil rights enumerated in the Basic Law[14] (Paterson and Southern 1991). In addition to the above functions, the Federal Constitutional Court has the special responsibility of protecting the constitutional and democratic character of the German state. In this role, the Court has the right to outlaw nondemocratic political parties attempting to use democratic procedures for the purpose of reestablishing an authoritarian regime in Germany.

The Constitutional Court consists of sixteen members elected in equal proportions by the Bundestag and the Bundesrat. A two-thirds majority of the respective chambers is required for the election of justices, a stringent requirement that has contributed to the high quality of the Court's members. The Court is divided into two chambers, one specializing in issues related to civil rights and the other in issues involving the constitutionality of legislative acts and intergovernmental relations.

The concept of a Supreme Court empowered to review the acts of the Government was an innovation adopted from the American experience by the framers of the Basic Law in the hope of placing yet another obstacle in the path of authoritarianism. With little prior experience to draw upon, no one was quite sure how much vigor the Federal Constitutional Court would display in executing its constitutional responsibilities.

---

[14]Judges are appointed by the state ministers of justice and constitute part of the Land bureaucracies. Most judges enter the bureaucracy as a career service, receiving appropriate bureaucratic ranks and salaries. As career civil servants, they remain judges or prosecutors for life, having little interaction with private-sector attorneys. The only courts at the federal level, aside from the Constitutional Court, are the five specialized courts and the Federal Court of Appeals. The five specialized Federal courts are the Administrative Court, the Labor Court, the Social Court, the Fiscal Court, and the Patent Court. Citizens having a grievance against a federal civil servant would seek redress in the Administrative Court, disputes over social security or health services would be considered by the Social Court, and so on. The Lander also possess a specialized network of labor, social, and fiscal courts, making for a very complex legal system.

After a slow start, the Federal Constitutional Court has emerged as a major actor on the German political scene. By 1990, the Constitutional Court had considered some 80,000 cases, more than 75,000 of which involved an interpretation of the Basic Law. Only 2 percent of the challenges to the Government's interpretation of the Basic Law were allowed, making the court a very conservative force in German politics.

The influence of the Court, moreover, is increasing. The use of German troops in United Nations peacekeeping missions had to be approved by the Court, as did Germany's ratification of the Maastricht Treaty. The Constitutional Court has also been playing a major role in sorting out problems resulting from the reunification of the two Germanies. The untangling of property rights in East Germany is a particularly knotty issue, as is the resolution of differences in "moral" legislation between the two Germanies. The East German policy of providing free abortions, for example, was struck down by the Court as contrary to the Basic Law (*NYT,* May 29, 1993).

The Federal Constitutional Court is a separate branch of the German government. As such, it possesses its own budget and is fully independent of the federal bureaucracy. The German judiciary, by contrast, is administered by the Lander, with more than 17,000 Land judges administering both local and federal law (Kloss 1991). While the German legal system is controlled by the Lander, the law they administer is the uniform legal code of the Federal Republic. In contrast to the American experience, the law on key issues such as criminal offenses, divorce, and custody is the same throughout the German Republic. Also, unlike the American experience, the German court system operates quickly, cheaply, and with minimal complexity. One reason for this is that Germany employs approximately nine times more judges than the United States on a per capita basis (Conradt 1986). Perhaps one reason that the Germans are so wedded to litigation is that their legal system is user-friendly.

Bureaucracy and Politics in Germany

The German civil service personifies the ideals of efficiency, precision, and dedication (Paterson and Southern 1991). It was the efficiency of the German (Prussian) bureaucracy that enabled Bismarck to transform a confederation of feudal principalities into the dominant military power of Europe (Smith 1990). It was the same efficiency that enabled Hitler to launch his quest for world domination. Today, the efficiency of the German bureaucracy supports the economic prosperity of the Federal Republic.

In terms of structure, the federal bureaucracy consists of approximately sixteen ministries, each of which is headed by a Cabinet minister appointed by the chancellor. Collectively, as noted earlier, they constitute the Government. Officials in each ministry fall into five basic categories: political officials, senior civil servants, upper-middle civil servants, intermediate civil servants, and lower-level civil servants.[15] The political officials are appointed by their respective ministers and represent the patronage level of the German bureaucracy. Falling in this category

[15]Germany possesses a large bureaucracy, with approximately one German in eight occupying a government position at the federal, Land, or local levels. Organizational and recruitment procedures are similar at all levels of government and problems of coordination are few. The federal bureaucracy is the smallest of the bureaucratic levels, with federal officials representing approximately 10 percent of the total number of German bureaucrats. The Lander employ slightly more than half of the bureaucrats, the various local governments the remainder (Paterson and Southern 1991). The small size of the federal bureaucracy reflects the dominant role of Land and local governments in implementing federal programs. Aside from areas of special expertise, lawyers dominate the ranks of the bureaucracy, reflecting a long historical tie between government service and the legal profession (Conradt 1986). Advancement in the upper levels of the bureaucracy is heavily influenced by performance and competence.

would be the "state secretaries" as well as the heads of each ministry's major departments or divisions. The political nature of Germany's top bureaucratic positions enables the Government to give direction to its policies. It also enables the ruling parties to reward key party officials.

The senior civil service includes subdepartment heads, section heads, and section assistants. Most officials in the senior and the upper levels of the German bureaucracy possess tenure for life and are accorded special status within German society. Indeed, it has been suggested that high-level German bureaucrats represent a distinct social class or guild, the members of which perpetuate their privileged position from one generation to the next (Jacob 1963). In return for this privileged status, they are expected to place their expertise above partisan and personal considerations (Kloss 1991).

The efficiency of the bureaucracy has contributed to the legitimacy of the Federal Republic by providing its citizens with a remarkably high standard of public services (Smith 1990). German trains run on time, as does almost everything else in Germany. It could be argued, of course, that the German bureaucracy is *too* efficient and that this same dedication to order has taken precedence over humanistic and moral concerns. The heart of this criticism was the remarkable efficiency of the German bureaucracy in implementing the programs of Hitler's Third Reich.

Senior bureaucrats are also important decision makers. The Government provides the broad guidelines for policy, leaving the details to be worked out by the senior bureaucrats. To some extent, political decision makers have little choice but to delegate large areas of decision-making authority to senior bureaucrats, for it is the senior bureaucrats who possess most of the information and expertise required to implement government policy (Paterson and Southern 1991). Senior bureaucrats, however, are also highly respected for their expertise, and their views are actively sought by the political leadership (Goetz 1997).

As decision makers, the German bureaucrats represent a very conservative force in German politics. Efficiency is a function of order and regimentation. Change, by contrast, is disruptive, shattering routine and forcing officials to take unwanted risks. If changes are to occur, from a bureaucratic perspective, they should be incremental changes that are easily incorporated into the system (Conradt 1993).

The conservative orientation of the German bureaucracy has created something of a paradox. On one hand, the efficiency of the German bureaucracy has few peers in today's world. On the other hand, the conservative orientation of the bureaucracy makes it poorly suited to the task of providing creative solutions to Germany's growing environmental, educational, and social problems, not to mention the problems associated with the reunification of the two Germanies and the integration of Germany into the European Union.

To some extent, this paradox has been resolved by creating a variety of planning agencies external to the bureaucracy. Most ministries now have planning staffs independent of the bureaucracy, as does the Chancellor's Office. Planning, however, remains a difficult task. Not only does tension exist between the planners and the bureaucracy, but federal planning is also beset by the multiple checks and balances of Germany's political system.

The Actors in German Politics: Elites, Parties, Groups, and Citizens

The political institutions reviewed above represent the core of the German political system. They are the formal mechanisms for deciding who gets what, when, and how. Political institutions, however, do not exist in a vacuum. Their operation is profoundly influenced by the values of the elites and officials charged with their operation. Democratic rules, no matter how elegant, are poorly served by authoritarian leaders. They are also poorly served by an apathetic public.

In order to understand the functioning of the political process in the Federal Republic of Germany, then, it is necessary to examine the elites that run the government, the political parties and groups upon which elites rely for their power, and the broader pattern of popular attitudes toward the government.

Elites and Politics in Germany

German history has been characterized by elitism (Dahrendorf 1959). Elites made policy, competent bureaucrats executed policy, and the masses obeyed policy.

The elites of the Federal Republic differ from earlier German leaders in two critical ways. *First, unlike Bismarck and Hitler, the leaders of modern Germany have demonstrated an unwavering commitment to democracy.* Indeed, during the early years of the Federal Republic, Germany's political elites were probably more democratic than the population as a whole. This argument is supported by the results of a 1951 opinion poll which indicated that 42 percent of the West German population and 53 percent of the West German population over the age of 35 considered the pre-war years of the Third Reich to be the best that Germany had experienced during the twentieth century (Conradt 1986). Elite commitment to democracy, then, played an important role in building support for democracy among the German masses.

A second critical difference between the elite structure of the Federal Republic and the elite structure of the Second and Third Reichs lies in its pluralistic nature (Dalton 1993). Hitler had consolidated all sources of political power under his personal control. Political power in the Federal Republic, by contrast, is divided among a wide variety of institutions, parties, and groups.

The *dominant political decision makers* or **elites** in the Federal Republic of Germany are the chancellor and the members of the Cabinet. Other members of the inner circle of political decision makers include the ranking members of the majority party in the Bundestag and their coalition partners. Members of the Constitutional Court are also included among the political elite, as are top-level bureaucrats and ranking members of the various Land governments. The presidency of a Land government often serves as a springboard to Federal leadership, with half of the Federal Republic's six chancellors having served as president-ministers of Land governments prior to becoming chancellor.

Leaders of the opposition party, although far less influential than the leaders of the governing party, also qualify as political elites. They play a major role in the policy-making process by publicizing the weaknesses of Government programs and proposing viable alternatives. Opposition leaders also derive considerable power from the closely contested nature of German elections. The opposition of today could well be the dominant party of tomorrow. More tangibly, the opposition party invariably controls important Land governments, thereby giving its leaders an active voice both at the Land level and in the Bundesrat. Should the opposition party control the Bundesrat, as is currently the case, its leaders possess the ability to block Government programs that fall within the purview of state's right.

If the German elite is defined in its broadest sense, the number of citizens qualifying for at least minor elite status is huge. As described by Russell Dalton (1993, 203–4),

A study of West German elites in the early 1980s illustrates the diversity of elite politics. The project first defined the most influential political figures…, producing a list of more than 3,000 individuals. A sample of this group was then asked who they themselves turn to for policy advice; when the names are added, the pool of "elites" nearly quadruples in size and greatly increases in diversity. These informal reference networks make up a core elite of individuals who are regularly consulted by other elites on national policy issues. This core group includes many different elites. Politicians comprise the largest group in the core (37.5 percent). Business representatives (19.1 percent) and union leaders (7.9 percent) make up two other large groups of core elites, but they certainly do not hold a monopoly of influence. Media figures, academics, and civil servants are important players in the policy process, which includes representatives of the military, various cultural institutions, and even non-Germans.

The political elites of the Federal Republic are closely linked to the German party system. Party leaders are assured safe positions on the party lists in both the federal and the Land elections. If their party is victorious, it is they who become members of the Government and otherwise dominate the policy-making process.

Given the dominant role of political parties in German politics, members of Germany's political elite have typically served a long apprenticeship in the party hierarchy (Dalton 1993). Most enter politics at the Land level before moving to the federal arena, and most have demonstrated both competence in office and loyalty to the party. By the time German politicians reach elite status, then, they are seasoned veterans with broad experience in the administrative and political realms. In the process of working their way up within the party hierarchy, moreover, most senior members of Germany's political elite have also established a strong base of popular support including links with a major pressure group such as the German Federation of Labor (GDB) or the Federation of German Industry (BDI) (Hancock 1989).

Parties and Politics in Germany

German political parties are of three varieties (Padgett 1993). At the first level are the **Christian Democratic Union** (CDU) and **Social Democratic Party** (SPD), Germany's two large **catch-all parties.** As indicated in Table 4.1, the CDU and the SPD accounted for approximately 78 percent of the popular vote in the 1994 elections and 76 percent in the 1998 elections. The CDU and SPD also dominate the Land elections, and thereby, the Bundesrat. It is either the CDU or the SPD that forms a Government, although the support of the smaller Free Democratic Party (FDP) is often required for either the CDU or the SPD to achieve an absolute majority in the Bundestag.

At the second level of the party structure one finds the Free Democratic Party and the Greens. Both generally possess enough support to meet the 5 percent rule for representation in the Bundestag, but neither is large enough to contend for power. As the major parties are seldom able to gain a clear majority in the Bundestag, a coalition with one of the smaller parties is often necessary to form a government. The role of balancer has traditionally been played by the Free Democrats, but following the SPD's victory in 1998, it was the Greens, a relatively new party, that played this role.

At the third level of the party structure one finds a small Communist Party as well as a spate of neo-Nazi parties. Neither the Communists nor the neo-Nazi parties enjoy sufficient popular support to surpass the 5 percent rule required for representation in the Bundestag, although there were fears that the economic hardships resulting from the unification process would enable one of the neo-Nazi parties to break the 5 percent barrier during the 1994 elections. This did not occur, and the neo-Nazi resurgence appears to have crested. The Communists, now reconstituted as the Democratic Socialists, by contrast, polled 5.1 percent of the vote on a national basis,

Table 4.1
The Results of the 1994 and 1998 Elections

Party	1994 Percent of Popular Vote	Seats in Bundestag	1998 Percent of Popular Vote	Seats in Bundestag
CDU	41.5	294	35.2	245
SPD	36.4	252	40.9	298
Green	7.3	49	6.7	47
FDP	6.9	47	6.2	44
Communist	4.4	30	5.1	35
Others	3.5		6.0	

Source: The Economist, Oct. 3, 1998, 37.

a result that entitled them to representation in the Bundestag. The surprisingly large Communist vote came largely from the states of the former East Germany and was viewed as a protest vote against the hardships and uncertainties caused by the reunification process. The 1997 local elections confirmed the strength of the Communists in the Lander of the former East Germany.

Even with their minor successes in recent elections, neither the fascists nor the communists pose a serious threat to German democracy. They would probably be written off as a nuisance in any other country, but Germany's past is too terrible to forget.

Both the Republican Party (the strongest of the neo-Nazi parties) and the Communist Party could be banned at the discretion of the Constitutional Court should their activities pose a potential threat to the regime. Whether the banning of the authoritarian parties would cripple or enhance their political influence is open to debate. On one hand, the outlawing of authoritarian parties deprives them of the opportunity to manipulate democratic procedures for authoritarian ends. On the other hand, merely outlawing an authoritarian political party does little to address the social forces that gave rise to its existence in the first place. Indeed, the very act of banning a political party may have the adverse effect of increasing its symbolic importance. Be this as it may, the Ministry of Interior has reluctantly banned several neo-Nazi groups in the name of preserving public security (*European,* July 15, 1993, 2).

German political parties, as noted earlier, are very cohesive and disciplined. Once a party position has been decided upon, members of the Bundestag are expected to support the party leadership regardless of their personal views. Members of the Bundestag vote their conscience only on issues that the party leadership has declared to be a "free vote."

The Christian Democratic Union. The Christian Democratic Union and its Bavarian counterpart, the Christian Social Union, emerged in the late 1940s as a broad coalition of centrist groups dedicated to the establishment of liberal democracy in Germany (Smith 1990). The Christian label was designed to unite Germany's Protestant and Catholic communities within the confines of a single party as well as to lend a moral tone to the political process. The Christian label was also designed to draw a clear line between the new party and its leftist counterparts, all of whom were manifestly anti-religious.

Victorious in Germany's first post-war election (1949), the CDU was soon forced to chose between a course of mild socialism on one hand and free enterprise on the other (Dalton 1993). Under the strong leadership of Conradt Adenauer, the CDU chose the path of free enterprise. Germany prospered and the CDU, in alliance with the smaller Free Democrats, would rule Germany for most of its existence as a democratic republic.

Once the CDU had made the decision to become the party of the center right, both its identity and that of its rivals took on greater clarity. The CDU was to become the party of business, proclaiming that a productive Germany would be a prosperous Germany. The CDU has also championed German participation in both a unified Europe and NATO, and it led the charge for German reunification. The achievement of unification transformed the image of Chancellor Kohl from that of a competent if unimaginative bureaucrat into a national hero. Ironically, the costs of digesting East Germany would quickly undermine his fleeting popularity, leading him to the brink of defeat in the 1994 elections. The costs of unification in conjunction with a staggering rate of unemployment—11 percent in the former West Germany; 16 percent in the former East Germany—spelled final defeat in 1998.

The CDU has traditionally drawn its support from practicing Catholics, the business community, women, older voters, and residents of Germany's smaller cities and rural areas (Smith 1990). In order to broaden its religious appeal, a number of seats on the CDU list are reserved for Protestants. In spite of its "big business" orientation, the CDU has also gone out of its way to accommodate German labor, many members of which vote for the CDU.

Although the CDU has dominated German politics throughout most of the Federal Republic's history, the growing urbanization of German society has strengthened the position of the SPD and the Greens, as has Germany's persistently high rate of unemployment.

To make matters worse, Helmut Kohl and most of those in key leadership positions in the CDU were implicated in a massive fundraising scandle that shook the Party to its core. In a bold move to regain its credibility, the Party selected Angela Merkel, an East German, to be its new leader, a dramatic move indeed (*NYT*, Apr. 11, 2000, www).

The Social Democratic Party. The Social Democratic Party (SPD) emerged during the Second Reich as a Marxist-oriented socialist party that was only slightly less radical than the communists. The SPD survived the persecution of the Hitler years with its leadership more or less intact, and was widely favored to win Germany's first post-war election (Paterson and Southern 1991; Berghahn 1987).

The 1949 elections, however, were won by the CDU. Germany prospered, and SPD appeals for the nationalization of German industry seemed antiquated, if not dangerous. Catholic workers were also offended by the hostility of the SPD to organized religion, and the Marxist orientation of the party raised lingering doubts about the ultimate loyalty of its members. Did their loyalties lie with Germany, or were they the unwitting tools of a Soviet Union committed to world domination?

Receiving only 30 percent of the popular vote in the 1957 elections, the SPD faced a critical choice. It could maintain its ideological purity and be relegated to the status of a minor party, or it could disavow Marxism and become a large catch-all party capable of challenging the CDU for the right to rule. It chose the latter course (Paterson and Southern 1991).

In 1959, the SPD dropped its demand for the nationalization of German industry, calling instead for a reasonable balance between economic growth and social welfare. The SPD also affirmed its support for NATO and pronounced socialism and Catholicism to be compatible doctrines. Marx was dead.

By 1966, the SPD had gathered sufficient public support to force a "Grand Coalition" with the CDU. The Grand Coalition, an unwieldy affair headed by the CDU, was to give way three years later (1969) to the first of several SPD Governments. The SPD would rule Germany without interruption for the next sixteen years (1969–1985).

Upon assuming power in 1969, the SPD moved rapidly to reassure the German business community that it was not hostile to capitalism. Labor was given an expanded role in corporate decision making, but Germany remained a bastion of capitalism. In point of fact, the German business community prospered under SPD rule. For all intents and purposes, the SPD had become a slightly left-of-center catch-all party, the major thrust of which was to offer voters a somewhat "kinder and gentler" approach to the business of government than the CDU. The 1998 elections, for example, saw the SPD platform call for gender equality, tax cuts for a large percentage of the German population, mild environmentalism, and a variety of government programs to solve Germany's unemployment problem by creating new jobs. Gerhard Schroder's performance in office has kept faith with his "new left" image and has been widely applauded by the German business community (*Businessweek Online,* May 1, 2000).

With an eye to the political center, the SPD was also careful to stress that "it wasn't going to change everything, merely do it better" (*Le Monde,* Sept. 29, 1998, 1). Much like Tony Blair and the Labour Party in Britain, then, the SPD had become a member of the **new left**, a *moderate, slightly left-of-center ideology* that at the turn of the century would be the dominant force in thirteen of the fifteen EU countries. The strategy was successful, and the SPD captured 298 seats in the Bundestag, a figure that enabled it to form a ruling coalition with the Greens (see Table 4.1) (Walker 1998). Gerhard Schroder, the new SPD prime minister, has made a remarkable metamorphosis from his early days as an anti-American, anti-nuclear radical in the youth wing of the SPD (Vincour 1998). More than the charisma of a dynamic Tony Blair–type leader, Schroeder's victory reflected the coming to power of a post-war generation that was untainted by the Hitler era. It is this generation—a generation of growth and prosperity rather than a generation of tragedy—that has now moved into ascendancy in Germany (*IHT,* Oct. 3, 1998, 2). Needless to say, the SPD victory was also underpinned by an 11-percent rate of unemployment, a figure that reached 16 percent in the Lander of the former East Germany.

Like the CDU, the SPD remains a pragmatic party whose policy positions are dictated largely by the desire to win elections (Markovitz and Gorski 1993). Placed in a comparative perspective, the SPD would be less doctrinaire than the British Labour Party, yet far clearer in its promotion of social justice than the Democratic Party of the United States.

As the position of the SPD would suggest, it finds a preponderance of its electoral support among younger, urban voters. The Party also draws considerable support from union members, and particularly from union members of secular orientation. The SPD, however, is not "owned" by the unions, and relations between the two groups often reflect considerable tension (Paterson and Southern 1991). Finally, the Party also attracts a disproportionate share of the Protestant vote.

The Free Democratic Party. The **Free Democratic Party (FDP)** attempts to occupy the middle ground between the Christian Democrats and the Social Democrats, but its positions are not always easy to define on a left-right spectrum. In recent years, for example, the FDP has been to the left of the CDU on foreign policy issues but has moved to its right on domestic issues involving social welfare. The members of the FDP are drawn disproportionately from the Protestant middle class and from farmers

Chancellor Gerhard Schroder represents the post–World War II generation that has come to power in Germany.

(Dalton 1993). Although small in size, never having garnered more than 13 percent of the popular vote, the FDP has traditionally played a pivotal role as a balancer between the larger CDU and SPD. Indeed, the FDP has served in more governments than either the CDU or SPD.

Unfortunately, from the perspective of the FDP, the middle ground between the CDU and the SPD has become increasingly narrow as each of the two major parties vies to dominate the political center. By the advent of the late 1980s, the FDP was struggling to surmount the 5 percent barrier and did so largely on the willingness of CDU voters to split their ticket to keep the FDP alive (Paterson and Southern 1991). The FDP also faced growing competition from the Greens, the success of which in the 1998 election suggested it was they, not the FDP, who had become Germany's "third party."

The Greens. The **Greens** emerged in the late 1970s in response to the growing deterioration of the German environment. Peace activists soon gravitated to the party, providing it with a dual focus: peace and the environment. Both issues commanded a vocal following in Germany.

To be concerned about the environment, however, was not necessarily to be opposed to a strong defense. While many students and intellectuals tended to support both issues, a large portion of the general population did not. As a result, many middle-class voters who were genuinely concerned about the environment found the Greens too radical for their liking (Kitschelt 1989; *IHT,* March 8, 1999). Following the unification of the two Germanies and the collapse of the Warsaw Pact, the environment has again dominated the Greens' agenda.

The Greens received 7.3 percent of the vote in the 1994 elections, a showing that forced the major parties, and especially the SPD, to place greater emphasis on environmental issues. While the dominant parties have shown greater sensitivity to environmental issues in recent years, neither could qualify as the party of the environment. The Greens captured 6.7 percent of the vote in the 1998 election (forty-nine seats in the Bundestag) and became the coalition partners of the victorious SPD. While the two parties have worked well together, tension remains over what the Greens consider to be Schroeder's lukewarm commitment to a strong environmental package. Particularly knotty is the Greens' demand for the abolition of Germany's program of nuclear energy. Schroeder has agreed in principle, but said that it will have to be worked out over the next twenty years.

Germany As a Party and Partisan State: The Role of Political Parties in the Political Process. The influence of political parties on German political life is so pervasive that Germany is often referred to as a "party state" (Smith 1990). In order to better understand this point, it may be useful to examine the diverse functions that the German party system performs.

First, as noted earlier, the party system plays a crucial role in recruiting and "educating" Germany's political elites. Before individuals assume leadership positions at the federal level, their mettle has been thoroughly tested. As a result of this process of political apprenticeship, Germany's leaders have generally displayed outstanding competence. Moreover, as democratic parties tend to select democratically inclined leaders, the recruitment process has provided the nation with almost five generations of political leaders committed to the democratic process.

Second, political parties provide a counterweight to the power of the chancellor. The chancellor is the party leader, but he or she is just one of several key party figures, all of whom possess an independent base of support. A chancellor who fails to keep in touch with the leadership core of his or her party risks a party rebellion or, in extreme cases, a vote of no confidence. In a parallel situation in England, it will be recalled, Margaret Thatcher was forced to resign by an internal revolt of the party leadership.

Third, the existence of two large and disciplined political parties lends responsibility to the German political process. The dominance of Germany's two major parties virtually assures that either the Christian Democrats or the Social Democrats will have sufficient votes in the Bundestag to form a Government, albeit with some assistance from the Free Democrats or the Greens. The majority party does possess the capacity to implement its electoral platform, and the German electorate expects it to do so.

Fourth, the cohesiveness of Germany's major political parties promotes coordination and harmony among the diverse units of a very complex political system (Paterson and Southern 1991). German federalism and the checks and balances inherent in the Basic Law were designed to fragment political power and, thereby, to preclude a return to authoritarian rule. The price of fragmenting power, however, is often confusion, indecision, and scapegoating as each branch of the government blames the others for its failings. The cohesion of German political parties helps to overcome these problems by providing members of the same party at all levels with a strong incentive for cooperation. This is not to suggest that party cohesiveness totally eliminates friction between the various units and levels of government, but it does make that friction considerably less evident than is the case in the United States.

Fifth, German parties provide the electorate with a meaningful choice of candidates and issues. Cynics might argue with this proposition, suggesting that the preoccupation of the two major parties with capturing the political center has blunted their role in providing the public with new options. Both major parties, they correctly point out, have become advocates of the status quo.

Sixth, the German party system provides citizens with an avenue of political participation that goes well beyond the regularly scheduled elections. German political parties encourage their members to get involved in all dimensions of the political process. Such political involvement, from the perspective of many political scientists, has strengthened German democracy by providing German citizens with a sense of political efficacy, i.e., a belief that the average citizen can make a difference. In this regard, it is interesting to note that actual membership in the two major parties has increased steadily over the course of the post–World War II era, a trend that bodes well for the future of German democracy.

Seventh, the German party system represents an important channel of communication between the political elites and the masses. Both of the major parties maintain a strong network of constituency organizations that enables their leadership to keep in touch with grassroots sentiment. In much the same manner, party meetings provide the leadership with the opportunity to explain the logic of its positions to the party faithful. This two-way communication process is an important element in German democracy.

Finally, the German party system plays an important stabilizing role in German society. The Weimar Republic, it will be recalled, operated on the basis of straight proportional representation. A party's seats in the Reichstag mirrored its popular vote. Any party, however narrow its appeal, was virtually assured a voice in parliament. The Weimar party system thus reinforced the fragmentation of German society by allowing each diverse segment to pursue its narrow self-interest at the parliamentary level. The party system of the Federal Republic, by contrast, aggregates the diverse segments of the German population into two large catch-all parties. Diverse regional, economic, religious, and ideological groups are forced to compromise their differences for the sake of electoral victory, thereby reinforcing the integration of German society (Jeffery 1998). In much the same manner, Germany's two-party system also encourages moderation. If parties are to win elections, they cannot adopt extreme positions (Smith 1990). The integrating role of German parties is particularly critical in the post-unification era, an era that finds many former East Germans attempting to cope with an alien political system in which they are treated as second-class citizens.

Pressure Groups and Politics in Germany

Germany possesses essentially the same array of economic, political, and social interest groups that exist in most Western democracies. As we shall see, however, the relationship between pressure groups and the government in Germany is very different from that in the United States.

Business. The German business community is represented by three large associations: The Federation of German Industry (BDI), the Federation of German Employment Associations (BDA), and the German Industrial and Trade Conference (DIHT). The BDI represents some 90,000 German firms, occupying a position roughly equivalent to that of the National Association of Manufacturers in the United States. The BDI is the most politically visible of the three business organizations and, as one might expect, maintains close ties with the Christian Democrats. The DIHT is the preferred organization of small businesses and independent craftsmen, and its members often have interests that differ from those of the industrial giants. The BDA serves as the business community's watchdog on wage policies and attempts to forge a unified policy toward labor.

> ### Success of German Unions
>
> German unions have been extraordinarily successful in pressing their demands, with German workers being the most highly paid of any of the major industrial powers. Many German workers also work thirty-six-hour weeks and receive up to forty days of vacation and sick leave per year, as well as generous pensions.

Labor. Labor, for the most part, expresses its views through the German Federation of Labor (GDB), Germany's major labor organization. Unlike the ideological unions of the Weimar era, the DGB follows the American pattern of placing economic goals above ideological concerns. Much of its activity in recent years has focused on *increasing worker participation in management decisions,* a process Germans refer to as **co-determination** (Kloss 1991). The DGB has also been increasingly concerned with protecting German workers from displacement by the influx of East European and Turkish "guest workers."

As in most countries of Western Europe, however, German labor is on the defensive (*Sunday Times,* Feb. 7, 1999, www). Only 40 percent of the labor force was unionized before unification, a figure that will be tested as the DGB attempts to reconcile the conflicting demands of workers in the two Germanies (Paterson and Southern 1991). The Government, moreover, has demanded give-backs by the unions, citing the need to keep Germany competitive in the world economic arena. Whatever its woes, the DGB continues to bargain for the wages of 90 percent of the German labor force (unionized or not)—a powerful position, indeed (Dalton 1993).

Institutional and Social Groups. German bureaucrats also constitute an important pressure group. German officials are encouraged to run for public office and are provided with six weeks of unpaid leave to do so. With about one-third of the members of the Bundestag being drawn from the ranks of the civil service, it is unlikely that the prerogatives of the German bureaucracy will soon be in jeopardy.

The Catholic and Protestant churches also possess formidable political influence, a fact well illustrated by the "church tax." Unless instructed otherwise, the government allocates 10 percent of an individual's income tax to a church. Religion also finds political expression through the Christian Democratic Party, a political organization expressly designed to integrate religion into the political process. Clearly, German citizens are less concerned with the separation of Church and State than their American counterparts.

All of the associations surveyed in the above discussion are **peak (or umbrella) associations**, each of which incorporates a multitude of smaller, more specialized organizations. All in all, Germany possesses some 20,000 associations, a figure that places it among the most organized societies in the world (Conradt 1986).

Most large peak associations find representation on a broad array of governmental councils and committees that enables them to review preliminary legislation before it is enacted into law. Most of Germany's professional organizations are also self-regulating. The German medical association, for example, licenses doctors and oversees the ethics of the medical profession.

In addition to their representation on semi-official councils, the dominant pressure groups are also well represented on the electoral lists of the two major parties, each of which trades "safe" positions on their lists for financial and electoral support. Indeed, some 50 percent of the Deputies in the Bundestag are employed in one capacity or another by a pressure group (Dalton 1993).

The CDU, quite logically, possesses stronger representation from the business community; the SPD, from labor. Both parties, however, strive to win at least some support from all of Germany's major groups. The CDU has successfully wooed the more moderate elements of the labor movement, particularly practicing Catholics.

Corporatism and Neocorporatism. The quasi-official role of German pressure groups stands in sharp contrast to the far more conflictive pattern of pressure group activity in the United States. To understand this difference, it is necessary to look at the differing group traditions of the two countries. American traditions have long stressed individualism and individual representation. German traditions, by contrast, have historically stressed group representation, or "**corporatism**" (Reich 1990). German craftsmen of the middle ages were organized into guilds that regulated the affairs of both the craft and its members. Entrance into a craft was closely regulated, as were ranks and wages. Eventually many guilds also took on the role of social organizations, attempting to care for the broader health and welfare of their members. The feudal leaders of the era soon found it convenient to provide the guilds with a self-regulating legal status in return for their political and financial support. Church leaders played similar roles, as did many labor groups in the era following Germany's belated industrialization.

Corporatism facilitated Hitler's rise to power by allowing him to win the support of large organizations by promising them that their interests would be secure. Following Hitler's 1933 victory, for example, the civil service and teaching professions joined the Nazi Party en masse (Grunberger 1971). The labor unions, in particular, were pressed into the service of the Nazi Party, trading their right to independent action for extravagant promises of a worker's paradise.

With the end of the Second World War and the emergence of the Federal Republic, authoritarian corporatism gave way to a democratic **neocorporatism** based upon voluntary cooperation between the Government and Germany's major pressure groups (Hancock 1989). Rather than the conflict that characterizes the pluralistic pattern of group representation in the United States, the emphasis in German politics is on finding broadly acceptable solutions to Germany's economic and social problems. German pressure groups articulate the interests of their members, but they do so in a manner that facilitates compromise. While some groups must ultimately win more than others, the emphasis is on precluding the alienation of any important segment of the population.

Neocorporatism remains an inherently conservative force in German society. Traditional corporate groups are "locked into" the system and possess far greater opportunity to shape legislation affecting their members than do the newer political interests that have emerged in the postwar era. Women, youth, environmentalists, and foreign workers, for example, all represent important segments of the German population that have been "*locked out*" of the established corporatist network.

Responding to under-representation, women, youth, and environmentalists have forged a variety of "citizen action groups" as a means of achieving their political objectives. These groups represent a new and expanding dimension of German politics that uses demonstrations, petitions, and marches to express their views on a broad variety of issues ranging from the environment and nuclear power to kindergarten reform and transit fares. Whether citizen action groups can compensate for the conservative nature of Germany's corporatist traditions remains to be seen.

Citizens and Politics in Germany

German citizens are among the most politically active in the world. Approximately 87 percent of the German electorate participated in the 1998 federal elections, a figure that dwarfs the 50 to 55 percent of the United States population that typically participates in presidential elections. Germans also participate in political parties, interest associations, and "citizen action" groups. As a result, Germany's leaders are well informed about the concerns of citizens.

In addition to the formal avenues of political participation, the opinions of the German population are assessed on a regular basis by a variety of polling organizations (Brettschneider 1997). Recent polls indicate the major concerns of German citizens. Of prime concern for 63 percent of all those questioned was the high unemployment rate in Germany. Following this was concern regarding crime among children and adolescents (52.3 percent), the lack of adequate training positions (51.2 percent), and the rising criminal rate (49.3 percent). One-third were unhappy about the high immigration rate (*Berliner Morgenpost,* Jan. 1, 1999).

The most important conclusion to be drawn from an analysis of election results and public opinion polls is that the Federal Republic enjoys the broad support of the German population (Dalton 1993). This was not always the case, questions of legitimacy having plagued the Federal Republic during the first decade of its existence. A public opinion poll conducted in 1951, for example, found that approximately one-third of the German population favored a return to a monarchial system similar to that of the Second Reich (Smith 1990). A 1953 survey also found potential support for neo-Nazi movements among 16 percent of the population. Such attitudes were, perhaps, to be expected, as the Federal Republic had been imposed upon Germany by the Allied Powers.

Questions concerning the legitimacy of the Federal Republic, however, were soon answered. By the 1970s, support for Nazi movements had dropped to 7 percent, a steady decline that would continue throughout the 1980s. The ability of the Federal Republic to establish its legitimacy among a skeptical population was undoubtedly a function of Germany's post-war prosperity. The Federal Republic not only provided for the well-being of its citizens, but it transformed Germany into one of the most prosperous states in the world.

Election results and opinion polls also indicate a relentless movement of German public opinion toward the center of the political spectrum. While fringe parties have enjoyed a brief revival in the post-unification era, the center of gravity of German politics has clearly shifted to the middle (Fuchs and Rohrschneider 1998).

Citizens of the former East Germany have yet to become full participants in German prosperity and remain somewhat distrustful of the federal government. It is they, more than any other segment of German society, who have been swayed by the appeals of the extremists.

This then, brings us to the question of mass influence on German politics. Does mass participation really make a difference? As in most Western democracies, public opinion matters most at election time (Dalton 1993). The primary goal of Germany's main parties is to win elections, and they can ignore public opinion only to their own detriment. Beyond question, it has been the force of citizen opinions that has pushed the locus of German politics to the political center (Jones and Retallack 1992).

The Context of German Politics: Culture, Economics, and International Interdependence

Politics is a reflection of a nation's institutions and the individuals and groups that give life to those institutions, but it is also influenced by the broader environmental context in which the political process occurs. As discussed in Chapter 1, political events are profoundly affected by the culture of the participants as well as by economic and international factors. This is certainly the case in Germany.

The Culture of German Politics: From the Authoritarian State to the Post-Industrial Society

It is the underlying cultural values of German society, according to cultural analysts, that are likely to provide the best guide to German politics over the long haul (Inglehart 1990). If the German masses are truly committed to human freedom and democracy, it would be difficult for a new dictatorship to emerge and survive. By contrast, if the German masses are primarily concerned with order and nationalism, the German government could well move in the direction of greater authoritarianism.

Sociological studies following the end of World War II found the German population to possess an abiding concern with authority. Many scholars questioned the compatibility of German culture with democracy (Smith 1990). The German population also displayed a far stronger devotion to rules and regulations than was evident in Anglo-American culture. Rules were rules, and they were to be obeyed. The German sociologist Dahrendorf (1959) also suggests that Germans possessed a low tolerance for ambiguity and social conflict. If problems exist, according to Dahrendorf, Germans attempt to resolve them immediately and then codify that resolution into law. This tendency, Dahrendorf continues, has resulted in the intense legalism and rigidity of German society. Once rules have been codified, they are difficult to change. Indeed, much of the German legal code is still based upon the laws of the Second and Third Reichs.

Not all Germans, of course, act or feel the same way, any more than all Americans act or feel the same way. Stereotypes are dangerous. **Political culture** merely suggests that certain values are more prevalent in some societies than in others. It would be difficult, for example, to argue with the observation that Germans, on average, tend to manifest a greater respect for rules and regulations than Egyptians, a topic to be explored in Chapter 10. It would be a mistake, however, to suggest that all Germans were overly concerned with rule compliance or that all Egyptians were not. At best, such cultural differences refer only to parts of the population, and then only to a degree.

Socialization and Cultural Change.   Cultural values are passed from one generation to the next, but they also change in response to new environmental realities (Inglehart 1990). The vast majority of today's Germans were either not yet born during Hitler's Third Reich or were in their infancy. Unlike their parents and grandparents, they have grown up in an environment of democracy and prosperity. The newer generations of German citizens are also far more educated and far more urban than prewar Germans, and they have been intensely socialized (indoctrinated) to believe in democratic values (Shafer 1991). One cannot, accordingly, assume that the values of today's Germans are the same as the values that predominated during the Second or Third Reich (Inglehart 1990).

What, then, are the dominant features of German political culture today? Until the advent of unification in 1990, both public opinion polls and election results indicated a persistent increase in democratic values over the course of the post-war era. While pockets of authoritarianism remained, the data indicated a commitment to democratic values equalling that of most other Western democracies.[16]

---

[16]Hastings and Payne (1990) report that German high school seniors are somewhat less democratic in outlook than a corresponding sample of American students.

The unification of East and West Germany put a temporary cloud on this otherwise rosy horizon (Minkenberg 1993). The former citizens of East Germany did not grow up in an environment of democracy and prosperity, and their political socialization continued to stress authoritarianism and compliance (Friedrich 1991). The economic burdens of reunification have done little to erode these values (Durr 1992). The reunification of Germany, then, involves far more than the collapse of the Berlin Wall. It also involves taking down a cultural wall that will remain for some time (Yoder, 1998).

Questions of democracy and legitimacy aside, Germans do seem to manifest a stronger commitment to rule compliance than do the citizens of many other societies. Other frequently cited traits of German political culture would include a strong sense of cultural identity, a high regard for organization and efficiency, and a belief that the good of the collective should come before the rights of the individual (Dalton 1993; Paterson and Southern 1991). Indeed, few countries in the world share the United States' pervasive concern for the rights of the individual.

German politics, moreover, is also influenced by the broader social and economic dimensions of German culture. Particularly important, in this regard, is the strong achievement orientation of German society. Germans, by and large, work very hard. They also place a premium on thrift and savings, as well as on organizational efficiency (Kloss 1991). Achievement is an economic trait rather than a political trait, but there can be little doubt that the strong performance of the German economy over the past four decades has played a central role in consolidating the legitimacy of the Federal Republic (Inglehart 1990).

Some German business leaders, however, now fear that Germany's famed work ethic has begun to fade as younger Germans are less willing to accept a deteriorating environment and the psychological stress of competition for the sake of a marginal increase in their paychecks (Ardagh 1991). Individual freedom, equality of the sexes, and grassroots democracy have also begun to rival efficiency as core social values (Dalton 1993). Prosperity remains an important concern, but not necessarily the most important concern (Fuchs and Rohrschneider 1998).

Political Economy and Politics in Germany

For political economists, the evolution of German politics has far more to do with the economy than with culture. The rise of Hitler, from the perspective of political economists, was the result of the collapse of the German economy during the Weimar era. Germans, in this view, were driven to authoritarianism by the inability of democratic political institutions to meet their basic needs. Hitler's program of rearmament and military expansion sparked an economic revival, lifting Germany from the depths of economic depression to the pinnacle of world domination (Borchardt 1991).

The economic success of West Germany has been heralded by neoclassical (capitalist) economists as a resounding demonstration of the superiority of free-market capitalism over socialism. East Germany and West Germany shared a common culture, but only the capitalist economy of West Germany brought prosperity.

Such conclusions, while inevitable, are not fully justified. The economy of East Germany was tied to that of the Soviet Union and would find it difficult to progress faster than the Eastern bloc as a whole. East Germany, however, was the most productive member of the East European economic bloc, suggesting that German culture did have an influence on productivity.

Debates over the relative merits of capitalism and socialism have now become passé, the communist bloc having collapsed. The most pressing debate today concerns

---

Relationship Between Prosperity and Democracy

The success of German democracy in the post–World War II era, from the political economic perspective, is a function of German prosperity. Prosperity doesn't guarantee democracy, but it does build support for democratic regimes that provide that prosperity. Had the economic circumstances of the Weimar Republic been more favorable, from the political economic perspective, the devastation of the Hitler era might well have been avoided.

---

the most effective form of capitalism: free-market capitalism or managed "state" capitalism in which the government plays a major role in stimulating economic growth and assuring that all strata of society share in the rewards of capitalist prosperity. The International Monetary Fund (IMF) and other institutions of international capitalism argue that prosperity is best achieved by a free market in which government intervention in the economy is kept to a minimum. This is also the official philosophy of the United States.

West Germany achieved its phenomenal record of economic success by a version of state capitalism that it refers to as **social market economy**. Under the system of social market economy, *government, business, and labor all cooperate to achieve two goals: growth and equity.* The Weimar Republic had been undermined by intense class conflict, as workers were pitted against the bourgeoisie in a drama straight from the pages of Marx. The social market economy was designed to assure that West German democracy would be free of class conflict. It has succeeded admirably.

Germany's economy possesses three basic components: (1) strong government efforts to assure economic growth; (2) cradle-to-grave welfare programs; and (3) government-mandated cooperation between labor and industry. Government efforts to assure economic growth are based on strong cooperation between government and industry. Economic growth is generated by providing the business community with a powerful voice in all phases of economic policy making via the neocorporate procedures described earlier. To some extent, the Minister of Economics is industry's representative in the Government (Paterson and Southern 1991). The German government also provides German industry with a technically trained labor force, something that is sadly lacking in the educational systems of both Britain and the United States. The famed German work ethic is matched by a high level of vocational competence.

The social dimension of the social market economy has taken the form of a comprehensive welfare system that assures that all Germans are provided with adequate housing, health care, education, unemployment benefits, and retirement pensions.

The social market economy stresses cooperation between government, industry, and labor. All have benefited. German firms also carry the cooperative process one step further by placing informal limits on intra-industry conflict. Competition is pursued, but it is not pursued to the point of destroying other German competitors. Industrial competition, moreover, stresses quality and service rather than low prices (Smyser 1992). German consumers pay more, but they also get more.

There can be little question that Germany's blend of capitalism and welfare has played a major role in sustaining both the stability and the democratic character of the Federal Republic (Dalton 1993). The German experience also indicates that "wise" government can be a very positive force in generating economic growth.

As positive as the German experience has been, three clouds loom on the horizon. Of these, the first is *the escalating cost of the social system.* Half of the West German population will soon be past retirement age and entitled to generous pensions (Geipel 1993). A falling birth rate, moreover, places increased pressure upon younger workers to fund the welfare system, something they have been increasingly reluctant to do, as German taxes are already among the highest in the First World. The unemployment rate in Germany also continues to hover around the 10 percent mark (16 percent in the former East Germany) and shows little sign of falling. The Government is now in the process of scaling back the welfare package.

The second cloud on Germany's economic horizon concerns *the unexpected and as yet incalculable costs of reunification.* The cost of bringing East Germany's infrastructure of roads, communications, and factories on par with those of West Germany will be staggering, and the stress of reunifying the two Germanies will mar the political landscape for several years to come.

The third cloud on Germany's economic horizon is *the pressure of competition from Asia and the United States.* German labor costs are currently the highest in the First World. To remain competitive, German factories are attempting to hold the line on salaries and scale back the number of their employees. While relations between labor and industry continue to stress cooperation rather than conflict, strikes have increased dramatically in the last few years. Indeed, labor unrest in the mid-1990s reached new post–World War II levels as workers struck to oppose cutbacks in their welfare benefits.

To make matters worse, the three crises confronting the social market economy are occurring simultaneously. The crowning achievement of the West German government was its ability to provide both economic growth and a high level of social welfare under a democratic system. That government is now attempting to scale down welfare payments at the same time that extremist political movements are making a comeback. Popular opposition to cutbacks in Germany's social welfare program clearly contributed to the defeat of the CDU in the 1998 elections.

International Interdependence and the Politics of Germany

Scholars in the field of international relations have long criticized students of comparative government for underestimating the interdependence of domestic politics and international politics (Pfetsch 1988). No country in the modern world, in their view, can escape the influence of either its regional neighbors or the larger international community. By the same token, individual countries often play a profound role in shaping their regional and international environments. Germany personifies both sides of the interdependence equation. Few states have been more directly influenced by international forces than Germany, and very few can rival Germany's capacity to shape its international environment.

The World and Germany. Germany, in many ways, is the creation of international forces. It was Napoleon's consolidation of the German principalities at the turn of the nineteenth century that stimulated the process of German state building. It was similarly the Franco-Prussian War of 1871 that facilitated the final unification of the German state. The harsh conditions of the peace treaty imposed upon Germany by the Allied Powers at the conclusion of World War I encouraged the rise of the Third Reich by undermining the economic viability of the Weimar Republic. Whatever chance the Weimar Republic may have had for success, moreover, was crushed by the Great Depression, control of which was far beyond the capacity of a single country. The rise of Hitler was also facilitated by the passivity of the Western powers. The British and French sought to buy peace by capitulating to Hitler's demands, while the United States was locked in an isolationist stupor (Churchill 1948).

External influence, moreover, was paramount in shaping the structure of the Federal Republic. The Basic Law was drafted under the watchful eye of the Allied Powers, as were educational and labor reforms designed to reshape German political culture (Dalton 1993).

Responding to the outbreak of the Cold War, the Western powers went out of their way to assure the economic and political stability of the Federal Republic. The stationing of Allied troops in West Germany, far from being the act of an occupying power, provided West Germany with a security umbrella under which its economy and its democracy could prosper. A West Germany unprotected from attack by Soviet troops stationed in Eastern Europe could not have become the economic and technological superpower that exists today.

More recently, the reunification of East and West Germany was made possible by the collapse of the Soviet empire. That collapse has also provided Germany with a new window of economic opportunity as the states of Eastern Europe seek German cooperation in the rebuilding of their shattered economies. On the negative side, the collapse of the Soviet bloc has resulted in Germany being inundated with refugees and migrants from all areas of Eastern Europe. How well Germany can cope with its refugee problem while struggling to integrate its East German population remains to be seen.

The European Union also exerts a profound influence on German politics. January 1999, for example, marked the entrance of the euro, a European single currency. The German mark will co-exist with the euro for a few years, but the economic policy of Germany will soon be made by European rather than German institutions. The political unification of Western Europe, while being pursued with less vigor, is also expected to occur within the next decade or two.

Finally, it should be recalled that the economic foundation of German politics is being threatened by growing competition from Asia and North America. German industry is being forced to trim its labor costs in order to remain competitive, and such cutbacks have already begun to increase the tension between labor and the government (Ardagh 1991).

Germany and the World. While German domestic policy is profoundly influenced by international forces, Germany also possesses a determining voice in shaping the broader contours of the international community. Germany is an economic superpower, its economic clout in world circles being surpassed only by that of the United States and Japan (Smyser 1993).

The influence of German economic policy on the states of Eastern Europe is profound (Hamilton 1993; Miller and Templeman 1997). Remittances from guest workers in Germany are vital to the economies of many Eastern European states and Turkey. If Germany continues to reduce its dependence upon guest workers, it will exact a heavy toll from an Eastern Europe struggling to recover from five decades of Soviet domination.

Concentrating on Germany's position as an economic superpower makes it easy to lose sight of the link between economic power and military power. While precluded by law from having a large military force independent of NATO, Germany maintains one of the largest military establishments in Europe, being eclipsed only by France, Turkey, and Russia (Geipel 1993). German firms have also been in the forefront of those states exporting nuclear, chemical, and missile technology to the less-stable states of the Third World, including Iraq, Iran, and Libya. There is no question of Germany's technical capacity to reestablish itself as the dominant military force in Europe should it choose to do so. Such an eventuality, of course, is forbidden by both law and treaty. Ironically, Germany now finds its former wartime adversaries calling upon it to play a greater military role

> ### Germany a Key Member of the European Union
>
> Germany's size, economic power, and central location make it the core state of an increasingly powerful European Union. Indeed, it is questionable whether the European Union could succeed without German participation. Germany has pushed for a stronger European Union, urging that progress toward a truly federated Europe not be held up by the reluctance of the British and the Scandinavians (Tewes 1998).

in sustaining the "new world order" (Clemens 1993a, 1993b). It has begun to do so by sending troops in support of UN peacekeeping efforts.

Challenges of the Present and Prospects for the Future

Germany currently ranks near the top of the world community in terms of the six indicators of good government outlined in Chapter 1: democracy, stability, human rights, economic growth, quality of life, and concern for the environment. As with all countries, however, Germany faces challenges in each of the six areas. These challenges are very real, and most have been increased by the unification of the two Germanies. Presumably, they will lessen as the former East Germany becomes better integrated into the social, political, and economic fabric of the former West Germany.

Democracy and Stability

Germany's transition from a totalitarian state to a liberal democracy has been one of the political success stories of the twentieth century. As similar transitions are currently taking place throughout the world, it may be useful to summarize briefly the most prominent factors underscoring Germany's success.

1. The Basic Law provided Germany with a political structure that achieved a workable balance between power and constraint. German chancellors possess the power to rule in a firm and decisive manner, but their powers are checked by those of the Parliament, the Lander, and the Supreme Court.
2. German political elites are intensely committed to democratic principles.
3. The preeminence of single-member districts in the German voting system has encouraged the growth of two stable and democratically oriented political parties that vie to capture the center of the political spectrum.
4. German pressure groups are overwhelmingly supportive of the political system and cooperate to assure its effectiveness.
5. The German population participates in the democratic process with exceptional vigor.
6. The German population appears to have internalized democratic values and bears little resemblance to the generation of Germans that created the horrors of the Third Reich.
7. The prosperity of the German economy has demonstrated that a democratic political system can meet the needs of its people.
8. The international community has provided strong political, economic, and military support for Germany's democratic regime.

In spite of the stability of German democracy over the course of the past four decades, doubts remain (*IHT,* Sept. 8, 1999, www). These concerns were expressed by Arthur Miller in *The New York Times Magazine:*

Does the Federal Republic of Germany arouse lofty democratic feelings in its citizens' minds, or is it a system that is simply a matter of historical convenience invented by foreigners? To be sure, this system has helped the nation to prosper as never before, but the issue is how deep the commitment is to its democratic precepts, how sacred they are, and if they will hold in hard times (Miller 1990, 77).

As if in answer to these doubts, the rise in neo-Nazi violence against foreigners has been matched by mass demonstrations demanding that its perpetrators be brought to justice. The German government has also moved to restrict the activities of extremist groups.

Human Rights

The most prominent victims of civil rights abuses in Germany are the members of its large foreign community (Blackshire-Belay 1990; *IHT,* Feb. 4, 1999, www). Guest workers, mainly from Turkey and the former Yugoslavia, were recruited to work in German factories and mines during the industrial boom of the early 1960s. Many have continued to live in Germany since that time, becoming German in everything but citizenship. The Turkish community, Germany's largest ethnic group, numbers some 1.8 million (*CSM,* June 9, 1993, 3).

Asylum-seekers from Eastern Europe have flocked to Germany since the collapse of the Communist Bloc. By 1993, more than 1,000 asylum-seekers per day were entering Germany, most of them seeking jobs in a country already staggered by a 10 percent rate of unemployment. Moved by popular pressure, the German government has recently engineered a constitutional amendment making Germany's asylum requirements among the most restrictive in Europe. The new law is being vigorously enforced, placing asylum-seekers under siege from both the neo-Nazis and the government. On the positive side, the German government has also moved to make it easier for long-term guest workers to become German citizens, a move extended by the new SPD Government.

Germany is also the most sexist of the major European states. It was not until 1977, for instance, that West German women were allowed to take a job without their husbands' permission (Ardagh 1991). Restrictions on night work for women prevailed until 1991, when they were declared unconstitutional. Women are also beginning to play a more active role in the political sphere, with females now occupying some 25 percent of the seats in the Bundestag. Among other things, this level of representation reflects the SPD's decision to establish quotas for women, a decision stimulated by the strong feminist position of the Greens. Female representation in Land parliaments and city councils is somewhat higher (Kiefer 1993).

Despite recent gains, informal sexism remains very much a part of German life. The traditional realm of females in German society was restricted to Kinder, Küchen, and Kirche (children, cooking, and church) (Ardagh 1991). Strong biases in this direction continue, with women constituting a lower percentage of the German work force than is the case in most other major European states. Women also tend to occupy lower positions than men, and many have only part-time employment. Indeed, only 5 percent of the top positions in Germany are held by females (Neumann 1998). Pregnant women or women with children find it particularly difficult to gain employment.

The restrictive status of women in West Germany came as a shock to East German women, some 95 percent of whom were employed and accustomed to free child care. They were also far more politicized than the women of West Germany. East German women have borne the brunt of unemployment as East German firms are either being closed or scaled back (Kiefer 1993). Progress toward equality of the sexes is being made, but it is being made in a very conservative manner.

Sustained Economic Growth and Quality of Life

Germany enters the twenty-first century as the world's third leading economic power, topped only by Japan and the United States. According to some estimates, Germans enjoy "what is probably the highest median standard of living in the world" (Geipel 1993). While German economic growth has been dampened by the problems of reunification, there can be little doubt that a fully integrated Germany will wield far greater economic power than West Germany alone (Treverton 1993).

Not only does Germany have a larger economic "pie" than most countries, but the German social market economy has assured that all Germans have an equal opportunity to achieve their economic goals (Rieger and Leibfried 1998). No country is totally free of economic classes, but Germany does better than most. Managing directors in Germany, for example, earn less than six times the salary of unskilled labor.

Three dimensions of German social policy are of particular interest, for they address problems with which the United States and many other industrial countries are currently grappling: health care, child care, and education.

The comprehensiveness of the German health care system is summarized in the following quotation suggesting that it is expensive, but it works:

> Health insurance is compulsory for all employed and self-employed people and their dependents. Under this system, you must belong to one of a range of statutory but semi-autonomous insurance agencies (Krankenkassen), or in some cases you can opt for a private one. By law each employee gives his agency 6.3 per cent of his income, and his employer adds a similar amount.... A patient is treated entirely free of charge (save that he pays 2 DM per prescription, and sometimes for 'extras' such as new spectacles) (Ardagh 1991, 229–30).

German education is both egalitarian and practical, with some 95 percent of German children attending public schools. All students receive a standard elementary education, followed, at approximately age eleven, by assignment to specialized schools at various levels. The brightest students go to college preparatory *Gymnasium,* while the midlevel advance on the technical training track. The lower group, some 35 percent of the German students, receive vocational training and apprenticeships (Ardagh 1991). The important point to be noted is that German children are both educated and provided with marketable skills. This is far less the case in the United States and Britain.

Germany's policy toward child care reflects its social and cultural values. Germany is becoming an elderly society and is very desirous of increasing its birth rate. It is also a very conservative society, with a majority of both sexes believing that young children should be cared for by their mothers, although more than 80 percent of the women sampled in a recent survey wanted to combine work and family responsibilities (Kiefer 1993). This mix of cultural values finds expression in a child care policy that provides exceptional benefits for childbearing but little in the way of day care centers for infants and young children (Kiefer 1993). The benefits for childbearing include fourteen weeks of paid maternity leave followed by three years of unpaid maternity leave. Some 95 percent of German parents also receive special child allowances that last until age 16 (Kiefer 1993). The German government wants women to have children, and it also wants the mothers to raise them.

While Germany is justifiably proud of its social welfare system, the cost of the system has become prohibitively expensive, with 40 percent of German salaries being deducted for social insurance (Wurzel 1996). Indeed, Germany's welfare benefits now equal one-third of the gross domestic product (GDP) (Wurzel 1996). Particularly problematic have been the aging of the German population, the burdens of absorbing the East German welfare system, and an unemployment rate that has

---

Germany Declares War on Pollution

Spearheaded by a broad and diverse coalition of political groups, Germany declared war on pollution. That war has been conducted with customary German thoroughness (Ardagh 1991). By the time of reunification, Germans were recycling some 42 percent of their newspapers and 70 percent of their old tires (Ardagh 1991). German laws on air pollution and hazardous waste are also among the strongest in the world.

---

continued to hover around the 10 percent mark in spite of the end of the economic recession that marked the first half of the 1990s (*IHT*, Aug. 6, 1999).

A Passion for the Environment

Germany is the most environmentally conscious of the major European states, a posture resulting from the severe deterioration of the German environment during World War II and the period of rapid economic growth that accompanied the establishment of the Federal Republic. By the 1980s, Germany's famed forests had begun to die, with the government declaring that more than one-third of Germany's trees were damaged from pollution-related diseases (Ardagh 1991).

Unfortunately, the quantity of hazardous waste being produced by German industry is increasing so rapidly that it may soon be difficult to keep under control. This is particularly the case as Germany has turned to nuclear energy in an effort to break its dependence on pollution-producing fossil fuels. Many Germans, however, find this cure to be worse than the disease, and the SPD Government has proposed a gradual program for eliminating Germany's nuclear program. Progress, however, has been slow. In addition to producing hazardous waste, nuclear energy also raises fears of a nuclear disaster. Germany is a densely populated country and memories of Chernobyl, the Soviet nuclear disaster, are fresh in the minds of its citizens. Many Germans are also nervous about the link between the peaceful and military uses of nuclear energy (Ardagh 1991). Perhaps with these thoughts in mind the new SPD/Green coalition has announced plans to "phase out" nuclear power over the next twenty-five years. The SPD was the relevant partner in this decision, and it is very likely that a conservative Government will be re-elected before it takes force.

Germany's pollution woes have been dramatically increased by the reunification of the two Germanies. While West Germany became "green" in the mid-1980s, East Germany, in a desperate attempt to keep pace with its more prosperous neighbor, operated in total disregard for its physical environment. Cleaning up East Germany is yet another cost of reunification.

Finally, it should be noted that many of Germany's pollution problems are not of its own making. Waves of air pollution drift over Germany from states of Eastern Europe that, like their East German counterpart, operated with total disregard for the environment. While no longer under communist rule, the leaders of these newly independent states are under tremendous pressure to jump-start their economies. Economic survival is taking precedence over preservation of the environment. To make matters worse, the industrial survival of the former communist states of Eastern Europe could well depend upon on their willingness to absorb high-pollution industries currently being forced out of the West. Germany's environmental problems, accordingly, cannot be solved without addressing the economic problems of its Eastern neighbors.

Prospects for the Future

Whatever its challenges, Germany is among the world's leaders in terms of democracy, stability, human rights, economic growth, quality of life, and concern for the environment. There is little evidence to suggest that this will change.

References

Almond, Gabriel, and Sidney Verba. 1965. *Politics: Civic Culture, Political Attitudes, and Democracy in Five Nations.* Boston: Little, Brown.

Anheier, Helmut, Friedhelm Neidhardt, and Wolfgang Vortkamp. 1998 (June–July). "Movement Cycles and the Nazi Party: Activities of the Munich NSDAP, 1925–1930." *American Behavioral Scientist* 41(9): 1262–1281.

Ardagh, John. 1991. *Germany and the Germans: After Unification.* New Revised Edition. London: Penguin Books.

Berghahn, V. R. 1987. *Modern Germany: Society, Economy, and Politics in the Twentieth Century.* 2nd ed. Cambridge, UK: Cambridge University Press.

Bertram, Christoph. 1998 (July–August). "Germany Moves On." *Foreign Affairs* 77(4): 186–194.

Blackshire-Belay, Carol. 1990. "The Foreign Workers and Foreign Workers' Germany." Unpublished paper.

Borchardt, Knut. 1991. *Perspectives on Modern German Economic History and Policy.* Translated by Peter Lambert. Cambridge, UK: Cambridge University Press.

Brettschneider, Frank. 1997 (Fall). "The Press and the Polls in Germany, 1980–1994: Poll Coverage as an Essential Part of Election Campaign Reporting." *International Journal of Public Opinion Research* 9(3): 248–265.

Brustein, William. 1998 (June–July). "The Nazi Party and the German New Middle Class, 1925–1933." *American Behavioral Scientist.* 41(9): 1237–1261.

Churchill, Winston. 1948. *The Gathering Storm.* New York: Houghton Mifflin.

Clemens, Clay. 1993a. "A Special Kind of Superpower? Germany and the Demilitarization of Post-Cold-War International Security." In *Germany in a New Era* (pp. 199–242), ed. Gary L. Geipel. Indianapolis: Hudson Institute.

Clemens, Clay. 1993b (Winter). "Opportunity or Obligation? Redefining Germany's Military Role Outside of NATO." *Armed Forces and Society: An Interdisciplinary Journal* 19(2): 231–251.

Conradt, David P. 1986. *The Germany Polity.* 4th ed. New York: Longman.

Conradt, David P. 1993. "Putting Germany Back Together Again: The Great Social Experiment of Unification." In *Germany in a New Era* (pp. 3–18), ed. Gary L. Geipel. Indianapolis: Hudson Institute.

Conradt, David P. 1996. *The Germany Polity.* 6th ed. New York: Longman.

Dahrendorf, Ralf. 1959. *Class and Class Conflict in Industrial Society.* Stanford, CA: Stanford University Press.

Dalton, Russell J. 1993. *Politics in Germany.* 2nd ed. New York: HarperCollins.

Detweiler, Donald. 1976. *Germany: A Short History.* Carbondale, IL: Southern Illinois University Press.

Durr, Karlheinz. 1992 (Jan.). "East German Education: A System in Transition." *Phi Delta Kappan* 73(5): 90–93.

Edinger, Lewis. 1977. *Politics: West Germany.* 2nd ed. Boston: Little, Brown.

Edinger, Lewis, and Brigitte L. Nacos. 1998 (Summer). "From the Bonn to the Berlin Republic: Can a Stable Democracy Continue?" *Political Science Quarterly* 113(2): 1279–91.

Flint, Colin. 1998 (June–July). "Forming Electorates, Forging Spaces: The Nazi Party Vote and the Social Construction of Space." *American Behavioral Scientist* 41(9): 1282–1303.

Friedrich, Walter. 1991 (Spring). "Changes in Attitudes of Youth in the GDR." *European Education* 23(1): 6–30.

Fuchs, Dieter, and Robert Rohrschneider. 1998 (April). "Postmaterialism and Electoral Choice Before and After German Unification." *West European Politics* 21(2): 9–30.

Fuller, Linda. 1998 (May). "The Socialist Labour Process, the Working Class, and the Revolution in the German Democratic Republic." *Europe-Asia Studies* 50, 50(3): 469–492.

Geipel, Gary L. 1993. "The Nature and Limits of German Power." In *Germany in a New Era* (pp. 19–48), ed. Gary L. Geipel. Indianapolis: Hudson Institute.

Gerth, Hans. 1940 (Jan.). "The Nazi Party: Its Leadership and Composition." *The American Journal of Sociology* 45: 526–27.

Goetz, Klaus H. 1997 (Winter). "Acquiring Political Craft: Training Grounds for Top Officials in the German Core Executive." *Public Administration* 75(4): 753–775.

Grunberger, Richard. 1971. *The 12-Year Reich: A Social History of Nazi Germany, 1933–1945.* New York: Ballantine.

Hamilton, David. 1993. "New Bargains: Germany as Europe's Central Power." In *Germany in a New*

Era (pp. 111–35), ed. Gary L. Geipel. Indianapolis: Hudson Institute.

Hancock, M. Donald. 1989. *West Germany: The Politics of Democratic Corporatism.* Chatham, NC: Chatham House.

Hastings, William L., and Kenneth A. Payne. 1990 (Nov.–Dec.). "Democratic Orientations Among High School Seniors in the United States and Germany." *Social Education* 54(7): 458–69.

Hucko, Elmar M., ed. 1987. *The Democratic Tradition: Four German Constitutions.* New York: St. Martin's.

Inglehart, Ronald. 1990. *Culture Shift in Advanced Industrial Society.* Princeton, NJ: Princeton University Press.

Jacob, Herbert. 1963. *German Administration Since Bismarck: Central Authority Versus Local Autonomy.* New Haven, CT: Yale University Press.

Jeffery, Charlie. 1998 (July–Sept.). "Electoral Reform: Learning from Germany." *Political Quarterly* 69(3): 241–51.

Jones, Larry, and James Retallack. 1992. *Elections, Mass Behavior, and Social Change in Modern Germany.* New York: Cambridge University Press (for the German Historical Institute).

Kiefer, Francine S. 1993 (Apr. 29). "Women in Today's Germany." *Christian Science Monitor*, 12–13.

Kitschelt, Herbert. 1989. *The Logic of Party Formation: The Structure and Strategy of the Belgian and West German Ecology Parties.* Ithaca, NY: Cornell University Press.

Kloss, Gunther. 1991. *West Germany: An Introduction.* 2nd ed. London: Macmillan.

Lipset, Seymour. 1960. *Political Man.* Garden City, NY: Doubleday.

Maor, Moshe. 1998 (July). "The Relationship Between Government and Opposition in the Bundestag and House of Common in the Run-up to the Maastricht Treaty." *West European Politics* 21(3): 187–207.

Markovitz, Andrei S., and Philip S. Gorski. 1993. *The German Left: Red, Green, and Beyond.* New York: Oxford University Press.

Miller, Arthur. 1990 (May 6). "Uneasy About the Germans." *The New York Times Magazine*, 46–47, 77, 84–85.

Miller, Karen Lowry, and John Templeman. 1997 (Feb.). "Germany's East Bloc: With Massive Flows of Investment and Aid, Bonn is Expanding its Clout in Central Europe." *Business Week* 3512: 5–7.

Minkenberg, Michael. 1993 (Oct. 1). "The Wall After the Wall: On the Continuing Division of Germany and the Remaking of Political Science." *Comparative Politics* 26(1): 53.

Neumann, Karin. 1998 (Winter). "Germany: Only 5% of Top Positions Held by Women." *WIN News* 24(1): 7.

Nove, Alec. 1992. *An Economic History of the USSR, 1917–1991.* 3rd ed. London: Penguin Books.

Padgett, Stephen. 1993. *Parties and Party Systems in the New Germany.* London: Dartmouth Publishing Co., Ltd.

Paterson, William E., and David Southern. 1991. *Governing Germany.* New York: W. W. Norton.

Pfetsch, Frank R. 1988. *West Germany, Internal Structures and External Relations: Foreign Policy of the Federal Republic of Germany.* New York: Praeger.

Pickel, Andreas. 1997 (April). "The Jump-Started Economy and the Ready-Made State: A Theoretical Reconsideration of the East German Case." *Comparative Political Studies* 30(2): 2–32.

Pond, Elizabeth. 1993. *Beyond the Wall: Germany's Road to Unification.* Washington, DC: The Brookings Institution.

Reich, Simon. 1990. *The Fruits of Fascism: Postwar Prosperity in Historical Perspective.* Ithaca, NY: Cornell University Press.

Rieger, Elmar, and Stephan Leibfried. 1998 (Sept.). "Welfare State Limits to Globalization." *Politics and Society* 26(3): 363–390.

Sargent, Lyman Tower. 1987. *Contemporary Political Ideologies: A Comparative Analysis.* 7th ed. Chicago: Dorsey.

Scheele, Godfrey. 1946. *The Weimar Republic.* London: Faber and Faber.

Schonhardt-Bailey, Cheryl. 1998 (April). "Parties and Interests in the 'Marriage of Iron and Rye.'" *British Journal of Political Science* 28(2): 291–332.

Shafer, Susanne M. 1990–91 (Winter). "Influences on Political Education in the Federal Republic of Germany." *International Journal of Social Education* 5(3): 72–91.

Smith, Gordon. 1990. *Democracy in Western Germany: Parties and Politics in the Federal Republic.* 3rd ed. London: Dartmouth Publishing Co., Ltd.

Smith, Robert B. 1998 (June–July). "Anti-Semitism and Nazism: Reconciling Fromm and Goldhagen." *American Behavioral Scientist* 41(9): 1324–1362.

Smyser, W. R. 1992. *The Economy of United Germany: Colossus at the Crossroads.* New York: St. Martin's.

Smyser, W. R. 1993. "The Global Economic Effects of German Unification." In *Germany in a New Era* (pp. 252–76), ed. Gary L Geipel. Indianapolis: Hudson Institute.

Tewes, Henning. 1998 (April). "Between Deepening and Widening: Role Conflict in Germany's Enlargement Policy." *West European Politics* 21(2): 11–27.

Treverton, Gregory F. 1993. "Forces and Legacies Shaping a New Germany." In *Germany in a New Era*, ed. Gary L. Geipel. Indianapolis: Hudson Institute.

Tuchman, Barbara. 1962. *The Guns of August.* New York: Macmillan.

Vinocour, John. 1998 (Sept.–Oct.). "Downsizing German Politics: Gerhard Schroeder, Man from the Plains." *Foreign Affairs* 77(5): 1–7.

Walker, Martin. 1998 (Oct.). "Social Democrats Win German Elections." *Europe* 380: S1–S3.

Wallach, H. G. Peter, and Ronald A. Francisco. 1992. *United Germany: The Past, Politics, Prospects.* Westport, CT: Praeger.

Weber, Max. 1947. *The Theory of Social and Economic Organization.* Translated by A. M. Henderson and Talcott Parsons. Copyright 1947, renewed 1975 by Talcott Parsons. Glencoe, IL: Free Press.

Wurzel, Eckhard, 1996 (Oct.–Nov.). "Germany: The Welfare System." *OECD Observer* 202: 45–47.

Yoder, Jennifer A. 1998 (June). "The Regionalization of Political Culture and Identity in Post Communist Eastern Germany." *East European Quarterly* 32(2): 197–219.

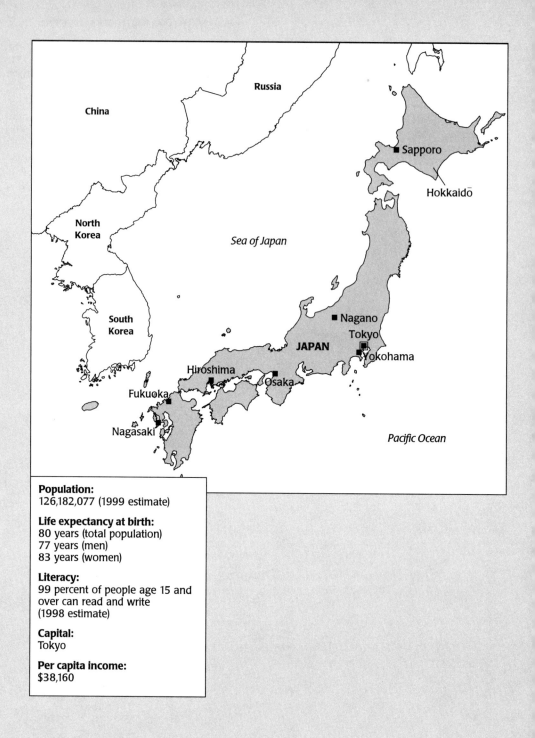

Population:
126,182,077 (1999 estimate)

Life expectancy at birth:
80 years (total population)
77 years (men)
83 years (women)

Literacy:
99 percent of people age 15 and over can read and write
(1998 estimate)

Capital:
Tokyo

Per capita income:
$38,160

5

Japan
The Politics of Economic Power

Until recently, Japan was the most aggressive economic power in the world. It was also the world's largest creditor and, by itself, accounted for some 15 percent of the world's gross national product. Indeed, the six largest banks in the world were Japanese banks (*Economist,* Aug. 5, 1995, 97). Japanese trade surpluses with the United States were staggering, a fact that led to charges of economic warfare (Thurow 1993). Some of Japan's severest critics went so far as to accuse it of attempting to destroy entire Western industries (McMillian 1985). The Japanese heatedly denied such charges, attributing their economic success to hard work, quality control, and the capacity to produce high-quality goods at a lower cost than their Western competitors. The Japanese also noted that their economic success was achieved despite the total devastation wrought by World War II, and that it was carried out within a democratic framework. Whatever the case, Japanese trade surpluses with the United States continue to be astronomical (*Japan Times*, Apr. 24, 2000, www).

Japan was also the only non-Western member of the First World, and its economic success forced Western scholars to rethink their theories of development, most of which maintained that the only path to democracy and prosperity was the Western model. *So great was the Japanese miracle that Western firms rushed to study Japanese management practice and courses on the Japanese "model" proliferated in US universities.* The Japanese, or so it seemed, had learned to build a "better mousetrap," and the West could ignore the Japanese experience only to its own detriment. The Japanese model of development, moreover, had been embraced by most of the emerging states of Asia, including South Korea, Taiwan, and the People's Republic of China. The Japanese government also conducted seminars on the Japanese model of development for officials of Third World countries (*Economist,* Jan. 14, 1995, 19).

As the twentieth century drew to a close, however, things in Japan started to go terribly wrong. Political scandals involving millions of dollars in bribes shook the government, and Japan's economy, once the envy of the world, began to unravel. Key banks and security firms collapsed, and with them the flow of credit required to drive Japan's industrial machine. By 1998, Japan was experiencing its worst economic crisis since the end of World War II. The Government seems incapable of action. The driving force behind Japan's economic miracle, it stood paralyzed while the country sank deeper into economic crisis.

Japan's woes, unfortunately, were not hers alone. As the second largest economy in the world, a strong and vibrant Japan was vital to the stability of the world economic system and particularly an Asian economic system teetering on the verge of collapse. It was quite possible that a collapse of the Japanese economy could trigger a world depression similar to that which had occurred during the 1930s. Japan is far from economic collapse, but it has clearly lost some of its former vibrancy.

In this chapter, we will examine the Japanese political system. We will also explore the economic and cultural circumstances that enabled Japan to compete so effectively in the world arena, as well as the factors that have placed the Japanese economy in crisis. Japanese politics, as we shall see, does have much in common with the politics of the West. It is, however, uniquely Japanese. In the words of one observer, "Japan is in the (Western) world, but not of it" (van Wolferen 1990, 408).

Japan in Historical and Cultural Perspective

Japanese politics draws its origins from cultural and philosophical traditions that are far removed from those of the West (Johnston, 1999). Western politics emerged from a Judeo-Christian tradition that was monotheistic. There was one God whose rules for eternal salvation were moral imperatives that admitted no contradiction. Individuals were enjoined to love one another and to work for the common good, but the ultimate contract was between the individual and an all-powerful god.

The religious underpinnings of Japanese culture, by contrast, emerged from a mélange of Confucian, Buddhist, and Shinto traditions that encompass multiple gods, many of whom take on remarkably human characteristics (Earhart 1982). All religions are considered to be of value by the Japanese, and it is not unusual for people to be married by priests of one religion and buried by those of another. In the case of Confucianism, there are no gods at all, merely intelligent rules for harmonious and orderly behavior. Confucianism will be discussed more extensively in Chapter 7.

This multiplicity of religious beliefs has made Japanese culture less absolutistic than that of the West. In Japan, one studies religious books to gain wisdom and to seek guidance in achieving the ultimate goal of social harmony (Dale 1990). Contradictions are part of social reality, and they are accepted as such. Eastern standards of good and evil, while very real, do not necessarily correspond to the absolutes that guide Western practice, a circumstance that has often led to cross-cultural misunderstandings.

A second important difference between Japanese and Western cultures lies in their differing views of the role of the individual in society. Western society, perhaps because salvation is a personal matter, tends to be intensely individualistic. The rights of individuals, as enshrined in documents such as the American *Declaration of Independence* or the French *Declaration of the Rights of Man and Citizen,* are considered inviolable and stand on par with the rights of society.

The Japanese, by contrast, often place the rights of the group above the rights of the individual. It is social harmony, from the Japanese perspective, that allows the individual to prosper, and people are expected to subordinate their own interests to those of the group.

The pervasive influence of culture on Japanese politics will be discussed throughout this chapter. The link between culture and politics, moreover, is not accidental. Emperor worship was added to Shinto rituals in the fourth century AD as the political leaders of that era sought to legitimize their rule by appeals to divine authority. Confucianism was added to Japanese culture in the fifth century in an effort to promote hard work and to enhance respect for hierarchical order. Buddhist doctrines stressing social obedience followed in the sixth century. *The Japanese practice of adapting foreign doctrines to fulfill political needs, then, has very deep roots*[1] (Earhart 1982).

Japan's cultural traditions were nurtured by a geographic isolation so complete that Japan's first sustained contact with the West would not occur until the middle of the nineteenth century. While Japan would eventually borrow Western technology and many of the overt characteristics of Western society, it would also remain supremely confident of the superiority of its own culture. This point is essential to understanding Japanese politics.

The political history of Japan is far too complex for easy recounting. Suffice it to say that the seventeenth century found Japan to be a loosely integrated state, the citizens of which were intensely proud of their ethnic uniqueness. Japanese religious beliefs reinforced this pride by placing Japan at the center of the universe. Racial purity continues to be cited by Japan's political leaders as one of the main reasons for Japanese economic dominance in the world today.

However much the Japanese population shared a common cultural identity, the Japan of the seventeenth century did not constitute a state in the modern sense of the word. Rather, the political system of the era was based upon feudal arrangements not unlike those of medieval Europe. Under these arrangements, a **shogun,** or *military warlord,* ruled Japan in the name of an emperor who had long ago become a symbolic figure (Duus 1976). The shogun ruled the central region of Japan directly, and the remainder of the country was divided into approximately 250 **daimyo,** or *feudal fiefdoms,* the leaders of which swore allegiance to the shogun. Both the boundaries of the shogun state and the allegiance of the daimyo would ebb and flow with the power of the shogun.

Feudal Japan also boasted *a large aristocracy of warriors* called the **samurai** (Wilson 1992). Much like the knights of medieval Europe, the samurai served their daimyo in exchange for land and financial allowances. Over time, they evolved into a hereditary military aristocracy that constituted some 6 percent of the Japanese population (Duus 1976). Not all samurai, however, were treated equally. While some enjoyed immense wealth and prestige, others found it difficult to survive on the allowances provided by the daimyo. As Japan approached the end of the feudal era, the samurai, as a class, had fallen on hard times.

> By 1800, ...the samurai were no more swashbuckling fighters than their lords were battle-hardened generals. Ever since the end of the sixteenth century, most samurai had been moved out of the countryside and into the castle towns of their daimyo. In the process, most had been "de-fiefed." Instead of living off income from land granted to them by their lords, they were given annual stipends of rice, the size of which indicated their rank. As the fires of feudal warfare faded to ashes most daimyo no longer needed their samurai retainers as fighters, but since the daimyo were still obliged to support their retainers, they found other uses for them in jobs as officials (Duus 1976, 35).

---

[1]While religion has played an important role in shaping Japanese culture, few observers find Japan to be an overtly religious society.

Commodore Matthew Perry is depicted meeting the Japanese imperial commissioners at Yokohama. In 1854, to the outrage of the Japanese public, the government signed a treaty permitting foreign vessels to obtain provisions in Japanese territory and allowing American ships to anchor at Shimoda and Hakodate.

The Japan of the early nineteenth century was a traditional society; Western advances in the areas of education, science, and industrialization had not yet reached the island kingdom. Political loyalties, while acknowledging the emperor as a deity, also remained localized.

The Meiji Restoration (1868–1912)

The gap between the strong sense of Japanese nationalism and the inherent weakness of the Japanese state was of little consequence as long as Japan remained an isolated kingdom (Milward 1979). In July of 1853, however, that isolation was shattered when a fleet of American warships entered Edo Bay and demanded that Japan open its ports to trade with the United States. The Japanese government, finding itself unable to resist the military power of an industrial state, capitulated. The resulting outrage of the Japanese public was so great that the country was pushed to the brink of civil war (Duus 1976). On January 3, 1868, military units from three of the larger daimyo seized the government, proclaiming the "restoration" of imperial rule. Popular support for the restoration was rallied under the slogan "Restore the Emperor and Drive Out the Barbarians!" The Emperor Meiji issued a decree abolishing both the daimyo and the samurai as the first step toward building a new court capable of challenging the West[2] (Duus 1976). The feudal period in Japan had come to an end.

---

[2]The daimyo received government bonds in exchange for their landholdings, while the more aggressive samurai became administrators in the new, modernizing bureaucracy. Many samurai also became involved in business organizations that were to become Japan's great corporations.

> ## Japan Absorbs Western Technology While Remaining Uniquely Japanese
>
> The success of the Meiji oligarchy in transforming Japan into a modern industrial power stands in vivid testimony to the capacity of a determined elite to modernize a traditional society. Even more remarkable was the fact that this was done by building upon traditional Japanese culture. Japan absorbed Western technology, but it remained uniquely Japanese. *This is a particularly important point, for it demonstrates that it is theoretically possible for the states of the Third World to modernize without becoming clones of the West.*

While the Emperor was rehabilitated as the symbol of political authority, all real power resided with the oligarchy that had seized power. This group included the daimyo who had overthrown the shogun, the more enlightened samurai, and educated commoners who were familiar with the West (Duus 1976). Although drawn from different backgrounds, the oligarchy was united by an all-consuming desire to transform Japan into a modern industrial state (Wilson 1992). Never again, they swore, would Japan be humiliated by a foreign power.

Under the Meiji reforms, every dimension of Japanese life was harnessed to the goal of modernization. The Japanese army was reorganized along Western lines, and the Japanese educational system was revamped to stress the Confucian virtues of obedience, loyalty, hard work, and patriotism. Japan's feudal bureaucracy was also modernized, becoming a skilled technocracy capable of transforming Japan into a modern industrial power.

Finally, and much later, the Meiji oligarchy would provide Japan with a **Diet**, or *parliament,* consisting of two houses. The *lower house,* the **House of Representatives**, was elected; the *upper house,* the **House of Peers**, *was reserved for a hereditary aristocracy consisting largely of former daimyo.* Although the Meiji oligarchy continued to rule the state in the name of the emperor, democracy had established a presence within the Japanese political consciousness (Duus 1976).

The Meiji reforms led to economic power, and economic power led to military power and expansionism. Japan began its occupation of Korea in 1887, and the colonization of China would follow in less than a decade. Far more dramatic, from the Western perspective, was the Japanese victory in the Russo-Japanese War of 1904–1905, a victory that shattered the myth of Western invincibility. The slogan "strong army, strong nation" became the order of the day.

The Era of Two-Party Government (1912–1931)[3]

By the early twentieth century, Japan was a country far different from what it had been on the eve of the Meiji restoration. Firmly established as an economic and military power, Japan had also made some progress, however limited, toward the establishment of parliamentary government.

Japanese politics, moreover, had begun to reflect the changing structure of Japanese society. Japan's industrial revolution had created a powerful business class, the influence of which soon rivaled that of the Meiji oligarchy. Particularly important was the emergence of **zaibatsu**, or *large business conglomerates controlled by a single interlocking directorate.* In time, the large zaibatsu would grow into integrated networks of mining, manufacturing, commercial, and banking firms, all under the control of a single board of directors.

---

[3]The era of two-party government did not come to an abrupt end but gradually gave way to growing military influence. Some scholars place the end of the era as early as 1926.

The industrial revolution had similarly created a middle class consisting of bureaucrats, white-collar workers, and merchants, as well as an industrial working class increasingly enamored of Marxist philosophy. Both would demand a greater voice in the governing of Japan, the middle class by forming political parties and the proletariat by taking to the streets. Reflecting the altered structure of Japanese society, the years between 1912 and 1931 would see Japan transformed into a quasi-democracy in which civilian political parties would share power with an emerging military-industrial elite.

The House of Representatives was dominated by two political parties, the Seiyukai and Minsei. Ex-bureaucrats occupied key positions in both parties, thereby extending the Meiji tradition of direct bureaucratic involvement in political affairs (Yakushiji 1992). Real power, however, belonged to political bosses who ruled from behind the scenes with lavish outlays of **pork barrel**[4] and patronage.

Although the two-party system gave the impression of democracy, this impression was more apparent than real. The first election based upon universal suffrage was not held until 1928, and even then, the left gained only 5 percent of the popular vote (Duus 1976). Charges of fraud were rampant. The power of the House of Representatives, moreover, was countered by that of the House of Peers, a nonelective body controlled by the Meiji aristocracy.

The era of two-party rule was profoundly unstable, with the Japanese economy alternating between periods of boom and bust. The gap between rich and poor was stark, as was the gap between the cities and the countryside. Marxism had become a popular force, and rioting and political violence were commonplace. Further complicating matters was the advent of the Great Depression. Japan required far-sighted and decisive leadership, but its quasi-democratic regime could provide neither.

Japan Prepares for War

The collapse of party government was precipitated by the escalating tension between the party bosses and the military. The military, arguing that Japan's economic problems were best solved by expanding its colonial empire, urged preparation for total war against any power that stood in the path of its colonial expansion. The party bosses, by contrast, attempted to ease Japan's economic woes by slashing the military budget. The conflict came to a head on September 18, 1931, when the Japanese military launched an unauthorized invasion of Manchuria. Divided among itself, the Government remained passive.

Government indecisiveness during the Manchurian crisis shifted the balance of power from Japan's civilian leadership to the Japanese military, and by 1936 the military had become the dominant force in Japanese politics. Now free of civilian restraint, the military began its long-sought preparation for total war. The early phases of the war effort would transform much of the Far East into what the Japanese would euphemistically call their "Asian co-prosperity sphere." Having consolidated its position in the North Pacific, Japan launched a brutal attack on Pearl Harbor on December 7, 1941. Only the United States, in the Japanese view, stood in the way of its unchallenged mastery of the Pacific basin.

Japan's preparation for total war was both psychological and economic. Psychologically, the military inflamed nationalist sentiments by transforming the emperor-god into a war god who would accept nothing less than total sacrifice

---

[4]"Pork barrel" refers to the funding of public works projects designed to enhance the political fortunes of politicians and their supporters.

The port city of Hiroshima was almost totally destroyed when the United States dropped an atomic bomb on the city on August 6, 1945. Nagasaki was bombed by the United States three days later.

from his subjects. The new cult of the emperor was referred to as State Shintoism (Earhart 1982).

Economically, the mobilization for total war saw the Japanese economy brought under the control of government planners, a pattern well established during the Meiji restoration. The military also intensified the transformation of Japanese business firms into paternalist organizations that provided their employees with lifetime job security and generous welfare benefits. The employees, in turn, were expected to sacrifice for the firm much as they would for their own families. Political indoctrination sessions became as common in the workplace as they were in the schools. In the present era, the large Japanese zaibatsu or conglomerates have refined the "company family" into something approaching a cult[5] (van Wolferen 1990).

Despite Japan's military dominance, Japanese politics during the Second World War remained divided and conflictual. The zaibatsu resisted state control, and both the party bosses and the aristocracy retained considerable influence in political affairs. Conflict between the army and navy was particularly intense, as each sought total command of the war (Duus 1976).

Japan's wartime leadership was able to mobilize the nation for war, but it was not able to prosecute the war with a single voice. The tragic consequence of this situation was that no one was able to stop a war that had been lost long before the dropping of atomic bombs on Hiroshima and Nagasaki in August 1945 (Duus 1976). Even then, it was the emperor, in a rare exercise of personal authority, who declared the war to be at an end.

---

[5]The transformation of firms into families had been pioneered during the turn of the century by the Ministry of Communications as a means of increasing the productivity and solidarity of the railroad workers. By 1920 the process had become widespread but voluntary. During the military period, it became state policy (Milward 1979).

American Occupation and the Framing of a New Constitution

The Japanese political system as we know it today was largely dictated by General MacArthur and American occupation authorities following the end of World War II (Herzog 1993). As in the case of Germany, the United States faced a critical choice. Many argued for the creation of a weak and fragmented Japanese state that would be incapable of further aggression, while others cautioned that a weak state would merely invite authoritarianism by falling prey to violence and instability (Kataoka 1992). There was also the Soviet threat to consider, not to mention the growing power of the communists in China.

In the end, Japan was provided with a political system that resembled the parliamentary systems of Europe. Executive power resides in a prime minister responsible before the popularly elected House of Representatives, the lower house of the Diet, or parliament. An upper house, the House of Councilors, is also popularly elected and serves as a check on the more powerful House of Representatives. A Supreme Court, although alien to Japanese culture, possesses the power to declare acts of the Diet unconstitutional and serves as Japan's final arbitrator of individual rights. The emperor, now stripped of his status as a deity, serves as the symbol of national unity, performing a role similar to that of the British monarch.

American efforts to engineer an institutional foundation for Japanese democracy were matched by equally pervasive efforts to reshape Japanese political culture, a process described by Joy Hendry:

> ...textbooks in use before the Second World War were banned by the Occupation Government because they helped to propagate the nationalistic fervour which led Japan into defeat. They taught Japanese mythology as history, encouraging all Japanese people everywhere to think of themselves as belonging to branch lines of the imperial line and thus descended ultimately from the imperial ancestress Amaterasu. Shinto ideology was also banned from schools in the immediate post-war period, and the values which were subsequently taught were for a while very Western, mostly American, with the lives of heroes such as Benjamin Franklin being held up as models for the children. Gradually, the courses have become more "Japanese" in content, and suitable Japanese heroes have been brought in to localise the value system being advocated. However, the content of school textbooks remains a topic of considerable controversy (Hendry 1991, 88–89).

The early years of the post-war era proved to be a violent free-for-all in which a conservative alliance of businessmen and bureaucrats vied with leftist unions for control of the political system. Wary of the growing radicalism of the left and stunned by the 1949 victory of the communists in China, the occupation authorities turned a blind eye as Japan's conservative politicians, many of whom had played a prominent role in the military regime, used less than democratic procedures to consolidate their power (Yakushiji 1992). Indeed, the CIA spent "millions" to keep the Japanese rightists in power during the 1950s and 1960s (*NYT,* Oct. 9, 1994, 1).

By the advent of the 1960s, Japanese politics had stabilized and the Japanese economic miracle had begun to take shape. Democratic attitudes also appeared to be taking root. All of these trends would continue to strengthen over the ensuing decades, transforming Japan into one of the world's leading democracies. Ironically, the West is now suggesting that it is time for Japan to upgrade its army and to perform its fair share of world peace-keeping duties.[6]

---

[6]Japan is precluded by its Constitution from sending troops abroad.

The only shadow on this otherwise serene picture is the fact that the Liberal Democratic Party (LDP), an alliance of conservative politicians, business leaders, and senior administrators, was the only party to govern Japan for a four-decade period stretching from 1955 until 1993. This, too, has now changed, with the 1993 general elections finding a much-fragmented LDP temporarily voted out of office for the first time in its history. The LDP, however, continues to be the dominant force in Japanese politics.

The similarity of Japanese political institutions to those of the West suggests that the political process in Japan is not markedly different from the political process in any other advanced industrial democracy (Richardson and Flanagan 1984). The Japan of today, it is argued, resembles the states of the West far more than it resembles the Japan of the prewar era. Japan's commitment to democracy has also been demonstrated by more than forty years of constitutional government. Popular interest in a military revival, moreover, has been virtually nil. The military, especially the Imperial Army, is widely blamed for the destruction of Japan during the Second World War.

Japan's similarity to the West has been challenged by Karel van Wolferen in a recent book entitled *The Enigma of Japanese Power.* Van Wolferen writes:

> The Japanese have laws, legislators, a parliament, political parties, labor unions, a prime minister, interest groups and stockholders. But one should not be misled by these familiar labels into hasty conclusions as to how power is exercised in Japan.
>
> The Japanese prime minister is not expected to show much leadership; labor unions organize strikes to be held during lunch breaks; the legislature does not in fact legislate; stockholders never demand dividends; consumer interest groups advocate protectionism; laws are enforced only if they don't conflict too much with the interests of the powerful... (van Wolferen 1990, 25).

Japan's political system "works" when a high level of consensus exists among its political, administrative, and business leaders, an alliance often referred to as **Japan Inc.** Complete agreement, for example, exists on the goal of economic growth, a goal that has been pursued for more than fifty years with untiring determination.

The Japanese system falters, however, when consensus is not present. This, unfortunately, occurs most often during times of crisis, as each power bloc within the ruling alliance vetoes the suggestions of the others. The present economic crisis, for example, has found the Japanese leadership paralyzed by internal conflict. Everyone recognizes the need for reform, but the dominant groups in the LDP and the Diet cannot agree on what should be done. Much in line with our earlier definition of politics as who gets what, when, and how, each group or faction wants its opponents to bear the brunt of reform while it protects its own turf (Hiwatari 1998).

The Japanese political system, then, has yet to achieve the elusive goal of decisive leadership. The prime minister is at the helm, but he lacks the ability to force his programs upon either his own ruling coalition or the administrative and business elites that provide the foundation of that coalition. *Some American and Japanese observers, accordingly, characterize Japan as an intensely centralized state with a vacuum in the middle* (van Wolferen 1990; Asada 1989). The situation is particularly frustrating to American trade negotiators who rejoice at Japanese promises to improve trade procedures, only to learn at a later point that the promises were goals rather than commitments.

The Political Institutions of Japan

In the pages that follow, we will discuss continuity and change within the Japanese political system. We will examine the forces that hold the system together, as well as those that are most likely to transform Japanese politics during the coming decade. Our discussion will begin with an examination of Japan's political institutions.

Elections and Politics in Japan

Until very recently, Japan possessed a complex electoral system that allowed any group able to garner 10 to 15 percent of the vote in an electoral district to elect its own member to the House of Representatives. Given the intense loyalty that Japanese workers feel toward their firms, many of the larger conglomerates were able to elect several members to the House of Representatives, most of whom were nominally affiliated with the LDP. The electoral system also strengthened the power of local political bosses who, as a result of their ability to control 10 percent or 15 percent of the vote in their respective districts, could literally sell a seat in the House of Representatives to the highest bidder (Cox and Thies 1998).

All dimensions of the Japanese electoral system, then, encouraged the lavish outlay of money. By the 1980s, the cost of running for office in Japan had become so prohibitively expensive that the average campaign for junior politicians cost some $2 million (*CSM,* Apr. 18, 1994, 22). Under these circumstances, it was difficult to run a successful campaign without illegal campaign contributions.

Between 1989 and 1991, for example, construction companies alone made more than $1 billion in illegal campaign contributions (*NYT,* June 30, 1993, A4). Particularly troublesome was a growing dependence upon campaign contributions from Japan's well-organized and quasi-legal crime syndicates. In early 1992, the magnitude of criminal involvement came to light when one of the LDP's most powerful leaders was forced to resign for accepting an illegal campaign contribution of $4 million from criminal elements. He publicly apologized and was fined $1,700 for his indiscretion (*NYT,* Oct. 15, 1992, A3).

Japan's leaders understood that escalating incidents of corruption and scandal were undermining their public support, but in line with the vacuum theory outlined previously, found it difficult to take decisive action until the situation had reached crisis proportions.

Eventually, the LDP's failure to address electoral reform precipitated the fragmentation of the party. Japan's first post-LDP Government created a new electoral system by dividing Japan into 300 districts, each of which elects a single member of the House of Representatives. An additional 200 members of the House of Representatives, however, continue to be elected by eleven proportional representation districts (*Economist,* Feb. 5, 1994, 31). Each voter thus has two votes: one for the single-member district to be cast for a candidate of choice, and one for the proportional-representation district to be cast for the political party of choice. The new electoral procedures were designed to force Japan's diverse political factions to come together for the sake of electing a single candidate who embodied their shared interests. It was also hoped that the new procedures would reduce the number of financial scandals by making it difficult for factional groups to buy seats in the House of Representatives.

Electoral procedures in the House of Councilors (HC) are also complex. Of the 252 members of the HC, 152 are elected in one of 47 multimember districts that correspond to Japan's prefectures or provinces. The remaining 100 members are elected by proportional representation on a national basis (Baerwald 1986). In this instance, Japanese voters cast two ballots: one for a national political party and one for a district candidate, each district being allocated from one to four members of the HC, depending upon the size of the district. Members of the HC are elected for fixed six-year terms, with half of the chamber being elected every three years (Baerwald 1986).

Executive Power in Japan: The Prime Minister

The Japanese prime minister is elected by the members of the Diet and serves for as long as he or she retains the confidence of the House of Representatives (HR) or until the four-year term of the HR expires. Between 1955 and 1993, the Liberal Democratic Party dominated the House of Representatives, with the cohesion and discipline of its "Dietmen" assuring that the president of the LDP would automatically become the prime minister.

Under these circumstances, the Japanese prime minister should have been among the strongest leaders in the First World. Like so much else in Japanese politics, however, executive authority in Japan does not conform to Western patterns. Rather than being the strongest prime minister in the First World, the Japanese prime minister is the weakest. Japan possesses a parliamentary political system, but the operation of that system is uniquely Japanese.

The weakness of the Japanese executive during the four decades of LDP rule found its origins in the fragmented nature of the ruling party (Ishida and Krauss 1989). Despite sharing a common vision of a stable and prosperous Japan, the competing factions of the LDP were intensely jealous of each other, with the slightest policy disagreements threatening to fragment the party and jeopardize its control of the Government. The prime minister, accordingly, was expected to be a coalition builder who would craft policies upon which the diverse factions of the LDP could agree. Policies lacking consensus were to be delayed until such time as a consensus could be achieved. Relations within the LDP were so sensitive that approximately one-half of the members of the Cabinet were changed on an annual basis as prime ministers scrambled to keep their coalitions intact (Richardson and Flanagan 1984). Prime ministers, moreover, were rarely elected for a second term, it being essential that each of the dominant groups in the LDP get its day in the sun (Hayes 1992). There were exceptions to this rule, but those exceptions were rare.

The temporary fall of the LDP in 1993 offered a chance for stronger political leadership in Japan, but instead the situation became even more confused. While LDP prime ministers had forged coalitions within a family of groups committed to a common principle, post-LDP prime ministers were now forced to forge ruling coalitions that spanned the breadth of the political spectrum (Shinoda 1998). The first post-LDP Government, for example, was an eight-party coalition that was voted out of office a few months after its formation. A more recent coalition Government consisted of a socialist prime minister supported by the conservative LDP, two parties of diametrically opposing philosophies. Japan continued to pursue policies that were in place, but its ability to alter those policies, which had never been strong, decreased. A list of Japan's coalition Governments is provided in Table 5.1.

Although Japanese prime ministers are less powerful than their Western counterparts, it would be incorrect to suggest that they are either weak or ineffectual individuals. This is not the case, as most prime ministers are consummate politicians who play a strong role in the shaping of policy decisions. The power of Japanese prime ministers, however, rests less on their ability to dictate policy than on their ability to broker between competing factions and parties within their ruling coalition. Prime ministers must also "broker" between different administrative agencies as well as between competing business interests (Richardson and Flanagan 1984). The success of a Japanese prime minister, then, is measured by his or her success as a political broker (Baerwald 1986).

The power of the prime minister and Cabinet also resides in their ability to either ratify or block policy initiatives generated by administrative agencies or powerful business interests. Policies must have the support of the prime minister and the

Table 5.1
Coalition Governments in Japan, 1983–1999

Date	Coalition
December 1983	The Liberal Democratic Party, led by Yasuhiro Nakasone, forms a governing coalition with the New Liberal Club to make up for its lack of a Diet majority. It lasts until the LDP's election victory in July 1986, after which the NLC disbands and most of its members return to the LDP.
August 1993	An anti-LDP alliance led by Morihiro Hosokawa topples the LDP from power for the first time in 38 years. Hosokawa steps down after nine months over a money scandal.
May 1994	Tsutomu Hata forms a minority coalition government after the Social Democratic Party (SDP) and New Party Sakigake pull out from the LDP alliance. Hata resigns in about two months under threat of a no-confidence vote.
June 1994	Tomiichi Murayama is elected prime minister by a surprise coalition of the LDP, longtime archrival SDP, and Sakigake.
January 1996	Ryutaro Hashimoto takes over as prime minister under the LDP-SDP-Sakigake coalition. SDP and Sakigake leave the Cabinet after Oct. 1996 Lower House elections but keep a non-Cabinet alliance until June 1998.
January 1999	Keizo Obuchi forms a coalition between the LDP and Ichior Ozawa's Liberal Party.

Source: Japan Times, Jan. 14, 1999, www.

inner circle of Cabinet if they are to see the light of day. Unfortunately, the prime minister often finds it easier to block the policies of others than to initiate new policies of his own (Richardson and Flanagan 1984).

As in most countries, the effectiveness of prime ministers depends on their relative power within the ruling party. In this regard, Shinoda suggests that Japan's prime ministers have fallen into four categories:

> …the Political Insider, the Grandstander, the Kamikaze Fighter, and the Peace Lover. The Political Insider (Sato Eisaku, Tanaka Kakuei, and Takeshita Noboru are the examples) is a leader with abundant internal sources of power who enjoys stable support within the ruling party and close ties with the bureaucracy and the opposition parties. The other three leadership styles lack such internal sources. The Grandstander (such as Hosokawa and Nakosone Yasuhiro) goes directly to the public and the media in his search for support of his policy goals to supplement his lack of internal sources of power. The Kamikaze Fighter (Kishi Nobusuke) tries to push through an unpopular policy by sacrificing his political leadership role, while the Peace Lover (Suzuki Zenko and Kaifu Toshiki) is an indecisive leader who fails to achieve controversial policy goals because he tries to please all the actors (Shinoda 1998, 13).

Legislative Power in Japan: The Diet

The Japanese Diet (Parliament) consists of two houses: the House of Representatives (HR) and the House of Councilors (HC). The prime minister and Cabinet—the Government—are elected by the Diet and serve at its pleasure. Should the HR and the HC disagree on the selection of a prime minister, a joint committee of the two chambers is given thirty days during which to work out a suitable compromise. Failing this, the candidate of the HR becomes the prime minister. The prime minister is responsible before the HR, a vote of no confidence among its members serving to

---

Big Bang Goes Bust

In 1996, Ryutaro Hashimoto (LDP) was named prime minister with carte blanche to clean up Japan's economic crisis. Proclaiming that "without reform Japan does not have a future," he outlined a comprehensive overhaul of the Japanese economy referred to as the "big bang" (*Economist,* A Survey of Japanese Finance, June 28, 1997). Two years later, the big bang had gone bust and Mr. Hashimoto had resigned from office (Leblanc 1998).

---

bring down a Government. Legislation requires the approval of both houses of the Diet, but an HC veto of an HR bill can be overridden by a two-thirds majority in the latter. Clearly, then, the House of Representatives is the dominant house of the Diet, and the most powerful of Japan's politicians are to be found in its ranks.

The House of Representatives. The 500 "Dietmen" of the House of Representatives (HR) are elected for four-year terms by the complex procedures discussed previously. Most bills are introduced by the Government, having been prepared in advance by the bureaucracy or the ruling coalition. Once introduced into the HR or the HC, they are sent to a standing committee for review. Committees do little to change the nature of a bill before sending it back to the floor for full debate.

Debate in the HR is vigorous, and the passage of Government legislation is far from automatic. Indeed, roughly one-half of the Government bills introduced into the Diet receive at least some modification. Others are withdrawn simply on the basis of a threatened fight by the opposition. This situation differs markedly from Western parliamentary practice in which Governments use their parliamentary majority to ram-rod bills through a hostile opposition. Why is this the case?

A partial answer to this question is to be found in Japan's historical and cultural heritage. *Conflict and individualism are accepted elements of Western culture and, ipso facto, of Western parliamentary practice. Japanese culture, by contrast, places enormous emphasis on harmony, accommodation, and collectivism.* Conflict is as much a fact of life in Japan as in the West, but the Japanese go to extreme lengths to avoid direct confrontation, battles being fought in private and losers being allowed to save face. In parliamentary practice, this cultural norm results in far greater emphasis on accommodation than occurs in the West. Consensus, not conflict, is the norm (Baerwald 1986).

Accommodation, however, also has a practical side. Coalitions are things of many parts, and most are exceptionally fragile. The Government reflects the dominant view within the ruling coalition, but each new bill also generates its own temporary coalition of Dietmen based upon regional and group interests. The cohesion and discipline of the ruling coalition, accordingly, is dependent upon the leadership's willingness to accommodate a broad array of entrenched interests, some of which may not be to its liking (Cox and Rosenbluth 1993). Cardinal to this dimension of Japanese politics is the concept of **fair share**. Japanese political leaders have traditionally promoted political stability by portraying Japan as one large family, all members of which are entitled to their fair share of the nation's wealth.[7] Important groups who can demonstrate they are not receiving their "fair share" will generally be accommodated in order to perpetuate this myth (Hayes 1992).

In addition to its legislative function, the HR serves as a check on the powers of the Government, investigating political malfeasance and using the question

---

[7]Japanese mythology maintains that all of Japan's citizens emanated from the same tribes.

period to force ministers to justify their policies. Neither has been effective in bringing ministers to heel. As Louis Hayes explains,

> In practice, the question-and-answer procedure serves the worthy goals of democratic discussion rather poorly. Instead, a ritual process takes place where often the minister himself does not answer but defers to a top bureaucrat from his ministry. The questions are generally known in advance, so prepared answers are given. The system is not without cost in that senior bureaucrats must spend a large part of their time "backing up" their ministers in the Diet rather than doing their administrative jobs. Since opposition politicians do not have access to the inner workings of the government, they are not informed about policy matters to an extent that they can regularly ask penetrating questions (Hayes 1992, 57).

The ultimate power of the HR, of course, lies in its ability to withdraw its confidence from the Government, a practice that has occurred with increased frequency in the post-LDP era.

The House of Councilors. The **House of Councilors** (HC) was designed to restrain the Government without actually crippling its ability to rule. As such, the 252 members of the HC can reject bills passed by the HR, but the HR can reassert its will by a two-thirds majority. The organizational structure and procedures of the HC parallel those of the HR.

While there can be little question that the HR is the dominant chamber of the Japanese Diet, the role of the HC is far from negligible. Three points, in this regard, are of particular importance.

1. It is not always easy for the Government to gain the two-thirds majority in the HR required to override a veto by the HC. This is particularly the case since the LDP has found its monopoly of power weakened.
2. The HC is sometimes controlled by a coalition different from that controlling the HR. In such circumstances, the Government must temper its legislation if a veto in the HC is to be avoided. This is an important consideration, for, as noted earlier, the Japanese prefer to avoid confrontation if at all possible.
3. An HC veto near the end of a HR session may stick for the simple reason that the HR does not have time to override it. Pending legislation is not carried over from one session to the next.

In the final analysis, then, *the power of the HC is inverse to the power of the ruling party or coalition in the HR.* Strong Governments override the HC with ease, while weak Governments bow to its demands. With the weakening of the LDP, the HC has become a far more significant factor in the Japanese political equation than it was in the past.

Bureaucracy and Politics in Japan

The structure of Japan's bureaucratic apparatus mirrors that of other Western democracies. Layers of clerks are supervised by a hierarchy of functionaries who reach their apex in a senior service of permanent secretaries and senior managers who work directly with Cabinet ministers in the formation of public policy. All bureaucratic positions are filled on the basis of merit.

Japan's bureaucratic elite is filled almost exclusively with graduates of the Tokyo University Faculty of Law and other prestigious institutions of higher learning. As such, it is largely indistinguishable from Japan's business and political elites, most of whom have also graduated from the same handful of elite institutions.

Bureaucratic elitism exists in many Western societies, but not to the degree that it exists in Japan. Neither the Oxbridge network in Britain nor the "enarques" of France approach the exclusiveness of the Japanese bureaucratic elite.

Japan also differs from its Western counterparts in the degree of power wielded by its bureaucratic elite. Senior administrative officials are part and parcel of Japan Inc., the three-way alliance of business leaders, bureaucrats, and conservative elites who have ruled Japan since the mid-1950s. *More than merely serving the power structure, Japan's bureaucratic elite is one of its major components* (Kato 1994).

Indeed, some authors suggest that politicians do little more than pump money into their constituencies while the senior bureaucrats make policy and manage the economy. In this view, it was the bureaucracy that orchestrated Japan's economic miracle, and it was the inflexibility of the bureaucracy that led to Japan's current economic debacle (Hartcher 1998). Particular blame is placed on the Ministries of Finance and International Trade

The Diet, moreover, generally sketches the broad outlines of policy, leaving the bureaucrats to work out the technical details. While this is the case in many countries, few can rival Japan in the level of discretion left to its senior bureaucratic officials. Even when legislation is relatively specific, the bureaucracy can resist policies that it opposes by simply out-waiting Governments, the average life of which is two years (Hayes 1992).

In addition to their considerable role in the drafting and implementation of legislation, Japan's senior bureaucrats also derive tremendous power from their role as economic managers. It was Japanese bureaucrats, it will be recalled, who orchestrated Japan's industrialization following the Meiji Restoration, just as it was bureaucrats who mobilized the country for total war during the era of military rule. Japan is not a "closed" or "command" society in the authoritarian sense of the word, but the Japanese economy is far more "managed" than its Western counterparts (Johnson 1989). Key ministries such as the Ministry of Finance and the Ministry of International Trade and Industry are particularly powerful, using their control over licenses, clearances, loans, and other fiscal instruments to force compliance with the national economic plans that have played such an instrumental role in orchestrating Japan's economic growth. Officials also play one firm against another, thereby manipulating the intense competition that exists among Japan's large business conglomerates. *Because of the strong influence of the bureaucracy in managing the economy, Japan's economic system is referred to as* **state capitalism.** Rather than being a passive bystander, the Japanese government is an active participant in the economic process.

The power of senior bureaucrats also emanates from "old-boy" networks that permeate the entire elite establishment, be it the bureaucracy, the LDP and its offshoots, or the business conglomerates. In order to appreciate the critical importance of the "old-boy" networks, it is necessary to understand that Japan is simultaneously the most formal and the most informal of societies. Economic relationships in Japan are complex, legalistic, and rigid. If all of the rules and regulations were followed to the letter, the Japanese economy would probably stop. The rules, however, are not followed to the letter. Rather, *most economic transactions in Japan take the form of informal agreements among elites sharing a common background*—a system that works to Japan's advantage in dealing with foreign competitors. While the "old boys" work things out informally, the foreigners are left to storm the castle of Japanese legalism (van Wolferen 1990). It is the bureaucrats, of course, who are the guardians of the rules.

The power of the bureaucratic elite also emanates from the "pork barrel" nature of Japanese electioneering. Politicians get elected by providing jobs, facilities, and related benefits to their constituents. Just as bureaucrats are the guardians of the rules, they are also the guardians of public spending on schools,

---

Informal Powers of Japanese Bureaucrats

The formal powers of Japanese bureaucrats are more than matched by their informal powers. Senior administrators constitute an integral part of the ruling elite. Many prime ministers and senior members of the Cabinet have come from bureaucratic backgrounds, and bureaucrats are the dominant occupational group in the Diet, a position generally occupied by lawyers in the West (Richardson and Flanagan 1984). The line between politics and administration in Japan is fine, indeed.

---

roads, public buildings, and related projects. The goodwill of a highly placed bureaucrat can do wonders for the career of a Japanese politician. The recent electoral reforms may have reduced the pork barrel power of the bureaucracy, but they have not eliminated it.

Finally, the power of bureaucratic elites is a function of Japanese culture. Acceptance of bureaucratic rules finds strong roots in Japan's Confucian and collectivist traditions (Drucker 1998). The Japanese are an orderly public that accord great respect to senior bureaucratic officials.

Perhaps because of their dominance, the power of the administrators is now being challenged by both politicians and business leaders, both of whom would like greater freedom from bureaucratic controls. Even intellectuals have joined the fray by questioning the competence of Japanese bureaucrats (Taichi 1998; Atsushi 1998). Ironically, the disarray of Japan's political system may have had the unintended effect of providing Japan's senior bureaucrats with more power than ever. Who else can fill the vacuum (Nakano 1998)? It is also interesting to note that senior bureaucrats played a major role in scuttling the economic reforms proposed by Prime Minister Hashimoto (Katsuji 1998).

Law and Politics in Japan: The Supreme Court

The Japanese legal system reflects the same intriguing blend of Western and Japanese traditions as the parliament and the bureaucracy. *In structure, it is very Western, but in practice, it is inherently Japanese.*

The Japanese Constitution provides for an American-style Supreme Court with the power to declare acts of the Diet unconstitutional. This power, however, is seldom used, and it does not constitute a major constraint on the power of the Government. The fifteen Justices of the Supreme Court are appointed for life, with the provision that their appointments be ratified by popular referendum at ten-year intervals. Ratification is largely pro forma, but the ratification process represents an interesting variation on American practice. In further variation from the US practice, only one-third of Japan's Supreme Court Justices are drawn from the ranks of the lower courts, the remainder being mostly senior bureaucrats who have passed the retirement age of fifty-five (van Wolferen 1990). Membership on the Japanese Supreme Court is also far more fluid than in the United States, with many Justices retaining their positions for only a few years.

The elite complexion of the Japanese Supreme Court makes it very much part of the system, and acts of the Diet are rarely overturned (Hayes 1992). The Supreme Court is also inclined to sustain the power of the Government in the face of challenges to its authority launched in the lower courts (Richardson and Flanagan 1984).

The Supreme Court also functions as the head of a highly centralized legal system that includes a variety of High Courts, District Courts, and Summary Courts (courts of first-instance). In a uniquely Japanese innovation, the legal system includes a broad network of **conciliation commissions** *designed to facilitate the* *out-of-court settlement of disputes whenever possible.* The conciliation commissions, in combination with the general Japanese abhorrence of public conflict, have resulted in a caseload for Japanese courts that is less than one-tenth that of courts in the United States and Europe (van Wolferen 1990).

Lawyers' fees are inordinately high in Japan, as entrance to the legal profession is highly regulated. In some years, less than 3 percent of the applicants pass the bar exam, as compared to some 70 percent in the United States[8] (*IHT,* Feb. 15, 1996, 4).

Aside from having a clear bias in favor of the political establishment, the legal system in Japan appears to work quite well. It is interesting to note that Japan has the lowest reported crime rate among the states of the First World (van Wolferen 1990). Is Japan's low crime rate related to its legal system or to aspects of Japanese culture? Perhaps it can also be attributed to Japan's economic prosperity or to a Japanese reluctance to report petty crimes.

The Actors in Japanese Politics: Elites, Parties, Groups, and Citizens

Political institutions are the arena of politics, but the actors in the political process give life to those institutions. In this section, we shall examine the four main types of political actors in Japan: elites, political parties, groups, and citizens. Each plays a critical role in determining who gets what, when, and how in Japan.

Elites and Politics in Japan

Japan is an intensely elitist society that is ruled by the conservative political, administrative, and business leaders who form the inner core of Japan Inc. (Rothacher 1993). As the three groups overlap, it is difficult to say which is dominant (Koh 1989). Although much power is exercised behind the scenes, participation in the Cabinet is a visible sign of elite status. To be named prime minister is the ultimate recognition of success. The heads of Japan's large conglomerates are also exceptionally powerful individuals, as are its senior bureaucrats. The power of senior bureaucrats, as noted in the preceding section, is also enormous. "Dietmen," most of whom speak for powerful interest groups, rank among the lower echelon of the elite, as do provincial governors and the mayors of the larger cities, the latter positions being stepping stones to higher office (Richardson and Flanagan 1984).

Japan is not unique in the fact that most of its policy decisions are made by a political elite. What is unique about Japan is the exceptionally narrow base from which its political elite is selected and the extraordinary ability of that elite to maintain itself in power (Johnson 1994).

Japan's political, administrative, and business leaders are recruited almost exclusively from a handful of elite universities headed by the Tokyo University Faculty of Law. In recent years some 60 percent of the LDP members in the House of Representatives have attended one of Japan's top five universities, a full 32 percent having attended Tokyo University Faculty of Law.[9] The picture is much the same in regard to Japan's administrative elites.

---

[8]The Supreme Court regulates the Japanese court system through its general secretariat of the Supreme Court. The secretariat supervises the appointment and promotion of judges and, according to some observers, assures that only supporters of the system will ascend the judicial ladder. Graduates of the Tokyo University Faculty of Law and other elite law schools do extremely well (van Wolferen 1990).

[9]Exceptions to this dominance, while rare, have occurred when successful entrepreneurs from outside of the political circle have used their wealth and talents to build powerful political machines. Such was the case of Yasuhiro Nakasone, one of Japan's most powerful politicians.

The tightness of Japan's ruling elite provides its members with an "old-boy" network that is virtually impenetrable. Tensions exist, but communications within the elite are open and fluid, allowing problems to be sorted out before they threaten the system (van Wolferen 1990). The elite club is also very close to becoming a distinct social class, as the rich are better able to afford the elite prep schools required for access to the elite universities. Japanese society, accordingly, is something of a paradox. Everything is based upon merit examinations, but it is mainly the rich and famous who can afford the elite training required to pass these tests (van Wolferen 1990). Some grants, however, are provided to merit scholars from poorer backgrounds.

Parties and Politics in Japan

Japan's first era of party rule (1912–1931) was a tumultuous one in which strikes and riots were commonplace (Duus 1976). Party politics was also riddled with corruption as party leaders pandered to special interests and used the public treasury to finance local political machines. One observer of the era likened the Diet to a bull ring and its members "to whores running after money and patrons" (Duus 1976, 172). Many Japanese recoiled from the electoral process, finding it abhorrent to Japan's traditions of harmony, decorum, and order (Duus 1976). All in all, Japan's first venture into Western-style democracy left much to be desired. It was, however, a beginning.

Party rule collapsed with the ascendence of the military but was revived during the United States occupation. The party map in the immediate post-war period included parties of every conceivable political persuasion, none of which were able to control more than a minority of the seats in the Diet (Calder 1988). Although the conservatives were the dominant force in the country, they were hopelessly divided among themselves. A pragmatic left, if cohesive, could easily have established itself as a powerful force in Japanese politics. The left, however, was also fragmented.

The conservatives chose the path of pragmatism, coming together in 1955 to form the Liberal Democratic Party (Masumi 1992). The parties of the left had earlier closed ranks to form the Japanese Socialist Party (JSP), but the JSP retained a strong Marxist orientation that was distrusted by a large segment of the Japanese population. This, among other things, allowed the LDP to rule Japan without interruption from 1955 until 1993.

Today, Japanese parties fall into roughly four categories:

▌ a large and powerful Liberal Democratic Party that continues to be the single largest party in the Diet;
▌ a handful of conservative parties that splintered from the LDP during the early 1900s;
▌ a Japanese Socialist Party (JSP) that has traditionally placed ideology above victory;
▌ and a multitude of minor parties, the nature of which is difficult to categorize.

Until the defeat of the LDP in the 1993 elections, Japan was referred to as a single-party-dominant system (Sartori 1992). While this may be less true today, Japan continues to be dominated by parties with a conservative ideology, of which the LDP is by far the most dominant. A list of Japan's major political parties is provided in Table 5.2.

The Liberal Democratic Party. Of Japan's diverse political parties, the **Liberal Democratic Party** (LDP) remains by far the most important. Until 1993, the

Table 5.2
Japanese House of Representatives Election Results for 1990, 1993, 1996, and Realignment of 1998

Parties	1990	1993	1996	1998 (Realignment)
Parties of the Right				
Liberal Democrats	275 (54%)	223 (44%)	239 (48%)	259
Japan New Party	0	35		
Japan Renewal (Shinseito)	0	55		
New Harbinger (Sakigake)	0	13		
New Frontier			156	
Union of Brotherhood				97
Union of Peace				46
Parties of the Center				
Komeito (Buddhist) Party	45	51		
Democratic Socialist	13	15		
United Social Democratic	4	4		
Other Center Parties and Independents	22	30	27	42
Parties of the Left				
Japan Socialist Party	136	70	52	15
Japan Communist Party	16	15	26	26
Independents/Others and Vacancies	22	30	7	15
Total	511*	511*	500	500

*Pre-Reform House of Representatives had 511 members.
Source: Table constructed by author based on information provided in diverse newspapers.

leadership of the LDP was the political leadership of Japan, the two entities being virtually inseparable. Accordingly, one cannot understand the growing complexity of Japanese politics today without reference to the LDP.

The Internal Politics of the LDP. The LDP is a large **catch-all party** that *aggregates a broad spectrum of business, administrative, and political interests,* its conservative philosophy not differing much from that of the Conservative Party in Britain or the Christian Democratic Party in Germany. Business is good for Japan, and the LDP is good for business. The pragmatic orientation of the LDP reflects a need to accommodate the three main elements that dominate the Party: the business community, the professional politicians, and the administrative elite, each of which must receive its due.

Big business demands strong support from the government in terms of tax breaks, subsidies, and protected markets. These are granted by LDP politicians who thrive on the lavish campaign contributions provided by the business community. Both business leaders and politicians, in turn, submit to rule by a powerful administrative technocracy that uses its vast spending and regulatory powers to promote the prosperity of its partners.

Beyond being a three-way alliance between big business, senior administrators, and conservative politicians, the LDP is also a party of personalities and factions, each of which vies for domination of the party apparatus. Each of the LDP's five to eight factions resembles a self-contained political party, and each is headed by a senior politician with a strong power base among the LDP's members in the Diet (Yakushiji 1992). Indeed, the fall of the LDP Government in 1993 occurred when several LDP factions simply declared themselves to be independent parties and withdrew their support from the LDP prime minister.[10]

Some of the dissident factions would later rejoin the LDP; others would form coalition governments with the LDP. So fluid is the formation and dissolution of LDP factions that in a single month of 1998, one new faction formed and four others merged. In the meantime, two of the smaller opposition parties had also merged to strengthen their position against the LDP (*Japan Times,* Nov. 7–13, 1998). Some observers have likened the growing struggles within the LDP to a civil war (Nagata 1998).

The formal leadership positions within the LDP are filled after tense and protracted bargaining among factional leaders. The same tense bargaining determines which factions will make Party policy and what the "fair share" of Cabinet positions allocated to each group will be when the Party is in power. Under this arrangement, ambitious "Dietmen" jockey to join a faction that will be strong enough to name a prime minister (party president) or stake a claim to important Cabinet positions. This, however, can be risky business as the fortunes of each faction ebb and flow with the course of events (Yakushiji 1992).

Even in the heat of battle, however, care is taken to assure that all factions receive at least minimal representation on the Cabinet when the Party is in power. This reflects the traditional Japanese concern with harmony. As the following quotation suggests, it also makes good political sense.

> A wise prime minister will also distribute a few posts in his cabinet even to the factions that opposed his candidacy. Such largesse may help to convince enemy factions to switch sides next time and in the interim may help to mitigate their maneuvering and dampen their criticism. After all, it is hard for factions to criticize the actions of a cabinet in which they hold office. The art of cabinet-making in Japan consists of being able to distribute just the right number and type of posts to satisfy one's factional allies, one's own faction, and opposing factions in the party (Krauss 1989, 49).

LDP factions are welded together by **patron-client networks** in which *the Party's junior members in the Diet are promoted to ever-higher positions within the Party in return for their support of a faction leader,* a process described by Brian Reading:

> The young politician starts by receiving help from his seniors. As he progresses up the political ladder, he is expected to raise more money himself. In time, it becomes his turn to help his juniors. Once he has been in the Cabinet, he is expected to make a significant personal contribution to his faction's funds. The faction leaders themselves must raise billions of yen each a year (sic), part of which are distributed to their younger followers. At oseibo, New Year, before elections and at other gift-giving times such as chugen in July, faction leaders hand out money to their followers, several million yen to each, nominally for "rice cakes" (Reading 1992, 238).

---

[10]The formal organization of the LDP is topped by its president, followed in turn by the secretary general, the chairman of the General Council (executive committee), and the chairman of the Policy Research Council. Next in line are the chairmen of the Committees of National Organizations, Public Relations, Finance, Diet Affairs, and so on (*Liberal Star*, Nov. 15, 1991). The secretary general is selected by the president to manage the Party, the president himself becoming the prime minister when the Party is in power (Flanagan et al. 1991). The LDP holds an annual convention, but its role is largely symbolic.

The occupants of the leadership positions reviewed above, along with the leaders of the Party's diverse factions, form its inner core. Chairs of lesser Party committees have generally served as vice-ministers and will form the next generation of Party leaders. All have served long apprenticeships in the Diet and are exceptionally skilled politicians.

The electoral clout of a faction within the LDP, as the above passage suggests, depends upon its access to financial support and bureaucratic largess. More than any other factor, Japanese elections are determined by the candidate's ability to finance a powerful local machine and to provide its constituents with subsidies, construction contracts, and related pork barrel projects (*Japan Times*, Apr. 25, 2000). It should come as little surprise, accordingly, that Japanese elections are among the most expensive in the world.

As elections became increasingly expensive, LDP factions sought to strengthen their relative positions by turning to illegal sources of funding, sources that included kickbacks on government contracts, rigging of the stock market, and contributions from Japan's quasi-legal crime syndicates. In one scandal, for example, no less than 130 members of the HR received an estimated $80,000,000 in illegal payoffs (Sterngold 1992). Perhaps the new electoral law will make Japanese politics less money-driven, but that remains to be seen. For the time being, the *Japan Times* has a regular feature entitled "Scandal Du Jour" (*Japan Times*, Mar. 25, 2000).

How the LDP Ruled, and Why It Lost Power (Temporarily). The total dominance of the LDP from 1955 to 1993 rested upon three key factors.

1. *The LDP was very flexible in accommodating potential challenges to the Party's dominance.* Any issue that reflected a broad base of voter support was embraced by the LDP, including most of the welfare programs originally proposed by the Japan Socialist Party.
2. *The LDP's alliance with Japan's administrative and business elites enabled it to outspend its opponents.* Money and "pork barrel" are the driving forces of Japanese electoral politics, and the LDP controlled both.
3. *The years between 1955 and 1993 were years of unparalleled prosperity in Japan.* Japanese voters seemed reluctant to change a system that worked so well. Scandals, while unfortunate, were tolerated as long as they did not alter the capacity of the system to operate effectively.

While the above factors were adequate to keep the LDP in power for almost forty years, the mid-1980s would find the Party showing increasing signs of internal disunity. The problems were many.

1. *Business leaders were becoming restive with the regulatory power of their administrative counterparts,* believing, at least to some degree, that Japan's system of state capitalism had outlived its usefulness. Such sentiments struck at the very heart of the LDP, which, for all intents and purposes, was an alliance between Japan's business and bureaucratic elites.
2. *The costs of elections and the corruption inherent therein had gotten out of hand.* Japanese voters were very tolerant of political scandal, but that tolerance was reaching its limits.
3. *The LDP was finding it increasingly difficult to buy off its challengers by assuring that they received their "fair share" of the state resources.* The LDP is a coalition designed to provide disproportionate benefits for its members. By attempting to do too much for too many, the LDP found it increasingly difficult to meet the demands of its own members. Fair share is a wonderful principle, but it is not an easy principle to implement.
4. *The LDP found it difficult to adjust to the changing demographics of Japanese society.* Four decades of unprecedented growth had resulted in a Japan that was far more educated, urbanized, and politically aware than the Japan of the immediate post–World War II era. Many LDP supporters, accordingly, began to

question a system that called for extraordinary sacrifices yet provided a relatively low standard of living for much of the middle and working class. Indeed, Americans living in Japan often wondered how the rank-and-file Japanese could afford to live in their own country (Sessions 1995; Kitching 1995).

5. *The LDP was suffering the same problems of "old age" that beset most dominant single parties that have ruled for long periods of time.* It was becoming complacent, corrupt, lethargic, and insensitive to the changing needs of the Japanese voter.

Despite the LDP's fall from grace in 1993, it would be premature to view the LDP as a declining force in Japanese politics. The LDP remains Japan's most powerful party, and it has been the dominant force in many of the coalition Governments of the post-LDP era. It is entirely possible, moreover, that the shock of its electoral defeat and the new electoral laws will serve as catalysts for working out a new formula that will bring the LDP in line with the social and demographic realities of today's Japan. This was certainly the message of the 1996 elections in which the LDP returned to power by capturing 48 percent of the seats in the House of Representatives. In particular, the LDP is concentrating its efforts on attracting urban voters, a group that has largely deserted the LDP in recent years (*Nikkei Weekly,* Aug. 24, 1998).

The New Frontier Party: Shinshinto. During the spring of 1992, one of the LDP's major factions announced that it was rejecting the "putrid politics" of the LDP and forming its own political party, the Japan Renewal Party. The fact that leaders of the Japan Renewal Party possessed long records of political corruption was seemingly irrelevant, as all major factions of the LDP possessed long records of corruption (*European,* July, 15–18, 1993, 7). Other factions soon followed suit. The platforms of the breakaway parties were virtually identical, all calling for electoral reform, an end to corruption, an enhancement of urban life, better trade relations with the United States, and a reduction in the power of Japanese bureaucrats (Ozawa 1993).

All of the new parties made respectable showings in the 1993 elections, but none showed much promise of becoming a major contender for power in Japan. In December 1994, accordingly, all of Japan's smaller political parties, with the exception of the Japanese Communist Party and the Japanese Socialist Party, merged to form the New Frontier Party (NFP), or Shinshinto. Only as a united force, they felt, could they challenge the power of the LDP.

The leaders of the Shinshinto proclaimed its formation to be the most significant event in Japanese politics since the end of World War II. In reality, however, the new entity varied little from the LDP. Decisions required consensus among diverse factions, each of which was, at least for a brief moment, an independent political party. If anything, the differences between the factions of the New Frontier Party were greater than those between the factions of the LDP. Also problematic was the absence of a clear ideological difference between the New Frontier Party and the LDP (Hiwatari 1998). Indeed, most groups in the NFP were formerly associated with the LDP.

These and related problems were too great for the new party to overcome, and it collapsed in December of 1997, giving way to six minor parties. At least for the moment, then, hopes of Japan evolving into a two-party state appear to have vanished. As indicated in Table 5.2, the Japanese party system is so fluid that only the LDP and the Communists have been able to maintain a clear identity. This in itself, has helped to assure the dominance of the LDP.

Political Left Has Little Influence on Japanese Politics

The dominant parties of the left are the Japanese Socialist Party and the Communist Party. The Japanese Socialist Party once provided the main opposition to the LDP, but was relegated to the position of Japan's "third" party by the 1996 elections, garnering only 52 seats in the HR. Subsequent realignments saw its representation in the HR dwindle to an insignificant 15 seats. The Japan Communist Party possesses a small (26 HR seats) but vociferous following. All in all, the political left has little influence on Japanese politics.

Pressure Groups and Politics in Japan

Japan possesses the same array of business, labor, and social pressure groups that are found in all modern industrial societies. In common with other features of Japanese politics, however, Japanese pressure groups are Western in form but Japanese in substance. Most pressure groups in the West, for example, are practical in nature, their members coming together to achieve a specific set of economic or social objectives. Individuals in the West seldom value pressure group membership as a social experience, and they often belong to several groups with competing objectives. As a result of such *conflicting loyalties* (**cross-cutting cleavages**), the cohesion of Western pressure groups is often weak.

The Japanese also form groups to achieve specific economic and social objectives. Unlike the situation in the West, however, pressure group participation in Japan is valued as an important social experience. The same intense loyalties that accrue to the family or the firm also accrue to the pressure group. The Japanese are also less likely to join groups with conflicting interests, a fact that makes Japanese groups far more cohesive than their Western counterparts.

Group leaders, moreover, command great respect in Japan. Decisions, once made, are generally obeyed by the rank and file. Translated into the broader political equation, this means that the political leaders of Japan are in a far stronger position to control and mobilize their population by making deals with their country's large pressure group associations than would be the case in the West, particularly in the United States.

Business Associations. *Business associations are the most powerful of Japan's pressure groups.* They include a variety of large peak associations such as the Federation of Economic Organizations, the Japan Committee for Economic Development, and the Japan Iron and Steel Federation (Fukushima 1989). The Federation of Economic Organizations possesses approximately 800 large corporate members, as well as more than 100 associational groups and federations. The Japan Committee for Economic Development brings together the company presidents of Japan's largest corporations, a powerful group indeed. The Japan Federation of Employers Organization and the Japan Chamber of Commerce represent a broad spectrum of business interests, regardless of size. Organizations also exist to express the specific interests of medium-sized and smaller businesses—interests that may or may not conflict with those of the industrial giants (Richardson and Flanagan 1984; Lamont-Brown 1995).

The National Federation of Cooperatives (NFC), in turn, represents a vast network of agricultural cooperatives, agrarian associations, and agri-business organizations. The NFC delivered the rural vote for the Liberal Democratic Party during its formative years and was rewarded for its support with protective measures that made Japanese produce the most costly in the world.

The farm lobby continues to be among the most powerful groups in Japan, but it has lost strength as a result of urbanization. Today, farmers amount to only 10 percent

Winners and Losers in Japanese Politics
Interest groups that belong to the conservative coalition are the winners in Japanese politics, their members receiving a disproportionate share of the state's resources. Key segments of Japanese society, however, are not part of the winning coalition, and it is they, relatively speaking, who are the political losers. Such groups include labor, women, Japan's small minority of Koreans, and indigenous outcasts.

of the Japanese population (Mulgan 1997). The exorbitant cost of food, moreover, has become increasingly burdensome to Japan's urban population, making continued price supports politically unpopular (Calder 1988). Also problematic have been demands from the United States for greater access to the Japanese food market, an area in which American products are more than competitive with their Japanese counterparts. Japan's large business corporations do not want to engage in a trade war with the United States over the question of agricultural subsidies, and they have begun to turn on their former allies (Calder 1988). Conflict over support for agriculture was one of the major issues leading to the fragmentation of the LDP.

Nevertheless, the farm lobby has been able to play a key role in blocking Japan's much-needed economic reform. In this they have been joined by Japan's massive construction industry and its large bureaucratic agencies. The former fears a curtailment of lucrative government construction contracts, while the latter fear a diminution of their massive regulatory power (Leblanc 1998).

Most of the associations discussed above are large peak associations that possess a multitude of group and corporate members. Doctors, lawyers, the police, and other professions are also represented by powerful peak associations, the leaders of which have figured prominently in the circles of the LDP and its conservative spin-offs. As a reward for their support of Japan Inc., professional associations have been allowed to regulate both their work rules and the ethics of their members. Not surprisingly, doctors' and lawyers' fees in Japan are astronomical, even by United States standards.

Labor Unions. Japanese labor emerged from the Second World War as one of the best organized forces in Japanese society and was expected to play a central role in Japanese politics. The failure of Japanese labor to live up to this expectation is attributable to a variety of factors. Japanese unions, like the socialist movement in general, remained preoccupied with questions of ideological purity. In line with their Marxist ideology, energies were spent on promoting class conflict rather than wage and benefit packages that would provide material benefits to Japan's workers. Problematic, also, was the cradle-to-grave embrace of Japan's larger firms, the comprehensiveness of which reduced the need for unions. The large conglomerates also viewed union membership as an act of disloyalty and usually provided their workers with a company union designed to solidify their loyalty to the firm. Finally, union activities were hampered by the large percentage of Japanese workers who found employment in small firms. In such cases, personal ties to the owner often precluded union participation (van Wolferen 1990). Given the above circumstances, it is not surprising that Japan loses fewer days to strikes than any other advanced industrial country (Hayes 1992). The number of strikes, moreover, has been declining.

In one way or another, then, Japanese unions have been deprived of the critical mass required to achieve political dominance. A labor movement that had unionized approximately 55 percent of the industrial labor force in 1949 would speak for only half of that number, 28 percent, by the mid-1980s (Hayes 1992).

Japanese unions have also been weakened by the recent privatization of the nation's railroads and telecommunications, two large public-sector organizations that employed many of Japan's unionized workers. Dealing with private organizations may prove far more difficult for Japan's unions than dealing with government corporations (Woodiwiss 1992).

The driving force in the Japanese labor movement is **Rengo**, a large umbrella organization created in 1987 to give focus to the labor movement. Rengo now speaks for approximately 65 percent of organized labor, or approximately 20 percent of the Japanese labor force. The Rengo strategy is to pursue a pragmatic, non-ideological approach to labor relations and to strengthen cooperation between the Japanese Socialist Party and other smaller parties of the center-left. As yet, this strategy shows little sign of being successful.

Women. By Western standards, Japanese women appear to be the most oppressed females of the First World. The post–World War II years have witnessed the economic emancipation of Japanese women, but economic liberation has not been matched by gains in the social and political arenas. Some 40 percent of Japanese women now work outside the home, but they are expected to work for less money than do men and to occupy minor positions. Japan possesses an "equal employment" law, but there are a few serious penalties for noncompliance (Leblanc 1998). Working wives are expected to assume primary responsibility for child rearing and to serve their families in the traditional Japanese manner. Women have also been systematically excluded from the inner circle of Japanese politics, with only 23 of the 500 seats in the 1996 elections to the House of Representatives being won by women. This, moreover, was a historic high (*Japan Times,* Oct, 1996).

Lacking direct access to the political system, feminists have launched a variety of civic action groups, the largest of which is **Chifuren**, *an association of Japanese housewives* (van Wolferen 1990; Pons 1998). Chifuren, which claims to represent some 6 million consumer-oriented housewives, focuses largely on economic issues such as fair product labeling.

Women are also forcing a change in Japanese society by more subtle means, not the least of which is the tendency of educated Japanese women to delay marriage or avoid it altogether. Some indication of the changing role of Japanese women is provided by Jane Condon:

> Although young Japanese women are still renowned for being *yasashii* (tender, kind, gentle), the days of total obedience are over. Young wives are less disposed to being nurses and maids at home. They want their husbands to help around the house, at least a little. They want the whole family to go out to eat at least once a month, if not once a week (hence the rise in the number of family restaurants). They are less likely to pack away their high fashion Japanese clothes when they marry. They buy new clothes less often, but they still want to look as nice as they did when they were *dokushin kizoku* (single aristocrats). They insist that their husbands talk with them more. And although young husbands may still be number one in the family, the idea of walking behind them strikes young wives as absurd (Condon 1985, 298).

It is not clear, however, that Japanese women are as vulnerable as Westerners believe. As discussed by Sumiko Iwao (1993):

> Today it is, in a sense, the husbands who are being controlled and the ones to be pitied. The typical Japanese man depends heavily on his wife to look after his daily needs and nurture his psychological well-being. The Confucian ethic of the three obediences formerly binding women could be rewritten today as the three obediences for men: obedience to mothers when young, companies when adult, and wives when retired. Recent television dramas have depicted the plight of salaried-worker fathers as their presence and power in the home fades; such men are estranged from their families by extended absences

(e.g., work assignments abroad or in other cities) and suffer from a syndrome known as "involuntary incapacity to go home [kitaku kyohi]." Their plight is only intensified by the stronger position of women in the home. These recent phenomena lead us to wonder whether it is not men, instead of women, who are being exploited in Japanese society today. The vast majority of men, however, remain largely unaware of their own vulnerability as they cling to the illusion that they are the respected superiors of society and belittle women's voices as nothing but emotional, unrealistic "female logic" (7–8).

Organized Crime As a Pressure Group. Particularly interesting is the political role played by *Japan's large and quasi-legal crime syndicates,* the **yakuza**. The syndicates claim some 90,000 members, approximately one-half of whom are members of Japan's three largest gangs. A 1992 law has sought to integrate the gangs more directly within the "system" by allowing district governments to register them as official **boryokudan** or *violence groups* (*Economist,* Feb. 29, 1992).

Organized crime presents the political leaders of all countries with three choices: to wage an expensive and endless war against the crime barons, to legalize everything, or to make organized crime a self-regulating part of the system (Nagashima 1990). The Japanese have opted for the third alternative, preferring to deal with organized crime rather than disorganized crime.

Japan's large criminal organizations are expected to regulate the activities of their members in the same manner as the Japanese Medical Association or any other professional group. A magazine published by one of Japan's foremost crime syndicates, accordingly, calls upon its members to do the following:

1. preserve harmony in order to strengthen the group;
2. love and respect people outside the group and remember what is owed to them;
3. always be courteous and always be aware of senior-junior relationships;
4. learn from the experience of seniors and work for self-improvement; and
5. show restraint in contacts with the outside world (van Wolferen 1990, 104).

The strategy of treating criminals as part of the Japanese family apparently works, for Japan has a lower reported crime rate than any other state of the First World (Sessions 1995; Kitching 1995). This strategy, however, is not without its dangers, for crime money has been finding its way into the electoral process. Japan's large crime families are also in the process of merging their operations with mainline economic enterprises, a process that may further blur the distinction between legitimate and illegitimate activities. Belatedly, the authorities are now beginning to assert themselves against organized crime and especially extortionists who target large companies (*NYT,* Aug. 11, 1999, www).

Citizens and Politics in Japan

Japan is a democracy, and the Japanese electorate possesses the ability to alter its political system if it chooses to do so. To date, however, the electorate has chosen not to do so, allowing a narrow conservative oligarchy to monopolize all vestiges of political and economic power in Japan. The LDP lost the 1993 elections, but the conservative elite, albeit more fragmented, won a record number of seats in the House of Representatives. By 1996, the LDP has again reasserted its dominance.

It would be a mistake, however, to suggest that the Japanese public was either totally passive or without influence. *One of the main reasons for the LDP's long domination of Japanese politics was its willingness to listen to public opinion and to respond accordingly.* In this regard, three indicators of public opinion are of particular importance: elections, public opinion polls, and civic action protests. Of these, election results are the most important, as they have a direct and immediate impact on the composition of the Diet (Flanagan et al. 1991).

When the electorate supported candidates favoring stronger environmental regulation during the 1960s and 1970s, for example, the LDP became the party of the environment, attacking Japan's environmental problems with characteristic Japanese vigor. Not only did the elite listen, but it acted. In the same manner, when voters demanded better care for the aging, the LDP became the party of the elderly. Treatment of the elderly, unlike the environment, did not stay a hot issue, and welfare programs for the elderly were scaled back (Campbell 1992).

Another reason for the LDP's power is economic: conservative leaders had provided the Japanese population with four decades of unprecedented economic prosperity. Few Japanese citizens were anxious to change a system that worked. That, however, may now be changing as Japan moves deeper into economic crisis. The 1998 election for the HC saw the LDP soundly defeated. Prime Minister Hashimoto resigned, attributing the LDP's poor showing to his mismanagement of Japan's economic reform (Leblanc 1998). It is interesting to note that a growing number of Japanese, 35 percent by some estimates, reject all political parties. This indicates a growing gap between the Japanese public and its political leadership (Leblanc 1998), a process that will clearly gain momentum if the economic crisis deepens.

Public opinion polls tell much the same story as the election results. Poll after poll indicates a preeminent popular concern with economic prosperity. Japanese polls, however, also indicate a growing concern with the intense pressures of Japanese life as well as the manifest corruption of the Japanese political system. Recent polls have also begun to reflect concern over Japan's economic position in the world, particularly in its relations with China. In a 1994 Japanese poll, for example, only 25 percent of the respondents felt that Japan would be the world's "premier economic power in the long term," a figure that was substantially lower than the 53 percent who had answered this question in the affirmative just three years earlier (*NYT,* Dec. 30, 1994, A4). Some 25 percent of the respondents believed that the world's dominant economy would eventually be China; only 4 percent saw the United States assuming this role. Recent polls reflect similar concerns, with Japan's youth becoming increasingly reluctant to embrace the austere lifestyle of their parents (Leblanc 1998).

By far the most visible expressions of Japanese public opinion are the civic action protests, sometimes violent, that have become an accepted part of Japanese politics. As with most other aspects of Japanese life, political protests are highly organized affairs. According to Patricia Steinhoff,

> Japanese bring to protest activity the same organizational style and skills that characterize Japanese corporations and community groups. Planning a demonstration is not very different from organizing a school outing or a large tour group, and publishing for a political protest movement requires the same skills as working for an advertising agency or daily newspaper.... Similarly, protest groups engage in the same sort of organizational rivalry and territoriality that are found throughout Japanese society (Steinhoff 1989, 177).

Protest demonstrations are generally organized by leftist groups and ultimately have little impact on policy. Some civic action protests, however, have been taken seriously and have led to the enactment of environmental and abortion rights legislation (Steinhoff 1989).

The Context of Japanese Politics: Culture, Economics, and International Interdepedence

What makes the Japanese system work? Why do Japanese voters maintain a conservative elite in power in spite of repeated and ever-worsening scandals? Why is Japanese society so self-regulating? Why are Japanese elites able to "trust" each other to honor informal agreements despite intense competition between groups? Why does the Japanese population trust bureaucrats to run things? Why is Japan outproducing the West?

Answers to these and similar questions tend to fall into two categories: culture and economics. We first examine the cultural bases of Japanese politics, and then turn to Japanese political economy. Both perspectives offer compelling explanations of "what makes Japan tick." We will also examine the extent to which Japanese politics is shaped by the country's interdependence with the other members of the world community.

The Culture of Japanese Politics

Cultural explanations of Japanese politics center on four themes: nationalism (racism), harmony (collectivism), acceptance of hierarchical authority, and an intense dedication to hard work. Each of the four themes finds its origins in the unique evolution of Japanese culture discussed in the introductory sections of this chapter.

Nationalism. The Japanese are intensely proud of being Japanese (Hendry 1991). They also have an infinite faith in their ability to succeed. To some observers, Japanese national pride borders on racism (van Wolferen 1990).

Japan's conservative leaders have used two nationalistic themes to build a broad base of popular support for their programs: pride and vulnerability. The Japanese have ample reasons to be proud of their accomplishments. In a few short decades, Japan has been transformed from a defeated ruin into an economic superpower. Paralleling nationalist pride, however, is a profound sense of vulnerability, a pervasive fear that Japan is too small to maintain its economic dominance and that its competitors are dangerously jealous of its success (Calder 1988). Japan's conservative elites have used this sense of vulnerability to solidify their control of Japanese politics, arguing that a radical change of leadership would jeopardize the nation's hard-won prosperity by aiding its adversaries.

While the perpetuation of nationalistic sentiments has strengthened the electoral appeal of Japan's conservative elite, it has also converted trade negotiations with the United States into a matter of national pride. This is not a matter of small concern, for Japan's trade surplus with the US continues to reach an astronomical level. Pride and fear are not uniquely Japanese emotions, but they do provide an essential clue to the success of the Japanese political system. Nationalism may be declining in the states of Western Europe as former enemies move in the direction of ever-greater unity, but it is not declining in Japan (Dale 1990).

The most recent manifestation of Japanese nationalism is a movement to rewrite the history of Japan's colonial expansion in the years leading up to World War II. The revisionist movement attempts to portray Japan's colonial expansion as a response to Western imperialism designed to protect the values of Asian culture. Revised manuals of history have sold over 250,000 copies since 1996, and their popularity is growing (Leblanc 1998).

As demonstrated by these junior high school students in Nishiki, Japanese students are responsible for keeping their schools clean. This is one of many practices that produce an orderly, safe, and rigorous, if regimented, educational system.

Harmony. *The cornerstone of Japanese political culture is its emphasis on collective harmony, or wa.* Western culture idealizes individualism, while Japanese culture idealizes the group. To be ostracized from the group is to lose one's sense of identity. More than that, it means losing one's entire system of social and psychological support. Ideal citizens in Japan are citizens who merge their identities with that of the group and who place group interest above self-interest (Moeran 1986). Interpersonal conflicts are often intense, but they are "brokered" to maintain the cohesiveness of the group (Nakane 1970).

The Japanese emphasis on social harmony provides the cultural underpinning for the concept of "fair share" that is so prominent in Japanese politics. Japan is viewed as one large family, all parts of which must, in some way or another, be kept within the system. The Japanese emphasis on collective harmony helps to explain the ability of Japan's political, economic, and administrative elites to "network" so effectively. Again, they are all part of the same family.

The cultural emphasis on harmony further underlies the self-effacing style of Japanese politicians, a style that makes it difficult for Western negotiators to pin down precisely who controls what. Everyone denies having power, and no decision can really be taken without the consensus of the larger group. Even when promises are made, these promises are contingent upon group approval.

Pressures for social conformity also strengthen the cohesion of Japanese pressure groups. Group members are under intense pressure to vote as a group, and conflicting group memberships (cross-cutting cleavages) are discouraged (Richardson and Flanagan 1984). Work groups also tend to become political groups. To accept employment in one of Japan's large conglomerates, for example, is to make a decision that will regulate the individual's economic, political, and social behavior for the remainder of his or her life. Japanese employees seldom change jobs and are expected to internalize the economic and political interests of their firms. It is the collective thing to do.

The Confucian Ethic: Hierarchical Authority and Hard Work. *Japanese political and economic culture also builds upon* **Confucian culture,** *four dimensions of which are particularly important: hard work, respect for hierarchical authority, rule by merit, and devotion to the group* (Hendry 1991; Dore and Sako 1989). These tenets of Confucian culture underscore the very foundation of Japan's political success in the post–World War II era. The Japanese are orderly, they follow the dictates of their leaders, most of whom are selected on the basis of merit, and they work hard. In so doing, they assure that the state will have ample resources to meet the economic needs of its people. Indeed, a recent survey reported that three out of four Japanese would prefer to work with a fever, rather than take sick leave (*Japan Times,* Jan. 11, 1999).

Culture also permeates the way Japanese do business. Table 5.3 outlines the profound differences between Eastern and Western management techniques.

Political Socialization and Cultural Change. Because Japanese cultural patterns are an important element in the Japanese political equation, they are carefully nurtured by Japan's political leaders. School curricula actively reinforce all of the cultural patterns cited above, downplaying cultural trends that the ruling elite deems "anti-Japanese." The socialization process is further reinforced by a mass media that is very much part of the "system" (van Wolferen 1990). This, moreover, is in spite of the fact that Japan is a media-saturated society with 121 daily newspapers with a combined circulation of 92 million. There are also some 2,400 magazines published on a monthly basis (Jain 1997). The intellectual community, too, seems to have been lulled into passivity by economic prosperity, being described as "disturbingly quiet and vacant" (Miyoshi and Harootunian 1989, ix–x).

Be this as it may, Japan is no longer an isolated community in which a narrow oligarchy can choose the values to which its subjects will be exposed. Two million foreigners now enter Japan on an annual basis, a figure that has been more than matched by the number of Japanese traveling abroad (Sugiyama 1992). In 1985, for example, approximately 4,000,000 Japanese citizens traveled abroad for reasons of business or tourism, a number that would approach the 9,000,000 mark by 1988 and nearly 14,000,000 by 1994 (Sugiyama 1992; *NYT,* Aug. 23, 1994, A3).

Particularly worrisome to Japanese leaders is the fear that Japan is becoming, however slowly, a post-industrial society. The pace of Japanese life is staggering, and many younger Japanese executives are "dropping out" of the rat race (Noguchi 1992; Leblanc 1998). The Japanese population that created the economic miracle is also becoming older, giving way to a generation of Japanese workers that may be less imbued with the work ethic of its elders. This, however, remains to be seen. No one expects radical changes in Japanese culture in the near future, but business leaders are nervous.

Also worrisome to Japan's business leaders is the low emphasis on innovation in Japanese culture. Toward this end, schools now display signs saying "Let us all be individuals," to which *The Economist* quipped, "All together now, repeat after me" (*Economist,* Mar. 21, 1998, 21).

Political Economy and Politics in Japan

Discussions of Japanese political economy generally have one of two basic themes. The first stresses the role of state capitalism in orchestrating Japan's phenomenal economic growth. The second focuses on the profound influence of economic factors in shaping the nature of Japanese politics.

Table 5.3
The Business Characteristics: A Comparison of American and Japanese
Management Practices

Characteristics of American Business	Characteristics of Japanese Business
I. Game Concept	**I. Mutual Trust**
1. Business is a game in pursuit of profits under the rules of laws and contracts. ▪ more arguments, documents, litigation, and trials ▪ high acting ability ▪ precedence of logic ▪ clear agreement and expression ▪ willingness to confront	1. Business is based on trusting relationships among people rather than on the rules of the game. ▪ fewer arguments, documentation, litigation, and trials ▪ low acting ability ▪ precedence of relationships among people ▪ ambiguous agreement and expression ▪ avoidance of confrontation
II. Individualism—Dignity as the Highest Priority	**II. Human Relations–Oriented**
2. The dignity of individuals and self-assertion ▪ active self-assertion ▪ individual decisions over consensus	2. "In the same boat" sensibility and mutual trust ▪ weak self-assertion ▪ dependence on consensus
3. Individual work	3. Teamwork
4. Refusal of individuals to be placed at a disadvantage	4. Reluctance to say "no"
5. A society excelling in creativity and versatility	5. Uniform society
6. An economy within which entrepreneurs with a high level of creativity are important	6. An economy in which entrepreneurs are less important
7. The existence of excellent professionals and their important social functions	7. Less important social functions for professionals
8. Priority of customer's benefit in sales	8. Salesperson loyal to employer
9. Exceedingly high mobility of labor	9. Exceedingly low mobility of labor
10. Lack of mutual dependence between employers and employees	10. Mutual dependence between employers and employees
III. Efficiency-Oriented—Simplicity, Clarity, and Speed	**III. Precision–Oriented—Dependence on Human Awareness**
11. Heavy dependence on machinery and technology vs. dependence on human resources	11. Heavy dependence on human resources
12. Binary way of thinking ▪ quick decision of yes or no, white or black ▪ increased efficiency and less precision	12. Decimal scale way of thinking ▪ consideration of various possibilities and careful decision making ▪ increased precision and decreased efficiency
13. Vertical way of thinking ▪ pursuit of efficient management through quick decisions ▪ danger of low precision	13. Horizontal way of thinking ▪ adoption of bottom-up management and teamwork ▪ careful decisions based on diverse considerations
14. A business-oriented stance ▪ realistic, straightforward, self-interested, and less consistent	14. Nonbusiness considerations taken into account ▪ heavy dependence on consistency
15. Approximate accuracy	15. Perfectionism
16. Limited loyalty and incentive-oriented work ethics	16. High loyalty and less incentive-oriented
17. Pursuit of profit accountability and operations ▪ short-term performance evaluation	17. Pursuit of profit accountability from mid-/long-term viewpoint ▪ mid-/long-term performance evaluation
18. Low service quality ▪ mechanical-service oriented	18. High service quality ▪ service with human touches
19. Easy dismissal of employees and selling of business	19. Lifetime employment and less selling of business
IV. Top-Down Management	**IV. Participation-Oriented Management**
20. Top-down management techniques by excellent managers ▪ management by forcing employees through authority rather than motivation	20. High degree of employee participation ▪ management by motivating employees through participation rather than forcing them

Source: World Link, "Special Report: Japan," vol. 5, no. 1, 1992, p. 61.

The United States and other advocates of **neoclassical economics** have scaled back the level of government involvement in economic matters, believing that this will increase productivity. Government interference, in their view, disrupts the law of supply and demand and results in reduced competition. Without competition, firms have little incentive to increase their efficiency, to improve the quality of their products, or to lower prices. Everyone loses: the state by a lack of revenue, and the consumer by the need to pay higher prices for inferior products.

The Japanese practice of state capitalism contradicts this logic, demonstrating that government intervention in the economic arena can promote dramatic economic growth (Sheridan 1993). Under the principles of state capitalism, the Japanese government uses the resources of the state to identify those areas in which Japan enjoys a competitive advantage in terms of resources, technology, and labor. The government then uses its control of loans, taxes, and import restrictions to stimulate industrial growth in these areas.

This does not mean that the Japanese are not capitalistic or that they are unconcerned with the need for economic competition. That is not the case. To the contrary, once the government has targeted an area of designated growth, Japan's fiercely jealous conglomerates compete for domination of that area. The automobile industry, for example, has long been favored by government incentives. Nevertheless, competition among Japanese automobile firms is intense. That competition has resulted in a product that is among the most efficient and the most reasonably priced in the world. The same is true of consumer electronics, optics, and an array of other products too numerous to mention.

The Japanese government, however, goes well beyond merely targeting areas of economic expansion. It also assures that Japanese industries receive favored treatment both at home and abroad. The Japanese, for example, have been reluctant to share their domestic market with their competitors, a policy that now threatens to set off a trade war with the United States. Japan also uses its massive foreign assistance program to promote sales in the states of the Third World. If Japan dumps its cars on the markets of the Third World in the guise of foreign aid, for example, it becomes very difficult for Western automakers to compete in these areas. Once entrenched, the quality of Japanese goods makes them very difficult to dislodge.

The Japanese model of economic growth, then, is a blend of private-sector initiative and government control. It is a partnership between the public and private sectors that pits Japan against its competitors. The nerve centers of Japan's system of state capitalism are the Ministry of Finance and the Ministry of International Trade and Industry, the senior administrators of which have the determining voice in deciding which areas are to be targeted for development (Johnson 1982; Bingman 1989).

It was this model of state capitalism that transformed Japan into the world's second leading economic power after the US (Hartcher 1998). The same model, however, is now blamed for Japan's economic crisis. Once praised for their foresight, bureaucrats in the Ministry of Finance and the Ministry of International Trade and Industry are now criticized for being inflexible, excessively theoretical, and heavy-handed, and accused of propping up weak companies and being more concerned with their own power than the good of the country (*Economist,* March 21 and June 28, 1998). While some state guidance promoted growth, too much political interference in the Japanese economy proved to be its undoing.

There were, of course, other factors undermining the Japanese economy as well. Marika Sugahara, a former senior official in the Prime Minister's office is quoted by *The Economist* as listing five key elements in what *The Economist* refers to as the Japanese disease. The elements are "a weakening of the Japanese work ethic; excessive homogeneity and conformity; a loss of creativity; a diminishing sense of public spirit; and a huge resistance to tapping the productive potential of

Intense activity in the Tokyo Stock Exchange reflects the vibrancy of the Japanese economy.

women and the elderly" (*Economist,* March 21, 1998, 21). Japan's economic crisis also coincided with the end of the Cold War and growing economic conflict with the US—Japan's largest market—now more concerned with its own economic problems than with the scourge of world communism. Japan's economic crisis further deepened with the collapse of many Asian economies, a phenomenon beyond the control of the Japanese alone. And finally, Japan's political leaders failed to act. This was less a failure of planning than a failure of political decision making. The "vacuum at the center" had struck again (Drucker 1998).

However much the Japanese economy has been shaped by its political system, the converse is equally true. Indeed, few political systems in the world have a stronger economic underpinning than that of Japan. Japan's ruling elite is preeminently an economic elite that has dedicated itself to making Japan the dominant economic power in the world. That elite, moreover, has used its control over the state's resources to maintain itself in office since 1955, the splintering of the LDP notwithstanding. Business groups make huge contributions to conservative candidates, and administrators assure that those candidates are favored in the allocation of public spending projects (Eisuke 1998).

Japanese voters, for their part, are very concerned about economic issues. The ruling elite has provided Japanese citizens with a steadily improving quality of material life, and Japan's citizens have responded accordingly. The elite, moreover, has been wise enough to assure that all segments of society share in that prosperity. *The principle of "fair share" is not just cultural; it is also smart politics* (Calder 1988). The sustained economic decline of the 1900s, in turn, was also blamed for the decline of the LDP and its loss of the House of Councilors election in 1998 (Kunii 1998).

Japan's economic elite have also benefited from the group emphasis in Japanese society. Workers in Japan's large conglomerates understand that they have a vested interest in voting for "company" candidates, and they are reluctant to become involved with parties and groups considered hostile to company interests. Economic intimidation is part and parcel of the Japanese political process (van Wolferen 1990).

From the broader perspective, political economists would also argue that the success of Japanese democracy is a reflection of Japan's economic success. The economic miracle of the 1950s and 1960s legitimized Japan's democratic institutions by demonstrating that they could meet the basic needs of the people. Four decades of prosperity have subsequently strengthened the foundations of that democracy. Questions arise, accordingly, concerning the stability of Japanese democracy now that the country has entered a period of prolonged economic decline.

International Interdependence and the Politics of Japan

Three dimensions of Japan's international environment have a profound impact upon its politics. *First, Japan lives by trade.* Any sustained diminution in its ability to export its goods and services will undermine a political system that has based its legitimacy upon economic growth. As noted in the preceding section, the line between economics and politics in Japan is often hard to find. *Second, Japan is a demilitarized country surrounded by powerful neighbors, not the least of which are China and Russia.* Indeed, Article 9 of the Japanese Constitution explicitly prohibits Japan from maintaining a military force capable of threatening its neighbors. Any sustained threat by Russia or China, accordingly, must inevitably cause a political crisis in Japan. *Third, many people argue that Japan's politics change only when it is faced with insurmountable pressure from abroad* (Leblanc 1998). The Meiji Restoration was triggered by the frigates of Admiral Perry, just as the foundations of Japanese democracy were put in place by the US victory in WWII.

From the end of World War II in 1945 until the end of the Cold War in 1990, both Japan's security and Japan's trade were guaranteed by the United States. Japan fell under the US's nuclear shield, and the US turned a blind eye to Japanese trade practices that it now complains are unfair. A strong Japan was vital to the US struggle against world communism, and if that required large trade deficits with Japan, so be it.

The end of the Cold War, however, brought a dramatic change in Japan's international environment. With the Cold War over, the US is far more concerned with reducing its staggering trade deficit with Japan ($5.16 billion in 1999) than it is with mopping up the final vestiges of world communism. In particular, the US has demanded that Japan open its markets to US products and that the Japanese government stop providing subsidies that allow Japanese firms to undersell their US competitors on the world market.

Japan heatedly rejects accusations of economic warfare. All states, Japan maintains, engage in protectionism in one guise or another (Hatakeyama 1992). This, of course, is true. The problem, according to the United States, is a matter of degree.

The crux of the situation, from the Japanese perspective, is that Japan, for largely cultural reasons, is able to outproduce its competitors. Western consumers prefer Japanese automobiles, electronics, and other products for the simple reason that they offer superior quality at a reasonable price (Ohsumi 1992). The Japanese also find Western workers to be lazy and their managerial staffs bloated and overpaid.

Whatever the relative merits of the argument, tensions involving trade relations between Japan and the West are reaching crisis proportions (*IHT,* Sept. 22, 1999, www). Japan would probably be the big loser in such a war, as more than 40 percent of its exports go to the United States alone. A trade war, however, would hurt all of the parties concerned and would undoubtedly hasten the deterioration of the strong bonds between the US and Japan that have developed over the course of the past fifty years.

US economic pressure on Japan, however, is about more than deficits. The US is attempting to force Japan Inc. to abandon the protectionist-state capitalist system

---

Japan's Nuclear Capacity

In 1994, the Japanese prime minister shocked the world by inadvertently mentioning that Japan possessed the capacity to build nuclear weapons (*NYT*, June 21, 1994, A5). The comment was later disavowed, but secret reports leaked from the Japanese Foreign Ministry confirm that Japan has possessed a nuclear capacity for some time, perhaps since the 1970s (*SCMP*, Aug. 6, 1994, 9). The United States admitted that it had been secretly supplying Japan with bomb grade plutonium for at least seven years prior to the 1994 disclosure (*NYT*, Sept. 9, 1994, A5). Japan's navy is rated as the region's best (*SCMP*, Oct. 22, 1994, 9), but its army is small (158,000) and has experienced recruiting problems (*IHT*, Nov. 28, 1995, 4).

---

that has provided the underpinning of its prosperity and political stability for the past fifty years. In point of fact, Washington is pushing Japan to adopt the free-market economic system of the United States. While making symbolic concessions to the US in an effort to avoid a trade war, Japan has largely refused to alter its economic practices, and tensions between the two allies have continued to build beneath a surface of civility that both sides are finding difficult to maintain.

For all of the tension between the two countries, however, Japan remains a vital element in US security arrangements for Southeast Asia. Some 22,000 US troops remain stationed in Japan as well as a contingent of 180 planes and a sizeable naval presence. The pact of military cooperation was renewed in 1997 with minimal debate on either side. The US is also counting upon Japan to play a major role in stabilizing the weak economies of the region, something that Japan has been reluctant to do. Rather, Japan has concentrated on building strong ties with China—a potential market of 1.6 billion consumers—and normalizing its relations with Russia. Not only would China provide Japan with a massive new market, but it would also provide an alternative market for Japanese goods in the event of a trade war with the United States or Western Europe. As might be expected, China is the largest recipient of Japanese foreign aid. It is also taking steps to establish itself as a regional power independent of the US.

Challenges of the Present and Prospects for the Future

The international community has increasingly defined "good government" in terms of six criteria: democracy, stability, human rights, quality of life, economic growth, and environmental concern. Japan is the only non-Western state to score in the top group in each of these six areas. Japan is a stable, prosperous, and egalitarian democracy whose citizens enjoy a broad range of human rights. Japan has also become a world leader in environmental legislation.

Even more remarkable than Japan's record in the six areas of good government is the fact that this record was largely achieved in the five decades following the end of World War II. Japan had industrialized well before the war, but its industrialization had brought little prosperity to the average Japanese citizen and had been orchestrated by authoritarian governments without regard for human rights, the quality of Japanese life, or the environment. Japan has experienced an economic miracle, but it has achieved a political miracle as well. The Japan of today bears little resemblance to the authoritarian Japan of an earlier era.

For all of Japan's accomplishments, critics suggest that Japan's political miracle is less miraculous than it seems. In particular, they argue that the Japanese view of democracy and human rights is far different from that of the West (Reading 1992; Herzog 1993). These and related topics will be discussed in the remainder of this chapter as we examine the challenges that confront Japan in each of the six areas of good government outlined above.

Democracy and Stability

Japan meets all of the procedural requirements for stable democracy discussed in the introductory chapter. Free elections are conducted at specified intervals; voters are provided with a meaningful choice of issues and candidates; issues are freely discussed; winners take office; and once in office, they rule. If voted out of office, political leaders step down without threat of revolution or violence.

Criticisms of Japanese democracy focus not on its procedures but on its practices. A single political party, the LDP, ruled Japan from 1955 until 1993. The LDP was finally voted out of office in 1993 but returned to power a few years later. The overwhelming dominance of a conservative elite does not, by itself, make Japan undemocratic. The escalating cycle of election scandals, however, does speak to the existence of a ruling elite that is more than willing to flout democratic procedures for the sake of remaining in power.

In addition to lavish outlays of money, the conservative elite is also accused of using its control of state institutions to suppress challenges to its authority (Reading 1992; Woronoff 1981). Indeed, everything in Japan seems to be micro-managed by Japan Inc., including the courts and the press.

However entrenched Japan's conservative elite may be, it is well within the capacity of the Japanese electorate to "vote the rascals out." They have done so rarely. In the view of some observers, popular acquiescence in conservative rule represents a clear sign that Japan has yet to develop a democratic political culture (Dale 1990). Acceptance of this criticism, however, is far from universal. As Louis Hayes put it, "To their critics, the Japanese are not really happy; they just think they are" (Hayes 1992).

The final years of the twentieth century saw Japan sink into a deep economic crisis that will test both its democracy and its political stability. Thus far, neither have faltered.

Human Rights

The Japanese Constitution delineates the rights of Japanese citizens in great detail. The concept of human rights in Japan, however, differs considerably from the concept of human rights in the United States and many other Western countries (Hendry 1991). Japanese culture stresses collectivism rather than individualism, viewing the rights of individuals as a set of reciprocal obligations within the group context (Hendry 1991). The group cares for the individual, but the individual is expected to subordinate his or her interests to those of the group.

Four dimensions of Japanese human rights practice are particularly worrisome to human rights groups in the West.

1. *The level of bureaucratic control is far greater in Japan than it is in most Western countries.* The government controls everything, and Japanese citizens find it very difficult to challenge the government. Japan, moreover, does not possess a freedom of information act. For the most part, Japanese citizens are ignorant of the content of their police dossiers. The Japanese legal system also provides few rights for defendants, but this would seem to be a matter of minor concern in a penal system that is one of the most forgiving in the world.

2. *Foreign minorities are severely disadvantaged in Japanese society* (Sellek and Weiner 1992; *Japan Times*, Apr. 11, 2000, www). The 700,000 members of Japan's long-established Korean community, its largest ethnic minority, enjoy few rights.

A prominent Japanese political leader has referred to Japan's "salarymen" as "commuter slaves in a commuter hell." The country's intense work ethic has been blamed for strained family relationships and increased rates of alcoholism.

Illegal immigrants have also become a problem for Japan, although to a lesser degree than in the United States and Western Europe (Sellek and Weiner 1992). The Government, moreover, is now under pressure from Japanese labor unions to reduce the number of guest workers (Nimura 1992).

3.   *The constitutional rights of Japanese women are severely restricted.* While the Japanese Constitution expressly states that "there shall be no discrimination in political, economic, and social relations because of race, creed, sex, social status, or family origin," the reality, as noted previously in this chapter, is quite different (Article III, Constitution). Japanese women, by Western standards, are the least liberated in the First World. Japan, for example, ranks 125th in the world in the number of women legislators (Leblanc 1998). Some 90 percent of the Japanese firms acknowledge problems with sexual harassment, but less than 6 percent have done anything about it (*CSM,* Apr. 14, 1998).

Moreover, many of the feminist gains made during the 1980s appeared to be slipping during the 1990s. A 1993 survey by the Labor Ministry, for example, found that most Japanese firms were reducing their recruitment of female graduates. The explanation for this practice was that males have a stronger commitment to their careers than females (*NYT,* May 27, 1994, A4). The education of women continues to lag behind that of men (*Japan Times,* Jan. 1, 1999 and Jan. 5, 1999).

Things are changing for Japanese women, but they are changing very slowly. The courts could alter this situation, but they have been reluctant to counter traditional practices. Ironically, it may be the aging of Japanese society that propels women to the fore in economic affairs. With its work force shrunk by retirement and a declining birth rate, Japan finds itself in desperate need of new workers. There may be little choice but to give women a greater role in economic affairs. It is unlikely, however, that this will translate into political rights.

4.   *The Japanese have shown little concern for human rights on a global scale.* Japan has not ratified UN treaties establishing a world standard for human rights, and flagrant human rights abuses in China are excused as being an internal matter rooted in Chinese culture (Herzog 1993). Clearly, Japan does not want criticism of

---

Japan's Welfare State Less Generous Than Europe's

Japan provides for the basic needs of its citizens. As John Campbell writes, however, the Japanese model of a welfare state is far less generous than those of Western Europe:

Japan is not a European-model welfare state: its 14.6 percent of national income devoted to social security in 1986 was greatly exceeded by Germany, France, and Great Britain (in the 25–36 percent range), let alone Sweden (40.7 percent); even the United States (16.2 percent) was higher. Japan has not fully embraced the idea of comprehensive cradle-to-grave security, and provides less than many other countries in such areas as personal social services, family allowances, special housing, and institutional care (Campbell 1992, 10).

China's human rights policies to stand in the way of growing economic cooperation between the two countries.

Economic Growth and Quality of Life

Japan's economic miracle has made it the world's second-largest economy after that of the United States. Economic prosperity, however, has not brought the average Japanese citizen a quality of life equivalent to that of the average citizen in the United States or Western Europe. Japanese workers earn as much as their Western counterparts, but the cost of living in Japan is so exorbitant that their money does not go as far as it would in the West. Indeed, the cost of living in Tokyo is more than twice as great as the cost of living in New York or London. Perhaps more damning is the fact that Japan's famed system of providing employees with a job for life is showing signs of strain as the unemployment rate has passed the 4 percent level, an acceptable figure for the US but a disastrous figure for the Japanese (*Sunday Times,* Jan. 3, 1999).

Economic growth has also had its psychological costs. The intense work ethic that has driven Japan's rise to economic dominance has also transformed Japan into a socio-psychological pressure cooker. The leader of one of Japan's political parties, for example, recently referred to Japanese "salarymen" as "commuter slaves in a commuter hell." Family life is strained, and alcoholism has become a national problem. Not unexpectedly, many younger Japanese are starting to question the "growth at any cost" philosophy preached by Japan's conservative elite (*Economist,* May 22, 1992, 81).

On the positive side, Japan's wealth is equitably distributed, and Japan boasts the longest life expectancy and the most highly educated population in the world (Hendry 1991). Japanese education also places an increasing emphasis on equality among individuals, albeit an equality that stresses uniformity and conformity (Cummings 1980; Hendry 1991; *Japan Times,* Mar. 23, 2000, www). By and large, Japan's students are being socialized to fit into an industrial system that will find them spending their entire lives working for a single employer. The sustained economic crisis of the late 1990s has called Japan's famed job security into question as the wave of bankruptcies continues to mount as does the rate of Japanese joblessness (*IHT,* Apr. 1, 2000, 1).

The Environment

Japan ranks among the most environmentally conscious of the major industrial powers, a distinction born of necessity. As described by Louis Hayes:

The process of environmental deterioration reached a peak in the 1960s, but the political and economic elites seemed indifferent to the problems. "The economic miracle became a noisy, smelly, overcrowded, unhealthy testament to human greed...." The initial response was to build taller smokestacks in order to disperse the pollutants over a wider area and thereby reduce their concentrations. Draining underground water supplies led to land subsidence and a threat to surface structures. Effluent discharged into the sea damaged fishing grounds and ultimately caused serious health problems (Hayes 1992, 122).

Today, Japan's environmental regulations are among the most stringent in the world, but this does not mean that Japan is an environmental paradise (Government of Japan 1990). It merely means that Japan, like the United States, has begun to attack its very substantial environmental problems. From the perspective of environmental activists, two major problems remain.

First, Japan is heavily dependent upon nuclear energy and plans to build twenty-five additional new nuclear facilities over the course of the next two decades. These plans have been temporarily delayed by international protests but will probably be revived in the near future (*NYT*, Feb. 22, 1994, A2; *CSM*, Feb. 24, 1993, 13). Nuclear plants entail the risk of radiation leaks within Japan, and they also require the storage of nuclear waste and the transnational shipment of lethal plutonium. The accidental sinking of a plutonium ship would be an unmitigated catastrophe for the regions affected. The Japanese have countered foreign criticism by stressing the exemplary safety record of their nuclear facilities. This record, however, was shaken in December 1995 by a "mishap" at an experimental "fast breeder" nuclear reactor. The mishap was all the more damaging to the government's nuclear program because of a botched attempt to hide it from the press (*CSM*, Dec. 29, 1995, 7). Other mishaps" have followed in rapid succession, and in 1999 Japan suffered the worst nuclear disaster in its history, being forced to seek technical assistance from the US and Russia. Nevertheless, it is unlikely that such setbacks will deter Japan's plans to become the world's first all-nuclear country.

The second area in which the Japanese have displayed a marked lack of environmental concern involves whales and other forms of marine life that figure prominently in the Japanese diet. With whales becoming an endangered species as a result of over-fishing, the International Whaling Commission has imposed a temporary ban on all whaling. The Japanese maintain that the ban on whale hunting has more to do with Western emotions that with the number of whales being harvested, and they have been pushing to have the ban lifted. They have, however, complied with its provisions.

Prospects for the Future

Does the above discussion suggest that Japan is somewhat less of a First World state than the United States and its Western allies? Not at all. What it does suggest is that Japan, like all states of the First World, is still a long way from meeting the ideal standards of good government expressed in the UN charter and related documents. The Japanese experience also suggests that countries possessing cultural and historical traditions different from that of the West will tend to approach concepts such as democracy, equality, and human rights from non-Western perspectives.

Japan is changing in the face of the domestic and external pressures outlined in this chapter, but the process of change is slow and evolutionary in character. The key question facing Japan as it enters the twenty-first century center on the ability of the Japanese government to address the pressures for change in a timely manner. If it does not, argues a leading Japanese economist, it could well find its economy stagnant by the year 2010 (Tadashi 1998). Political problems would increase apace.

References

Asada, Akira. 1989. "Infantile Capitalism and Japan's Postmodernism: A Fairy Tale." In *Postmodernism and Japan*, ed. Masao Miyoshi and H. D. Harootunian. Durham, NC, and London: Duke University Press.

Atsushi, Yamada. 1998 (Jan.–Mar.). "Change-Proof Finance Ministry." *Japan Quarterly* 45(1): 37–41.

Baerwald, Hans H. 1986. *Party Politics in Japan*. Boston: Allen and Unwin.

Bingman, Charles F. 1989. *Japanese Government Leadership and Management*. London: Macmillan.

Calder, Kent E. 1988. *Crisis and Compensation: Public Policy and Political Stability in Japan, 1949–1986*. Princeton, NJ: Princeton University Press.

Campbell, John C. 1992. *How Policies Change: The Japanese Government and the Aging Society*. Princeton, NJ: Princeton University Press.

Condon, Jane. 1985. *A Half Step Behind: Japanese Women Today*. Tokyo: Charles E. Tuttle Co.

Cox, Gary W., and Frances Rosenbluth. 1993 (Sept.). "The Electoral Fortunes of Legislative Factions in Japan." *American Political Science Review* 87(3): 577–89.

Cox, Gary W., and Michael F. Theis. 1998 (June). "The Cost of Intraparty Competition: The Single, Nontrasferable Vote and Money Politics in Japan." *Comparative Political Studies* 31(3): 267–292.

Cummings, William K. 1980. *Education and Equality in Japan*. Princeton, NJ: Princeton University Press.

Dale, Peter N. 1990. *The Myth of Japanese Uniqueness*. London: Routledge.

Dore, Ronald P., and Mari Sako. 1989. *How the Japanese Learn to Work*. London: Routledge.

Drucker, Peter F. 1998. (Sept.–Oct.). "In Defense of Japanese Bureaucracy." *Foreign Affairs* 77(5): 68–81.

Duus, Peter. 1976. *The Rise of Modern Japan*. Boston: Houghton Mifflin.

Earhart, H. Byron. 1982. *Japanese Religion: Unity and Diversity*. Belmont, CA: Wadsworth.

The Economist. 1997. "A Survey of Japanese Finance."

Eisuke, Sakakibara. 1998 (Feb.) "Moving Beyond the Public Works State." *Japan Echo* 25(1): 31–36.

Flanagan, Scott, Bradley Richardson, Joji Watanuki, Ichiro Miyake, and Shinsaku Kohei, eds. 1991. *The Japanese Voter*. New Haven, CT: Yale University Press.

Fukushima, Glen S. 1989. "Corporate Power." In *Democracy in Japan* (pp. 255–80), ed. Takeshi Ishida and Ellis S. Krauss. Pittsburgh: University of Pittsburgh Press.

Government of Japan, Environment Agency. 1990. *Quality of the Environment in Japan: 1990*.

Hartcher, Peter. 1998. *The Ministry*. Cambridge: Harvard Business School Press.

Hatakeyama, Noboru. 1992. "A More Assertive Voice." *World Link* 1: 58–59.

Hayes, Louis D. 1992. *Introduction to Japanese Politics*. New York: Paragon House.

Hendry, Joy. 1991. *Understanding Japanese Society*. London: Routledge.

Herzog, Peter J. 1993. *Japan's Pseudo-Democracy*. Sandgate, Kent, England: Japan Library.

Hiwatari, Nobuhiro. 1998 (Oct.). "Adjustment to Stagflation and Neoliberal Reforms in Japan, the United Kingdom, and the United States: The Implications of the Japanese Case for a Comparative Analysis of Party Competition." *Comparative Political Studies* 31(5): 602–633.

Ishida, Takeshi, and Ellis S. Krauss. 1989. *Democracy in Japan*. Pittsburgh: University of Pittsburgh Press.

Iwao, Sumiko. 1993. *The Japanese Woman: Traditional Image and Changing Reality*. New York: Free Press.

Jain, Purnendra. 1997 (Nov.). "Media and Politics in Japan." *Australian Journal of Political Science* 32(3): 481–82.

Johnson, Chalmers. 1982. *Miti and the Japanese Economic Miracle*. Stanford, CA: Stanford University Press.

Johnson, Chalmers. 1989. "MITI, MPT, and the Telecom Wars: How Japan Makes Policy for High Technology." In *Politics and Productivity: The Real Story of Why Japan Works* (pp. 177–239), ed. Chalmers Johnson, Laura D. Tyson, and John Zysman. New York: Ballinger.

Johnson, Chalmers. 1994. *Japan: Who Governs? The Rise of the Developmental State*. New York: Norton.

Johnston, Eric. 1999 (Jan. 6). "Century of Change: Foreign Press Find Japan Tough to Figure." *Domestic News*, p. 5.

Kataoka, Tetsuya, ed. 1992. *Creating Single-Party Democracies*. Stanford, CA: Hoover Institution Press.

Kato, Junko. 1994. *The Problem of Bureaucratic Rationality: Tax Politics in Japan*. Princeton, NJ: Princeton University Press.

Katsuji, Yoshida. 1998 (Jan.–Mar.). "The Administrative Reform Debacle: Hashimoto's Nemesis." *Japan Quarterly* 45(1): 30–37.

Kitching, Leslie. 1995 (Feb.). Interview with author.

Koh, B. C. 1989. *Japan's Administrative Elite*. Berkeley, CA: University of California Press.

Krauss, Ellis S. 1989. "Politics and the Policy-Making Process." In *Democracy in Japan* (pp. 39–64), ed. Takeshi Isheda and Ellis S. Krauss. Pittsburgh: University of Pittsburgh Press.

Kunii, Irene M. 1998 (July 27). " 'I Hate the LDP': Japanese Voters Sent the Party a Message. Will It Get Through?" *Business Week* (3588): 40–42.

Lamont-Brown, Raymond. 1995 (April). "Japan's Quartet of Important Advisors." *Contemporary Review* 266(1551): 196–99.

Leblanc, Claude. 1998. *Le Japoscope 98*. Paris: Editions Ilyfunet.

Masumi, Junnosuke. 1992. "The 1955 System: Origin and Transformation." In *Creating Single-Party Democracies* (pp. 34–54), ed. Tetsuya Kataoka. Stanford, CA: Hoover Institution Press.

McMillian, Charles J. 1985. *The Japanese Industrial System*. New York: De Gruyter.

Milward, R. S. 1979. *Japan: The Past in the Present*. Kent, England: Paul Norbury.

Miyoshi, Masao, and H. D. Harootunian, eds. 1989. *Post-Modernism and Japan*. Durham, NC: Duke University Press.

Moeran, Brian. 1986. "Individual, Group and *Sishin*: Japan's Internal Cultural Debate." In *Japanese Culture and Behavior* (pp. 62–79), ed. Takie S. Lebra and William P. Lebra. Honolulu: University of Hawaii Press.

Mulgan, Aurelia G. 1997 (Dec.). "Electoral Determinant of Agrarian Power: Measuring Rural Decline in Japan." *Political Studies* 45(5): 875–900.

Nagashima, Atsushi. 1990. "Criminal Justice in Japan." In *Crime Prevention and Control in the United States and Japan*, ed. V. Kusuda-Smick. Dobbs Ferry, NY: Transnational Juris Publications.

Nagata, Jiro. 1998 (Sept.–Oct.). "LDP Civil War." *The International Economy* 12(5): 29–32.

Nakane, Chie. 1970. *Japanese Society*. Berkeley, CA: University of California Press.

Nakano, Koichi. 1998 (March). "The Politics of Administrative Reform in Japan, 1993–1998: Toward a More Accountable Government?" *Asian Survey* 38(3): 291–310.

Nimura, Kazuo. 1992. "The Trade Union Response to Migrant Workers." In *The Internationalization of Japan* (pp. 246–68), ed. Glenn D. Hook and Michael A. Weiner. London: Routledge.

Noguchi, Yoshi. 1992 (Mar. 1). "Dropping Out of Tokyo's Rat Race." *The New York Times*, p. F11.

Ohsumi, Haruyasu. 1992. "The Business Characteristics." *World Link* 1: 61.

Ozawa, Ichiro. 1993 (Spring). "My Commitment to Political Reform." *Japan Echo* 20(1): 8–12.

Pons, Philippe. 1998 (Mar. 22–Sept.). "Le Japon dans la Lumíere des Femmes." *Le Monde*, 17.

Reading, Brian. 1992. *Japan: The Coming Collapse*. London: Orion Books, Ltd.

Richardson, Bradley, and Scott Flanagan. 1984. *Politics in Japan*. Boston: Little, Brown.

Rothacher, Albrecht. 1993. *The Japanese Power Elite*. New York: St. Martin's.

Sartori, Tani. 1992. "The Japan Socialist Party Before the Mid-1960s." In *Creating Single-Party Democracies*, ed. Tetsuya Kataoka. Stanford, CA: Hoover Institution Press.

Sellek, Yoko, and Michael A. Weiner. 1992. "Migrant Workers: The Japanese Case in International Perspective." In *The Internationalization of Japan*, ed. Glenn D. Hook and Michael A. Weiner. London: Routledge.

Sessions, Dillon David. 1995 (Feb.). Interview with author.

Sheridan, Kyoko. 1993. *Governing the Japanese Economy*. Cambridge, England: Polity Press.

Shinoda, Tomohito. 1998 (July). "Japan's Decision Making Under the Coalition Governments." *Asian Survey* 38(7): 703–24.

Steinhoff, Patricia G. 1989. "Protest and Democracy." In *Democracy in Japan* (pp. 171–98), ed. Takeshi Ishida and Ellis S. Krauss. Pittsburgh: Pittsburgh University Press.

Sterngold, James. 1992 (Feb. 23). "Another Scandal in Japan." *The New York Times*, E3.

Sugiyama, Yasushi. 1992. "Internal and External Aspects of Internationalization." In *The Internationalization of Japan*, ed. Glenn D. Hook and Michael A. Weiner. London: Routledge.

Tadashi, Nakamae. 1998 (March 21). "Views from 2020." *The Economist* 346(8060): 25–27.

Taichi, Sakaiya. 1998 (Feb.) "The Myth of the Competent Bureaucrat." *Japan Echo* 25(1): 25–31.

Thurow, Lester. 1993. *Head to Head: The Coming Economic Battle Among Japan, Europe, and America*. New York: Warner Books.

van Wolferen, Karel. 1990. *The Enigma of Japanese Power*. New York: Vintage Press.

Wilson, George. 1992. *Patriots and Redeemers in Japan*. Chicago: The University of Chicago Press.

Woodiwiss, Anthony. 1992. *Law, Labour and Society in Japan: From Repression to Reluctant Recognition*. London: Routledge.

World Link. 1992 (Jan./Feb.). "Special Report: Japan." *World Link* 5(1): 50–69.

Woronoff, Jon. 1981. *Japan: The Coming Social Crisis*. Tokyo: Lotus Press.

Yakushiji, Taizo. 1992. "Japan's Political Change Towards Internationalization." In *The Internationalization of Japan*, ed. Glenn D. Hook and Michael A. Weiner. London: Routledge.

Part Three

The Decline of Communism

Transitions to Democracy and Capitalism

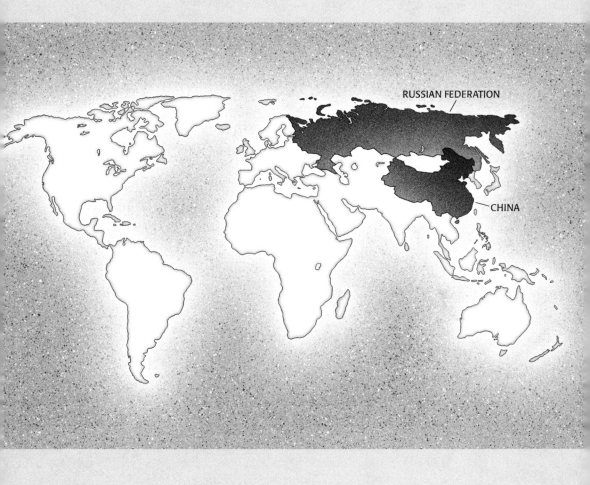

RUSSIAN FEDERATION

CHINA

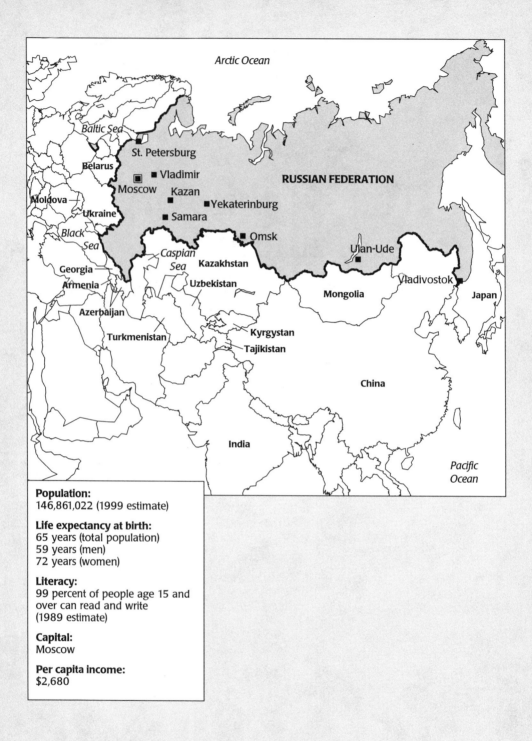

Population:
146,861,022 (1999 estimate)

Life expectancy at birth:
65 years (total population)
59 years (men)
72 years (women)

Literacy:
99 percent of people age 15 and
over can read and write
(1989 estimate)

Capital:
Moscow

Per capita income:
$2,680

6

The Russian Federation
The Transition to Democracy and Capitalism

The collapse of the Soviet Union[1] in August 1991 ranks high among the most dramatic events of modern history. As the world looked on, one of the most powerful nations on earth—a military superpower—simply disintegrated into fifteen independent states.

Of the new states created by the collapse of the Soviet Union, a reemergent Russia is by far the most imposing. Russia inherited 77 percent of the land area of the former Soviet Union; 51 percent of its population (147,400,000); 58 percent of its gross national product (GNP); and more than half of its military forces, including some 2,000,000 troops and 27,000 nuclear warheads. In the euphoria following the collapse of the Soviet Union, it is easy to forget that Russia continues to be a military superpower. The Soviet Union has collapsed, but Russia has not.

Having reemerged as an independent state after seventy years of Soviet rule, the Russian Federation, the official name of Russia, is attempting to make a transition from authoritarianism to democracy and from socialism to capitalism. The degree to which Russia succeeds in this transition will determine the course of world events for decades to come. A democratic and capitalist Russia would be a major force in sustaining the new world order now being forged by the United States and its allies. An authoritarian Russia, by contrast, could reopen the superpower conflict of an earlier era.

Russia's transition to democracy and capitalism, unfortunately, has not been smooth. Economic reforms have slowed and democracy is being challenged by a virulent Russian nationalism. Russia will not return to the communism of old, but it could well lapse into an authoritarianism reminiscent of Nazi Germany (Plutnik and Filimonov 1998; Gregor 1998).

---

[1]The former Union of Soviet Socialist Republics, or USSR, was commonly referred to as the Soviet Union.

If this were to happen, the West could find the new Russia even more dangerous than the Soviet Union that it replaced.

In the ensuing discussion of Russian politics, we will begin by examining the politics of the Russian Empire and the Soviet Union, respectively. In so doing, we will explore historical continuities that may be helpful in understanding the uncertainties of Russian politics today. Next, we will examine ongoing efforts to transform Russia into a democratic, free-market society. Particular stress will be placed on Western efforts to facilitate the transition process, some of which may have done more harm than good.

Russia in Historical and Cultural Perspective

Every political system is, to some extent, a prisoner of its past. In the case of modern Russia, this past was one of brutal authoritarianism as a Russian empire forged by autocratic tsars gave way to the world's first experiment in state communism. It is this legacy that the citizens of Russia must now overcome if they are to make a successful transition from dictatorship and socialism to democracy and capitalism. One cannot understand the difficulty that this transition entails without some familiarity with Russia's tsarist and communist legacies.

Tsarist Russia

It is difficult to date the origins of Russia with great precision. By the ninth century, Rus tribes had established a rudimentary state in the area that now constitutes the Ukraine and Western Russia. That state, however, did not endure and was overrun by Mongol tribes in the mid-thirteenth century (Hoetasch 1966). The fifteenth century witnessed the reestablishment of the Russian state in Muscovy, the general area surrounding Moscow. This new state did endure. Over the course of the next four hundred years, the Russian Empire gradually expanded to become the largest country on earth, bordering the United States on the east, Japan and China on the southeast, India and Afghanistan on the south, Iran and Turkey on the southwest, and Poland and Finland on the northwest.

Russia also became the center of the Orthodox Christian Church, with Moscow proclaiming itself the "Third Rome" following the Muslim conquest of Constantinople in 1453. There was no separation of church and state in imperial Russia, and the **tsars** used religion to legitimize an authoritarian system. By embracing Eastern Orthodoxy, Russia was also set apart from both the Renaissance and the Protestant Reformation, two intellectual currents that were to stimulate the evolution of democracy in Western Europe (Billington 1966).

The Russian Empire was built through the gradual absorption of its neighbors, a process that would find Russia's leaders attempting to weld each new conquest into the body politic of the Russian state.[2] The forced integration of its smaller neighbors created a Russia that was as complex and fragmented as it was large. Indeed, the end of the nineteenth century would find Russians a minority in their own empire (Pipes 1964). Most of Russia's more than 100 "nationalities" (as ethnic minorities were referred to) had its own language or, at the very least, its own national dialect. Many had their own religions, with approximately one-third of the empire's population being Muslim.

---

[2]Eastern Europe and Afghanistan were ruled through puppet regimes.

The Russian Empire, then, evolved as a volatile mix of ethnic and religious communities unified only by the power of the central government. The larger and more complex the empire became, the greater the force that was required to keep it together. It is not surprising, accordingly, that the three hallmarks of the Russian Empire were authoritarianism, centralization, and bureaucracy—the same three hallmarks that best describe the government of the Soviet Union. Russian tsars held absolute power; all policy decisions, however small, were made in Moscow and implemented by the massive tsarist bureaucracy. In spite of the modernization of Russia by Peter the Great (1682–1725) and some of Russia's other more enlightened tsars, the Russian people would not be granted a popularly elected parliament until 1905 (Massie 1980). Even then, the power of the tsars remained close to absolute (Salisbury 1978).

For all of its centralization and bureaucracy, Russia remained a largely feudal society until the eve of its collapse. Authoritarian tsars ruled with the support of an aristocracy of bureaucrats and landed gentry, all of whom lived off the labor of Russia's peasants.[3] Many of Russia's peasants were virtually owned by the aristocracy. The serfs (indentured peasants) were freed in the mid-1800s, but few enjoyed true autonomy (Blum 1964).

Russia would be the last of the major European states to industrialize, doing so largely in response to a growing military threat from the West. Napoleon's invasion of Russia in 1812 was repulsed, but it demonstrated both the weakness of the tsarist regime and the growing military power of Russia's industrialized neighbors. Some fifty years later, war with Britain in the Crimea would again demonstrate that Russia's peasant-based economy lacked the resources to fight a sustained war against an industrial power. Fearing further attack from the industrialized states of the West, Russia's leaders launched an aggressive program of industrialization. Nevertheless, by the beginning of the twentieth century, more than 90 percent of Russia's population still consisted of illiterate peasants.

It is important to note that Russia's industrialization was promoted by the state rather than by an emerging middle class or bourgeoisie. The weakness of the middle class accentuated the huge gap between the impoverished masses and the wealthy aristocracy, and it deprived Russia of a middle group capable of wresting democratic concessions from an all-powerful monarch.

Despite its efforts to industrialize, Russia was humiliated in 1905 in a brief war with Japan, a country far weaker than Russia's adversaries to the west. The Russo-Japanese War underscored the profound weakness of the tsarist regime and sparked a wave of mass protest that Lenin would call a "dress rehearsal" for the communist revolution of 1917. Order was restored by the tsar, but not without granting political reforms that included the establishment of a parliament, or Duma. Defeat by the Japanese also impelled a shaken tsarist regime to launch a program of forced industrialization that would transform Russia into the world's fifth largest industrial power within a decade. Russia remained the least developed of the European powers, but it was a power nonetheless (Nove 1992).

Ironically, it was an industrialization program designed to strengthen the tsarist regime that led to its undoing (Diller 1992). Peasants flocked to industrial centers in search of wealth, only to find themselves working for pitiful wages in appalling conditions reminiscent of the early days of industrialization in Britain and France. Labor unions, first introduced into Russia following the political reforms of 1905, became a

---

[3]Unlike the pattern of feudalism in England and France, the power of Russia's landed aristocracy was limited by Ivan the Terrible's use of the *oprichnina,* a historical forerunner of the secret police. The aristocracy did, however, form a privileged class that was expected to finance the monarchy and keep the peasants in check (Green 1994).

Roadside scene from a Russian peasant village near the end of the nineteenth century. In feudal Russia, the bureaucrats and landowners lived off the labor of the peasants, many of whom were virtually owned by the aristocracy.

fertile breeding ground for Marxists and other radical groups. Government repression was brutal, but it served only to hasten the politicization of a proletariat that now consisted of some 4,000,000 industrial workers. The more the regime attempted to crush its opponents, the more it pushed the country toward the brink of revolution.

The final decade of the monarchy was a time of intense intellectual activity as the opponents of the tsarist regime plotted its downfall. Moderate forces advocated a British-style constitutional monarchy, while anarchists argued that political authority was both unnecessary and undesirable (Coker 1934). Few doctrines, however, were more intensely debated than those of Karl Marx.

The interplay of political and intellectual forces leading to the collapse of the tsarist monarchy is far too complex to be recounted in a few paragraphs. Suffice it to say that Russia's entry into World War I strained the tsarist regime to the breaking point. Losses were heavy, and the burden on the Russian people was immense. In the spring of 1917, massive food riots erupted in St. Petersburg and other major cities. Soldiers mutinied, and *popular councils* called "**soviets**" seized control of local governments. Tsar Nicholas II abdicated on March 3, 1917, bringing the tsarist monarchy to an end (Wolfe 1964). He and his family were killed shortly thereafter.

Soldiers and workmen took control of the Duma (parliament) in Petrograd during the Russian Revolution in 1917.

The collapse of the tsarist monarchy gave way to a confused period in which power was shared between the Duma and the soviets. The Duma attempted to implement something approaching liberal democracy, while the leaders of the soviets plotted revolution (Sakwa 1989). Lenin, the brilliant leader of a faction of the communist movement referred to as the **Bolsheviks**, soon gained control of the soviets in Moscow, St. Petersburg, and other major industrial cities, a base that would enable him to seize control of the Russian government on October 24, 1917 (Pipes 1964). The Soviet Union was born.[4]

The Union of Soviet Socialist Republics (USSR)

The goal of Lenin and the Bolsheviks was to transform the Russian Empire into a powerful industrial state capable of spearheading a global proletarian revolution. Lenin was under no illusions concerning the enormity of his task. The legacy of the empire was heavy, and Russia's industrialization lagged far behind that of the West. The communist leadership also expected the capitalist powers to crush the young Marxist state in order to prevent communism in Russia from spreading throughout the world. Such fears would dominate Soviet policy throughout its history.

Lenin's immediate concern was not world revolution but the consolidation of his own revolution. The old Russian Empire was disintegrating as soldiers deserted the front and ethnic nationalities pressed for independence. Unless the situation could be brought under control, the communists would be consumed by the revolution that they had been so instrumental in fomenting. In order to bring the war to an end, Lenin signed a disadvantageous peace treaty with Germany in 1918. He had little choice in the matter.

The collapse of the tsarist regime found the Bolsheviks to be a party of no more than 25,000[5] members, their influence coming less from their numbers than from

---

[4]Technically, the USSR, or the Soviet Union, was formally established by the Constitution of 1918.
[5]Figures vary according to source.

their organizational discipline. The Bolsheviks, however, enjoyed strong support among the urban workers, nearly 200,000[6] of whom would join the communist ranks between the collapse of the tsar in March 1917 and the October Revolution of the same year (Baradat 1992).

A rapid increase in party membership enabled Lenin to seize control of Moscow and other major cities, but the countryside remained in the hands of his opponents. The irreconcilable positions of the two sides plunged Russia into a civil war of devastating ferocity that would rage for more than two years. In the process, the communists forged a political and military organization that would enable them to dominate the Russian Empire in a manner undreamed of by the most ambitious of the tsars.

Lenin had provided much of the intellectual, spiritual, and organizational genius of the Bolshevik movement, and his stature in the annals of world history would rank with that of Lincoln, Churchill, Gandhi, and others who left an indelible stamp on the history of their era (Shub 1966). Two other individuals, however, were also to play a crucial role in shaping the course of the Soviet state (Wolfe 1964). The first was Leon Trotsky, a dazzling intellect who forged the Red Army. It was that army, some 5,000,000 strong by the end of the civil war, that assured the victory of the Bolsheviks (Sakwa 1989). The second was Joseph Stalin, a skilled and ruthless party organizer who used his position as general secretary of the Party to build a foundation of personal power within the Party's administrative apparatus. When Lenin suffered a dehabilitating stroke in1932, power passed to Stalin.

Lenin refused to name a successor, choosing instead to offer critical evaluations of his two colleagues. Trotsky, in Lenin's assessment, was excessively self-assured and preoccupied with administrative details. As for Stalin, Lenin wrote, "Comrade Stalin, having become General Secretary, has concentrated enormous power in his hands, and I am not sure whether he will always be capable of using that authority with sufficient caution" (Lewin 1989, 60).

The Politics of Totalitarianism. Having consolidated their power, the Bolsheviks (renamed the Communist Party of the Soviet Union) faced the task of transforming the Soviet Union from a nation of illiterate peasants into a modern industrial power. That task, as Trotsky would write in his *Defense of Terrorism,* could only be achieved by the use of overwhelming force:

> No organization except the army has ever controlled man with such severe compulsion as does the state organization of the working-class in the difficult period of transition.... The state, before disappearing, assumes...the most ruthless form (and) embraces authoritatively the life of the citizens in every direction (Trotsky 1934, 157).

The Communist Party's ruthless pursuit of industrialization and military power would be matched only by the Nazi regime in Germany, if then. Indeed, Stalinist rule was to introduce a new concept to the realm of political discourse: **totalitarianism.** No area of human endeavor was to escape the scrutiny of the all-pervasive state.

Totalitarianism, Soviet-style, rested on five key elements: party dominance in the political realm, socialism in the economic realm, creation of a "New Soviet Man" in the socio-cultural realm, and thought control in the psychological realm, all of which were underscored by the pervasive use of terror.

The foundation of totalitarian rule in the Soviet Union was party supremacy. Suspected opponents of the Communist party were either shot or sent to forced labor camps (gulags), a policy that would apply to opponents of Stalin as well (Rigby 1992). Soviet military commanders, while invariably ranking members of

---

[6]Figures vary according to source.

The Great Terror

During the Stalinist era, an average of 8,000,000 citizens were incarcerated in the Soviet labor camps at any given time. The purges of 1937 and 1938, often referred to as the "great terror," witnessed the arrest of more than 5,000,000 Soviet citizens, 1,000,000 of whom are assumed to have been shot (Wheatcroft 1981; Rosefielde 1981; Conquest 1971).

---

the Party, were paired with a corresponding political commissar, military orders requiring the approval of both. In much the same manner, no social groups, however innocuous, were allowed to exist independent of the Communist Party. Soviet logic was simple: sustained political opposition is essentially a group affair, and any group, however innocent its pretext, possesses the capacity to serve as a nucleus for opposition to the regime. The partial exception to this principle was the Orthodox Church; religious activity was discouraged but not eliminated.[7] To be religious, however, was to be looked at with suspicion.

The economic realm requires little elaboration, for the very essence of Marxism is the belief that economic power is the source of political power. *All factories, farms,*[8] *mines, and other means of production were nationalized by the communist regime,* their activities being micro-managed by economic planners in Moscow. Any form of capitalist activity, however minor, was condemned as counter-revolutionary and its perpetrators sent to labor camps.

In the social, cultural, and psychological realms, the Stalinist regime demanded the mobilization of Soviet citizens in mind as well as in body. Soviet artists, writers, schools, mass media, unions, and youth organizations were all mobilized to create a "New Soviet Man" who was "disciplined, working steadily and consistently, puritanical in conduct and motivation" (Bauer, Inkeles, and Kluckhohn 1956, 162). All information was managed by the state; Soviet citizens received only news that supported the regime and its objectives.

The Terror. Underpinning the edifice of totalitarian rule was a terror so pervasive that Soviet citizens would come to distrust their closest friends. Informers were everywhere, and children were even encouraged to spy on their parents and relatives (Bauer, Inkeles, and Kluckholn 1956). In many instances, individuals were arrested simply for fitting the wrong profile:

> A person may be arrested not because he has done something, but because his "objective" characteristics suggest that he *might* do something—e.g., a member of his family may have been declared an "enemy of the people," he may have lived in German-occupied territory under compromising circumstances, he may have been a member of a group which has fallen into disfavor or the associate or protege of some deposed political figure, or in the earlier years of the regime his "social origins" may have been suspect. Any sign which may point to a person's loyalty being *potentially* weak—even if only because the state has done him an injustice—can serve as the basis for… arrest (Bauer, Inkeles, and Kluckholn 1956, 79).

The purpose of the terror was to atomize the Soviet population by making individuals afraid to communicate with one another. Party control over social organizations, then, was reinforced by a profound sense of psychological isolation (Ticktin 1992; Arendt 1951). Soviet citizens, moreover, soon discovered that the best way to avoid the terror was to display exaggerated support for the regime and its policies.

---

[7]Religion was too deeply ingrained among the Russian population to be totally eliminated.
[8]Peasants were allowed to retain small plots of land.

Huge rallies and a swelling Communist Party membership created the illusion that the Soviet regime enjoyed far broader popular support than was actually the case. Illusion or not, thoughts of revolt became both dangerous and futile.

The Stalinist regime was to score impressive economic, social, and military gains, but it was not to achieve its goal of creating a "New Soviet Man." Terror designed to force compliance with the goals of the regime merely pushed the population into greater passivity. Russians marched when ordered and stopped when the pressure stopped. Informal "mutual-support" groups also emerged to ease the harshness of Soviet life (Bauer, Inkeles, and Kluckhohn 1956). Some informal groups took the form of **patron-client networks** in which a senior official looked after the interests of his clients in return for their political support. The fall of a patron, needless to say, was a disaster for all concerned. Other groups were less structured, serving merely to share food and favors and to break the unbearable strain of psychological isolation. The regime also failed to create a classless society; an aristocracy of tsarist bureaucrats had merely given way to an aristocracy of communist bureaucrats (Armstrong 1959).

World War II. Stalin believed that a clash between the communist state and its capitalist adversaries was inevitable, yet the first foreign attack on the Soviet Union did not occur until June 1941. It was on that date that Hitler, having conquered most of Europe, broke an earlier nonaggression pact with Stalin and unleashed his armies against the Soviet Union. Heroic resistance by the Red Army and the harshness of Russia's winters combined to stall the German advance at the gates of Moscow, but the costs of World War II were immense. As described by Nove:

> After decades of silence, it is now possible to cite fairly reliable estimates of human losses, which vastly exceeded those of World War I. Close to 8 million were killed, over 5 million captured by the enemy, many of whom died in prisoner-of-war camps. Altogether, the evidence points to demographic losses of about 27 million people, that is to say the population at the end of 1945 was 27 million lower (on comparable territory) than it was in June 1941, but this includes civilian losses (a million in the siege of Leningrad alone, and over a million Jews slaughtered by the Germans)....
>
> Of the 11.6 million horses in occupied territory, 7 million were killed or taken away, as were 20 out of 23 million pigs. 137,000 tractors, 49,000 grain combines and large numbers of cowsheds and other farm buildings were destroyed. Transport was hit by the destruction of 65,000 kilometers of railway track, loss of or damage to 15,800 locomotives, 428,000 goods wagons, 4,280 riverboats, and half of all the railway bridges in occupied territory. Almost 50 per cent of all urban living space in this territory, 1.2 million houses, was destroyed, as well as 3.5 million houses in rural areas (Nove 1992, 291).

Even after sustaining such massive losses, the USSR emerged from World War II as one of the world's two superpowers, its immense land armies threatening to over-run a war-battered Europe. The United States countered Soviet superiority in land-based troops with the formation of the North Atlantic Treaty Organization (NATO), a military alliance of the West's major industrial powers. NATO forces were also placed under the nuclear shield of the United States, an attack on Western Europe being tantamount to an attack on the United States. The result was a Cold War in which each side threatened the other with the possibility of nuclear annihilation.

Political power in the Soviet Union was totally dominated by the Communist Party, a vast organizational network that concentrated authority in the hands of its "secretary general." The secretary general "consulted" with a **Politburo**, or *executive committee comprised of powerful political and military leaders.* A far broader committee, the Central Committee, represented the Soviet Union's second echelon of elites. Parallel organizational structures existed at the provincial and local levels of the Soviet Union, each responding to orders from on high. Dissent of any form was not allowed.

The Party's ability to totally dominate Soviet society was facilitated by its control of the nation's social and professional organizations (Baradat 1992). Young children joined the Octoberists, teens the Young Pioneers, and young adults the Komsomol, or Communist Youth League. Workers, lawyers, farmers, veterans, writers, artists, scientists, and managers all possessed their own Party-sponsored unions, as did virtually every other group in Soviet society. Nothing escaped the purview of the Party, its labor unions alone enrolling more than 130,000,000 members (Baradat 1992). The Party also kept an eye on its citizens via a vast network of Party inspectors. These, in turn, were supported by voluntary citizen inspectors as well as other party activists (Theen 1993).

The Evolution of the Soviet Union. The basic political structure described above was put in place by Stalin and changed little over the next four decades. The substance of Soviet politics, however, changed substantially over the years.

First, the "terror" of the Stalinist era was sharply curtailed by his successors, with rule by fear giving way to a more benign form of administrative authoritarianism (Hauslohner 1989). The capacity for terror, however, remained, and dissidents (often referred to as *refuseniks* because of their unwillingness to accept the Party) were routinely sent to labor camps or mental hospitals.

Second, Stalin's heirs attempted to create a set of "informal" rules that would preclude the emergence of a new Stalin (Rigby 1984; Hauslohner 1989). Henceforth, the Party would be ruled by what the Soviet elite referred to as "collective leadership." While the rules of collective leadership were not explicit, something approaching a "balance of power" would emerge within the Politburo and the Central Committee (Kelley 1987). The new rules also made the general secretary more accountable to the Politburo and the Central Committee and increased the institutional stability of the Soviet System.

Third, post-Stalinist leaders attempted to increase the legitimacy of the communist regime by improving the quality of Soviet life. A true welfare state was created in which the vast majority of Soviet citizens were provided with employment, housing, education, and health care. The quality of services was poor by Western standards, but it was a clear improvement over the Stalinist and tsarist eras. Greater stress was also placed on the production of consumer goods (Hauslohner 1989).

The evolution of the Soviet system in the post-Stalinist era was guided by the leadership of three men: Nikita Khrushchev, Leonid Brezhnev, and Mikhail Gorbachev.

The Khrushchev Era (1957–1964). Nikita Khrushchev assumed the mantle of Soviet leadership in 1957, vowing to modernize the Soviet economy and revitalize the Communist Party. The Khrushchev era was to witness some dazzling successes, including the 1957 launching of Sputnik, the world's first space satellite. Stalin was also denounced, giving hope for a more humane political environment. Khrushchev, however, was unable to revive a moribund Soviet economy, and his efforts to reform the Party apparatus resulted in his removal from office. Few Party members at any level were willing to have their security jeopardized by the magnitude of reform that would have been necessary to truly revitalize the Soviet system (Kelley 1987). Khrushchev was not executed, but he became a "non-person" whose existence was purged from the Soviet history books.

The Brezhnev Era (1964–1982). Khrushchev was followed in office by Leonid Brezhnev, a Politburo member less enamored of radical reform than his predecessor.

Brezhnev offered Party bureaucrats increased job security in exchange for increased performance. The compromise failed (Kelley 1987).

All in all, the Brezhnev era was a time of remarkable stability, the Khrushchev reforms were pushed aside and business within the mammoth bureaucracy continued much as usual (Kelley 1987). That stability, however, was illusory, as the Soviet economy continued to deteriorate and the Soviet population became increasingly alienated from a system that had trouble meeting their basic needs (Hauslohner 1989; Lapidus 1989; Bahry and Silver 1990).

The Gorbachev Era (1985–1991). By 1985, the balance of power in the Politburo and Central Committee had shifted to the side of the reformers, paving the way for the appointment of Mikhail Gorbachev as general secretary.[9] Opposition to Gorbachev's appointment was intense, but the time for reform had arrived (Bialer 1989).

The Gorbachev reforms began with a call for *greater openness and democracy within the Soviet system,* a process conveyed by the Russian term **glasnost**. The logic of glasnost, according to Gorbachev, was simple. The terror of the Stalinist era and the administrative suffocation of the Brezhnev years had created a population that was alienated from its political system. Mass apathy, moreover, had led to the stagnation of the Soviet economy. The situation had now reached crisis proportions and could only be reversed by energizing the Soviet masses and renewing their faith in the system. To accomplish this, the masses would have to be empowered, regardless of what that might mean for the Party and its bureaucratic apparatus (Bialer 1989). These were powerful words for an ardent communist, but the salvation of the Communist Party, in Gorbachev's view, required no less.

Glasnost was part of a broader process called **perestroika**, or *structural reform. The goal of perestroika was to break the grip of the government and party bureaucracies on the Soviet economy* by giving factory managers increased flexibility in the management of their plants (Hewett and Winston 1991). Managers, in turn, were expected to make a profit and to increase the quality of their products. Changes in the political system were equally sweeping, with elections to government councils at all levels featuring multiple candidates elected by secret ballot following an extended period of free and open discussion.[10] Experimentation with small-scale capitalism was also encouraged (Spulber 1991).

Gorbachev declared the Cold War to be over and pledged world peace in exchange for Western cooperation in rebuilding the Soviet economy. Matching his words with deeds, Gorbachev relaxed Soviet controls over its client states in Eastern Europe, allowing each to form its own government independent of Moscow. Some former communist regimes collapsed in the face of popular revolts, while others moved toward greater democracy of their own accord. No symbol of the end of the Cold War, however, was more poignant than the collapse of the Berlin Wall in 1989 and the subsequent reunification of Germany, a country that had been responsible for some 27 million Soviet deaths during the Second World War.

Gorbachev's reforms, however profound by Soviet standards, came too late to save a system well on its way to collapse (Mandel 1992; Duch 1993). Hardline conservatives scuttled Gorbachev's reforms from within, while the leaders of the

---

[9]Between 1982 and 1985, Gorbachev was preceded in office by Yuri Andropov and Konstantin Chernenko, both of whom died shortly after taking office.

[10]A Congress of People's Deputies was added to the parliamentary structure, one-third of its membership being chosen in free elections. The members of the Congress of the People's Deputies, in turn, were charged with electing both the president of the republic and the members of the Supreme Soviet, a body now reduced to some 400 members (Bialer 1989). Gorbachev was duly elected president, assuming control of both the Party and state apparatus.

"nationalities" used the new democracy to press for ever-greater autonomy (Willerton 1992). Lithuania and the other Baltic states forcibly annexed by the USSR during World War II proclaimed their independence from the USSR in 1991, but Gorbachev was reluctant to crush the Baltic revolts for fear of jeopardizing promised economic aid from the West. He may also have been apprehensive about using the army against Soviet citizens, as it had become increasingly clear that the Marxist state was withering away.

The Commonwealth of Independent States (CIS). On December 8, 1991, Russia, the Ukraine, and Belorussia proclaimed their independence as sovereign states and signed a treaty forming the Commonwealth of Independent States (CIS). Most other former Soviet Republics would follow suit (Willerton 1992). The Soviet Union had ceased to exist. The new states created by the breakup of the USSR are illustrated in Figure 6.1.

The Commonwealth of Independent States was a voluntary association formed to preserve the benefits of economic and military integration that had existed under the Soviet system[11] (Diller 1992). The Commonwealth Treaty remains in place, but its effectiveness is limited at best. Economic agreements are honored in the breach, and conflict over the control of former Soviet weapons has shattered any serious hope of forging a unified military command.[12]

Hopes for an effective commonwealth have also been dampened by ethnic conflicts within and between the newly independent republics. Several countries erupted in civil war as competing nationalities attempted to create ethnically pure states, while other republics attacked their neighbors in the hope of resolving boundary disputes. The reconstitution process will take decades to sort itself out, and the ultimate outcome is uncertain.

The Soviet Union: A Postmortem and a Legacy. Why did a superpower as overtly successful as the Soviet Union simply collapse? It is doubtful that the debate surrounding this question will ever be fully resolved, yet certain factors hold particular importance. Of these, four are remarkably similar to the factors that led to the collapse of the tsarist empire (Smith 1992).

First, the Soviets, like their tsarist counterparts, had failed to solve the "nationalities" problem. The Soviet Union had been integrated economically, but it had not been integrated either culturally or politically. Indeed, most of the Soviet Union's more than 100 ethnic groups retained a strong sense of "national" identity and resented Russian dominance (Bremmer and Taras 1993). In the words of one senior Russian official, there was a common perception "that the USSR is an empire in which Russia is the metropolis and the national republics the colonies" (Kux 1990, 17). Once the Soviet system began to weaken, the pressure for greater "national" autonomy became irresistible.

A second similarity between collapse of the tsarist empire and the collapse of the USSR is to be found in the alienation and passivity of the Soviet masses. The totalitarian regime could force the Soviet population into submission, but it could not force them to embrace the system.

---

[11]Latvia, Lithuania, Estonia, and Georgia did not join the Commonwealth of Independent States.
[12]Russia originally demanded approximately two-thirds of all Soviet weapons but settled for less (*CSM,* Oct. 13, 1992, 2; *Economist,* Mar. 25, 1992; *Economist,* May 30, 1992). Nuclear weapons were to have been returned to Russian territory, a process initiated by Gorbachev during the final years of the USSR, but the collapse of the USSR would find nuclear arsenals in four former Soviet republics: Russia, the Ukraine, Kazakhstan, and Belarus. Also problematic are the stockpiles of enriched uranium and laboratories required to support a nuclear arsenal (*Economist,* Mar. 14, 1992). The nuclear question has yet to be fully resolved.

Figure 6.1
States of the Former Soviet Union

A third area of similarity between the collapse of the tsarist empire and the collapse of the USSR is to be found in the rigid and parasitic nature of their respective bureaucracies (McAuley 1992). As discussed by Hillel Ticktin, there was little that Gorbachev could do to alter the situation:

Gorbachev…embarked on wholesale dismissals of ministers, the closing down of entire ministries, the merging of ministries, and the devolution of tasks down to enterprises. The simple effect of removing the old corrupt bureaucrats and replacing them with new, dynamic corrupt bureaucrats undoubtedly stirred people up and compelled management to find ways of forcing workers to work better, but this could only last a short time. Workers and managers became increasingly tired of exhortations and threats. Gorbachev could not imprison the large numbers incarcerated under Stalin in order to increase

The Western Response to Gorbachev

The United States and its allies were not casual bystanders in the reform process. Gorbachev pleaded for Western assistance in his reform effort, but the Western response was as confused as Gorbachev's reforms themselves. Gorbachev was honored as a hero, but little aid was forthcoming, the West being unsure of how to assist a decaying economic system that remained largely socialist in orientation. While some Western leaders urged massive loans for the Gorbachev regime, others cautioned that it made little sense to pour money into a sinking ship. Still others argued that it was best for the ship to sink; why should capitalist powers attempt to salvage a communist regime? Whatever the reasons, Gorbachev was left to dangle in the wind.

production; he was compelled simply to rant along about "making life harsh for those who do not work" (Ticktin 1992, 155).

A fourth similarity between the collapse of the tsarist empire and the collapse of the USSR is to be found in "the Western problem." The USSR, like the tsarist empire before it, labored under a pervasive fear that its survival was threatened by the technological superiority of the West. The longer the arms race continued, the greater the technology gap between the two power blocs became. America's "star wars" initiative, however fanciful, threatened to put the technology race out of reach. The economic burden of the arms race with the West placed excessive strains on a weak Soviet economy and deprived its population of basic necessities.

It would be a mistake, however, to draw too close a parallel between the collapse of tsarist Russia and the collapse of the Soviet Union. The essence of the Soviet system was **socialism**: *the belief that state ownership of the means of production could provide a more rational allocation of a society's resources than capitalism. The most fundamental reason for the collapse of the USSR was that socialism, at least as practiced in the USSR, did not result in the rational allocation of the Soviet Union's resources.* Control of the economy was placed in the hands of a massive, centralized bureaucracy that lacked the capacity to address the complex needs of the largest country on earth (Campbell 1992). Delays, confusion, and shortages became the norm as managers of factories and collective farms struggled to meet unrealistic production goals established by State planners in Moscow (Nove 1992). Managers also responded to pressure from Moscow by placing quantity above quality, a problem that had existed from the earliest days of the Soviet regime.

The collapse of the USSR was also hastened by the decay of the Communist Party, the leadership of which had become immobilized. Wedded to the past, Soviet leaders were reluctant to chart a new course for the future. This was particularly the case during the Brezhnev era. The problem, however, was not merely one of leadership. Seventy years of unchallenged rule had dulled the zeal of Party members and transformed one-time revolutionaries into self-serving bureaucrats (Kelley 1987).

Finally, many observers place the blame for the breakup of the Soviet Union on the reform process itself. Gorbachev was committed to reforming the Soviet system, but there is little evidence that he had a clear plan in mind or that he appreciated the severity of the USSR's economic woes (Nove 1992; Bialer 1989). The first two years of the reform effort were a period of trial and error. In some instances, reforms that met strong resistance were replaced by others of a less threatening nature. In other instances, cautious reforms were strengthened to increase their effectiveness. The result was a confusion of half-hearted and sometimes contradictory policies that sought a middle ground between socialism and capitalism and between democracy and authoritarianism (Dowlah 1992; Kux 1990). Such middle ground, however, was not to be found (Nove 1992).

President Boris Yeltsin makes a point after leaving a Moscow polling place, while his wife, Naina, looks on.

Russia Reborn

If Mikhail Gorbachev presided over the collapse of the USSR, it would be Boris Yeltsin, his one-time supporter, who would guide the rebirth of the Russian state (Morrison 1991).

Yeltsin, a mining engineer by training and the First Secretary of a regional Party organization, was brought to Moscow as part of Gorbachev's effort to instill new life in the Party apparatus. Yeltsin soon became a key figure in the Central Committee, being a tireless worker and an outspoken advocate of Gorbachev's reforms. Gorbachev made Yeltsin a candidate member (junior member) of the Politburo in 1986, using him to lead the charge against his conservative opponents. Yeltsin's commitment to reform, however, far outpaced that of an unsure Gorbachev, and his thinly veiled attacks on Gorbachev's "hesitancy" weakened Gorbachev's position within the Politburo. Gorbachev responded by removing Yeltsin from the Politburo in 1987, a move which, under normal circumstances, would have spelled the end of Yeltsin's political career. Circumstances, however, were far from normal, and 1991 would see Yeltsin become the first democratically elected president of the Russian Republic (province).

Yeltsin would use his position as president of the Russian Republic to accelerate the pace of reform within the Soviet Union and to demand ever-greater independence for the Soviet Union's fifteen republics (provinces). Yeltsin's efforts brought him tremendous popularity, and his personal stature quickly surpassed that of Gorbachev. They also spelled the end of the USSR.

The Transition to Democracy and Capitalism. With the breakup of the Soviet Union later in 1991, Boris Yeltsin would proclaim the newly independent Russian Federation (Russia's formal designation) to be a democratic republic. Russia's socialist economy, Yeltsin said, would be transformed into a free-market economy within the broader framework of a world capitalist system. Gorbachev's reforms, in Yeltsin's view, had failed because they sought a compromise between Party control and democracy and between socialism and capitalism. The new Russia, he said, would not make the same mistake.

The transition to democracy and capitalism, however, would prove difficult. No one was absolutely sure what should be done or how to go about it. Theories abounded, but theories are often wrong, and much would depend on the results of trial and error. Russia may have been reborn, but it was not starting with a clean slate. The leaders of the new Russia were reformed communists, and the best-organized groups in the new Russia were the remnants of the old Communist Party. The citizens of the new Russia, moreover, had been socialized into politics under the Soviet system, and nothing in their prior experience had prepared them for either democracy or capitalism. In addition, citizens in the Soviet Union were brought up under an economic system that, whatever its failings, provided them with a great deal of economic security. Their standard of living was below that of the West, but people did have jobs and enough food to eat. It was not clear that the Russian electorate would be willing to jeopardize that security for the vague promise of capitalist prosperity somewhere down the road. This was not an insignificant worry, for the transition to capitalism promised to be extremely painful. The transition process, then, was not starting from zero. Much of what had been done under the communist regime would have to be undone by its successors.

Under socialism, providing jobs was more important than making a profit, and most Soviet factories had far more workers than they needed. If a factory didn't make a profit, the government merely provided subsidies to keep it afloat. Few Russian firms showed a profit in the Western sense of the word. Soviet workers also had little incentive to work hard; their wages were low, and raises and other benefits were more or less automatic. With the transition to capitalism, Russian firms would need to become profitable. Excess employees would be laid off and unprofitable firms closed down. Job security and a cradle-to-grave welfare system would also become relics of the past. The harsh side of capitalism, then, was a source of grave concern to many Russians who, while welcoming a capitalist lifestyle, were reluctant to jeopardize the economic safety net provided by socialism. Indeed, as rational actors, it would be logical for the Russian electorate to use its new democratic freedom to vote for a continuation of socialism. Capitalism would have to prove its utility in a hurry or suffer the consequences.

Institution Building in Democratic Russia. Russia emerged from the breakup of the USSR with a political system that was as bewildering to the politicians as it was to the general public (Hahn 1992). By and large, its new leaders made up the rules as they went along (Bremmer and Taras 1993). As long as Yeltsin's popularity remained intact, there was little the Parliament could do to oppose his policies. Indeed, the Parliament granted Yeltsin the power to rule by decree during Russia's first year of independence. They had little choice, for without a strong leader, Russia would have dissolved into chaos. *Yeltsin used his emergency powers to implement a sweeping program of capitalist reforms suggested by his American advisors. Often referred to as "shock therapy," the reforms were designed to dismantle the old socialist economy in the shortest time possible.* The sooner Russia embraced capitalism, the American argument went, the sooner it would be placed on the path to economic growth and prosperity. There would be hardships for Russia's workers, but that was the price of cleaning up the economic mess created by seventy years of socialism. Proceeding slowly would merely prolong the pain.

The rapid pace of Yeltsin's economic reforms soon encountered strong opposition throughout Russian society, it being one thing to talk about reform but quite another to do it. *While a minority of Russians prospered under the capitalist reforms, the majority feared losing the social safety net that they had long taken for granted.* After one year of reform, Yeltsin himself would be forced to admit that things were getting worse rather than better (*NYT,* Dec. 2, 1992, A8).

The stage was thus set for a confrontation between the forces of political and economic reform embodied in the person of Boris Yeltsin and the forces of resistance embodied in the Parliament.

Irregular forces loyal to the Parliament stormed key government buildings in a move that was broadly interpreted as an attempted coup. Army divisions loyal to the Parliament were also rumored to be on the outskirts of Moscow. They failed to materialize, and Yeltsin ordered the Parliament evacuated. The conservative deputies, however, refused to leave the Parliament building and challenged Yeltsin to evict them by force (*NYT,* Sept. 29, 1993, A6). Supporters of both sides poured into the streets, and Yeltsin, perhaps fearing civil war, ordered the army to shell the Parliament. It did so, albeit reluctantly, bringing the crisis to an end on October 5, 1993. Yeltsin would rule by decree until the convening of the new Parliament, or Duma, in January 1994 (*NYT,* Oct. 6, 1993, A4).

Elections: 1993, 1995, 1996, 1999. Elections were duly held on December 12, 1993, with Russia's voters being asked to elect a new Parliament and to approve a new Constitution that had been designed by Yeltsin a few months earlier. As a democratic exercise, Russia's first post-Soviet election left much to be desired. Electoral procedures were not agreed upon until a few days before the election, making electoral strategy rudimentary at best. The draft Constitution, itself, would not be presented to the voters until about a month (thirty-three days) before the election, hardly adequate time for serious debate in a country as large and diverse as Russia.

The electoral system that evolved was similar to that of Germany, with half of the 450 seats in the lower house, now renamed the State Duma, being elected by single-member districts and the other half being elected by party lists—confusing stuff for a nation with little experience in democratic practice.[13] Few of the parties involved in the election, moreover, were more than a month or two old, and voters were unfamiliar with the programs and the candidates.

Approval of the Constitution was a victory for Yeltsin, but the results of the parliamentary election were not. The Russia's Choice Party, the main party supporting Yeltsin's economic reforms, remained a minority in a Duma dominated by anti-reform parties ranging from the very conservative to the profoundly anti-democratic. The most startling result of the parliamentary elections was the emergence of the neo-fascist "Liberal Democratic Party" as the second-largest party in the Duma. Vladimir Zhirinovsky, the party's leader and an announced candidate for the 1996 presidential elections, was widely referred to as the Russian Hitler (*CSM,* Jan. 10, 1994, 2). The Communist Party had also made a strong showing. The 1995 legislative elections saw a revitalized Communist

---

[13]If a party received 20 percent of the vote, it received 20 percent of the 250 seats to be elected by the parties. Those seats would be filled by names on a list prepared by each party, starting at the top of the list. This assured that party leaders would be well represented in the Duma.

Party emerge as Russia's largest vote-getter, but Zhirinovsky continued to make a strong showing with approximately 10 percent of the vote. Either way, Russian democracy was showing signs of strain.

The Communists continued to show strength in the months preceding the 1996 presidential elections, and early polls gave the Communist candidate, Gennady Zyuganov, a ten-point lead over a faltering Yeltsin (*Economist,* April 13, 1996, 42). Fears of a Communist victory were also fueled by continuing questions concerning Yeltsin's health. Indeed, a series of apparent heart attacks in 1995 cast doubt on Yeltsin's capacity to run at all. Moscow was also rife with rumors that the elections would be postponed, the more virulent of which accused the military of plotting a coup d'état (*IHT,* June 22, 1996, 5).

Yeltsin won the 1996 presidential election, but serious questions remained concerning his health and his ability to rule. Many but not all of the presidential powers were temporarily granted to the prime minister as Yeltsin prepared for heart surgery in 1996. Had Yeltsin passed away, new presidential elections would have been held within three months. Had Yeltsin merely lost the capacity to rule, power would have been shifted to the prime minister. This was not a simple proposition, however, for according to a member of the Constitutional Court, it was Yeltsin who would decide at which point he was no longer capable of ruling in an effective manner (*CSM,* Sept. 24, 1996, 7).

Because of this uncertainty, the remainder of Yeltsin's term in office would be characterized by profound **immobilism** as Yeltsin would collapse in illness only to reassert his power by sacking those whom he had appointed to key positions during earlier periods of lucidity. Emboldened by Yeltsin's sagging popularity—a reported 2 percent expressed confidence in Yeltsin in a 1998 poll—his opponents in the Duma sparked a constitutional crisis by rejecting his choice for prime minister on two successive occasions (*Le Monde,* Oct. 13, 1998, 4). Had they rejected his candidate a third time, Yeltsin would have suffered a humiliating defeat and his capacity for leadership would have been largely destroyed (*Le Monde,* Sept. 2, 1998, 3). A last-minute compromise between the two sides was worked out with the selection of Yevgeny Primakov, an old-time communist and ex-spy-master, as the new prime minister. He would be the first of at least five prime ministers appointed by Yeltsin during the next two years (*IHT,* Aug. 17, 1999, www). All promised reform, but little was forthcoming, as Russian politics and the Russian economy entered a holding pattern that would last until the next presidential election constitutionally mandated for the year 2000. Meanwhile, the Russian economy neared collapse as banks folded and workers and soldiers remained unpaid for months. Yeltsin, himself, surprised the world community by resigning on New Year's Eve, 1999. Vladimir Putin, prime minister and Yeltsin's personal choice to succeed him, became acting president the following day.

One of Putin's first acts was to grant Yeltsin immunity from prosecution. Simultaneously, he began removing Yeltsin's cronies, including his daughter, from positions of influence. To a large extent it was they who had been running things during Yeltsin's long periods of incapacity.

Chechnya: A Nasty Little War. Shortly after the proclamation of the Russian Federation as an independent country, one of its component parts, the small Muslim state of Chechnya, declared its independence from the Russian Federation. The turmoil of the era precluded Yeltsin from taking action against the breakaway state, and the event went largely unnoticed outside of Russia. From Yeltsin's perspective, however, the secession of Chechnya, if left unchallenged, would trigger similar action by other states dominated by non-Russian minorities. It was not merely the loss of one minor state that was at stake, in his view, but the continued viability of the Russian Federation as a whole (*Economist,* Jan. 14, 1995, 43).

With the 1993 elections behind him and his power consolidated, Yeltsin turned his attention to the Chechnya problem. Dispatching troops to the border of the breakaway republic in the autumn of 1994, Yeltsin demanded that the Chechnyan leaders end their secession. They refused, and Russian troops began a half-hearted and erratic march toward the Chechnyan capital of Grozny. Once the battle was joined, Chechnyans fought with uncommon valor, while the Russian forces hardly fought at all (*NYT,* Dec. 25, 1994, 1). Indeed, confusion reigned as the Russian army seemed incapable of crushing a rebellion sustained by a few thousand poorly equipped Chechnyan forces with no air cover.

With Yeltsin's victory in the 1996 elections, a tentative peace was reached with the Chechnyan forces, a peace that was generally considered a defeat for the Russian forces. The problem, however, has continued to fester, and in the summer of 1999, rebels in the neighboring province of Dagestan proclaimed their independence. Much of their support came from Chechnya. Russian troops would enter Chechnya a few months later, blaming Islamic groups in Chechnya for a series of terrorists attacks in Russia and reasserting Russia's position that Chechnya remain part of the Russian Federation. In the meantime, Russian security officials arrested some 20,000 suspects, mostly from Chechnya and its neighboring provinces, in an attempt to stem the wave of terrorist bombings. Vladimir Putin, who served as prime minister during the final months of Yeltsin's reign and then became acting president with Yeltsin's surprise resignation, gained tremendous popularity by pursuing the war with a brutality reminiscent of Joseph Stalin. Chechnya was recaptured but only at a horrific cost that saw the province's major cities obliterated. Even then, most of the resistance fighters merely retreated to their mountain hideaways, launching a fierce guerrilla war against Russian forces.

Who Is Vladimir Putin? The Russian victory in Chechnya was tremendously popular in Russia, and Putin, a totally unknown individual prior to being named prime minister by Yeltsin in the final months of 1999, was catapulted into the political limelight. Other than his brutal suppression of the Chechnyan rebellion, Putin's few months in office had done little to indicate the direction of his political and economic views. Indeed, all that was known of him was that he was young (forty-seven years old) and tough, an ex-KGB spy, and the former director of the Federal Security Service, the successor to the KGB. Putin's decisive action in Chechnya, however, was credential enough for a population reeling from the near chaos of Yeltsin's final years in office, and he scored a first round victory in the 2000 presidential elections with approximately 52.5 percent of the popular vote (*NYT,* Mar. 28, 2000, www). Putin had also bolstered his image as a "tough guy" by flying his own jet to inspect the situation in Chechnya and publicizing his expertise in judo.

The question, however, is not Putin's "toughness"—a fact that now seems well established—but his commitment to democracy, economic reform, and international cooperation. His resume is blank on the topic, but an article posted on his website stated that "It will not happen soon, if it ever happens at all, that Russia will become the second edition of, say, Britain, in which our liberal values will have deep historic traditions" (*NYT,* Jan. 17, 2000, www).

Much of the information on Putin seemed to come from former East German intelligence officers who worked closely with Putin during his fifteen-year tenure in East Germany. Among other things, they reported that Putin did not drink alcohol and was a strong supporter of Gorbachev's economic and social reforms (*NYT,* Jan. 10, 2000, www). However optimistic such reports may be, the real values of Vladimir Putin will not be known for some time.

The Political Institutions of Russia

Political institutions are the arena of politics. It is the executives, legislatures, courts, bureaucracies, and other agencies of government that authoritatively allocate the resources of the state. In this section, we shall examine the political institutions of Russia, of which the executive is by far the most important.

The Constitution of Russia

The Yeltsin Constitution has much in common with the Constitution of France, upon which it is patterned (Belyakov and Raymond 1994). Its centerpiece is a very strong president, a bicameral parliament called the **Federal Assembly**, and a Constitutional Court. The 450 members of the *lower house of parliament* (**Duma**) are elected directly by the populace, while the **Federation Council**, or *upper house,* consists of 178 members (two apiece from each of the 89 regions that constitute the Russian Federation).[14] The president shares executive power with a chairman (prime minister) named by the president with the consent of the Duma. The new Constitution also provides Russia's citizens with a broad array of civil rights, including freedom of thought, speech, and religion. A free press is also guaranteed, as is the right to form groups and parties. In addition to these and other rights taken for granted in the United States, the Constitution guarantees all Russian citizens the right to housing, education, health care, and an old-age pension (Constitution, Articles 39–43).

Popular support for the Constitution remains a matter of conjecture, inasmuch as it was ratified under extraordinary circumstances. But then, so was the Constitution of France, both constitutions having been dictated by strong leaders in countries on the brink of civil war. The French, however, possessed deeply rooted democratic traditions. The Russians do not.

Executive Power in Russia: The President and the Prime Minister

Much like the Constitution of France, the Russian Constitution creates a dual executive. Unlike France, however, the dominance of the Russian president is unlikely to be challenged by his prime minister.

The President. The formal powers accorded to the Russian president by the Yeltsin Constitution are awesome. The president is the commander-in-chief of the armed forces and is charged with protecting both the Constitution and the integrity of the State. If either is endangered, the president is empowered to declare a state of emergency and to rule by decree. He also nominates the prime minister and must approve the members of the Cabinet. The president, moreover, is Russia's chief legislator, possessing the right to introduce legislation and to veto acts of Parliament. Beyond this, the president may also issue presidential decrees that have the force of law if they are not declared unconstitutional by the Constitutional Court or overruled by the Parliament (Remington, Smith, and Haspel 1998). If the Parliament does pass new legislation overriding a presidential decree, that legislation is also subject to a presidential veto and must be overridden by a two-thirds majority in both houses. The president can also bypass Parliament altogether by taking his case directly to the

---

[14]The original members of the Federation Council were elected. Subsequent members will be appointed by the regional governments.

Charismatic Authority

Charismatic authority, as noted in the earlier discussions of de Gaulle and Hitler, is a particularly powerful force in circumstances of anomie or social disorganization—circumstances that are very much in evidence in today's Russia. With their political and social institutions in disarray, moreover, many Russians find that the best way to get along is to side with a strong leader until the air clears. Yeltsin originally served as a charismatic father figure, but this role faltered as he became debilitated by illness. Whether Russia's new president can play that role remains to be seen.

people via a referendum. And, if all else fails, he can dissolve the Duma, thereby initiating a new round of legislative elections.

The president, moreover, is Russia's chief bureaucrat. In this capacity, he nominates and removes heads of government departments. Yeltsin has carried out both tasks with great vigor in an effort to make the state bureaucracy more responsive to his wishes. Putin has followed this tradition with a vengence. The president also nominates judges, including those of the Constitutional Court.[15]

The formal powers of the Russian president, then, are profound, perhaps taxing the limits of democratic practice. Were it not for a constitutional provision limiting presidents to two four-year terms of office, the powers of the Russian president would rival those of the latter tsars.

The informal powers of the president are also formidable, three of which are of particular importance. First, because the president dominates both the legislative and administrative processes, interest groups must curry his favor if they are to achieve their objectives. Very little gets done in Russia without presidential approval. Second, because the president is Russia's chief dispenser of patronage, it is his supporters who will dominate Russia's administrative and legal structure. Legislators wanting programs for their constituents will also be under intense pressure to join the president's team. Finally, the president is the focal point of public opinion. He is the mover and shaker in Russian politics, and everything he does is noteworthy. The ability of the Russian president to control the media also appears to be far greater than it is in most Western democracies, a fact that became evident during the 2000 presidential campaign.

As the following passage suggests, the Russian president is surrounded by a massive support team.

> The world may see a single individual, the aged and enfeebled Boris Yeltsin, in the eye of Russia's political storm. But Russia's executive branch consists of far more than one man. The presidency is supported by a mighty and extensive administration. Founded on the American model in the days before the unsuccessful coup against Mikhail Gorbachev in August 1991, the office under Yeltsin has grown into a vast industry encompassing everything from a private airline to a Kremlin pharmacy. A gauge to the size of the apparatus is a presidential telephone directory that runs 227 pages with tens of thousands of entries in departments as varied as the Presidential Archive and the Presidential Guard. It may be the only compass available for navigating the labyrinth, yet there are only 3,000 copies of the "little green book," as it is known to its proud possessors (Meier 1998).

The president's combination of formal and informal powers provides him with extraordinary influence over the future of Russian politics. Although the new Russian Constitution embodies many of the theoretical checks and balances of the

[15]Presidential nominations for the Constitutional Court require the approval of the Federation Council, or upper house of the Parliament.

United States Constitution, it has yet to be demonstrated that those checks pose a serious obstacle to a determined president. If Russia's social and economic circumstances continue to deteriorate, Yeltsin's successors could well be tempted to cross the thin line that separates Russian democracy from dictatorship.

The Prime Minister and Cabinet. The president names the prime minister (Chairman of the Duma) with the approval of the Duma.[16] The prime minister presides over the Cabinet, most members of which have also been selected by the president. Indeed, the most powerful members of the Cabinet, including the Ministers of Defense, Interior (Police), and Foreign Affairs, report directly to the president rather than to the prime minister, as do special intergovernmental committees on espionage, frontier guards, information, and the media. Yeltsin had no intention of creating a prime minister who could challenge his authority in any way, a view clearly endorsed by Putin.

The Cabinet consists of approximately twenty-five ministers, most of whom supervise large bureaucratic departments and are responsible for drafting policy in their domains. Cabinet ministers represent a core element in the new Russian elite, but given the uncertain nature of Russian politics, their power is often fleeting.

Legislative Power in Russia: The Federal Assembly

The Federal Assembly consists of two houses: the State Duma, a name adopted from the abortive parliaments of the tsarist era, and the Federation Council (Hahn 1995). The Duma is the popularly elected house of the Russian Parliament; the Federation Council is designed to provide representation for Russia's 89 regions, each of which is accorded two seats. Both chambers must approve legislation for it to become law. A two-thirds majority in each chamber is also required to override a presidential veto—a daunting task indeed.

The Duma. While both houses of the Federal Assembly must approve legislation before it can become law, the Duma alone has the power to force the resignation of a Government (prime minister and Cabinet) via a **vote of no confidence**. Votes of no confidence have been frequent, but no government has fallen. The Duma also confirms the presidential nominations for the head of the central bank as well as many other senior positions.

The Duma's ability to bring down a Government makes it the focal point of partisan conflict in Russia. This is all the more the case because half of the 450 members of the Duma are elected on the basis of party lists, a procedure that makes the Duma a barometer of party support among the Russian electorate. The other half of the Duma's members are elected in single-member districts, a process that often finds partisan identification being clouded by local and ethnic considerations. Nevertheless, most of the members of the Duma elected in single-member districts soon affiliate with the party that best reflects their ideological views.

The partisan composition of Russia's first post-Soviet Duma sent a particularly chilling message to advocates of democratic and economic reform, with many of the Duma's largest parties opposing Yeltsin's reforms. As indicated in Table 6.1, moreover, this trend was strengthened by the 1995 elections, with some 50 percent of the Duma's members belonging to either the fascist or communist parties. Many of the deputies wearing the independent label also incline toward the extremist camp

---

[16]If the Duma rejects three candidates nominated by the president, or if it withdraws its confidence from a sitting prime minister, the president has the option of dissolving the Duma and calling for new elections.

Table 6.1

Parties in the Duma and Their Ideological Positions in the 1995 and 1999 Elections

	Number of Seats in the Duma	
Party	**1995**	**1999**
Radical Reform		
Democratic Choice	9	
Union of Right Forces		29
Moderate Reform/Populist		
Yabloko	46	21
Fatherland	–	66
Our Home	55	7
Unity		72
Communist		
Communist Party (KPRF)	155	113
Agrarian	20	(see Independents and Others)
Far Right/Ultra Nationalist		
Liberal Democrat/Zhirinovsky Bloc	50	17
Independents and Others	115	125
TOTAL	450	450

Sources: Moscow News (50), Dec. 22–28, 1995, p. 2; Wilfried Derksen, *Elections in Russia*, Jan. 16, 2000, www. Ideological categories based upon *Russia Today: Election 2000*, Jan. 22, 2000, www.

(*Moscow News,* No. 50, Dec. 22–28, 1995). To put things in perspective, imagine the situation in the United States if 40 percent of the members of Congress openly advocated the overthrow of the American political system.

The main strength of the Duma lies in the budget-making process. To date, parliamentary squabbling has resulted in budgets that have been both delayed and confusing. The Duma, moreover, seldom votes a major piece of legislation up or down. Rather, the legislation is introduced in different guises until a reasonable consensus can be reached. The 1995 budget, for example, went through thirteen votes before it was finally passed by the Duma (*NYT,* Dec. 28, 1994, A4). Subsequent budgets under the Yeltsin regime were equally traumatic (*Le Monde Economie,* Sept. 8, 1998).

Except on rare occasions, however, the parties in the Duma have found it difficult to provide sustained opposition to the president (Haspel, Remington and Smith, 1998; Barber 1997). Not only are the president's powers awesome, but the parties of the Duma are fragmented by both ideological and personality conflicts. Much the same is true of individual parties, including the Communists (*Moscow News,* Feb. 12, 1998, 2). Indeed, some elements of the Communist Party openly attempted to jump on Putin's bandwagon in the final days of the 2000 election campaign despite the fact that the Communist candidate was Putin's main challenger (*NYT,* Mar. 21, 2000, www).

The Federation Council. The Federation Council participates in all phases of the legislative process except the naming and censure of Governments. Its special powers include confirmation of a state of emergency, approval of the use of Russian troops on foreign soil, and acceptance of presidential nominations for judges and the public prosecutor. The Federation Council must also approve boundary changes within the Russian Federation. Given the ethnic complexities of Russia's diverse regions, the latter task may prove challenging. The early experience of the Federation Council suggests that it is more inclined to cooperate with the president than is the Duma. If this trend continues, Russian presidents should be able to weaken further the powers of the Parliament by playing one chamber against the other.

The powers of the president and the Parliament, then, are far from equal. The Parliament plays an important role in the legislative process, but that role is largely a passive one of responding to presidential initiatives. There is little that the Parliament can do to force legislation on a reluctant president. There is also little the Parliament can do to check the powers of the president, short of outright impeachment. Impeachment, however, requires the participation of both houses of the Federal Assembly and is a long and complicated process. Because of the dominant role of the presidency, much of the burden of building democracy in Russia will rest with its president.

Law and Politics in Russia: The Constitutional Council

The **Constitutional Council** (Supreme Court) consists of nineteen judges appointed for life by the president. The Council is empowered to review the constitutionality of laws and presidential degrees, and it must consent to the initiation of impeachment proceedings against the president. The Constitutional Council also arbitrates disputes between the president and the Parliament and may hear cases brought by the member states of the Russian Federation and by individual citizens.

The concept of judicial review, which states that courts can declare acts of government unconstitutional, is totally foreign to Russian practice (Butler 1992). The Soviet Union possessed a Constitutional Court, but its role was to regulate a subservient legal system rather than to pass judgment on the wisdom of Soviet leaders. In the confusing days following the collapse of the Soviet Union, however, the old Constitutional Court was placed in the position of arbitrating the conflict between Yeltsin and his opponents. Leaning first toward one side and then the other, the Court did establish the precedent of declaring the acts of both Parliament and the president unconstitutional (Sharlet, 1997). Be this as it may, it is unlikely that the new Constitutional Council will soon be in a position to check the power of the president.

While its power may be far from absolute, the Constitutional Council will not suffer from a lack of business. Russia's commercial law is being totally rewritten, and boundary disputes between Russia's eighty-nine states (republics), the demarcation of which was often arbitrary, will also crowd the Council's agenda. Also to be resolved are disputes arising from the reform of Russia's criminal justice system, including the institution of jury trials. This will not be an easy task, for both Russian law and Russian jurists are holdovers from the Soviet Union.

Federalism in Russia

The Yeltsin Constitution divides Russia into eighty-nine republics or states, each of which sends two members to the Federation Council (upper house of the Russian Parliament). Of the eighty-nine republics, twenty-one are ethnic republics that give special autonomy to a particular minority group. The remainder are administrative republics. Many of Russia's smaller ethnic groups are also demanding special status as ethnic republics.

As the Chechnyan conflict illustrates, *the potential for ethnic conflict in Russia remains very high and, if left unchecked, could lead to the fragmentation of the Russian Federation.* Ethnic Russians are a minority in approximately half of the Federation's republics and can be outvoted in local elections by ethnic minorities, most of whom

Reflecting the changing role of the Russian military, the massive tank formations of the past are being dismantled and replaced by a greater reliance on rapid deployment capabilities and "smart" weapons.

resent Russian domination (Diller 1992). Most ethnic republics (states) have used their autonomy to press for ever-greater independence from Moscow, and many have also passed legislation prejudicing the rights of ethnic Russians (Theen 1993; Dowley 1998). Moscow has relied on legal maneuvers to curb both tendencies but may eventually be compelled to maintain the integrity of the Russian state by force. This was certainly the message of the war in Chechnya. Strained relations between the central government and the republics, then, represent yet another obstacle that must be overcome if the reformers are to lead Russia to the promised land of democracy and capitalism (McAuley 1997; Tolz and Busygina 1997).

The Military and Politics in Russia

The Soviet Union was ruled by the Communist Party and sustained by the Soviet military. The Soviet military was a highly professional military that occupied a powerful and privileged position within Soviet society (Garthoff 1966; Garthoff 1992).

After the collapse of the USSR, efforts were made to transform the Soviet military into the collective military of the Commonwealth of Independent States (CIS), thereby providing the members of the CIS with an element of stability during a period of profound uncertainty in both regional and international affairs. The breakaway states, however, distrusted Russian dominance of the old Soviet military, and cooperation gave way to conflict as each new country, however poor, established its own army.

Russia's share of the Soviet military became the Russian military, much of it stationed in Eastern Europe and the former Soviet republics. Finding itself the object of fear and scorn, the military began a slow withdrawal into the Russian heartland, retreating from a war that it had not lost. Russia, moreover, had few facilities for its returning forces, the housing for which had been provided by the "host countries" of Eastern

Europe. Compounding matters was the collapse of the Russian economy. Military spending for example, fell from $246,000,000 in 1985, the beginning of the unraveling of the USSR, to some $40,000,000 in 1992 (*NYT,* Nov. 26, 1993, 3).

Even more problematic was the military's loss of a mission. With the Cold War at an end, Russia no longer needed a Soviet-type military. Sensing a military in disarray, few conscripts bothered to show up for duty. Some estimates placed the level of draft-dodging at more than 90 percent, while others suggested that the Russian military would soon have more officers than enlisted men (Schmemann 1993). Both trends were aggravated by the Chechnya War. Indeed, Army Day in 1995 was marked by a Yeltsin warning that the Russian military was on the verge of disintegration (BBC, Feb. 23, 1995).

The collapse of the USSR brought changes in the political sphere as well. Rather than being excluded from the political fray, the military became its arbiter. During the early years of independence, the military supported Yeltsin and the reformers, with the military's shelling of the old Parliament signaling the final collapse of the old regime. The military, however, exacted its price, demanding increased military spending and a slower pace of economic reform.

The full extent of the military's politicization, however, would not become apparent until the Chechnya War of 1994. Several generals resigned in protest over the war, while others were openly critical of the manner in which it was being prosecuted. Such actions, which would have been unthinkable during Soviet days, suggested that the military viewed Yeltsin as a weak and ineffective leader.

The situation continued to deteriorate during 1996 as Alexander Lebed, then Russia's security chief, warned that the army was "on the brink of mutiny" as a result of unpaid wages (*IHT,* Oct. 7, 1996, 11). The quasi-victory in Chechnya provided a boost in army morale, but not to the extent of stemming the tide of draft dodgers that has become a torrent (*IHT,* Apr. 13, 2000, 4). Not only was the army short of recruits, but those to honor their draft notices were poorly educated and lacked the technical skills of which the army was in urgent need (ibid.).

The Russian military is now in the process of redefining its role in the new Russia. This involves changes in both the military's mission and the relationship between the military and Russia's civilian leaders.

The process of redefining the military's mission began late in 1993 when Yeltsin, after extensive consultation with military leaders, announced a new military doctrine that declared Russia to be free from the threat of foreign invasion. Henceforth, the role of the military will be to insulate Russia from the regional conflicts that have engulfed the former states of the USSR. In line with its new mission, the military will concentrate on developing rapid deployment forces rather than relying on the massive tank formations that were its hallmark during the Soviet era. Decreases in troop strength will be balanced by increased technological sophistication and by greater reliance on smart weapons (*NYT,* Nov. 3, 1993, A6). While the mission of the military has been redefined, it will take years to complete the transformation process. It will also take time to rebuild the military's badly shaken morale (*CSM,* Oct. 15, 1993, 1). Precisely because the Russian military has lost its capacity to fight a major land war with the West, greater reliance is being placed upon nuclear weapons (*Washington Post,* Jan. 15, 2000, www).

Redefining civilian-military relations also poses a challenge that will take years to resolve, the problem being twofold. First, the military remains a potent pressure group. The more the Russian president depends upon military support, the more the military's demands for improved salaries and equipment will have to be accommodated. *Second, it is not clear that the military speaks with a single voice.* All branches of the military share a common interest in receiving increased salaries and improved weaponry, but political issues such as economic reform have proven to be highly contentious. Also contentious is the issue of using military forces against civilian populations. The more the military is called upon to quell domestic violence, the more likely it is to divide into pro-government and anti-government factions. This message was made abundantly clear by the war in Chechnya.

If Russia's fragile political balance begins to deteriorate, dissension and conflict within the military could lead to a coup. Yeltsin was well aware of this possibility and went out of his way to assure that troops loyal to his presidency were concentrated in the Moscow region. Lack of stability within the Russian military will unquestionably cloud Russian politics for some time to come (Ulrich 1998).

Bureaucracy and Politics in Russia

No matter what happens within Russia's decision-making institutions, the country's day-to-day affairs continue to be managed by the huge state bureaucracy inherited from the USSR. Privatization may eventually reduce bureaucratic control of the economy, but the process will be slow. Russia has not had a private sector for more than seventy years, and it will take at least a decade to develop a new class of capitalist managers capable of transforming Russia's antiquated state enterprises into effective private-sector firms.

Continued dependence upon a large state bureaucracy poses two major threats to democratic and economic reform in Russia. *First, the Russian bureaucracy is the same corrupt and self-serving bureaucracy that contributed to the stagnation of the Soviet Union* (Mellor 1997). There is little reason to believe that its behavior will change under the new regime. *Second, it appears that most segments of the bureaucracy are opposed to economic reform.* It could hardly be otherwise, as government officials possess a vested interest in maintaining a bureaucratic regime. Indeed, Russia's bureaucrats attempted to stall the reform process during much of Yeltsin's presidency in the hope of gaining a reprieve in the 2000 elections. It was well within their power to do so, for bureaucratic clearances continue to be required for most forms of economic activity in Russia today. Whether Putin can shake the bureaucracy from its lethargy remains to be seen.

Yeltsin made little secret of his frustration with the bureaucracy, referring to it as an "army of rapacious and bumbling officials" (*NYT,* Feb. 25, 1994). Unfortunately, there may be little that Russian leaders can do to alter the situation. Russia continues to be a bureaucratic state and, aside from removing a few senior officials, they have little option but to rely on the bureaucracy to carry out their programs. The Russian bureaucracy, moreover, is a seamless web of patron-client networks, each level receiving support from another. The more a president attacks the bureaucracy, the more rigid and uncooperative it becomes (Afanasyev 1998).

The Actors in Russian Politics: Elites, Parties, Groups, and Citizens

Political institutions are the arena of politics, but the actors in the political process mold and shape those institutions. They are the "human" element in the political process. In this section, we shall examine the four main types of political actors in Russia: elites, parties, groups, and citizens. Each plays a critical role in determining how Russia's scarce resources are allocated.

Elites and Politics in Russia

Russia inherited the elite structure of the Soviet Union. As such, virtually all members of the new elite were former members of the Communist Party. Some, including Boris

Yeltsin and his followers, became advocates of democracy and capitalism. Others remained faithful to the ideals of communism or embraced Russian nationalism with a fervor that bordered on fascism. Putin appears to be a cautious reformer, but the jury is still out.

The centerpiece of the Russian elite structure is the presidency created by the Yeltsin Constitution. No other political institution in Russia, singly or in concert, can effectively challenge the decision-making power of the presidency. It is Putin, accordingly, who must set the pace of democratic and economic reform in Russia. If they falter, reform will falter.

The next rung on the elite hierarchy is occupied by the president's inner circle of policy advisors. The more one has the president's ear, the greater one's influence in shaping policy. Defined in these terms, the inner circle of the Russian elite would certainly include presidential favorites in the Cabinet as well as the president's informal policy advisors. Of particular importance in this regard are six oligarchs, a less than affectionate name given to the six tycoons who dominate the Russian economy and who played a major role in keeping Yeltsin in power (Freeland 1998). As *Newsweek* quips, they "made their money the old-fashioned way—through sweetheart deals, buying up state assets at bargain prices not available to others and then receiving more state property in exchange for short-term loans to the government" (*Newsweek,* Sept. 7, 1998, 31). Coullaudon (1998) also stresses the same theme:

> …the Russian elite is progressively creating a clan-like mentality. Many Russian scholars and political analysts argue that it is these clans, as opposed to formal political institutions, that exercise real power. In 1996, in an interview with *Moscow News,* Grigory Yavlinsky claimed that the ministers of the Yeltsin government are agents of large monopolies and various oligarchic clan groups in Russia. Even First Deputy Prime Minister Boris Nemtsov agrees with the notion that an oligarchic capitalism rules the country. A growing number of articles in the Russian press are devoted to this topic. As one Moscow newspaper pointed out earlier this year, "the main threat to Russia comes neither from communists nor from fascists, but from the rise of an oligarchy."

Also ranking high on the elite hierarchy are those military commanders in whom Putin has confidence and who continue to be the guarantors of his regime. This area, too, remains shrouded in mystery.

At the secondary level, the Russian elite structure includes the leaders of the Federal Assembly, senior bureaucrats, senior military officers, managers of Russia's huge public-sector factories, and powerful regional and ethnic leaders (Hughes 1997). These secondary elites have little to say about the formation of public policy, but they have been very effective in blocking programs that they oppose. Yeltsin was in control of the Government, but it was not clear that he was in control of Russia.

The Russian elite system, as presently constituted, poses several obstacles to the emergence of a stable, democratic, and capitalistic Russia.

1. *There is little consensus among Russia's elites concerning either the rules of the game or the need to work out their differences by democratic means.* It is unlikely that Russia will be able to create stable democratic institutions without increased elite support for those institutions.
2. *The intense fragmentation of the elite structure threatens to polarize Russia's citizens into hostile camps.* To date, this polarization has focused largely on the pace of capitalist reform, but the broader issues of Russian nationalism and ethnic autonomy have also generated intense conflicts that will be difficult to reconcile by democratic means.
3. *The obstructionist orientation of much of Russia's secondary elite can only be overcome by forceful and consistent leadership from the president.* Yeltsin

attempted to work within the framework of democracy, but his leadership was vacillating and indecisive. Putin's leadership suffers from neither.

4. *The immense power of the Russian president virtually assures that a change of presidents will result in sweeping and dramatic shifts in policy.* This is a source of concern for the supporters of Russian democracy, for there are few democratic heroes on the horizon.

Parties and Politics in Russia

Political parties are such an integral part of the democratic process in advanced industrial societies that it is difficult to visualize a democratic government without them. Russia, however, was forced to begin its transition to democracy without the benefit of an established party system. Under the Soviet system, only one party was allowed to exist: the Communist Party.

The task of building a democratic party system in Russia is progressing, but it has been hampered by a variety of factors, two of which are particularly important. *First, many of Russia's emergent political parties have little interest in either democracy or democratic procedures.* Party conflict in Russia, accordingly, is not a contest between democratic alternatives, but a contest between democracy and authoritarianism. *Second, establishment of a viable system of democratic political parties has been hampered by a lack of democratic experience among the Russian public.* The new political system is poorly understood, as is the role of political parties therein.

Reflecting the above problems, Russia's first parliamentary elections were contested by a broad spectrum of political parties, ranging from the communists on the far left to the fascist Liberal Democrats on the far right. Most had been pieced together only a few weeks prior to the election and possessed little in the way of a formal structure.

The picture was much the same in the 1995 Duma elections, with some forty-three parties fielding candidates for elected office. Of these, only four exceeded the 5 percent rule required for representation in the Duma.

By and large, Russia's new political parties fall into four groups: the radical reformers, the moderate reformers, the communists, and the fascists. *The radical reform bloc advocates a rapid transition to capitalism, whatever the human costs of that transition may be.* The sooner Russia "bites the bullet," from the perspective of the radical reformers, the sooner it will be able to reap the benefits of rapid economic growth. The Russia's Choice Party emerged as the single largest party in the 1993 Duma but received less than 5 percent of the popular vote in the 1995 elections. It merged with the Union of Right Forces in the 1999 elections, but the radical reformers gained only twenty-nine seats in the Duma. The radical reformers have been intensely critical of the war in Chechnya and have been beset by internal divisions (Cherkasov and Rodin 1997; *Russia Today: Election 2000,* Jan. 22, 2000, www).

The moderate reformers are headed by the Unity Party, the Fatherland Party, and the Yabloko Party (a title compiled from the names of its three leaders). *The moderate or centrist parties accept the need for capitalism but believe that capitalist reforms should be implemented in a humane manner that minimizes the pain of unemployment and the loss of government subsidies. They advocate phasing in the reform program over a number of years.* As capitalist industries take root and grow, according to the moderate reformers, they will absorb the unemployment resulting from the gradual closure of government enterprises. The pace of the transition to capitalism will be slower, but capitalism will come.

The radical and moderate reformers represent the democratic core of the emerging Russian party system. They are opposed by two extremist blocs, the communists and the fascists. *The **Communists** admit that mistakes were made in the past, but stress that communism did provide for the basic needs of the Russian population.* They also argue that a reformed Communist Party would be far more efficient than the old Soviet Party and that it would be free of the burden of supporting the poorer regions of the USSR. This, in itself, they say, would guarantee prosperity.

The Communist message appeals to the many Russians who benefited from the old system. It also strikes a responsive chord among Russians fearing unemployment and economic hardship. The Communist Party emerged as the single largest party in the 1995 and 1999 Duma elections and finished second in the presidential elections of 1996 and 2000. Ultimately, the future of the Communist Party will depend upon the success of Russia's transition to capitalism. If things get better, the appeal of communism should fade. If they do not, memories of a secure past may take on a new urgency (Christensen 1998). The Communists, however, are also weakened by internal discord (Krasnikov 1998).

Far more scary is the **fascist** doctrine of the Liberal Democratic Party headed by Vladimir Zhirinovsky. Among other things, the fascist campaign in the 1993 elections called for a strong army, continued government management of Russia's industries, liquidation of the "5000 gangs that control the economy," arms sales to any country or group that wants to buy them, deportation of non-Russians, avoiding the mistakes of Hitler in dealing with the West, "nuking" the Japanese if they continued to pressure Russia to give back some small islands occupied since the end of World War II, a strong dose of anti-semitism, and finding husbands for all unmarried women (*Economist,* Dec. 18, 1993, 45, 46). The Party's platform was much the same in the 1995 and 1999 elections, but its vote total decreased from 22 percent to 11 percent. It fell even further in the 1999 elections.

Taken as a whole, the Russian party system possesses four characteristics that must be overcome if it is to play a strong role in building a democratic Russia (Fish 1995; Golosov 1998).

1. *The party system is too fluid* (McFaul and Petrov 1997). Most of the parties contending in past elections will undoubtedly undergo several transformations before the next election, a process that will produce even greater confusion among the Russian electorate (*IHT,* Aug. 18, 1999, www). The fluidity of the party system has been further aggravated by the fact that many of the candidates elected in the single-member districts were independents who gained victory on the basis of personal and ethnic appeals rather than any clear ideological program.

2. *Russian parties are dominated more by personalities than by ideologies.* The personalization of Russia's parties makes it difficult to establish strong and disciplined party organizations capable of sustaining a Government in the Duma.

3. *Russian parties have little in the way of grassroots organizations.* This is a function of their newness, but it is equally a function of their fluidity and their fragmentation into personality cliques. Whatever the case, it is not clear that Russia's parties are serving as a true conduit for mass participation.

4. *The Russian party system is too polarized to permit the reconciliation of competing political and economic interests* (Evans and Whitefield 1998). How, for example, does one reconcile the interests of the capitalist reformers with those of the communists? The problem, unfortunately, is far broader than a simple question of competing interests. While political parties in the First World campaign for the right to guide legitimate political institutions, those of Russia are struggling to redefine the very nature of their political system.

Strikes in Russia

Strikes, once illegal, have become commonplace, providing the labor movement with a powerful weapon in slowing the pace of reform. Some 264 strikes occurred in 1993, for example, with 288 strikes occurring in the first four months of 1994 alone (*Business Week,* June 6, 1994, 51). Strikes by Russian miners have proven particularly disruptive and continue to increase in severity as workers go months without pay (Ferguson 1998).

Pressure Groups and Politics in Russia

The eventual structure of Russia's party system will reflect the balance of competing interests within Russian society. The major pressure groups under the old regime were fairly easy to enumerate: the party apparatus, the state bureaucrats, the military, the KGB, the economic managers, the intelligentsia, and, at least theoretically, the workers and peasants. All formal pressure groups were tightly controlled by the Communist Party.

The advent of democracy has led to a veritable explosion of group activity: workers now strike, intellectual societies abound, and ethnic minorities have forged their own national associations. Indeed, the number of pressure groups in Russia now rivals that of most Western countries.

The most visible groups in Russia today are the Union of Industrialists and Entrepreneurs, the new capitalist class, organized crime, the labor unions, the bureaucracy, the military, the ethnic minorities, the intellectuals, women, and the Russian Orthodox Church. Much like Russia's fledgling political parties, most pressure groups must start from scratch, as any independent group activity was outlawed by the Soviet regime. Also, as in the case of political parties, the group dynamic of Russian politics remains fluid, with the relative strength of the combatants yet to be worked out.

The Union of Industrialists and Entrepreneurs represents the old industrial elite of the USSR. Its members control much of Russia's heavy industry, and while not opposed to change, t*hey have a vested interest in "slow" change and in the preservation of a strong public sector within the Russian economy.* The Union of Industrialists appears to have a strong voice in the Duma.

The Federation of Independent Trade Unions, which is a remake of the old Communist Labor Federation, claimed a membership of some 65 million workers in 1992 but has seen that figure drop to less than 40 million (2000 RFE/RL, Jan. 13, 2000). *It is strongly opposed to the economic reform program,* as are most of the nonaffiliated unions that have mushroomed during the recent era (*Economist,* Aug. 8, 1992; Diller 1992).

Efforts to create a new *Russian capitalist class* began with the privatization of Russia's collective farms and some of its state-owned industries. For the most part, this was accomplished by simply distributing shares of the newly privatized firms to the Russian population. A small minority of Russian entrepreneurs also began their own businesses.

While the entrepreneurs represent a true capitalist class, this is far less the case for the Russian citizens who simply received a packet of vouchers in the mail. While they technically own most of Russia's industries, they have not invested their own money in those industries. The whole concept of stock ownership, moreover, remains new and confusing, and it could take a long time for Russia's new capitalist class to acquire the level of political awareness possessed by its Western counterparts.

Unfortunately, much of the new entrepreneurial activity is illegal in nature, with some estimates suggesting that *criminal elements control 40 percent of the Russian economy* (Urban, Irgrunov, and Mitrokhin 1997). Not only has organized crime

---

The Feminist Movement in Russia

Aside from the Women of Russia Party, Russia possesses little in the way of a feminist movement. As late as the mid-1990s, there was no feminist newspaper and only one women's magazine other than a Russian version of *Cosmopolitan* (*NYT*, Apr. 17, 1994, 7). Indeed, some estimates suggest that the position of women has declined since independence. In 1991, women earned approximately 75 percent as much as men. That figure has since dropped to 40 percent (*NYT*, Apr. 17, 1994, 7). The task of establishing a feminist movement will be difficult. The theoretical equality of women under the Soviet system has given way to increased sexism and job discrimination during the Yeltsin era (Gray 1989; Atkinson, Dallin, and Lapidus 1977). Sexual harassment is blatant and is broadly accepted as normal behavior (*NYT*, Apr. 17, 1994, 7). Russian women have also borne the brunt of the layoffs that have accompanied Russia's transition to a market economy with more than 70 percent of Russia's officially unemployed being women (Human Rights Watch: World Report 2000, Section on Women's Rights, www).

---

become a critical political group, it has also established strong links with corrupt political figures at all level of government (Kramer 1998).

Intellectuals, meaning anyone with a college education, have traditionally occupied a middle stratum between the elite and the workers. Numbering more than 15,000,000, this group is in the best position to take advantage of the opportunities offered by democracy and capitalism. Intellectuals, however, represent a broad and diverse spectrum of Russian society, and they are unlikely to speak with a single voice (Ticktin 1992; Ostapchuk 1997). *While most welcome the greater political freedom offered by democracy, many also cling to the economic security offered by their bureaucratic positions.*

The Women of Russia Party captured twenty-three seats in the 1993 election, serving notice that Russian women will vote as a bloc in order to achieve feminist objectives such as job equality and child care. This message was muted in the 1995 and 1999 elections.

The Russian Orthodox Church was saved from near extinction by the collapse of communism. It too is attempting to adjust to the realities of the new Russia. The task will not be easy, for seventy years of communist rule transformed Russia into a largely secular society in which religion was the preserve of the aged. *The Church is also divided into conservative and modernizing factions, the former being wary of becoming too Western too rapidly.* The Russian Orthodox Church has gone into business, supported by large tax breaks granted by Yeltsin. Among other things, the Church is a large oil exporter and in 1996 imported 10 percent of the cigarettes sold in Russia (*The Sunday Times,* Jan. 17, 1999).

Whatever the Church's problems, recent estimates suggest that there are some 60,000,000 Orthodox "believers" in Russia, although a far lower number attend church on a regular basis. An indication of the Church's revived political influence was its ability to persuade the Duma to pass a law restricting the activities of Protestant evangelists such as Billy Graham and Jimmy Swaggart (B. A. Robinson, "Religious Intolerance in Russia," Dec. 17, 1999, www). Whether the Church's influence will extend beyond purely religious affairs remains to be seen. Priests, however, have been forbidden to run for office (*Russia Today,* June 4, 1999, www).

The interests of Russia's *ethnic minorities* were discussed earlier, as were the interests of the bureaucracy and the military. Little is to be gained by recounting the earlier discussion other than to note that all three groups add an element of profound uncertainty to Russian politics.

The birth of Russian democracy, then, has been accompanied by a growing pluralism. Many of Russia's better-organized interest groups oppose a rapid shift from socialism to capitalism. Some groups also seem lukewarm to the prospect of increased democracy. For the most part, the opponents of economic and democratic reform are the same groups that dominated politics during the Brezhnev era. Understandably, they are attempting to salvage what they can of their privileged status. Over time, the influence of the old groups should give way to the growing power of those groups that do benefit from the reforms, not the least of which is the emerging capitalist sector. The transition, however, will take time and could turn violent. Limited pluralism is a positive force for democracy, but extreme pluralism marked by irreconcilable views is not. At the moment, Russia appears to be moving in the latter direction.

Citizens and Politics in Russia

Citizen participation is the essence of democracy, and Russia's citizens will have to display strong support for their new political institutions if those institutions are to succeed. Russia's citizens, however, have had little experience with democracy, and many seem overwhelmed by its complexities (Remington 1992). The oppression of the Soviet regime also remains fresh in the minds of Russia's citizens, and many are reluctant to speak openly in what continues to be an uncertain political environment. In many rural areas, moreover, the old elites are still in charge. Mass participation, in such areas, may have more to do with regimentation than with conscience.

Not unexpectedly, the results of the opinion polls and the elections conducted during the early years of the transition process were confusing (Finifter and Mickiewicz 1992). Russians remained nationalistic yet seemed resigned to the loss of an empire. They supported economic reform, but not at the price of personal deprivation. *Surveys conducted on the eve of the 1995 elections showed an overwhelming concern with economic issues and quality of life, followed in turn by worries over crime and disorder* (*Economist,* Dec. 16, 1995, 20). Perhaps this helps to explain the strong showing of the Communists and other extremist parties in these elections.

More recent polls continue to reflect the same concerns, with fear of anarchy becoming a pre-eminent concern and a growing number of Russian citizens losing faith in their government (Betaneli 1998). In this respect, *a 1997 poll found the Russian population to be split into two roughly equal camps: those willing to bet on a better future via capitalism and democracy, and those inclined to return to the stability of the past* (Levinson, Gorzev, Andreyev, and Bout 1997). Did half of Russia's citizens really want to return to an authoritarian form of government, or were they merely protesting the rapid pace of economic reform? While Western scholars debated the broader meaning of the extremist vote, Yeltsin was under no illusions, abandoning his shock therapy approach to capitalist reform and joining the ranks of the gradualists. At the very least, Russia's masses had made their voice heard. Putin's election is difficult to interpret as other than a vote for stability and national dignity, his brutal pursuit of the war in Chechnya being a symbol of both.

The strong showing of Fascists and Communists in Russia's elections poses a serious dilemma for advocates of economic reform. *Should free expression be encouraged even if it threatens Russia's transition to capitalism, or would it be better to have a prolonged period of guided democracy in which a strong but democratically elected leader uses less than democratic means to carry out what must ultimately be very painful reforms?* This dilemma continues to dog Western leaders.

Mass participation, moreover, is not limited to elections and public opinion polls. Strikes and protests have become more frequent, sometimes threatening to turn violent. Mothers' marches undermined the war effort in Chechnya, and demonstrations of all varieties increased during the period leading up to the 1996 and 1999/2000 elections. Finally, it should be noted that the masses do not have to be politically active in order to influence the political process. *Mass apathy undermined the power of both the tsarist empire and the Soviet Union. It continues to undermine Russia's fragile democracy.*

The Context of Russian Politics: Culture, Economics, and International Interdependence

While the actors in Russian politics play a vital role in determining who gets what, when, and how, the behavior of those actors is often influenced by the broader environmental context in which Russian politics occurs. In this section, we examine three dimensions of Russia's environmental context: political culture, political economy, and the influence of the international arena.

The Culture of Russian Politics

Russia inherited the political and economic institutions of the Soviet Union. It also inherited Soviet political culture. It is relatively easy to craft new institutional structures, but the task of reshaping the values, attitudes, and predispositions of the individuals who give life to those institutions is a far more difficult task (Smith 1991).

In this regard, observers of Russian politics have noted a variety of *cultural traits likely to slow Russia's transition to democracy and capitalism,* many of which originated during the era of tsarist rule (Gorer and Rickman 1962). It is not suggested that all Russians share these traits, but only that their prevalence makes them politically relevant. Russians, for example, have traditionally displayed *an intense concern for order and stability.* As discussed by Archie Brown:

> Another central value of the dominant Soviet political culture is the emphasis placed upon order (poryadok). Indeed, the extent to which fear of disorder, or chaos, has been one of the strongest bonds of unity, drawing together all social groups—workers, peasants, intellectuals, and power-holders—in the Soviet Union has been remarked upon by both Western analysts and by perceptive observers within the USSR (Brown 1985, 19).

Russians are also said to be predisposed toward authoritarianism, a trait that could well find them seeking salvation from their political and economic woes in a charismatic father figure (Brown 1985; Rainone 1998). Support for Boris Yeltsin clearly fits this mold, as does the now-fleeting popularity of Vladimir Zhirinovsky. The socialization programs of the Stalin era, moreover, actively sought to inculcate Soviet youth with the virtues of authoritarianism. The official Stalinist guide to child-rearing provides interesting insights into this process:

> In relation to children, parents must be unremittingly vigilant, exacting, and consistent in disciplinary demands and in the imposition of duties; no relaxation of effort on the parents' part is permissible for fear that the child may fall under bad influences and be controlled by antisocial elements. While parents should show warmth, affection, and understanding, they should not permit excessive intimacy, which might undermine their authority. Parents must not be all-forgiving, for conduct deviations in children cannot be tolerated (Calas 1955, 107).

Still other prominent features of Russian culture include *apathy and a sense of psychological disengagement from the political system.* As stated previously, widespread political apathy played a key role in undermining both the tsarist empire and the Union of Soviet Socialist Republics (Tucker 1987). In both instances, political apathy was reinforced by a profound mutual distrust between the elites and the masses. The masses resented the capriciousness of a harsh political system, and the political elites feared the hostility of the masses (Brown 1985).

Although they may care little for their political institutions, Russians are intensely *nationalistic* (Tolz 1998). They resent Russia's decline as a world power and remain suspicious of the West and its motives (Dunlop 1993). The ultra-nationalist Liberal Democratic Party played upon nationalist themes in the 1993 elections, gaining control of almost one-fourth of the seats in the Duma. Nationalist themes have also struck a responsive chord in the military, with some Russian officers openly advocating a return to the empire.

Cultural factors are likely to slow Russia's emergence as a capitalist power as well. *The socialist policies of the Soviet Union created a culture of dependence by encouraging people to rely on the state rather than on themselves* (Smith 1992). Russians will accept capitalism if it improves their standard of living, but they will find it difficult to accept a reduction in personal welfare. In short, the Russian population is likely to expect the best features of both capitalism and socialism (Alexander 1998). For the moment, it has neither.

Further complicating matters is *the persistence of a socialist work ethic that saps the productivity of Russian workers.* This negative work ethic evolved in response to the Soviet practice of giving all workers more or less the same salary, regardless of how hard they worked or the quality of their output. The lack of incentives, combined with a guaranteed job, resulted in a work force that was sluggish, at best. The socialist work ethnic also found strong cultural support in the traditional peasant emphasis on equality: better that all suffer than only one succeed. Whatever the case, productivity lagged, innovations were few, quality was poor, and upkeep of facilities was neglected (Smith 1992). Perhaps capitalism and the profit motive will alter this situation, but culture changes slowly. It will take time to generate an achievement ethic similar to that which has promoted the tremendous productivity of Germany and Japan.

Finally, Russians must cope with the stress of collapsing social, political, and economic institutions, a situation often referred to as **anomie**. People can adjust to new rules if they know what the rules are, but the rules in Russia continue to be in a state of turmoil. No one is quite sure where to turn or what the future will bring. Simply stated, *Russia is currently suffering from a crisis of authority.* Laws are passed in Moscow, but they are often ignored by those in outlying regions. Gangs and local "bosses" have emerged to fill the vacuum. In many areas, local police officials have become petty warlords.

Escalating levels of crime, drug abuse, and drunkenness reflect this state of social disorganization. Alcoholism, for example, increased dramatically during the latter Brezhnev years, with the average Soviet citizen consuming three times more alcohol than a resident of Western Europe (Diller 1992). It has continued to increase during the Yeltsin years, with one commentator suggesting that Yeltsin has used cheap vodka as a means of muting public dissent (Ivanov 1998). Crime, moreover, has become so pervasive that it is now threatening Russia's transition to capitalism. Business people have become the preferred targets of Russia's proliferating gangs, as they are the ones who have the money.

The main themes of Russian culture, then, are apathy, distrust, authoritarianism, alienation, and uncertainty, themes that are not conducive either to democracy or to rapid economic development. Cultural predispositions change, but they change slowly, sometimes over the course of several generations. Dramatic cultural change, moreover, will require an active and far-reaching program of resocialization. The old "cultural map" must be redrawn and Russia's educational curriculum must be totally revamped to forge a political culture based upon democratic and capitalistic values (Frost and Makarov 1998; Urban 1998). These values must also be stressed by the media, labor unions, youth groups, political parties, parents, and other agents of political socialization. To date, steps in this direction have been minimal and haphazard.

Political Economy and Politics in Russia

Cultural analyses of Russian politics focus on the values, attitudes, and predispositions of the average Russian citizen. Political economists, by contrast, are more inclined to focus on their economic motivations. If individuals benefit from capitalism, from the political economy perspective, they will support capitalism. If they do not, they will not. The same logic applies to Russian democracy. If democratic institutions can solve Russia's mounting economic problems and improve the economic well-being of the average citizen, they will be embraced by the Russian electorate. If the present economic uncertainties are allowed to prevail, Russian voters will increasingly seek economic security in a return to an authoritarianism of one form or another. This was certainly the message of Russia's parliamentary elections. Russia's rising crime wave is equally the product of growing economic uncertainty.

Few experts contest the proposition that some form of capitalist economic reform is essential if Russia is to solve its economic problems and evolve into a stable democracy (Rutland 1992; *Economist,* Jan. 18, 2000). The question is how to go about the process of reform.

The reformers argue that time is of the essence. The sooner capitalism can be put in place, the sooner Russia can put the trauma of the reform process behind it. New factories would replace the old, prices would moderate, and Russia would begin to enjoy Western-style prosperity. Equally important, shock reform would preclude Russia's politicians from changing their minds and giving way to the pressures of public opinion.

The moderates, by contrast, believe that it would be a grave mistake to attempt to move from socialism to capitalism in one fell swoop. Many conservative Russians, moreover, feel that socialism was not all bad, suggesting that Russia should establish a mixed economy in which capitalism and socialism co-exist. Responding to the trauma produced by the early years of shock therapy and the strong extremist vote in the 1993 and 1995 elections, most Russian politicians now argue for a more gradual transition to capitalism.

The fate of Russian democracy will depend to a large degree on the success of its economic reforms. Thus, it may be useful to briefly examine some of the obstacles that those reforms must overcome if they are to succeed. Six of these obstacles hold particular importance.

The first obstacle to economic reform is the absence of a coherent reform strategy applied with consistency over time. However desirable the IMF's shock treatment may be from an economic point of view, it is politically unfeasible. The option of moderate or slow reform, however, is equally problematic; to date, moderate reform has been more of a slogan than a program. Even if the proponents of moderate reform can come to an agreement on what it means or how to go about it, moderate reform will require more staying power to implement than the Russian political system currently possesses. The worst of all possibilities would be no economic reform strategy at all, a situation that is perilously close to being the case in today's Russia (Goldman 1994; *NYT,* Jan. 7, 1994, 1). Recent banking scandals have only added to the malaise (*IHT,* Feb. 12, 1999, www).

A second obstacle to economic reform has been the reluctance of Russia's privatized firms to operate on the model of capitalist firms in the West (Economist, Oct. 8, 1994, 21). Privatization was achieved simply by distribution of shares of state-owned enterprises to the Russian population on a more or less random basis. In some cases, the firms were sold to their employees at unrealistically low prices. Whatever the case, the management remained the same, as did problems of overstaffing, underproduction, and poor quality control. Some firms are now beginning to act like capitalists, but the process of change is slow, and resistance to layoffs is high.

Third, economic growth has been slowed by the persistence of a hostile and rigid bureaucracy. Not only do rules and regulations cover all forms of economic activity, but those rules are constantly changing. This is a particularly difficult problem for foreign firms wishing to invest in Russia (Hanson 1998; Brovkin 1998). Bureaucratic problems, however, are not merely a matter of obstructionism. The Russian bureaucracy is also profoundly inefficient and has found it difficult to provide the infrastructure services required for rapid economic reform. Particularly disconcerting has been its inability to collect a large percentage of the taxes owed to the debt-ridden state.

Fourth, progress toward economic growth has lagged because of Russia's uncertain political environment. Not only did Yeltsin vacillate in his commitment to reform, but as his health continued to deteriorate, many investors, both domestic and foreign, chose to wait on the sidelines until the picture came into better focus. Worse yet, many Russian investors are investing their money in the West rather than in their own country. Perhaps Putin's very firm hand can reverse this trend.

Fifth, successful economic development is hampered by the sheer magnitude of the task. Many of Russia's largest industrial establishments are geared to a defense industry that has now collapsed, while others are outdated by Western standards. Indeed, economists argue that much of Russia's heavy industry is beyond salvation and that efforts to keep it alive are merely wasting scarce resources. Russia's leaders, however, have refused to close unprofitable industries for fear of the political consequences. As things currently stand, the export of raw materials is the bright spot in the Russian economy.

Finally, economic reform faces severe problems on the international front, as foreign assistance from the First World has been trickling in much more slowly than expected. As many poor states have found to their dismay, pledges are one thing, and hard cash is another. When aid does arrive, it often seems to fall into the hands of organized crime (*NYT,* Aug. 19, 1999, www).

Russia's political uncertainties have made the West increasingly wary of investing in Russia, while the 1998–99 collapse of the Asian economies and the decliningprice of oil, one of Russia's main exports, further depressed the economic picture (*Le Monde Economie,* Sept. 8, 1998).

Russia's economic woes are amenable to solution, but that solution will not be rapid, nor will it be achieved without firm and consistent leadership from Russia's political leaders (Frye 1997). For better or for worse, politicians will remain Russia's primary economic decision-makers for some time to come (Afanasyev 1998).

International Interdependence and the Politics of Foreign Aid

Russia may no longer be an economic power, but it is very much a nuclear power, having inherited much of the nuclear arsenal of the Soviet Union. A brief outline of Russian military strength is provided in Table 6.2. New alarms have also been raised about Russia's continued development of biological weapons (*NYT,* Dec. 28, 1998). Russia's cooperation in forging a new world order is based upon two premises: that it will share in the prosperity of that new world order and that it will play a major role in shaping the affairs of the world community. If either premise is not sustained, the world could again find itself divided into hostile camps.

Table 6.2
Russian Military Strength

	Weapons	**Warheads**
Intercontinental ballistic missiles	1,040	4,260
Submarine-launched ballistic missiles	832	2,696
Battle tanks	25,000	

Source: Based on figures provided by the International Institute for Strategic Studies and reported in a variety of news sources. The figures reported are for 1995. Other reports suggest that Russia may have as many as 22,000 nuclear weapons (Lisa Ledwidge, "Living (still) with Nuclear Dangers," *Foreign Policy in Focus*, www, July 30, 1999, Vol. 3, No. 27).

Under the confused circumstances surrounding the collapse of the Soviet Union, the easiest way for the West to assure Russian cooperation in the creation of a new world order was to support Boris Yeltsin. It was hoped that Yeltsin's tremendous popularity would enable him to impose the radical economic reforms that Western economists believed were essential to the revival of the Russian economy. Once the economic reforms were in place, in their view, it would only be a matter of time before a prosperous and democratic Russia took its place as a full member in the world capitalist system. The West, however, wanted the economic reforms in place before it pumped huge amounts of money into the fragile Russian economy.

Yeltsin, for his part, wanted the aid first, citing the need to build political support for the transition process. Russia was also reluctant to open its markets to Western firms, fearing that Russian factories would be unable to compete with foreign products. Both sides were correct in their assessment of the situation, the West being guided by economic logic while the Russians acted on the basis of domestic political logic. By the end of the millennium, accordingly, Russia and the West had yet to agree on a common reform strategy.

The United States and its allies would thus find themselves in a quandary. To provide Russia with massive foreign assistance before capitalism is in place would be to prop up a failed economic system (Blackwill, Braithwaite, and Tanaka 1995). Not to provide Russia with massive foreign assistance, however, would be to undercut Russia's democrats and risk a return to military confrontation between the two superpowers. The strong showing of the Fascists and the Communists in recent elections adds urgency to the Western dilemma.

Reacting to the 1993 Communist electoral gains, the United States softened its push for shock reform, fearing an even greater popular backlash in years to come. The radical reformers felt betrayed, but the United States could not risk destabilizing a Yeltsin regime upon which it had placed its hopes for world stability. To make matters worse, much of the aid that the West has provided has simply disappeared without a trace (*NYT,* March 19, 1999, www). Some of it has been used to support Putin's brutal war in Chechnya (BBC, Jan. 12, 2000, www).

The West, then, could well find itself pumping money into Russia largely for the sake of keeping a friendly, pro-Western regime in power. *Western aid to Russia is politically motivated, and it will continue to be forthcoming as long as the West retains a vital interest in keeping Russia in friendly hands,* even though the funds may be supplied at a far slower pace than the Russians would prefer (Yavlinsky 1998). In the final analysis, then, economics will take a back seat to politics.

Challenges of the Present and Prospects for the Future

This final segment in our discussion of Russian politics focuses on the challenges facing the reborn Russian state in each of the six main areas separating the First and Third Worlds: democracy, human rights, stability, economic growth, quality of life, and environmental concerns. The challenges are grave, and Russia's ability to overcome them is still very much in doubt (Evans 1998). Russia's challenges, however, are not hers alone. They are also matters of concern to the world community. No state would pose a greater threat to the security of the United States and its allies than an authoritarian Russia inflamed by nationalist extremism.

Democracy

With the 2000 presidential elections, Russia had met the minimal procedural requirements of a democratic state. Its leaders had been elected by the Russian population in reasonably fair elections from among a meaningful choice of candidates.[17] Elected leaders did take office, and they did rule. One can quibble over the minimal powers accorded to the Parliament, but Russia had clearly taken a major step toward democracy.

To be classified as a democracy, however, a political system must stand the test of time. No one can say how long that time must be, but it is clearly more than one or two elections. The success of a democracy also depends upon the support of an elite committed to democratic principles, a system of democratic political parties, a free press, a prosperous economy, and a political culture that stresses compromise and tolerance (Gibson 1998).

All of these considerations raise doubts about the ability of Russia's democracy to stand the test of time (Pipes 1997). *Virtually all of the political leaders in Russia are former communists, and their experience with democratic procedures is minimal at best.* Putin appears to be committed to democracy, but it is not a democracy for the faint of heart. Between 1993 and 1998, no less than six members of Parliament were assassinated (Gessen 1998). The democratic credentials of other leading politicians are suspect; in fact, the leaders of the fascist and communist blocs have made little secret of their scorn for the present system. Democratic leadership, moreover, extends beyond the president and the leaders of the Parliament. It also must be provided by the bureaucrats responsible for implementing government policy, by the leaders at the regional andlocal levels, and by the soldiers who sustain the state. It is not clear just how much democracy has penetrated at these levels (Bahry, Boaz, and Gordon 1997).

The ability of the Russian party system to sustain the new democracy also remains unclear. Those political parties that have evolved to date are simply too fluid, too unstructured, and too lacking in popular support to play a vital role in the democratic process. To make matters worse, the Communists and the Nationalists are among the best organized of Russia's political parties. Money also plays an important role in the election process, but money is only one part of a very complex political process (Treisman 1998).

On the positive side, Russia appears to possess a relatively free press (Benn 1992). Indeed, a major milestone in freedom of the media came during the first phase of the Chechnya War as Russian TV viewers were treated to the spectacle of Russian officers refusing to advance on Chechnyan forces. They also watched as the corpses

---

[17]Boris Yeltsin was elected president of the Russian Republic prior to the collapse of the USSR. He was the first democratically elected leader of the era.

of Russian soldiers were pulled from downed tanks and helicopters, something that never could have happened during Soviet rule. This, unfortunately, did not extend to the 1999/2000 campaign to retake Chechnya. The 2000 presidential elections have also witnessed a clear Government bias in the Russian press as Putin's opponents have been tied to "Jews, gays, and foreigners" (*NYT*, Mar. 24, 2000, www). Indeed, the eve of Putin's inauguration would see a major Moscow paper leak documents claiming that Putin had ordered the successor to the KGB to block journalists who stood in the way of his control of Russian politics (*IHT*, May 5, 2000).

Perhaps with some justification, the Government has complained that the opposition press is less than responsible. While some papers are objective in reporting the events of the day, the fascists and other extremist groups have used the press to undermine democracy and to cultivate dissension among the population. The Government, accordingly, finds itself in a dilemma. To deny nondemocratic parties access to the media would be to compromise democratic principles. Not to do so could place Russia's democracy in jeopardy.

The intense fragmentation of Russia's group structure is equally problematic. While group pluralism is generally viewed as a positive sign for democracy, the abiding distrust that separates Russia's main interest groups may be difficult to reconcile by democratic means. Relations between ethnic Russians and the country's ethnic minorities are particularly tense, as are relations between the new capitalist class and the advocates of a welfare state.

Russia's broader cultural, economic, and international environments have also offered little encouragement to the proponents of democracy. Russian political culture inclines toward authoritarianism and apathy, and Russia's partially reformed economy has done little to justify faith in democratic leadership. In part, of course, this was the fault of an international community that forced Russia to adopt capitalist economic reforms far more rapidly than the realities of Russian politics would allow. The international community has also equivocated on its promises of economic aid.

For all of its problems, Russian democracy—if such it is—continues to survive. Whether it can continue to do so with the passing of Yeltsin remains to be seen.

Stability

The advent of Soviet rule brought stability to a Russian Empire that was on the verge of anarchy. The collapse of the Soviet Union returned much of that empire to a state approaching anarchy. Other than war in Chechnya, the Russian Federation has escaped the civil turmoil that has engulfed many of its neighbors. Nevertheless, a rising tide of crime and lawlessness, moreover, threatens to rob Russia's citizens of their newly won freedoms. Indeed, Russian security forces report the existence of some 3,000 mafia-like gangs (*Economist*, Aug. 28, 1993, 46). Yeltsin and Putin have issued sweeping decrees to bring crime under control, but the severity of those decrees threatens to undermine Russia's very real progress in the area of civil rights. Among other things, police are now allowed to hold suspected criminals for up to a month without showing cause. For many of Russia's citizens, these anti-crime measures are uncomfortably similar to those of the Stalinist era. They also seem to be of little avail, as criminal elements now control some 40 percent of the Russian economy—hardly a stabilizing situation.

The causes of political instability in Russia have been discussed at length throughout this chapter. They include a declining economy, uncertain decision making, bureaucratic strangulation, fragmentation of the military, mass unfamiliarity with democratic institutions, ethnic conflict, foreign pressures to reform faster than political circumstances will allow, insufficient foreign assistance, and a host of lesser problems too numerous to mention. Russia's uncertain democracy has also contributed to the nation's political instability by providing the fascists and the communists with unlimited opportunities to obstruct the effective operation of the government. Each of the above sources of political instability feeds upon the others, making its resolution that much harder. It is difficult to solve Russia's economic problems, for example, without firmer political leadership than the Yeltsin regime displayed. Yeltsin's ability to provide firm leadership, however, was crippled by the need to follow democratic procedures as well as by the irresponsible rhetoric of the extremists. The cycle has become increasingly vicious in the years since independence, and it shows few signs of easing. One cannot blame the Russian population if it voted overwhelmingly for Putin in an effort to return an element of stability to Russian politics.

Human Rights

For the first time since the founding of the Union of Soviet Socialist Republics, Russia's citizens are free to express their opinions, organize into political action groups, affiliate with the religion of their choice, and move freely from one part of the country to another. The right of private property is also being restored.

As dramatic as the revolution in human rights has been, excessive optimism remains premature. Again, the problems are many. Russia has retained the large law and order establishment inherited from the USSR, albeit in reorganized form and in reduced size. The Soviet KGB, for example, has become the Federal Counter Intelligence Service. The task of instilling the revamped security forces with a new human rights ethic could take several generations.

Human rights are also being stained by the precarious balance between democrats and extremists in the Duma. Restricting the activities of the fascists and the communists may be necessary to stabilize Russia's fragile democratic institution, but the precedent is a dangerous one.

The human rights of ethnic minorities have come under increasing challenge in post-Soviet Russia. A clear prejudice exists against non-Russians living in Moscow and other major cities, but ethnic Russians also suffer human rights abuses in regions in which they are a minority. The complaints of ethnic Russians, however, are far more likely to receive a warm hearing in Moscow than those of the minorities.

Finally, the rights of Russian women lag far behind those of Russian men (Attwood 1991). Few women fill highly paid positions of authority, and sexual harassment is commonplace. Indeed, since the advent of capitalism, job ads in the private sector openly solicit young, attractive, and unmarried female applicants.

Economic Growth and Quality of Life

The early years of independence have been difficult for most Russians. Progress toward the establishment of a capitalist economic system has been made, but it has been slow and erratic. Many Russians have prospered from the reforms, but many others have suffered greatly. To make matters worse, the promised cuts in employment have yet to materialize as a nervous government continues to subsidize its large state enterprises. Underemployment, however, has risen dramatically as factories, their markets depressed, have been operating on partial shifts. Even then, many workers must wait months for their salaries.

Some measure of the plight of the Russian population is to be found in the length of time individuals must work in order to purchase basic goods. In 1994, for example, the average Russian citizen had to work approximately 2.5 hours to buy a pound of sausage, while the corresponding time for an American worker was only 12 minutes. Similarly, a Russian citizen had to work well over an hour to buy a gallon of gasoline, while a United States citizen could accomplish the same feat in 8 minutes. Disparities, moreover, are substantially greater for durable goods. Russians had to work 71 days to buy a TV set, as opposed to a mere 6 days for United States citizens. Even purchasing a fifth of vodka in Russia required a half day's wages (*NYT*, Oct. 16, 1994, 5).

Russia's transition to capitalism has also created growing disparities in wealth between the emerging capitalist class and the vast majority of Russians who continue to subsist on state salaries. Theoretically, anyone can become a capitalist, but few Russians have developed the skills or possess the capital to do so. Training in capitalism is being provided by Western donors, but this is a long-range process that will take years to reach fruition. In the meantime, the average Russian is made acutely aware of his or her plight by the flashy success of those who have made it. Greed may be a powerful stimulus for economic growth, but envy is a powerful stimulus for political instability.

The Environment

During the Soviet era, industrialization was viewed as both the key to military power and the standard by which socialism would demonstrate its superiority to capitalism. Managers of factories and collective farms (industrialized agriculture) were under intense pressure to meet or exceed the production quotas decreed by Moscow, and environmental concerns were largely irrelevant to a bureaucracy that thrived on production statistics. The wastefulness and inefficiency of Soviet industry were legendary. The situation was equally bad on the collective farms as managers attempted to boost productivity by the extravagant use of fertilizers and pesticides.

It was the Chernobyl nuclear disaster of April 26, 1986, however, that alerted the world to the magnitude of the USSR's environmental problems. On that day, the melt-down of a flawed nuclear reactor blanketed both the USSR and its neighbors with a cloud of radioactive dust. Most of the USSR's nuclear reactors remain vulnerable to accident, and a new Chernobyl is not out of the question.

The full scope of the Soviet ecological disaster, however, would not be known until after the collapse of the USSR and the opening of its former territories to Western inspectors (Edwards 1994). The picture is not pretty, with some 70 million former Soviet citizens being exposed to air pollution so severe that some form of respiratory disease is all but inevitable. Three-fourths of the surface water in the former Soviet Union is also severely polluted, with the former Soviet Union dumping twice as much nuclear waste in the oceans as the rest of the industrial world combined (*NYT*, Apr. 27, 1993, A1).

The Russian federation has been very straightforward in publicizing its environmental problems, but it lacks sufficient funding to address them in an effective manner. It also fears that the enforcement of strict environmental codes will cripple an already lagging economy. For the time being, issues of political and economic survival take precedence over concern for the environment. The world community has been invited to clean up the mess, and it may have little option but to do so. Pollution does not respect national boundaries.

Prospects for the Future

The challenges facing Russia are of a magnitude unknown among the states of the First World. The situation is far from hopeless, but parallels have been drawn

What was once a forest has become a polluted wasteland in the Montschegorsk region, illustrating the environment degradation wrought by decades of Soviet industrialization.

between the situation in today's Russia and that of Germany in the years preceding the rise of Hitler (Shenfield 1998). The success of Zhirinovsky in the 1993 elections and the communists in recent elections has given credence to these comparisons, raising fears that the Russian masses will embrace a new form of authoritarianism if their economic and political circumstances do not improve dramatically in the near future. Such parallels, however, are dangerous, for the political and economic environment of today's world is far different from that which prevailed between the two world wars. Russia is changing, but the direction of that change remains to be seen. In the meantime, Russia's future remains profoundly uncertain.

References

Afanasyev, Yuri. 1998 (Dec.). "We're Still Tied to Socialism." *Moscow News* 50: 4.

Alexander, James. 1998 (May). "Uncertain Conditions in the Russian Transition: The Popular Drive Towards Stability in a 'Stateless' Environment." *Europe-Asia Studies* 50(3): 415–44.

Arendt, Hannah. 1951. *The Origins of Totalitarianism.* New York: Harcourt, Brace.

Armstrong, John A. 1959. *The Soviet Bureaucratic Elite: A Case Study of the Ukrainian Apparatus.* New York: Praeger.

Atkinson, Dorothy, Alexander Dallin, and Gail Warshofsky Lapidus, eds. 1977. *Women in Russia.* Stanford, CA: Stanford University Press.

Attwood, Lynne. 1991. *The New Soviet Man and Woman.* Bloomington, IN: Indiana University Press.

Bahry, Donna, Cynthia Boaz, and Stacy Gordon. 1997 (August). "Tolerance, Transition, and Support for Civil Liberties in Russia." *Comparative Political Studies* 30(4): 484–515.

Bahry, Donna, and Brian D. Silver. 1990 (Sept.). "Soviet Citizen Participation on the Eve of Democratization." *American Political Science Review* 84(3): 800–47.

Baradat, Leon P. 1992. *Soviet Political Society.* 3rd ed. Englewood Cliffs, NJ: Prentice-Hall.

Barber, John. 1997 (Autumn). "Opposition in Russia." *Government and Opposition* 32(4): 598–614.

Bauer, Raymond A., Alex Inkeles, and Clyde Kluckhohn. 1956. *How the Soviet System Works.* New York: Vintage.

Belyakov, Vladimir V., and Walter J. Raymond. 1994. *Constitution of the Russian Federation: With Commentaries and Interpretation by American and Russian Scholars.* Lawrenceville, VA: Brunswick.

Benn, David Wedgwood. 1992. "Glasnost and the Media." In *Developments in Soviet and Post-Soviet Politics* (pp. 174–99), ed. Stephen White, Alex Pravda, and Zvi Gitelman. London: Macmillan.

Betaneli, Nugzar. 1998 (Feb. 25). "Polls Show Public Distrusts Politicians." *The Current Digest of the Post-Soviet Press* 50(4): 7–9.

Bialer, Seweryn. 1989. "The Changing Soviet Political System: The Nineteenth Party Conference and After." In *Politics, Society, and Nationality Inside Gorbachev's Russia* (p. 234), ed. Seweryn Bialer. Boulder, CO: Westview Press.

Billington, James H. 1966. *The Icon and the Axe: An Interpretive History of Russian Culture.* London: Weidenfeld and Nicolson.

Blackwill, Robert, Rodric Braithwaite, and Akihiko Tanaka. 1995. *Engaging Russia.* Washington, DC: The Brookings Institution.

Blum, Jerome. 1964. *Lord and Peasant in Russia: From the Ninth to the Nineteenth Century.* New York: Atheneum.

Bremmer, Ian, and Ray Taras, eds. 1993. *Nations and Politics in the Soviet Successor States.* Cambridge: Cambridge University Press.

Brovkin, Vladimir. 1998 (Summer). "Fragmentation of Authority and Privatization of the State: From Gorbachev to Yeltsin." *Demokratizatsiya* 504–505.

Brown, Archie. 1985. *Political Culture and Communist Studies.* Armonk, NY: M. E. Sharpe.

Butler, William E. 1992. "The Rule of Law and the Legal System." In *Developments in Soviet and Post-Soviet Politics* (pp. 107–46), ed. Stephen White, Alex Pravda, and Zvi Gitelman. London: Macmillan.

Calas, E. 1955. "Appendix B: Summary of Conclusions of Research on Soviet Child Training Ideals and Their Political Significance." In *Soviet Attitudes Toward Authority*, by Margaret Mead. New York: William Morrow.

Campbell, Robert W. 1992. *The Failure of Soviet Economic Planning.* Bloomington, IN: Indiana University Press.

Cherkasov, Gleb and Ivan Rodin. 1997 (Oct. 8). "Strife-Ridden 'Our Home' Elects New Duma Leaders." *The Current Digest of the Post-Soviet Press* 49(36): 5–7.

Christensen, Paul T. 1998 (Dec.). "Socialism After Communism? The Socioeconomic and Cultural Foundations of Left Politics in Post-Soviet Russia." *Communist and Post-Communist Studies*, 31(4): 345.

Coker, Francis W. 1934. *Recent Political Thought* (p. 217). New York: Appleton-Century-Crofts.

Conquest, Robert. 1971. *The Great Terror.* London: Pelican.

Coulloudon, Virginie. 1998 (Summer). "Elite Groups in Russia." *Demokratizatsiya* 535.

Diller, Daniel C., ed. 1992. *Russia and the Independent States.* Washington, DC: Congressional Quarterly Inc.

Dowlah, A. F. 1992. *Soviet Political Economy in Transition.* New York: Greenwood.

Dowley, Kathleen. 1998 (Dec.). "Striking the Federal Bargain in Russia: Comparative Regional Government Strategies." *Communist and Post-Communist Studies* 31(4): 359–60.

Duch, Raymond M. 1993 (Sept.). "Tolerating Economic Reform: Popular Support for Transition to a Free Market in the Former Soviet Union." *American Political Science Review* 87(3): 590–608.

Dunlop, John. 1993. "Russia: Confronting a Loss of Empire." In *Nations and Politics in the Soviet Successor States* (pp. 43–74), ed. Ian Bremmer and Ray Taras. Cambridge: Cambridge University Press.

Edwards, Mike. 1994 (Aug.). "Soviet Pollution." *National Geographic* 186(2): 70–99.

Evans, Alfred B., Jr. 1998 (Sept.) "Russia's Politics of Uncertainty." *American Political Science Review* 92(3): 733–34.

Evans, Geoffrey, and Stephen Whitefield, 1998 (Sept.). "The Evolution of Left and Right in Post-Soviet Russia." *Europe-Asia Studies* 50(6): 1023–43.

Ferguson, Rob. 1998 (May). "Will Democracy Strike Back? Workers and Politics in the Kuzbass." *Europe-Asia Studies* 50(3): 445–69.

Finifter, Ada W., and Ellen Mickiewicz. 1992 (Dec.). "Redefining the Political System of the USSR: Mass Support and Political Change." *American Political Science Review* 86(4): 857.

Fish, M. Steven. 1995. *Opposition and Regime in the New Russian Revolution.* Princeton, NJ: Princeton University Press.

Freeland, Chrystia. 1998 (Oct. 12). "Not-so-Badfellas." *The New Republic* 219(15): 18–19.

Frost, Sheri and Denis Makarov. 1998 (Dec.). "Changing Post-Totalitarian Values in Russia Through Public Deliberation Methodology." *PS: Political Science and Politics* 31(4): 775–82.

Frye, Timothy. 1997 (Oct.). "A Politics of Institutional Choice: Post-Communist Presidencies." *Comparative Political Studies* 30(5): 523–53.

Garthoff, Raymond. 1966. *Soviet Military Policy.* London: Farber and Farber.

Garthoff, Raymond. 1992. *Deterrence and Revolution in Soviet Military Doctrine.* Washington, DC: Brookings Institution.

Gessen, Masha. 1998 (Dec. 14). "St. Petersburg Dispatch: Pistol Politics." *The New Republic* 10–11.

Gibson, James L. 1998 (March). "Putting Up with Fellow Russians: An Analysis of Political Tolerance in the Fledgling Russian Democracy." *Political Research Quarterly* 51(1): 37–69.

Goldman, Marshall. 1994. *Lost Opportunity.* New York: W. W. Norton.

Golosov, Grigoril. 1998 (Autumn). "Who Survives? Party Origins, Organizational Development, and Electoral Performance in Post-Communist Russia." *Political Studies* 46(3): 511–44.

Gorer, Geoffrey, and John Rickman. 1962. *The People of Great Russia: A Psychological Study.* New York: W. W. Norton.

Gray, Francine du Plessix. 1989. *Soviet Women: Walking the Tightrope.* New York: Doubleday.

Green, Barbara. 1994. *The Dynamics of Russian Politics: A Short History.* Westport, CT: Greenwood Press.

Gregor, James. 1998 (Mar.). "Fascism and the New Russian Nationalism." *Communist and Post-Communist Studies* 31(1): 1–14.

Hahn, Jeffrey W. 1992. "State Institutions in Transition." In *Developments in Soviet and Post-Soviet Politics*, ed. Stephen White, Alex Pravda, and Zvi Gitelman. London: Macmillan.

Hahn, Jeffrey W. 1995. *Democratization in Russia: The Development of Legislative Institutions.* Armonk, NY: M. E. Sharpe.

Hanson, Philip. 1998 (Summer). "Governance and the Russian Economy." *Demokratizatsiya* 587.

Haspel, Moshe, Thomas Remington, and Steven Smith. 1998 (May). "Electoral Institutions and Party Cohesion in the Russian Duma." *The Journal of Politics* 60(2): 417–39.

Hauslohner, Peter. 1989. "Politics Before Gorbachev: De-Stalinization and the Roots of Reform." In *Politics, Society and Nationality Inside Gorbachev's Russia* (pp. 41–90), ed. Seweryn Bialer. Boulder, CO: Westview Press.

Hewett, Ed A., and Victor H. Winston, eds. 1991. *Milestones in Glasnost and Perestroyka: The Economy.* Washington, DC: Brookings Institution.

Hoetasch, Otto. 1966. *The Evolution of Russia* (pp. 7–12). Translated by Rhys Evana. San Diego, CA: Harcourt Brace Jovanovich.

Hughes, James. 1997 (Sept.). "Sub-National Elites and Post-Communist Transformation in Russia: A Reply to Kryshtanovskaya and White." *Europe-Asian Studies* 49(6): 1017–37.

Ivanov, Mikhail. 1998 (April). "The Kremlin and the Bottle." *Russian Life* 41(4): 16–22.

Kelley, Donald R. 1987. *Soviet Politics from Brezhnev to Gorbachev.* New York: Praeger.

Kramer, John M. 1998 (Oct.). "The Politics of Corruption." *Current History* 97(621): 329–35.

Krasnikov, Yevgeny. 1998 (Mar. 11). "The Split is Yet to Come." *The Current Digest of the Post-Soviet Press* 50(6): 12–14.

Kux, Stephan. 1990. *Soviet Federalism: A Comparative Perspective.* Boulder, CO: Westview.

Lapidus, Gail W. 1989. "State and Society: Toward the Emergence of Civil Society in the Soviet Union." In *Politics, Society and Nationality Inside Gorbachev's Russia* (pp. 121–47), ed. Seweryn Bialer. Boulder, CO: Westview Press.

Levinson, Aleksei, Boris Gorzev, Yevgeny Andreyev, and Georgy Bout. 1997 (Feb. 5). "Who's Adapting to New Russian Reality? Three Takes." *The Current Digest of Post-Soviet Press* 49(1): 1–4.

Lewin, M. 1989. Cited in *Soviet Politics: An Introduction* (p. 60), by Richard Sakwa. London: Routledge.

Mandel, David. 1992. "Post-Perestroika: Revolution from Above v. Revolution from Below." In *Developments in Soviet and Post-Soviet Politics* (pp. 278–99), ed. Stephen White, Alex Pravda, and Zvi Gitelman. London: Macmillan.

Massie, Robert K. 1980. *Peter the Great: His Life and World.* New York: Ballantine.

McAuley, Mary. 1992. *Soviet Politics: 1917–1991.* Oxford: Oxford University Press.

McAuley, Mary. 1997. *Russia's Politics of Uncertainty.* Cambridge: Cambridge University Press.

McFaul, Michael, and Nikolai Petrov. 1997 (Nov.). "Russian Electoral Politics After Transition: Regional and National Assessments." *Post-Soviet Geography and Economics* 38(9): 507–50.

Meier, Andrew. 1998 (Sept. 21). "Yeltsin's Mighty Presidential Web." *Time International* 150(3): 80.

Mellor, Rosemary. 1997 (Sept.). "Through a Glass Darkly: Investigating the St. Petersburg Administration." *International Journal of Urban and Regional Research* 21(3): 481–503.

Morrison, John. 1991. *Boris Yeltsin: From Bolshevik to Democrat.* New York: Dutton.

Nove, Alec. 1992. *An Economic History of the USSR: 1917–1991.* London: Penguin Books.

Ostapchuk, Anna. 1997 (Dec. 25). "Intelligentsia Spilt in Two." *Moscow News* 51–52: 4.

Pipes, Richard. 1964. *The Formation of the Soviet Union.* Cambridge, MA: Harvard University Press.

Pipes, Richard. 1993. *Russia Under the Bolshevik Regime.* New York: Alfred A. Knopf.

Pipes, Richard. 1997 (Sept.–Oct.). "Is Russia Still an Enemy?" *Foreign Affairs* 76(5): 65–79.

Plutnik, Albert and Dmitry Filimonov. 1998 (July 22). "Why Such Apathy about 'Fascistization' of Russia?" *The Current Digest of the Post-Soviet Press* 50(25): 7–9.

Rainone, Zebulon T. 1998 (June). "Democracy Stalled: Evaluating the Russian Federation Today." *East European Quarterly* 32(2): 269–81.

Remington, Thomas F. 1992. "Towards a Participatory Politics?" In *Developments in Soviet and Post-Soviet Politics* (pp. 147–73), ed. Stephen White, Alex Pravda, and Zvi Gitelman. London: Macmillan.

Remington, Thomas, Steven Smith, and Moshe Haspel. 1998 (Oct.). "Decrees, Laws, and Inter-Branch Relations in the Russian Federation." *Post-Soviet Affairs* 14(4): 287–322.

Rigby, T. H. 1984. "Khrushchev and the Rules of the Soviet Political Game." In *Khrushchev and the Communist World* (pp. 39–81), ed. R. F. Miller and F. Feher. Totowa, NJ: Barnes and Noble.

Rigby, T. H. 1992. "Reconceptualising the Soviet System." In *Developments in Soviet and Post-Soviet Politics* (pp. 300–19), ed. Stephen White, Alex Pravda, and Zvi Gitelman. London: Macmillan.

Rosefielde, Steven. 1981 (Jan.). "An Assessment of the Sources and Uses of Gulag Forced Labour, 1929–1956." *Soviet Studies* 33: 1.

Rutland, Peter. 1992. "Economic Crisis and Reform." In *Developments in Soviet and Post-Soviet Politics* (pp. 200–26), ed. Stephen White, Alex Pravda, and Zvi Gitelman. London: Macmillan.

Sakwa, Richard. 1989. *Soviet Politics: An Introduction.* London: Routledge.

Salisbury, Harrison. 1978. *Black Night, White Snow: Russia's Revolutions 1905–1917.* New York: Doubleday.

Schmemann, Serge. 1993 (Nov. 28). "A Once Proud Force Finds Itself Impoverished and Demoralized. *The New York Times*, p. 1.

Sharlet, Robert. 1997 (July–Sept.). "The Politics of Constitutional Amendment in Russia." *Post-Soviet Affairs* 13(3): 197–200.

Shenfield, Stephen. 1998 (Oct.–Dec.). "The Weimar/Russia Comparison: Reflections of Hanson and Kopstein." *Post-Soviet Affairs* 14(4): 355–69.

Shub, David. 1966. *Lenin.* Middlesex, England: Penguin.

Smith, Gordon B. 1992. *Soviet Politics: Struggling with Change.* 2nd ed. New York: St. Martin's.

Smith, Hedrick. 1991. *The New Russians.* New York: Random House.

Spulber, Nicolas. 1991. *Restructuring the Soviet Economy.* Ann Arbor, MI: University of Michigan Press.

Theen, Rolf. 1993 (Winter). "Russia at the Grassroots: Reform at the Local and Regional Levels." *Indepth* 3(1): 53–90.

Ticktin, Hillel. 1992. *Origins of the Crisis in the USSR.* Armonk, NY: M. E. Sharpe.

Todaro, Michael P. 1989. *Economic Development in the Third World.* New York: Longman.

Tolz, Vera. 1998 (Sept.). "Forging the Nation: National Identity and Nation Building in Post-Communist Russia." *Europe-Asia Studies* 50(6): 993–1023.

Tolz, Vera, and Irina Busygina. 1997 (Dec.). "Regional Governors and the Kremlin: The Ongoing Battle for Power." *Communist and Post-Communist Studies* 30(4): 401–26.

Treisman, Daniel. 1998 (Oct.). "Dollars and Democratization: The Role and Power of Money in Russia's Transitional Elections." *Comparative Politics*, p. 1.

Trotsky, Leon. 1934. Adapted from *Recent Political Thought* (p. 157), ed. Francis W. Coker. New York: Appleton-Century-Crofts.

Tucker, Robert C. 1987. *Political Culture and Leadership in Soviet Russia: From Lenin to Gorbachev.* Brighton, England: Wheatsheaf Books.

Ulrich, Marybeth P. 1998. "The Search for Stability in the Russian Army." In Danopoulos, Constantine and Daniel Zirker (eds.) *The Military and Society in the Former Eastern Bloc.* Boulder, CO: Westview Press.

Urban, Michael. 1998 (Sept.). "Remythologising the Russian State." *Europe-Asia Studies* 50(6): 969–93.

Urban, Michael, Vyacheslav Igrunov, and Sergei Mitrokhin. 1997. *The Rebirth of Politics in Russia.* Boston, MA: Cambridge University Press.

Wheatcroft, S. 1981 (Apr.). "On Assessing the Size of Forced Concentration Camp Labour in the Soviet Union, 1929–56." *Soviet Studies* 33(2): 265–95.

Willerton, John P. 1992. "Executive Power and Political Leadership." In *Developments in Soviet and Post-Soviet Politics* (pp. 44–67), ed. Stephen White, Alex Pravda, and Zvi Gitelman. London: Macmillan.

Wolfe, Bertram D. 1964. *Three Who Made a Revolution.* New York: Dial.

Yavlinsky, Grigory. 1998 (May–June). "Russia's Phony Capitalism." *Foreign Affairs* 77(3): 67–90.

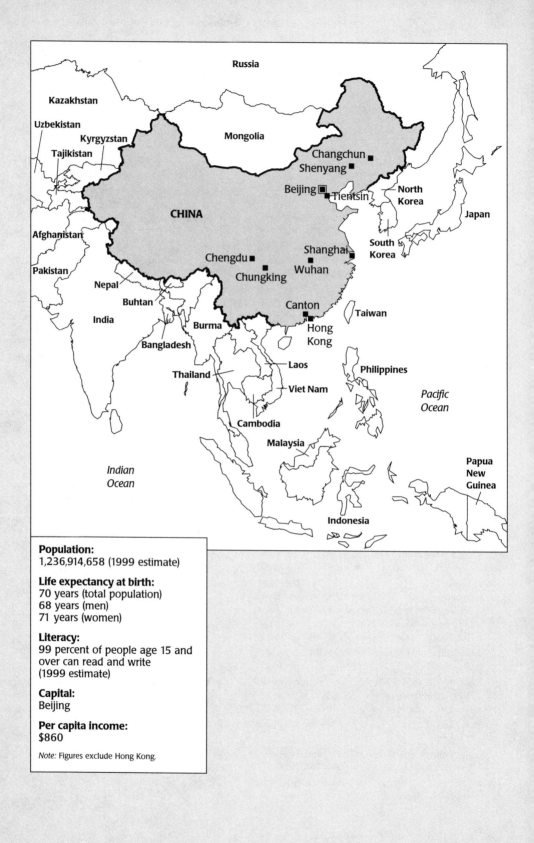

Population:
1,236,914,658 (1999 estimate)

Life expectancy at birth:
70 years (total population)
68 years (men)
71 years (women)

Literacy:
99 percent of people age 15 and
over can read and write
(1999 estimate)

Capital:
Beijing

Per capita income:
$860

Note: Figures exclude Hong Kong.

7

The People's Republic of China
The Politics of Impending Change

With more than 1.2 billion citizens, China is the world's most populous nation. Indeed, its population is larger than that of Western Europe and North America combined. China is also the only remaining member of the communist bloc capable of posing a sustained military threat to the new world order being forged by the United States and its allies, a threat underscored by China's status as a nuclear power. China, moreover, is a permanent member of the Security Council of the United Nations. Collective action by that body is virtually impossible without the support of the Chinese leadership. Finally, it should be noted that China may soon possess the world's largest economy (Overholt 1993). Wishful thinking aside, there can be no new world order without the active participation of China. Many observers now expect the twenty-first century to be the century of China (Nicholas and Wu Dunn 1994).

Despite ongoing tensions, relations between China and the United States have improved dramatically in recent years. The United States wants access to the huge Chinese market. It also believes that increased trade between China and the West will erode communist dogma and place China firmly on the path to capitalist development. This assumption is supported by China's begrudging transition from socialism to state capitalism. China, for its part, desperately needs First World technology and has turned to foreign investment as a means of acquiring that technology. Be this as it may, China remains very much an authoritarian state. Whether it will continue to be a communist state remains to be seen (Cheng and White 1998).

In this chapter we will examine the politics of China, placing special emphasis upon Chinese efforts to develop a capitalist economic system while simultaneously retaining a Marxist political system. Can capitalism serve the will of Marxist leaders, or will capitalism destroy communism from within? We will begin by reviewing recent Chinese history and then move to an examination of China's political institutions. This accomplished, we will look at the actors and environments of Chinese politics. We will conclude by examining the challenges that face China in the areas of democracy, stability, human rights, quality of life, economic growth, and environmental concern.

China in Historical and Cultural Perspective

The history of modern China begins with the proclamation of the Republic of China in 1912. Prior to that date, China had been ruled by a succession of feudal dynasties, the authority of which ebbed and flowed with the military power of the emperor. Periods of unity were crowned by unparalleled cultural and technical achievements. The invention of printing, gunpowder, and paper money all stand in testimony to Chinese creativity. Periods of unity, however, were often short-lived and gave way to civil wars, many lasting fifty years or more (Sivin 1990; Gernet 1982).

As in the case of Japan, the collapse of feudalism in China was precipitated by conflict with the West. The early nineteenth century found British merchants selling large quantities of India-grown opium in China. The emperor's attempt to stem the flow of opium from British India into China threatened the lucrative opium trade and was used by Britain as a pretext for war with China, albeit a war that involved little more than a small flotilla of ships. The "Opium War" (1839–1842) forced the Manchu (Qing) Dynasty to open China's coastal cities to foreign trade and to cede Hong Kong to Great Britain. Other Western powers joined Britain in extracting concessions from China's decaying regime, feudal armies being unable to resist the modern weapons of the West (McAleavy 1967).

Much as in the case of Japan, defeat by Western forces undermined the legitimacy of China's political institutions. Unlike the Japanese case, however, the ancient regime failed to collapse. Rather, the emperor would preside over more than half a century of decay, disintegration, foreign humiliation, famine, disease, rebellion, and civil war. The Taiping Rebellion (1850) alone resulted in some 20,000,000 deaths (Liu 1986).

The Western penetration of China unleashed two contradictory responses among the Chinese masses. The first response was a rush to acquire Western education and technology. Foreign schools flourished in China's main cities, giving birth to a Westernized middle class. The modernizers urged reform upon the collapsing regime, but to no avail. Many were put to death for their efforts, while others formed secret revolutionary organizations (Liu 1986).

The second reaction to foreign penetration was anti-foreign nationalism or xenophobia. To many Chinese, particularly those of lower class origins, foreigners were responsible for bringing death and destruction to their country. Symbolic of China's xenophobic reaction to foreigners were the "Boxers," a band of peasant mystics who dedicated themselves to the destruction of everything foreign. The Boxers, who claimed to possess magical powers that rendered them invincible to Western bullets, soon found broad support among China's illiterate masses. In 1900, the Boxers were officially blessed by the emperor and ordered to rid Beijing of its foreign population. The Western community dispatched a joint expeditionary force to quell the rebellion, destroying much of Beijing and leaving China an occupied country (McAleavy 1967).

Suggesting the magnitude of the opium trade, vast quantities of the drug await export from an opium factory in Patima, India, during the 1880s. Opium smuggling upset the balance of trade and destroyed China's economy.

Confucianism

The core of traditional Chinese culture is **Confucianism**. Confucius (511–479 BC) was a senior official in one of the minor Chinese mini-states of his era (Wei-Ming 1990). Forsaking his government position, he became a great educator, preaching that wise government was a gift of heaven and that it was the responsibility of governments to act in a meritorious and responsible manner. Rulers were encouraged to care for their citizens and to promote social harmony within their realms. Government officials, moreover, were to be selected from among the most learned members of society. It was the wise who were to rule. The masses, for their part, were instructed to be socially responsible.

Social responsibility, according to Confucius, was built upon four key elements: (1) compliance with the laws of the land, (2) loyalty to one's family, (3) responsibility toward others, and (4) a continual striving for self-improvement. The overarching values of Confucianism, then, were order, hard work, and harmony. If everyone played his or her role properly, society would be both prosperous and peaceful. Hard work and rule by the wise would assure prosperity, and social responsibility would promote peace and harmony (Pye 1991).

Confucianism, then, is a secular religion that appeals to a universal desire for order and harmony. While its ideals of a just and ordered society were seldom achieved in the tumultuous world of feudal China, its underlying principles continue to have a profound appeal throughout much of the Asian continent. Confucianism is clearly the dominant cultural-religious force in China today (*SCMPI,** Oct. 1, 1994, 6).

---

*SCMPI stands for South China Morning Post International.

Sun Yat-sen and the Kuomintang

The aspirations of China's Westernized reformers found expression in the works of Sun Yat-sen, a Chinese physician and intellectual who had traveled widely in the West. Sun Yat-sen's philosophy stressed three principles: democracy, nationalism, and people's livelihood. Democracy, according to Sun Yat-sen, would give expression to the will of the Chinese masses, but it was to be an orderly democracy in keeping with Chinese concerns for order and stability. China was also to be an independent nation free of foreign domination, as well as a caring nation that stressed social equality and the fair distribution of land. Sun Yat-sen's principle of "people's livelihood" stopped short of a call for socialism, but his writings were warmly embraced by the socialists of the era.

Feudal China gave way to a military uprising on October 10, 1911, and Sun Yat-sen was proclaimed president of the Republic of China. Although it had collapsed with scarcely a whimper, Chinese feudalism left a profound legacy. China's feudal dynasties had forged a unified Chinese state and created a bureaucratic apparatus capable of administering that state. The feudal era, moreover, had nurtured a deeply rooted sense of Chinese cultural identity. However tumultuous their political environment, the Chinese were confident of the superiority of their culture (Fairbank 1971).

Sun Yat-sen had been selected to head the revolutionary government, but most power was retained by the military. Sun Yat-sen resigned the presidency in 1912 but remained the spiritual guide of the revolution (Liu 1986; Linebarger 1969).

Upon Sun Yat-sen's resignation from the military government, his followers formed the **Kuomintang (KMT)**, *a nationalist movement designed to give expression to his revolutionary vision* (Liu 1986; Linebarger 1969). The KMT rapidly became the dominant political movement in Chinese politics, but it suffered from fragmentation and the lack of a clear ideology. While intellectuals argued for a democratic path to modernization, the military wing of the party called for a modernizing dictatorship on the Japanese model. The latter emerged supreme, but it failed to provide the KMT with a coherent organizational structure (Liu 1986; Linebarger 1969).

Lacking the support of Sun Yat-sen and the KMT, the revolutionary government soon dissolved into anarchy. Rival military commanders pillaged Beijing in a futile quest for emperorship, while bandit gangs terrorized the countryside. A powerful KMT could have seized power at this point, but the movement lacked the organizational capacity to do so.

Chiang Kai-shek

During the mid-1920s, the leadership of the KMT passed to a young general by the name of Chiang Kai-shek. Chiang Kai-shek provided the KMT with the organizational structure that it had previously lacked and immediately set about building a military force that would make him the leader of China. Once in power, his first task would be to bring order to Beijing. His second task would be to destroy China's newly formed Communist Party, a party with which the KMT had previously maintained a tenuous alliance.

For a brief period, it seemed as if Chiang Kai-shek would succeed on both counts. Beijing was seized in 1928, and the Communists were put to flight. To control Beijing, however, is not to control China. Warlords maintained control over large areas of China, while the Communists established themselves in others. As late as 1937, the KMT was in full control of only four of China's provinces (Liu 1986; Fairbank 1987).

Left to its own devices, the KMT may well have crushed its Communist rivals. It was clearly the stronger of the two organizations. China, however, was not left to its own devices. The Japanese attacked China in 1931, occupying the northeastern section of the country and placing the KMT forces on the defensive. Lacking the capacity to fight both the Communists and Japanese, Chiang Kai-shek reluctantly joined the Communists in a united front against the Japanese. In retrospect, this was a mistake. While Chiang Kai-shek's forces were exhausted by the struggle against the Japanese, the Communists, under the leadership of Mao Zedung, emerged from the conflict with a disciplined and battle-tested army.

Communism in China

The end of World War II would witness a desperate struggle between the KMT and the Communists for control of China. It was both a war between armies and a psychological struggle for the hearts and minds of the Chinese people. The Communists would win both wars. Not only had Chiang Kai-shek's troops become exhausted by their long struggle against the Japanese, but the KMT had become a corrupt and self-serving organization. Chiang Kai-shek was well aware of the problem, establishing special "tiger-beating squads" to fight the corrupt officials, or "tigers," who preyed upon innocent citizens (Chang 1991, 85–86). His efforts were to no avail, for KMT officials expressed the same disdain for the Chinese masses as the emperors of old.

The Communists, by contrast, seized every opportunity to build strong links with the peasantry. Party officials were given strict orders to treat the peasants with courtesy and respect. They also expropriated the property of the large landowners and distributed it to the peasants, a process called "the land returning home" (Chang 1991, 166). In much the same manner, the Communists treated captured nationalist soldiers, most of whom were unwilling conscripts, with leniency (Chang 1991). Many switched allegiances and joined the ranks of the Communists.

By 1949, Communist troops controlled most of China, forcing Chiang Kai-shek and his remaining KMT forces to take refuge on the Chinese island of Taiwan. The civil war thus ended with the existence of two Chinas: *mainland China,* referred to as the **People's Republic of China**, and *Taiwan,* referred to as the **Republic of China**. Each claimed to be the legitimate government of China, with Chiang Kai-shek and his US-supported armies posing a constant threat to the security of the communist state.

The Communist Party of China: Its Origins. The Communist Party of China (CCP) was formed in 1921 with the active encouragement of the Soviet Union. For the most part, its members were drawn from the same base of students and intellectuals that had earlier formed the KMT. Many of China's young Communists were former members of the KMT who had become disillusioned with that organization's lack of direction. Others were attracted to the party by the power of Marxist philosophy and the success of the Russian Revolution.

While space does not allow for a full recounting of the devastating struggle between the KMT and the CCP, suffice it to say that 1934 found the communist forces on the verge of collapse. Faced with annihilation, Mao Zedung, the leader of the CCP, led most of his remaining troops on a forced march to a remote region of China where they would be inaccessible to Chiang Kai-shek's army. The famed "long march" covered some 8,000 miles, with only 20 percent of its participants surviving the ordeal (Liu 1986).

In desperation, Mao realized that intellectuals and China's small labor movement could not be relied on to defeat the KMT and transform China into a communist society. *China's illiterate peasants—the overwhelming majority of the Chinese population—would have to be transformed into a revolutionary force.*

Many Marxists scoffed at Mao's assertion that illiterate peasants could be welded into a viable revolutionary force. Marxist doctrine was based upon the class consciousness of industrial workers, a consciousness engendered by years of capitalist exploitation. China's peasants lacked such revolutionary consciousness. For the most part, they were conservative and superstitious. Mao, himself, had called them "blank" (Schram 1970, 352).

Mao, however, was to demonstrate that intense socialization (indoctrination) could transform peasants into ardent Communists. This was particularly true of peasants who had been uprooted by decades of war and social disintegration. Mao's peasant recruits were taught to read and write, and indoctrination in Marxist theory was paralleled by instruction in practical skills. The formation of communist work groups also fostered a sense of solidarity and collective belonging. As described by Alan P. L. Liu:

> In every village Chinese Communists organized "poor peasants" associations to facilitate land distribution. After that, every group of peasants, regardless of age and sex, was organized into some useful auxiliary for the CCP. There were, for example, the Red Defense Army (adult males), Young Pioneers (teenage youth), and Children's Corps. These were assigned tasks, such as sentry duty, scouting, policing, transporting, road repairing, and caring for the wounded (Liu 1986, 26).

Central to Mao's revolutionary strategy was the doctrine of guerrilla warfare. Frontal attacks on the KMT had proven disastrous. Hit-and-run tactics, by contrast, enabled the CCP to keep the stronger KMT forces at bay. Part and parcel of this strategy was the infiltration of KMT strongholds by communist supporters. It was this same strategy that would provide the foundation of communist victory in Vietnam (Godwin 1988).

The CCP and the KMT joined forces in 1937 to resist the Japanese invasion of China, but they resumed their battle for control of China at the war's end. The battle was an unequal one, with the Communist Party now boasting more than a million members as well as an army of 1.2 million regular soldiers. These, in turn, were supported by more than 2 million irregular forces. Mao claimed victory in December of 1949 as KMT forces retreated to the island of Taiwan.

The Communists Take Over. The Chinese Communist Party had been forged as an instrument of revolutionary struggle. It now faced the challenge of transforming the world's most populous state into a Marxist society. The task would be difficult, for the Chinese mainland had been devastated by more than a decade of war and rebellion. The communist leadership, moreover, feared an American-backed "counter-revolution" by KMT forces on Taiwan and was forced to divert scarce resources into military production.

The most enduring obstacle to communist success, however, was neither the wartime devastation of China nor the hostility of the United States. Rather, it was the superstitious nature of China's illiterate peasants and their attachment to the land. The peasants, comprising more than 80 percent of China's population, knew nothing of the modern world, and their attitudes toward the political system were a blend of fear and hostility. The success of communism would depend ultimately upon Mao's ability to transform China's masses into a modern political and economic community. The task would not be easy.

On the plus side, the Communists had emerged from the civil war with a political-military apparatus that was both large and battle-tested. A decade of war and revolution, moreover, had created an intense desire for peace and stability among the Chinese masses. China was ready for a strong, centralized government (Liu 1986). Finally, Mao also benefited from the support of the Soviet Union. From the Soviet perspective, the victory of communism in China represented a turning point in world revolution. It could not be allowed to fail.

The USSR, however, was not without misgivings toward its communist neighbor. The Soviets welcomed the emergence of China as a client-state subservient to Soviet interests, but they did not welcome the emergence of a potential competitor for the leadership of the communist world. China, after all, possessed almost three times the population of the USSR. The situation was delicate (Ogden 1992). The honeymoon between the two communist powers would be short-lived, as Mao lost little time in demanding that the Soviets return "illegally" occupied territory. By the mid-1970s, the Sino-Soviet border had become a war zone (Godwin 1988).

Consolidating the Revolution. Whatever his problems with the USSR, Mao could not begin the task of transforming China into a modern industrial power until he had consolidated the revolution. Consolidation of the revolution required four critical steps:

1. The CCP had to crush the remaining opposition to communist rule.
2. The CCP had to transform its revolutionary institutions into institutions of governance.
3. The economy had to be nationalized.
4. The population had to be revolutionized.

Of the four steps required to consolidate the revolution, the destruction of the opposition was the most immediate. Mao's dictum on the topic left no room for ambiguity: "Power," he said, "grows out of the barrel of a gun." Known opponents of the regime were either slaughtered or sent to work camps. Intellectuals and members of the bourgeoisie were closely watched, many being sent to forced labor camps for "re-education" (Chang 1991). No unions or mass associations of any type were allowed to exist other than those sponsored by the Communist Party.

The transformation of the Communist Party from a party of revolution into a party of governance was accomplished by imposing the Soviet model on China. This model consisted of three main elements: the Communist Party, the state apparatus, and the military, all of which will be described shortly. The Communist Party made policy, the state apparatus executed policy, and the military kept the party in power and enforced its dictates. All important figures in the state apparatus and the military were also ranking members of the Communist Party. Despite this elaborate framework, effective decision-making power during the first two decades of communist rule was concentrated in the hands of Mao Zedung.

Steps to consolidate Party control over the Chinese economy were equally pervasive (Harding 1981). All of China's industrial, commercial, and financial establishments were nationalized, and all farms were collectivized. Economic development was attacked with military precision as roads, dams, and other projects were constructed by forced labor, much of it drawn from the ranks of China's political prisoners.

Mao also moved rapidly to "revolutionize" China's population. The problem was twofold. *First, China's peasants had to be shaken from their political indifference.* China was a nation of peasants, and there could be no modernization without their active participation. *Second, China's urban population had to be cleansed of its anti-revolutionary tendencies.* Among other things, this included cynicism, survivalism, and strong inclinations toward capitalism.

Sayings of Chairman Mao

■ "The socialist system will eventually replace the capitalist system; this is an objective law independent of man's will. However much the reactionaries try to hold back the wheel of history, sooner or later revolution will take place and will inevitably triumph" (Mao 1967, 13).

■ "We should rid our ranks of all impotent thinking. All views that overestimate the strength of the enemy and underestimate the strength of the people are wrong" (Mao 1967, 46).

■ "We must see to it that all our cadres and all our people constantly bear in mind that ours is a big socialist country but an economically backward and poor one, and that this is a very great contradiction. To make China rich and strong needs several decades of intense effort, which will include, among other things, the effort to practice strict economy and combat waste, i.e., the policy of building up our country through diligence and frugality" (Mao 1967, 105).

■ "We must affirm anew the discipline of the Party, namely:
(1) the individual is subordinate to the organization;
(2) the minority is subordinate to the majority;
(3) the lower level is subordinate to the higher level; and
(4) the entire membership is subordinate to the Central Committee."

■ "Whoever violates these articles of discipline disrupts Party unity" (Mao 1967, 144–45).

Mao attacked traditionalism in a campaign against the "four olds": old ideas, old habits, old cultures, and old customs. Unrevolutionary behavior, in turn, was attacked by a campaign against the "five evils": bribery, tax evasion, theft of state intelligence, cheating on state contracts, and theft of state property (Chang 1991).

Through these and similar campaigns, Mao aspired to transform China into a totalitarian society on the Stalinist model. All dimensions of economics, society, culture, and psychology were to be brought under the control of the Party (Pye 1968). Nothing less would suffice in Mao's drive for domination and development.

Mao's authority came from five sources. *First, Mao was Chairman (Secretary General) of the Chinese Communist Party, the most powerful position in China.* Mao used his position as party chairman to assure that his supporters dominated all key positions in the Party, state, and the military.

Second, Mao was adroit at manipulating the various "tendencies" and cliques within the governing apparatus. As described by Jung Chang:

> Mao had to scheme hard to preserve his power. In this he was a supreme master. His favorite reading, which he recommended to other Party leaders, was a classic thirty-volume collection of Chinese court intrigues. In fact, Mao's rule was best understood in terms of a medieval court, in which he exercised spellbinding power over his courtiers and subjects. He was also a maestro at "divide and rule," and at manipulating men's inclination to throw others to the wolves (Chang 1991, 228).

Third, Mao went out of his way to maintain strong support within the military. Then, as now, the military was the ultimate guarantor of political leadership.

Fourth, Mao went to extraordinary lengths to transform himself into a charismatic demi-god (Dittmer 1987; Chang 1991). By the mid-1960s, *The Little Red Book* of Mao's sayings had become the main guide to policy and politics in China. In near-religious litany, political discourse was couched in the sayings of Chairman Mao.

The sayings of Chairman Mao were reinforced by the thousands of "miracles" ascribed to Mao. Miracles were an important element in Mao's charisma, for the masses of Mao's era were illiterate peasants predisposed to mysticism and magic. The more they believed in Mao's magic, the more likely they would be to follow his commands. The older Mao became, the more magnificent his miracles, for an admission of weakness would break the spell of his power.

The Miracles of Mao

- "The success of the P.L.A. 3016 Unit's Mao Tse-tung's thought propaganda team of medical workers in curing deaf-muteness proves once again that people armed with Mao Tse-tung's thought have the greatest combat effectiveness, and can surmount all difficulties and perform miracles" (Urban 1971, 20).

- "One of our guides never fastened her seat belt; she told me that no safety precautions were necessary because the pilot could make no mistake, inspired as he was by Chairman Mao. The air hostesses even danced in the corridors of the aircraft, and on several occasions led communal singing of their favorite Maoist tunes. Mao the helmsman was a great favourite and very infectious at that" (Urban 1971, 29).

- "...Mai-Hsien was unconscious or semi-conscious for quite a long time after being admitted to hospital. People anxiously awaited his regaining consciousness. The nurse tested reactions by showing him a pictorial magazine. As she turned over the pages she noticed his lips quivering. His eyes were concentrated on a picture of Chairman Mao. With great effort he managed to raise his left hand, which had remained useless since his admission to hospital, and with trembling fingers he touched the picture....He suddenly exclaimed 'Chairman Mao!' It was the first time since he had been in hospital that he had spoken so clearly" (Urban 1971, 144).

Finally, Mao ruled by fear. Once again quoting Jung Chang,

Fear was never absent in the building up of Mao's cult.... A popular song went: "Father is close, Mother is close, but neither is as close as Chairman Mao." We were drilled to think that anyone, including our parents, who was not totally for Mao was our enemy. Many parents encouraged their children to grow up as conformists, as this would be safest for their future (Chang 1991, 262).

Personality and Politics: The Cult of Mao Zedung. The more political power is concentrated in the hands of a single individual, the more the personality of that individual will shape his or her policy decisions. In this regard, Mao's personality blended a dogmatic belief in Marxist philosophy with an insatiable thirst for power and a profound distrust of intellectuals.[1]

The various dimensions of Mao's personality would find expression in an endless succession of mass "campaigns" that were to become the hallmark of Maoist rule. Of these, three were of paramount importance: the "Hundred Flowers Blooming" campaign of 1957, the "Great Leap Forward" campaign of 1958–1960, and the "Great Proletarian Cultural Revolution" campaign of 1966–1969.

The harshness of the communist drive to consolidate power caused intense resentment in China. It also stifled creativity and innovation, both of which were essential for China's economic development (Liu 1986). It is hard to be creative when the slightest offense to government officials can land you in jail. In May 1957, accordingly, Mao moved to stimulate greater innovation and popular support by calling upon the Party to "let one hundred schools of thought contend; let one hundred flowers bloom" (Pye 1991, 244).

The period of the "Hundred Flowers Blooming" was short-lived. Stunned by the intensity of mass criticism, Mao's flirtation with free discussion was terminated before the end of the year, giving way to a new "anti-rightist" campaign. A rightist, in Mao's view, was anyone who complained about the government or the Party. Deng Xiaoping, a subsequent ruler of China, was placed in charge of an

---

[1]A particularly interesting portrait of Mao's personality is provided by his personal physician, Dr. Li Zhisui, in his book *The Private Life of Chairman Mao*, translated by Tai Hung-chao. New York: Random House, 1994.

A smiling Chairman Mao stands in the midst of a group of students at the Shaoshan School in 1959. Mao Zedung ruled China with a combination of charisma, manipulation, and intimidation.

anti-rightist campaign in which some 100,000 counter-revolutionaries were killed and millions of other were sent to the countryside for "re-education" (Pye 1991, 244). By and large, this meant working in rice paddies from dawn to dusk.

Mao's second grand campaign was the "Great Leap Forward" of 1958–1960. Earlier experiments with economic planning had proved disappointing as industry lagged and agriculture was in disarray. In a classic effort to place mind over matter, Mao ordered unrealistic increases in economic productivity. Workers were forced to work double shifts, machine tools were driven to the breaking point, and coal and other natural resources were consumed with little concern for cost or conservation (Pye 1991). By the end of the campaign, some 20 million Chinese peasants had been forced to leave the countryside and work in Mao's new factories (Liu 1986, 44).

Mao's Accomplishments and Their Human Costs

Mao Zedung's successes were many. He had forged the Chinese revolution, and he had made major contributions to Marxist-Leninist theory by demonstrating that the states of the Third World could bypass capitalism in their transition from feudalism to socialism. Such contributions, while archaic to the Western mind, continue to strike a responsive chord in many areas of the Third World.

Mao must also be credited with establishing a political system that provided the Chinese population with a minimally acceptable level of health, education, and nutrition. Most Chinese were employed, and most received at least rudimentary housing. These were no small achievements in a country of 700,000,000 citizens, most of whom were plagued by illiteracy, disease, and starvation.

Despite these accomplishments, however, the human costs of Mao's revolution were staggering. Millions of Chinese citizens died in Mao's Cultural Revolution and related campaigns, and the Chinese economy continues to suffer from the devastation of the Great Leap Forward.

Both the optimism and the chaos of the Great Leap Forward are epitomized by Mao's dream of transforming even rural villages into "backyard" steelworks.

> As for the "backyard furnaces," the peasants, who were forced by their leaders to build steel furnaces about which they knew nothing, hastily contrived structures that often blew up or did not function at all.... Thus, under the supervision of cadres anxious to overfulfill production quotas that the central government said other communes had fulfilled, the peasants ripped out the metal heating units in their buildings, tore down metal fences, and threw excess pots, pans, and shovels into the furnaces (Ogden 1992, 43).

The economic chaos created by the Great Leap Forward weakened Mao's power and placed him on the defensive (Dittmer 1987). Mao responded in classic Chinese style by strengthening his personal alliances within the Party and the military.

The Great Proletarian Cultural Revolution of 1966–1969.[2] With his power solidified, Mao began a relentless attack on reformers, the "capitalist rightists" as he called them, that would culminate in the Great Proletarian Cultural Revolution of 1966–1969. The Cultural Revolution began in early 1966, with Mao making an emotional appeal to his supporters to "sweep out the monsters and ghosts." The educational establishment was attacked first, with students sacking professors and administrators and replacing them with ad hoc revolutionary committees manned by Maoist students. Later in the same year, Mao called upon throngs of hysterical students to uproot the enemies of the revolution wherever they found them, thus giving birth to the famed "red guards." Waves of high school and college youth wearing red armbands attacked bureaucrats and factory managers, denouncing them as traitors and rightists (Chang 1991). Death estimates were enormous, but no one knows exactly how many were killed (Liu 1986).

The Cultural Revolution threw China into chaos, decimating the Party and replacing the government with a system of revolutionary committees beholden only to Mao. Economic activity had come to a standstill. Of China's political institutions, only the army remained intact (Godwin 1988).

By 1969, the Party had reasserted its authority, appointing Deng Xiaoping, the pragmatic economic reformer, to rebuild China's shattered economy. Mao had survived the Great Cultural Proletarian Revolution but was in ill health and died on September 9, 1976.

---

[2]Some vestiges of the Cultural Revolution remained until 1976.

The Era of Deng Xiaoping: Reform Begins. The struggle for succession was a complex process that far exceeds the scope of the present discussion. Suffice it to say that by 1978, Deng Xiaoping and the reformist wing of the Party were in ascendence. The challenges facing Deng Xiaoping were many. The military was challenging the authority of the Party leadership and had to be depoliticized. Conservative elements remained deeply entrenched in the Party apparatus and had to be neutralized. The Party and state bureaucracies, having become rigid, top-heavy, and corrupt, were reluctant to lead the charge of economic reform. Finally, Deng Xiaoping faced a gerentocracy crisis (Yu-lin 1991). The Chinese leadership had been forged in an era of revolution that had begun in the 1920s. Now very old men, China's leaders clung tenaciously to their positions of power. Deng himself was in his mid-seventies upon assuming power.

In many ways, Deng's approach to leadership was the opposite of Mao's (Goodman 1994). Mao was ideological, placing theory above reality. Deng, by contrast, was pragmatic, bending theory to the needs of reality. Mao distrusted intellectuals and foreigners, but Deng was comfortable with both. Mao struggled to keep China in a state of revolutionary fervor, while Deng stressed the need to build order and stability (Pye 1991). In one critical area, however, the two men were in complete agreement: the Communist Party was to remain dominant.

Under the slogan "Learn the Facts," Deng launched a program of sweeping economic reform. Peasant agricultural plots were extended, light industry was given priority over heavy industry, small-scale capitalism was encouraged, foreign investment was welcomed, and workers were free to seek jobs of their own choosing. In addition, special industrial zones were created in several of the coastal cities that had traditionally provided China's window on the West. These industrial zones, now free of suffocating bureaucratic regulations, became the focal point of China's experiment in guided capitalism.

Economic reform was paralleled by education reform in which Mao's emphasis on ideology gave way to Deng's "Four Modernizations": agriculture, industry, science, and the military (Ogden 1992). Bureaucratic control over China's schools was relaxed, but the Party organs maintained a high profile (Ogden 1992).

The Tiananmen Square Massacre. Deng Xiaoping was an economic reformer, not a democratic reformer. The two processes, however, are difficult to disentangle. Economic development requires an educated work force, relatively free communications, foreign investment, entrepreneurial risk-taking, a reasonably free market, and the opportunity for individuals to acquire wealth. The same conditions, however, make political control difficult.

Deng allowed limited political reform for the sake of reviving the Chinese economy (Zhibin 1991). Political reform, however, is a difficult process to monitor. By 1986, student demonstrations demanding greater political freedom had spread throughout China's major cities. Deng may have inadvertently triggered these demonstrations by reviving Mao's slogan of "Let a Hundred Flowers Bloom" (Pye 1991). Deng, solicitous of increased foreign investment, was reluctant to crush the demonstrations with force. Encouraged by Deng's restraint and the presence of foreign reporters, the spring of 1989 would see student protesters occupying Tiananmen Square, the Chinese equivalent of Red Square in Moscow. Demanding sweeping democratic reforms, the students erected barricades and challenged the government to evict them. Deng offered minor concessions, but the Party elders remained divided over both the seriousness of the event and the proper way of dealing with it (Chang 1993). The students, perhaps emboldened by the political disarray in the Soviet Union, demanded more.

Economic Reform Versus Political Control

It is difficult

■ to train technicians without raising political aspirations,

■ to facilitate economic communication without facilitating political communication,

■ to allow people to accumulate wealth without tempting them to use that wealth for political ends,

■ to permit decentralized economic decision making without undermining state planning,

■ to invite economic risk-taking without inviting political risk-taking, or

■ to invite foreign investment without opening the door to foreign values.

Both sides, moreover, became preoccupied with "saving face." The students wanted to be honored as patriots who had played a historic role in moving China toward democratic reform, but the Government refused. Honoring the students would be a sign of government weakness and would merely invite further demonstrations (Chang 1993). Army troops surrounded the square but seemed reluctant to act. When they did act, they displayed incredible brutality. Tanks opened fire on the barricades, massacring the students who manned them (Wasserstrom and Perry 1992; Oxenberg, Sullivan, and Lambert 1990). Thousands were arrested. Much to the dismay of the Chinese leadership, the drama was broadcast on Western television (Oxenberg, Sullivan, and Lambert 1990).

Reform Revisited. The years following the massacre would find Deng Xiaoping reasserting his control over the Party apparatus. Capitalistic reforms were pursued with renewed vigor, unleashing a period of spectacular economic growth. Students no longer protested, but visitors to the Chinese mainland found life to be freer of political constraints than at any time during the Communist regime (Chang 1993).

By 1992, Deng's policy of limited capitalism, now dubbed "socialism with Chinese characteristics" or "market socialism," had become Party doctrine. Indeed, the Fourteenth Party Congress of 1992 praised Deng Xiaoping's theory of building socialism with Chinese characteristics as being "a legacy of Mao Zedung thought" (*China Daily,* Sat., July 10, 1993, 1).

As Deng's health began to fade during the early 1990s, party factions and the military began to jockey for position in a post-Deng world (Wo-Lap Lam 1994). Deng, for his part, had quietly promoted pro-Deng forces within the military to assure the smooth transfer of power to President Jiang Zemin, his hand-picked successor. Early in 1994, for example, Deng convened a secret meeting of China's top generals, most of them his own appointees, and urged then to "rally round comrade Jiang Zemin as the core of the new leadership," and to "uphold political stability at all costs." The military was also called on to "provide help to the Party and the Government in maintaining social order" and to "bolster central authority and check the growth of regionalism"[3] (*SCMPI,* July 2, 1994, 7).

The transition from Deng to Jiang Zemin was orderly, as supporters of the latter gradually assumed key positions in the Party and the army. By the end of the century,

---

[3]According to the official *People's Daily,* the transfer of power from the second generation of revolutionaries led by Deng to the third level of revolutionaries led by Jiang Zemin took place in 1994 (*SCMPI,* Oct. 8, 1994, 6).

Jiang was firmly in control of the Chinese leadership, holding the key positions of president of China and chairman of the Central Military Commission (positions to be discussed shortly). Nevertheless, his power would seem to be less absolute than either of his predecessors, Mao or Deng (Taylor 1998).

Jiang and Zhu Rongji, the new prime minister elected in the Fifteenth Party Congress of the Communist Party (1997), extended Deng's reforms. Among other things, Jiang promised sweeping reforms of China's industrial sector:

■   China's large and medium-sized state enterprises will be converted into independent corporate entities that will be insulated from the meddling of bureaucrats. They will still be owned by the state, but they are expected to follow scientific management practices and will be judged by their ability to compete in competitive market conditions. Smaller corporation will be privatized. Enterprises that cannot compete will be merged or closed down.

■   Salaries and rewards for workers will be based on performance.

■   Foreign investments will be encouraged. Indeed, "China will take an active stance in the world by improving the pattern of opening up in all directions, at all levels and in a wide range, developing an open economy, enhancing our international competitiveness, optimizing our economic structure and improving the quality of tits national economy" (*China Daily,* Sept. 15, 1997).

■   Corruption will be eliminated and people will be encouraged to "get wealthy through honest labor and lawful operation..." (*China Daily,* Sept. 15, 1997). In this regard, the honest investment of capital was to be encouraged.

These are powerful words from China's leading communist.

The capitalistic reforms introduced by Deng and extended by Jiang and the moderate faction within the Communist Party are essential to China's economic development. They are not, however, without their dangers. By moving in the direction of greater capitalism, the Party is losing touch with its ideological roots. What is the justification for a Communist Party in a capitalist society? If present trends continue, the Chinese regime will become little more than a classic Chinese dictatorship masquerading under the guise of communism. For better or for worse, China is becoming a post-communist society in everything but name.

More fundamentally, China's capitalist reforms have created—or revived—the bourgeoisie or capitalist class, the arch-enemy of communism. This class, buoyed by its increasing wealth and strong external contracts, must inevitably demand a greater voice in the running of China. Potential conflicts between the ruling class and the new capitalist class, however, should not be exaggerated. Many of the new capitalists are the friends and relatives of Party officials and bureaucrats. Indeed, one of Deng's daughters became an ardent capitalist, investing in a chain of fitness salons.

The military has also become a bastion of capitalism, using its facilities to turn out a broad range of consumer products ranging from soft drinks to bicycles. It is also becoming a major force in real estate. Recent estimates suggests that the Chinese military, sarcastically referred to as the PLA Inc., may own as many as 30,000 companies (*CSM,* June 3, 1998, 2). This, too, has come under attack by Jiang.

Even when communist officials are not involved in capitalist activities they are often the recipients of massive bribes. Both the communist establishment and the bourgeoisie, then, are benefiting from the present arrangement. This had little to do with communism, but it has a great deal to do with human nature.

Rapid economic growth has brought other problems as well, not the least of which is skyrocketing inflation. Government salaries are no longer adequate to sustain a meager existence for China's bureaucrats and workers. Labor unrest, long outlawed as counter-revolutionary, has become commonplace. China's impoverished Government has promised higher salaries but lacks the money to provide them. The situation in the countryside is little better as peasants, once confined to their villages, flock to the cities in search of work. Seldom successful, the migrants from the rural areas now form a huge "floating population," taxing the resources of China's already congested cities (*SCMPI,* Nov. 19, 1994, 6). Crime and social unrest have increased apace (*CSM,* Sept. 22, 1994, 6).

The plight of China's poor has been made all the more stark by the growing prosperity of the private sector. Under Mao, poverty was uniform. Some regions were more prosperous than others, but differences among individuals were minimal. That has now changed as state workers see their counterparts in the private sector enjoy a lifestyle that is far superior to their own. The poverty of the many is being made increasingly bitter by the prosperity of the few.

Regional disparities have also increased. The coastal economic zones have become boom towns of incredible wealth, while the economies of the interior regions remain stagnant. Leaders from the interior regions are demanding greater equity, but the leaders of the free economic zones are reluctant to share their newfound wealth. Reflecting this fact, the Fifteenth Party Congress stressed the need to focus foreign investment in the poorer interior provinces (*China Daily,* Sept. 12, 1997).

It would be inaccurate to suggest that the Chinese government is losing its capacity to rule or that the Chinese Communist Party will soon go the way of its Soviet counterpart. This does not appear to be the case. The problems besetting the Chinese leadership, however, are very real, and they will not be easily solved without firm and consistent leadership (Harding 1998).

The Political Institutions of China: The Party, the State, and the Military

The Communist Party rules China through three instruments of power: the Party apparatus, the state apparatus, and the military (see Figure 7.1). The three bodies are interlocking, with senior positions in the state apparatus and the military being occupied by ranking members of the Party. Labor unions, youth associations, and all other large organizations are also under the direct control of the Party. In fact, very little exists in China that is not under the direct control of the Communist Party.

Power in China: The Communist Party

The organizational structure of the Chinese Communist Party (CCP) is similar to that of the Communist Party of the Soviet Union, upon which it is based (Dreyer 1993). In theory, the CCP is remarkably democratic. Members of the Party elect delegates to a National Party Congress that theoretically meets at five-year intervals, although this has seldom been the case in practice. The National Party Congress, in turn, elects a Central Committee of some 200 to 300 members to manage its affairs during the periods in which the Congress is not in session,

View of a Party Congress in the Great Hall of the People. The National Party Congress is a largely symbolic entity, used mainly to announce changes in Communist Party policies and leadership.

i.e., most of the time. The Central Committee, being too large to operate as a coherent unit, elects an executive committee or Politburo of some twenty to twenty-five members to manage its affairs on a daily basis. Of the members of the Politburo, five or six form a core leadership group referred to as the Standing Committee. Other key organs of the CCP, as indicated in Figure 7.1, are the Central Discipline Inspection Commission and the Military Commission.

The National Party Congress is the least powerful of the Party organs, meeting irregularly, depending upon the needs of the moment and the whims of the leadership. Delegates to the National Party Congress are selected rather than elected, and they vote as instructed.

While largely symbolic affairs, Party Congresses are often used by Party leaders to announce major changes in the Party line. They also showcase the rise and fall of key officials, thereby providing foreigners with a partial view of intra-Party conflicts. The Fourteenth Party Congress of 1992, for example, signaled Deng's return to dominance in the post-Tiananmen era by announcing that his policy of "socialism with Chinese characteristics" had become official Party doctrine. The Fifteenth Party Congress of 1997, in turn, was used to further consolidate Jiang's power by reducing that of his adversaries, a process that remains incomplete (Cheng and White 1998). As noted earlier, the Congress also proclaimed an extension of the economic reform process.

The Central Committee of the Communist Party represents a "Who's Who" of influential leaders throughout all segments of Chinese society, including the military, the Party apparatus, the state apparatus, and the provincial Party organizations. Most real power, however, is concentrated in the hands of the Politburo and its standing committee.

The day-to-day affairs of the Communist Party are managed by the General Secretariat of the Communist Party. The general secretary of the Secretariat (organi-

Figure 7.1
Chinese Communist Party Organizations

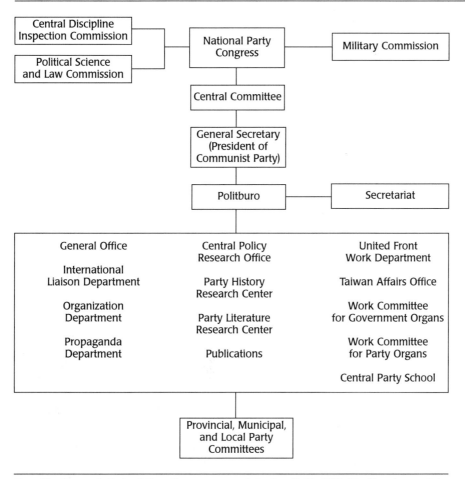

Note: The Fourteenth National Party Congress convened October 12–18, 1992. The first plenum of the Fourteenth Congress convened October 19–20, 1992; the second plenum, March 5–7, 1993; and the third plenum, November 11–14, 1993. This chart represents the organization of the Chinese Communist Party as of February 1, 1994.
Source: Central Intelligence Agency.

zational apparatus) was usually the single most powerful individual in China. This was clearly the case during Mao's tenure as Party secretary and was equally the case during much of the 1980s when the post was occupied by Deng's hand-picked supporters.[4] The position of general secretary was subsequently abolished, being replaced by the president of the Communist Party.

At the sub-national level, the Communist Party is divided into provinces, prefectures, cities, counties, and townships. The provincial party apparatus (including

---

[4]The Military Commission is charged with overseeing the military, assuring military subservience to the Party, and establishing military policy. Membership includes China's military elite, as well as dominant civilian members of the Party.

The Central Discipline Inspection Commission (CDIC) is charged with assuring that Party members faithfully execute the Party line as determined by the Party elite. The CDIC also serves as the Party's "high court," albeit a court that is unlikely to render a verdict that conflicts with the opinions of the Party leadership (Ogden 1992). Most recently, the CDIC has been placed in charge of combating corruption within Party ranks. Although corruption was always a problem, the temptations produced by China's guarded transition to capitalism have seen corruption within the Communist Party reach epidemic proportions (*SCMPI*, Nov. 25, 1995).

Four Critical Functions of Party Cells

■ *First, they serve as a constant reminder of the Party's omnipotence.* "Big brother" is everywhere, noting all manner of suspicious activities including the coming and going of "non-residents."

■ *Second, they provide a communication channel.* The Party line is explained to the masses, and the public mood is conveyed to the relevant superiors.

■ *Third, they are the "missionaries" of the Party* (Liu 1986). They preach Party doctrine and generally facilitate the Party's socialization and recruitment efforts.

■ *Fourth, they play a critical role in maintaining the "esprit de corps" of Party members.* As in any large organization, the effectiveness of the CCP must inevitably reflect the morale of its members. The morale of Party members was devastated by the Cultural Revolution and is currently being undermined by the rapid pace of capitalist reform.

---

autonomous regions and a few major cities) parallels that of the national party, with each province having its own party congress, central committee, and administrative apparatus.[5] At the bottom of the Party hierarchy one finds a network of "primary organizations" or "cells" that permeate the fabric of Chinese society. In this regard, the Party's constitution states that party cells are to be "formed in factories, shops, schools, offices, city neighborhoods, people's communes, cooperatives, farms, townships, towns, companies of the People's Liberation Army, and other basic units, where there are three or more full party members" (Liu 1986). Each primary organization, in turn, is divided into three levels: the primary party committee, the party branch, and the general party branch. Each has a secretary and conducts regularly scheduled meetings of the membership (Liu 1986).

Cadres: The Core of the Party. The heart of the communist system is the **cadre**. As discussed by Lucian Pye:

> The ideal cadre (ganbu) is a Communist Party member who works with endless vigor and complete self-sacrifice for the goals of the revolution. As an activist he is part of the elite, sensitive to the rationale of the correct Party line. At the same time he is completely in tune with the masses, aware of their interests and their problems. He is a paragon of Communist virtues, always striving to improve himself, constantly sensitive to his own failings, and completely obedient to the demands of the Party... (Pye 1991, 184–85).

The Communist Party of China now possesses approximately 60 million members, a figure that constitutes approximately 5 percent of the Chinese population (*China Today*, Jan. 2, 2000, www). Based upon past trends, less than half of these will qualify as cadres (Liu 1986). Because of their superior discipline and presumed dedication to the Party, cadres fill most positions of responsibility in China, including all sensitive positions in the military and the state apparatus. Cadres are divided into various ranks and levels. Some flavor of the class distinction within cadre ranks is provided by Fox Butterfield:

---

[5]The provincial party is headed by a first secretary or chairman. Provincial first secretaries are the most powerful individuals within their respective provinces, and they enjoy membership on the Central Committee of the CCP. Vacancies in the national party leadership are generally filled from the ranks of the provincial first secretaries (Liu 1986).

The structure of the national Party organization is also paralleled at the local level, executive decisions being made by a local council (central committee) headed by a first secretary. First secretaries at lower reaches of the Party hierarchy have enormous power over the lives of the local inhabitants and have often come under Party criticism for being "local emperors" (Liu 1986). Local first secretaries generally serve on the central committees of the provincial party organization, thereby assuring a continuous flow of information from the national to the local level.

Only cadres above grade thirteen are allowed a leather swivel chair, like those used by Western executives. Officials in grades thirteen to sixteen range get a soft upholstered chair with springs and a velvet-covered seat. Grade seventeen cadres are entitled to a wooden chair with a cushion; those below that, only a plain wooden seat (Butterfield 1983, 67).

The original cadres were born out of revolution, their idealism and ideological commitment being forged in battle. Today's cadres, however, manifest little of the zeal of an earlier era, forty years of communist rule having transformed revolutionaries into bureaucrats. Indeed, senior officials have long complained of both corruption and "feudalism" among the cadres, feudalism referring to the tendency of cadres to transform themselves into minor demigods (Liu 1986). As described by Jan Wing:

> Like many grassroots-level party secretaries, Mr. Shen, who has a third-grade education, is mayor, police chief, judge, welfare dispenser, businessman, and father confessor rolled into one. As the top Communist official in town, he labels his critics "counter-revolutionaries" and uses the village militia to suppress them (*SCMPI*, May 14, 1994, 6).

It is interesting to note that the first major attack on cadre corruption was Mao's "three evils" campaign of 1951, a campaign attacking corruption, waste, and bureaucratism. The problem has only worsened with time.

Moving Up the Party Hierarchy.   Advancement within the Chinese Communist Party is by **co-optation**. That is to say, *members of higher committees select the members of the lower committees who are to be elevated to a higher rank.* Elections, to the point that they exist, are pro forma.

Three criteria are of particular importance in the promotion process: performance, loyalty, and patronage. Each Party member possesses a personnel file that evaluates his or her performance record, with particular stress being placed on the individual's loyalty to the Party. Performance is important, but dedication to the Party is more important. More important than either performance or loyalty is the support of a powerful patron. Senior officials are anxious to promote individuals who share their ideological views and who can be counted on to support them in their factional struggles. A patron-client bond is thus forged in which both the security and the advancement of lower officials is linked to the power of their patron. If the patron falls, so do his clients.

Ideology is an important component in patron-client relationships, for the CCP is fragmented into competing Maoist, conservative, and reformist tendencies. Each must stick together if it is to survive. Regional, family, and historical links also enter into the picture (Nathan 1990).

In large part, advancement as a cadre requires agility in toeing the Party line. This is not always an easy task, for the Party line shifts with both the needs of the moment and the composition of the leadership. Supporting the Party line during the "Hundred Flowers Blooming" campaign, for example, was condemned as treason during the Great Proletarian Cultural Revolution, and the more ardent "bloomers" found themselves in labor camps. The Party line now calls for capitalism, but that, too, could change if the merging capitalist class posed a threat to the Party control. It is interesting to note, in this regard, that Party control was a dominant theme of the Fifteenth Party Conference.

The State Apparatus

The state apparatus in communist China is remarkably similar to that of any other modern state. A Constitution provides for a National People's Congress, a symbolic president, a premier, and a State Council (Cabinet). The Constitution also provides for a variety of human rights but leaves little doubt that China is a socialist state guided by the principles of communist democracy. The Constitution is easily amended, its provisions being altered to reflect major ideological shifts within the communist hierarchy. The core of the state apparatus is the massive state bureaucracy, most of which is devoted to managing China's socialist economy.

The role of the state apparatus is to execute policies made by the leadership of the Communist Party. In this regard, the Chinese make a clear distinction between "Party line" and the rules and regulations required to implement the Party line. The Communist Party leadership, by way of example, recently established a new Party line on energy policy, calling for the damming of China's major rivers and placing greater reliance upon atomic energy. The state bureaucratic apparatus will be responsible for designing and executing both projects, albeit under the watchful eye of the Party apparatus.

While the state apparatus is inferior to the Communist Party, it is a vital part of the Chinese political system. As the above example suggests, Party guidelines provide the state apparatus with broad scope for maneuvering. They also provide its leaders with ample opportunity to reward their clients.

The National People's Congress is a symbolic parliament that does little more than ratify decisions of the Communist Party hierarchy. Should the Communist Party weaken, however, it could take on new significance. This, it will be recalled from Chapter 6, was the precedent set during the collapse of the Soviet Union.

The most powerful position in the state apparatus is that of premier or prime minister. The premier is a very powerful and highly visible figure and is selected by the Party leadership from among the ranking leaders of the Communist Party. This does not mean that relations between the Party leadership and the premier are either smooth or cordial. In the aftermath of the Tiananmen Square massacre, for example, Deng Xiaoping was forced to appoint Li Peng, the leader of the conservative faction, to the position of premier. In so doing, he enabled the conservatives to use the state apparatus as a platform for attacking his reforms. Li Peng was replaced as head of the state apparatus (prime minister) in 1998 by Zhu Rongji, a senior official more in accord with the reformist politics of Jiang. Nevertheless, Li Peng was named president of the National People's Congress and continued to be listed as the "number two" man in China (*IHT,* Mar. 17, 1998, 1).

The list of ministries in the State Council is similar to that of any cabinet. The Ministries of Defense, Foreign Affairs, Finance, and Planning are particularly influential, being followed in turn by lesser ministries such as Health and Communication. Cabinet ministers in China generally have less flexibility than their counterparts in Western societies, as most policy initiatives come from the Party. Nevertheless, each minister controls a slice of the huge state bureaucracy and thereby possesses immense opportunities for patronage. Indeed, the opportunities for patronage within the state bureaucracy are so immense that the 1980s found the State Council with more than 1,000 ministers and deputy ministers. Everyone wanted a piece of the action. The number was sharply reduced by Deng Xiaoping, and Zhu Rongji has promised to reduce the number to 29, hardly a popular move (Taylor 1998; Jinghuai and Xia 1998).

The state apparatus, however, is far more than its leadership structure. It is also the seven million bureaucrats charged with administering the country and controlling its massive economy. As the state owns almost everything, the bureaucracy manages almost everything. Progress in China, accordingly, depends upon the effectiveness of its bureaucracy. The problems of bureaucracy in China were discussed in reference to the cadres and need not be repeated at this point. Suffice it to say that the rigidity, corruption, and ineptness of China's bureaucrats have played a major role in the stagnation of the Chinese economy (Zhibin 1991; Lawrence 1998).

Jiang has responded to China's continuing bureaucratic woes by threatening to fire half the bureaucracy, a dramatic if unlikely move that would place some

People's Liberation Army (PLA) troops listen to speeches at a farewell ceremony shortly before traveling to Hong Kong.

2,000,000 ex-bureaucrats on the unemployment rolls (*IHT,* Mar. 31, 1998, 1). Attacks on bureaucratic corruption also took prime billing at both the 1997 Congress of the Communist Party and the parallel National People's Congress (*China Daily,* Sept. 24, 1997).

The Military and Politics in China

The position of the People's Liberation Army in the Chinese system is summed up by Mao's dictum that "political power grows out of the barrel of a gun." The Chinese Communist Party could not have seized power without a strong army, and it cannot remain in power without the support of that army.

In theory, the People's Liberation Army (PLA) is subservient to the Party, and like all organizations in Communist China, it is expected to follow the Party line. In reality, however, relations between the Party and the PLA are far more complex than the Party would like, and it could well be the military that dictates the Party line during the coming era.

Military policy is made by the Military Commission, one of the key centers of power within the communist system. The level of military representation on important leadership councils such as the Central Committee, the Politburo, and the all-important Standing Committee of the Politburo reflects the balance of power between the military and the Party. Military representation of the Central Committee peaked at 43 percent during the collapse of the Cultural Revolution and then declined to 23 percent with Deng's consolidation of power in 1982 (Liu 1986). By the turn of the century, the military had fallen on hard times, the Fifteenth Congress of the Communist Party (1997) having reduced military representation on the Central Committee to 8 percent. Military influence on the Politburo also declined and there was no member of the military in the Standing Committee of the Poliburo (Cheng and White 1998). Plans were also announced to trim 500,000 personnel

Problems in the Military

As in the case of other cadre-led organizations, the military has lost much of its revolutionary zeal in the post-revolutionary era. The leadership of the Chinese military has grown old, and the military suffers the same factionalization that has beset the Party as a whole but to a lesser extent (Godwin 1988). Rivalries between diverse military regions are intense, as are rivalries between the different branches of the military. Corruption also reached new proportions, forcing China's top generals to celebrate the sixty-sixth anniversary of the founding of the PLA by launching an attack on "corruption, money worshipping, and hedonism" (*London Guardian*, July 30, 1993, 11). A massive effort is now underway to improve the public image of the army by showing soldiers rescuing victims of China's devastating floods and otherwise serving the public (*IHT*, Aug. 28, 1998, 5).

from the PLA and "take the road of fewer but better troops…who know the art of modern war" (*China Daily*, Sept. 24, 1997). Be this as it may, the PLA still has 2,820,000 troops on active duty (BBC, July 20, 1999, www).

The fusion of civilian and military authority also extends to the regional and provincial levels, with China being divided into seven "great military regions" (BBC, July 20, 1999, www). These, in turn, are divided into some 27 military districts, more than 200 sub-districts, a nearly equal number of garrison commands, and more than 2,000 departments (Godwin 1988, 45). Each military region, district, and sub-district is headed by both a military commander and a political commissar. Each also possesses its own Communist Party replete with an executive committee and Party organization. The role of the political commissar is to assure that military commanders conform to the Party line. They also keep Party officials abreast of military affairs via a special political department that spans all levels of the military establishment (Godwin 1988). In most instances, the role of the political commissar is filled by the first secretary of the appropriate Party organization (Liu 1986). The intricacies of the Chinese military are poorly understood in the West, and their exact structure and their operation is the subject of considerable uncertainty. The important point to be noted is that the Party has spared no effort to assure that the command of the PLA remains firmly under Party control (Jencks 1992). This is becoming an increasingly difficult task. This, too, was a major theme of the 1997 Party Congress (*China Daily*, Sept. 24, 1997).

The relationship between the military and the Party remains complex. Five dimensions of this relationship are particularly important to the shaping of China's future.

1. *China's military leaders are dedicated Party members.* As such, they possess a vested interest in the survival of the system.
2. *Factionalism within the Party extends to the military.* Indeed, each Party faction has sought to bolster its position by recruiting military allies. The military, then, does not speak with a single voice (Jencks 1992).
3. *The military leadership appears to be less factionalized than the Party leadership.* As such, it has been able to shape policy by arbitrating between Party factions. It was military support for Deng, for example, that allowed his economic reforms to continue. This continues to be the case under Jiang.
4. *The military has displayed signs of "warlordism" as regional commanders carve out personal fiefdoms.* Warlordism is a contravention of Party discipline and poses a clear threat to Party dominance.
5. *The military represents a corporate pressure group.* Like other pressure groups, the members of the military are united by a common interest in extending their power, benefits, and social status. The military is also vitally interested in attaining modern weapons.

The multifaceted relationship between the military and the Party makes it difficult to predict how relations between the two pillars of communist authority will unfold under Jiang Zemin as China continues its course of dramatic change. Depending upon the circumstances, each one of the five factors outlined above could play a determining role in shaping the behavior of China's military leaders.

Before leaving the topic of the military, it should be noted that China possesses a large People's Militia, an organization roughly akin to the National Guard in the United States. It also possesses a large People's Armed Police. In theory, the People's Militia is under the control of the PLA, but this has not always been the case. Mao politicized the Militia during his various campaigns, threatening to turn it into a counterweight to the army. The Militia has now been returned to PLA control, with recent estimates placing its size at more than 4.3 million (Liu 1986, 220). The armed militia is also supported by a broader inactive militia of some 6,000,000 members (Godwin 1988, 157). The People's Armed Police, in turn, perform a role similar to that of the police in most countries. They are, however, very much part of the state security apparatus, and never more so than in the post-Tiananmen era.

The Actors in Chinese Politics: Elites, Groups, and Citizens

Political institutions are the arena of politics, but it is the actors in the political process that give life to those institutions. To a great extent, it is these actors who determine who gets what, when, and how. In this section, we will look at three main groups of political actors in China: elites, groups, and citizens. (China's single political party, the Chinese Communist Party, has already been discussed extensively.)

Elites and Politics in China

The elite hierarchy in China is topped by the members of the all-powerful Standing Committee of the Politburo, many of whom also serve on the Central Military Commission. They are followed in order of importance by the lower-ranking members of these key party organs. Provincial first secretaries, the commanders of the Grand Military Regions, and the leaders of the state apparatus are also powerful individuals. Most are members of the Central Committee, a sure sign of elite status. Ironically, Deng Xiaoping occupied no formal positions during the final years of his rule, choosing instead to rule through his protégés. Jiang Zemin has rapidly consolidated his hold on the presidency and clearly occupies the top rung in the hierarchy of Chinese elites.

Two aspects of China's elite structure are particularly visible. First, a very small number of individuals wield extraordinary power. Second, those individuals are very old. On the eve of the Fourteenth Party Congress (1992) Deng Xiaoping was 87; Chen Yun, his arch foe, was 86; and Yang Shangkun, the president of the Republic, was 85 (*Economist,* Feb. 1, 1992, and Mar. 21, 1992). Even the new generation of party elites is old by Western standards.

With the advent of the Fifteenth Party Congress, however, technocrats moved to the fore. As described by Cheng and White:

> With the departure of Deng Xiaoping and other communist veterans, Chinese politics is entering a new era. The ascent of technocrats to dominance of the leadership is now clearer than ever in the composition of the new Fifteenth Central Committee (CC) of the Chinese Communist Party (CCP). All seven members of the Standing Committee of the CCP's Politburo, the most powerful group in the country, are technocrats. **Technocrats** may be defined as *people who have three traits: technical educations, professional experience, and high posts.* They vie for power on all available grounds but cohere as a political elite

party because of their notion that technical professionalism confers some right to rule. Eighteen of the 24 Politburo members are engineers by training, and technocrats in this sense also constitute a majority of the 344-member CC. These engineers-turned-politicians are now the people running China (Cheng and White 1998, 1).

The extraordinary power that resides in the hands of a few individuals means that the personalities of those individuals have an inordinate impact on policy decisions, Mao's rule being a case in point. Most attempts to predict the future of Chinese politics, accordingly, place strong emphasis on the personalities of the combatants. As Jiang Zemin has been successful in consolidating his position, China's capitalist reforms will more than likely continue. An upswing in the political fortunes of Li Peng and the conservative wing of the Party, however, would signal a return to the hard-line policies of the past.

As in all societies, China possesses a huge network of secondary elites. Cabinet ministers and junior ministers, once more than a thousand in number, fall in this category, as do other senior Party, administrative, and military figures. Local Party and administrative leaders exercise almost total power within their localities. The secondary elites do not set the Party line, but they have a great deal to say about how the Party line will be executed. The rigid and self-serving nature of China's secondary elites has contributed markedly to China's bureaucratic woes. The old secondary elite, however, is also giving way to a new technocratic elite. Progress toward democracy has been limited, but the technical competence of the elite has clearly improved since the mid-1980s (Chen 1998; Li 1998).

Recent capitalist reforms are also creating a new capitalist elite, the continued evolution of which could pose a serious challenge to Party rule in coming decades. This is particularly the case in the coastal regions which have been the focal point of China's guided transition to capitalism. The more this process continues, the more difficult it will be for the Jiang leadership to consolidate its authority.

Groups and Politics in China

The only formal pressure groups allowed in China are those sponsored by the Communist Party. Among others, these include the All-China Federation of Trade Unions, the All-China Women's Federation, the Communist Youth League, and the Young Pioneers (ages nine to fifteen). All professionals also have their own Party-sponsored organizations.

These and other "mass organizations" perform five functions in the communist system: control, socialization, communication, mobilization, and recruitment. Along with the police and various intelligence organizations, they assist the Party in keeping tabs on key segments of Chinese society. They instruct their members in the dogma of Marx, Lenin, and Mao and otherwise strengthen support for the Party and its objectives. In their role as communicators, they convey the Party line to the masses and help the Party leadership keep in touch with public opinion.

Mass organizations also play an important mobilization role. In Mao's "Great Leap Forward," for example, the mass organizations took the lead in working double shifts and otherwise forcing increased productivity. Popular demonstrations supporting Party policy, including the Tiananmen Square crackdown, are similarly orchestrated by the mass organizations.

Finally, the mass organizations are an important avenue of recruitment for the Communist Party. This is particularly true of the youth organizations, but "activists" in all Party organizations are likely to be noticed by Party officials.

In spite of the Party's efforts to corral all segments of society into its mass organizations, the CCP has not been successful in eliminating the influence of special interests from Chinese politics. Rather, it has forced those special interests to take a different form. In this regard, four types of interest or pressure groups are of particular importance to Chinese politics. At the broadest level, one finds the competing tendencies and factions within the Party, the three most dominant of which are the reformers, the conservatives, and the Maoists. The reformers believe that capitalistic reforms and bureaucratic decentralization offer the best hope for revitalizing communist rule in China. The conservatives, by contrast, argue that capitalist reforms will inevitably undermine communist authority by creating a bourgeois counter-elite with strong ties to the capitalist world. Once established, it would be but a matter of time before this new bourgeois elite would use its wealth and influence to topple the communist regime. The solution to China's problems, from the conservative perspective, is Party-led state capitalism. Capitalism would be allowed to exist, but it would be carefully monitored and not allowed to challenge the regime. The difference between the moderates and the conservatives, then, is one of degree. The new generation of conservatives is described as follows by Wo-Lap Lam:

> Pedigree, connections, energy, and education are on the side of the xinbaoshou neophytes, many of whom are sons of party elders who have engineering or business-administration degrees from Western universities....
>
> For them, the co-habitation of some form of market economies and the CCP police-state apparatus is not a contradiction in terms. In fact, it is a magic formula for maintaining stability (*SCMPI*, Oct. 22–23, 1994, 11).

The Maoists, in turn, oppose reform of any variety and are overwhelmingly preoccupied with uprooting the enemies of the revolution. These, in their eyes, constitute no less than 10 percent of the population, and include both the new capitalist class and its supporters in high places (Zhibin 1991, 62). The Maoists are now in decline but could revive if continued economic reform leads to internal disorder on the scale of Tiananmen Square (Chang 1992; Metzger 1998).

Underlying factional interests are China's all-pervasive **patron-client networks.** As described by Andrew Walder, patron-client networks were part of the communist system from its very beginning:

> Despite its totalitarian pretensions, local political rule in the Mao era was in practice a clientist system. The local party and its representatives selected loyal supporters on political grounds, provided them with careers and privileges, and relied on these loyal subordinates to push through party policies. Cadres inevitably used the economic resources at their disposal to reward the loyal, and through time the mutual support of cadres and activists grew into a web of personal loyalties radiating out from party branches (Walder 1991, 358–59).

The military, the state bureaucracy, and the Party bureaucracy also constitute important pressure groups. The military is now putting intense pressure on China's leaders for increased resources and authority, while the Party and state bureaucracies have similarly closed ranks in resisting government efforts to reduce corruption and routinization. Bureaucrats occupy a privileged position in Chinese society, and they have no desire to see that position eroded. Much the same is true of local leaders, many of whom enjoy enormous power and wealth (Zhibin 1991).

Finally, post-Maoist reforms have revived a variety of "counter-revolutionary" interests. Particularly alarming, from the Party's perspective, were the student protests that culminated in the Tiananmen Square massacre. The Tiananmen Square riots demonstrated just how quickly organized opposition to Party rule can take root. They also demonstrated that the communist regime had lost touch with the students. As described by Stanley Rosen:

Carrying a baby on her back, a peasant woman rakes grain she is drying on woven mats in a village near Xingguo in south China. Recent decades have brought greater prosperity to urban entrepreneurs, but China's 850 million peasants have seen their livelihood become increasingly precarious.

If the regime's ideology has lost a great deal of its appeal to youth, a similar argument could be made for its key political organization, the Communist Youth League. Membership within the CYL has become virtually universal among college students. Unlike the pre-Cultural Revolution period…today's CYL offers neither glory nor obvious benefits. Membership therein is merely pro forma. Indeed, the regime has ample evidence of the league's decline (Rosen 1992, 177–78).

In the aftermath of the Tiananmen Square uprising, all student groups independent of the Party were banned (again) and university administrators were told to increase their supervision of student activities (Rosen 1992). China's leaders are rightly concerned about the disaffection of the students. Students are the most articulate and daring segment of Chinese society, and surveys indicate that they are overwhelmingly committed to the Westernization of China (Rosen 1992). In particular, it is the students who fuel the pro-democracy movement that continues to embarrass the Chinese regime in the Western press.

China's long-suffering peasants also have begun to find their political voice (White 1987). Pressed by Mao to make ever-greater sacrifices for the industrialization of China, the peasants looked to Deng's reforms as the road to greater prosperity. The reforms did bring greater prosperity, but that prosperity took the form of IOUs issued for products that the peasants were forced to sell to the government. The reforms also brought higher costs and taxes, spurring violent protests throughout the rural areas. In earlier days, peasant protests would have invited repression. In the post-Tiananmen era, the government has been reluctant to use the army to quell mass unrest for fear that the military might side with the masses. The army acted harshly in the Tiananmen riots, but it acted slowly. The government, accordingly, has promised to pay its IOUs promptly and has launched a vigorous public relations campaign designed to convince the peasants—still a large percentage of the Chinese population—that their concerns are being addressed by the Chinese leadership (*China Daily,* June–July 1993).

Urban workers have also become increasingly active. Strikes, although officially illegal, have become commonplace (*SCMPI,* Nov. 5, 1994, 7). The government has responded to increased labor unrest by allowing the Party's trade unions greater scope in bargaining for wages and benefits. It has also moved to strengthen Party control over those unions (Wo-Lap Lam 1993).

Perhaps more distressing for the Chinese leadership was the emergence of the Falun Gong spiritual sect toward the end of the 1990s. The cult, a blend of Taoism, Buddhism, and various folk religions, quickly generated a following in excess of 10 million and was banned, without success, by Party officials in 1999 (*IHT,* Apr. 14, 2000). In an official spate of self-criticism, an official magazine attributed the needs of the common people for spiritual security in the environment of profound change that is accompanying China's shift to a capitalist economy (ibid.). The movement reportedly has more than seventy adherents worldwide (*NYT,* May 1, 2000, www).

One way or another, then, the once-monolithic facade of communist China is displaying a growing pluralism. The more this trend persists—and there is plenty of evidence that it will—the more difficult it will be for the new generation of Party leaders to reestablish the authoritarianism of an earlier era. Indeed, the growing pluralism of Chinese society could well threaten the very existence of the communist state.

Citizen Politics: Political Participation and Public Opinion in China

The Communist Party goes to great lengths to perpetuate the fiction that the masses are the source of political authority in China. The Party Congress and the National People's Congress, the Chinese equivalent of a parliament, are heralded as a direct expression of the popular will. Also, as noted earlier, one of the main functions of the Party apparatus at the local level is to keep tabs on the public "mood," thereby allowing the leadership to moderate policies that generate excessive resentment. The Party cannot wait for demonstrations to occur before adjusting its policies, because in the Chinese system demonstrations represent a breakdown in Party control.

For the average Chinese citizen, four avenues of public opinion are of particular importance: the wall poster, the "side lane news" (gossip), demonstrations, and passive withdrawal. Wall posters[6] provide for the relatively free expression of personal sentiments during periods of intellectual opening such as Mao's "Hundred Flowers Blooming" campaign and are closely watched by the Party (Pye 1991).

Writing wall posters is limited to the literate, but "side lane news" or gossip is available to all. It is also pervasive and dangerous. In the absence of reliable information, rumors, however false, can result in panic and destruction. Rumors also tend to spread rapidly and are very difficult for the regime to counter.

Demonstrations and petty rebellions have also been a persistent form of public expression in China, with Mao's attempts to communalize Chinese agriculture meeting with intense mass resistance. The student demonstrations culminating in the Tiananmen Square massacre, moreover, ushered in a new era of mass protest. Although the Tiananmen demonstrations were crushed, the ensuing years have witnessed a sharp upsurge in protests by workers and peasants. Such protests have focused upon immediate economic grievances rather than questions of political philosophy and, as such, have been tolerated by the regime. The line between economic protest and political protest, however, is extremely fine (Wasserstrom and Perry 1992).

---

[6]They were outlawed in the 1980s but have subsequently made a revival.

The citizens of communist China, it must be stressed, do not engage in demonstrations lightly. When demonstrations do occur they signal a far more intense level of mass discontent than would be conveyed by similar actions in the West. They may also indicate that the masses sense a weakening of the Party's leadership.

Public opinion polls have also made their appearance in China, although their reliability remains suspect (Lau and Wang 1992–93). Interestingly enough, a 1994 poll of Chinese youth showed Chairman Mao to be a more popular figure than Deng. Some 97 percent of the respondents expressed dissatisfaction with government anti-corruption measures, while large majorities decried a decline in social ethics and law and order. Most of the respondents approved of China's market reforms.[7] Other surveys found Beijing's citizens to be worried about education, money, and the shortage of electrical appliances.[8]

In addition to the above avenues of public expression, China now boasts more than 8.9 million users of the Internet, a figure that will soon number in the tens of millions as cheap technology brings the Chinese masses on line (CNN, Jan. 19, 2000, www). Even China's newspapers are becoming somewhat more open as they compete for the advertising dollars of the private sector (Hong 1998).

Perhaps the most significant manifestation of public opinion, from the perspective of China's economic development, has been the passivity of its citizens. They do what they are forced to do and little more. Psychological involvement in the system continues to be minimal. Even the cadres and Party members appear to be motivated as much by opportunism as by conviction. Conversely, the remarkable productivity displayed by China's peasants on their private plots has sent a clear and unambiguous message to the Party leadership: the profit motive works. The spectacular revival of the private sector has reinforced that message.

The Context of Chinese Politics: Culture, Economics, and International Interdependence

The actors in Chinese politics play a vital role in determining who gets what, when, and how, but the behavior of those actors is often influenced by the broader environmental context in which Chinese politics occurs. In this section, we will examine three dimensions of that environmental context: the culture of Chinese politics, the political economy of Chinese politics, and the influence of the international arena on Chinese politics.

Culture and Politics in China

Chinese politics reflects deeply entrenched cultural patterns. Some of these cultural patterns paved the way for the communist regime, while others became its enemies (Li, Mark, and Li 1991). China would become communist, but communism would also become Chinese. *Of the cultural patterns that paved the way for the Maoist regime, none was more important than the Chinese predisposition toward strong government* (Ogden 1992). Chinese history, it will be recalled from the earlier discussion, was marked by alternating periods of strong and weak governments. Strong governments brought order and prosperity, while weak governments brought civil war and carnage. The victory of the communists in 1949 brought an end to

---

[7]The survey (*n* = 6,150) was conducted by the *China Youth Daily* and was reported in the *South China Morning Post International,* Jan. 28, 1995, 7.

[8]The survey (*n* = 2,000) was conducted by the China Academy of Social Sciences (*SCMPI,* Jan. 28, 1995, 7).

decades of war and revolution, and most Chinese welcomed the prospect of a strong regime, whatever its ideological trappings.

During the years of revolutionary struggle, *the communists built upon the Confucian values of order and obedience and went out of their way to honor the Confucian principles of compassion for the masses and the selection of leaders on the basis of merit.* While communism was an alien ideology, its organizational requirements were compatible with much of Chinese culture.

The communist regime was also able to build upon the strong sense of Chinese nationalism. The Chinese were very much aware of themselves as Chinese, an awareness buoyed by an inherent sense of cultural superiority (Watson 1992). Indeed, early Chinese emperor worship was founded on the belief that the emperor was the celestial link between heaven and earth, with China being the center of the earth, a middle kingdom to which all other countries paid tribute (Ogden 1992). This profound sense of Chinese nationalism was to become the cornerstone of communist efforts to mobilize the Chinese population against its foreign enemies. Communism was an alien ideology, but nationalism was not.

Just as the communists drew upon Chinese culture, so Chinese culture shaped the nature and operation of the communist regime. *Nowhere is the influence of culture on communist practice more evident than in the profound respect for age that permeates the Party hierarchy.* Until recently, most of China's senior leaders were well into their 80s, with the second echelon of leaders being almost as old. The entrenched authority of China's elites has severely limited mobility within the Party hierarchy, advancement often taking decades.

Chinese culture also undermined the secular logic of Marxist-Leninist thought by transforming Mao into a new emperor-god. In the words of Zhibin,

> Traditionally, the Chinese government, as well as the entire Chinese nation, has revolved around a paramount leader. Only under such a superman can China's unity be secured.... The need for a single paramount leader, who sits high in the palace and decides on all affairs, big or small, is felt as urgently today as yesterday. All the officials are his employees and any of them can be dismissed at any time at his pleasure.... As a popular Chinese saying declares, "A family cannot be without a master for a day; a nation cannot be leaderless for a day" (Zhibin 1991, 89–90).

Whether this tendency will continue in the future remains to be seen.

Culture As the Enemy of Modernization. Mao and the Communist Party were products of Chinese culture, yet they also viewed that culture as an obstacle to the modernization of China. In order to understand Mao's hostility toward traditional culture, it must be recalled that the China of the 1920s was very much a traditional society. Rural peasants constituted more than 80 percent of the population, industry was poorly developed, and communications were rudimentary. Most Chinese, urban and rural, were illiterate. Superstition and mysticism were rife.

In common with pre-industrial populations everywhere, Chinese culture was a family-centered culture in which family members worked as a group. The family cared for its members in adversity and old age, arranged their marriages, and protected them from their enemies. Indeed, it was the family that defined the individual's very identity. You were what your family was (Chang 1991).

The family-centered nature of Chinese society ran counter to Mao's version of a modern Marxist society. Mao demanded that loyalty to the state supersede loyalty to the family, that conflict between clans give way to communal cooperation, and that superstition and mysticism be replaced by "scientific" Marxism. Communism, as preached by Mao, was to become the new religion of China.

Be this as it may, there is little evidence to suggest that traditional culture has been replaced by a modern culture. Rather, the majority of China's population has bent to the communist system without embracing it. Nowhere was this situation more visible than in Mao's attempts to communalize agriculture. The government could force the peasants to live in communes, but it could not force them to abandon their traditional ways. Production collapsed, and the grand experiment in social communism had to be moderated.

Socialist Work Culture. For more than four decades, mainland China has been ruled by a socialist system in which individual initiative was stifled. Employment was guaranteed, with everyone in the same class receiving essentially the same wage regardless of how hard they worked. Much as in the case of the Soviet Union, Chinese workers soon developed a **socialist work culture** *characterized by low productivity and poor quality control.* The vitality of Government enterprises, according to the official *China Daily,* is "depressed by the rigid labor and personnel systems, overloaded welfare programs, old equipment and out-of-date technology, low wages, and incompetent management" (*China Daily,* June 29, 1993, 4). The same theme was reported during the Fifteenth Party Congress in 1997. It is this socialist culture that China's reformers must now battle in their effort to revive China's battered economy and to make China competitive on a world scale. The challenge is a perplexing one, for China's reformers must rekindle capitalist behavior without being overwhelmed by it (Wade 1990; Barme 1998).

In sum, China's current leaders are confronted with a difficult cultural environment as the "four olds," "three evils," and "five antis" remain very much in evidence (Chang 1991). China cannot go back to what it was on the eve of the revolution; the impact of communism has simply been too great. The question is whether the melange of traditional, transitional, and socialist attitudes will preclude it from moving forward.

Political Economy and Politics in China

Mao Zedung and other leaders of China's communist movement were ardent political economists who firmly believed Marx's dictum that political power flowed from economic power (Selden 1988). Whoever controlled the means of production, in their view, would control the government. They also believed that class conflict was the inevitable and irreversible unfolding of history.

The appeal of Marxism to the young Chinese intellectuals of the early twentieth century is easy to understand. China was a backward society on the verge of collapse. Its masses lived in squalor and its elite was preoccupied with its own luxury. Marxism offered both modernity and social equality. Marxism also placed Mao and other members of the Communist Party in the vanguard of a powerful movement. It was they who would lead revolutionary China. Once in power, Mao followed Marxist doctrine to the extreme. Industries and commercial establishments were nationalized, farms were collectivized, capitalism gave way to centralized planning, and heavy industry replaced agriculture as the cornerstone of the Chinese economy.

What went wrong? Why is China now turning to capitalism in order to cure its economic ills? The explanations are many. In part, China's economic woes of today can be traced to Mao's erratic economic policies, not the least of which was the Great Leap Forward. Attempts to terrorize the workers into greater productivity merely produced inflexibility and routinization (Teiwes and Sun 1998).

The CCP, moreover, does not distinguish between economic leadership and political leadership. Political leaders make all of the major economic decisions,

---

Economic Influences on Chinese Politics

Philosophical issues aside, the role of economic factors in shaping the direction of Chinese politics is beyond question. In this regard, four points are of particular importance.

■ *First, the growing political unrest in China today is essentially economic unrest.* Strikes, although formally outlawed by the Party, have become commonplace. China's peasants, moreover, are in a state of near-revolt. While urban income increased by 7.8 percent during 1994, rural income fell by 5 percent (*SCMPI*, Jan. 28, 1995, 7). Rural taxes have been slashed in an effort to accommodate the peasants, but circumstances are so desperate that many Party leaders believe that peasant unrest constitutes the greatest single threat to the security of the communist regime (*SCMPI*, Jan. 28, 1995, 7).

■ *Second, the growing pluralism of Chinese politics is essentially economic pluralism.* For the first time in the history of the People's Republic, labor unions and peasant associations are asserting their independence of the Party. The recent emergence of business associations also represents an entirely new challenge for the Party leadership.

■ *Third, economic pressures have forced China's leaders to seek foreign investment.* Doing this has made the Party leadership vulnerable to foreign pressures and opened the Chinese mainland to foreign influences.

■ *Fourth, China's phenomenal economic growth during the 1990s is almost exclusively the result of private-sector activity.* The productivity of government factories and government farms remains stagnant. From a practical perspective, it is doubtful that the Party could rescind the reforms even if it wanted to. The result would be economic catastrophe. The debate of the future is not between reform and a return to Maoist economics. Rather, it is a debate about the pace and nature of economic reform.

---

regime survival being considered more important than economic development. Deng Xiaoping emphasized economic reform, but as the tragic events of Tiananmen Square illustrated, not to the point of jeopardizing Party supremacy. Economic reform would gain new momentum in the post-Tiananmen era, but not until the Party had reasserted its political authority.

Neoclassical political economists attribute China's economic problems not merely to Mao but to Marxism in general. Any governmental distortion of the free market, in their view, reduces productivity. The more the Chinese leadership interfered with the natural operation of the market, the worse things became. Empirical support for this argument is striking, for the relaxation of government economic-controls produced the fastest-growing economy in the world during the last decade of the twentieth century.

Marxist-oriented political economists acknowledge that bureaucratic rigidity and cults of personality crippled China's economic growth (Gregor 1995). These, in their view, were vestiges of China's inadequate preparation for socialism, not attributable to Marxism itself. Marxist-oriented political economists also blame China's economic failure on the West's refusal to provide the communist state with the markets and technology required for its economic development.

China is experiencing a revolution of rising expectations as its citizens become increasingly aware of the vast chasm separating their lives from those of the citizens of Taiwan, Hong Kong, and Singapore. The contrast between the lives of the average Chinese citizen and those citizens in China's coastal cities is also becoming increasingly stark. If the communist regime can meet the economic expectations of its population, it will survive. If it cannot, it will go the way of the Soviet Union.

It is this logic that is propelling capitalist reforms in China (Totten and Shulian 1992). The communist elite has turned to state capitalism in a desperate effort to maintain its power. This is a dangerous strategy. By allowing limited capitalism, the communists have created a capitalist class whose interests are diametrically opposed to their own. They have also empowered that class by providing it with great wealth. Beyond empowering their enemies, the communist regime is undermining whatever legitimacy it may enjoy by violating the egalitarian principles of the Marxist-Maoist philosophy that it has preached since its inception. As expressed in a popular Chinese rhyme, "The economic reforms (made) the peddlers rich, the coastal areas fat, and the officials drunk (from too many feasts), but left the salary earners starved" (Hsiung 1990, 36). Reflecting this changing reality, Party ideology is downplaying Marxism and replacing it with strong doses of nationalism and "spiritual civilization" (*SCMPI,* June 16, 1996, 6).

International Interdependence and the Politics of China

With the shattering of China's isolation in the mid-1800s, its domestic politics would increasingly be shaped by the pressures of the outside world. Of these, none was greater than the West's reaction to the victory of the communists in 1949.

The United States responded to the communist victory by encircling the Chinese mainland with a ring of military bases that stretched from Japan to the Philippines. It also rebuilt Chiang Kai-shek's forces on Taiwan, thereby presenting the communist regime with the constant threat of renewed war. China turned to the Soviet Union for protection but found its alliance with the USSR to be a difficult one. Indeed, tensions between the two communist states soon rivaled those between China and the United States.

The hostility of China's international environment played upon Mao's "siege mentality," a trait deeply ingrained during the formative years of revolutionary struggle. China became a garrison state, a "bamboo curtain" isolating the middle kingdom from the modern world. Relations with the West improved with the passing of Mao, but the Chinese leadership remains cautions (Segal 1990).

China is more vulnerable to foreign pressure today than at any point during the history of the communist regime. Four dimensions of this vulnerability are particularly noteworthy.

1. *China continues to be encircled by hostile forces in Japan, Taiwan, South Korea, and, perhaps, Russia.* Western weapons are also far more sophisticated than those of the Chinese. While few people expect the West to invade the Chinese mainland, many of China's aged Cold Warriors remain unconvinced. Continuing tension between China and Taiwan, in particular, reinforces Chinese fears of the West (Freeman 1998).

2. *The collapse of the USSR has left China isolated in its struggle with the capitalist world.* Relations between the USSR and China were hostile, but the Soviets could not allow the destruction of a communist power in China without weakening their own security. That has changed as Russia is being integrated into the West.

3. *China's leaders now realize that they cannot develop their economy without Western technological assistance and access to Western markets* (Johnson 1991). Indeed, China's trade surplus with the US now exceeds that of Japan. The price of that cooperation will be pressure for increased economic (capitalistic) and political reforms, the nature of which could well undermine the communist regime (Hsiung 1990).

4. *The security of the communist regime is being eroded by the huge prosperity of the Chinese mini-states of Taiwan, Hong Kong, and Singapore, all of which possess capitalist economic systems.* * Indeed, some dependency theorists suggest that the West promoted the economic development of Taiwan, Hong Kong, and Singapore as part of a deliberate strategy to undermine popular support for the Marxist government.

---

*Hong Kong reverted to China in 1997.

Table 7.1
Military Strength of the US and China

	Active Troops	Reserve Troops	Planes	Major Warships	Budget (billions)
US	1,547,000	2,045,000	11,189	239	$265
China	2,930,000	1,200,000	6,100	117	$32

Source: Center for Defense Information, Washington, D.C.

Whether or not this is the case, there can be no doubt that the expectations of China's citizens are being shaped by the prosperity of their smaller neighbors (Rabushka 1987). This trend can only increase as trade between the island states and the mainland continues to grow.

Although China is increasingly vulnerable to external pressure, it would be a mistake to believe that Chinese leaders lack the ability to fight back (Carroll 1990; Shuja 1998). China is a nuclear power, albeit at a less advanced level than the USSR or the United States. A ranking of the world's nuclear powers in the mid-1990s, for example, found the nuclear arsenals of both the United States and Russia to be twenty times larger than the nuclear arsenal of China. Nevertheless, China is the world's fourth leading nuclear power in terms of warheads (behind France) and the world's third leading nuclear power in terms of total explosive yield. China has also developed its own nuclear submarine. The balance of troops, by contrast, is heavily in the favor of the Chinese, with China having almost twice as many people on active military duty as the United States (*CSM,* June 23, 1998, 4) (see Table 7.1).

China also has been expanding its influence in the Third World, particularly among states that are attempting to forge a military capacity independent of the West (Ding 1991). Algeria, Argentina, Brazil, India, Iran, Iraq, North Korea, Pakistan, South Africa, and Syria, for example, have all been involved in nuclear transactions with China. All, including China, deny that the nuclear technology in question will be used for military purposes, but Western experts remain skeptical. The list of states receiving military assistance of a nonnuclear nature is considerably larger. In many ways, then, China remains locked in a Cold War with the West.

The message inherent in Chinese foreign policy is clear: the West must cooperate in the economic development of China if it desires Chinese cooperation in the maintenance of world peace (Ding 1991; Shuja 1998). Adding to China's influence is its status as a permanent member of the United Nations Security Council (Johnson 1991). The UN cannot act effectively without Chinese cooperation, a fact that is well understood by Chinese leaders in their dealings with Japan and the West.

External pressure on China is also softened by competition within the capitalist world for entry into the Chinese market. That market is immense. China will deal with those states of the First World that offer the most technology at the least cost in terms of political reform. Japanese business leaders are well positioned on both counts, and the United States is not far behind. Indeed, prior to the Tiananmen Square massacres, the United States was the largest foreign investor in China (McDonald 1990). It is now attempting to regain that position. Be this as it may, China's trade surplus with the US is astronomical (see Figure 7.2).

Finally, the very size and potential of China provides it with global influence. Direct military confrontation with China seems very unlikely, and the capitalist powers seem content to use their economic leverage as a means of forcing reforms that

Figure 7.2
U.S. Trade with China

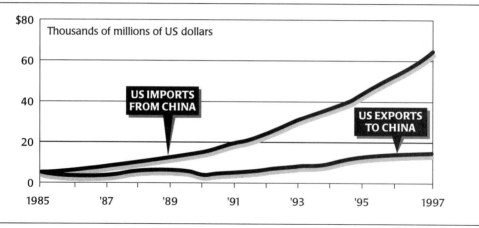

Source: U.S. Department of Commerce.

will either transform China into a capitalist democracy or lead to a Soviet-style collapse. The Chinese leadership, for its part, hopes to strengthen its domestic position by absorbing Western technology. The Party will bend the rules of Marxism in order to acquire Western technology, but it will use that technology for its own purposes.

Challenges of the Present and Prospects for the Future

China is now undergoing a profound transformation that must inevitably influence its attitudes toward democracy, human rights, quality of life, economic growth, and the environment. This transformation will also have much to say about the continued stability of the People's Republic of China (Harding 1997). In the concluding section of this chapter, we will examine the challenges that confront China in each of these six areas of "good government."

Democracy and Stability

China meets none of the procedural requirements of a Western-style democracy. Free and fair elections are not held at regular intervals, and when elections do occur, there is no meaningful choice between candidates. The picture is equally bleak in regard to the facilitators of democracy. Free speech is precluded, political parties other than those beholden to the Communist Party are not allowed, and pressure groups are controlled by the Communist Party.[9] The Party is very worried by the collapse of the Soviet Union following the introduction of democratic reforms (Harding 1998). China's broader political environment, moreover, provides little support for the emergence of a true democracy. Chinese culture, for example, stresses conformity, order, and submission rather than the free expression of popular views. China's citizens are desperately poor. For most, economic survival is probably of greater urgency than the fine points of electoral choice (Nathan 1997; Dickson 1997).

[9]Several minor political parties that were allies of the Communists during the early days of the revolution continue to exist. They are totally controlled by the Communist Party and have no influence on Chinese politics. Their sole function is to facilitate the illusion of democracy.

For all of the harshness of the Chinese regime, several factors point to a less authoritarian China in years to come (Oksenberg 1998). Of these, the strongest is the link between capitalist reform and political reform. Capitalism does not require political democracy, but it does require that people be able to move about and communicate with relative ease. Economic pluralism, moreover, also produces political pluralism. A viable private sector is emerging in China and, if present trends continue, it will clearly possess the economic resources to challenge the authority of the communist regime. Workers and peasants, as noted earlier, are also showing increased signs of political life. Particularly important in this regard have been systems of self-government established by Chinese peasants (Wandi 1998; Chen 1998; White 1998). China's leaders have been forced to create a façade of greater freedom to attract the trade and investment so essential to their nation's economic development. Finally, optimism for greater political freedom in China is buoyed by the persistence of the democracy movement. Despite government repression, the democratic movement will not go away, as each new generation of students renews its call for democracy.

Ironically, *the same forces that are pushing China in the direction of greater democracy may also be pushing it toward greater political instability.* The regime's ambivalence about the scope and pace of its capitalist reforms, for example, has resulted in a growing sense of political indecisiveness. This indecisiveness was already evident in the buildup to the Tiananmen Square massacre as an uncertain regime failed to suppress the students for fear of jeopardizing Western support. When it finally acted, it overreacted, treating the world to a grisly display of army tanks firing on unarmed students. This was not the behavior of a government in control; it was the behavior of a confused government acting out of desperation (Sullivan 1992). Another Tiananmen is not out of the question as competing wings of the Party and the army struggle for dominance and survival in the post-Deng era.

The symptoms of the regime's deteriorating position, moreover, are everywhere. Labor and peasant unrest are increasing, the coastal provinces are asserting their independence from Beijing, military bosses in remote regions are becoming warlords, ethnic and religious conflicts have increased, corruption is blatant, and crime and lawlessness are epidemic. According to the *China Daily,* each year brings "10 million people seeking jobs in towns and cities. Many of them come from surplus factory worker forces which stand at a staggering 20 million... An estimated 8.14 million workers were laid off last year" (*China Daily,* Sept. 15–24, 1997).

The symptoms of China's growing instability leave little doubt that something is wrong with the Chinese political system. Few observers, however, predict the collapse of the regime.

Human Rights

Human rights advocates applaud China's halting progress in the direction of greater political liberalization, but they caution that the communist regime continues to rule by force. Suspected opponents of the regime are routinely sent to forced labor camps, as are advocates of greater autonomy for China's ethnic minorities. Hopes that China's human rights situation would improve under Deng were shattered by the slaughter of pro-democracy advocates at Tiananmen Square. While some limited economic protest is now tolerated, political expression is constrained (*IHT,* Jan. 1999). The Chinese Parliament (National People's Congress) has recently passed new civil rights legislation, but most observers find it to be little more than a cosmetic device designed to facilitate the process of foreign investment (*SCMPI,* Dec. 3, 1994, 6). Much the same appears to be true of China's 1998 decision to sign the United Nations Accord on Human Rights (Benewick 1998).

A man holding a child walks past a propaganda poster that advises, "Practice birth control to bene-fit the next generation."

China's disregard for human rights, moreover, is not limited to the political realm. Faced with an exploding population, China limits couples to one birth every four years. Women who violate this rule are either fined or forced to undergo abortions. Many women who have already given birth to a child are forcibly sterilized. Some 12 million women were sterilized in 1991, and an additional 6 million in 1992 (*NYT*, July 21, 1993, A6). In recent years, the more severe measures have been relaxed, but the pressure for small families continues to be intense (*IHT*, Nov. 3, 1998, 5). The average Chinese woman now bears 1.9 children, down from 2.5 in 1988 (Cheng 1992). The figures may be far higher, however, as many second and third children go unreported as a result of bribes to local officials (*NYT*, Apr. 14, 2000, www).

China has responded to criticisms of its human rights record by attacking the inequality of an international system that forces a majority of the earth's population to live in conditions of squalor and poverty and by maintaining that it is neither realistic nor fair to judge states of the Third World by Western standards. China also argues that its human rights record should be judged by its ability to provide for the basic needs of its population rather than by its treatment of a few individuals (*China Daily*, June 17, 1993; BBC, Oct. 5, 1998).

China's leaders now find themselves in a dilemma. To jeopardize China's very profitable trade with the United States would be to threaten its economic revival. Indeed, China's trade surplus with the United States in 1992 was $23 billion, a figure that approached the $50 billion mark by the end of 1997 (*CSM*, June 23, 1998, 1). As important as US trade may be, the communist regime cannot afford to lose face by bowing to American pressure. To do so would be a public display of weakness, encouraging opponents of all varieties to grandstand in front of the Western press. Chinese nationalism, moreover, would be insulted. This dilemma was played out in curious but predictable fashion during the spring of 1994. Warren Christopher, the American Secretary of State, visited Beijing to negotiate a new trade pact designed to increase US exports to China. Prior to his visit, he "got tough" with China by publicly criticizing its human rights record. Improved trade relations between China and the United States, Christopher said, would be contingent upon a tangible improvement in the regime's human rights policies (*CSM,* Mar. 14, 1994, 3). The Chinese regime responded by arresting pro-democracy advocates who had been released from prison during the prior year. Thus, both sides were placed in a quandary. China wanted to retain its trading status with the United States, while the United States wanted to stake out its share of the huge Chinese market before it was consumed by the Japanese and the Germans. The damage was repaired behind the scenes, and the Clinton White House altered its position to argue that trade, not confrontation, was the most effective strategy for promoting human rights in China. US policy remains much the same today, as business meetings open with a toast to human rights.

Economic Growth and Quality of Life

Maoist philosophy placed the collective development of China above the interests of individual citizens. As China prospered, its citizens would share equally in that prosperity. How well, then, have the Communists fared in building a prosperous and egalitarian society?

The answer to this question depends to a large extent upon one's point of comparison. Is the People's Republic of China to be evaluated in comparison to pre-revolutionary China or to the Chinese mini-states of Taiwan, Hong Kong, and Singapore? A third alternative would be to evaluate the success of China in comparison to neighboring India, the world's second-largest country. China pursued an authoritarian path to socialist development, while India pursued a democratic path to socialist development (see Chapter 8).

If evaluated by comparison to pre-revolutionary China, the communist regime has been a huge success. China was stabilized, plague and famine were largely eliminated, some 95 percent of the population were employed, and most Chinese citizens have access to education and health care, however basic it may have been. These were not mean accomplishments for a country that possesses almost a billion and a quarter citizens.

Communist rule has also produced a more egalitarian society than that of pre-revolutionary China, with huge gaps in wealth being eliminated. Advances were also made in the area of women's rights, although much remains to be done. While women represent some 38 percent of the Chinese labor force, for example, they fill only 6 percent of the higher-level positions (*SCMPI,* Dec. 18, 1993, 10). Women also do all of the housekeeping chores, which, according to some estimates, translates into an additional 5.4 hours of work per day (*SCMPI,* Dec. 18, 1993, 10). Nevertheless, the principle of sexual equality is an important step for a society that traditionally bound the feet of women to assure their subservience to men (Chang 1991).

Concern over economic inequality, however, are now giving way to concern over rapid economic growth. By opening its coastal cities to foreign investment, the communist regime has created huge disparities in wealth between its provinces. Per capita income in Beijing and Shanghai, now tops $750 per year, while that of the poorer interior provinces is well below $200. Limited capitalism has similarly produced stark differences in personal wealth.

China also scores well in comparison to India, its GNP per capita growing at a pace of 7.8 percent during the past decade while that of India for the same period was 3.2 percent. Life expectancy is also higher in China, as are literacy rates, employment figures, and virtually all other quality-of-life indicators. India, of course, is a democracy. While its social and economic progress has been somewhat slower than that of China, its citizens have not suffered the regimentation and repression of their Chinese counterparts.

For many of China's citizens, however, the standard by which the communist regime is being judged is neither pre-revolutionary China nor India. The communist regime is being judged in comparison to the Chinese island states of Taiwan, Hong Kong, and Singapore. The comparisons are devastating for the communist regime. Prior to being returned to China in 1997, the GDP per capita in Hong Kong was $18,520 per year. The corresponding figure for mainland China was under $1,000. Similar differences exist across the broad range of social and economic indicators. Parallel figures for Taiwan and Singapore, although less dramatic, tell essentially the same story. *Communist development has been vastly inferior to capitalist development, albeit capitalism with a high level of state involvement.*

The Environment

The preeminent goal of the communist revolution was to transform China into a modern industrial society. Human rights and democracy were sacrificed to that goal, as was China's environment. Mao's Great Leap Forward pillaged the Chinese environment in a fanatical drive to gain industrial parity with the West. The present rush to capitalist growth now threatens to do the same (Bouchuan 1991; Dasgupta, Wang, and Wheeler 1997).

The figures on China's industrial pollution are staggering. In 1991, China poured some 25 billion tons of industrial waste into its rivers and coastal waters (*NYT*, Feb. 28, 1993, A11). The same year saw acid rain cause an estimated $2.8 billion in damage to China's farms and forests, much of it resulting from the fact that China is the world's largest coal burner (*NYT*, Feb. 28, 1993, A11). By 1999, nine of the world's ten most polluted cities were in China (*IHT*, June 18, 1999, www). The air quality in many of China's older industrial cities is seven times worse than the quality of air in New York City (World Bank 1992). The situation, moreover, is deteriorating (US Govt. Embassy Beijing, Feb. 1998, www). The desire for rapid industrialization has also found China turning to nuclear power to bolster its energy resources. China's nuclear technology, unfortunately, is not known for its sophistication, and neither are its procedures for storing nuclear waste (*NYT*, Apr. 19, 1993, A7).

China's environmental crisis is also a function of its exploding population. In spite of the draconian birth control practices enforced by the communist regime, China's population is expected to increase by more than 100 million within a decade. The rate of population growth is low, but China's population base is so large that even a low birth rate produces a catastrophic increase in the number of people to feed, house, and employ. As China's population has exploded, moreover, urban sprawl has consumed neighboring farmlands, thereby increasing the already excessive use of fertilizers and pesticides (*NYT*, Mar. 27, 1994, 1). To make matters worse, it is now being predicted that China, with some 22 percent of the earth's population but only 7 percent of its arable land, may again face critical food shortages (Brown 1995).

Not only is China's population expanding, but it is becoming increasingly motorized. A country that was propelled by bicycles is gradually becoming a country propelled by motorscooters and automobiles. The polluting capacity of hundreds of millions of motorized vehicles, most without pollution control devices, staggers the imagination. Nevertheless, Chinese leaders have announced that automobile production will be one of the four key areas of industrial expansion stressed during the coming decade[10] (*IHT,* Sept. 23, 1994, 11).

The picture is much the same in regard to China's limited water resources. China's official news agency recently acknowledged that millions of Chinese citizens suffer from water poisoning (*SCMPI,* Apr. 2, 1994). The situation is particularly critical in China's major cities, 250 of which are now experiencing water shortages (*NYT,* Jan. 2, 1994, E4). In order to alleviate water shortages in the more arid north, China is preparing to build an 860-mile aqueduct to transport water from the south of the country. The project, originally conceived by Mao Zedung, is viewed as an environmental nightmare by the West.

Until recently, environmental legislation has not been allowed to stand in the way of economic growth. That, however, may be changing, for in 1995 serious pollution was made punishable by death (*SCMPI,* Nov. 25, 1995, 7). China's environmental problems, unfortunately, have also become the problems of its neighbors. In fact, China's growing pollution may soon pose a greater threat to the world than its armies.

Prospects for the Future

China is rapidly becoming a post-communist society. While the Party continues to rule through the mechanisms described in this chapter, Marxist dogma is rapidly giving way to pragmatic capitalism. The capacity of the Communist Party to survive this transition is a question of heated debate among Sinologists. Some find China's current problems to be of a transitory nature and predict that the twenty-first century will be the century of China. Others see a China on the verge of a Soviet-style collapse. Still others believe that China is entering a prolonged period of political instability as a much-divided Communist Party clings desperately to power. It is the latter possibility that may pose the greatest danger to the world community.

References

Barme, Geremie R. 1998 (Sept.). "Spring Clamor and Autumnal Silence: Cultural Control in China." *Current History* 97(620): 257–62.

Benewick, Robert. 1998 (Autumn). "Towards a Developmental Theory of Constitutionalism: The Chinese Case." *Government and Opposition* 33(4): 442–62.

Bouchuan, H. E. 1991. *China on the Edge: The Crisis of Ecology and Development.* San Francisco: China Books.

Brown, Lester R. 1995. *Who Will Feed China?* New York: W. W. Norton.

Butterfield, Fox. 1983. *China: Alive in the Bitter Sea.* New York: Bantam.

Carroll, John. 1990 (May). "Are We Overestimating China's Potential?" *Across the Board* 27(5): 48–51.

Chang, Jung. 1991. *Wild Swans: Three Daughters of China.* London: HarperCollins.

Chang, Jung. 1993. Interview by Monte Palmer, July 9, 1993.

Chang, Mari Hsia. 1992 (Jan.). "What Is Left of Mao Tse-tung Thought." *Issues and Studies* 28(1): 18–38.

Chen, Shi. 1998 (July). "Leadership Change in Shanghai: Toward the Dominance of Party Technocrats." *Asian Survey* 38(7): 671–87.

Chen, Weixung. 1998 (Sept.). "Politics and Paths of Rural Development in China: The Village Conglomerate in Shandong Province." *Pacific Affairs* 71(1): 25–39.

Cheng, Chaoze. 1992 (Feb.). "Socioeconomic Influences on Fertility Decline in Mainland China." *Issues and Studies* 28(2): 103–27.

Cheng, Li, and Lynn White. 1998 (March). "The Fifteenth Central Committee of the Chinese Communist Party: Full-Fledged Technocratic

---

[10]The other areas are telecommunications, computers, and petrochemicals.

Leadership with Partial Control by Jiang Zemin." *Asian Survey* 38(3): 213–64.

Dasgupta, Susmita, Hua Wang, and David Wheeler. 1997 (March). "Surviving Success: Policy Reform and the Future of Industrial Pollution in China." A Policy Research Working Paper, The World Bank.

Dickson, Bruce. 1997. *Democratisation in China and Taiwan*. New York: Oxford University Press.

Ding, Arthur S. 1991 (Aug.). "Peking's Foreign Policy in the Changing World." *Issues and Studies* 27(8): 17–30.

Dittmer, Lowell. 1987. *China's Continuous Revolution*. Berkeley, CA: University of California Press.

Dreyer, June Teufel. 1993. *China's Political System: Modernization and Tradition*. New York: Paragon House.

Fairbank, John K. 1971. *The United States and China*. 3rd ed. Cambridge, MA: Harvard University Press.

Fairbank, John K. 1987. *The Great Chinese Revolution, 1800–1985*. New York: Harper & Row.

Freeman, Chas. W., Jr. 1998 (July–Aug.). "Preventing War in the Taiwan Strait: Restraining Taiwan—and Beijing." *Foreign Affairs* 77(4): 6–11.

Gernet, Jacques. 1982. *A History of Chinese Civilization*. Translated by J. R. Foster. London: Cambridge University Press.

Godwin, Paul H. D. 1988 (June). *The Chinese Communist Armed Forces*. Maxwell Air Force Base, Alabama: Air University Press, Center for Aerospace Doctrine, Research and Education.

Goodman, David. 1994. *Deng Xiaoping and the Chinese Revolution*. London: Routledge.

Gregor, James A. 1995. *Marxism, China, and Development*. New Brunswick, NS: Transaction Publishers.

Harding, Harry. 1981. *Organizing China: The Problem of Bureaucracy, 1949–1976*. Stanford, CA: Stanford University Press.

Harding, Harry. 1997 (Nov. 15). "The Complexity of China's Reform." *Vital Speeches* 64(3): 77–78.

Harding, Harry. 1998 (Jan.). "The Halting Advance of Pluralism." *Journal of Democracy* 9(1): 11–17.

Hong, Liu. 1998 (Jan.). "Profit or Ideology? The Chinese Press Between Party and Market." *Media, Culture and Society* 20(1): 32–41.

Hsiung, James C. 1990 (June). "Mainland China's Paradox of Partial Reform: A Post Mortem on Tiananmen." *Issues and Studies* 26(6): 29–43.

Jencks, Harlan W. 1992. "China's Army, China's Future." In *China in the Nineties: Crisis Management and Beyond*, ed. David Goodman and Gerald Segal. Oxford: Clarendon Press.

Jinghuai, Liu and Hai Xia. 1998 (Sept. 14). "Restructuring of the State Council General Office." *Beijing Review* 41(37): 12.

Johnson, Chalmers. 1991 (Aug.). "Where Does Mainland China Fit in a World Organized into Pacific, North American, and European Regions?" *Issues and Studies* 27(8): 1–16.

Lau, Tuen-yu, and Jiangang Wang. Winter 1992–93. "Editor's Introduction." *Chinese Law and Government* 25(4): 3–29.

Lawrence, Susan V. 1998 (Aug. 20). "Excising the Cancer." *Far Eastern Economic Review* 161(34): 10–13.

Li, David D. 1998 (May). "Changing Incentives of the Chinese Bureaucracy." *American Economic Review* 88(2): 393–97.

Li, Peter, Stephen Mark, and Marjorie Li. 1991. *Culture and Politics in China*. London: Transaction Books.

Linebarger, Paul. 1969. *Sun Yat-sen and the Chinese Republic*. New York: AMS Press.

Liu, Alan. 1986. *How China Is Ruled*. Englewood Cliffs, NJ: Prentice-Hall.

Mao, Tse-tung. 1967. *Quotations from Chairman Mao Tse-tung*. New York: Bantam Books.

McAleavy, Henry. 1967. *The Modern History of China*. London: Weidenfield and Nicholson.

McDonald, T. David. 1990. *The Technological Transformation of China*. Washington, DC: National Defense University Press.

Metzger, Thomas A. 1998 (Jan.). "Sources of Resistance." *Journal of Democracy* 9(1): 18–26.

Nathan, Andrew J. 1990. *China's Crisis*. New York: Columbia University Press.

Nathan, Andrew. 1997. *China's Transition*. New York: Columbia University Press.

Nicholas, Kristof, and Sheryl Wu Dunn. 1994. *China Wakes*. New York: New York Times Books.

Ogden, Suzanne. 1992. *China's Unresolved Issues: Politics, Development, and Culture*. 2nd ed. Englewood Cliffs, NJ: Prentice Hall.

Oksenberg, Michel. 1998 (Jan.). "Confronting a Classic Dilemma." *Journal of Democracy* 9(1): 27–35.

Overholt, William H. 1993. *China: The Next Economic Superpower*. London: Weidenfeld & Nicholson.

Oxenberg, Michael, Lawrence R. Sullivan, and Marc Lambert, eds. 1990. *Beijing, Spring 1989: Confrontation and Conflict*. New York: M. E. Sharpe.

Pye, Lucian. 1968. *Mao Tse-tung: The Man and the Leader*. New York: Basic Books.

Pye, Lucian. 1991. *China: An Introduction*. 4th ed. New York: HarperCollins.

Rabushka, Alvin. 1987. *The New China: Comparative Economic Development in Mainland China, Taiwan, and Hong Kong*. Boulder, CO: Westview Press.

Rosen, Stanley. 1992. "Students and the State in China: The Crisis in Ideology and Organization." In *State and Society in China: The Consequences of Reform* (pp. 167–218), ed. Arthur Lewis Rosenbaum. Boulder, CO: Westview Press.

Schram, Stuart R. 1970. *The Political Thought of Mao Tse-tung*. New York: Praeger.

Segal, Gerald, ed. 1990. *Chinese Politics and Foreign Policy Reform.* London: Kegan Paul for Royal Institute of International Affairs.

Selden, Mark. 1988. *The Political Economy of Chinese Socialism.* Armonk, NY: M. E. Sharpe.

Shuja, Sharif M. 1998 (Oct.). "China in Search of a Dominant Role." *Contemporary Review* 273(593): 169–78.

Sivin, Nathan. 1990. "Science and Medicine in Chinese History." In *Heritage of China* (pp. 164–96), ed. Paul S. Ropp. Berkeley, CA: University of California Press.

Sullivan, Roger W. 1992 (Feb.). "Trade, Investment, and the Fear of 'Peaceful Evolution.'" *Issues and Studies* 28(2): 51–66.

Taylor, Ian. 1998 (June). "China's New Prime Minister." *Contemporary Review* 272 (1589): 291–94.

Teiwes, Frederick C., and Warren Sun. 1998. *China's Road to Disaster: Mao, Central Politicians, and Provincial Leaders in the Unfolding of the Great Leap Forward, 1955–1959.* New York: M. E. Sharpe.

Totten, George, and Zhou Shulian, eds. 1992. *China's Economic Reform: Administering the Introduction of the Market Mechanism.* Boulder, CO: Westview Press.

Urban, George, ed. 1971. *The "Miracles" of Chairman Mao.* Los Angeles: Nash Publishing.

Wade, Robert. 1990. *Governing the Market: Economic Theory and the Role of Government in East Asian Industrialization.* Princeton, NJ: Princeton University Press.

Walder, Andrew G. 1991. "Social Structure and Political Authority: China's Evolving Polity." In *Two Societies in Opposition: The Republic of China and the People's Republic of China After Forty Years* (pp. 358–59), ed. Ramon H. Myers. Stanford, CA: Hoover Institution Press, Stanford University.

Wandi, Jiang. 1998 (March 16). "Fostering Political Democracy from the Bottom Up." *Beijing Review* 41(11): 11–14.

Wasserstrom, Jeffrey N., and Elizabeth J. Perry, eds. 1992. *Popular Protest and Political Culture in Modern China: Learning From 1989.* Boulder, CO: Westview Press.

Watson, James. 1992. "The Renegotiation of Chinese Cultural Identity in the Post-Mao Era." In *Popular Protest and Political Culture in Modern China: Learning from 1989* (pp. 67–83), ed. Jeffrey N. Wasserstrom and Elizabeth J. Perry. Boulder, CO: Westview Press.

Wei-Ming, Tu. 1990. "The Confucian Tradition in Chinese History." In *Heritage of China* (pp. 112–37), ed. Paul S. Ropp. Berkeley, CA: University of California Press.

White, Gordon. 1987. "Riding the Tiger: Grassroots Rural Politics in the Wake of Chinese Economic Reforms." In *The Re-Emergence of the Chinese Peasantry,* ed. Ashwani Saith. London: Croom Helm.

White, Tyrene. 1998 (Sept.). "Village Elections: Democracy from the Bottom Up?" *Current History* 97(620): 263–68.

Wo-Lap Lam, Willy. 1993. "Beijing in Bid to Overhaul Unions." *South China Morning Post International Weekly*, July 10–11, 1993, 7.

Wo-Lap Lam, Willy. 1994. *China After Deng Xiaoping: The Power Struggle in Beijing Since Tiananmen.* Hong Kong: P. A. Professional Consultants.

World Bank. 1992. *World Bank Report, 1992: Development and The Environment.* New York: Oxford University Press.

Yu-lin, Yu. 1991. "Change and Continuity in the CCP's Power Structure Since Its Thirteenth National Congress: A Line Approach." In *Two Societies in Opposition: The Republic of China and the People's Republic of China After Forty Years* (pp. 57–73), ed. Ramon H. Myers. Stanford, CA: Hoover Institution Press, Stanford University.

Zhibin, Gu. 1991. *China Beyond Deng: Reform in the PRC.* Jeffrey, NC: McFarland and Co.

Part Four

The Politics of Development

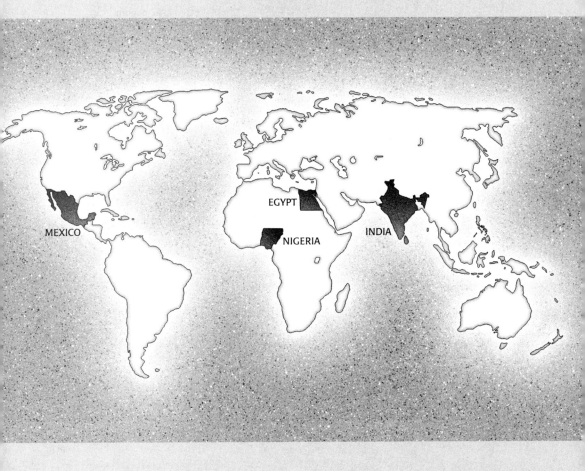

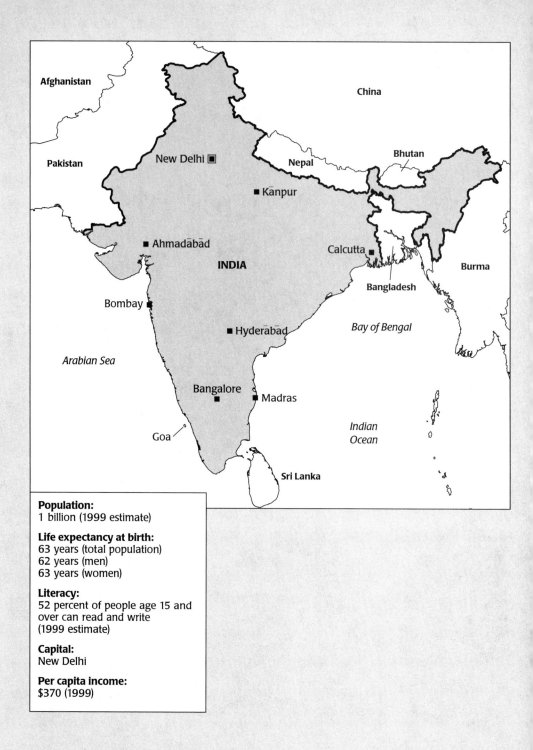

Afghanistan

China

Pakistan

New Delhi ▣

Nepal

Bhutan

■ Kānpur

■ Ahmadābād

Calcutta ■

Burma

INDIA

Bangladesh

Bombay ■

Arabian Sea

■ Hyderābād

Bay of Bengal

Bangalore
■

■ Madras

Indian
Ocean

Goa

Sri Lanka

Population:
1 billion (1999 estimate)

Life expectancy at birth:
63 years (total population)
62 years (men)
63 years (women)

Literacy:
52 percent of people age 15 and
over can read and write
(1999 estimate)

Capital:
New Delhi

Per capita income:
$370 (1999)

8

India
Democracy in Turmoil

India is the world's largest democracy. With a population of more than 1 billion, its electorate is larger than that of the United States, Canada, Great Britain, France, Germany, Italy, and Japan, *combined.* The most remarkable aspect of India's democracy, however, is not its size but its very existence. Political scientists have long maintained that democracy requires a literate electorate and a substantial level of economic development (Lipset 1960). India, however, began its existence as an independent country without meeting either of these conditions. India's first task, said its first prime minister, would be "to free India through a new constitution, to feed the starving people, and to clothe the naked masses" (Shah 1988, 263). India has made tremendous strides in education and economic development in the five decades since it achieved its independence. Nevertheless, it remains among the poorest countries in the world.

For the most part, theories suggesting that democracy requires an educated and reasonably prosperous electorate would seem to be valid. Among the major states of the Third World, India alone has succeeded in maintaining a democratic political system throughout the course of its history as an independent country.[1] While much of the Third World is now moving toward greater democracy, India's democracy is beginning to show signs of strain. The most consistent themes in current analyses of Indian politics are "institutional decay" and the "crisis of governability" (Kohli 1990; Vanaik 1990; Rudolph and Rudolph 1987).

The special focus in this chapter will be on India's unique ability to maintain a democratic political system under social and economic conditions that have fostered dictatorship in other areas of the Third World.

---

[1]Some scholars would add Costa Rica and a few island states to this list. These states, however, are very small.

The Taj Mahal stands in testimony to the artistic brilliance of pre-colonial India.

India in Historical and Religious Perspective

The richness of India's early history defies easy summary. By the advent of British rule in 1818, the Indian subcontinent, an area that includes the current countries of India, Pakistan, Bangladesh, Burma, Nepal, and Tibet, had witnessed the rise and fall of some 100 major dynasties (Mansingh 1986). The last of the great empires, the Mughal Empire, began in the early 1500s and lasted, at least in name, until the mid-1800s. By that time, however, the Indian subcontinent had long since fragmented into a mosaic of princely mini-states, some 562 of which were allowed to retain quasi-independent status within the context of British rule. Not only did the fragmentation of India make it easier to rule, but the British found the principalities to be "a pleasant backwater of feudalism and flattery, of pomp and circumstance" (Mansingh 1986, 43).

Two legacies of India's early history are of particular importance to the study of modern India. The first was the emergence of a distinctively Indian culture that found Indians having more in common with each other than they did with their neighbors. The second was the adoption of the Hindu religion by approximately 80 percent of the Indian population.

Hinduism

The major religions of the West teach that the souls of the righteous will reside in heaven. Hindus also believe that the souls of the righteous will reside in heaven, but

---

Karma

According to Hindu doctrine, each soul possess **karma**, *the predisposition for good or evil*. Karma is a particularly difficult concept to pin down, being described as everything from a cosmic force to luck or destiny (Benderly 1986). Wise individuals use their karma to increase their purity and their cosmic knowledge.

---

their version of heaven is substantially different from that depicted in the Torah, Bible, or Koran. For Hindus, heaven is a cosmic soul that embodies the true harmony of the universe. Eternal peace for the human soul can only be achieved by *uniting with the cosmic soul,* a process referred to as attaining **nirvana**. The goal of salvation is not to remain an individual soul but to become part of a greater soul.

Attainment of nirvana demands such an exceptional level of purity and religious knowledge that it can only be achieved after a prolonged cycle of birth and rebirth in different life forms. Believing that the reincarnation of the soul often occurs in animal form, many Hindus refrain from eating meat. Cows maintain a special status in the Hindu religion, symbolizing motherhood, fruitfulness, and exceptional purity. To injure a cow is to commit a major transgression against Hindu beliefs (Fuller 1992).

Souls reborn in human form enter one of five levels, depending upon their record of knowledge and purity: the **Brahman**, or *priestly caste;* the **Kshatriya**, or *warrior caste;* the **Vaishya**, or *trader caste;* the **Sudra**, or *artisan caste;* and the **untouchables**, *individuals who lack standing in one of the four castes.* Untouchables are expected to clean sewers and execute other "impure" tasks, thereby allowing members of the four castes to maintain their ritual purity (Deliege 1999).

The four castes are further broken down into *more than 2000 sub-castes,* or **jati,** the members of which share a common occupation and station in life. It is now possible for individuals to escape from the social and economic limits of their caste and jati, but most do not (Nyrop 1986).

Hinduism contains an incredibly rich pantheon of gods and goddesses, the role of which is to inspire individuals to strive toward ever-greater purity and cosmic knowledge (Fuller 1992). Of these, the three dominant gods are **Brahma**, the *god of creation;* **Vishnu**, the *god of preservation;* and **Siva**, the *god of destruction.* These gods are joined by innumerable lesser gods and goddesses, the nature of which varies from region to region. The holy books of Hinduism describe the deeds of the major deities as a means of providing guidance in the attainment of nirvana.

Because Hindu gods and goddesses are viewed as "guides to knowledge" rather than as the central force in the universe, Hinduism has been able to incorporate a far greater range of religious beliefs than monotheistic religions such as Islam, Christianity, and Judaism (Benderly 1986).

Hinduism, as the above discussion suggests, is far more than a religious system. It is also a social system, a political system, and an economic system.

- As a *social system,* Hinduism divides societies into specific classes and assigns a prescribed role to each class.
- As a *political system,* Hinduism specifies which classes are to rule and which are to serve.
- As an *economic system,* Hinduism establishes a highly complex division of labor and provides a religious justification for the unequal distribution of wealth.

For all of its venerable traditions, many scholars now view Hinduism as an obstacle to India's modernization. The problems are twofold. *First, the caste system perpetuates inequality between individuals and groups.* As such, it conflicts with modern notions of democracy and human rights. *Second, the caste system restricts the types of economic activity in which groups can engage.* In so doing, it restricts mobility between groups and forces individuals to pursue the same occupation as their parents. For traditional Hindus, economic activity is not a matter of merit and energy, but of birth.[2]

In India, as in all societies, some people are more religious than others. The caste system has been eroded by five decades of secular rule dedicated to economic equality and social justice. Many untouchables have also converted to Buddhism and Christianity, religions that advocate equality. Nevertheless, Hinduism remains a strong component of India's political culture.

The Religious Minorities

Islam, India's second religion, will be discussed at some length in Chapter 10, "The Arab Republic of Egypt." For the moment, suffice it to say that Islam shares much in common with Christianity and Judaism. According to Islam, the fate of mankind is determined by a single, all-powerful God, and there is no concept of reincarnation. A particularly interesting aspect of Islam is the belief that pigs are impure, if not a manifestation of the devil.

Islam and Hinduism, then, represent opposing religious systems with little scope for compromise. In times of communal passions, the cow and the pig have become highly charged political symbols; Muslims[3] have taunted their adversaries by killing cows, while Hindus have thrown pigs into mosques (Muslim houses of worship).

Muslims represent only 14 percent of the Indian population (see Table 8.1), but that percentage translates into 137 million citizens, most of whom are concentrated in India's northern states. The geographical concentration of India's Muslims increases their political influence and has led to persistent demands for greater regional autonomy. Besides Hinduism and Islam, India also contains sizeable Christian, Sikh, and Buddhist communities.

In addition to its diverse religions and castes, India is further fragmented into hundreds of linguistic groups, fifteen of which have been recognized as official languages. Not only is India divided into a vast mosaic of religions, castes, and ethnic and regional groups, then, but each tends to speak its own language.

British India

The **British East India Company**, *a private British corporation, established trading posts in India during the early 1600s.* Over the course of the next 250 years, it would transform the Indian subcontinent into a private colony. Huge fortunes were made in India, most of which found their way back to England. In the view of some historians, it was the wealth of India that financed Britain's industrial revolution (Thompson 1980).

As the British East India Company expanded, it became inevitable that the British government would be drawn into the governance of the subcontinent. In part, government involvement was triggered by Company demands for financial assistance in ruling a geographic area several times larger than the British Isles.

---

[2]For a contrary view, see Lloyd I. Rudolph and Susanne H. Rudolph, 1967, *The Modernity of Tradition* (Chicago: University of Chicago Press).
[3]Members of the Islamic faith are referred to as Muslims.

Table 8.1
The Religions of India

Religious Affiliation	Percent	Millions
Hindu	80.0	787.0
Muslim	14.0	137.0
Christian	2.4	23.0
Sikh	2.0	19.0 ·
Buddhist	0.7	6.8
Other	0.9	8.0

Source: The CIA Factbook, 1999.

The involvement of the British government in Indian affairs was also precipitated by a public outcry over the Company's inhuman exploitation of the Indian population. The Company's goal was to make money, and it pursued that goal with ruthless efficiency.

Far greater than its concern for the Indian masses was the British public's outrage over the "heathen" practices of the Indian population. Of these, none was more offensive to the British population than the practice of **sati,** or *wife-burning at funeral ceremonies.* Given the logic of the day, the wife's spirit was sent to join that of her departed husband (Hardgrave and Kochanek 1993). Vivid portrayals of this and other alien customs were provided to the British public by returning missionaries, who, unswerving in their belief in the superiority of the Christian faith, demanded that the British Government join their struggle against the devil.

Public revulsion against the greed of Company directors and the heathenism of the Indian population led to the India Act of 1784, a law which imposed a British-style legal system on those areas of the subcontinent controlled by the Company. It also called for the creation of an Indian Civil Service based upon merit examinations. A tradition was thus established in which the best and brightest of the British middle class would establish a career in the Indian Civil Service (ICS). In so doing, they would attain a lifestyle of power and splendor normally reserved only for royalty (Collins and Lapierre 1975).

The transition from Company rule to colonialism was triggered by the Sepoy[4] Rebellion of 1887, a rebellion ignited by rumors that newly introduced British artillery shells had been sealed with a mixture of cow and pig fat (Mansingh 1986). The underlying causes of the Sepoy Rebellion, of course, were far more complex. The Indian population had been increasingly impoverished by the exploitive practices of the British East India Company, and Government reforms had only confused an unstable situation by undermining the authority of local rulers. Anti-British sentiments were also fueled by the clash of Christian and Hindu cultures and the overzealous activities of Christian missionaries (Mansingh 1986). Whatever the case, the rebellion of the Sepoys was crushed by British forces, and India became the crown jewel of the British Empire. Three-fifths of the subcontinent was placed under direct British rule, while the remainder was ruled indirectly through some 562 princes and maharajahs. British rule would remain in effect until 1947.

---

[4]Sepoys were native soldiers employed by the British East India Company.

Colonialism and Its Consequences

The advent of direct colonialism accelerated a process of social change that had begun with Company rule. Some of these changes made a positive contribution to India's emergence as a modern state, while others would condemn the new nation to decades of conflict and poverty.

On the negative side, the Indian economy was restructured to meet the economic needs of England (Tomlinson 1992). India provided Britain with raw materials, and Britain used India as a protected market for its manufactured products. British industries flourished while India's industrial development was stunted. The colonies were designed to serve Britain, not to compete with its industries (Mansingh 1986).

Colonial rule also unleashed a Pandora's box of social problems that continue to plague Indian society today. Foremost among these problems was an explosion of the Indian population. Traditionally, a large family was vital to survival in India, providing hands for the field, power within the local community, and security in old age. Indian culture, accordingly, glorified large families. A woman's status depended upon her ability to bear children, particularly male children. The "real" man was a man who could produce a large family. The cultural emphasis on childbearing was made all the more urgent by the fact that disease killed most babies before they reached adulthood. Colonialism revolutionized Indian health practices by introducing modern medicine and sanitation procedures, but it did not alter the cultural emphasis on large families. People lived longer, but they also continued to have large families. The result was a population explosion that continues today.

British rule also disrupted traditional social and cultural patterns by imposing British law upon a society that had little in common with British traditions. This was particularly the case in regard to land ownership and inheritance. Land and property in India were often owned collectively by an extended family or clan. British commercial law, by contrast, stressed individual ownership based upon written deeds. Efforts to force the British tenure system upon India, as a British official of the era would admit, were catastrophic:

> Our rigid and revolutionary methods of exacting land revenue have reduced the peasantry to the lowest extreme of poverty and wretchedness, and the procedures of our settlement courts have been the means of laying upon them burdens heavier than any they endured in former times (Mansingh 1986, 38).

As a result of the population explosion and the disruption of established agricultural practices, famine became commonplace. India could not produce enough food to support its rapidly expanding population.

While some Indians embraced British values, many more clung to their traditional ways. A large segment of the Indian population, however, found themselves torn between the two extremes. The security of traditional ways was collapsing, yet the laws and customs of the British were difficult to grasp. In many instances, they seemed profoundly inappropriate. In sociological terms, a large segment of Indian society, particularly in urban areas, was becoming **marginalized**, *its members belonging neither to the old world nor to the new.* Caught in the conflict between two cultures, their primary goal became one of survival. India today remains very much a **transitional society**, *a society in which a large segment of the population is struggling to find security among the conflicting demands of tradition and modernity* (Naipaul 1990).

Colonialism, for all of its exploitive characteristics, also gave much to India. British colonialism strengthened the unity of India by providing the subcontinent with a *powerful cadre of administrators,* the Indian Civil Service (ICS). It also provided India with an *infrastructure of roads, railroads, currency, and communications* far superior to that found in most of the Third World. Perhaps more importantly, India was

A nineteenth-century painting from Punjab depicts a European learning to shoot a tiger that is clawing an elephant.

provided with *a language that would transcend the linguistic boundaries that isolated its diverse groups.* That language was English.

The colonial experience was also to provide India with a *Westernized political elite.* Acknowledging that India was too vast to be ruled by the British alone, the British East India Company soon determined "to form a class who may be interpreters between us and the millions whom we govern; a class of persons, Indian in blood and color, but English in taste, in opinions, in morals, and in intellect" (Mansingh 1986, 40). Over time, the members of this Westernized political elite began to guide India's struggle for independence.

Finally, the colonial era provided India with *almost fifty years of democratic experience*. Popular elections, however limited in scope, introduced the Indian population to the principles of democracy and facilitated the development of modern political organizations. Of these, the most prominent were the Congress Party and the Muslim League.

The **Congress Party** began in 1885 as a regular gathering of Westernized intellectuals from various parts of the Indian subcontinent. Over the course of the next four decades, the Congress Party evolved from a loose debating society concerned with securing greater Indian representation on provincial councils into a highly sophisticated political organization capable of mobilizing mass opposition to British rule throughout the subcontinent. The Congress Party, however, was to become far more than a mere political party. It was to become India's independence movement: its symbol of hope, democracy, and development (Sisson and Wolpert 1988). Indeed, the Congress Party would be the subcontinent's only "all-India" political organization. To a large extent, it remains the only "all-India" political party in India today.

The rise of the **Muslim League** paralleled that of the Congress Party, albeit in predominantly Muslim areas of the continent. The Muslim League, like the Congress Party, consisted largely of Westernized intellectuals from upper class backgrounds. Both organizations pressed for self-government and occasionally cooperated for the achievement of that end. Each increase in self-government, unfortunately, sparked growing conflict between the two communities. The Muslims, then some 25 percent of the population, feared domination by the Hindu majority (Gilmartin 1998). By the dawn of independence, communal conflicts had become so intense that civil war could only be averted by dividing the subcontinent into two independent states, India and Pakistan. Even with the partitioning of the subcontinent, millions of Muslim and Hindu refugees would die in the desperate struggle to reach safe borders. In spite of the creation of Pakistan as an independent Muslim state, many Muslims chose to remain in India. For them, as for the Hindus, India was their home and the home of their ancestors.

How then, does one evaluate India's colonial experience? Was India helped or hindered by its colonial heritage? The answer depends upon one's point of view. The British emphasize colonialism's legacy of democracy, national unity, and infrastructure development. Many Indians, by contrast, believe that colonialism locked them in a cycle of poverty and economic dependence from which they have yet to escape. They also blame today's ethnic and religious tensions on a colonial strategy that stressed the principle of "divide and rule." Britain did not create India's ethnic tensions, but its colonial policy clearly exacerbated them. Whatever one's point of view, today's India is very much a product of its colonial past.

Forging the Indian State

Of India's Westernized elite, two individuals would leave an indelible stamp on India and on the world as a whole. These individuals were Mahatma Gandhi and Jawaharlal Nehru.

Mahatma Gandhi. Mahatma Mohandas Karamchand Gandhi was born into a devoutly Hindu family in 1869, shortly after India's emergence as a British colony. His Hindu upbringing would be tempered by the study of law in Britain and South Africa and by an insatiable interest in philosophical currents as diverse as Christianity on one hand and Thoreau and Tolstoy on the other (Mansingh 1986). In many ways, Gandhi embodied the intellectual turmoil of an Indian population torn between the spiritual superiority of India's past and the material superiority of the

West. The challenge for Gandhi, as for India itself, was to use Western advances in the areas of health and education to build a new India that embraced the best of both worlds, the traditional and the modern. The first step in meeting that challenge, in Gandhi's view, was to end the exploitive colonial system that was destroying the inherent goodness of traditional India.

Gandhi returned to India in 1915, having spent more than twenty years in South Africa. He assumed the leadership of the Congress Party shortly thereafter, setting himself the herculean task of liberating India from British rule while simultaneously improving the health and welfare of the Indian population. While much attention has been devoted to Gandhi's hunger strikes, far less mention is made of his tireless campaigns to introduce sanitary health practices to rural India, campaigns that often found Gandhi and his entourage lugging a portable toilet from village to village in order to teach rural villagers the principles of modern sanitation (Collins and Lapierre 1975).

The four pillars of Gandhi's political philosophy were *tolerance, human dignity, self-reliance, and nonviolence.* Colonialism, in his view, was inherently wrong, but so was the plight of the untouchables or "scheduled" classes. Hoping to spare India the devastation of class warfare, he called upon the rich to give generously of their wealth and the poor to be moderate in their demands.

Gandhi preached that human violence could be attributed to seven causes:[5]

1. Wealth without work
2. Pleasure without conscience
3. Knowledge without character
4. Commerce without morality
5. Science without humanity
6. Worship without sacrifice
7. Politics without principles

Gandhi's political strategy, in turn, focused on three fundamental points: *transforming the Congress Party from a debating society into a mass-based political organization, teaching the masses to oppose colonialism by nonviolent means, and using himself as a model of sacrifice and self-denial.* Gandhi's policies of nonviolence were a combination of passive resistance, protests, boycotts, noncooperation, and tax avoidance, depending upon the needs of the moment. When the British increased the tax on salt, for example, Gandhi called for a boycott on salt purchases and taught his followers how to extract salt from sea water. Gandhi's moral appeals were reinforced by a policy of self-denial that often found him wearing little more than a loincloth and going on hunger strikes that riveted the world's attention on the plight of Indian masses and their struggle for independence (Fischer 1954).

As Gandhi's program took root, Gandhi himself acquired almost saintly stature among the Indian masses. The name *Mahatma,* literally translated, means "Great Soul." The British government, as might be expected, cared little for Gandhi and his tactics. Winston Churchill referred to him as "a half-naked fakir" (Tully and Mansani 1988).

Some flavor of Gandhi's campaign of noncooperation is provided by Louis Fischer's description of Gandhi's "spinning wheel" campaign, a campaign directed against the purchase of British-made clothes. Indians, Gandhi preached, should become self-reliant by spinning their own clothes, however crude they might appear. The spinning wheel would subsequently become the symbol of Gandhi's movement.

---

[5]*CSM,* Feb. 1, 1995, "Interview with Arun Gandhi," 14.

Gandhi's long propaganda journey for nonco-operation…had all the attributes of religious revivalism. He told audiences they must not wear foreign clothing, and when they applauded he asked them to strip off all wearing apparel made abroad and pile it in front of him. To this heap of shirts, trousers, coats, caps, shoes, and underwear Gandhi then set a match, and as the flames ate their way through the imported goods, he begged everybody to spin and weave their own clothing.

During those strenuous seven months of travel all of his meals, three a day, were the same and consisted of sixteen ounces of goat's milk, three slices of toast, two oranges, and a score of grapes or raisins (Fischer 1954, 69).

Jawaharlal Nehru. Jawaharlal Nehru, the son of a prominent Congress Party leader, was born in 1889 into the Brahman or aristocratic caste. Educated in the finest of British schools, he was assured a successful career in law or business. Nehru, however, chose to become a disciple of Gandhi, embracing his views on equality and nonviolence. He was also deeply influenced by the social views of the British **Fabians,** *a group of British intellectuals who advocated democratic socialism as the means of achieving a just and democratic society.* Human misery, in the Fabian view, was the result of tyranny and economic inequality. A democratic political system was the remedy for tyranny and a socialist economic system the antidote to inequality.

Although he was devoted to Gandhi, Nehru's vision of a modern India was to diverge markedly from that of his mentor. Gandhi advocated a fusion of traditionalism and modernity, glorifying the Indian village as the model of social harmony. Nehru, while retaining the essence of Gandhi's message of tolerance and nonviolence, visualized a modern, industrialized, and totally secular India. The India of the past, in Nehru's view, had little choice but to give way to the India of the future.

Nehru worked tirelessly for independence, his exceptional oratorical skills and his vision of a prosperous and modern India transforming him into a charismatic figure whose popularity would eventually rival that of Gandhi himself. If Gandhi was the spiritual force of the independence movement, Nehru would become its symbol of hope.

In spite of their differing visions of India's future, the personal bond between the two men remained unshakable (Fischer 1954). As independence approached, Gandhi urged the Congress Party to name Nehru as his successor. It was Nehru who would head the new nation. Gandhi, tragically, was assassinated by a Hindu fanatic in 1948 during the communal strife that accompanied the partition of the subcontinent into Hindu and Muslim countries (Tully and Masani 1988). In the view of many, it was the horror of Gandhi's death that quelled the will to violence. In death, he had performed one last service for his country (Tully and Masani 1988).

Nehru assumed the leadership of India with a vision of democracy, mild socialism, secularism, equality, and nonalignment.[6] Universal suffrage was proclaimed, expanding the Indian electorate from some 14.2 percent of the population to all adult citizens (Tully and Mansani 1988). The free-market economic policies of the colonial period were overlaid by socialist economic planning. While some capitalism remained, government policy dictated a path toward self-reliant industrial development. *Locally produced goods were to replace foreign imports, even if the quality of local goods proved to be inferior.* The important thing was for India to

[6]Neutrality in international politics.

Jawaharlal Nehru's vision of India's future differed from that of Mahatma Gandhi (shown in paint-ing behind Nehru), but Nehru shared Gandhi's belief in the value of tolerance and nonviolence.

develop its own industrial base and its own core of technical expertise. This policy is referred to as **import substitution**.

India's new Constitution proclaimed India to be a secular country. Discrimination on the basis of caste or religion was banned, and a quota system was introduced to assure that the untouchables and other "scheduled" or disadvantaged classes[7] received fair access to educational and employment opportunities. At the international level, Nehru proclaimed that India would follow a policy of nonalign-ment, preaching nonviolence at the international level much as Gandhi had preached nonviolence to the Indian masses.

Nehru's policies were the policies of India's Westernized elite, but they did not necessarily reflect the views of the masses (Embree 1990). The majority of India's population remained locked in the isolation of their rural villages, poverty-stricken and illiterate. Traditional ways were the only ways that they knew. The situation was little better in the sprawling slums of urban India (Mamoria and Doshi 1966).

The masses accepted Nehru's policies out of faith more than understanding. The Congress Party had liberated India from British rule, and its leaders were not to

---

[7]A good breakdown of India's disadvantaged groups is to be found in Ghanshyam Shah, "Grass-Roots Mobilization in Indian Politics," in *India's Democracy* (225–63), ed. Atul Kohli (Princeton, NJ: Princeton University Press, 1988).

be doubted. The rhetoric of the independence struggle, moreover, had painted a glowing picture of an independent India that offered prosperity to all. It was a time of great optimism. Finally, Nehru's policies were accepted for the same reason that government policies had always been accepted: docility and passivity. As later events would indicate, however, acceptance did not mean commitment.

Despite Nehru's personal popularity, opposition to his policies came from all fronts. Many Westernized intellectuals doubted the wisdom of allowing illiterate peasants to vote. In the words of Nehru's cousin, B. K. Nehru:

> And now 100 percent of the adult population has suddenly got the vote. The consequence is that the representatives they send to parliament or the state legislatures have no idea of how the British constitution, which we regard as the model for our behavior, functions, or what the rule of law involves, or what the position of the permanent civil services is in a modern state.... That being lacking, the institutions themselves get eroded (Tully and Mansani 1988, 24).

Religious and regional tensions also remained intense, with mass protests forcing Nehru to redraw the boundaries of India's states to reflect the linguistic and religious backgrounds of their inhabitants. Nehru's hopes of making Hindi the unifying language of the Indian state were also to fade. Hindi was the language of the northern elite, and its dominance was resented by inhabitants of India's other regions. While Hindi retained its premier position, fourteen additional languages also received sanction as official languages (Brass 1992). English continues to be India's "common" language, although it is spoken mostly by the educated classes.

Nehru was also to experience reverses in the economic sphere. Socialism proved to be a disappointment as economic development got bogged down in bureaucratic red tape and failed to keep pace with mass expectations. As a result, the optimism of the independence era began to give way to disillusionment, eroding popular support for the Congress Party and its programs. Within a decade of independence, the Communist Party would win sweeping victories in Kerala, a key industrial state, while regional parties were increasing their strength throughout the country.

Particularly disappointing to Nehru were his failures in the international arena. Nehru had hoped to transform the "nonaligned" movement of newly independent countries into a "moral force" that would ease Cold War tensions and bring the superpowers to their senses[8] (Gordon 1992). This, however, was not to be. War flared with Pakistan, and the situation along India's poorly demarcated border with China became increasingly tense. Nehru had hoped that the border disputes between the two countries could be resolved within the framework of the nonaligned movement, but this was not to be. War erupted in 1962, and the Indian military suffered a humiliating defeat at the hands of the Chinese.

Nehru suffered a stroke in 1964, passing away a few months thereafter. His close associates believed that his spirit had been broken by the war with China, a war that had shattered his belief in the capacity of the Third World to resolve its own problems in a peaceful and cooperative manner (Tully and Mansani 1988).

Indira Gandhi. Worried by the steady erosion of its popular support following Nehru's death, the inner core of the Congress Party, the "Syndicate," sought a candidate who would be both popular and pliable. There was only one logical choice who met both criteria: Nehru's daughter, Indira Gandhi.[9]

---

[8]The nonaligned movement was a coalition of Third World states that met periodically to discuss common strategy in dealing with the United States and the Soviet Union. They pledged to avoid joining alliances with either nation. Nehru also hoped that the nonaligned movement would become a strong moral force in world politics.

[9]Indira Gandhi was not related to Mahatma Gandhi but had taken her husband's last name. Gandhi is a common name in India.

Indira Gandhi sits beneath a portrait of her father, Jawaharlal Nehru, about three years after his death.

The Syndicate had accurately assessed Gandhi's popularity. The Congress Party won the ensuing election (1967), and Indira Gandhi was sworn in as India's third prime minister. The Syndicate, however, had grossly misjudged Indira's pliability. She kept her own counsel and largely excluded the Syndicate from the decision-making process.

By 1969, tensions between Indira Gandhi and the Syndicate had reached the breaking point. The Syndicate stripped Gandhi of the party leadership and calledupon the Parliamentary Congress Party (the Congress Party's Members of Parliament) to elect a new prime minister. They refused to do so, thereby splitting the Party into two factions: the Congress (R) and the Congress (O). The situation remained ambivalent until the 1971 general elections, in which Gandhi's Congress (R) scored a resounding victory. The Congress (R), for all intents and purposes, was the Congress Party.

The 1971 elections placed Indira Gandhi firmly in control of both the Congress Party and the Parliament, the masses having reaffirmed the magic of the Nehru legacy. Her personal popularity further increased with the crushing defeat of Pakistan in the third Indo-Pakistan war. Gandhi seized the moment to place her close supporters in key positions, not the least of which was the position of Chief Justice of the Supreme Court.

The more powerful Indira Gandhi became, however, the more her problems seemed to mount. The thrill of independence had worn off, and inflated hopes of sudden prosperity had been dulled by a stagnating economy. Rampant corruption in high places fostered mass cynicism and tarnished the image of the Congress Party.

Even nature seemed to turn against Indira as droughts caused mass famine. In mid-1973, the army was called in to crush food riots.

Gandhi's problems were also of her own making. Nehru had used the Congress as a sounding board for diverse opinions. Things got worked out and tensions were kept in check. Gandhi, by contrast, ruled the Congress (R) with an iron hand, alienating key figures in the Party's state and local organizations (Manor 1992). Equally disconcerting was the growing political influence of Sanjay Gandhi, Indira Gandhi's youngest son and heir apparent to his mother's power. Many observers believed that it was Sanjay, not Indira, who was ruling the country. Whether or not this was the case, Sanjay and his "friends" were at the core of the mounting corruption scandals. Some flavor of the situation is provided by the following conversation between Indira Gandhi and Romes Thapar, one of her close friends and supporters.

> I began a series of collisions with Mrs. Gandhi over all this corruption. She used to get very indignant and say: "You know that I don't do anything like this, and it's absurd." I said: "Well, if you're not prepared to accept what people are feeling, then we'll call it a day." "No, no," she said, "I'm not saying that. I'm just saying that you must discipline yourself and think of all the problems I have to face." So I said: "Well, I'm just telling you that people think you're corrupt." She said: "I am not." I said: "They say you're the queen bee that sends them out to make the collection." She was very upset, and so we started meeting less frequently (Tully and Mansani 1988, 117).

The crisis came to a head in June 1975, when an Indian court convicted Indira Gandhi of minor election fraud and ruled that she was to be replaced as prime minister. Gandhi denounced the court decision as a conspiracy against Indian democracy and invoked the "emergency powers" of the Constitution. The elections were postponed, and the press was placed under strict censorship. More than 100,000 opposition leaders were also "detained" by the police.

Presumably under Sanjay's influence, Gandhi also used her emergency powers to introduce sweeping social reforms including slum clearance, reforestation, the abolition of dowries, literacy programs, and mass sterilization (Seekins 1986). In many ways, the reforms were precisely what the stagnating country required to regain its momentum. India was being denuded of its forests, dowry conflicts fueled bride-burning, slums perpetuated subhuman living conditions, illiteracy depressed development, and overpopulation precluded India from breaking its cycle of poverty and despair.

However appropriate Sanjay's reforms may have been in theory, the result was chaos. Traditional Hindus (and other sects) resented the abolition of dowries, slum dwellers were evicted from their hovels merely to become homeless, and sterilization programs were directed largely at untouchables and Muslims. The clash between Nehru's vision of secular modernity and the reality of traditional values had become the cutting edge of Indian politics. Rumors that Gandhi would soon assume dictatorial powers swept the country.

Just as hope for democracy faded, Gandhi declared the emergency to be at an end. Among other things, she was upset by Western portrayals of herself as a dictator and the corresponding implication that India had ceased to be a democracy. The emergency powers, in her view, had been invoked to save Indian democracy, not destroy it. She also believed that she was far more popular than was actually the case and that her decision to impose emergency rule would be vindicated by the electorate. The illusion of popularity was propagated by advisors anxious to curry favor and could not be contradicted in the press because of the emergency decrees. Whatever the case, elections were scheduled for March 1977, and Indira Gandhi and the Congress (R) were defeated.

For the next two years, India was ruled by a fractious coalition government headed by Morarji Desai of the Janata Party. It was the first non-Congress Government in India's history. The transition from the Congress to the Janata was carried out in the best of democratic traditions.

The Desai coalition was a patchwork of diverse parties and individuals unified solely by their opposition to Gandhi's rule. Lacking common political values and wracked by personality conflicts, the Desai coalition collapsed of its own weight in 1979, and new elections were scheduled for June of the following year.

Indira Gandhi, in the meantime, had been rebuilding the shattered Congress (R), now rechristened the Congress (I) or Congress Indira. The Congress (I) swept to victory in 1980, returning Indira Gandhi to the prime ministership. Sanjay, his influence now dominant, waited in the wings (Manor 1992). A Sanjay reign, however, was not to be. He was killed in an airplane accident later the same year, and Rajiv, his elder brother, reluctantly became the heir apparent of the Nehru dynasty.

The next four years would see Indira Gandhi face a crisis of center-periphery relations as religious, regional, and linguistic minorities throughout India pressed for greater autonomy from the central government (Manor 1992). Particularly knotty were Sikh demands for a "Sikh Autonomous Region" loosely attached to the Indian state. The central government, if the Sikhs had their way, would retain responsibility for defense, currency, communications, and foreign affairs, but little more (Seekins 1986).

When Gandhi refused, extremist elements within the Sikh community launched a campaign of terror against the regime, killing government officials and destroying government facilities. The government responded with overwhelming military force, forcing the extremists, now fearing annihilation, to take shelter in the Golden Temple, the holiest shrine in the Sikh religion.

The situation had become critical. To violate the sanctity of a holy shrine would risk inflaming political tensions among India's religiously sensitive population. Capitulation to Sikh demands for a Sikh Autonomous Region, however, would invariably provoke similar demands among other communal groups. The crisis came to a head in 1984 when the army assaulted the temple with force, perhaps excessive force, causing hundreds of casualties and severely damaging the Golden Temple (Dua 1992). Indira Gandhi was assassinated by her Sikh bodyguards in November of the same year.

Rajiv Gandhi. Rajiv Gandhi assumed the leadership of the Indian government following the assassination of his mother, and he led the Congress (I) to a sweeping victory in the national elections held later that year. His margin of victory was the largest in Indian history, possibly reflecting a large sympathy vote resulting from the assassination of his mother. Be this as it may, the campaign was also the most expensive in Indian history (Noorani 1990).

Rajiv Gandhi seemed to be the right person at the right time. He was more a technocrat than a politician, and his reputation for honesty restored popular confidence in the government. He was also far more flexible than his mother and used his persuasive powers to rebuild the party organization at the state and local levels (Seekins 1986).

Rajiv Gandhi's rule was marked by a turn toward increased capitalism as taxes were reduced and the door was opened to limited foreign investment. The economy flourished, as did the Indian business class, raising hopes that India would soon "take off" on the path to rapid economic growth.

All, however, was not well. Gandhi's reforms were timid, leaving control over most areas of the economy in the hands of the bureaucracy. The upsurge in private-sector investment, while benefitting the business community, broadened the gap between rich and the poor and triggered an inflationary spiral that crippled the lifestyle of India's salaried middle class. Regional and religious tensions also mounted as extremist groups of all varieties tested the resolve of the Government.

Faced with the need for decisive leadership, Gandhi proved indecisive (*Economist,* "A Survey of India," 1991 and 1995). His image of honesty had also been scarred by the blatant corruption of his close supporters (Noorani 1990). Rajiv Gandhi and the Congress were voted out of office in 1989 and two years later, Rajiv would fall to an assassin's bullet.

Perhaps in reaction to the assassination, the Congress was returned to power in 1991, but was again defeated in 1996 with the Congress Party receiving the lowest percentage of the popular vote in its illustrious history. Power passed to the hands of the pro-Hindu Bharitiya Janata Party, but the BJP was unable to secure a majority in the lower house of Parliament and resigned after thirteen days.

Power then passed to the leftist-oriented United Front, a coalition of some thirteen parties. The reign of the United Front lasted less than two years and saw the Indian political system thrown into even greater confusion as no Government could hold the unwieldy coalition together for more than a few months. The return of the BJP following the 1998 general elections, represented India's fourth Government in twenty-two months (*IHT,* Mar. 30, 1998, 4). The return of the BJP in 1998 did not offer much greater hope for stability. With only 178 or 33 percent of the 540 seats in the Lok Sabha, the lower or popular house of the Indian parliament, the BJP could rule only by piecing together an eighteen-party coalition, fragile stuff indeed (Kohli 1998). Even then, it lacked a clear majority in the Lok Sabha (*Economist,* May 2, 1998, 39). A new round of national elections took place in the fall of 1999, with the BJP and its allies receiving a clear majority. The Congress Party had suffered its third successive loss (*Times of India,* Oct. 11, 1999, www).

Grim Realities for India. Whatever their ideological persuasion, Indian leaders face awesome challenges as they enter the twenty-first century. As expressed by R. K. Mishra, the director of a major Indian newspaper, "Never before since independence did India face such frightening convergence of a grim economic crisis, acute social tensions and widespread violence and disturbing political uncertainties" (*NYT,* June 23, 1991, E3). The "grim realities" to which Mishra referred include a population of 1 billion, about half of whom have an income of less than $30 per month, the minimum income required to support a healthy adult in India (U.N. Human Development Report, 1999). In China, by way of comparison, only 30 percent of the population is believed to be below the poverty level.

Illiteracy and disease in India's poorer regions, as one might expect, are endemic. Civil rights and political order in these regions are also on the verge of collapse. As described by a correspondent for *The Economist:*

> Atrocities continue with nauseating regularity. Most often they are the work of small landowners trying to make untouchables work their fields without payment.... The untouchables know there is no hope of those guilty being punished by the courts. There are no reliable figures for how many people die this way each year in Bihar, but one local journalist reckons it may be close to 4,000 (*Economist,* Apr. 6, 1991, 6).

Even more distressing is the growing involvement of criminals in politics. To again quote *The Economist:*

> Law-breakers should not be law-makers, says India's election Commission. It reckons that 40 members of Parliament in Delhi and 700 members of state assemblies face charges or have been convicted of offenses ranging from murder to rape to theft and

extortion. Of the 13,952 candidates who contested the general election last year, the commission thinks around 1,500—more than one in ten—were facing criminal charges (*Economist,* Sept. 27, 1997, 45).

India's escalating political violence is symptomatic of the growing sense of political uncertainty that has accompanied the end of the Nehru/Gandhi dynasty and the decline of the Congress Party (Anderson 1992). Between 1989 and 1998, India suffered through six separate Governments, a pattern that promises to be the trend of the future. The results of the 1998 elections were described thus by Thakur:

> For the first time in more than 50 years since Independence, India is to be led by a right-wing party with an ideology rooted in Hindu nationalism. When the greatest need of the hour was for a clear electoral result, India was again saddled with a fragmented political verdict, a fractured political elite, a deeply divided Parliament, and a hydra-headed government. India's watershed twelfth general election was held over 13 days in four stages, starting on February 16, 1998. The scale of the exercise is mind-boggling. There were 4,750 candidates chasing 605 million eligible voters, up from 593 million in 1996. Just one state, Uttar Pradesh (UP), has over 100 million voters. The largest electorate, Outer Delhi, has 2.8 million voters; the smallest is Lakshadweep with 37,000. Over 2.5 million ballot boxes and almost 774,000 polling stations were used for the elections, the total cost of which was Rs 6.4 billion (about $166 million). The voter turnout was 62.2 percent an increase of over 3 percent from 1996 (Thakur 1998, 1).

The picture was much the same in the 1999 elections.

Political uncertainty in India is also a function of a stagnant economy and a decaying bureaucracy. The "steel frame" of professional administration inherited from the British has given way to a bureaucracy known largely for its corruption and rigidity (D'Souza 1990). Government-run industries are outmoded and inefficient, while the private sector's growth continues to be choked by over-regulation (*Economist,* "A Survey of India," 1995). Progress is being made in India's transition from socialism to capitalism, but it is slow and uncertain.

Many Indians resent public criticism of their country's social and economic problems, suggesting that they distort the tremendous progress that India has made in the four decades since independence. Despite a growing gap between rich and poor, they note, their country now boasts a rapidly increasing middle class whose lifestyle is very similar to that of the West. While the ravages of poverty cannot be overstated, wealth is no longer the province of the few. They also point with justifiable pride to the fact that India, whatever its social and economic problems, has maintained a democratic political system for half a century. With one or two minor exceptions, India is the only state of the Third World that can make this claim.

The Political Institutions of India

In crafting the political institutions of independent India, Nehru and the leaders of the Congress Party were guided by five overriding considerations. First, *India was to be a democracy.* This point was nonnegotiable. Second, *India required a government strong enough to tackle the massive problems confronting the new state,* not the least of which was the growing threat of civil war between the subcontinent's Hindu and Muslim populations. Third, *the rights of India's citizens had to be protected* from the whims of a strong government. Fourth, the new political institutions had to *correct the ravages of the caste system* and other inequities of Indian society. Finally, India's political institutions had to *be responsive to the profound regional and cultural diversity* of the subcontinent.

The resulting government structure was a complex blending of British and American practice, the heart of which was a British-style parliamentary democracy. India's leaders had profound respect for the British system, and they believed that a prime minister supported by a strong majority in Parliament would give them the power they needed to tackle the herculean problems confronting the new state. (As mentioned in Chapter 2, a prime minister supported by a majority in Parliament has virtually unlimited power.)

The leaders of the Congress Party, however, well understood that India was not Britain and that communal tensions posed a constant threat to the rights of India's citizens. India, accordingly, was provided with a written constitution that enumerated the rights of its citizens and created a system of checks and balances.

The Constitution of India

The checks and balances provided by the Indian Constitution include the fragmentation of power between the prime minister and a president; the creation of two houses of Parliament—the **Lok Sabha** (*House of the People*) and the **Rajya Sabha** (*Council of States*); the establishment of a Supreme Court empowered to declare acts of parliament unconstitutional; and the implementation of a federalist system that divides power between the central government and the states. The Constitution also addressed the inequities of Indian society by abolishing untouchability and by reserving seats in the Parliament for members of the scheduled minorities (untouchables and primitive tribes) in proportion to their share of the population. Bureaucratic positions were also reserved for the "scheduled classes" consistent with the requirements of efficiency.

While impressive in scope, India's political institutions were alien to Indian culture. They had evolved in England to meet the needs of a culture radically different from that of the Indian subcontinent. India's institutional development, accordingly, has witnessed constant tension between the ideals of Nehru's secular democracy and the reality of India's social, religious, and economic environment. The political system envisioned in the constitution of 1950 is far different from the Indian political system today. The form remains, but the substance is evolving to meet the realities of Indian life.

Many observers find the India of today to be far more chaotic than the India of the Nehru era, and they view the evolution of its political institutions as a process of decay. Others see it merely as a process of adjustment. India is India, in their view, and its political institutions must reflect its own cultural traditions. Whatever the case, Nehru's vision of a secular and socialist India is being severely tested, a theme to be examined throughout the remainder of this chapter (Rudolph and Rudolph 1987 and 1998; Tully and Mansani 1988; Ganguly 1998).

Executive Power in India: The President and the Prime Minister

Executive power in India is divided between the president and the prime minster. The president is elected indirectly by an electoral college consisting of both houses of the Indian parliament and all state legislatures. The prime minister is elected by a majority vote in the Lok Sabha, the popularly elected house of Parliament.

The President. By custom, the role of India's president is largely symbolic, often being compared to that of the German president or the British monarch. Unlike the

Chronology of Indian Prime Ministers

1947	India is granted its independence. Jawaharlal Nehru becomes India's first prime minister.
1948	Mohandas (Mahatma) Gandhi is assassinated.
1964	Nehru suffers a stroke and passes away shortly thereafter. Lal Bahadur Shastri becomes prime minister.
1966	Indira Gandhi is sworn in as prime minister upon the death of Lal Bahadur Shastri.
1967	Indira Gandhi leads the Congress to victory in national elections, reaffirming her position as prime minister.
	Indira Gandhi and the "Syndicate" are locked in a power struggle for control of the Congress. The party will split two years later.
1969	The Congress Party splits into two factions: an Indira Gandhi faction [Congress (R)] and opposition faction [Congress (O)]. Indira Gandhi remains prime minister.
1971	Indira Gandhi and the Congress (R) win a two-thirds majority in national elections (lower house). (March)
1973	Indira Gandhi strengthens her hold on the Indian political system by appointing a loyal supporter as the Chief Justice of the Indian Supreme Court. Her move breaks tradition and undermines the independence and impartiality of the Supreme Court.
1975	Indira Gandhi is found guilty of corrupt electoral practices and activates the "emergency" provision of the Constitution, ruling by decree. (June)
1977	Elections are held. Indira Gandhi and the Congress (R) are defeated. The Congress is out of office for the first time since independence.
	Morarji Desai of the Janata Party becomes India's first non-Congress prime minister.
1979	The Janata Government falls. A caretaker Government is formed.
1980	Indira Gandhi is reelected prime minister.
	Sanjay Gandhi, Indira Gandhi's son and heir apparent to the position of prime minister, is killed in an airplane accident.
1984	Indira Gandhi orders the Indian army to attack the Golden Temple, the holiest site of India's Sikh minority. (June 5, 6)
	Indira Gandhi is assassinated by her Sikh bodyguards. Her son, Rajiv Gandhi, assumes leadership of the Congress (I) Party. (Oct. 31)
	Rajiv Gandhi and the Congress (I) win the largest majority in Indian history. The Party begins a gradual move away from socialism.
1989	National elections deprive the Congress (I) of a majority in Parliament. Rajiv Gandhi resigns as prime minister. (November)
	V. P. Singh of the Janata Dal Party forms a minority government.
1989/1990	Chandra Shekhar, the leader of a small factional party, becomes prime minister with the support of Rajiv Gandhi and the Congress (I).
1991	Conflict between Shekhar and Gandhi precipitates the collapse of the Shekhar Government and a call for new elections.
	Rajiv Gandhi is assassinated.
	The Congress (I) wins a marginal victory in national elections. Narasimha Rao is sworn in as prime minister. (June 1) The Nehru dynasty ends.
1996	The BJP emerges from the 1996 elections as the largest party in the Lok Sabha. Its leader, Atal Bihari Vajpayee, is asked to form a Government. Unable to garner a majority in the Lok Sabha, he resigns after 13 days. A 13-party coalition referred to as the United Front rules for almost two years but changes prime ministers every few months.
1998	The BJP wins a plurality in the 1998 elections and Vajpayee heads a coalition Government consisting of 18 diverse parties.
1999	The BJP (and allies) win a clear majority in the 1999 elections. Vajpayee returns as prime minister.

British monarch, however, the Indian president possesses formidable constitutional powers. The president appoints the prime minister in accordance with the will of the Lok Sabha. If one party possesses a majority in the Lok Sabha, the appointment of its leader as prime minister is purely pro forma. If the Lok Sabha is deadlocked, however, the president may play a determining role in the appointment process. The president also appoints the governors of India's states and territories, the justices of the Supreme Court, and most other high officials. The president serves as the commander-in-chief of India's armed forces and, in times of emergency, can suspend the Government and rule by presidential decree. The president can also suspend state governments if, in his or her view, the state government has lost the power to rule effectively.

The Constitution requires the president to *seek* the "aid and advice" of the prime minister and Cabinet in the exercise of the above powers, a provision that was amended in 1976 to read that the president *will seek the advice of the prime minister and act in accordance with that advice.* Much of the president's theoretical power, accordingly, now resides with the prime minister. As the president of India declared bluntly in granting Indira Gandhi the right to rule by emergency decree,"India is Indira, and Indira is India" (Tully and Mansani 1988, 119). Nevertheless, the situation could easily change. With the power of the Congress Party on the wane and the opposition fragmented, a series of weak prime ministers could well force the president to play a more decisive role in Indian politics.[10] This was very much the case in the 1996 elections when the Indian president asked Atal Bihari Vajpayee, the leader of the pro-Hindu BJP, to form a Government. No single party possessed anything near a majority in the Lok Sabha, and he could have just as easily asked the leader of the leftist United Front to do so. This was not a matter of small concern, for the BJP and the United Front are at opposite ends of the political spectrum (*India Today,* June 15, 1996, 24). A similar scenario was played out following the 1998 elections.

The Prime Minister. The formal role of the Indian prime minister is to propose legislation to the Parliament, to guide that legislation through the parliamentary process, and to administer the programs approved by the Parliament. In practice, if not in theory, the prime minister also exercises most of the powers reserved for the president, including the power to appoint governors, Supreme Court justices, and most other major officials. It is also the prime minister who determines when a national state of emergency should be declared or when state governments should be removed for violating the Constitution. The appointment powers usurped from the presidency provide the prime minister with abundant patronage at both the national and state levels. Friends and supporters fill key positions; opponents find their careers truncated.

The formal powers of the prime minister, then, are formidable. As the experience of Indira Gandhi well illustrated, no other single branch of the Indian government can long resist the will of a powerful prime minister. Indira Gandhi weakened the presidency, undermined the authority of the Supreme Court, and crushed state governments hostile to her programs (Moog 1998). It was during the reign of Indira Gandhi that the "decay" or "adjustment" of India's political institutions began in earnest.

---

[10]In addition to the powers discussed above, the president also plays a minor role in the legislative process, having the power to withhold his or her assent from a bill, thereby forcing the Parliament to reconsider it. As the Government presumably enjoys the support of the Parliament, such "vetoes" constitute little more than a delaying tactic.

The formal powers of the prime minister, moreover, are augmented by a variety of informal powers. The Nehru Dynasty, for example, derived extraordinary powers from both the organizational dominance of the Congress Party and the charisma of the Nehru-Gandhi name. The prime minister is also the focal point of the mass media and is better positioned to shape public opinion than any other agency of the Indian government.

With the passing of the dynasty, one would expect Indian politics to be less influenced by issues of charisma and personal popularity, but this may not be the case. Personality continues to play a profound role in the electoral process, as do charismatic religious movements, not the least of which is a resurgent Hindu fundamentalism (Tully and Mansani 1988). The Congress Party, itself, made Sonia Gandhi, Rajiv Gandhi's Italian-born wife, president of the Party in an effort to recapture the magic of the Gandhi name (Ganguly and Burke 1998). The strategy proved unsuccessful, and the Congress Party lost in the 1999 elections—its third loss in three years.

The Council of Ministers (Government). The prime minister heads the Council of Ministers, the Indian equivalent of Britain's "Government." The Council of Ministers consists of three layers: the Cabinet, non-Cabinet ministers, and deputy ministers. The Cabinet usually consists of approximately twenty of the ruling party's most senior politicians, and it is they who advise the prime minister on key issues of public policy. Of these, the holders of prestige ministries such as Foreign Affairs, Finance, and Defense are the most powerful. Non-Cabinet ministers are individuals waiting to work their way into ministerial positions.

The Council of Ministers (Government) as a whole may have more than 100 members, as each incoming prime minister uses appointments to the Council as a means of building parliamentary support. Coalition governments are under even greater pressure to make large numbers of appointments to the Council, for each segment of the coalition must have its share of the spoils (*Times of India,* Jan. 15, 1999, www).

As the size of the Council of Ministers makes it too unwieldy to meet as a collective body, most work is done by committees in consultation with the prime minister. This increases the power of the prime minister, for only the prime minister possesses a complete picture of what is going on.

During the era of the Nehru Dynasty, prime ministers dominated the Cabinet, leaving its members little scope for independent action. The experience of India's coalition governments has been exactly the opposite, with prime ministers being elected only after exhaustive negotiations among coalition partners, all of whom were well represented on the Cabinet. As the slightest affront to a coalition partner risked bringing down the Government, prime ministers were reluctant to take decisive stands on key issues. The result was frustration and conflict as each faction in the coalition blamed the others for the Government's failings (*Times of India,* Jan. 7, 1999, www). If the tendency toward coalition governments continues, the most fundamental challenge to Indian democracy may be finding a pattern of leadership that is both decisive and stable.

Legislative Power in India: The Indian Parliament

Legislative power in India is divided between two houses of parliament, the Lok Sabha, or lower house, and the Rajya Sabha, or upper house. Both houses of parliament are important to the political process, but the Lok Sabha is dominant.

The Lok Sabha. The Lok Sabha is the focal point of parliamentary democracy in India. Much as in England, voters in each of India's 543 single-members, simple-plurality electoral districts elect one member to the Lok Sabha.[11] The members of the Lok Sabha elect the prime minister who, in turn, forms a Government (Council of Ministers). Once appointed, the Council of Ministers serves at the pleasure of the Lok Sabha. A vote of no confidence "brings down" the Council of Ministers. This forces either the dissolution of the Lok Sabha or the reconstruction of a new Council of Ministers that is capable of winning a majority therein.

Parliamentary procedures leading to the passage of a bill are similar to those of Great Britain (see Chapter 3), with each bill receiving several readings before being sent to the president for the official stamp of approval. During the four decades of the Nehru Dynasty, the prime minister dictated both the content and priority of legislation. Opposition parties used debates and the Question Hour to embarrass the Government, but such tactics, while often animated, had little influence on policy.

Reflecting this tradition of domination by the prime minister, the Indian Parliament now epitomizes the decay of India's political institutions (*Times of India,* Dec. 24, 1998, www). As described by Hardgrave and Kochanek:

> Most Members of Parliament have no knowledge or training in the legislative process, fail to do their homework and lack technical competence. Absenteeism has increased as members cultivate their home constituencies or pursue varied extra-parliamentary interests. They are indifferent to executive abuse of the system, ignore poor drafting of legislation, and provide minimal scrutiny of the budget. As a result, complex bills are rushed through in mere minutes, perfunctory replies to questions are provided without challenge, and grants for an increasing number of ministries and departments are passed without discussion. The decorum of Parliament has often been disrupted by rowdy confrontations between the majority and opposition MPs (Hardgrave and Kochanek 1993, 81–82).

The Rajya Sabha. The upper house of the Indian Parliament, the Rajya Sabha, is elected by the state legislatures. The Rajya Sabha is roughly equal to the Lok Sabha in its legislative authority, but it cannot bring down a Government. The prime minister and Council of Ministers (Government) are responsible before the Lok Sabha alone. The members of the Rajya Sabha, much like senators in the United States, are elected for six-year terms, with a third of the membership standing for election at two-year intervals. The 250 seats of the Rajya Sabha are allocated in rough proportion to the population of India's states and territories,[12] with smaller states faring slightly better than their larger counterparts. Twelve of the members of the Rajya Sabha are nominated by the Indian president for meritorious service to the state.

If the Lok Sabha and the Rajya Sabha pass differing versions of a bill, the bill is shuttled back and forth between the two chambers until agreement is reached. If a mutually acceptable bill cannot be reached by this process, the president may call a joint session of Parliament to work out the differences.

During most of the past five decades, the Congress Party dominated both the Lok Sabha and the Rajya Sabha, thereby limiting conflict between the two houses (Hardgrave and Kochanek 1993). This pattern is now changing as the growing strength of regional and communal parties has made the Rajya Sabha

---

[11]Two additional seats in the Lok Sabha are reserved for the Anglo-Indian community.
[12]The maximum number of seats is 250. The actual number of seats may vary slightly.

the focal point of efforts to reassert state rights. The ability of a revitalized Rajya Sabha to reverse the decay of India's political system remains open to question. On the positive side, an assertive Rajya Sabha would breathe new life into both the Indian Parliament and India's federal system. On the negative side, a strong Rajya Sabha could cripple the ability of the Indian government to take decisive actions against religious and regional groups intent on destroying the unity of the Indian political system.

Law and Politics in India: The Supreme Court

The Indian political system represents a fusion of British and American practice. India's leaders preferred a parliamentary system patterned after that of Great Britain, but they were fearful that Britain's "unwritten" constitution would be unworkable in the tumultuous environment of Indian politics. India's citizens, accordingly, were provided with a broad array of constitutionally guaranteed rights, all of which were protected by an American-style Supreme Court empowered to declare acts of parliament unconstitutional. A fundamental tension was thus established between the British concept of parliamentary supremacy and the American concept of constitutional/judicial supremacy.

The inherent tension between the Supreme Court and the Parliament came to a head when the Supreme Court declared many of Indira Gandhi's social programs unconstitutional. The battle was an unequal one, as Indira Gandhi, supported by large majorities in the Parliament, merely amended the Constitution to gain her objectives. This was a relatively simple process, for an amendment to the Indian constitution generally requires little more than a majority vote in the two houses of Parliament.

The real weakness of the Supreme Court, however, proved to be political rather than legal. Faced with the prospect of the Supreme Court's continued opposition to her policies, Indira Gandhi merely "stacked" the court with friends and supporters.[13] The 1977 defeat of Indira Gandhi found the Supreme Court "restacked" by the Janata Party, only to be again restacked by Gandhi following her return to office in 1980.

The Supreme Court survived, but its integrity had been severely compromised. The Court is now attempting to reestablish a position of impartiality and independence, a goal that may be easier to achieve in the era of weak coalition governments (Moog 1998). In point of fact, India's elected politicians have begun to complain of the Supreme Court's growing activism, claiming that it is attempting to become a third house of Parliament (*India World,* Jan. 17, 1999, www).

The broader India court system is best described as overwhelmed, a fact that legal experts say is destroying the justice system. On average, Indian courts now take 6.6 years to process a case (*Times of India*, Apr. 3, 2000, www).

Federalism in India

In addition to the existence of a Supreme Court, American influence on the Indian Constitution is also evident in the federal structure of the Indian political system. Powers such as defense, foreign affairs, currency regulation, and other matters of overriding national importance are reserved for the federal government. Education,

---

[13]Gandhi forced the appointment of one of her close allies to the position of chief justice. This was a critical move, for it is the chief justice who appoints the remaining members of the court.

welfare, and police security are largely controlled by the states. In areas such as economic planning, the federal and state governments enjoy concurrent authority. The states also possess direct representation in the Parliament via their ability to appoint members to the Rajya Sabha.

Although power is divided between the federal and state governments, the powers of the federal government are clearly superior to those of the states. The Constitution empowers the federal (Union) government to override state legislation on issues requiring national uniformity and to remove state Governments (governor and cabinet) that violate the Constitution. Prime ministers have used this constitutional provision to remove antagonistic state Governments on several occasions, often for political rather than constitutional reasons (Hardgrave and Kochanek 1993). As things currently stand, the powers of the states have been weakened so much that they can do little without the approval of the central government (Manor 1998).

Bureaucracy and Politics in India

India entered independence with a core of senior civil servants who were among the finest in the world (Braibanti 1966). It was the Indian Civil Service, variously referred to as the "steel frame" or "permanent government," that enabled India to make a smooth transition from colonialism to independent rule. India, thus, was twice blessed. It was blessed with an experienced political elite committed to democracy, and it was blessed with an exceptionally qualified administrative elite capable of executing government policies in an efficient manner.

With the pressures of independence, the quality of the ICS, now renamed the Indian Administrative Service (IAS), began to erode. As a colonial service, the responsibilities of the ICS were largely those of collecting taxes and maintaining law and order (Tummala 1982). With independence, the IAS was suddenly expected to provide the Indian population with a full range of health, education, and welfare services, not to mention the management of a complex socialist economy. The task of the IAS was made all the more difficult by the mediocre nature of the lower levels of the Indian bureaucracy. Unlike the elite senior service, the rank-and-file members of the Indian bureaucracy had not been trained in Britain, nor did they necessarily accept Nehru's ideal of a Westernized India. Most were merely intent on personal survival. No matter how talented they may have been, the elite core at the top of the administrative pyramid could not compensate for weaknesses at the pyramid's base.

The IAS was to suffer other problems as well. Many Indians resented the elitist, upper-caste, "Anglo" nature of the IAS. A democratic state, in the view of many, should have a democratic bureaucracy that was open to all. As discussed in the Indian press,

> The present bureaucracy under the orthodox and conservative leadership of ICS with its upper class prejudices can hardly be expected to meet the requirements of social and economic changes along socialist lines. The creation of an administrative cadre committed to national objectives and responsive to our social need is an urgent necessity (Sekhar and Dharia 1969, 110).

Much as in the case of the Supreme Court, a tension soon developed between the ideological goals of India's political leaders and the "efficiency" goals of the IAS. Political leaders wanted to relax the standards for entrance to the IAS, but the IAS resisted, arguing that a lowering of entrance standards would open the civil service to less qualified and less politically neutral applicants. The choice between efficiency and democracy is not an easy one, and as in the case of the

Supreme Court, efficiency was sacrificed to politics. Entrance standards to the IAS were relaxed, and performance declined.

Much of the political pressure on the IAS took the form of pure bullying, a process described by Nehru's cousin, B. K. Nehru:

> Suspension, denial of promotion and transfer are the three powers that have been used to bend civil servants to the Minister's will. What does a married man with children do if he's told to do something and says "I won't"? So the next day he finds himself transferred. Now his children can't get admission to schools, he can't get a house; it causes complete dislocation to his life. So it's not surprising that so many have succumbed to these pressures (Tully and Mansani 1988, 49).

A former Minister of Commerce blames this situation on the politicization of the bureaucracy:

> The parliamentary system has worked well in countries which have a seasoned and committed bureaucracy. In India, the bureaucracy has peen politicized. Bureaucrats change with the change of every government. This practice is bad since our bureaucrats, unlike their counterparts in America who are hired and fired, are permanent servants. Our bureaucracy has become not only insensitive and irresponsible to the aspirations of the people, but to an extent it has become irresponsible and lethargic. Political parties are mainly responsible for this. If a bureaucrat is left to himself, he would certainly behave better (*Times of India,* Dec. 1, 1998, www).

Despite movement toward a free market economy, the Indian bureaucracy continues to serve as a break on economic development. The Indian bureaucracy also continues to grow (*India Times,* Apr. 20, 2000, www).

The Actors in Indian Politics: Elites, Parties, Groups, and Citizens

Political institutions are the arena of politics, but the actors in the political process play a critical role in determining who gets what, when, and how. In the present section, we shall examine the four main types of political actors in India: elites, parties, groups, and citizens.

Elites and Politics in India

The transformation of India's political institutions is often attributed to the changing nature of India's political elites. This argument is both simple and persuasive. India is an elite-directed society in which the masses, most of whom are poorly educated, follow the path outlined by their leaders. If the elites are democratic, the masses will be democratic. If the elites incline toward fragmentation and demagoguery, the masses will offer little opposition. One way or the other, it is the elites who determine the direction of the Indian political system.

Over the course of the past five decades, the Indian elite system has progressed through three stages: the independence stage, the nationalist stage, and the professional politician stage (Rudolph and Rudolph 1987). *The elite structure during the independence stage was dominated by Mahatma Gandhi, Nehru, and other leaders of exceptional vision.* That vision was one of a secular and democratic India. It was Gandhi and Nehru who created the Indian political system, and it was Nehru, supported by an elitist Indian Civil Service, who made the system work during its formative years.

The nationalist stage in the evolution of the Indian elite structure featured Indira Gandhi and other "second-generation" leaders of the Congress Party. Indira Gandhi's vision of India focused squarely on the creation of a strong centralized government in which overwhelming power would reside with the prime minister. As the dominance of Indira Gandhi increased, the creativity and resourcefulness of other leadership positions decreased proportionally. Leaders became survivors.

The present elite structure of India, the professional politician stage, is increasingly dominated by a class of professional politicians who attained office by virtue of their close association with the Nehru dynasty and its successors (Guru 1991). India's current generation of professional political elites, according to its critics, lacks the vision, commitment, and energy of either the independence or the nationalist elites. Their primary interest appears to be perpetuating a status quo from which they are the primary beneficiaries.

An elite structure drawing its power from politicians and the higher civil service, moreover, is now finding its authority increasingly challenged by a new wave of business, religious, and regional elites. The latter are demanding that Nehru's vision of a secular, socialist democracy give way to the realities of Indian culture and the pressures of a new world order dominated by the capitalist powers, a process increased by the 1998 victory of the pro-Hindu BJP.

Parties and Politics in India

The Indian political system was long classified as a single-party-dominant democracy. The Congress Party, with the exception of two brief experiments in coalition rule, ruled India for almost fifty years. The 1996 elections, however, saw the Congress receive only 28 percent of the popular vote, the lowest vote total in its illustrious history. Perhaps more damning, the Congress was relegated to third place in the Lok Sabha, its membership in the lower house of the Indian Parliament trailing that of both the BJP and the United Front.

If India's political institutions are experiencing decay or adjustment, it is because the Congress Party is also experiencing decay and adjustment. India is also becoming an increasingly complex society that may have simply outgrown its single-party system. Whatever the case, India may soon become a true multiparty democracy (Chhibber and Petrocik 1990; Singh 1992).

The Congress Party. The early dominance of the Congress Party had four sources: the charisma of Gandhi and Nehru, the prestige that accrued to the Party as the vehicle of the independence movement, the Party's broad base of local and regional organizations, and the Party's flexibility in absorbing a broad range of ideological, regional, and communal groups. Most groups simply found that some influence within the Congress was preferable to no influence outside of the Congress. From time to time, groups would leave the Congress, only to return to the fold at a later point (Weiner 1957).

Those, however, were the early days of independence. The Congress Party remains the dominant political force in Indian politics today, but the foundations of its power are rapidly being eroded. The Dynasty is now gone, and the optimism of the independence era has given way to an awareness of the harsh realities of Indian life.

The problems besetting the Congress (I), moreover, are not limited to the loss of a charismatic leader or to the weakness of its organizational structure. The Party is also developing a split personality. The Congress has traditionally championed Nehru's vision of a secular socialist state that stressed equality for all religions and

Huge posters of historical leaders overshadow a meeting of India's Congress Party, which ruled the country for more than half a century.

social classes. This made its appeal particularly strong among the Muslims, Sikhs, Christians, the scheduled castes, and the other "disadvantaged" groups that constitute some 35 percent of the Indian electorate. Bearing in mind that slightly more than 40 percent of the vote is sufficient to secure a majority in the Lok Sabha, a strong minority vote could almost guarantee dominance of the Congress. The importance of the "secular" vote was also heightened by the tremendous diversity that existed within the broader Hindu community. Minorities tended to vote as a bloc, but Hindus were less likely to do so.

Five decades of secular politics, however, have increasingly galvanized India's Hindu majority into a politically conscious voting bloc, and the pro-Hindu Bharatiya Janata Party (BJP) now represents the fastest-growing political movement in India (Thakur 1998).

In response to this trend, some leaders of the Congress now argue that the Party should adopt a "Hindu" strategy as a means of countering the growing popularity of the BJP. By placing greater emphasis on Hindu values and by downplaying aid to the disadvantaged, they argue, the Congress would simultaneously undercut the BJP and strengthen its own electoral position. India's minorities, particularly the Muslims, are now fearful that the Congress Party will desert them in the hope of capturing a higher percentage of the Hindu vote, although the Congress is now moving to allay these fears (*Times of India,* Jan. 22, 1999, www).

The Congress Party is also having difficulty deciding if it is the party of socialism and equality or the party of capitalist growth. Thus far, the party has vacillated on both issues, conveying the image of a party without a clear vision of India and its future. It is also increasingly perceived as the party of the rich.

Why, despite all of its problems, does the Congress Party continue to be a powerful force in Indian politics? One answer to this question is that the Congress is still the Congress. Old attachments die slowly. Another explanation is that the Congress remains the only "all-India" party in terms of its ability to appeal to a broad range of the Indian electorate. Finally, the Indian opposition

Table 8.2
Seats in the Lok Sabha

Party	Seats in 1999
BJP (and allies)	298
Congress (and allies)	136
Third Front (and allies)	103
Vacant or Pending	6
TOTAL	543

remains factious and fragmented. It is not clear that a coalition of diverse opposition parties is capable of ruling India in a coherent manner over a sustained period of time.

Opponents of the Congress Party. The overwhelming dominance of Nehru and the Congress Party during the early years of Indian independence crippled the emergence of strong opposition parties. Even today, most of India's opposition parties continue to revolve around "key" personalities, many of whom were once members of the Congress. Indian opposition parties also tend to be fluid and ephemeral, emerging to meet the needs of one election, only to fade or reconstitute themselves before the next. Even India's communists have found it difficult to form a single party. The original Communist Party of India split into two factions, one—the CPM—more Marxist than the other. They, in turn, have been joined recently by a Communist Party Marxist-Leninist (CPML) (*Times of India,* Jan. 8, 1999, www).

The Bharatiya Janata Party. The party most likely to challenge the Congress during the coming decade is the pro-Hindu Bharitiya Janata Party (BJP). Prior to the 1991 elections, the BJP ranked second in strength to the Congress, with 86 seats in the Lok Sabha. The BJP doubled its popular vote in the 1991 elections and emerged as the largest party in the Lok Sabha following the 1996 elections. While the BJP's victory was impressive, the Party fell well short of a majority in the Lok Sabha and failed in its bid to form a ruling coalition. It achieved this goal in 1998 and again in 1999. (See Table 8.2.) The appeal of the BJP is quite simple. To paraphrase BJP statements:

> India is a predominantly Hindu state much as the states of North America and Western Europe are predominantly Christian states. Caste Hindus have been unjustly deprived of their rights by government policies designed to accommodate minorities and various disadvantaged groups. The time has now come for the majority to assert its political voice (*NYT,* June 9, 1991, Y10).

In spite of the BJP's recent successes, the realities of India's communal mosaic make it unlikely that the BJP will replace the Congress as the dominant force in Indian politics. Non-Hindus and the disadvantaged classes (untouchables and tribes) constitute almost 40 percent of the electorate. This, when added to the 25 percent of the electorate that belong to the lower castes, makes a total of 65 percent of the population that would likely be disadvantaged by BJP rule.

Recent state elections, moreover, have indicated that the so-called "backward caste," a group composed largely of farm workers and small artisans, has begun to generate its own leadership rather than following the lead of the BJP (*Far Eastern Economic Review: Asia 1995,* 125). The commentary of *The Times*

The Paradox of the Leftists

The leftist opponents of the Congress and the BJP represent something of a paradox. Collectively, they possess the power to defeat the Congress. Their internal divisions, however, make it difficult for them to sustain a Government that can remain in office long enough to implement a coherent program of action. This will continue to be the case for the foreseeable future, inasmuch as the ideological differences that separate them are not easily bridged. Equally problematic are the intense personality conflicts that divide the leaders of India's opposition parties, as well as their lack of strong constituency organizations (*Times of India,* Dec. 27, 1998 and Jan. 8, 1999, www).

---

of India was particularly biting, saying that the BJP had been rejected by all but the backbone of its supporters—the entrenched trading classes and the educated upper caste urban rich. The BJP is now attempting to portray a more populist image, hoping to convince lower-caste Hindus that a BJP victory would not jeopardize their rights. It is also working hard to establish alliances with regional parties in an effort to strengthen its electoral base (Singh 1998).

In addition to cultivating a more populist image, the BJP has also attempted to consolidate its support among lower-caste Hindus by building upon the cult of Ram. Ram, the war god of a Hindu epic, was a pious, yet militant defender of Hindu virtues. He was regal, yet mixed easily with Hindus of all castes. It is this image of a Hindu party united by a militant piety that the BJP is attempting to convey. Implicit in the cult of Ram is the threat to Hindu piety posed by both India's large Muslim minority and the political resurgence of the disadvantaged classes[14] (*Far Eastern Economic Review: Asia 1995,* 125–26).

The Parties of the Left: A Third Front? The decline of the Congress Party over the past several decades was accompanied by the rise of a variety of socialist parties advocating greater equality of opportunity and increased taxation of the rich (Crossette 1992). The unity of the left was fleeting, however, and, more often than not, brief electoral alliances were shattered by personality conflict and internal bickering.

By the advent of the 1996 elections, however, the diverse parties of the left had organized themselves into a third force capable of challenging the Congress and the BJP for the right to rule. As described by *India Weekly* shortly after the election:

> The NF-LF (National Front-Left Front) previously known as the Third Front—and now calling itself the United Front—has gathered up a dozen other small and regional parties, making a total of 13. This jelly-like formation has no common point or programme other than pulling down the new BJP (Bharatiya Janata Party) government. The various elements of the combine were enemies before the election, but were forced to sink their differences for the "down with the BJP" mission. If in point of fact that combine does come to power after May 31, the various elements will promptly start pulling one another down for the sake of the loot which is the reason why they seek office. This should be all the easier for them, since the NF-LF have been screaming about the bad effects of the economic reforms introduced by the Congress (I) during the last five years. Sections of the Congress (I) involved in these reforms now face the prospect of embracing the NF-LF as political allies (*India Weekly,* May 25, 1996, 1).

As a practical matter, *India's diverse parties tend to coalesce into three blocs or alliances: a center alliance dominated by the Congress Party, a rightist alliance*

---

[14]The cult of Ram turned violent in 1990 when supporters of the BJP laid siege to a small Islamic mosque in Ayodhya, the presumed birthplace of Ram. After having destroyed the mosque, they were driven off by the police. Both sides were thus offended.

dominated by the BJP, and a leftist alliance increasingly referred to as the United Front (Kumar 1991). The leftist bloc advocates socialism and higher job quotas for minorities and the disadvantaged classes, while the rightist alliance stresses greater capitalism and the transformation of India into a Hindu state. The Congress and its allies are desperately seeking middle ground between these two irreconcilable extremes. The task is a daunting one.

India's party system, moreover, has been made all the more complex by the emergence of increasingly strong regional parties. Regional parties gained more than 15 percent of the national vote in 1989 and some 12 percent of the national vote in 1991. This trend continued in 1996, with the United Front drawing much of its support from regional parties (*India Today,* June 15, 1996, 25). The strongest of the regional parties are those associated with regional and religious movements demanding greater autonomy from New Delhi (India's capital).

Groups and Politics in India

India possesses a more complex group structure than any other country on earth. All of India's groups, moreover, are politically relevant. In order to understand this point, it is necessary to recall that the traditional social order of India was based upon a system of castes and sub-castes, each of which possessed specific rights and obligations depending upon its hierarchical position within the Hindu religion.

The Muslim invasion added complexity to India's communal mosaic by introducing a religion that stressed social equality and the worship of a single, all-powerful God. Lesser challenges to Hindu dominance would also be posed by India's smaller Christian and Buddhist communities. In a country as populous as India, however, few groups are truly small.

Both caste and religious communities, in turn, are fragmented by linguistic differences. *Indians speak some 1,652 diverse languages, of which Hindi is the most prominent* (Krishna 1992). Large segments of the country, however, do not speak Hindi and resent persistent efforts to make Hindi the national language. The issue is far more than a matter of pride, for imposing Hindi as the national language would give Hindi speakers a political and economic advantage over Indian citizens who do not speak Hindi.

The British occupation further fragmented Indian society by pitting Western values against traditional Hindu and Muslim values. It thus became common to speak of "forward-looking" groups and "backward-looking" groups (Frankel 1988). *Foremost of the forward-looking groups were the new elites created by the British, elites that would eventually form the Congress Party. The backward-looking groups, by definition, were any groups that opposed the Westernization of the subcontinent.*

The British occupation also witnessed the emergence of Western-style interest groups ranging from business associations and labor unions to student groups and human rights organizations. Conflict between economic classes, once clouded by religious dogma, was also brought into sharper focus by the colonial experience (Shah 1988; Vanaik 1990).

As things stand today, the list of politically relevant pressure groups includes castes, jati, social classes, religions, tribes, linguistic groups, business and labor organizations, peasant movements, student groups, women, regional movements, and institutional interests such as the bureaucracy and the military (Shah 1990).

Business and Labor. The Indian Chamber of Commerce (FICCI), the main peak organization of Indian business, was founded in 1927, a full two decades before the granting of Indian independence in 1947. The FICCI is well financed and uses both formal and informal procedures to lobby for its policies (Misquitta 1991). At the formal level, the FICCI and its component organizations are represented on an endless array of official advisory boards and commissions designed to reconcile differences between the public and private sectors of the Indian economy. The councils are also designed to build harmony between business and labor. At the informal level, the FICCI makes its point by lavish campaign contributions (Misquitta 1991).

As is true of most Indian organizations, the effectiveness of the FICCI has been undermined by internal conflict. In part, this conflict is the result of competition between India's large industrial families. It is also the result of growing dissension between exporters who favor free trade and local industrialists demanding continued protection from foreign competition. Tensions have also emerged between the giants of India's industry and their smaller competitors, a problem that led to the creation of rival business organizations such as the Indian Merchant Chamber (Misquitta 1991). Whatever its internal strains, the business community is rapidly becoming a dominant force in Indian politics. The continued liberation of the Indian economy can only increase this trend.

Labor unions, like business organizations, are deeply rooted in the colonial era. Indeed, the eve of independence would find India with no less than 457 labor unions of one form or another (Misquitta 1991). The Indian labor movement has sought to press its demands through a combination of strikes and collective bargaining, but neither strategy has enjoyed much success. It is very difficult to bargain effectively or to conduct a sustained strike in an environment of severe unemployment. Those strikes that do occur are usually crushed by the Government. Finally, the effectiveness of the Indian labor movement has been undermined by its lack of unity. Rather than confronting business and government as a unified front, Indian labor has allowed itself to be fragmented into a variety of conflicting regional and ideological units (Misquitta 1991; *Times of India,* Feb. 2, 2000, www). Be this as it may, strikes continue, with a 1998 "general strike" producing mixed results. While the financial sector and some mines were temporarily paralyzed, most other businesses remained open (*Times of India,* Dec. 12, 1998, www). Effects on India's massive rail network were also limited. Despite its limited success, the pace of labor unrest will invariably increase as India moves toward privatization and the scaling back of its huge and largely unprofitable state-owned industries. Indeed, strikes may become increasingly violent as India's workers face increased unemployment and the loss of their social safety net.

Students. More than 4 million strong, India's students are at the forefront of most political demonstrations. Not all students are politically active, but those who are active are very active. Student protests have brought down state governments on several occasions and have often forced the federal (union) government to change course on politically sensitive issues. India's colleges and universities are routinely closed down as a result of student activism (Hardgrave and Kochanek 1993). Needless to say, politicians attempt to exploit the students to suit their own purpose. As a recent affair at Lucknow University is described by the *Times of India:*

> The BJP-led government...is not the first or only government to have extended such generous patronage to student leaders. Samajwadi Party too had earlier been guilty of extending similar favours to the chosen few. Increasing interference by successive

governments, full-time politicians and contractors using the union to fuel their political ambitions, the growing indifference among students to the affairs of the union and alienation of the main body of students are some of the ills afflicting the students' body, calling for a review of the union and its election. In the last election, the eventual winner of the post of union president is believed to have spent a cool two lakhs of Rupees on his campaign, most of which or even more would have been collected from politicians, engineers, contractors and through plain extortion. The Indian Industries Association in fact was forced in April this year to write a letter to the Vice Chancellor, suggesting that immediate steps be taken to modify the ground rules and restrict the role of political parties, money and muscle power (*Times of India,* Dec. 20, 1998).

Student protests are motivated both by the idealism of youth and by frustration with a political system that will doom many students to either unemployment or a low-paying government job. Some estimates suggest that as many as 35 percent of Indian students now face the prospect of prolonged unemployment (*CSM,* Dec. 22, 1992, 6).

The effectiveness of student protests is a function of several factors. Student protests are loud and noisy and have also become increasingly violent. Perhaps more importantly, student protests serve as the catalyst for broader mass protests, the growing volatility of which is an unwelcome prospect for any Government, state or national. Despite their effectiveness in stimulating protests, students are too fragmented by class, caste, religious, or other differences to stay the course (*CSM,* Dec. 22, 1992, 6). They also manifest a profound lack of discipline, personality often being more important than ideology.

Women. Women's groups have become increasingly active in Indian politics, and not without cause. In 1992, almost 5,000 women were killed by their husbands for not providing adequate dowries (*NYT,* Dec. 23, 1993, A5). *The Times of India* blames parents as well as husbands:

> Studies now confirm that the seeds of violence against the daughter are sown in her parental home right at birth. This merely worsens after her marriage...In most dowry death cases, the parents have pressured the daughter to return to her marital home, often knowing that she may even be murdered (*Times of India,* Jan. 27, 1999, www).

Wife-beating is routine. For many females, suicide is the only escape from an unhappy marriage (Calman 1992; *Times of India,* Jan. 27, 1999, www). Even in happy families, women are totally subservient to men. Women in the more traditional areas of northern India continue to be secluded, wearing a veil when in the presence of unrelated males (Basu, Alaka, 1992). The condition of Indian women is described by Leslie Calman:

> The battering and harassment that culminates in thousands of cases in murder result from women's subordination in the family and in society, a subordination that state structures uphold....
>
> Despite these poor stacked odds, it is almost unthinkable for an Indian woman of any community not to marry. As a *Hindustan Times* editorial lamented, one thing that all the religious communities in India can agree on is that marriage for a woman is a sine qua non. "A woman living alone is viewed with hostility and contempt even when she is supporting herself." Divorce is also gravely frowned upon. Two thousand years ago the Hindu law-giver Manu wrote that "A woman must never be independent." This dictum is largely believed today; worse, it is acted upon by those in authority (Calman 1992, 124).

Indian women, then, are not merely fighting political injustice. They are fighting cultural norms that severely undervalue the role of women. Women's organizations tend to be divided between groups attempting to fight political injustice and groups that provide support for battered and abused wives. Those groups attempting to fight political injustice face a particularly difficult task, for India's laws already stress the equality of all citizens, male and female. This was part of Nehru's vision of a modern secular India. Those laws, unfortunately, are rarely enforced with vigor, as neither the government nor the police are inclined to alter practices that are broadly accepted by society. In the final analysis, political oppression and cultural oppression are difficult to separate.

The effectiveness of the women's movement in India is further undermined by the same caste, class, regional, and political differences that fragment most pressure groups in India. Also problematic is the passivity of many Indian women. A recent survey of women in two diverse areas of India found that "an astonishingly high proportion (more than 95 percent) of women from both regional groups maintained that they were generally happy and contented with life" (Basu, Amrita, 1992, 231). As the author of the survey poignantly concluded: "Either ignorance really is bliss or we need to use much more culture-specific notions of individual welfare and aims…" (Basu, Amrita, 1992, 231).

While much of the writing on Indian women focuses on violence and political rights, it is important to stress that those issues will be difficult to address without a far greater emphasis on the broader feminist problems of inferior education, health care, and economic opportunity. The position of educated upperclass women, it should be noted, is far superior to that of poor women, particularly women living in rural areas. In gender relations, as in most everything else, India is becoming a dual society: a society of abundance and increasing opportunities for the rich, and a society of scarcity and increasing despair for the poor.

The Disaffected: Secessionists and Peasants. Groups that have found the Indian Government unresponsive to their demands have turned to violence. Sikh extremists in the Punjab are in open rebellion, as are the Muslims in Kashmir and the Tamils in the south of India. Four Indian provinces are either now or have recently been under direct military control.

The rural poor, lacking a responsive ear in Delhi and the state capitals, have also turned to violence (Karna 1989). As described by Ghanshyam Shah:

> The rural poor are not stupid. They protest and revolt against injustice. A large number of their protests are spontaneous and sporadic and take forms ranging from outcry to so-called 'social banditry,' from strikes to armed struggle. More often than not, these collective actions are impulsive and lack organizational planning. Unable to sustain themselves against local powers acting in collusion with political bosses and government administrations with access to resources and police power, they peter out in a few days. Local bosses bribe, split, co-opt, mesmerize and terrorize the poor (Shah 1990, 299).

Increasingly, however, peasant rebellions are taking on a more organized character (Mishra 1980). Local peasant parties have emerged in several areas of rural India, and secessionist groups are now establishing peasant associations in an effort to broaden their popular base (Sahasrabudhey 1986). The growing militancy of India's peasants can be traced to the "green revolution" of the 1960s (Misquitta 1991). Landed farmers used government support and advanced agricultural technology imported from abroad to make India self-sufficient in the production of food. Those farmers who prospered used their newfound wealth to purchase the lands of less successful peasants, turning the latter into a rural proletariat forced to work for little more than a subsistence wage (Mittal 1986).

Five Axes of Political Conflicts in India

In spite of the existence of *multiple memberships* (**cross-cutting cleavages**), political conflict has increasingly polarized the Indian electorate along five axes: rich/poor, centralization/decentralization, socialist/capitalist, Western/traditional, and Hindu/minority.

- *The rich/poor axis is manifest in the growing gulf between India's rich and poor.* Indeed, it has become commonplace to speak of two Indias: the dynamic and prosperous India of the middle classes and the destitute India of slum dwellers and landless peasants (Bonner 1990). As in most countries, it is the poor who are the least successful in making their voices heard.

- *The centralization/decentralization axis pits the bureaucracy, the Government, and most other elements of the national political establishment against a bewildering array of religious, regional, and linguistic groups demanding greater autonomy from Delhi rule.* Only the most extreme groups advocate outright secession, but all demand a shift of power from the center to the periphery.

- *The socialist/capitalist axis places the bureaucracy, labor unions, and welfare organizations in conflict with business interests.* India's business leaders, although divided on the issue, increasingly view economic liberalization (capitalism) as the path to prosperity and development. Bureaucrats, labor groups, and welfare recipients, by contrast, fear that greater capitalism will lead to unemployment and the dismantling of India's social welfare network.

- Political conflict in India also continues to revolve around a *Western/traditional axis. The Indian Constitution, as discussed earlier, imposed a British-style political system on a society with radically different cultural traditions* (Embree 1990). The conflict between those competing traditions continues today, finding its most visible expression in religious fundamentalism of several varieties, Sikh and Muslim fundamentalism as well as Hindu fundamentalism (Singh 1998).

- Finally, political conflict in India continues to be shaped by a *Hindu/minority axis. The divide between the Hindus and Muslims, always problematic, has been sharpened by a growing Hindu assertiveness.* India, in the view of Hindus, is a predominantly Hindu society and should reflect Hindu values. This view is not limited to Hindu fundamentalists but has been fueled by broadbased resentment over the sweeping affirmative action programs designed to improve the socio-economic status of India's disadvantaged groups. All parties, however, are playing the religious card.

Their recent militancy notwithstanding, the peasants remain divided by class, caste, religion, language, and region. The poorer peasants also tend to be illiterate, making them easy prey for unscrupulous land barons who employ private armies to keep them in line.

Are Group Loyalties Becoming Stronger or Weaker? Most Indians are members of an organized religion, a status group within that religion, a linguistic group, a professional group, a social class, and a region. With so many attachments pulling in so many different directions, it is difficult for any single group to claim the total allegiance of most of India's citizens. Middle-class bureaucrats spar with middle-class businessmen over the pace of economic reform. Poor Hindus are torn between religious obligations that stress the rewards of the hereafter and the opportunity to achieve a better life in the present (Gould 1990). Caste and religious attachments, accordingly, are no longer adequate to assure political dominance.

Citizens and Politics in India

One of the major criticisms of the elitist perspective of politics is that it assumes an almost mindless pliability among the masses. This model may have been valid during the era of independence when India was overwhelmingly rural and illiterate, but it is less applicable today. India possesses an educated, highly politicized, and prosperous middle class that now constitutes as much as 20 percent of the Indian population (Dubey 1992, 146). Indeed, it is the urban middle classes

Calcutta police and soldiers attempt to keep order as voters line up to cast their ballots. The Indian electorate has become increasingly politicized in recent years as a result of educational attainment, urbanization, and frustration with the country's social and economic problems.

that now form the bulwark of Western democracy in India (Dubey 1992). India's lower classes, moreover, are also becoming politicized, placing ever-increasing demands for social justice on a political system that, despite its socialist rhetoric, has done little to meet their needs.

The growing politicization of the Indian population is partially attributable to increased education and urbanization. It is also a function of an Indian press that is as "vivid" as it is intense. Except for a few premier papers, the line between fact and conjecture in India's more than 4,000 newspapers is often difficult to distinguish. Politicization, however, has also been increased by mass frustration over corruption, violence, and the failure of India's leaders to come to grips with the country's pressing social and economic problems. A majority of India's population is "hurting," and they want solutions to their problems.

Election studies provide two diverse views of Indian public opinion. The first view is provided by the platforms and campaign rhetoric of India's political parties, and the second by the voting patterns of the Indian electorate.

A comparison of party platforms suggests that the five issues of primary concern to the Indian public are violence, rising prices, poverty, corruption, and economic growth (Chaube 1992). Similar concerns are reflected in public opinion polls. Each of the five issues has reached crisis proportions in India, and each touches the lives of most Indian citizens.

While all of India's political parties promise an end to violence, inflation, poverty, and corruption, recent campaign rhetoric also reveals the growing polarization of the Indian public. Hindu fundamentalism and increased capitalism have become the central themes of the political right, while the political left continues to advocate socialism and ever-increasing job quotas for the disadvantaged classes. The left also continues to stress the need for land reform and economic development in the rural areas.

The expression of public opinion, however, encompasses far more than elections and public opinion polls. Public opinion is also reflected in the escalating cycle of communal violence and crime that continues to erode the fabric of Indian society. The use of violence as a form of political expression is also increasing (Kohli 1990). Violence underscored the 1991 electoral campaign, rendering voting problematic in several areas.

> The elections left a trail of blood. Former Prime Minister Rajiv Gandhi assassinated on the last leg of a comeback campaign. Five Lok Sabha candidates and 21 assembly candidates killed. Another 350 lost their lives in election-related violence. Hundreds of others were injured. Muscle power ruled in a number of constituencies. Booths were captured, voters terrorized and either forced to vote for a particular candidate or not allowed to vote at all, as men with criminal records, dacoits and mafia dons jumped into the poll fray. Money, muscle and machine-guns became the deciding factor in quite a few areas, pushing issues and personalities to the background (Kumar 1991, 23).

Strict security measures have made recent elections more peaceful, with relatively few election-related deaths. Be this as it may, new votes had to be reordered in 599 of India's 350,000 polling districts during the 1998 elections as a result of fraud (*IHT*, Feb. 18, 1998). The picture was much the same during the 1999 elections.

For all of their problems, Indians scored remarkably high on the "Happiness Barometer," a survey of twenty-two countries. The US led the list with 46 percent of American citizens saying they were "very happy" with India's 37 percent being not far behind and well ahead of the French and the British (*Times of India*, Apr. 14, 2000, www).

The Context of Indian Politics: Culture, Economics, and International Interdependence

India has remained a democracy throughout its five decades of independence. As we have seen in the preceding discussion, this impressive record has been achieved inthe face of overwhelming odds. India's democracy, however, is showing signs of strain, and an increasing number of observers now speak of a crisis of governability (Kohli 1990).

Why has India become so difficult to govern? Some explanations are cultural in nature, suggesting that many Indians have yet to embrace Nehru's vision of a secular, democratic state. Other explanations are economic, suggesting that the roots of India's political crisis lie in its inability to meet the basic needs of its people. Still other explanations focus on the existence of an international system that places India at a disadvantage in its dealings with the First World. Each offers important insights into India's crisis of governability.

The Culture of Indian Politics

Cultural analyses of India's crisis of governability tend to focus on the concept of a **civic culture** (Almond and Verba 1963). The concept of a civic culture suggests that the citizens of a democratic state must do more than merely follow their leaders. They must *be committed to democratic values, understand how their political institutions work, and believe in their ability to influence those* *institutions.* Barring this, it will be impossible for citizens of a state to assure the accountability of their leaders. A civic culture also implies that *loyalties to the state are stronger than loyalties to ethnic, religious, and other parochial groups and that the good of the state will take precedence over the good of its parts.* A state in which loyalties to parochial groups are stronger than loyalties to the state is doomed to a nightmare of communal conflict. This at least has been the message of Bosnia, Lebanon, Northern Ireland, the states of the former Soviet Union, and much of Africa.

India did not possess a civic culture at the time of its independence. Its largely rural and illiterate population possessed little understanding of modern democratic practice, and most individuals lived and worked within the confines of their jati or related groups. Not only was their personal identity a product of the group, but it was an identity that they could not escape. They were what their group was. Under such circumstances, it was only to be expected that group attachments would surpass loyalties to the state or to the concept of a united India. Tolerance of other groups was minimal, at best.

The challenge of Nehru and the Congress Party, then, was to create a civic culture in India by making the lofty ideals of the Indian Constitution part of India's political culture. Their successes were many. Indians vote, participate in political campaigns, and discuss politics with a ferocity seldom found in the democratic states of the First World. They are also intensely conscious of being Indian and are justifiably proud of their democratic traditions.

Political Economy and Politics in India

Political economists find India's crisis of governability to be essentially an economic crisis (Jannuzi 1989). It is unrealistic, in their view, to expect people to support a political system that cannot meet their basic needs (Roy and James 1992). The growing conflict between communal groups that has become endemic to Indian politics, from the political economic perspective, is a struggle for the control of scarce resources (Madan 1989). The more scarce the resources, the greater the violence. Electoral conflict is also viewed as being largely economic in nature, with the more prosperous Hindus voting for the BJP and the minorities and the disadvantaged groups voting for either the Congress or the parties of the left. Indians, like most other people, tend to be rational economic actors.

While political economists agree that India's crisis of governability is economic in origin, they disagree violently on the cure. Neoclassical economists urge a total liberalization of the Indian economy. They would clip the wings of the India's powerful bureaucrats (often referred to as the "License Raj") and allow Indian businesses to operate free of government regulation. The massive Indian bureaucracy would be radically downsized, and state subsidies on food and other necessities would be curtailed. Curtailed, too, would be social legislation that precludes employers from firing employees for poor performance (Tomlinson 1992).

In support of their argument, **neoclassical economists** point to the substantial growth in the Indian economy that has accompanied the country's modest shift to capitalism in recent years. With a truly capitalist economy, they argue, India would more than keep pace with the economic miracles of South Korea and Taiwan. To be sure, economic disparities between advantaged and disadvantaged groups would increase in the short run. Inefficient government enterprises would have to be trimmed of excess workers, and the weaker government firms would probably have to be closed. The gap between rich and poor would also increase as capitalists reaped the benefits of their investments. Capitalists, however, create jobs. In the long run, all groups would be better off than they are today.

Leftist economists reject the capitalist argument, pointing to the inequalities that accompany economic liberalization. More than ever, from their perspective, India would be transformed into a dual society in which a modern, technologically advanced India would coexist with an India of backwardness and poverty. Leftist political economists also point with pride to the tremendous economic progress that India has made in recent decades, arguing that it is possible for India to develop economically while simultaneously caring for the health and welfare of its population. While some tightening up of bureaucratic laxity may be in order, they say, socialism has not been a failure (Vanaik 1990).

A third group of political economists, generally referred to as "**growth with equity**" **economists**, seeks a balance between the goals of rapid economic growth and social welfare. (Growth with equity is one of several versions of state capitalism.) Free-market capitalism would be encouraged, but the state would continue to assure that all major elements of society were cared for (Todaro 1989). As expressed by former Prime Minister Rao, "Governments do not have the right to go overboard and plunge large amounts of people into mass misery" (*NYT,* Jan. 15, 1995, 4).

India's politicians are moving toward the "growth with equity" position more out of necessity than conviction (Inoue 1992). They understand that increased capitalism is necessary to stimulate a faster pace of economic growth, but they fear that a rapid transition to capitalism would strain the fabric of Indian politics beyond the breaking point. In typical Indian fashion, they have sought a midpoint between the two extremes. The Government, for example, has reduced the bureaucratic red tape that has traditionally choked capitalist activity in India. It has also eased the barriers to foreign investment in India. By the same token, however, the Government still prevents private-sector firms from laying off their excess employees. It also maintains a broad range of public-sector industries, most of which are noncompetitive on the world market and survive by the grace of protective tariffs and government subsidies (*Economist,* "A Survey of India," Jan. 21, 1995).

This blend of reform and protectionism has been sufficient to stimulate an upswing in the Indian economy, but it has not produced the economic miracle that has occurred in South Korea, Taiwan, Malaysia, and India's other neighbors that have taken the fast track to capitalism. Ironically, even China, a presumably communist state, seems to be embracing capitalism with greater zeal than India.

The difference between India and her neighbors, of course, is democracy. South Korea, Taiwan, and the other rapidly industrializing states of Asia carried out their transitions to capitalism under the auspices of authoritarian or quasi-authoritarian regimes. They did not have to worry about being voted out of office by an electorate fearing unemployment or distraught by the removal of subsidies on food, rent, and other necessities. Once capitalism was in place, these states moved, however grudgingly, in the direction of greater democracy. India, by contrast, is a democracy, and the proponents of economic reform must face the wrath of voters worried by an environment of growing economic insecurity.

In a classic political-economic trade-off, then, India's leaders must balance the need for economic growth against the need to get elected. India's transition to capitalism, accordingly, has been slow and erratic, but such is the price of democracy. Many Indians feel that it is a price worth paying.

International Interdependence and the Politics of India

The above discussion has focused on the domestic underpinnings of India's political crisis. Many Indians believe that their political and economic woes also have much to do with an unfavorable international environment. This point of view, generally referred to as dependency theory, argues that the major economic powers of the First World have little interest in stimulating economic development in India or in any other state of the Third World.

While the merits of dependency theory continue to be debated, it is difficult to dispute the dominance of rich states in establishing the terms of trade with their less-developed counterparts. In what has come to be known as the North-South Dialogue,[15] the poorer states of the world, most of which lie in the Southern Hemisphere, are demanding that the wealthy states of the Northern Hemisphere commit themselves to the economic and social development of the Third World. The states of the North have shown some willingness to do so, but only at a price.

In the case of India, the price of that help is the abandonment of India's predominantly socialist economic system and the opening of the Indian economy to multinational corporations. This may be a difficult price for India's leaders to pay, for many Indian firms may find it difficult to compete with the more sophisticated products of the West. The huge government factories, in particular, may be forced to lay off a large percentage of their work force if they are to become competitive on a global scale. While this may make economic sense, it will be a tough pill to swallow for the politicians faced with mounting unemployment and political instability. Pressure for economic reform is made all the more pressing by the economic growth of Taiwan and South Korea, both of which have been major recipients of Western aid and both of which have instituted state capitalist economic systems on the Japanese model.

India's domestic policies are profoundly influenced by external pressures. India, however, is also a major international actor in its own right. Three points, in this regard, are of major importance.

■ *First, India is a leader in Third World efforts to forge a more equitable distribution of wealth between the predominantly rich states of the North and the predominantly poor states of the South.* Although such efforts have yet to bear fruit, the states of the North may soon realize that the political and economic instability of the Third World threatens their own peace and prosperity.

■ *Second, and of far greater practical importance, India is a member of the nuclear club.* India's democratic leaders remain dedicated to the nonproliferation of nuclear weapons and the peaceful uses of nuclear energy, but neither India nor Pakistan have signed the United Nations Nuclear Non-Proliferation Treaty. Indeed, 1998 nuclear tests by India and Pakistan have raised very real fears of a nuclear arms race in the region.

■ *Third, a revived Indian economy could well transform India into one of the dominant economic powers in the world.* Along with China, a prosperous India has the potential to be an economic superpower of the future.

---

[15]See Chapter 1.

Challenges of the Present and Prospects for the Future

In Chapter 1 we outlined six standards of good government that find wide acceptance among the nations of the international community: democracy, stability, human rights, quality of life, economic growth, and environmental concern. Nehru's vision of a modern India personified these six standards. India was to be a stable democracy that guaranteed the human rights of all its diverse citizens. It was also to be a state that provided its citizens with an improving quality of life. Although India was a poor state, all Indians would have an equal opportunity to share in its development. Economic growth required no less. Although Nehru spoke little of environmental concern, the logic of his philosophy projected an India that would live in harmony with its physical universe.

To what extent, then, has India lived up to Nehru's vision of a stable democracy committed to human rights, an equitable quality of life, economic growth, and environmental harmony?

Democracy and Stability

There can be no ambiguity about India's status as a democracy. Free and fair elections are held at regularly scheduled intervals, and the winners of those elections take office and rule. Political parties and pressure groups abound, and the Indian press is free and vigorous. India's political elites also remain overwhelmingly committed to democracy. Unlike the situation in neighboring states, democracy is not being forced upon a reluctant leadership by a restive population.

While meeting all of the established criteria of a democratic state, India's practice of democracy has often differed from that of the West. Until very recently, India was a one-party democracy in which several parties contested for power but only the Congress Party ruled (Chhibber and Kollman 1998). Indian democracy is also a rough-and-tumble democracy in which the fine points of electoral decorum are not always observed (Austin 1995). Voting is conducted on different days in different regions in order to assure the maximum deployment of security forces. Four Indian states remain under virtual military rule.

India is now evolving into a multiparty democracy, a process which, while making India appear more democratic to Western observers, risks the destabilization of the Indian political system. Also undermining India's democracy is the decay of its political institutions. India's citizens once had faith in the fairness of their political institutions, but this faith has since been eroded. As discussed by Atul Kohli:

> India is still, of course, a functioning democracy, but increasingly it is not well governed. The evidence of eroding political order is everywhere. Personal rule has replaced party rule at all levels—national, state, and district. Below the rulers, the entrenched civil and police services have been politicized. Various social groups have pressed new and ever more diverse political demands in demonstrations that often have led to violence. The omnipresent but feeble state, in turn, has vacillated; its responses have varied over a wide range: indifference, sporadic concessions, and repression (Kohli 1990, 5).

Ramakrishna Hegde echoes these sentiments:

> The present system, especially during the past 20 years, has moved the country close to disintegration. The parliamentary system gives unlimited scope for horse-trading, floor-crossing and corruption. It is also responsible for the emergence of casteist (sic) and regional forces. It has led to political instability because of frequent elections (Hegde 1998).

In the final analysis, *the success of India's democracy will depend upon the ability of its leaders to stem the violence, economic stagnation, and institutional decay that have become endemic to Indian politics* (Austin 1995). In attempting to achieve this goal, India's democratic leaders have sought a compromise that will reconcile the widely divergent positions of the left and the right. To date, these efforts have produced timid policies that border on immobilization. In the meantime, India's social and economic problems continue to escalate. Because of these problems, there have been proposals to transform India into a presidential rather than a parliamentary system (*Times of India,* Feb. 2, 2000, www).

Human Rights

The Indian Constitution enumerates an impressive list of civil rights including the rights of free speech, religious expression, and assembly. All Indian citizens are equal before the law, regardless of race, creed, color, language, or gender. The Constitution addresses past grievances by reserving jobs, educational opportunities, and seats in Parliament for members of India's scheduled classes and tribes. In so doing, the Indian Constitution addresses group rights as well as individual rights. Ironically, the guarantee of group rights often contradicts the guarantee of individual rights. The Constitution, for example, gives preference to religious law in areas such as marriage, divorce, and inheritance. Muslim women are governed by more restrictive personal statutes than their Hindu counterparts, a clear violation of their individual rights as Indian citizens.

The situation of the disadvantaged groups is also problematic. The enforcement of group rights has fared much better than the enforcement of individual rights. Disadvantaged groups do receive enhanced educational and employment opportunities, but the picture is far from perfect. Most members of the disadvantaged groups find employment at the lowest levels of the bureaucracy, a fact that is attributable to a high rate of illiteracy among these groups (Madan 1989). Progress, however, is being made.

Rural workers also enjoy few rights in Indian society, with many in the more traditional states such as Bihar living in conditions of near-servitude. As local governments are controlled by the landowners, little has been done to alter that situation. The courts have sided with the landowners, citing the constitutional right of private property.

Growing religious and ethnic violence have placed a particular strain on India's attempts to guard the civil rights of minorities, with violence against Christians becoming pronounced in recent years (*Times of India,* Dec. 16, 1998; Apr. 20, 2000, www). Illegal searches and seizures are becoming commonplace, and in extreme cases, soldiers have fired upon civilian crowds. Such atrocities have been particularly frequent in government efforts to control the Sikhs in the Punjab and Islamic extremists in Kashmir. Indeed, the Terrorist and Disruptive Activities Act now enables the army and police to carry out mass arrests free of normal constitutional constraints. In the mid-1990s, for example, some 70,000 people were being held in preventive detention (*NYT,* Jan. 22, 1995, 6). The Indian government acknowledges these unfortunate occurrences but generally views them as an exception to an otherwise strong record on human rights.

Economic Growth and Quality of Life

Nehru viewed economic growth and the provision of an equitable quality of life as part of the same package. Both were to be achieved by a socialist economic system in which India's resources, however meager, would be allocated in a rational and just manner. As India developed, so would the prosperity of all of its citizens.

As noted in earlier discussion, five decades of socialism have produced dramatic improvements in the quality of Indian life. India is now the seventeenth largest economy in the world and manufactures everything from cars and buses to nuclear weapons. Its green revolution has also assured self-sufficiency in grains for a country that long suffered from famine. The Indian middle and upper classes, moreover, are both highly skilled and prosperous.

The quality of life enjoyed by the middle and upper classes, unfortunately, is not shared by India's poor, a group that includes some 55 percent of the Indian population, depending on how one defines poverty (United Nations, Human Development Report, 1999). By and large, the poor are illiterate, poorly fed, have little access to medical attention, and live in conditions of squalor (Dhadve 1989; Deolalikar 1992). While all of India's poor live in penury, the rural poor are truly the wretched of the earth. The more India seems to develop, moreover, the greater the gap between the two Indias seems to become (Hardgrave and Kochanek 1993). Despite all of its accomplishments, the Indian economy now lags far behind that of its Asian neighbors, including the People's Republic of China.

The Environment

India's environmental record mirrors the duality of its record in regard to quality of life and human rights. Its environmental legislation is exemplary, but the enforcement of that legislation often leaves much to be desired (Khator 1991). India's environmental crisis received worldwide attention in 1984 when an explosion at the Union Carbide plant in Bhopal resulted in some 4,000 pollution-related deaths (*NYT,* Mar. 25, 1993, A7). Poor adherence to environmental regulations was blamed for the disaster. The potential for similar catastrophes exists throughout India. Indian cities are also choked with pollution, with New Delhi believed to be the fourth most polluted city in the world (*Hindustan Times,* Dec. 17, 1998, www).

In part, India's environmental crisis finds its origins in the same tension between economic development and environmental concern that faces most countries of the Third World. Rapid economic growth, although it is destructive to the environment, provides much-needed jobs. It also provides the monies that the state requires to provide its citizens with an acceptable quality of life. Enforcement of environmental legislation slows economic growth. The cruel choice between rapid development and environmental concern was summarized very concisely by Indira Gandhi:

> The environmental problems of developing countries are not the side effects of excessive industrialization but reflect the inadequacy of development. The rich countries may look upon development as the cause of environmental destruction, but to us it is one of the primary means of improving the environment for living, or providing food, water, sanitation and shelter; of making the deserts green and the mountains habitable.... On one hand the rich look askance at our continuing poverty—on the other, they warn us against their own methods. We do not wish to impoverish the environment any further and yet we cannot for a moment forget the grim poverty of large numbers of people. Are not poverty and need the greatest polluters? (Gandhi 1972; Khator 1991, 22–23).

As with so much else in India, poor environmental enforcement is also a function of bureaucratic laxity. As Renu Khator (1991) has noted, the environmental bureaucracy is too politicized to function effectively.

The phenomenal growth of India's population makes the choice between economic growth and protecting the environment all the more difficult. An India of 360 million in 1947 has become an India of one billion today. A vigorous birth control program has slowed the rate of population growth to 1.8 percent per annum, but that figure translates into 16 million new citizens each year. Most will be born into poor and illiterate families (Khator 1991, 10–11).

Prospects for the Future

As India has moved grudgingly in the direction of greater capitalism, Western economists have begun to speak of an awakening Indian tiger whose economic muscle will rival that of its Asian neighbors. As the Indian economy grows, in their view, all Indians will benefit. The rich will get richer, but the increased wealth will "trickle down" to even the lowest rungs of Indian society (*Economist,* "A Survey of India," 1995).

Such optimism rings hollow to those familiar with the depths of India's political and social problems. Increased capitalism has produced increased wealth, but there is little evidence of that wealth trickling down to India's poor. In fact, India's social problems have grown worse rather than better. If the violence and political instability caused by India's social problems continue to increase, both Indian democracy and the integrity of the Indian state could be called into question.

Pessimism, however, is nothing new in India. Prophecies of despair have accompanied each stage of India's political evolution, yet Indian democracy has continued to survive despite formidable odds. More than likely, this strength and resilience will continue to sustain India in the years to come.

References

Almond, Gabriel, and Sidney Verba. 1963. *The Civic Culture.* Princeton, NJ: Princeton University Press.

Anderson, Walter. 1992. "Lowering the Level of Tension." In *India Briefing, 1992* (pp. 13–46), ed. Leonard A. Gordon and Philip Oldenburg. Boulder, CO: Westview Press.

Austin, Dennis. 1995. *Democracy and Violence in India and Sri Lanka.* New York: Council on Foreign Relations Press.

Basu, Alaka Malwade. 1992. *Culture, the Status of Women, and Demographic Behaviour: Illustrated with the Case of India.* Oxford: Clarendon Press.

Basu, Amrita. 1992. *Two Faces of Protest: Contrasting Modes of Women's Activism in India.* Berkeley, CA: University of California Press.

Benderly, Beryl Lieff. 1986. "Religious Life." In *India: A Country Study* (pp. 131–76), ed. Richard F. Nyrop. Washington, DC: U.S. Government Printing Office.

Bonner, Arthur. 1990. *Averting the Apocalypse: Social Movements in India Today.* Durham, NC: Duke University Press.

Braibanti, Ralph, ed. 1966. *Asian Bureaucratic Systems Emergent from The British Imperial Tradition.* Durham, NC: Duke University Press.

Brass, Paul R. 1992. "Language, Religion and Politics." In *Foundations of India's Political Economy* (pp. 60–92), ed. Subroto Roy and William E. James. New Delhi: Sage.

Calman, Leslie J. 1992. *Toward Empowerment: Women and Movement Politics in India.* Boulder, CO: Westview Press.

Chaube, S. K. 1992. "The Campaign and Issues." In *Lok Sabha Elections 1989: Indian Politics in the 1990s* (pp. 72–85), ed. Mahendra Prasad Singh. Delhi: Kalinga Publications.

Chhibber, Pradeep K., and Ken Kollman. 1998 (June). "Party Aggregation and the Number of Parties in India and the United States." *American Political Science Review* 92(2): 329–342.

Chhibber, Pradeep K., and John R. Petrocik. 1990. "Social Cleavages, Elections and the Indian Party System." In *Diversity and Dominance in Indian Politics* (pp. 105–22), ed. Richard Sisson and Ramashray Roy. New Delhi: Sage.

Collins, Larry, and Dominique Lapierre. 1975. *Freedom at Midnight.* New York: Simon and Schuster.

Crossette, Barbara. 1992 (May 19). "India's Descent." *New York Times Magazine.*

Deliege, Robert. 1999. *The Untouchables of India.* Trans. by Nora Scott. London, England: Berg Pub., Ltd.

Deolalikar, Anil. 1992. "Nutrition and Health." In *Foundations of India's Political Economy: Towards an Agenda for the 1990s* (pp. 242–73), ed. Subroto Roy and William E. James. New Delhi: Sage Publications.

Dhadve, M. S. 1989. *Sociology of Slum*. New Delhi: Archives Books.

D'Souza, Victor S. 1990. *Development Planning and Structural Inequalities: The Response of the Underprivileged*. New Delhi: Sage.

Dua, Baghwan D. 1992. "Problems of Federal Leadership." In *Foundations of India's Political Economy: Towards an Agenda for the 1990s* (pp. 91–111), ed. Subroto Roy and William E. James. New Delhi: Sage.

Dubey, Susan. 1992. "The Middle Class." In *India Briefing, 1992* (pp. 137–64), ed. Leonard A. Gordon and Philip Oldenburg. Boulder, CO: Westview Press.

Embree, Ainslie T. 1990. *Utopias in Conflict: Religion and Nationalism in Modern India*. Berkeley, CA: University of California Press.

Fischer, Louis. 1954. *Gandhi: His Life and Message for the World*. New York: Mentor Books.

Frankel, Francine R. 1988. "Middle Classes and Castes in India's Politics." In *India's Democracy* (pp. 225–63), ed. Atul Kohli. Princeton, NJ: Princeton University Press.

Fuller, C. J. 1992. *The Camphor Flame: Popular Hinduism and Society in India*. Princeton, NJ: Princeton University Press.

Gandhi, Indira. 1972. "On Environmental Politics in India." Speech at the opening session of the United Nations Conference on Human Environment, Stockholm.

Ganguly, Meenakshi, and Greg Burke. 1998 (March 2). "That Gandhi Magic." *Time International* 150(27): 28.

Ganguly, Sumit. 1998 (Feb.). "India in 1997: Another Year of Turmoil." *Asian Survey* 38(2): 126–134.

Gilmartin, David. 1998 (July). "A Magnificent Gift: Muslim Nationalism and the Election Process in Colonial Punjab." *Comparative Studies in Society and History* 40(3): 415–36.

Gordon, Sandy. 1992. "Domestic Foundations of India's Security Policy." In *India's Strategic Future: Regional State or Global Power?* (pp. 6–34), ed. Ross Babbage and Sandy Gordon. London: Macmillan.

Gould, Harold A. 1990. *The Hindu Caste System, Vol. 3: Politics and Caste*. Delhi: Chanakya Publications.

Guru, Shyama Prasad. 1991. *Political Socialization of the Urban Political Elites*. New Delhi: Discovery Publishing House.

Hardgrave, Robert L., and Stanley A. Kochanek. 1993. *India: Government and Politics in a Developing Nation*. 5th ed. New York: Harcourt Brace Jovanovich.

Hegde, Ramakrishna. 1998 (Dec. 1). "Partisan of Good Politics." *The Times of India* 1–3, www.

Inoue, Kyoko. 1992. *Industrial Development Policy of India*. Tokyo: Institute of Developing Economies.

Jannuzi, F. Tomasson. 1989. *India in Transition: Issues of Political Economy in a Plural Society*. Boulder, CO: Westview Press.

Karna, M. N. 1989. "Studies in Peasant Protests and Agrarian Relations in India: A Trend Analysis." In *Peasant and Peasant Protests in India* (pp. 1–20), ed. M. N. Karna. New Delhi: Intellectual Publishing House.

Khator, Renu. 1991. *Environment, Development and Politics in India*. New York: University Press of America.

Kohli, Atul. 1990. *Democracy and Discontent: India's Growing Crisis of Governability*. Princeton, NJ: Princeton University Press.

Kohli, Atul, 1998 (July). "Enduring Another Election." *Journal of Democracy* 9(3): 7–20.

Krishna, Sumi. 1992. "The Language Situation: Mosaic or Melting Pot? In *Federalism in India: Origins and Development* (pp. 64–86), ed. Nirmal Mukarji and Balveer Arora. New Delhi: Vikas Publishing House PVT, LTD.

Kumar, Arun. 1991. *The Tenth Round: Story of Indian Elections 1991*. Calcutta: Rupa Co.

Kux, Dennis. 1992. *India and the United States: Estranged Democracies, 1941–1991*. Washington, DC: National Defense University Press.

Lipset, Seymour M. 1960. *Political Man*. New York: Doubleday.

Madan, N. L. 1989. *Indian Political System: Socio-Economic Dimensions*. Jawahar Nagar, Delhi: Ajanta Books International.

Mamoria, C. B., and S. L. Doshi. 1966. *Labour Problems and Social Welfare in India*. Delhi: Kitab Mahal Private.

Manor, James. 1992. "The State of Governance." In *Foundations of India's Political Economy: Towards an Agenda for the 1990s* (pp. 37–59), ed. Subroto Roy and William E. James. New Delhi: Sage Publications.

Manor, James. 1998 (July). "Making Federalism Work." *Journal of Democracy* 9(3): 21–35.

Mansingh, Surit. 1986. "Foreign Relations." In *India: A Country Study* (pp. 459–502), ed. Richard F. Nyrop. Washington, DC: U.S. Government Printing Office.

Mishra, Sachida Nand. 1980. *Political Socialization in Rural India: Social Change and Leadership Patterns in a Bihar Gram Panchayat*. Delhi: Inter-India Publications.

Misquitta, L. P. 1991. *Pressure Groups and Indian Democracy*. New Delhi: Sterling Publishers.

Mittal, S. P. 1986. "Perspectives of New Peasant Movements in India." In *The Peasant Movement Today* (pp. 135–45), ed. Sunil Sahasrabudhey. New Delhi: Ashish Publishing House.

Moog, Robert. 1998 (April). "Elite-Court Relations in India." *Asian Survey* 38(4): 410–423.

Naipaul, V. S. 1990. *India: A Million Mutinies Now.* New York: Viking Press.

Noorani, A. G. 1990. *Indian Affairs: The Political Dimension.* Delhi: Konark Publishers.

Nyrop, Richard F. 1986. *India: A Country Study.* Washington, DC: U.S. Government Printing Office.

Roy, Subroto, and William E. James, eds. 1992. *Foundations of India's Political Economy: Towards an Agenda for the 1990s.* New Delhi: Sage.

Rudolph, Lloyd I., and Susanne H. Rudolph. 1987. *In Pursuit of Lakshmi: The Political Economy of the Indian State.* Chicago: University of Chicago Press.

Rudolph, Lloyd I., and Susanne H. Rudolph. 1998 (March 16). "Organized Chaos." *The New Republic* 218(11): 19–20.

Sahasrabudhey, Sunil. 1986. *The Peasant Movement Today.* New Delhi: Ashish Publishing House.

Seekins, Donald. 1986. "Government and Politics." In *India: A Country Study* (pp. 375–458), ed. Richard F. Nyrop. Washington, DC: U.S. Government Printing Office.

Sekhar, Chandra, and Mohan Dharia. 1969. "Committed Bureaucracy." *Hindustan Times* (New Delhi, December 1, 1969), cited in "Higher Civil Service in India" in *Administrative Systems Abroad* (pp. 96–126), ed. Krishna K. Tummala. Washington, DC: University Press of America.

Shah, Ghanshyam. 1988. "Grass-Roots Mobilization in Indian Politics." In *India's Democracy* (pp. 225–63), ed. Atul Kholi. Princeton, NJ: Princeton University Press.

Shah, Ghanshyam. 1990. *Social Movements in India.* New Delhi: Sage.

Singh, Gurharpal. 1998 (April). "India's Akali–BJP Alliance." *Asian Survey* 38(4): 398–409.

Singh, Mahendra Prasad, ed. 1992. *Lok Sabha Elections 1989: Indian Politics in the 1990s.* Delhi: Kalinga Publications.

Sisson, Richard, and Stanley Wolpert, eds. 1988. *Congress and Indian Nationalism.* Berkeley, CA: University of California Press.

Thakur, Ramesh. 1998. "A Changing of the Guard in India." *Asian Survey* 38(6): 603–623.

Thompson, Edward. 1980. *The Making of the Indian Princes.* Columbia, MO: South Asia Books.

Todaro, Michael. 1989. *Economic Development in the Third World.* New York: Longman.

Tomlinson, B. R. 1992. "Historical Roots of Economic Policy." In *India's Political Economy* (pp. 275–305), ed. Subroto Roy and William E. James. New Delhi: Sage.

Tully, Mark, and Zareer Mansani. 1988. *From Raj to Rajiv: 40 Years of Indian Independence.* London: BBC Books.

Tummala, Krishna K. 1982. "Higher Civil Service in India." In *Administrative Systems Abroad* (pp. 96–126), ed. Krishna K. Tummala. Washington, DC: University Press of America.

Vanaik, Achin. 1990. *The Peaceful Transition.* London: Verso.

Weiner, Myron. 1957. *Party Politics in India.* Princeton, NJ: Princeton University Press.

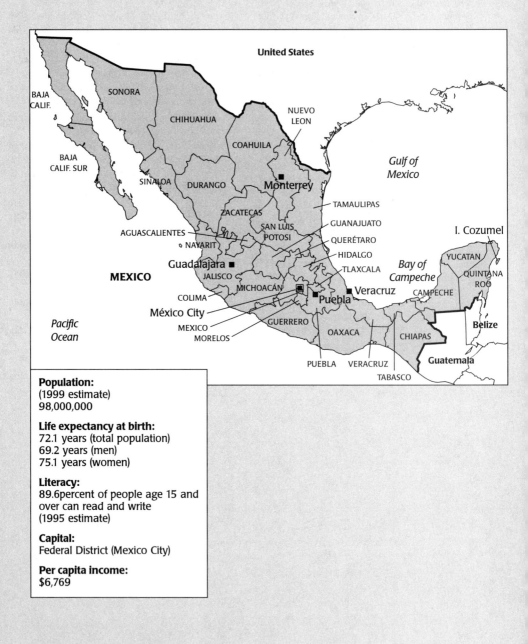

United States

BAJA
CALIF.

SONORA

CHIHUAHUA

NUEVO
LEON

COAHUILA

*Gulf of
Mexico*

BAJA
CALIF. SUR

SINALOA

DURANGO

■ Monterrey

ZACATECAS

TAMAULIPAS

GUANAJUATO

I. Cozumel

AGUASCALIENTES

SAN LUIS
POTOSI

QUERÉTARO

ο NAYARIT

HIDALGO

YUCATAN

Guadalajara ■

TLAXCALA

*Bay of
Campeche*

QUINTANA
ROO

MEXICO

JALISCO

COLIMA

MICHOACÁN

■
Puebla

■ Veracruz

CAMPECHE

México City

*Pacific
Ocean*

MEXICO

GUERRERO

MORELOS

OAXACA

CHIAPAS

Belize

Guatemala

PUEBLA

VERACRUZ

TABASCO

Population:
(1999 estimate)
98,000,000

Life expectancy at birth:
72.1 years (total population)
69.2 years (men)
75.1 years (women)

Literacy:
89.6percent of people age 15 and
over can read and write
(1995 estimate)

Capital:
Federal District (Mexico City)

Per capita income:
$6,769

9

Mexico
The Politics of Crisis and Change

Stephen D. Morris

Mexico has undergone fundamental and intriguing changes in recent years. After decades of stability, the country endured during the 1990s a guerrilla insurrection, economic recession, the assassination of a presidential candidate, the exiling of a former president, and the jailing of his brother for murder and corruption. The long-ruling Institutional Revolutionary Party (**PRI**) has lost much of its power, challenged by the growing appeal of the National Action Party (**PAN**) on its right and the Party of the Democratic Revolution (**PRD**) on its left. The once-dominant Mexican presidency has also yielded power to a more emboldened Congress, a more assertive PRI, and a more viable and active civil society. Mexican social organizations, once largely controlled by the government or the PRI, have pried open political space, pressing their demands while checking the power of government. Meanwhile, the traditional ideological pillars that once legitimized the regime have withered, crystallizing intense debates over the nature of political power, the nation, and the meaning of being Mexican. Even electoral fraud and repression, once relied upon to help keep the PRI in power, have lost much of their capacity to stem the tide of opposition. These recent changes have been neither easy nor smooth, punctuated instead by deep economic and political crises, conflict, and, all too often, violence and repression. Though change offers hope, Mexico enters the new millennium facing an uncertain political and economic future.

Referred to as "one of the seven political science wonders of the world" (Blum 1997, 34), the Mexican political system has puzzled observers for years. Because the system that emerged from the chaos of the 1910–1917 Revolution fused characteristics of pluralist democracy (a progressive constitution, formal division of powers, and elections) with authoritarian practices (extreme concentration of power in the presidency, single-party dominance, repression, and electoral fraud) it was difficult to classify the system as either democratic or authoritarian. So while some analysts stressed the regime's democratic credentials, labeling it "semi-democratic," others emphasized the system's authoritarian properties, discounting the elite's persistent promises to "perfect" the system's democracy. Even today, analysts disagree over how much the system has truly changed and where it may be heading, since the current political transition combines and confuses signs of democratic breakthrough with strong remnants of an authoritarian order and thinking.

Much of the bewilderment and amazement enveloping Mexican politics reflects the uniqueness of the Mexican case. Unlike other Latin American countries known for instability, military coups, repression, and democratic-authoritarian cycles, Mexico has enjoyed stable, civilian-led institutions for most of the twentieth century. It has kept the military at bay and largely out of politics, and it has never had to rely extensively on open or brutal repression to control the population. Unlike other authoritarian regimes, the Mexican system has incorporated a wide spectrum of societal interests, proved itself somewhat responsive to the people's needs, and transferred political power by using elections that combine fair (opposition parties) and unfair (fraud) tactics to legitimize the PRI's rule. In full control since its formation in 1929, the PRI still clings to its record as the longest-ruling party in the world. Today, Mexico's pattern of change continues to set it apart from other countries. In contrast to the democratic transitions in Latin America and Eastern Europe, in Mexico the old institutions and interests have remained largely intact, providing the framework for political change.

This uniqueness alone makes the study of Mexican politics exciting, and the country has attracted considerable scholarly attention. But the country's salience to the US and world bolsters its importance. Mexico shares a porous 1,952-mile border with the US—the longest border between a First and Third World country. Thanks in large part to the 1994 North American Free Trade Agreement (NAFTA)[1] that inaugurated a free trade zone linking Mexico, the US, and Canada, Mexico now ranks as the second-largest trading partner of the US and the greatest source of legal and illegal immigrants—a trend that is transforming the demographic and cultural landscape of both countries. Moreover, because an estimated 75 percent of the illegal drugs entering the US pass through Mexico's arid and mountainous terrain, the country figures prominently in the US-led war on drugs.

But Mexico is also important in its own right. It is the thirteenth largest country by area—roughly the size of the United Kingdom, France, Spain, Italy, and Germany combined—and the eleventh most populous (94.3 million in 1997). It is the largest Spanish-speaking country in the world. It has the fifteenth largest economy, and it is the sixteenth largest trader on the global market, the eighth largest producer of crude oil, the second largest recipient of foreign investment among developing countries, and a diplomatic leader among Third World nations. Though poor when compared to developed countries (US per capita income is approximately ten times that of Mexico), Mexico places at the higher end among developing countries. The site of the first Olympic games to be held in a developing country, Mexico has produced Nobel winners in literature (Octavio Paz), chemistry (Mario Molina), and peace (Alfonso Garcia Robles), and has made notable contributions to the worlds of art (Frida Kahlo, Diego Rivera, Rufino Tamayo, David Siquerios, and José Clemente Orozco), music (Plácido Domingo, Augustin Lara,

---

[1]NAFTA is a lengthy accord designed to lower tariffs and trade barriers between Mexico, the US, and Canada. The agreement went into effect January 1, 1994, and will eliminate virtually all tariffs by 2009.

Gabriel Ruiz, and Luis Miguel), literature (Octavio Paz and Carlos Fuentes), and sport (Oscar Chávez, Fernando Valenzuela, Vinny Castillo).

Our exploration of Mexican politics will highlight the system's unique features and also describe recent changes and trends. We begin with a brief overview of the nation's history. Mexico's history features a rich indigenous past, political instability and revolution, foreign invasion, and the fracturing and loss of territory. Next, we will examine the country's main political institutions as they have developed since the Revolution, drawing a crucial distinction between the "formal" legal/constitutional order and the actual operations of the system. Our next focus of attention will be the main actors in the political drama, and we will examine the "informal" rules that have long structured the elite-dominated political game, the major political parties and the nature of elections, the politics of groups and citizens, and the changing roles of the various political actors in recent years. Shifting our focus somewhat, we will explore the broader context of Mexican politics with brief discussions of Mexican political culture, economic policy, and the country's all-important relationship with the US. In the concluding section we will look at Mexico's political challenges and prospects for the future, raising a series of critical questions: Despite ongoing political problems, will Mexico be able to construct a functioning democratic system and extend the protection of basic human rights to all? Will the PRI's reign come to an end during the presidential election of 2000, as some suggest? And if so, what will become of the PRI? Will NAFTA and the neoliberal economic reforms of the past decade pave the way for sustainable and equitable growth?

Mexico in Historical Perspective

Pre-Columbian History

As most visitors to the country soon realize, Mexico is an archeological treasure, featuring a rich history dating as far back as 10,000 BC and incorporating an array of indigenous cultures. The Olmecs, best known for their colossal carved stone heads and cult of the jaguar, were among the first, flourishing in the eastern-central region of the country around 1200 BC. The classic period, stretching from 200 BC to AD 1000, featured the resplendent cultures of the Teotihuacán in the valley of Mexico, the Monte Albán in what is today the state of Oaxaca, and the Maya in the Yucatán peninsula. Perhaps better known are the groups that thrived in the post-classic period, such as the Toltecs, the Zapotecs, and later the Mexica or Aztecs whose empire encompassed most of the central and southern portions of the country by the sixteenth century.

The numerous archeological sites and anthropological museums dotting the landscape and attracting millions of tourists each year bear witness to the nation's indigenous heritage. Mexico's indigenous past and present inform popular legends, beliefs, and practices. For the majority of Mexico's **mestizo** or mixed Spanish-Indian population, their indigenous roots serve as a source of pride and a component of personal and national identity—a sentiment nurtured by the government's promotion of the ideas of *mexicanidad* and *indigenismo* in the 1920s and 1930s. Even today, according to the 1995 census, 8.5 million indigenous people remain culturally distinct from the mestizo mainstream, speaking one of among one hundred different indigenous languages heard throughout the country. Most of the indigenous Mexicans live in the southern regions and sadly, suffer the worst levels of poverty, social discrimination, and political repression of any

---

The Aztec Founding of Tenochtitlán

Legend has it that the Aztecs set out from the north sometimes after 1100 AD to establish a city on the site where, according to prophecy, they were to find an eagle devouring a snake while perched atop a cactus in the middle of a lake. After years of wandering, their search ended when they entered the valley of Anahuac and gazed out upon Lake Texcoco. After years of struggle with rival tribes, they established on that site the glorious city of Tenochtitlán: a city rivaling the great cities of Europe by the time of the conquest. Since then, Tenochtitlán, now known as Mexico City, has been the political, economic, and cultural center of Mexico, and the symbol of the eagle on the cactus adorns the Mexican flag. The Aztecs also provided the country with its modern-day name, while words from the Aztec language, including *chocolate, coyote*, and many others, inform more than just Mexican Spanish.

---

social group—an irony given the important place of indigenous peoples in the nation's history and psyche. The deplorable conditions of the present-day indigenous helped trigger the uprising in 1994 by the *Ejército Zapatista de Liberación Nacional* (**EZLN**) (Zapatista Army of National Liberation) in the southern state of Chiapas and their struggle since then, through more peaceful and political means, to assert the political and cultural rights of indigenous peoples.

Conquest and Colonization

The great Aztec city of Tenochtitlán—now the site of Mexico City—fell to Hernan Cortez in 1520, converting him into Mexico's greatest villain and ushering in three centuries of Spanish colonial rule. The legacies of colonial rule over what was then called New Spain are many. The Spanish imposed a strong, centralized authoritarian state upon indigenous Mexico, with power concentrated in the hands of the viceroy; they enthroned an all-powerful and privileged Catholic Church that instilled Christianity, the Spanish language, and attitudes of intolerance toward those who disagreed with the Church's teachings; they erected an economic order that turned Mexico's abundance, particularly its mineral resources, into Spanish wealth; and through miscegenation, they created the bronze race of the mestizo. The colonial system rested atop a strict racial and cultural hierarchy. Those of Spanish descent enjoyed the highest positions; the mestizos were relegated to an ambiguous legal-social status, and the indigenous provided the physical labor. Though the crown officially abolished Indian slavery in the 1550s, the various systems of forced labor prevailed long afterwards. Colonialism even fostered a legacy of corruption. Because laws were made in distant Spain and not only took time to reach the colony but failed to reflect local conditions, a culture of disrespect for the law and corruption took hold.

In many ways, Mexico's three centuries of colonialism transformed the land and its people. The Spanish built mining camps to extract Mexican silver; introduced European crops, draft animals, and technology; altered production and trade; and developed ranching on huge estates, particularly in the drier northern regions of the country, taking land from the indigenous communities. But among the many transformations wrought by the Spanish, none was more devastating than the introduction of diseases such as smallpox and measles against which the indigenous population had virtually no defense. Though estimates vary widely, Mexico's indigenous population fell drastically from around 30 million at the time of the conquest to fewer than 1 million less than a century later. Mexico would not reach the 30 million population mark again until the middle of the twentieth century.

Shown here is a detail from a mural of the ancient Aztec city of Tenochtitlán, on the site of present-day Mexico City.

Independence and Instability: The Nineteenth Century

As in other Latin American countries, Napoleon and war in Europe unleashed Mexico's struggle for independence. Stretching from 1810 to 1821, Mexico's independence movement left a unique legacy of popular, mass-based uprisings that failed to achieve their objectives but produced some of the nation's most important heros and ideals. Initiating the *Grito de Dolores* (Cry from the town of Dolores) on September 16, 1810 (recognized as independence day in Mexico), Father Miguel Hidalgo and later Father Jose Maria Morelos (the fathers of Mexican independence) spearheaded peasant/indigenous-based mass uprisings under the banner of the Virgin of Guadalupe. Their peasant armies attacked Spanish citizens and property, demanding liberty, an end to slavery, and modest social reforms. But both leaders were captured by royal forces and executed. Only after years of intermittent struggle in 1821 would Mexico finally attain its independence, but not in a mass-based popular movement nor for such progressive goals. Instead, a conservative general from the colonial army, General Augustin de Inturbide, switched sides and joined other reformist rebels to expel the Spanish rulers and establish himself as Mexico's first emperor, a post that lasted only a year and a half.

Throughout much of the nineteenth century, political instability, foreign intervention, and economic turmoil engulfed Mexico, scarring the country for years to come. In the aftermath of the bloody independence struggle, and with the economy in ruins, conflict erupted between two main elite factions: the Conservatives and Liberals. The Conservatives favored centralized authority, respect for traditional Spanish values, and protection of the position and privileges of the Catholic

---

The *Virgin de Guadalupe*

The Virgin of Guadalupe is the most important religious and cultural symbol of Mexico, worshiped by Mexicans throughout the world. According to legend, the dark-skinned Virgin appeared to the Indian peasant Juan Diego on December 9 and 12, 1531, on the hill of Tepeyac outside Mexico City, a site where Indians had always worshiped Tonantzin, the mother of gods. Unable to convince the bishop of the apparition, Juan Diego returned to the site, where the Virgin called out his name. This time the Virgin gave Juan Diego roses, a rarity to the region, and instructed that he carry the roses in the fold of his shirt to the bishop. When Juan Diego unfurled his peasant shirt to present the roses, the shirt bore the likeness of the Virgin. In her honor, a shrine was erected that is still visited by millions. The legend of the dark Virgin hastened the Christianization of the indigenous, and the Virgin became the symbol for the nation. Just as Hidalgo and Morelos fought for Mexican independence under the banner of the Virgin of Guadalupe, her image adorns the homes of millions of modern-day Mexicans. During his 1998 visit to Mexico, Pope John Paul II recognized the importance of the Virgin of Guadalupe to Mexico and all Hispanics.

Church. Liberals, influenced by the ideals of the French and American Revolutionaries, rejected Spanish traditions, embraced republican and free-market ideals, and sought to curtail the overwhelming economic and political power of the Church. The deep split led to almost constant conflict, and the periodic emergence of military strongmen who could provide a semblance of order. It also set the stage for foreign intervention.

Holding the huge, sparsely populated country together amid such turmoil proved particularly difficult during the first half of the nineteenth century. Soon after independence, the country faced the fracturing of its territory in the north and in the Yucatan peninsula. Though the government put down the quest for independence in Yucatan, it was unable to prevent American settlers in the north from establishing an independent Texas in 1836. Eleven years later when Texas joined the American union, the US, long desirous of Mexican land and drunk on the ideas of Manifest Destiny, launched an all-out war against Mexico. When the fighting ended with the US invasion of Mexico City (hence the line in the US Marine Hymn: "From the Halls of Montezuma"), Mexico was forced to relinquish half its territory to its northern neighbor, ceding the lands of current-day California, Arizona, New Mexico, Nevada, and parts of Colorado. No country in modern times has lost as much territory. The event greatly wounded the nation's pride, feeding a sense of anti-Americanism that has held for years. Indeed, the *niños heroes* or child heros—the young cadets who leaped to their death at Chapultepec Castle in Mexico City rather than surrender to invading US forces—still rank as important national heroes officially recognized on September 13.

But the war with the US was not the only episode of foreign invasion and instability during this period. Following the victory of the Liberals behind Benito Juárez[2] in the War of the Reform (1858–1861), Spanish, French, and British forces took control of the port of Veracruz in 1861 to collect on past loans. England and Spain withdrew following negotiations, but the French, encouraged by Mexico's Conservatives, launched a war of occupation. Though defeated temporarily in the battle of Zaragoza on May 5, 1862—the famous Cinco de Mayo celebration of today—Napoleon's troops eventually gained control, placing the Austrian duke Maximilian on the throne in 1864. Civil war ensued as the Liberals, exiled in the US, struggled to overturn the monarchical order and reestablish republican rule. In 1867, after years of struggle, the most widely revered of Mexican heroes, Benito Juárez, aided by the US, proved triumphant, defeating the French and returning to power.

---

[2]Benito Juárez served as president of Mexico from 1858 to 1872. He is popularly viewed as the greatest Mexican president in history.

Historians Michael Meyer and William Sherman (1995) cite the victory of Juárez in 1867 as the beginning of modern Mexico. During his three terms as president, Juárez—and Sebastian Lerdo following Juárez's death in 1872—reestablished liberal policies that stripped the Church of its political and economic power, opened a free internal market, broke up the communal landholdings of the Indians to encourage private land ownership, strengthened the power of the state, and promoted secular education and development. But divisions within the liberal ranks led to revolt in 1871 when General Porfirio Díaz, in one of Mexico's greatest historical ironies, assailed the practice of indefinite re-election. He rose up in rebellion and took control of the nation in 1876.

The Porfiriato and the Mexican Revolution

Stressing order as necessary for development, Díaz consolidated his grip on political power and ruled Mexico for more than three decades, a period known as the **Porfiriato.** During this authoritarian period, Díaz promoted the development of agricultural exports by large landowners—foreign and domestic—who pushed peasants off the land, leaving millions landless. He opened the country to foreign businesses and oversaw the construction of the nation's first railroads, the revitalization of the mining industry, and the drilling of vast oil fields. Maintaining a sham of democracy that selected a string of powerless presidents, Díaz ruled with a combination of political mastery and an iron fist, relying on the army and the rural police to keep order. By the turn of the century, Mexico could indeed point to many achievements under Díaz: political stability, economic growth, an increase in the population, improvements in health and sanitation, the beginnings of industry, and a boom in the nation's cultural and intellectual life. Yet Mexico remained basically a rural society with land concentrated in the hands of a few and a mass peasant population living in conditions worse than those of their ancestors. Under the system of *haciendas,* for example, fifteen of the richest Mexican landowners owned more than three hundred thousand acres each.

Despite the economic advances under Díaz, by the first decade of the twentieth century the dictator faced severe opposition. In a dramatic call to arms, Francisco Madero, the leader of the Anti-Re-electionist Party,[3] spearheaded a revolt on November 20, 1910—celebrated as the Day of the Mexican Revolution. This opened one of the bloodiest chapters in the history of the nation and the first social revolution of the twentieth century. Rebel armies sprang up in towns throughout the country and by May 1911, Díaz resigned and fled to Europe. Madero was then elected president in what most considered to be a relatively free election, but fell two years later in a military coup led by Victoriano Huerta and supported by the US. Once again, the revolutionary generals, some of whom had continued to fight despite Madero's victory, rose up in arms against Huerta's reactionary government and each other. The major protagonists in the drama included Generals Venustiano Carranza and Alvaro Obregon of the Constitutionalist army in the north, Pancho Villa from the northern state of Chihuahua, and Emiliano Zapata in the state of Morelos just south of Mexico City. By 1915, anarchy reigned as civil war engulfed large parts of the country. By 1917, more than a million and a half Mexicans were dead, many more were left homeless, and the economy was devastated. Those who would eventually become the nation's Revolutionary heroes—Madero, Carranza, Villa, Zapata, and Obregon—would all meet violent deaths.

---

[3]Recall that Díaz's rise to power was also based on the idea of no re-election.

General Porfirio Diaz ruled Mexico with an iron fist for more than three decades, promoting industrialization at the expense of indigenous peasants.

Upon gaining the upper hand militarily, Carranza organized a constituent assembly that met in Querétaro in 1917 to draft a new constitution. The document, which despite many changes remains in force today, defined the Mexican Revolution and shaped Mexican political thought for years to come. Designed to satisfy as many interests as possible, it contained strong anti-clerical language, greatly restricting the role of the Church in politics and society; it promised land to the peasants in response to the abuses under the Porfiriato and the demands of Zapata's agrarian guerrillas; it granted the state exclusive rights to exploit the subsoil in contrast to Díaz's policy of turning mines over to foreigners; it provided extensive rights to workers, including an eight-hour work day, a minimum wage, and equal pay for equal work; it established an array of political freedoms; and, reflecting perhaps the primary problem of the Díaz period, it banned re-election.

But despite the new constitution and the Carranza victory, conflict continued to rack the country. Carranza was ousted and killed by his once-trusted advisor Alvaro Obregon, who himself was gunned down years later by a lone assassin. In a bid to quell such conflict, consolidate control, and provide for an orderly transfer of power among the Revolutionary elite, President Plutarco Elias Calles (1924–1934) brokered an agreement among the elite to establish the Party of the National Revolution (PNR) in 1929—the forerunner of today's **PRI**. Established from the seat of political power, the young party demonstrated during the 1929 presidential election its capability to mobilize and even use fraud to gain victory. Though Calles ruled from behind the scenes for more than a decade—a period known as the Maximato—the PNR became the nation's preeminent political vehicle, incorporating and channeling the aspirations and demands of politicians. As such, it brought needed political stability to the country and ended the violence of the Revolutionary period.

The term of Lázaro Cárdenas (1934–1940), one of Mexico's most popular presidents, capped what is often referred to as the Revolutionary Phase in Mexican

In response to the abuses of the Porfiriato, *Mexican revolutionaries sought to improve conditions for workers and peasants. Political conflict continued for years, leading to the formation of the Party of the National Revolution (PNR) in 1929.*

politics. During this period, Cárdenas greatly strengthened the power of the presidency and the state. He forced Calles into exile and incorporated the nation's major labor and peasant organizations into the dominant party, turning them into "official" and privileged sectors of the party. Known at the time as the PRM (Party of the Mexican Revolution), the dominant party not only monopolized political power, but represented both ideologically and organizationally the nation's major labor and peasant groups. At the same time, Cárdenas began to implement with unprecedented vigor the more radical, socialist components of the Constitution, further broadening the power and scope of the state. He took land from wealthy landowners and gave it to peasants organized into state-controlled cooperatives known as **ejidos**; he nationalized the foreign oil companies following a labor dispute, creating the state-owned oil company Pemex (*Petróleos Mexicanos*); and he promoted the state's role in developing infrastructure, particularly in the countryside, providing a foundation for the nation's industrial growth. Building on Calles's accomplishments, he also promoted a strongly nationalistic and socialistic ideology rooted in the ideals of the Mexican Revolution, a glorification of the nation's indigenous past, and a cultural renaissance.

The Institutionalized Revolution

The unique political edifice built in the aftermath of the Revolution provided the foundation for an unprecedented period of political stability and economic prosperity in Mexico that stretched from the 1940s to the late 1970s. The president's authority was largely unquestioned, and the dominant party—which by 1946 became known as the PRI—channeled popular demands, mobilized the vote, and distributed political spoils and the rewards of economic growth. Meanwhile, the constitutional prohibition on re-election ensured presidential authority and fluidity of leadership. With such political stability in effect, the government downplayed many of the more radical, socialist ideals of the Revolution and focused its energies on developing the country economically along more capitalist lines. Like other governments of the region during this time, the Mexican government rejected the notion that free trade and free markets alone could pull the country out of its poverty and underdevelopment. The government thus took the lead in promoting economic development by using its extensive powers to build infrastructure, encourage local industry and foreign investment, and restrict foreign competition.

In many ways the strategy of development paid off. For more than thirty years, the economy grew at an average annual rate of 6 percent, transforming Mexico from a predominantly rural, agrarian-based, and illiterate society into an urban, largely industrial, and literate country. The lives of millions of Mexicans improved. And for the first time in its history, Mexico enjoyed a large increase in its population, which skyrocketed from 22 million in 1945 to more than 70 million by 1980.

The relationship between political stability and economic development is complex. On the one hand, Mexico's decades of economic growth, known as the "Mexican Miracle," clearly contributed to its remarkable political stability. Growth supplied real benefits that could be distributed to those incorporated into the PRI, particularly the privileged labor, peasant, and bureaucratic organizations; it kept the nation's business elite satisfied and thus "out of politics"; and it provided sufficient spoils to reward government officials who chose to play by the rules of the political game. Economic growth also fostered a measure of popular legitimacy that prompted many to overlook the lack of true democracy, the corruption, the electoral fraud, or the selective repression of the regime's opponents. Yet, on the other hand, economic growth and development also set the stage for change by giving rise to new social organizations and interests that would increasingly stand outside of the PRI-dominated political framework, thereby straining the political system. Demands by workers, students, business, and the growing educated middle class for greater autonomy, liberty, and free elections grew more insistent during the period, often triggering repression. In 1968, weeks prior to the opening of the Olympic Games in Mexico City, students, joined by middle-class citizens and workers, staged massive protests against the government. They carried signs protesting government repression, the denial of basic rights, and the massive poverty of the people. The government responded brutally, killing hundreds of protesters and arresting thousands more. The event—a watershed in Mexican political history—revealed some of the failings of the political system and underscored the need for fundamental political change.

Crisis and Change

In many ways, the stability of the Institutionalized Period flowed more from the capacity of the regime to overcome crisis than from the absence of crisis. By the 1980s, however, the regime began to lose much of its capacity to overcome periodic crises. Facing growing budget deficits and balance-of-payment problems, the government incurred significant debt during the 1970s and early 1980s. Though oil exports provided a surge of growth from 1978–1981, global economic conditions turned sour in 1981, as oil prices dropped and interest rates rose. By August 1982, the Mexican government was bankrupt, unable to meet its obligations to foreign banks. Economic growth, long the source of regime legitimacy, plummeted. Climbing out of the recession and maintaining economic growth proved difficult as the country embarked on a rocky road spiked with the multiple challenges of economic and political crisis and change. In response to the deep economic crisis, Presidents Miguel de la Madrid (1982–1988) and Carlos Salinas de Gortari (1988–1994) downplayed the more progressive tenets of the

Revolutionary ideology and began to dismantle the economic model of the "Miracle" years. They removed trade restrictions, joined the General Agreement on Trade and Tariffs (GATT—currently the World Trade Organization), negotiated free trade agreements with the US and Canada (NAFTA) and others, privatized hundreds of state-owned industries, opened the economy to foreign investment, and cut back drastically on social programs and government spending.

In the midst of economic crisis, pressures for political change mounted. Opposition parties, once pacified by being allowed minor representation in Congress, mobilized for free and open elections, gained popular support, and challenged the PRI's hold on power at the polls. An array of new social organizations, human rights groups, and indigenous groups, together with existing business and labor organizations, clamored for a greater role in the system, challenging the state's and the PRI's controls over society. As the government struggled to pay off its massive foreign debt, it had few spoils to distribute to shore up support. Even once tolerable levels of corruption among political leaders began to draw a firestorm of criticism in the wake of economic crisis, further undermining the legitimacy of the PRI-controlled government. By the late 1980s, such pressures unleashed deep divisions within the ranks of the PRI itself as Cuauhtémoc Cárdenas (and many others) quit the party of his famous father to challenge the PRI's contender, Carlos Salinas, in the 1988 election. Although officials declared Salinas the victor with barely 50 percent of the vote, the election was so marred by fraud that the outcome further robbed the regime of its legitimacy (the true results of that election may never be known).

Political conflict reached new heights in 1994. In January, a group of indigenous rebels seized control of a series of small towns in the southern state of Chiapas. Two months later, the PRI's presidential candidate, Luis Donaldo Colosio, was gunned down in open daylight in Tijuana. Though the fighting in Chiapas soon gave way to prolonged negotiations, the EZLN nonetheless challenged the PRI's hold on power in the state, raised difficult questions about indigenous rights, and increased the popular pressures on the government to make true democratic reforms. And despite the fact that President Salinas handpicked a replacement candidate who was able to win the August election, divisions among the political elite continued to fester. Together, such pressures forced the government to engage in a series of step-by-step changes that would gradually begin to dismantle the basic features of the political system. Most notably, the government passed a series of electoral reforms that made elections freer and campaigns more equal, thus enabling the opposition in subsequent years to win almost a third of the nation's gubernatorial seats and, in 1997, a majority in the lower house of Congress, the Chamber of Deputies. So by century's end, the once-stable political system was struggling to handle political transition and democratization, wrestling with the prospects of an end to the PRI's long reign, and confronting new political and economic challenges.

The Political Institutions of Mexico

To understand Mexican politics, it is necessary to distinguish between the system's formal rules and the way it actually operates. The gap between the ideal and the reality not only provides a partial explanation for the confusion over the nature of Mexican politics noted at the outset, but also adds to the tension that shapes political developments. As we will see, many recent political changes have centered on pushing the system closer to the way it is supposed to operate and away from the way it has functioned in the recent past.

The Constitution

Mexico is a highly legalistic society, a trait it inherited from Spain and the medieval period. This means that acts must be justified and grounded in law, and dealing with the government usually entails a mountain of paperwork and regulations. The Mexican Constitution, drafted in 1917 and amended frequently since then, lays out the basic parameters of the political system and serves as a guide to the legitimizing ideals and goals of the system (if not its operation). The Constitution may not define what actually happens, but it at least specifies what "should" happen.

The Mexican Constitution resembles the US Constitution in several ways. It establishes a democratic form of government and divides power between executive, legislative, and judicial branches; it enshrines the principle of popular sovereignty through multiparty elections; it creates a federal system whereby each of the nation's thirty-one states operates under its own constitutional framework and exercises certain powers; it mandates a separation of church and state; and it provides for extensive individual freedoms. The Mexican Constitution differs from the US document, however, in two fundamental ways. First, the Mexican Constitution mandates a strong governmental role in the economy and society. Article 27, for instance, grants the government exclusive rights over the exploitation of the subsoil, which broadly interpreted sanctions the state's right to determine the limits and functions of private property. Article 123 establishes the state's role in protecting the rights of workers, going so far as to mandate profit-sharing and to specify the number of paid vacation days. Second, in the electoral arena, the Constitution creates a mixed system of proportional representation and district seats and, most importantly, prohibits re-election. Deeply ingrained in the lessons of history, the ban on re-election applies not just to the executive, as might be expected, but to all elected officials at the federal, state, and local levels. Legislators, however, may repeat, but not consecutively.

Executive Power in Mexico

As set out under the Constitution, the executive branch of the Mexican government is headed by the president, who is elected for a six-year term, and includes seventeen cabinet-level departments and certain agencies within the Mexico City government. The extended cabinet also includes state-owned firms such as *Petróleos Mexicanos* (Pemex), *Comisión Federal de Electricidad* (CFE), the Social Security Institute, Central Bank (Banxico), *Nacional Financiera* (Nafin), the *Banco Nacional de Comercio Exterior* (Bancomext), and several others. Though the Constitution establishes a system of separation of powers and provides for checks and balances, in practice, the Mexican president has enjoyed almost unlimited powers, prompting literary comparisons with dictators, Spanish viceroys, and Aztec chiefs.

In relation to other institutions of government or society, the Mexican president truly "rules." Within the executive branch, the president delegates authority to trusted colleagues but maintains tight control over budgetary and policy matters. Until 1997 when the PRI lost its majority in the Chamber of Deputies, the president dominated the legislative branch, naming congressional leaders, dictating the agenda, and gaining routine approval of his legislative proposals. Even today, the president still plays the major role in initiating legislation and controlling the flow of information. The president holds similar control over the judiciary, the federal bureaucracy, and state and local governments. And given the extensive power of the state over the economy, and the PRI's control over societal organizations, the president's power reaches even further and deeper. Historically, this awesome presidential power goes so far as to include the power to hand-pick a successor.

Much of the extraordinary power of the Mexican president, or what is commonly referred to as **presidentialism**, stems from the PRI's political dominance in a context of no re-elections and a weak to nonexistent civil service system. As political head of the PRI, the president has long held the authority to determine the party's nominations for the vast number of elected seats at the federal and state levels, a prerogative that helps ensure party discipline and personal loyalty. The PRI's long-time control of federal and state legislatures, in turn, has not only enabled the president to dictate to a basically rubber-stamp Congress, but has also permitted the president to count on the number of votes needed to alter the Constitution, or remove judges or state governors. Few, at least within the PRI, have ever dared to challenge presidential authority or initiatives, thereby making meaningless the institutional checks on the power of the presidency set out in the Constitution. Even beyond the formal branches of government, the PRI's incorporation of peasant, labor, and other social organizations has long placed the president at the center of power, enabling him to determine leadership in these critical organizations, reward loyalty, and punish his opponents. As might be expected, the absence of checks on presidential authority has also given rise to corruption and the abuse of power within the executive and bureaucratic ranks.

Though the president remains the most powerful actor in the Mexican political drama, however, recent reforms and developments have chipped away at presidential authority. In contrast to his predecessors, President Ernesto Zedillo (1994–2000) has had to negotiate with a Congress no longer dominated by the PRI; he has had to bow to a central bank and electoral authority that has gained a certain degree of autonomy, a judiciary that struggles to become more autonomous, a PRI that is far more undisciplined than in the past, and a range of social organizations that escape the controls of the PRI or are increasingly immune from political pressures. Somewhat to his credit, Zedillo has generally acknowledged these changes, though the pattern is not clear and important tests remain. Such changes are explored in greater detail below.

Legislative Power in Mexico

The bicameral Mexican Congress includes the **Chamber of Deputies** and the Senate. The Chamber is composed of 500 members elected for a term of three years: 300 *diputados* (deputies) represent electoral districts in a winner-take-all contest, while 200 are party representatives elected through a system of proportional representation. The Senate, in turn, counts 128 members, or four from each of the nation's thirty-one states and the Federal District (Mexico City) elected to a six-year term: three are elected "at-large" in the state and one seat is given to the runner-up party in that state. In accordance with the Constitution, the Chamber has exclusive powers over questions of finance, commerce, public education, health, and defense, while the Senate has such additional functions as approval of treaties, ratification of diplomatic and consular appointments, naming of provisional governors, and authorization of Supreme Court appointments. Both houses meet from September 1 to December 31 and can be called together for extraordinary sessions. A sort of joint executive committee known as the *Gran Comisión* handles the functions of the Congress when the larger body is not in session.

For years, the Mexican Congress played a subordinate role in Mexican politics. The PRI's huge majority routinely amended the Constitution, passed legislation, and approved executive appointments, whenever the president wanted, often with no debate, opposition, or input. Since the introduction of proportional representation seats designed specifically for representatives of opposition parties in 1963,

---

Political Corruption

From high-level politicians leaving office with millions of dollars to the payment of bribes to police and bureaucrats, corruption has long plagued Mexican politics. According to one observer,"corruption is not a characteristic of the system, it *is* the system" (*NYT*, Feb. 15, 1996, 1A). In fact, in a 1994 word association poll, *corruption* emerged as the term most often associated with the word *government*, testifying to low levels of public confidence in the government and particularly the police (Beltran et al. 1997).

In many ways, corruption in Mexico reflects the traditional authoritarian judicial system. More recently, much corruption stems from the rise of drug trafficking. In the early 1990s, the attorney general claimed that perhaps as much as 80 percent of the police force was under the pay of drug traffickers. This peaked with the arrest a few years later of the chief of Mexico's anti-narcotics police for collusion with the drug traffickers.

Among the more spectacular cases in recent years involves Raul Salinas, the brother of the former president, who was arrested on charges of murder, drug trafficking, and the laundering of hundreds of million of dollars in overseas accounts under false names as well as the discovery of police in the state of Morelos leading a kidnapping ring. Despite government efforts over the years to deal with corruption, little progress has ever been made. By fostering greater accountability and reducing the scope of governmental regulations, recent political and economic changes offer some basis for hope.

Congress began to serve as a forum for the opposition to criticize the president, though the body's policymaking power remained limited. Congress was one of the few areas where the opposition was permitted a role in politics, however.

As the crises of the 1980s and 1990s strengthened the presence of opposition parties in Congress, the role of the institution began to change. In 1988, when the PRI's majority in the Chamber of Deputies slipped to a meager four votes (at the same time, the PRI lost four seats in the then sixty-four-seat Senate for the first time), the PRI found itself unable to act alone to alter the Constitution (which requires a two-thirds majority vote), forcing President Carlos Salinas (1988–1994) to negotiate and strike legislative bargains with the opposition, particularly the PAN. This tendency took a more decisive turn following the 1997 elections, when the PRI lost its absolute majority in the Chamber of Deputies (Figure 9.1). Though the PRI continues to be the largest party in the Chamber, the combined opposition holds enough votes to sway any legislative outcome. This turnabout further undercut presidential authority while enhancing legislative autonomy. Congress now began to debate and even alter presidential initiatives, initiate investigations into wrongdoing by members of the executive branch, and expose information about government operations and presidential politics that had long been kept under wraps. Today, the Congress and the president battle publicly over a range of policy matters, and the rules of engagement are not yet clear. Indeed, one of the big challenges facing the country is to work out the mechanics of executive-legislative relations. Within that context, many now see the prohibition on re-election in Congress at least as a measure that greatly weakens the institution, preventing it from developing the expertise needed to match presidential authority.

The Mexican Judiciary

Constitutionally, the Mexican judicial system includes the Supreme Court of Justice composed of 11 ministers, the circuit courts (*Tribunales Olegiados de Circuito, Tribunales Unitarios de Circuito*), district courts (*Juzgados de Distrito*), and, as of 1995, a Judiciary Board charged with carrying out the administrative duties of the courts. Like the legislature, however, the Mexican judiciary has historically played a limited role, subordinate to the president, though some change in recent years can be detected. Unlike the US, Mexico has a civil or Roman law system whereby judges do not have the power to "make law" through judicial

Figure 9.1
Party Composition of the Chamber of Deputies (1997–2000)

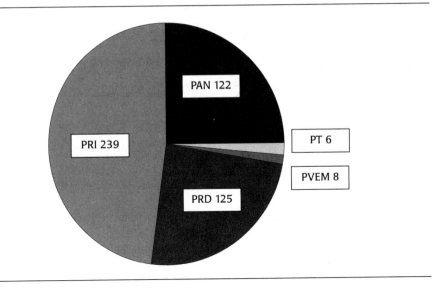

interpretation or "unmake law" by ruling on the constitutionality of laws or acts of government. This in itself weakens the court's power to check presidential authority. Judges do play a more extensive role in normal criminal and civil cases, however, working with public ministers (lawyers for the state) and defense attorneys to collect and present evidence, decide which laws might be applicable to a given situation and what evidence is relevant, and determine guilt or innocence and assign punishment. The fact that Mexican presidents have historically controlled judicial appointments and been able to bring about the votes in Congress to remove judges virtually at will has further undermined the power of the judicial branch.

Yet some things have changed on the judicial front in recent years. In 1995, Zedillo promoted a major reform of the judiciary that in theory strengthened the legal autonomy of the courts. The reform even allows the Supreme Court some power to rule on the constitutionality of laws if petitioned to do so by the attorney general or one-third of the legislature that passed the law in question. The reform also created a professional judicial council to handle lower-level appointments, the administrative aspects of the judicial branch, the professionalization of the courts, and the judiciary's budget. It is too early to tell the degree to which these reforms will truly alter the functioning of the Mexican judiciary, however.

One unique feature of the Mexican legal system is the *amparo*. Akin to an injunction, an **amparo** is an order issued by a judge that temporarily restrains or prevents the government from continuing a particular action against an individual or corporation. Within Mexico's highly legalistic context, such a device can be used—and abused—to protect individual rights. In fact, the amparo system has received both praise as a check on the power of government and criticism because of the corruption that enables the legal device to be employed to undermine the legitimate functions of the government and to enrich judges.

The Mexican Bureaucracy

Often characterized as inefficient and politicized, the many agencies and bureaus of the vast Mexican bureaucracy have limited political autonomy and yet enjoy a degree of power not found in the bureaucracies of most industrialized nations. First, Mexican bureaucrats have limited job security. There is no civil service system based on merit per se, though aspects of such a system do operate for the diplomatic corps, within the financial departments, and at the lowest levels of the government. This means that most bureaucrats serve at the pleasure of higher-ups and can be removed virtually at will. Even the bureaucrats' labor union is part of the PRI, thus restricting the bureaucrats' freedom. Within this politicized context, subordinates develop a strong loyalty to their superiors, as opposed to the organization or outside constituents, and tend to refer decisions upwards to the highest levels, thereby avoiding the risk of making a decision that might upset the higher-ups. Because almost all appointments are political and rooted in trust, there is also much turnover within the bureaucracy. One study, for instance, showed that about a third of government positions changed hands every six years, suggesting a complete turnover every eighteen years (Smith 1979). Of course, this turnover has occurred among supporters and members of the same political party.

Yet despite this lack of autonomy vis-à-vis the president, the Mexican bureaucracy has nonetheless enjoyed considerable power because of the prominent role of the Mexican state in society. Extensive regulations over the economy, social organizations, and everyday life in Mexico—reflecting the legalistic nature of Mexican society—enhance the power of bureaucrats and politicize the implementation of policy. With few concerns except satisfying the interests of their superiors, bureaucrats have long enjoyed extensive discretionary authority that can be used or abused according to their own personal and political interests. With few channels to influence public policy, individuals in society also focus on bureaucrats' discretionary power to try to alter what the government does. Both situations, of course, enhance the degree of inefficiency, corruption, and individualized policy solutions. Though presidents have often promised and even attempted piecemeal administrative reform, the Mexican bureaucracy has proved highly resistant to change and riddled by corruption.

One area of the Mexican bureaucracy that merits particular focus is the Federal Electoral Institute (**IFE**). Established in 1990 following intense political battles over elections and electoral fraud, the IFE organizes elections and implements laws regulating parties, campaigns, and the vote. In stark contrast to the past, when the PRI's representatives established and implemented the electoral rules to their own advantage, IFE now enjoys almost exclusive authority and autonomy in this all-important political realm. Unique among government institutions, IFE is run by a General Council composed of eight electoral "citizen" councillors nominated by the delegations of the political parties and approved by a two-thirds vote in the Chamber of Deputies. Though the parties and the legislature are represented on IFE's board of directors, only the citizen councillors have voting rights. For many, IFE represents a fourth branch of the government.

Federalism in Mexico

The Mexican Constitution mandates a federal system with the government in each of the nation's thirty-one states structured along the same lines as the federal government, though with a unicameral as opposed to bicameral legislature. Governors are elected to six-year terms and state legislators, representing a combination of district and proportional representation seats, serve for three years. The lowest administrative unit is the *municipio,* which resembles county governments in the US. The some 2,400 municipios in the country are run by a mayor or municipal president and a local assembly, all elected to three-year terms.

In theory, state and local governments have a certain degree of autonomy; however, in practice federalism has tended to take a back seat to a strong central government and presidency. Many of the functions assigned to state governments in the US, such as overseeing education and health care, are carried out by the federal government in Mexico. Moreover, state and local governments in Mexico have limited control over financial resources. The federal government takes in about 80 percent of all government revenues and from this transfers approximately 18 percent of total expenditures to the state/local governments. This concentration of fiscal power in the federal government weakens the capacity of state/local governments to develop their own programs or to pursue a policy line distinct from that of the federal government. The president's control over PRI nominations and his ability to use the PRI's congressional majority to remove governors also has restricted the autonomy of state and local governments. President Salinas, for example, removed a total of sixteen governors for a variety of reasons during his six-year term.

There have been some efforts in recent years to strengthen the role of state government, a tendency coinciding with the decline of the PRI and presidentialism. Moves to grant greater autonomy to municipal governments and decentralize such administrative tasks as education to the state level, for example, have shown some progress, but results have remained rather limited. At the same time, through such means as instituting a local property tax, some state and local governments have begun to tap into their own resources in an attempt to cut their reliance on federal funds, though again the impact has been quite limited. Perhaps the most important move in bolstering the autonomy of state and municipal governments has been the rise of opposition parties. Beginning in the early 1980s, the PAN began to win a string of municipal elections, particularly in the northern states, a trend capped by the party's first gubernatorial win and the PRI's first state-level loss in Baja California in 1989. Since then the PAN and the center-left PRD, in coalition with smaller parties, have won control of almost a third of the nation's states as well as some of the country's most important cities including Mexico City, Guadalajara, and Veracruz. As with the Congress, this turn of events has weakened the president's ability to dictate to state governments, forcing more negotiations and greater compromise, though the federal government still controls most of the purse strings.

Mexico City is a unique case. Until recently, the city administration was treated as a unit within the federal government, under the full authority of the president. The president appointed city officials, including the mayor and attorney general, while the federal Congress handled the city's laws and budget. Facing growing political pressures for greater representation in the 1980s, however, the government established a Representative Assembly to advise and oversee operations of the city. Subsequent reforms increased the assembly's role as a policy-making body and called for the popular election of a mayor or chief of government. In 1997, for the first time, the city elected its mayor, and though many of the administrative and decision-making functions remain in the hands of the federal government—in fact, the situation remains in a state of legal limbo—the reforms have strengthened the autonomy of the federal district. Now under the leadership of PRD leader Cárdenas, the Mexico City government represents an important base for the party to develop its skills at governing.

To summarize, many political changes have occurred within Mexico's institutional setting. Though the presidency is still the most powerful institution, it has relinquished some of its power to increasingly assertive and autonomous legislative and judicial branches and state governments. But the decline of the all-powerful presidency has also opened power vacuums and uncertainty as the details of executive-legislative, executive-judiciary, and intergovernmental relations in this new era have yet to be worked out. Today, these provide much of the fodder of political conflict.

The Actors in Mexican Politics: Elites, Parties, Groups, and Citizens

Elites and Political Recruitment

Since the Revolution, Mexican politics has remained an exclusive game among a political class whose members are loosely organized into informal networks and who bow to a set of informal political guidelines. As a general rule, patterns of political recruitment in any country tend to reflect the way the political system operates, and in Mexico this has long centered on the presidency, the electoral dominance of the PRI, and the absence of re-election. Though candidates for public office are formally selected by the party, the president has always played the dominant role in selecting PRI candidates, who until recently were virtually assured victory. For lower-level positions at the state level or for the Chamber of Deputies, the president might defer the power to others, but could intervene to shape the outcome if he wished. Many of the individuals selected to run on the PRI's ticket for office come from the party's many affiliated organizations. As part of the PRI's organization, officials of major labor unions or other social organizations who have demonstrated their abilities to abide by the rules of the political game and the capacity to deliver support to the PRI are rewarded with political office. Rarely, given the absence of re-election, do PRI candidates have strong local bases of support outside the party or their organizations.

The power of the president in recruitment extends all the way to the presidency itself: in a process known in Mexico as the **dedazo** (literally "big finger"), the outgoing president has been able to hand-pick his successor. Normally, the selection process begins more than a year prior to the general election as potential candidates vie for the president's attention while secretly engaging in a type of high-level back-stabbing. The president's/party's selection is usually announced at a party convention with party officials voting to confirm the "nomination." Historically, the person selected to run atop the PRI ticket has been a member of the cabinet and, as would be expected, a close associate of the outgoing president.

Studies of recruitment patterns in Mexico from 1884 to 1991 by Roderic Camp (1996) show the nation's top political officials during that time to have been somewhat of a homogenous bunch, though changes have occurred over the years. Military backgrounds predominated during the early years, but by the 1950s this was no longer the case and a true political class began to emerge. The majority of the country's top officials during the Institutionalized Period were middle-class males who had attended the national university and had climbed the ranks of the Mexican bureaucracy. Few of the top leaders followed electoral routes to power through either Congress or state and local governments. More recently, top government officials, often referred to as technocrats, have come disproportionately from the Mexico City area, pursued graduate degrees abroad, spent time in the financial/economic agencies of the federal government, and have accrued very limited electoral experience. In fact, none of Mexico's last three presidents had any electoral experience prior to running for the nation's top post. President Zedillo, for instance, received a graduate degree in economics from Yale and served in the Bank of Mexico, the Department of Programming and Budgeting, and a brief stint as Secretary of Education before being selected by outgoing President Salinas to lead the nation.

One distinctive feature in the workings of the political elite is the *camarilla*. As Camp (1996, 114) describes it, a **camarilla** is a "group of people who have political interests in common and rely on one another to improve their chances within the political leadership." Camarillas are essentially informal teams or networks of politicians who work together to pursue their political objectives and careers. The links extend well beyond one government agency and encompass generations of politicians. All successful politicians are members of of a camarilla, and these networks provide much of the fluidity of recruitment and continuity that characterizes Mexican politics. Loyalty holds these elite teams together as politicians carry their groups of supporters with them from one position to another.

Since so much is decided by those at the top, rising to the top in Mexican politics has meant participating in such teams and abiding by certain "informal" rules. As elaborated by Peter Smith (1979), the "informal," often "unwritten" rules of the system include the following: never openly criticize the president; once a decision is made by the president, support it; show loyalty to the party and practice a rhetoric based on the principles of the Revolution; all the spoils of power go to those within the PRI family; be patient and wait your turn to enjoy the spoils of power; do not try to undermine the system; and finally, the president must renounce any prospect of re-election.

Like other features of Mexican politics, recruitment methods and other rules of the game are changing, though slowly and in often unpredictable ways. Since being tapped as the PRI's candidate is no longer a guarantee of victory, the party has taken greater care in recent years to select individuals who are not only faithful to the system, but can mount an effective campaign and compete in more meaningful contests. More importantly, facing a decline in the party's appeal, some party activists have sought to curtail the power of the president to select the party's nominees for public office. Though no pattern has been firmly established, the PRI has experimented with using party conventions and open primaries to select their candidates, although in many cases the results have left many party members crying fraud and actually dropping out of the party in protest. Thus far, the efforts to reform the party's procedures for selecting candidates have created almost as many problems as they have resolved, pitting many of the party's technocrats against the traditional politicians known as the *políticos*. Some limitations have reached to the highest level. Reflecting serious factional splits, the party's rank-and-file pushed a series of measures in 1996 that restricted the president from simply naming his successor. The new rules require a selection process to be carried out and mandate that the candidate have some electoral experience. As part of this climate of change, President Zedillo has promised not to exercise the historic power of the dedazo: a move that has created a severe power vacuum at the top. As of this writing, the PRI planned to hold a national primary in November 1999 to select among a list of pre-candidates. While some see the process as bringing a degree of internal democracy to the party, many others believe the president has a "favored" candidate: a type of disguised dedazo. What is clear is that internal turmoil has replaced much of the stable elite game that once characterized the PRI.

Within the opposition parties, whose members now occupy important positions in the federal Congress and at the state and local levels, recruitment patterns are somewhat distinct from those found within the presidency and the PRI. Reflecting their key constituencies, PAN representatives tend to have backgrounds in the world of business, while PRD officials trace their roots to the PRI or to the array of social organizations providing the base of PRD's support. Many members of the PRD are teachers, leaders of independent unions, or administrators of NGOs (non-governmental organizations). Generally, the candidate selection procedures of opposition parties are more open than those of the PRI. The PAN, in particular, has substantial experience conducting democratic party conventions to select candidates, often touting these as "lessons in democracy" for the PRI. The younger PRD has also experimented with conventions, local primaries, and even allowing non-party members, or social candidates, to run on the PRD ticket, though factional divisions and accusations of fraud plague the PRD.

For most of this century, the nation's economic elite has remained separate from the political class, although the distinctions are beginning to blur somewhat. Because of the extreme levels of inequality and the structure of Mexican business, the nation's economic elite includes a relatively small cohort of the leaders of large economic groups with vast industrial and financial holdings throughout the country. Respecting an unwritten accord with the government, the economic elite has generally shied away from the political mainstream and sought to influence policy from behind the scenes, usually through corporate-based negotiations or bargaining directly with the executive. Until recently, the government has kept its side of the bargain by ensuring stability and a propitious business climate.

Parties and Elections

As in most societies, parties have played a critical role in the political life of Mexico. They have helped educate citizens, recruit and train leaders, mobilize voters, formulate solutions to the nation's problems, and govern. Nevertheless, Mexican parties have been unique in many ways, primarily because of the PRI and its incredible hold on power. Created by President Calles as a device to resolve disputes among the revolutionary elite and ensure their continuation in power, the PRI was designed not to compete for power but rather to protect it. For decades the party has totally dominated the electoral scene, winning virtually every contest and securing almost monopolistic control over the government.

The Role of the PRI. *A number of factors have contributed to the PRI's incredible record. First, from its beginnings, the party has striven to be inclusive and to incorporate important groups, offering them a means to express their demands in exchange for the opportunity to partake in the spoils of power.* Initially, the party brought together the revolutionary elite: local strongmen, revolutionary generals, the military, and the political class. Later, under President Cárdenas, the party expanded to incorporate the nation's major labor unions, peasant leagues, and popular organizations, giving it the corporatist structure that it relies on today. Such a strategic move not only expanded the party's representation, but also undercut the ability of other political parties or organizations to mobilize these interests against the government. As shown in Figure 9.2, the PRI is not a true party of individuals, but rather a party of affiliated organizations grouped since 1946 into three broad sectors: labor, peasant, and popular wings. Workers, for instance, who must join the labor union where they work, become a part of the PRI by virtue of belonging to the union. From this organizational framework, leaders of the many affiliated organizations represent a pool from which the party selects its candidates for office, relying on their organizations to help mobilize the rank-and-file and deliver the vote to the PRI. To keep the rank-and-file happy, the government has used these organizational channels to distribute the fruits of economic prosperity and to implement public policy.

A second contribution to the PRI's long success has been the regime's ideology. An outgrowth of the ideals of the Mexican Revolution, the party has long stressed the progressive principles of social justice, equality, the struggle of labor against capital, land reform, and nationalism. With strands of anti-Church, anti-business, and anti-foreign sentiments thrown in, the PRI's ideology virtually defined and represented the interests of the nation itself. Even if the government failed to realize the lofty goals of the Revolution, the party nonetheless represented those ideals and the nation. The sheer ideological strength and nationalist charm of the party conveniently undercut the appeal of other parties or the regime's opponents, whom the PRI labeled anti-Revolutionary and, hence, anti-Mexican.

Figure 9.2
The PRI's Corporate Structure

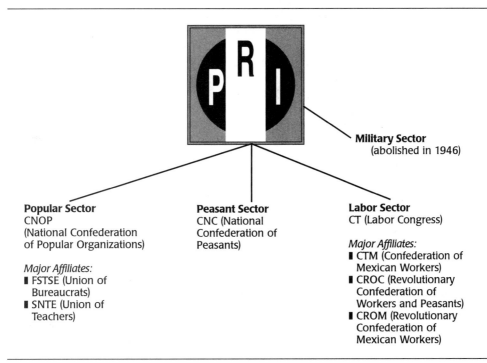

Military Sector
(abolished in 1946)

Popular Sector
CNOP
(National Confederation
of Popular Organizations)

Major Affiliates:
▮ FSTSE (Union of
Bureaucrats)
▮ SNTE (Union of
Teachers)

Peasant Sector
CNC (National
Confederation of
Peasants)

Labor Sector
CT (Labor Congress)

Major Affiliates:
▮ CTM (Confederation of
Mexican Workers)
▮ CROC (Revolutionary
Confederation of
Workers and Peasants)
▮ CROM (Revolutionary
Confederation of
Mexican Workers)

A third factor promoting the PRI's ability to maintain power derives from the party's unique relationship to the government. Through a variety of mechanisms, the government, controlled by members of the PRI, crafted and manipulated policy to favor the PRI, helping to ensure its electoral dominance. The government, for instance, backed the founding and funding of small parties in the 1950s and 1960s that supported the PRI (referred to as satellite parties) to help give the appearance of democracy and water down the presence of the true opposition; it routinely dismissed allegations of fraud directed at the PRI; and it drew electoral districts in ways that played on the PRI's strengths. Similarly, the government incorporated and rewarded PRI-affiliated organizations, such as labor unions, making life difficult for "independent" unions. This usually made PRI affiliation beneficial to those abiding by the rules of the game, despite the lack of autonomy or internal democracy. The government also provided substantial financial, human, and material resources, including its controls over the media, to enable the PRI to run massive and effective campaigns. This, of course, gave the PRI a further edge over any competitor.

Though the government favored the PRI and the PRI provided the personnel for the government, it is important to distinguish "rule by the party" from "rule over the party." In contrast to the old Soviet Union or China, in which the Communist Party effectively controlled the government and determined policy ("rule by the party"), Mexico's PRI has never truly controlled the Mexican government, made policy, or selected the nation's leaders. Instead, the PRI has been controlled by the Mexican president, who has employed the party as an electoral machine to discipline the political elite and mobilize popular support for the government ("rule over the party"). In short, it has been the president, rather than the PRI, who has shaped policy and picked the nation's leaders. So while the PRI has dominated the electoral scene in Mexico, it has remained somewhat weak outside the electoral arena.

Of course, this creates a paradox—a dominant party participating in a democratic game—and raises questions for the various participants. For opponents, why compete in a game that is, in a large sense, rigged? For citizens, why vote if the outcome is a foregone conclusion? And for members of the PRI, how is it possible to bow to the ideals of democracy and yet participate in a system that is anything but democratic? To answer these questions, it is important to recognize the underlying tensions this basic paradox has created in Mexico. The opposition faces the dilemma of whether to promote change from within the system or from outside it. The government, meanwhile, must try to balance the need to maintain "democratic" legitimacy against the need to protect its "authoritarian" power.

Elections and the Role of Opposition Parties. Because the constitution sets up a democracy and the government calls itself democratic, elections must be held, and opposition parties must be allowed to participate. It is within this context that opposition parties have long been allowed to exist in Mexico, although they have clearly faced an uphill battle. In a sense, the opposition was allowed to participate, but not to win. This meant that over the years opposition parties have had to struggle on two fronts: push the government to abide by the rules of democracy and play fair, and try to gain votes. Among the first parties to carve out an independent course and contest the PRI and the government was the PAN. Founded in 1939 in opposition to the left-leaning policies of Cárdenas, the PAN attracted a modicum of support among the emerging middle class, particularly in the northern and western portions of the country. Since its inception, the PAN has mounted public campaigns challenging the government to make elections fair and eliminate fraud, engaging in protests designed to expose the regime's failings and raise questions about the system's democratic credentials. It has at various times boycotted elections, boycotted Congress, and organized public protests to expose fraud, some of which have even turned violent. To maintain its democratic legitimacy and keep the upper hand in the face of these constant pressures, the government has had to offer reforms that would open the system, but it has done this slowly, reluctantly, and in a manner it could control. Eventually, however, these changes would gradually set the stage for the PAN to take some of the PRI's power by either winning an election outright or by mounting sufficient pressures to force the government to recognize its victories. During the 1980s, and amidst widespread discontent over the economic crisis, the PAN won a host of state and local elections. This trend, whereby pressures would stimulate electoral reforms, followed by more opposition wins, continued through the 1990s.

Besides facing pressures from the PAN, the government also faced the problem of abstentionism. Why should people vote if the outcome is known beforehand and the process is clearly unfair? By the 1960s many failed to see a reason to vote, and more people stayed home on election day than voted for the PRI. Since this, too, undermined the legitimacy of the PRI's hold on power, the government dealt with abstentionism by changing the rules to ensure greater participation by opposition parties (helping to give the appearance of competition) and to reduce fraud. Among many changes, the government established seats in Congress for the opposition parties based on a system of proportional representation. This ensured parties a minor say in government and more importantly their participation in the elections, providing voters an outlet for their political emotions. The competition, in turn, gave greater meaning to the government's claims of democracy, but without really threatening the PRI's hold on power.

Among the various reforms, the political/electoral reform of 1977 legalized a number of independent leftist parties. The measure not only helped the government bolster its democratic credentials but it did so while diluting the opposition within

Political Parties of Mexico

Major Parties

PRI (Institutional Revolutionary Party). Founded in 1929 as the PNR (National Revolutionary Party), the PRI became an all-encompassing, umbrella party incorporating a broad range of interests, ideas, and individuals. Yet, because of its subordination to the president, the PRI lacks independence and autonomy. Officially, the PRI represents the ideals of the Mexican Revolution, though each president has tended to stress certain ideals while downplaying others. The party's corporatist structure encompasses large segments of the nation's poor, while the stability the party guarantees has helped it maintain the support of much of the nation's economic elite. The PRI still holds the greatest number of seats in Congress and a majority of governorships. As of this writing, Francisco Labastida Ochoa was campaigning as the party's presidential candidate for the 2000 election.

PAN (National Action Party). Founded in 1939 in opposition to the leftist policies of President Cárdenas, the PAN has long posed the strongest challenge to the PRI. Though incorporating principles of Christian democracy in the early years, the party considers itself today a center-right organization emphasizing democratic political reform and a pro-business economic platform. The party draws particularly well among the middle class, business, and conservatives, and enjoys its greatest levels of support in the northern and western states. As of early 1999, the PAN held governorships in five states (Aguascalientes, Baja California, Guanajuato, Jalisco, and Nuevo Leon), and in one state (Nayarit) in a broad coalition of opposition parties. With Vicente Fox as its candidate, the PAN has a chance of unseating the PRI in 2000.

PRD (Party of the Democratic Revolution). The PRD was formed in 1989 in a political alliance that brought together an array of small independent leftist parties and dissident members of the PRI. A large part of its success stems from the popularity of Cárdenas who, along with others, broke from the PRI in 1987. The PRD classifies itself as center-left, opposes the government's neoliberal economic policies, though the party does not support a socialist platform, and often engages in confrontational tactics to pressure the government for political reform. The party draws support from the nation's poor and working-class sectors and enjoys its greatest support in Mexico City and the poorer states of the south. As of early 1999, the PRD held the important post of Mexico City mayor and governorships in three states (Baja California Sur, Tlaxcala, and Zacatecas), and in one state (Nagarit) in a broad coalition of opposition parties. As he has for the past two contests, Cardenas will lead the PRD ticket for the 2000 election.

Minor Parties

PT (Workers Party). The PT was formed in 1990 by local political groups primarily in the states of Chihuahua, Durango, and Zacatecas. It promotes popular mobilization, and its platform calls for a socialist, pluralist, and democratic society. It has regional strength in the central state of Durango and has worked in coalition with the PRD at times.

PVEM (Mexican Ecologist Green Party). Beginning as the Mexican Green Party (PVM) in 1986, the PVEM was founded in 1993. The PVEM represents an ideological movement with a social base interested in the preservation of nature and the environment. It draws much of its support from the Mexico City area.

the PAN: a strategy of divide and conquer. Though the emergence of the new parties provided a legal and peaceful channel for leftist opponents, thereby weakening the appeal of guerrilla or terrorist routes to change that had emerged in the early 1970s, such parties drew only minimal support. This situation changed in 1988 when much of the left united behind the candidacy of Cuauhtémoc Cárdenas following his departure from the PRI. In a stunning and controversial outcome, Cárdenas officially received 38 percent of the vote in the fraud-marred election. One year later, Cárdenas established the PRD, formally uniting an array of leftist factions and former members of the PRI.

As electoral trends indicate (see Figure 9.3), support for the PRI has slowly waned as support for the opposition has waxed. Today, the PRI, PAN, and PRD, along with a few minor parties, compete in elections that tend to be freer and fairer than in the past, thanks to the reforms in the mid-1990s that established an autonomous IFE. Table 9.1 also depicts this growing competitiveness, showing the number of competitive electoral seats in the country. Over a short period of time, the majority of electoral districts have gone from being controlled fully by the PRI to

Figure 9.3
Electoral Trends: The Decline of the PRI

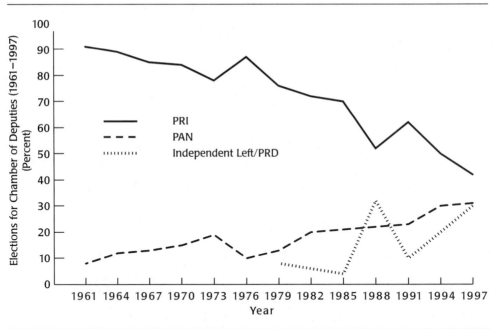

being competitive. But as Joseph Klesner (n.d.) indicates, Mexico does not yet have a truly three-party system, but rather a segmented two-party system. The PRI and PAN compete in certain areas of the country, and the PRI and PRD battle in other parts. Generally, the PAN enjoys its greatest strength in the northern and western states and in the Yucatan, while the PRD draws well in the south and Mexico City area. Though the combined strength of the opposition is greater than that of the PRI, the PRI remains the strongest party nationwide and is still the only party that effectively covers the entire country.

The three major political parties differ not only in their geographic and social bases, but also in their ideals. Though historically the PRI has represented a position somewhat on the left emphasizing nationalism and supporting the interests of peasants and workers, since the 1980s the party has shifted its focus to a center-right position stressing free market reforms, a dismantling of the state, promotion of business interests, and economic integration with the US. The ideological shift has created divisions within the party, prompting many of the party's left-wing members to either leave the party to join the ranks of the PRD or challenge the president's authority internally. Ideologically the PAN has long emphasized the principles of democracy and good government, calling for an end to political corruption. It favors free-market economics, paying special attention to the interests of small and medium-sized businesses, and has historically represented traditional Catholic and conservative values. The PRD, by contrast, occupies the center-left position along the ideological spectrum, though like the PRI it promotes a range of ideals. The PRD stresses capitalism with a more human face, emphasizing social justice, equality, and the interests of the "popular class" (a term that refers to the large working and poor classes in Latin America).

Interestingly, this overall mix of goals often finds the PAN siding with the PRI on economic questions while working with the PRD on political matters. In recent years, for instance, PAN–PRI coalitions have been instrumental in passing many of the major economic reforms, while PAN–PRD cooperation in Congress helped to strip the PRI of its control of the institution. Extensive talks were held in 1999 to

Table 9.1
The Rise of Electoral Competitiveness
Federal Electoral Districts by Number of Parties Competing (1979–1997)

Number of Parties (Index)	1979	1985	1991	1997
Tripartite (3-party) (PRI v. PAN v. PRD)	0	3	1	56
Plural Bipartisan (PRI v. others combined)	5	27	20	112
Pure Bipartisan (PRI v. PAN or PRI v. PRD)	53	71	92	107
Hegemonic (non-competitive) (PRI only)	242	199	187	25
TOTAL	300	300	300	300

Source: Klesner (n.d.).

create a PAN–PRD electoral coalition for the 2000 presidential election. However, the attempt failed and the two parties backed their own presidential candidates. Such a "showdown" could spell the end of the PRI's long reign.

Recent developments such as these present broad challenges to all three of the major parties. The PAN and the PRD wrestle with the problems associated with their rapid growth, ranging from organizational challenges to those related to moving from being the opposition to running or co-running the government. The PRI faces even more formidable tasks. Though it is still the best organized and best financed party, it faces the challenges of arresting its declining popularity, maintaining the support of the traditional corporate sectors, and competing in freer and fairer elections. As a result of these pressures, divisions have erupted within the PRI and discipline has eroded as competing factions battle for control of the party. Critical of the government and the party's shift to the right since the mid-1980s, many party leaders have sought to restrict the president's control over the PRI and to force the party to reassert its more traditional ideological roots. Given the stakes, this internal struggle has come to center on the critical battle over selection of the party's presidential candidate for 2000. In late 1999, the PRI conducted an internal primary to select its presidential candidate for the 2000 election. Initial indications suggest that this unprecedented move helped ease the internal divisions and bickering within the party and garner a measure of popular legitimacy.

Pressure Groups and Politics in Mexico

Groups provide much of the raw material of politics. Traditionally, most Mexican organizations have been tied to the system through official or unofficial mechanisms—a feature that adds to the system's authoritarian credentials. Such organizational links may be with the PRI, with the government, or both; but the basic corporatist structure has long allowed the government to restrict the freedom of social organizations and to control social mobilization. Yet, as in other areas, recent political changes have spawned new groups and actors, new rules and procedures, and new issues and problems.

Groups Controlled by the PRI and the Government. **Corporatism** refers to *a formalized system of bargaining between the state and state-designated or controlled organizations. As part of this arrangement, organizations exercise control over their particular domains but lose a degree of autonomy.* Different levels within this corporatist

President Ernesto Zedillo addresses a gathering of the ruling PRI, calling for reforms within the party.

structure can be noted. At one level, as outlined in our discussion of the elite and the PRI, a number of organizations are fastened to the official party, the PRI. Labor, peasant, and popular organizations, as shown in Figure 9.2 above, form the base of the PRI, gaining representation for their organizations in return for following the rules of the party. At another level, corporatism finds the government (rather than the PRI) incorporating privileged organizations into policy-making arrangements. The government, for example, places representatives of the major labor confederations on local labor arbitration and conciliation boards and similar agencies that implement labor and social policy. Such agencies not only rule on the legality of strikes, internal union politics, and the distribution of funds for housing and other social programs, but they act in ways that favor and hence reward organizations that support the president and the party.

Labor unions and popular organizations coalesce within the PRI, while organizations outside the PRI's reach have traditionally been tied to the government through a variety of techniques, facilitating government control. Government-mandated entities such as the CONCANACO (Confederation of National Chambers of Commerce), CANACINTRA (National Chamber of Industries of Transformation[4]), CONCAMIN (Confederation of Chambers of Industry), and the ABM (Mexican Bankers Association), for instance, have offered a framework for government-business bargaining, while the government's extensive controls over the economy provided it with the wherewithal to discipline business demands. Facing the need to secure government licenses for virtually everything or a market structured by government-controlled enterprises, most businesses recognize the importance of cooperation. The government has often used these corporatist channels and controls to

[4]"Transformation" normally referred to industries that enjoyed government assistance in some way or were beneficiaries of the government's industrialization policy.

hammer out public policy, consulting both labor and business to work out the details of policy. Indeed, with Congress historically insignificant, policy has centered on such corporatist-based arrangements.

Government controls (sometimes subtle, sometimes not) over social organizations can also be seen with respect to the press. Though the Constitution calls for a free press, the government has historically limited that freedom using a variety of mechanisms. For the visual media, the government is in charge of granting the concessions, thus ensuring that the nation's major television stations are held by supporters of the PRI-led government. The major television network, *Televisa,* for instance, once a virtual monopoly, was created by a government concession in the 1950s to two families with close ties to the ruling elite. Even *Televisa's* main competitor today, *Television Azteca,* emerged as the result of a government auction in the 1990s. Governmental controls over the written press have included everything from the placement of government advertisements (a critical source of revenue for the press) and the government's subsidized sale of imported newsprint, to under-the-table payments to journalists for favorable coverage. Though such controls have historically nurtured self-censorship within the press, the government has also occasionally applied strong-arm tactics to remove recalcitrant editors or outright repression to destroy forays into opposition journalism.

"Independent" organizations such as "unofficial" labor unions exist, but since they do not enjoy "favors" from the government, their ability to provide benefits to their members has remained limited. In addition, such organizations have often suffered outright repression. A wave of strikes in the late 1950s, led by the electrical workers' union, for example, ended with the military arresting strikers. The government used a similar tactic to cripple the massive protests led by students in 1968 and by teachers in the 1970s. Historically, repression has been used to discourage the creation and activities of "unofficial" organizations that seek influence outside the normal corporatist channels or seek to instill democratic reforms within the PRI-controlled organizations. Labor's struggle to democratize the official unions tied to the PRI, for instance, has proved particularly difficult over the years.

Nevertheless, recent political changes have opened some political space for social organizations while at the same time raising the political costs to the government of outright repression. Though the nation's major labor organizations remain shackled to the PRI, some independent labor unions have emerged in the 1990s to challenge the "official" unions and the government. Following the death of long-time leader of the Confederation of Mexican Labor (CTM) Fidel Velázquez in 1997 (he had held power for more than forty years) the UNT (National Workers Union) was founded, incorporating important unions such as the telephone workers and calling for an end to authoritarian and corporatist controls over labor. Business organizations have similarly become more active politically since the 1980s, exerting their independence and influence. Facing economic decline and economic policies detrimental to their interests, big business launched the CCE (Coordinating Council of Enterprises) and COPARMEX (Employers Council) to better represent their interests in dealings with the government. Breaking the nonpolitical pattern of the past, these organizations actually began to channel some support to the PAN. Presidents de la Madrid, Salinas, and Zedillo were able to stem this trend only by embracing a series of economic measures favorable to big business. Even the press in recent years has sometimes eluded government controls, becoming more independent and critical of the PRI and the government.

The Rise of NGOs. Other societal organizations have also blossomed in recent years, further hastening the nation's move from authoritarian corporatism to pluralist democracy. Fueled by the economic decline of the times, the earthquake of 1985, and the fraudulent election of 1988, in particular, a range of **NGOs** (*non-governmental organizations*) have emerged to play ever more important roles in training citizens, channeling popular demands for political change, and asserting vigilance over the government in the areas of human rights, elections, and the environment. Since 1991, organizations such as Civic Alliance have lobbied for electoral reform, monitored polling places on election day, coordinated quick counts to help expose "unbelievable" results, and collected and disseminated data on the media's treatment of the parties. In 1994, Civic Alliance coordinated more than 83,000 election observers, including more than 900 foreign observers. In the area of human rights, similar social organizations have emerged to monitor the government's progress. In 1994, more than 200 human rights organizations operated throughout the country, employing the national and international media to expose human rights abuses and pressure the government for action. Such organizations are playing an ever-increasing role in raising citizen consciousness and involvement while checking the power of government.

Guerrillas. In recent years, the political scene has been rocked by the emergence of guerrilla/political organizations. In 1994, the **EZLN** took control of a handful of local towns in the southern state of Chiapas. Violence soon gave way to a cease-fire and negotiations, but the talks broke down in 1996 after the government backtracked on a deal brokered by a congressional delegation. In 1996, the *Ejército Popular Revolucionaria* (EPR) emerged, carrying out a series of attacks on official targets in the states of Oaxaca and Guerrero. Although these organizations struggle through primarily political channels to pressure government for political change, particularly the rights of peasants and the indigenous, the presence of these groups has led to the growing militarization of these regions, spawning government-supported paramilitary organizations and triggering repression. Clashes among supporters of these organizations, often in alliance with the PRD, and supporters of the PRI have become all too common. Authorities have reacted particularly harshly to members and suspected members of the EPR. In September 1996, for example, the government carried out a series of raids in San Augustin Loxicha, detaining 127 people and carrying out illegal searches, torture, and five executions.

Drug Traffickers. A different challenge emerges from drug organizations. According to estimates by the US State Department, the portion of cocaine entering the US through Mexico went from around 10 percent in the mid-1980s to about 70 percent a decade later as Colombian cartels turned to Mexico as a major port of entry. In addition, it is estimated that 20 to 30 percent of the heroin consumed in the US and 80 percent of the imported marijuana comes from Mexico. Estimates of Mexico's earnings from the drug trade range from $7 billion to $30 billion a year. Through corruption, violence, and the threat of violence, drug trafficking organizations have come to enjoy significant influence over government officials and government policy, operating with virtual impunity in various parts of the country. Reflecting the growing influence of the drug cartels in the 1990s, Mexicans have begun to use terms such as "narco-democracy," "narco-politicos," and "narco-violence" in their daily lexicon. Combined with the changes noted earlier, the drug trade further weakens the nation's political institutions and seriously undermines social order.

Citizens and Politics in Mexico

Given the unique nature of the Mexican political system, citizens have historically been politically active, but usually in tightly controlled government or PRI-sponsored

In a US-owned garment factory just over the Texas border, a Mexican worker assembles designer clothing.

activities. The government, for instance, supported the formation of peasant organizations and labor unions, sponsoring marches and mobilizing the rank and file to manifest their support for government policy. Even in the face of opposition pressures during late 1980s and early 1990s, the government, through a program called Solidarity, organized citizens to tackle development problems. The government donated materials, while the local organizations provided the labor (and presumably votes for the PRI in appreciation). As might be expected, the PRI has played a particularly strong role in mobilizing citizen participation. Tapping into its extensive organizational network, the PRI has periodically orchestrated national campaigns to rejuvenate the people's faith in the system and PRI-led change. In one example of this pattern, official unions (those affiliated with the PRI) have always staged massive marches on May Day (Labor Day) capped by speeches and cheers praising the benefits of economic prosperity and the stability fathered by the PRI.

Citizens' Rights. Extensive inclusion of citizens in the government and the PRI has helped ensure a degree of social control and arguably even reduced the need for repression, but the power of the government-PRI alliance has left individual citizens with few means to protect themselves against political abuse. Repression, abuses, and impunity have prevailed, and individuals facing repression or extortion by police have had almost no effective recourse. Even when clear evidence of governmental wrongdoing surfaces, whether in terms of corruption or repression, those responsible for the abuse have rarely been prosecuted.

Paradoxically, recent political changes have opened the way for both greater citizen involvement and more abuses. Citizens now actively participate in opposition parties and social organizations, they are better informed, and they are far more likely today to challenge the government and stand up for their rights. Yet, perhaps because of the heightened conflict and the power vacuums hastened by the erosion of old institutions, evidence points to a rise in the abuse of human rights by the government.

As documented by national and international human rights organizations, police, military, and paramilitary forces have been responsible for the torture, disappearance, and deaths of hundreds of citizens in recent years. The PRD claims that 580 militants of the party have been killed since the party's inception in 1989, particularly in states such as Guerrero where PRI and PRD supporters often face off in violent struggles. According to *Systemic Injustice,* a 1999 report by Human Rights Watch,

> Torture, "disappearances," and extrajudicial executions remain widespread in Mexico despite numerous legal and institutional reforms…[This reflects] the justice system's ineffective protection of individual guarantees and its lax approach to human rights abuses.

The Role of Women. Generally, official politics continues to be a male-dominated game in Mexico. Only three women have served in the Cabinet (the highest-ranking female official is Rosario Green, the current Secretary of Foreign Relations) and three have served as state governors. Women are often involved in social movements and popular organizations, however, particularly organizations that seek to provide support to the poor. In many indigenous communities, women play a major role in running commerce. Although women enjoy legal and constitutionally mandated equality, many civil codes still maintain male marital power, and the general culture continues to view the family as the woman's primary responsibility. The drop in the average number of children per family from six to fewer than three during the past two decades, combined with economic crisis, has prompted more women to enter the work force. Mexican women now constitute 35 percent of the work force but are generally paid less than males and work overwhelmingly in the service sector, particularly in education, health services, and family care. Women continue to constitute a majority of the work force in the **maquiladora** or *assembly-plant sector of the economy,* where they receive low wages and face various types of discrimination such as forced pregnancy exams (Fernandez Poncela 1996).

The Context of Mexican Politics: Culture, Economics and International Interdependence

The Culture of Mexican Politics

Mexican Nationalism. Prior to the Mexican Revolution, one could hardly speak of a Mexican nation. No common identity or sense of belonging prevailed; rough terrain and limited communications separated regions of the country; indigenous communities were isolated from the mainstream mestizo society; and class and racial divisions were well defined. The Revolution and the cultural programs that followed in the 1920s and 1930s changed much of that. In what was dubbed by President Calles as a "cultural revolution," the government sponsored public education, commissioned public murals by artists such as Diego Rivera, and developed a rhetoric that instilled a sense of unity and a common ideology. Since that time, Mexicans have felt a strong sense of national identity and pride in being Mexican. Much of that common identity is rooted in shared ethnic/religious/cultural values and manifests itself in a sense of pride in *mestizaje,* or the people's mixed European/indigenous ancestry. Part of this, as noted earlier, involves positive images of the nation's indigenous past and a reverence for the Virgin of Guadalupe. Identity rooted in ethnicity ensures unity by downplaying class differences. Mexican nationalism also incorporates a civic/historical component represented by social and economic ideals and principles of the Revolution. This includes belief in the rights of peasants to own the land they work and workers to share in the fruits of their labor, a preference for an activist state charged with the task of defending the rights of the nation against foreigners, and strong feelings that the Church, business, and foreigners should stay out of politics.

A critical component informing Mexico's political culture and the ideology of the Mexican Revolution is the perception of mistreatment and threat from the US. History has taught Mexico to remain cautious and suspicious of its extremely powerful neighbor to the north, a posture reflected in the popular Mexican saying attributed to Porfirio Diaz: "Poor Mexico, So Far from God, So Close to the US." This defensive attitude shapes Mexican foreign policy and has made national unity more urgent. According to analysis by Jorge Castañeda (Pastor and Castañeda 1989, 28), the prime lesson contained in Mexico's history textbooks is that "the nation is lost, easily dominated by the Americans, when it is divided."

For years, most Mexicans shared these views, creating a strong sense of unity. Although the government failed to realize its Revolutionary objectives, as we have seen, at least the populace agreed on what the objectives should be. But as in other areas, recent changes have challenged the foundations of the nation's identity and many of the tenets of the Revolution. Economic reforms since the 1980s have not only replaced the more revolutionary programs designed to protect the workers and the peasants, but have strengthened ties to the US and business—groups previously excluded from the ideological equation. By challenging past thinking, NAFTA and the sale of state-owned enterprises have raised questions about the nature of Mexican nationalism and the goals and objectives of the state. Consequently, many see the current leadership as "selling out" the country, while others express concerns that closer ties to the US threaten the nation's cultural identity. In a similar vein, the Zapatista guerrillas pose questions about the situation of the nation's indigenous. Current-day Indians are demanding that their languages and cultures be respected, thereby challenging past notions of national unity and disrupting traditional perceptions of being Mexican. The idea of multiculturalism seems oddly out of place in a country that has long considered itself unified both racially and culturally. By exposing new divisions and debates and by weakening the foundations of political agreement and cooperation, these cultural trends complicate the current political transition.

Beyond issues of national identity, Mexican political culture is also noted for attitudes of mistrust and cynicism toward the government and politicians, and an underlying desire for political and democratic change. While institutions such as the family and the Church tend to enjoy positive ratings, few trust the government. Popular evaluations of unions, Congress, and the police are particularly negative. Within this context, Mexicans harbor a clear desire for political change, greater levels of democracy, and a more prominent role for opposition parties in the government, and popular opinion supports peaceful and gradual change. In many ways, such views bode well for Mexico's emerging democracy, though the lack of trust and low levels of respect for political institutions suggest that the country still has a long way to go to make democracy work.

Mexico's Social Values. On a much broader plane, Mexican culture stresses the importance of personal relationships, the family, hierarchy, and Catholicism. Mexicans attach an almost spiritual importance to nurturing human relationships, downplaying materialism. As a result, needs involving human relations generally take precedence and greater emphasis is placed on the humanistic pursuits of philosophy, literature, and the arts than on other subjects. Mexicans consider the bonds of family sacred, and family members tend to rely upon one another for personal advancement more than in the US. Within both the family and society as a whole, Mexicans also stress hierarchy.

A Sample of Public Opinion in the 1990s

- 76 percent are "very proud" of being Mexican.*

- 12 percent said others respect the law "a lot," 42 percent said others respect the law "sometimes," 31 percent said others respect the law "a little." *

- Percent expressing positive evaluations of select social institutions:*

Family	84	Church	62	Schools	60
Congress	16	Unions	14	Police	12

- 51 percent felt the government should change its ideals, while 30 percent believed that the government should continue to support the ideals of the Revolution.***

- 76 percent disagreed with the idea of priests talking politics during religious services.***

- 53 percent said Mexico today is worse than when their parents grew up; 22 percent said today's Mexico is better.*

- 34 percent felt their vote would be respected; 34 percent said it would not.*

- 88 percent said corruption is widespread; 77 percent agreed that corruption prevails because the guilty go unpunished; and 58 percent disagreed with the statement that the current government was doing a lot to combat corruption.*

- 20 percent expressed "trust" in the US; 50 percent "distrusted" the US.****

- 69 percent considered foreign influence in the area of music and arts as positive; 36 percent labeled foreign influence in economics and finance as positive.*

Sources: * Gutierrez Vivó (1998); **Este País* (August 1991); ***Beltran, et al. (1997); ****Inglehart, et al. (1996).

Authority and respect in Mexico are usually to tied to one's position, and titles are used frequently to indicate prestige and status. Finally, Mexicans are solidly Catholic, though far fewer attend Church on a regular basis. Owing to historic conflict and the resulting constitutional restrictions, the Church has played a very limited political role in the country, though it has occasionally spoken out against human rights abuses and electoral fraud. In 1991, President Salinas reformed Church-State relations, recognizing the Vatican and allowing Catholic Church officials to participate more actively in politics. Some Church officials have become important figures in promoting political change in the southern part of the country. Bishop Samuel Ruiz, for instance, mediated the conflict with the Zapatistas in Chiapas. With the path now clear, the political role of the Church should increase in years to come.

Political Economy

In Mexico, as in most developing countries, the economy is the most significant influence on politics. For Mexico, political stability coincided with a period of solid economic development and growth that lasted for decades. Mexico enjoyed a growth rate averaging 6 percent per year from roughly the 1940s to mid-1970s. During this time, known as the "Mexican Miracle," the country moved from being an illiterate agrarian society relying on the exportation of products such as silver, cattle, and coffee to an urban, literate society producing a range of industrial goods for domestic consumption. Standards of living rose, and people began to enjoy opportunities and wealth unknown to their parents.

A policy package known as **import substitution industrialization** guided this period of prosperity. Seeking industrialization, the government, among other measures, imposed high tariffs to discourage imports and promote domestic production, channeled funds through state-controlled development banks into infrastructure and industrial development, offered incentives to encourage foreign companies to set up shop in Mexico, kept taxes low to promote the growth of business, and even controlled the demands of labor to help reduce the costs of doing business. As a complement to the large and growing private sector, the government owned and operated numerous companies: oil and gas, electric power, transportation, telephone, and eventually even steel, chemicals, and vehicle producers, often providing their products at subsidized prices to private business.

Political stability was both a contributor to and a byproduct of Mexico's prosperity. Political stability allowed the government to target resources to economic development, while economic growth supplied the government with resources to reward its supporters, particularly labor and other organizations tied to the PRI, and to keep business satisfied with the political arrangement. Though some expressed concern about corruption or democracy, economic growth helped ensure the legitimacy needed to paper over the cracks—clear proof that the PRI and the government, Mexico's unique political alliance, provided good things for some of the people. Even though widespread poverty persisted and the gap between the nation's few rich and many poor remained wide, at least the trends and the prospect for change remained, nurturing the hope that the lives of all would someday improve. The policies of import substitution, moreover, solidified a coalition among labor, business, and the government while providing government with many sticks and carrots to help maintain the allegiance of its coalition partners.

By 1976, however, prosperity and the state-business-labor alliance it sustained began to break down, giving way to periodic economic crises that would threaten popular support for the PRI and government and fuel political conflict and change. Facing huge trade deficits and demands for social programs, the Mexican government borrowed heavily during the 1970s, expanding the size and reach of the state. This debt-led strategy maintained growth for a few years, bolstered in large measure by the government's discovery of significant reserves of petroleum which it sought to develop at an almost break-neck pace using even more foreign loans, but global economic conditions turned sour in the early 1980s and the bottom fell out of the Mexican economy. In August 1982, Mexico announced that it was bankrupt. The announcement sent shock waves throughout the world, triggering Latin America's debt crisis and initiating what would become known throughout the region as "the lost decade."

Saddled with a massive foreign debt, high interest rates, low petroleum prices, and international banks reluctant to lend more money, Mexico faced hard choices and hard times. Under pressure by the US and international financial organs such as the IMF, the government responded by slashing government spending on everything from infrastructure to social programs, by enforcing drastic cuts in real wages through repression of labor unions and allowing inflation to outstrip wage increases, and by tightening monetary policy. The economy slipped into a deep recession. As problems persisted, the government went even further, dismantling import substitution policies and replacing them with a program of neoliberalism. It auctioned off or closed state enterprises, reducing the number of such entities from 1185 in 1982 to 185 by 1997. It opened trade by cutting tariff rates and negotiating free trade agreements with, among others, the US, Canada, Central America, Columbia, Chile, and the European Union. It liberalized the financial sector, privatizing the banks that had been taken over by the state in 1982 and erasing scores of restrictions on foreign investment. In addition, it removed price controls, reduced or eliminated subsidies to the poor and middle class, and slashed industrial promotion programs. These policies continue today, with ports and electric companies slated for privatization.

The dramatic policy shift transformed the structure of the Mexican economy. In a decade or so, Mexico went from a relatively closed economy to a much more open one. Whereas just 3.5 percent of overall production went to exports in 1975, by 1990 that figure had climbed to 23.9 percent (Pastor and Wise 1998). From less than $40 billion in 1980, total trade skyrocketed to more than $200 billion by 1998. Within this context, Mexico shifted from its reliance on the exportation of oil to being a major exporter of manufactured goods. Though oil remains the nation's largest export item, manufactured goods now make up more than 80 percent of total exports. At the same time the country received billions of dollars in direct and portfolio investments from the US and other countries, with the former feeding the boom in export manufacturing, particularly maquiladora production, and the latter creating mini-booms in the Mexican stock market. Many large businesses, both foreign and domestic, have grown at spectacular rates, enjoying tremendous profits and producing a handful of billionaires.

But despite the clear structural transformation, the results have been mixed and have fallen short of expectations. Modest levels of economic growth were restored in the late 1980s and early 1990s and some individuals did quite well, yet by 1995 the government, facing a huge trade deficit and high debt, was forced to devalue the currency again. The move triggered a new wave of capital flight and more hard times. The economy plummeted, reaching new lows. In response, the US brokered an international bailout in the amount of $40 billion (a loan Mexico paid back a few years later) while the Mexican government deepened the neoliberal reforms and austerity. On the positive side, the reforms have been largely successful at taming inflation and reducing government spending. Negotiated pacts with business and labor to freeze wages, prices, and the exchange rate, and curtailing government spending, reduced inflation to less than 20 percent. Mexico was thus able to avoid the bouts of hyperinflation that crippled the Argentine and Brazilian economies during this time.

Yet, despite the dramatic increase in exports, the taming of inflation and government spending, and the growing number of billionaires, other indicators point to severe and continuing problems as the result of political crises and neoliberal reforms. (See Figure 9.4.) Real wages have decreased drastically, poverty levels have increased, and the distribution of income, already inequitable in comparison to other countries, has worsened. Growing numbers of Mexicans are working in the informal sector—from selling tacos on the sidewalks to washing windshields on the street—and the number of working children has risen. A study by the National University, shows that the average working family in the late 1990s spends 67 percent of income on basic foodstuffs compared to just 14.5 percent ten years earlier. From just 1994 to 1996, the number of poor increased by 13 million, with 40 million Mexicans, or 41.6 percent of the population, living in poverty (Cevallos 1998). Meanwhile, the gaps between the rich and poor have widened. The share of income going to the richest 10 percent of households increased from 34 percent in 1984 to 41 percent in 1994, while the portion accruing to the poorest 40 percent of households fell from 13 percent to 10 percent (Inter-American Development Bank 1998).

Just as the earlier period featured the happy marriage of economic and political stability, the deteriorating economy in recent years has gone hand-in-hand with political crisis and change. Problems associated with the growing number of poor, the increasing levels of inequality, rising underemployment and unemployment, the fall of real wages, and the inability of small and medium businesses to compete against cheap imports or enter the export market, have all created growing demands on the government, contributed to the rise of new social organizations, and hastened the loss of the PRI's and the government's popularity. Today, the country faces the difficult task of correcting the problems created or left unaddressed by its neoliberal reforms.

Figure 9.4
Economic Indicators: Trends Since the 1980s

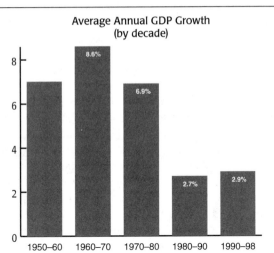

Average Annual GDP Growth
(by decade)

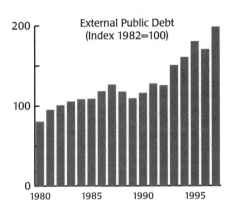

External Public Debt
(Index 1982=100)

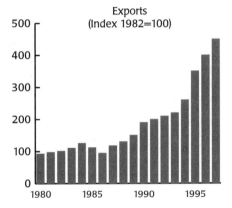

Exports
(Index 1982=100)

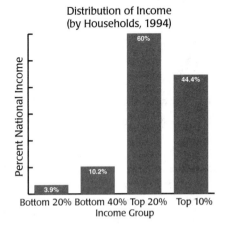

Distribution of Income
(by Households, 1994)

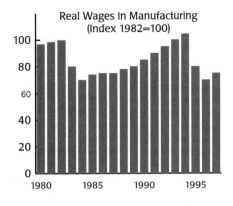

Real Wages in Manufacturing
(Index 1982=100)

Sources: Inter-American Development Bank (1998); Lustig (1998); Pastor and Wise (1998).

International Interdependence: Relations with the United States

Mexico's proximity to the powerful and wealthy US has affected tremendously all aspects of the nation's life, from national identity to economic policy and even the country's unique political experiment. Indeed, the country's relationship with its northern neighbor dominates Mexico's domestic and foreign policies.

Living in the shadow of the US has never been easy for Mexico, presenting the country with a complex mix of risks and opportunities. On the one hand, Mexico has historically suffered at the hands of the US. It has been invaded by the US on more than one occasion, lost more than half its territory to US expansionism, and has often felt the meddling presence of the US in its internal politics. For good or ill, its economy has long been dominated by US interests, whether by US companies, trade, or financial bailouts. Even today, 80 percent of Mexican trade is with the US and large chunks of key industries are held by US investors. Even in the field of culture, US companies provide much of the programming for television, radio, and theaters—compromising, according to many, the nation's distinct cultural identity. At the same time, Mexicans in the US suffer discrimination and abuse owing to their status as "illegals." Reflecting these concerns, some polls show a majority of Mexicans expressing a lack of trust in the US.

Arising from these concerns, the Mexican government has long sought to contain US influence. In foreign policy matters, the government has emphasized basic principles of international law such as a country's right to self-determination and the principle of non-intervention in the affairs of other countries, and has tried to pursue a course largely independent of the US. Contrary to other countries of the region, for instance, Mexico rebuked the US lead in breaking relations with Cuba in the 1960s, maintaining a close political relationship with the Castro regime ever since and denouncing the US embargo in the international arena. During the 1980s when conflict racked Central America, Mexico led the way in opposing US policy and seeking a peaceful, negotiated solution to the conflict. Even Mexico's domestic economic policy has historically ensured a certain distance from the US, with constitutional provisions, regulations, and policies restricting foreign ownership of Mexican properties.

At the same time, however, Mexicans have also held a more positive image of the US and a peaceful, constructive relationship, even taking advantage of the country's proximity to pursue economic development through means unavailable to others. Just as polls show a lack of trust toward the US, they also show that Mexicans respect the nation's economic and political successes. Despite their critical views of the US government and US policy, moreover, most Mexicans are open and polite toward US citizens. Because of cultural and demographic trends, many Mexicans have family in the US and/or have visited the US; most are familiar with the country. As part of these trends, data from Inglehart, Nevitte, and Basañez (1996) show a degree of convergence of Mexican and US social values. Within this context, Mexicans have enjoyed a peaceful and pragmatic relationship with their northern cousins. Working through diplomatic channels, the US and Mexico have peacefully resolved a series of conflicts, ranging from the expropriation of US oil companies in 1938 to territorial disputes in the 1960s. Indeed, despite the rhetoric, cooperation—not conflict—best characterizes the country's relationship with the US.

In the wake of the economic crises and neoliberal reforms of the 1980s and 1990s, the Mexican government has pursued a policy of greater cooperation and integration with the US. The Mexican economy, in particular, has become closely integrated with the US economy as thousands of maquiladoras along the border assemble US-made parts and export the finished products back across the border. In many ways, Mexico has become the new industrial belt of the US, enhancing the importance of Mexico's economic well-being to the US—a realization that made the US-sponsored financial bailout in 1995 quick and necessary.

The Mexican-U.S. relationship is complex and multifaceted, touching on many emotions and actors, and mixing aspects of cooperation and conflict. It incorporates not only trade and financial matters, but the problem of drug trafficking and money laundering. The Mexican government cooperates with the US in addressing these issues, yet often resents US pressures for more action. Ironically, the growing economic integration with the US actually facilitates the drug trade. With an estimated 2.8 million trucks crossing the border every year, only a small percentage can possibly be searched (Andreas 1996). The US provides funds and training in the effort, but both governments face an uphill battle. The relationship also involves the delicate matter of Mexicans going north in search of jobs and their treatment in the US. Given the country's economic woes, immigration represents an escape valve, relieving some of the economic pressures, but it also exposes Mexicans to discrimination and abuse. The complex bilateral relationship also involves problems and political cooperation along the 1,952-mile border, where local governments struggle with everything from shortages in infrastructure to toxic wastes.

In many ways, Mexico has become as much a matter of domestic policy in the US as "foreign policy" and vice versa. From treasury to commerce, drug enforcement agencies to immigration officials, the relationship involves a wide range of actors on both sides of the border. Given the complexities, the relationship has become highly institutionalized in recent years. Meetings between officials on both sides are common, while scores of agreements have been reached that set out specific procedures to resolve conflict. NAFTA, for instance, establishes trilateral institutions to resolve trade disputes and disagreements over labor and environmental issues. In labor and environmental areas, the US and Mexico work together to monitor and ensure the enforcement of their own labor and environmental laws.

Challenges of the Present and Prospects for the Future

As we have seen, Mexico has undergone many changes in recent years. Not all of the changes are positive, and the country continues to confront serious political and economic problems. Some stem from the continuation of old authoritarian patterns and attitudes and the struggle for democracy; others reflect the setbacks of the economic crises of the 1980s and 1990s and the nature and implementation of recent reforms. Though Mexico is clearly in a period of transition, the outcome is uncertain. Some trends encourage a positive outlook, but others occasion a more cautious evaluation.

Democracy and Stability

On the democratic front, Mexico has enjoyed perhaps its greatest level of progress in recent years. This is particularly true in relation to elections and dispersal of presidential power. Though electoral fraud remains a problem at the local level, elections are generally cleaner, more open, and more competitive than in the past. Mexicans have come to recognize elections as the legitimate means to select a government and pursue political change. As elections have increased in importance, so too have the roles of political parties and Congress. The nation's major parties now offer the public a clear choice, working more effectively to represent the people's interests, and they work together in government to deal with the nation's problems. Even the PRI, still the largest party, has shown signs of adapting to a more democratic and competitive environment. At the same time, Mexico has made significant strides in curtailing the authoritarian power of the presidency. The new Congress has increased its oversight powers, while recent reforms have paved the way for a more powerful judiciary and a more active civil society.

In some ways, Mexico's progress toward democracy has meant greater political stability. The country is no longer racked by massive protests over electoral fraud, and support for using violence to promote change remains limited. But progress on the electoral front has also opened up a range of issues and created problems that threaten stability. Since policy is no longer made by the president acting alone, gridlock has emerged. In 1998, for instance, the government struggled for months to hammer out an agreement on the budget and other matters. Such problems make it difficult for the country to address its many social and economic problems. Political changes have also led to power vacuums. In a sense, the old institutions are eroding, but new institutions have yet to be built. This is particularly true within the PRI. The assassination of PRI candidate Luis Donaldo Colosio and other top officials in the 1990s as well as the deep divisions over how to select its 2000 presidential candidate have greatly eroded the once-cohesive PRI. Whether and how the PRI will survive its internal difficulties is thus one of the key factors shaping the outcome of the current transition.

Democracy involves more than elections. Democracy also demands respect for the rule of law and accountability. Despite its progress in the electoral arena, Mexico desperately needs to create effective, more efficient government institutions, instill the rule of law, and respect the rights of its citizens. Law enforcement and the judicial system remain weak, marred by deep-seated corruption and widespread abuse of authority. Though in theory greater democracy and pluralism should set the stage for stronger checks and balances and less corruption, recent trends are not encouraging. The rise of narco-money and organized crime, in particular, has added to the instability created by the erosion of the authoritarian institutions, triggering political violence, crime, and corruption. A major priority for the country in the near future must therefore be to improve the implementation of the nation's laws, especially in relation to the government itself.

Human Rights

Concern over the rule of law is directly related to the issue of human rights. Despite electoral improvements, the country continues to make slow progress in protecting human rights. As documented by a variety of national and international organizations, torture and disappearance as well as impunity continue. The government has been slow to reform the judiciary and law enforcement agencies, and the reforms that have been adopted have brought limited results. The spread of crime, the existence of paramilitary organizations, and the activities of narco-traffickers all seriously complicate these efforts.

Although the abuse of human rights spans the country, it is a particular problem in conflict-ridden and impoverished states such as Chiapas, Oaxaca, and Guerrero. With more than 50,000 government troops and scores of paramilitary organizations supported by local PRI officials, the political situation in Chiapas, in particular, has deteriorated, with violence becoming all too commonplace. Shortly before Christmas in 1997, for instance, forty-five Indian peasants were massacred by a paramilitary organization with ties to the local government in the town of Acteal. Investigations revealed the complicity of state officials, and some in fact have been prosecuted, but tensions and the potential for further violence remain high. Rather than respond with greater protections, moreover, the government initially reacted by restricting the activities of human rights workers in the area.

Table 9.2
Quality-of-Life Comparisons

	GDP/pc (1995)	Life Expectancy (Years) (1995)	HDI (1995)	Population Without Access to Safe Water (%) (1990–96)	GDI (1995)	Political/ Civil Rights (Scale 1–7) (1998–99)	Corruption Ranking (Scale 10–1) (1996)
Brazil	$5,928	66.6	.809	24	.751	3/4	2.96
China	$2,935	69.2	.650	33	.641	7/6	2.43
Kenya	$1,438	53.8	.463	47	.459	6/5	2.21
Mexico	**$6,769**	**72.1**	**.855**	**17**	**.774**	**3/4**	**3.30**
US	$26,977	76.4	.943	nd	.927	1/1	7.66

GDP/pc = Real Gross Domeastic Product per capita
HDI = Human Development Index
GDI = Gender Development Index

Source: Human Development Report 1998; Freedom House; and Transparency International Corruption Rating.

Economic Growth and Quality of Life

Despite the severity of the 1995 recession, Mexico's economy bounced back quickly and relatively well. By the end of the decade, economic growth had been restored and inflation held in check. Given that it took the country years to recover from its 1982 crisis, most economists see the recent recovery as proof that the country's economic foundation is solid and that recovery and sustainable growth are on the horizon. The drop in world oil prices and the Asian and Brazilian financial crises in 1998, however, weakened expectations and slowed the rate of growth. Growth is expected to be moderate, at around 3 to 5 percent for the next few years.

But while the macro indicators suggest economic health, problems at the micro level remain, raising questions about the people's quality of life. Though generally better off than most in the Third World (see Table 9.2), Mexicans have faced intense economic hardship since the 1980s and, as noted earlier, many are worse off today than they were before the rocky road of crisis and change began. With as much as 40 percent of the population in poverty, deep-seated inequality, and a million new workers entering the job market each year, the government faces massive challenges in improving the people's quality of life. The expected modest rates of economic growth will hardly make much headway. It is estimated that at the current rate of economic growth it will take forty to sixty years to eradicate poverty in Mexico (Interpress Service, February 17, 1999). Overcoming its economic problems, then, will not be easy for Mexico.

The Environment

In addition to rule of law, human rights, and economic issues, Mexico also faces many environmental problems including the loss of biodiversity, deforestation, groundwater depletion, and pollution. Low levels of economic development, high poverty rates, extreme inequality, rapid population growth, uncontrolled urbanization, and a concentration of industry in the Mexico City area have all contributed to these problems, and the country has a long way to go to make up for years of neglect and abuse. Typical of the pattern highlighted throughout our discussion, the government has an extensive legal framework of environmental protections and even relatively strong organizations, yet it faces serious shortcomings in terms of trained personnel, limited resources, and lack of enforcement. Historically, society has given greater priority to other matters than to the environment.

Two particular problems are air quality in Mexico City and environmental problems along the border. Mexico City is home not only to 18 million inhabitants, but to a large portion of the nation's older industrial plants and more than a million autos that average twelve years of age and collectively spew tons of wastes into the atmosphere. The fact that the city sits in a valley surrounded by mountains with periods of insufficient rainfall produces a situation referred to as thermal inversion, greatly exacerbating the level of contamination. In recent years, the government has responded by restricting autos from circulating one day of the week and by instituting a series of emergency measures to close harmful industrial plants temporarily. Results have been somewhat limited, though they have probably slowed the city's slide into environmental disaster.

The government also faces severe environmental problems in the border region. Among the fastest-growing cities in the country, border towns face environmental stress due to the uncontrolled growth of maquiladora industries and the resulting population pressures. Though maquiladoras are required to handle toxic wastes properly, such practices are rarely followed. According to many, substantial pressures exist for officials to "overlook" environmental violations because of the need for jobs. In the meantime, the infrastructure, including sewage and sanitation systems, has been stretched well beyond its limits. Local and federal governments lack the resources to compensate for years of neglect.

Recent political changes, however, bode well for improvement in efforts to protect the environment, though the country clearly has a long way to go. Economic changes have helped build up industry outside the Mexico City region, while political changes have given birth to a range of environmental organizations and greater governmental oversight. NAFTA's environmental side agreement provided an institutional framework whereby greater international attention and pressures could be brought to bear to ensure that the country abides by its own environmental laws. The agreement also establishes the North American Development Bank (NADBank) to help finance clean-up measures along the border. It remains to be seen, however, how effective these measures will be. Most agree that both the urgency and attention to environmental issues in Mexico will grow considerably in the near future, though existing measures remain limited.

Prospects for the Future

For years, Mexican politics have manifested a wide breach separating democratic ideals from an authoritarian reality: the country had elections, but a single dominant party; nominal checks and balances, but an all-powerful president; constitutional rights and freedoms, but repression and impunity. Though almost everyone agreed on the need to reduce this gap, politics pivoted on the struggles among political actors employing a mix of cooperative and confrontational tactics over how to close the gap, how fast, at what cost, and to whose benefit.

Periodic political and economic crises reflect and feed on the tensions created by this breach, creating political challenges, risks, and opportunities for change. In managing crisis and change, Mexico has clearly made progress, gradually closing the political fissure. The crises and reforms of the 1980s and 1990s, in particular, have clearly fostered progress: elections are cleaner and more competitive; the president enjoys less discretionary authority than his predecessors did; and the pressures on the government to be accountable, to strengthen the rule of law, to improve governance, and to achieve a level of social justice are much greater than in the past.

On Sunday, July 2, 2000, in perhaps the nation's most contested and freest election, the Mexican electorate peacefully voted the PRI from power. The candidate from the PAN-PVEM coalition (the Alliance for Change), Vicente Fox, an entrepreneur and former governor from the state of Guanajuato, received 42.54 percent of the vote followed by the PRI's candidate, Francisco Labastida, with 36.10 percent, and the PRD-led coalition candidate (Alliance for Mexico) Cuauhtemoc Cardenas with 16.65 percent.

Many factors contributed to the PRI's loss. At one level, the people simply wanted a change. According to exit polls, the young and the better educated strongly backed Fox. Second, Fox ran a highly effective campaign that focused and energized this popular desire for change. Breaking rules along the way, the charismatic Fox built an effective grassroots organization and used modern marketing techniques to craft his image. Finally, the electoral process was managed by a truly independent and autonomous electoral authority, the IFE, a product of the electoral reforms of 1996.

On December 1, 2000, Mexico will enjoy the first peaceful transfer of power from one party to another in over a century, opening a new chapter in the evolution of the Mexican political system. Though basic political institutions remain intact, the PRI's defeat creates the possibility of fundamental change in the way Mexican political institutions have functioned for years. Vicente Fox will face many challenges, but there is a new sense of optimism in the country.

References

Andreas, Peter. 1996. "US–Mexico: Open Markets, Closed Border," *Foreign Policy* No. 103 (Summer 1996): 51–69.

Beltran, U., F. Castaños, J. I. Flores, Y. Meyenberg, and B. H. del Pozo. 1997. *Los Mexicanos de los Noventa*. Mexico: UNAM.

Blum, Robert E. 1997. "The Weight of the Past." *Journal of Democracy* 8(4): 28–42.

Camp, Roderic A. 1996. *Politics in Mexico*. New York: Oxford University Press.

Cevallos, Diego. 1998. "Minimum Wage Does Not Provide Enough." *InterPress Service,* December 9, 1998; reprinted in *Mexico NewsPak* 6(22): 10.

Fernandez Poncela, Anna M. 1996. "The Political Participation of Women in Mexico Today." In *Changing Structure of Mexico: Political, Social, and Economic Prospects* (pp. 307–14), ed. Laura Randall. Armonk, NY: M. E. Sharpe.

Freedom House. 1998. *Freedom in the World.* (Internet)

Gutiérrez Vivó, José, ed 1998. *El otro yo del mexicano.* México: Oceano.

Inglehart, Ronald F., Neil Nevitte, and Miguel Basañez. 1996. *The North American Trajectory: Cultural, Economic, and Political Ties Among the United States, Canada, and Mexico.* New York: Aldine de Gruyter.

Inter-American Development Bank. 1998. *Facing Up to Inequality in Latin America: Economic and Social Progress in Latin America, 1998–1999 Report.* Washington, DC: Inter-American Development Bank.

Human Development Report 1998. New York: United Nations.

Human Rights Watch. 1998. *Systemic Injustice: Torture, "Disappearance," and Extrajudicial Execution in Mexico.* New York: Human Rights Watch.

Klesner, Joseph. (no date). "Electoral Politics and Mexico's New Party System." Unpublished manuscript.

Lustig, Nora. 1998. *Mexico: The Remaking of an Economy.* 2nd ed. Washington, DC: Brookings Institution Press.

Meyer, Michael C., and William L. Sherman. 1995. *The Course of Mexican History.* 5th ed. New York: Oxford University Press.

Pastor Jr., Manuel, and Carol Wise. 1998. "Mexican-Style Neoliberalism." In *The Post-NAFTA Political Economy: Mexico and the Western Hemisphere* (pp. 41–81), ed. Carol Wise. University Park, PA: Pennsylvania State University Press.

Pastor, Robert A., and Jorge G. Castañeda. 1989. *Limits to Friendship: The United States and Mexico.* New York: Vintage Books.

Smith, Peter H. 1979. *Labyrinths of Power: Political Recruitment in Twentieth-Century Mexico.* Princeton, NJ: Princeton University Press.

Transparency International. 1996. "International Corruption Ranking, 1996." Gottingen University (Internet version).

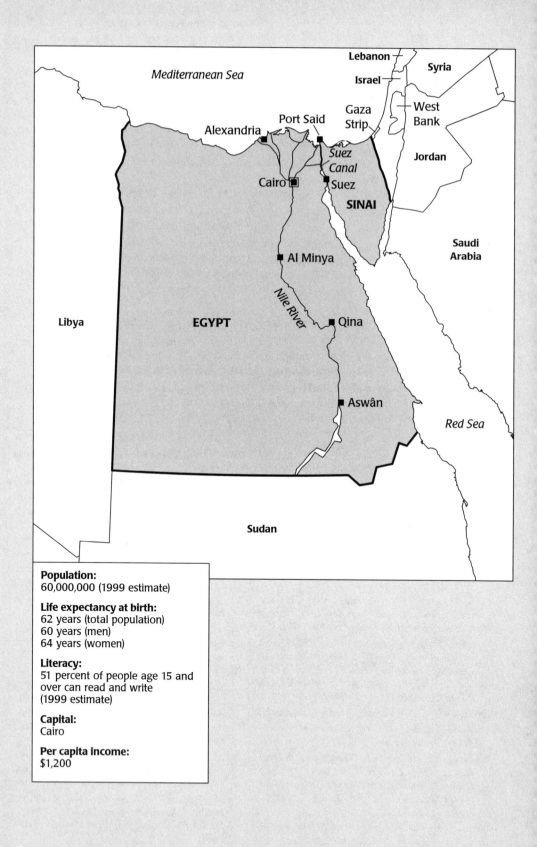

Population:
60,000,000 (1999 estimate)

Life expectancy at birth:
62 years (total population)
60 years (men)
64 years (women)

Literacy:
51 percent of people age 15 and
over can read and write
(1999 estimate)

Capital:
Cairo

Per capita income:
$1,200

10

The Arab Republic of Egypt
The Politics of Indecision

Egypt is the core state of the Arabic-speaking world, a world that includes more than twenty states located in the Middle East and North Africa. Egypt possesses the dominant army, the strongest industrial base, and the largest population of the Arab world. Egypt is also host to the Arab League, a regional organization designed to promote political, military, and economic cooperation among the Arab states. All in all, no other Arab state approaches Egypt in terms of its regional and international influence.

Egypt's dominant position within the Arab World is summed up by the Arabic expression "um Al Arab"—mother of the Arabs. Little happens in Egypt that does not have a direct impact on its Arab neighbors. During the 1950s and 1960s, for example, Egypt was the focal point of an Arab resurgence that ignited anti-Western revolutions in Lebanon, Jordan, Iraq, and Syria. Not all of the revolutions were successful, but American interests in Saudi Arabia and other oil-producing states were placed in jeopardy, as was the security of Israel.

Politics in the Middle East, however, are subject to abrupt and startling changes. During the 1980s and 1990s, Egypt became the champion of regional cooperation, making peace with Israel and promoting the stability of Saudi Arabia and other oil-producing states of the region. Egyptian cooperation remains vital to maintaining order in what is probably the most volatile region in the world.

Understandably, the United States and its Western allies are struggling to assure that Egypt remains a bastion of moderation and regional cooperation. Toward that end, the United States provides Egypt with some $2 billion in foreign assistance each year. Other countries also provide foreign aid to Egypt, as do the World Bank and the International Monetary Fund. Egypt is the largest single recipient of foreign assistance in the Third World.[1] In return for providing aid, the United States and other international donors have pressured Egypt to increase the pace of its transition from a socialist dictatorship into a capitalist democracy. A democratic and capitalist Egypt, in their view, is essential to the stability of the Middle Eastern region.

Progress toward democracy and political moderation, unfortunately, are being undermined by Egypt's poverty and by a population that is growing more rapidly than the country's fragile economy. Foreign aid has kept the Egyptian economy afloat, but it has failed to solve Egypt's fundamental economic problems. The Egyptian population is losing patience with its government, and radical Islamic (Muslim) Fundamentalist groups are vowing to transform Egypt into an Islamic government somewhat similar to that of Iran.[2] Indeed, fair and open elections in Egypt could well result in a Fundamentalist victory.

In this chapter we will trace Egypt's circuitous path toward democracy and capitalism, placing particular emphasis on two topics: the rise of Muslim Fundamentalism and the limits of America's ability to impose political and economic reform on its client states. Problems encountered in stimulating political and economic reform in Egypt could presage similar frustrations in America's much-heralded plan to transform other countries of the Third World into capitalist democracies.

Egypt in Historical and Religious Perspective

The glories of Pharonic Egypt require little recounting. Egypt was the cradle of Western civilization, its pyramids and monuments standing in testimony to a people of dazzling creativity. The Pharonic period, however, came to an end well before the Christian era, and Egypt would succumb to a seemingly endless succession of foreign invaders, including the Babylonians, Persians, Greeks, Romans, Arabs, Crusaders, Turks, French, and British. Indeed, Egypt would not reclaim full control of its own destiny until 1952. Be this as it may, modern Egyptians remain intensely proud of their Pharonic heritage. They are Arabs in language and culture, but they are also profoundly aware of their uniqueness as Egyptians.

Islamic Egypt

Of the long procession of foreign invasions, none had a more lasting influence on Egyptian society than the Arab invasions of the seventh century. Fired by zeal for the new Islamic (Muslim) religion, tribal armies from the Arabian Peninsula[3] imposed their language, culture, and religion on a vast territory that stretched from Spain in the west to India in the east. Arabic would become the language of Egypt and Islam the religion of more than 90 percent of its population. Of the non-Muslims, most would be Coptic Christians[4] (Carter 1986).

---

[1]Russia is rapidly overtaking Egypt as the major recipient of foreign assistance from the world community. Israel also receives more aid from the United States than Egypt does, but Israel is usually considered a First World country.

[2]Adherents of the Islamic faith are referred to as Muslims.

[3]Today, this region is Saudi Arabia.

[4]The Coptic Church centers on the Patriarchate of Alexandria, one of the four major centers of early Christianity, the others being Rome, Constantinople, and Antioch. Egypt also possessed a substantial Jewish minority.

Both a mosque (religious temple) and a university, Al-Azhar in Cairo is the world's oldest and most renowned center of Islamic learning.

Islam shares much in common with both Judaism and Christianity. The God of the Jews and the Christians is also the God of the Muslims. Indeed, "Islam" means "submission to God's will." Islam acknowledges the prophets of the Jews, and Christ is recognized as a major prophet but not as the Son of God.

By the tenth century, Egypt had become the political center of the Islamic Empire, a position that it maintained for some two hundred years. The splendors of Cairo dazzled visitors of this era.

> I saw a series of buildings, terraces, and rooms. There were twelve adjoining pavilions, all of them square in shape.... There was a throne in one of them that took up the entire width of the room. Three of its sides were made of gold on which were hunting scenes depicting riders racing their horses and other subjects; there were also inscriptions written in beautiful characters. The rugs and hangings were Greek satin and moire woven precisely to fit the spot where they were to be placed. A balustrade of golden latticework surrounded the throne, whose beauty defies all description. Behind the throne were steps of silver. I saw a tree that looked like an orange tree, whose branches, leaves, and fruits were made of sugar. A thousand statuettes and figurines also made of sugar were also placed there (Nasiri Khusraw in Behrens-Abouseif 1990, 7).

It was during this era that the Al-Azhar mosque, the world's oldest and most famous center of Islamic learning, was established. Al-Azhar is both a mosque and a university, and its sheikh (rector) is one of the most influential political figures in modern Egypt.

The Suez Canal, officially opened in 1869, brought in royalties that were quickly squandered by the royal family.

Modern Egypt

The modern history of Egypt begins with the reign of Mohammed Ali, an Albanian adventurer sent to Egypt in 1789 as part of a joint Turko-British military operation designed to end the French occupation of Egypt.[5] The French were evicted, and Mohammed Ali surfaced as the head of an Egyptian government nominally loyal to the Sultan of Turkey. Mohammed Ali, however, dreamed of an empire and felt little loyalty to the Sultan of Turkey or to any other power (Marsot 1984). Egypt was to be the base of his empire. Welding Egyptian fellah (peasants) into the strongest army of the Middle East, Mohammed Ali was able to conquer much of the region that now constitutes the Sudan, Israel, Jordan, and Saudi Arabia (Goldschmidt 1988, 19). On two occasions, he threatened to conquer Turkey itself, but both efforts were stymied by the British and French (Lawson 1992).

The line of Mohammed Ali proved to be an undistinguished one. The royal family, supported by an aristocracy of large landowners, lived in oriental splendor while the Egyptian peasants were reduced to lives of servitude (Ayrout 1962). The political and economic structure of Egypt during this period was remarkably similar to the feudalism of medieval Europe, with an aristocracy of large landowners providing financial support to the monarchy in exchange for the right to rule their fiefdoms as they saw fit. How they achieved these objectives was of little concern to the royal family (Lane 1954).

The profligate lifestyle of the royal family soon exhausted Egypt's meager financial resources. The construction of the Suez Canal in 1869 provided the Egyptian government with royalties from canal traffic, but even this new source of

---

[5]Napoleon I had invaded Egypt shortly after the French Revolution in 1789, hoping to add the North African state, a possession of Turkey, to the French Empire. Ever fearful of French power, the British joined with the Turks to frustrate the venture.

revenue could not satisfy the appetites of the monarch. Short of cash, the king sold Egypt's 44 percent share in the Suez Canal to British and French investors.[6] When the money had been squandered, the heirs of Mohammed Ali turned to deficit financing (Longgood 1957). Possessing little in the way of new resources, Egypt defaulted on its loans. England and France responded by seizing the Egyptian custom houses, depriving the king of Egypt's most reliable form of taxation and sparking a brief rebellion (1882) that led to the British occupation of Egypt.

By the early 1920s, hostility to British occupation would find expression in two political movements. The first was the **Wafd Party**, *a broad coalition of nationalist groups dedicated to liberating Egypt from British rule* (Berque 1967). The Wafd would remain Egypt's major political party throughout the era of the monarchy. The second organization was the **Muslim Brotherhood**, *a secret religious organization dedicated to the creation of an Islamic state in Egypt* (Husaini 1956). The Muslim Brotherhood remains one of the strongest political forces in Egypt today. There was considerable overlap between the two movements, as the Muslim Brotherhood was also violently opposed to the British presence in Egypt.

The British granted Egypt independent status in 1922 but retained the right to station troops on Egyptian soil. Egyptian politics throughout the inter-war period would remain a three-way struggle between the British Embassy, the king, and the Wafd (Youssef 1983).

The end of World War II ushered in a period of profound political instability as the British sought to remain a key force in Egyptian politics while Farouk, a particularly corrupt and inept leader, struggled to rule as an absolute monarch. The Wafd continued to press for greater democracy, but the party had lost much of its nationalist zeal, becoming the party of the wealthy (Berque 1967). The influence of the Muslim Brotherhood had been weakened by the assassination of its founder.

The Egyptian Revolution of 1952

It was in this environment that Farouk sent his army to war against the newly proclaimed country of Israel in the misguided belief that the Jews couldn't fight. Victory assured, Jerusalem would be ruled from Cairo (as per interviews with Hassan Pasha Youssef, Head of the Royal Diwan, 1983). Poorly led and poorly armed, the Egyptian forces suffered huge losses, liberating only the Gaza strip, a sparse coastal area adjacent to the Egyptian border.

Smarting from their defeat at the hands of the Jews and frustrated by the ineptness of their political leaders, a small group of junior army officers headed by Gamal Abdul Nasser formed the Free Officers, a secret military organization dedicated to the modernization of Egyptian society. The group seized power in July 1952 (El-Din 1995).

Their task would not be an easy one. The Egyptian population, largely illiterate, was mired in poverty and disease and was growing at a rate that outpaced Egypt's meager resources. More people meant more starvation. The security of the revolution, moreover, was threatened by both a narrow aristocracy of large landowners and a large contingent of British troops who continued to be stationed on Egyptian territory. The presence of foreign troops was particularly worrisome for the new regime, for the United States and Britain threatened to overthrow any Arab regime that posed a direct threat to Western interests.

---

[6] Britain and France now controlled 100 percent of the shares of the Suez Canal.

The first two years of the revolutionary era were relatively uneventful as Nasser and the Free Officers remained in the background, allowing formal power to be exercised by General Naguib, a respected military leader with moderate political views. The appointment of a figurehead president was designed to reassure both the West and Egypt's established elite that the new regime did not pose a threat to their interests. Nasser and the Free Officers, moreover, needed time to figure out how best to modernize Egypt and its population. None of Egypt's new leaders possessed broad experience in either government or economics; they would have to learn by trial and error. Efforts were also made to work with the Wafd and other political groups in order to place Egypt on the path to democracy, but these efforts went poorly. The military demanded unity and sacrifice, while Egypt's civilian politicians sought little more than a continuation of the corrupt and divisive policies of the old regime. The experience left Nasser with a profound distrust of political parties and the politicians who led them. Egypt needed sacrifice and discipline, not chaos (Dekmejian 1975).

General Naguib chafed under the figurehead role assigned to him and challenged Nasser for leadership of the revolution. He was removed from office in 1954, some two years after the July revolution, and Nasser ascended to the presidency (Woodward 1992).

The Political Revolution Becomes a Social Revolution: Nasser (1954–1970)

The Nasser who replaced General Naguib possessed a far clearer picture of Egypt and its future than the younger officer who had deposed the hapless King Farouk some two years earlier. Egypt's future, in Nasser's view, required a program of rapid industrialization that would bring the country and its population on par with the nations of the West. The West was invited to cooperate in Egypt's modernization, but only on the condition that Egypt be treated as a sovereign and independent country. Foreign troops would no longer be welcome on Egyptian soil.

The centerpiece of Nasser's modernization plan was to be the Aswan Dam, a towering structure that would span the narrows of the Nile River in a sparsely populated region not far from the Sudanese border. Electric power generated by the dam would fuel an economic miracle, providing jobs for Egypt's masses and transforming Egypt into a modern industrial state. The dam would also control the Nile's floods, thereby producing a dramatic expansion of Egyptian agriculture. The Aswan Dam, however, was to be more than an economic venture. It would also symbolize hope and progress, legitimizing the revolutionary regime and eliciting popular support for its programs.

The West applauded Nasser's goal of economic development and promised support for the construction of the Aswan Dam. The honeymoon between Nasser and the West, however, was to be short-lived. Nasser demanded the evacuation of British troops from Egyptian soil, a demand reluctantly agreed to by a Britain still clinging to dreams of empire. Clashes between Israeli forces and Palestinian refugees seeking shelter on Egyptian soil soon escalated into clashes between Israeli forces and the Egyptian army. Nasser asked the West for arms to resist Israeli incursions, but the West refused. Nasser responded by purchasing arms from the Soviet bloc, a move that shattered the West's monopoly of power in the Middle East. For the first time in its history, the Soviet Union had gained entree into the Middle East and the Mediterranean basin. Fearful that Western security would be placed at risk, the United States demanded that Nasser rescind the communist arms deal. When he refused, the United States cancelled its aid for the Aswan Dam (Gorst and Johnman 1997). Nasser, in turn, responded by nationalizing the Suez Canal.

It was at this point that Israel, fearful of Nasser's escalating popularity in the Arab world, conspired with Britain and France to bring down the Nasser regime. Israeli forces stormed the Suez Canal in October 1956, while Britain and France demanded the right to occupy the canal under the pretext of protecting international shipping. The second Arab-Israeli war had begun. When Egypt refused to cede the canal, it was occupied by British and French forces. The three conspirators, however, had failed to consult with an American administration that was attempting to counter Soviet influence in the Third World by stressing America's history as a revolutionary, anti-colonial power (Brands 1993). Eisenhower sided with Egypt, forcing French, British, and Israeli forces to withdraw from Egyptian territory. Nasser reigned victorious.

In a period of two brief years, Nasser

- evicted British troops from Egyptian soil,
- shattered the Western arms monopoly in the Middle East,
- nationalized the Suez Canal, and
- defeated (albeit politically) the combined forces of Israel, France, and Britain.

In the eyes of Egypt and the entire Arab world, Nasser had become a charismatic hero of towering proportions, well fitting Weber's description of a charismatic leader "endowed with supernatural, superhuman...powers" (Weber 1947).

Arab Nationalism. Nasser's near-defeat in the Arab/Israeli war of 1956 convinced him that Egypt would never be free from external threat as long as his Arab neighbors remained subservient to the West. His resentment of foreign domination, moreover, was shared by thousands of students, military officers, and intellectuals throughout the Arab world. Indeed, Arab nationalism was rapidly becoming the dominant political ideology of the region.

The message of Arab nationalism was both simple and powerful (Farah 1987; Doran 1999): The Arabs are one people united by a common history, a common culture, a common language, and for the most part, a common religion. Once powerful, the Arabs now find themselves fragmented into a multitude of petty states manipulated by Western imperialists and Israel. All that is required for a resurgence of Arab power is the reunification of the Arab people into a single state.

However potent its message, the Arab nationalist movement had historically lacked a dominant leader capable of marshaling its diverse and conflicting wings (Gershoni 1981). Nasser provided that leadership.

A union of Egypt and Syria was forged in 1958. Pro-Nasser coups also overthrew the pro-Western monarchs of Iraq, Yemen, and Libya, and Nasser's supporters came within a hairsbreadth of toppling pro-Western regimes in Saudi Arabia, Jordan, and Lebanon. As soon as the Arab world was united, Nasser vowed, the humiliation of 1948 would be redressed and Israel would be returned to the Palestinians.

On the domestic front, Nasser transformed Egypt's political system into a military dictatorship. The quasi-parliamentary institutions that had evolved under the monarchy were abolished. Abolished too, were the Wafd and other political parties of the era. The Muslim Brotherhood was driven underground and remained dormant throughout much of the Nasser era. All effective power would reside in Nasser and the Revolutionary Command Council, a group of Nasser's most trusted associates among the Free Officers. Nasser would later create a single political party, the Arab Socialist Union, in an effort to mobilize popular support for his regime and its objectives.

Changes in the economic and social arena were equally dramatic. Egypt's largest farms were expropriated by the government and their lands redistributed among the peasants. All banks, insurance companies, factories, and large commercial establishments were also nationalized, transforming Egypt into a predominantly socialist economy. Only small firms employing a handful of employees were allowed to remain in the private sector. Schools and health clinics mushroomed as the government sought to eliminate the scourges of illiteracy and poverty. Graduates of the new schools and universities were guaranteed a job with the government.

Egypt, however, was not a communist state. Its ideology was Arab nationalism. Nasser's goal was the creation of an Egypt that was as equitable as it was prosperous. Socialism and military rule were merely the means to that end (Hosseinzedeh 1989). Capitalism and party politics, in the view of Nasser and his colleagues, had brought Egypt little more than poverty, inequality, and conflict. Egypt's military leaders would use their authority to assure that Egypt's scarce resources were allocated in a just and productive manner. Once economic and social development had been achieved, Egypt would become a true democracy in which educated and prosperous Egyptians could make wise and judicious choices.

Both Arab unity and economic development, however, were to prove elusive. The union with Syria was short-lived, and pro-Western regimes in Lebanon, Saudi Arabia, and Jordan were stabilized by the United States and Britain. The 1960s also found Egypt embroiled in the Yemeni Civil War, a disastrous involvement that paralleled the American experience in Vietnam. Egyptian forces controlled the major cities but could not subdue the tribes that dominated Yemen's impenetrable countryside. The morale of the Egyptian forces sank as defeat became inevitable. The collapse of the Yemeni venture was followed in short order by the outbreak of the June War of 1967. This, the third of the Arab-Israeli wars, would see Israel rout Egyptian forces in less than six days.

The domestic situation was equally bleak. Dramatic progress had been made in the areas of education and public welfare, but Egypt's economy lagged as funds that might have been used for economic development were sapped by war and the quest for Arab unity (Abdel-Fadil 1980; Beattie 1994). Efforts to provide all Egyptians with employment, moreover, were overwhelmed by Egypt's continuing population explosion. There were simply too many people for too few jobs. The shift to socialism, for its part, served only to swell the size of an unproductive bureaucracy (Waterbury 1978; Ayubi 1980).

The Revolution Changes Course: Sadat (1970–1981)

Nasser, long in ill health, died in 1970, bringing to an end the most dramatic era in modern Arab history. Nasser was succeeded in office by Anwar Sadat, his vice-president and a charter member of the Free Officers (Heikal 1975). The picture facing Sadat was bleak (Baker 1990). Egyptian forces faced the Israelis across the Suez Canal, the economy was depressed, and the Egyptian population was demoralized. The military, once viewed as the saviors of Egypt, was in disgrace (Abdul-Hamid 1992; Kechichian and Nazimek 1997). Arab nationalism and socialism were equally victims of the war. Both had proven to be false gods.

Anwar Sadat, moreover, possessed none of Nasser's charisma. Many Egyptians believed him to be a weak individual who had been placed in office as a figurehead president until more powerful forces could sort out the course of the revolution (Heikal 1983). The Soviet Union also distrusted Sadat, preferring that the Egyptian presidency go to an Egyptian military leader with communist leanings. Even American officials had little faith in Sadat, assuming, as others did, that his tenure in office would be a brief one (Heikal 1983).

Egyptians pour into Cairo for the funeral of Gamal Abdul Nasser, Egypt's president from 1954 to 1970. Nasser's popularity extended beyond the borders of Egypt, with his supporters proclaiming, "We Arabs all are Nasser."

Sadat, however, proved to be a remarkably resilient individual. He crushed an attempted coup in 1971, expelled Soviet military advisors in 1972, and temporarily drove the Israelis from the Suez Canal in the October War of 1973. That war, the fourth Arab-Israeli war in a quarter of a century, saw Egyptian forces score dazzling victories against an Israeli army that had humiliated the Egyptian army some five years earlier.[7] The October War, referred to as the Yom Kippur War by the Israelis, made Sadat a hero in his own right. He had masterminded the first Egyptian military victory of the modern era. Sadat was now the unquestioned ruler of Egypt.

The course of Egyptian policy under Sadat was to bear little resemblance to that of the Nasser era. Sadat had little interest in either Arab unity or world revolution, a position that gained him the strong support of both the United States and Saudi Arabia. Neither the United States nor its oil-rich allies wanted to contend with a new Nasser. The cornerstone of Sadat's foreign policy, moreover, was to be peace with Israel. The October War was followed during the mid-1970s by a negotiated withdrawal of Israeli troops from the Sinai Peninsula. The Camp David peace accords between Egypt and Israel were agreed to in 1978, bringing Israel peace with the most powerful of its Arab neighbors. The Arab world, needless to say, felt betrayed. The headquarters of the Arab League was moved from Cairo to Tunisia, and Arab financial assistance to Egypt was terminated. Egypt, now severed from its natural base of support, became dependent upon economic and military assistance from the United States.

---

[7]The outcome of the war was inconclusive, with Israeli forces (backed by strong support from the United States) regaining lost territories.

Gamal Abdul Nasser (left) pushed for rapid industrialization, seeing it as Egypt's key to a prosperous future. Anwar Sadat (center), who advocated economic and political reforms, was killed by Muslim extremists. Hosni Mubarak (right) maintained Sadat's reforms and strengthened Egypt's ties with the Arab world.

Policy changes on the domestic front were equally dramatic. In 1974, Sadat launched his **infitah**, or *shift to capitalism* (Gillespie 1984). Henceforth, Egypt would possess a mixed economy in which private-sector firms were free to compete with the public sector. American aid and Western investment, Sadat promised, would make Egypt the economic hub of the Middle East (Fahmy 1988). Egypt, moreover, had traded guns for butter. The "peace dividend" would allow Egypt to scale back its military expenditures and concentrate on economic development. Prosperity was assured. Economic reforms were matched by halting steps toward democracy. Although Sadat remained the absolute leader of Egypt, political parties re-emerged and the Egyptian Parliament was allowed to debate issues of minor importance.

Sadat's dream of capitalist prosperity fared little better than Nasser's vision of a socialist utopia. The newly revived capitalist sector concentrated on quick-profit projects that did little to strengthen the overall economy, while huge sums of money found their way into the pockets of Sadat's friends and family (Springborg 1989). Although a minority of Egyptians prospered, the majority sank deeper into poverty (Gillespie 1984). Egypt's economic and social problems continued to multiply, as did its population. Democratic reforms were cancelled as Sadat's popularity plummeted, with many of the disaffected joining the Muslim Brotherhood and other Islamic groups. In September 1981, Sadat ordered the arrest of more than 1,500 political activists, many of them Muslim Fundamentalists. He was assassinated a month later by Muslim extremists within the military.

The Revolution in Retreat: Mubarak (1981–   )

Sadat was succeeded in office by Vice President Hosni Mubarak, the current President of Egypt. Mubarak, a leader with a reputation for honesty and caution, has extended Sadat's reforms in the areas of democratization and capitalism and maintained Sadat's policies of friendship with the United States and Israel. Mubarak, however, has also reestablished Egypt's ties with the Arab world. The headquarters of the Arab League has returned to Cairo, as has foreign assistance from Saudi Arabia and the oil-producing states of the Arab/Persian Gulf. Egypt has once again become the center of the Arab World.

The Egypt of today, moreover, bears little resemblance to the Egypt of the Nasser era. Revolutionary Councils have given way to a constitutional structure not dissimilar to that of France. Executive power is divided between a strong president and a weak prime minister selected by the president. Legislative authority resides in a Parliament elected in a quasi-fair election, and a Constitutional Council (Supreme Court) possesses the power to declare acts of the Government unconstitutional. It has done so on several occasions but usually with the implicit agreement of the president. The single-party apparatus of the Nasser era has been replaced by a multiparty system, albeit a multiparty system in which the government party always wins. The Egyptian press is freer than at any time since the Nasser Revolution of 1952, and the rigid socialism of the earlier era has been challenged by a growing private sector (Kays 1984).

Nevertheless, the Egypt of today is very much the product of the Nasser era. The president of the Egyptian Republic is still a military officer, as are his major advisors. The Parliament and the Court, while vigorous in the execution of their responsibilities, pose little challenge to the presidency. Despite some progress toward privatization and economic reform, the Egyptian economy continues to be micro-managed by a massive bureaucracy (Harik 1997).

The Egypt of today has also inherited the problems of the past (McDermott 1988). The population explosion continues, with the 20 million Egyptians of the revolutionary era having become nearly 60 million today. That figure, moreover, is expected to reach 125 million by the year 2020. Poverty continues, although few Egyptians are threatened with starvation. Housing shortages are critical, as are levels of unemployment and underemployment. Official estimates place the unemployment figure in the 10 to 13 percent range, but unofficial estimates are much higher. From one-third to one-half of all working Egyptians, moreover, are underemployed, a euphemistic term for disguised unemployment.

The capitalist reforms of the Sadat and Mubarak eras have also created new problems. While a minority of the Egyptian population enjoys unparalleled prosperity, most Egyptians find life increasingly more difficult. Many Egyptian intellectuals also feel that Egypt is in danger of becoming dependent on the United States. While this may or may not be the case, the $2 billion in foreign aid that the United States provides to Egypt on an annual basis does assure that American views will receive a careful hearing in Cairo. The growing strength of the Islamic Fundamentalists also threatens to undermine the viability of Egypt's quasi-democratic political institutions. It is in this environment, then, that we examine Egyptian politics and its quest for democracy, stability, and prosperity.

The Political Institutions of Egypt

Political institutions are the arena of politics. It is the executives, legislatures, courts, bureaucracies, and other agencies of government that authoritatively allocate the resources of the state. In this section, we shall examine the political institutions of Egypt, of which the executive is by far the most important.

Executive Power in Egypt: The President and the Prime Minister

Much as in the case of France, whose constitution served as a pattern for the Egyptian constitution, Egypt possesses both a president and a prime minister. It is here, however, that similarities stop, for the Egyptian prime minister possesses only the power that the president allocates to him.

The President. The Egyptian president stands at the pinnacle of a political system that is intensely centralized. The Egyptian president is commander-in-chief of both the military and the internal security forces. He appoints the prime minister, the Cabinet, a variety of vice-presidents, and all senior members of the bureaucracy and the military.[8] Interestingly, Mubarak has refused to appoint a vice-president, a fact that has caused concern among his supporters as he begins his fourth term in office (*Agency France Presse,* Sept. 28, 1999). The president may dissolve Parliament at will, and he is also empowered to rule by decree during periods of emergency. President Sadat ruled by emergency decree for much of his decade (1970–1981) in office, as does Mubarak today (*Cairo Times,* Feb. 29, 2000, www). More recently, however, Mubarak has encouraged the Egyptian Parliament to play a more vigorous role in governing Egypt. Growing tensions between the government and the Islamic Fundamentalists, unfortunately, threaten to force a reversal of this policy.

The formal powers of President Mubarak are augmented by formidable informal powers. Of these, five are of particular importance.

1. *President Mubarak possesses strong support within the ranks of the officer corps.* Whatever its progress toward democracy, Egypt remains a quasi-military regime.
2. *Mubarak is supported by the resources of the Presidential Office.* The Presidential Office is a special bureaucracy of several thousand members who assist the president in political and security matters. It also includes a special intelligence service and a presidential army, the Republican Guards.
3. *The president is the leader of the National Democratic Party (NDP), the semi-official party of the Egyptian political system.* The NDP's near-total dominance of the Egyptian Parliament assures that the president's program will be enacted into law.
4. *The president enjoys tremendous patronage power by virtue of his control over Egypt's massive state bureaucracy.* All military or civilian appointments of consequence require presidential approval, and permits are required for everything. There is no dimension of politics in Egypt that escapes the attention of the Egyptian president and his appointed representatives.
5. *The president and his accomplishments are glorified by the mass media, much of which is state-controlled.* Even the press, while technically free, exercises remarkable self-restraint in criticizing a president who seemingly can do no wrong.

For all of his quasi-dictatorial powers, the Egyptian president is far from being a free agent. The Presidential Office, the military, the NDP, and the bureaucracy each attempts to increase its own power by "manipulating" the president. The Presidential Office, for example, serves as a "gatekeeper," regulating access to the president and controlling the information the president receives on key issues. Given his multiple responsibilities, the Egyptian president is far too busy to see everybody or read everything. It is the Presidential Office that decides what the president needs to know.

The military, for its part, maintains the regime in power, and its voice remains the strongest single voice in Egypt today (Kechichian and Nazimek 1997). The senior members of the Presidential Office, for example, are selected from the military, as are key governors and administrative personnel. Military access to the president is direct and immediate.

In much the same manner, the National Democratic Party is Mubarak's link to the civilian power structure at the national and local levels, a power structure of ever-increasing importance as Egypt moves in the direction of greater democracy. The advice of its leaders must be heeded if Mubarak is to stay in touch with an increasingly

---

[8]Many senior appointments are suggested by the prime minister and approved by the president, but the president's voice is dominant.

politicized population. The bureaucracy, in turn, absorbs most of Egypt's budget and determines how efficiently the president's policies will be implemented. Presidential decisions are not self-executing, and the president needs the cooperation of the bureaucratic elite to get things done.

The agencies of presidential power in Egypt, then, are not passive. They provide the president with the organizational apparatus that he requires to govern, but they also place demands on him that are not easily ignored. All Egyptian presidents, in turn, have attempted to avoid manipulation or "capture" by any single agency by pitting one agency against another (conversation between the author and Salwa Gomaa, 1993). This grand balancing act provides the president with multiple sources of information but also creates confusion within the ranks of the government.

The Prime Minister and Cabinet. As the above discussion suggests, the position of prime minister is not a powerful one. The prime minister is selected by the president, serves at the will of the president, and can be dismissed at the whim of the president. His[9] major responsibility is guiding the president's program through a subservient Parliament dominated by the semi-official National Democratic Party. The president makes the major decisions, and the prime minister and Cabinet work out the details (Bahgat 1991). Quite frequently, a change in prime ministers reflects a major change in policy. If the new policies are successful, the president takes the credit. If the policies fail, the prime minister and Cabinet take the blame and give way to a new "team."

Legislative Power in Egypt: The Majlis As-Shab and the Majlis As-Shoura

The Egyptian Parliament consists of two separate and independent bodies: the People's Assembly (**Majlis As-Shab**) and the Consultive Assembly (**Majlis As-Shoura**). The members of the People's Assembly are elected for five-year terms by universal suffrage. Half of the members of the Consultive Assembly are popularly elected, and the remainder are selected by the president. The Consultive Assembly, as its name suggests, is an honorific debating society designed to air issues of public importance (Bianchi 1989). Its sessions are often broadcast on Egyptian television, but the body has little legislative authority. Indeed, cynics refer to it as a rest home for "burned-out" officials (Springborg 1989).

The theoretical powers of the People's Assembly, by contrast, are formidable. All laws of the land must be approved by the People's Assembly, including the annual budget. As in the United States, moreover, a presidential veto can be overridden by a two-thirds vote of its members, although this has yet to happen. Laws enacted by the president during periods of emergency rule must be submitted to the People's Assembly for ratification after the emergency period has ended. Both the prime minister and the members of his Cabinet are responsible before the People's Assembly, and confidence may be withdrawn from the Government as a whole or from an individual minister. In the latter instance, the minister in question is forced to resign, but the Government remains in place.[10] Members of the People's Assembly also possess the right to interrogate ministers and senior members of ministerial staffs. Finally, the People's Assembly plays an important role in the nomination of the president. If a president dies, resigns, or is incapable of fulfilling his presidential responsibilities, the president of the People's Assembly serves as the head of government while the members of the Assembly nominate a new candidate

---

[9]There has yet to be a female prime minister in Egypt.
[10]This is an unlikely event because the Government always has a majority in the Assembly.

for the presidency. Only one person is nominated for the presidency, and that person is presented to the public by means of a **plebiscite**. *The public may vote for acceptance or rejection.* If the public rejects the nomination, the People's Assembly will nominate a second candidate who will again be presented to the public in a plebescite. This has yet to happen.

The constitutional powers of the Egyptian Parliament, unfortunately, are largely theoretical. It is the leader of the National Democratic Party, President Mubarak, who has the final say on what legislation the Assembly will pass. Somewhat fair legislative elections, moreover, have become a feature of Egyptian politics only within the last few years, and even these elections have been structured to assure overwhelming victories by the semi-official NDP. Until recently, the most popular political movements, the Muslim Fundamentalists and the Nasserites, were banned from direct political participation, and even today the position of the Muslim groups remains uncertain. Voting turnout is low, and opposition parties often choose to boycott elections as a symbolic means of protesting questionable electoral procedures.

Does this mean that the Egyptian Parliament is irrelevant? Not entirely. The existence of a functioning parliament and the holding of reasonably fair parliamentary elections are important steps in the democratic process. Whether this process will continue to grow remains to be seen. The 1995 elections were not encouraging (Mustafa 1995).

The Parliament also allows the opposition an opportunity to provide vocal criticisms of Government policy. In the session of the Majlis As-Shab that convened in February 1999, for example, the opposition complained that Egypt's economic reforms had increased the wealth of the rich while further impoverishing the poor. They also complained bitterly of corruption in local government, suggesting that many local districts had been transformed into the private fiefdoms of local officials (*Al-Ahram,* Feb. 14, 1999, 13).

Law and Politics in Egypt: The Constitutional Court

The Egyptian Constitution provides for an independent judiciary as well as a Constitutional Court that supervises the judicial system and possesses the right to declare laws and other acts of government unconstitutional. The Constitutional Court also interprets the meaning of laws judged to be ambiguous. The broader structure of the Egyptian legal system is based upon French (Napoleonic) canon law, with adjustments being made for the predominantly Islamic character of Egyptian society. Islamic law takes precedence in marriage, divorce, and other areas referred to as personal statutes. The Islamic Fundamentalists would like to see the Koranic role in Egyptian law greatly expanded, and the Mubarak regime seems to be moving, however grudgingly, in this direction.

How, then, does a Western-type legal system operate in a quasi-dictatorial state? On routine matters, the Egyptian courts operate with reasonable efficiency and are generally free of political influence. Politically sensitive issues are more problematic, as the Constitutional Court's power to review government decisions can be overridden by the president's emergency powers.

The president has the option of sending issues of state security to military courts rather than to civilian courts. Islamic Fundamentalists charged with attacks on foreign tourists, for example, have been tried by military courts, a procedure that deprives them of their constitutional rights. The military has its own legal system and is not subject to civilian law.

These limitations aside, the Constitutional Court has played a vigorous role in strengthening Egyptian democracy. Unfair election laws have twice been declared unconstitutional by the Court, and the Court has also played a vigorous role in blocking Government attempts to restrict the activities of political parties. The Constitutional Court cannot rival the presidency as a source of political power, but it has developed at least some precedents for independent action. The president has also allowed unpopular policies to be overridden by the Court as a means of saving face. Rather than backtracking in the face of popular opposition, he can claim to be strengthening Egyptian democracy. Recently, for example, the Court invalidated a very controversial law prohibiting female students from wearing Islamic dress to schools. The government capitulated in the name of democracy, thereby freeing itself from a policy that would have been difficult, if not dangerous, to enforce. More recently, the courts have been in the forefront of attacking corruption in the People's Assembly, a fact that has created tension between the two branches of government (*Al-Ahram,* Sept. 4, 1999, 16).

Bureaucracy and Politics in Egypt: The Emergence of a Bureaucratic State

The Egyptian bureaucracy, in common with most bureaucracies of the Third World, performs two basic functions:

- First, it maintains an ever-increasing array of services essential to the day-to-day operation of the state.
- Second, it bears primary responsibility for the economic and social development of Egyptian society.

If one is to judge by the comments of President Mubarak, the Egyptian bureaucracy has failed on both counts. In a 1985 speech, he complained that

> We had before us (upon assuming office) the prospect of crumbling public services and utilities. The situation was the result of years of accumulated paralysis and neglect. Citizens complained of the situation from the moment they opened their eyes in the morning until they returned from work. The flow of water was inadequate and irregular. Electric current fluctuated, and extended blackouts were common. Communications moved at a snail's pace. Roads were impassable. Television was limited. The decay of the sewer system turned some streets and quarters into swamps....
>
> Medical equipment in public hospitals is old and in short supply. Public services (bureaucracy) oppress the citizens with routine and delay. Free education has lost much of its effectiveness, and the expense of college education is oppressive to Egyptian families. Then there are the problems of housing shortages, rising prices, vanishing goods, and of houses collapsing on their inhabitants. The list of problems our people complain of is endless, yet they are forced to put up with them (Mubarak, 1985, Address to the Egyptian Parliament, *Al-Ahram,* Nov. 14, 1985).

The situation is little better today. Indeed, the Egyptian bureaucracy is now viewed as a major obstacle to the economic and social development of Egyptian society (Palmer, Leila, and Yassin 1988; *Al-Ahram,* Sept. 2, 1999, 11).

The criticisms of the Egyptian bureaucracy are both numerous and varied. Government employees in Egypt are said to be self-serving, lazy, corrupt, rigid, lacking in creativity, insensitive to the public, and fearful of taking responsibility. One study estimated that the average Egyptian official "works" somewhere between twenty minutes and two hours per day (Ayubi 1982). Unless bureaucratic performance improves dramatically, the quality of life of the average Egyptian will continue to slide. Political stability and hopes for democracy will deteriorate apace.

The International Monetary Fund (IMF), USAID, and the World Bank have all demanded that Egypt scale down the size of its bureaucracy. Egyptian intellectuals and the Egyptian press have joined the chorus, blaming the bureaucracy for most of Egypt's social and economic woes. As yet, however, reform remains elusive. The Mubarak government, as the Nasser and Sadat governments before it, depends upon the bureaucracy to provide a safety net to the ever-increasing number of unemployed graduates. Mubarak also needs a patronage system to reward supporters of the regime.

The Actors in Egyptian Politics: Elites, Parties, Groups, and Citizens

Political institutions are the arena of politics, but it is the actors in the political process who determine who gets what, when, and how. In this section we will look at the "human" element of Egyptian politics by examining the political influence of Egypt's elites, parties, groups, and citizens.

Elites and Politics in Egypt

Political power in Egypt is concentrated in the hands of the president. Parliaments and political parties exist, but their ability to constrain the authority of the president is largely symbolic. Elite status in Egypt, accordingly, is determined by access to the president.

The concentration of political authority in the hands of the Egyptian president makes the decision-making process inordinately dependent upon the values, style, and personality traits of a single individual. The concerns of one president, moreover, are not necessarily those of the next. In a period of a few years, for example, Egypt was transformed from Nasser's vision of Egypt as a socialist state allied with the Soviet Union and dedicated to the cause of Arab unity into Sadat's vision of Egypt as a mixed socialist/capitalist state allied with the United States and disparaging of Arab unity. Mubarak, in turn, has tried to stake out a middle ground between the two extremes. Should Egypt's gradual march toward democracy lead to a victory for the Islamic forces, the transformation of Egyptian politics would be total.

Predicting the course of Egyptian politics, then, has much to do with analyzing the personality style of the man in power. In this regard, Salwa Gomaa suggests that the personality styles of Egypt's three presidents have been radically different (Gomaa 1991). Nasser, for example, saw himself as a guide and teacher. Sadat's self-image, by contrast, was that of the patriarchal father. He viewed Egypt's citizens as his children and felt it was his duty to take care of them. Others have suggested that Sadat viewed himself as something of an English gentleman, smoking his pipe while shaping the course of world history (McDermott 1975). Both Nasser and Sadat, according to Gomaa, had large egos. Both felt that they could change the course of history and were anxious to do so. Mubarak, by contrast, appears to view himself as a senior bureaucrat assigned the responsibility of guiding the ship of state through troubled waters.

Differences in self-image are paralleled by differences in decision-making styles. Sadat gloried in the element of surprise, making sweeping decisions with blinding speed. He hated details, and he made many decisions on the basis of oral reports and poorly documented information. He also seemed to place greater faith in foreign advisors than in his own people. This was particularly true in the area of foreign affairs. Mubarak, by contrast, is far more cautious than his predecessor. He proceeds slowly, making careful, step-by-step decisions based upon consultations with a wide variety of groups. He also tends to read reports in great detail and doesn't like surprises. Nasser fell between the two extremes. He was careful by nature but reacted swiftly to external events. Mubarak's personality style, then, lends itself to moderation. It is not clear, however, that his incremental mode of decision making is conducive to solving Egypt's massive social and economic problems. Massive problems often require radical solutions.

As powerful as the Egyptian president may be, he ultimately shares power with a variety of sub-elites or secondary elites who assist in the formulation and execution of his policies (Akhavi 1975). This group includes senior military commanders, vice-presidents (if they exist), senior members of the presidential office, senior Cabinet ministers, and the leadership of the NDP. The elite circle would also include governors of Egypt's most populous provinces, a limited number of business leaders, and Egypt's senior religious leaders.

Sadat attempted to break his dependence upon the secondary elite by keeping it in a perpetual state of flux. He was also reluctant to share the limelight with his subordinates, many of whom he believed to be of questionable loyalty (El Gamassy 1989). Mubarak, by contrast, has made minimal alterations in the structure of the secondary elite over the past decade. Mubarak is also less inclined to go it alone than Sadat, preferring instead to broker between competing policy alternatives suggested by his subordinates. Both factors make the secondary elite under Mubarak far more powerful than the secondary elite under Sadat.

The secondary elites, in turn, head a cadre of "influential" military officers, party leaders, and senior bureaucrats that form the backbone of Egypt's presidential system. Although not qualifying as an elite in the grand sense of the term, they clearly represent a privileged "political" class. As such, they coexist with both the new entrepreneurial class spawned by the infitah and the older aristocratic class, both of which also enjoy privileged status in Egyptian society.

Parties and Politics in Egypt

Political parties have a relatively brief history in Egypt. We will look at how the party system evolved and where it stands today.

The Evolution of Egyptian Political Parties. Egypt's revolution was a "revolution from above" (Trimberger 1978). The military had seized power in the name of the masses, but it had no direct link with the masses. Having abolished Egypt's traditional political parties within a few months of seizing power, Nasser would soon find it difficult to rule without a political organization of some type. An Egyptian population benumbed by centuries of oppression and foreign domination had to be energized if the revolution were to achieve its goals. This was the task of a political party.

Nasser needed a political organization to mobilize the Egyptian masses, but he remained deeply opposed to the revival of a multiparty system. Party conflict, from Nasser's perspective, would merely reinforce the divisiveness of an Egyptian society already fragmented by conflict and distrust. He also feared that a strong political party would represent a challenge to the authority of the military regime. Nasser wanted a political organization capable of defending the revolution and mobilizing the masses on its behalf, but he did not want an independent political organization that would constrain his own authority.

Nasser, accordingly, resolved to create a single, mass-based political organization: the Arab Socialist Union. The Arab Socialist Union (ASU) would be open to all Egyptians other than the enemies of the revolution—a category that included wealthy landowners, communists, and the Muslim Brotherhood. The new party would penetrate all echelons of Egyptian society from the remotest villages to the slums of Cairo (Baker 1978). Its members would be the revolution's cadres. They would mobilize the

Egyptian masses in support of the revolution's goals, and they would also be the eyes and ears of the revolution, constantly vigilant to the machinations of its enemies. The new party was to have other functions as well. It would serve as a forum for debate, a channel of communication, an agent of political socialization, and a conduit for recruiting the "best and the brightest" into the service of the revolution.

The ASU, however, was not to become the revolutionary instrument that Nasser had envisioned (Baker 1978). Fearing any independent source of political authority, Nasser and his supporters kept the ASU on a tight leash. Equally problematic was a shortage of cadres willing to dedicate their lives to the revolution and its objectives. While some Egyptians joined the ASU out of revolutionary fervor, most were motivated by expediency and opportunism. Membership in the ASU increased one's chances of securing a good position in the bureaucracy and provided political connections. It was also the avenue to power at the local and regional levels. Opportunists, unfortunately, make poor cadres. Their dedication was to themselves, not to the revolution. The ASU would thus become a self-serving political bureaucracy not unlike the Communist Party bureaucracy of the Soviet Union.

If the ASU had served Nasser poorly, it served Sadat not at all. The leaders of the ASU opposed Sadat's presidency in 1970 and subsequently used the ASU apparatus to undermine his authority. In 1971, the leadership of the ASU was implicated in an abortive attempt to overthrow Sadat.

Sadat would eventually revive the Arab Socialist Union, albeit with a leadership loyal to himself. Sadat, like Nasser, had hoped that the reformulated ASU would provide broad-based support for his regime. It did not. Much as before, the revived ASU served as little more than a machine for distributing patronage to Sadat's supporters, and the public remained apathetic.

Shaken by riots in 1977, Sadat promised the Egyptian population a return to democracy. Egypt, Sadat declared, would have three independent political parties: a party of the left, a party of the capitalist right, and a party of the center. Sadat disavowed membership in any of the three parties, claiming to stand above politics. Virtually all government officials, however, became members of the centrist party, as it was well understood that this was the party of Sadat, his protestations to the contrary notwithstanding. The Wafd Party also resurfaced in 1977, calling itself the New Wafd Party. Egypt had thus evolved into a qualified multiparty state, although the communists and Nasserites were still proscribed from forming an independent political party, as was the Muslim Brotherhood.

In July 1978, Sadat made yet another about-face, announcing the creation of the National Democratic Party (NDP), of which he would be president. Members of the centrist party, barely a year old, resigned to become members of Sadat's new party. Sadat's National Democratic Party took over the buildings and organizational network of the defunct ASU, providing a remarkable continuity in membership and party organization between Sadat's ASU and the NDP. The more things changed, the more they stayed the same. Egypt had become a multiparty state, but only one party counted.

Political Parties and Mass Movements in Egypt Today. Mubarak's era of quasi-democracy has witnessed a proliferation of political parties. Some have deep roots in Egyptian society, while others are little more than empty shells left over from the Sadat era. The picture is made even more complicated by the fluidity of Egyptian parties. Parties merge in an effort to make a stronger electoral showing, only to splinter as a result of personality conflict or ideological differences.

For all its complexity, the Egyptian party system is dominated by four distinct tendencies: the left, the center, the capitalist right, and the Islamic (Muslim) right.

Egyptian Party System

Tendency	Dominant Party	Type of Government
Left	Nasserites, Tagumma	Socialism
Center	National Democratic Party	Guided democracy
Capitalist right	New Wafd	Free-market democracy
Religious right	Muslim Brotherhood	Islamic state

The parties of the left, now dominated by the Nasserites and the Tagumma (Communists), advocate a return to the socialism of the Nasser era, albeit a socialism administered in a more efficient and less corrupt manner. The parties of the capitalist right, and the **New Wafd** in particular, call for a complete break with Egypt's socialist past, including the privatization of the public-sector enterprises that constitute a large percentage of the Egyptian economy. The religious right, of which the Muslim Brotherhood is the quasi-legal representative, would transform Egypt into an Islamic theocracy but is not opposed to capitalism. Spanning the middle of these seemingly irreconcilable tendencies is the ruling National Democratic Party. Its ideological position, such as it is, calls for some socialism, some capitalism, and some religion. However vague its ideology, the NDP is the only party that counts. Aside from the Muslim Brotherhood, to be discussed shortly, the other parties are ephemeral to the political process.

The National Democratic Party is the successor of the Arab Socialist Union as reconstituted by Sadat, and it embodies essentially the same membership and organizational structure as the ASU. Village and neighborhood organizations form the base of the NDP's organizational pyramid, followed in turn by organizations at the district and provincial levels. This elaborate organizational structure is capped by a national secretariat headed ultimately by President Mubarak, the head of the Party.[11]

Despite its democratic trappings, the NDP remains a highly centralized organization controlled by President Mubarak. Its role is to provide Egypt's quasi-military regime with resounding majorities in the Parliament, a role accomplished by the lavish use of "wasta" (political patronage). Much like the old ASU, the NDP is the regime's primary dispenser of patronage. The members of the NDP enjoy greater access to government jobs and receive preferential treatment in their dealings with Egypt's pervasive bureaucratic apparatus. Both concerns are of vital importance in a country where little can be accomplished without "connections" of one form or another.

The NDP also assures its dominance by co-opting local landowners, businessmen, and other notables into the Party apparatus. The notables use their considerable influence to encourage voting for the NDP. The NDP reciprocates by assuring that the interests of the notables are taken care of and by providing them with patronage to reward their supporters. The stronger the base of the notables, the stronger the position of the NDP.

Finally, election laws have been manipulated in favor of the NDP. Until recently, for example, election laws required that a party receive 8 percent of the vote to be represented in the Parliament. The votes of parties receiving less than 8 percent automatically went to the majority party—the NDP. The huge electoral

---

[11]Party policy, in theory but not in practice, is determined by periodic Party Congresses. The Party Congress also elects a Central Committee to guide party activities between Congresses. The NDP emphasizes its credentials as the party of the revolution by requiring that at least half the delegates to Party Congresses and half the members of the Central Committee be workers and peasants.

victories of the NDP result from other factors as well. Many Egyptians feel that opposing the NDP is useless, so they refrain from voting. This has made voter turnout in Egypt among the lowest in the world.

The NDP's domination of the People's Assembly has enabled Mubarak to rule under the guise of parliamentary democracy without fear of serious opposition to his policies (*Middle East Times*, 2000, Issue 7, www). Indeed, the NDP maintains an array of specialized committees, the membership of which is remarkably similar to the membership of the legislative committees in the People's Assembly. What the party committees decide is essentially what the parliamentary committees recommend. Although opposition delegates can (and do) chastise Government policy, the Government's position is never in doubt (*Middle East Times*, 2000, Issue 14, www).

Islam and Politics in Egypt

To understand the role of the Islamic right in Egyptian politics, it is important to recall that Islam does not recognize a clear distinction between church and state. The Koran (the holy book of Islam) is the law of God as revealed to the Prophet Mohammed. The Koran speaks of a world of peace and a world of war (Khadduri 1955). Muslims, the adherents of Islam, live in the world of peace. As such, they constitute an Islamic nation to be guided by Islamic law. Western notions of nationalism are contrary to the concept of a unified nation of believers, for loyalty to a state contradicts loyalty to God.

Egypt is a predominantly Islamic country, with approximately 90 percent of its citizens adhering to the Islamic faith. Divorcing Islam from Egyptian politics is a virtual impossibility. The political influence of Islam manifests itself in at least five ways.

First, Islam provides the moral underpinning of Egyptian society. Egyptian politicians are very careful not to offend Islamic sentiments. Even in the heady days of revolutionary nationalism, every effort was made to find an Islamic justification for Nasser's policies. Egyptian socialism was not Marxist socialism. Rather, it was Islamic socialism, legitimized by the principles of social equity contained in the Koran.

Second, much of the current political debate in Egypt centers on the extent to which Islamic law should be incorporated into Egyptian secular law. Islamic groups are pushing hard to have the Koran implemented as the legal Constitution of Egypt. At the minimum, they demand a sharp curtailment of bars, imprudent dress, and other Western practices offensive to Islamic law.

Third, the mosque provides a focal point of Islamic opposition to the Mubarak regime. The Government can ban the Fundamentalists from forming political parties, but it cannot close the mosques. Sermons in the mosque are often political, suggesting indirectly or not so indirectly that Egypt's problems would be fewer if the Government followed Islamic principles. Informal conversations before and after the prayers also provide Islamic Fundamentalists with ample opportunity to proselytize in support of their goal of an Islamic state. Sadat made an abortive attempt to bring Egypt's mosques under government control, but he was assassinated for his efforts. The Mubarak regime has now renewed this endeavor (Zaqzug 1999). As the Minister of Religious Endowments charged with implementing the policy explained, "The Friday sermons are not a political broadcast" (Zaqzug 1999). Whether it will succeed or not remains a matter of conjecture, for it is estimated that Egypt possesses some 60,000 mosques, many beyond the control of the state. The government also lacks a sufficient number of "qualified" preachers to service the vast numbers of non-governmental mosques (Mustafa 1995). (Non-governmental mosques are operated by private individuals, while government mosques are owned and operated by the Egyptian government.)

Tens of thousands of Muslims kneel in prayer at dawn in front of Cairo's Mustafa Mahmoud Mosque at the start of Eid al-Adha, a four-day feast commemorating the life of the prophet Abraham. Nine out of ten Egyptians are Muslim.

Fourth, Islamic groups now control the "street." In Egypt, as in most other countries of the Third World, street demonstrations often turn violent, testing the Government's resolve and threatening to trigger broader religious and class violence. More often than not, such demonstrations begin in the universities and spread to labor unions and other groups. The Fundamentalists have now gone far beyond street demonstrations, assassinating government officials and foreign tourists. In 1995 an attempt was made to assassinate Mubarak, but it failed. Fundamentalist violence has eased for the moment as fundamentalist groups attempt to go mainstream, but it could reemerge at any time (Rose al-Yousef, Dec. 2, 1999; *Middle East Times,* Jan. 2000, www).

Finally, Islam stands as an alternative to the established model of a Westernized state. The Islamic Fundamentalists are minimally concerned with reforming the Egyptian political system. Their goal is the destruction of the present system and the creation of an Islamic state, a process that occurred in Iran in 1979. The creation of an Islamic state has considerable appeal to many Egyptians. Since the present system isn't working, what do they have to lose?

The Islamic forces in Egypt, although formidable, do not speak with a single voice. Rather, one finds three separate claimants to the Islamic mantle: the traditional Islamic religious establishment, the Muslim Brotherhood, and the Islamic Fundamentalists (Mustafa 1995).

The Islamic Establishment. The most important figures in Egypt's formal Islamic establishment are the Minister of Religious Endowments, the Grand Mufti or Judge, and the Rector of Al-Azhar, Cairo's renowned Islamic university (Barraclough 1998; Ismail 1998). These, in turn, are surrounded by a variety of religious leaders collectively referred to as the Ulema. The government plays a dominant role in the appointment of senior religious officials, thereby assuring that the religious establishment is headed by men whose positions are compatible with the views of the president. Under Nasser, the Islamic establishment was headed by religious scholars who shared the regime's reformist views. Under Sadat and Mubarak, it has become more conservative. Despite their differences, all Egyptian governments have sought the blessing of the Ulema for their policies.

The Muslim Brotherhood. The Muslim Brotherhood is the oldest and most visible element of the Islamic Right. Created in the 1920s by Hassan Al-Banna, the Brotherhood preached a message that was both simple and poignant. Egypt's plight, according to the Brotherhood, was caused by the decadence of the ruling elite and by the foreign influences that sustained that elite. God's word, as revealed by the Prophet Mohammed, was both clear and unequivocal. To follow the word of God was to achieve eternal salvation; to ignore it was to court damnation. It was the duty of all Muslims to forge a government based on Islamic principles. The main tools of the Brotherhood were teaching and preaching, providing welfare service for the poor, and assassination (Husaini 1956).

Anwar Sadat and many other Free Officers were members of the Muslim Brotherhood before seizing power in July 1952 (Abdula 1990). Indeed, relations between the Free Officers and Brotherhood were not to become fully clarified until the Brotherhood attempted to assassinate President Nasser in 1954. Nasser's revenge was swift and brutal. The Brotherhood was driven into remission, but its organizational roots remained intact. Sadat revived the Brotherhood in 1971 in an effort to curb the growing influence of his leftist opponents.

The tacit acceptance of the Brotherhood as a quasi-legitimate political organization provided it with increased scope for political activity. Electoral alliances were forged with the New Wafd and other parties of the capitalist right. More recently, the Brotherhood has simply incorporated the Socialist Labor Party and the much smaller Liberal Party. The Brotherhood also dominates Egypt's most important student and professional unions and has deepened its mass base by opening a vast network of Islamic schools, clinics, and investment companies (Aly 1989; Fahmy 1998). Some estimates now suggest that as much as 10 percent of the Egyptian population uses the services provided by the Brotherhood and related organizations (Mustafa 1995). In many ways, the Islamic elements are creating a social infrastructure parallel to that of the state. The Egyptian government is now attempting to curb the activities of the Muslim Brotherhood (*Middle East Times*, 2000, Issue 15, www).

The Fundamentalist Right. Legitimacy has had its costs. The growing moderation of the Brotherhood has made it passé for many younger Fundamentalists, who, while fragmented into disparate groups, share a common belief that the existing political system is beyond reform. It must, in their view, be destroyed and replaced by an Islamic government.

Assessing the strength of the Fundamentalist movement is a difficult task.

▍ It was they who assassinated Sadat, and it is they who continue to pose the most serious threat to the survival of the Mubarak regime. During the 1990s, extremist groups have attacked tourist buses, forcing at least a 40 percent drop in Egypt's tourist revenues. The attacks have now eased, but the Fundamentalists have not given up their goal of establishing an Islamic state. Merely the strategy has changed (Barakat and Sadiq 1998).

■ What is known of the Fundamentalist leaders is that they tend to be young, well educated, and frustrated by the decadence and inequities of Egyptian society (Ibrahim 1980; Ansari 1985; Ayubi 1982, 1983, 1989). They also find much support among the poor.

■ The Fundamentalists are well funded and have a broad base of support throughout all areas of Egyptian society, including the military, the police, and the educational system. In the autumn of 1994, for example, the Government began a purge of pro-Islamic teachers from Egypt's 25,000 schools, a venture that was doomed to failure before it began (*NYT,* Oct. 4, 1994, A4).

■ While no one knows the exact size of the Fundamentalist movement, its numbers will only be increased by the growing gap between the rich and the poor in Egyptian society (Kienle 1998; Springborg 1998).

Pressure Groups and Politics in Egypt

In addition to political parties and Islamic organizations, a variety of other groups exercise varying degrees of influence on Egyptian politics. We will look at several of these groups, including workers and peasants, business associations, the military, and social groups.

Workers and Peasants. The latter years of the monarchy had witnessed the emergence of a wide variety of labor unions, business organizations, professional associations, and other Western-type pressure groups in Egypt. With the advent of revolutionary socialism in the early 1950s, the business groups disbanded, while the labor, peasant, and professional associations were tied to the government in a corporatist arrangement similar to that described in the discussions of German politics (Beinin and Lockman 1987; Binder 1978). Egypt's unions, weak by European standards, supported the Nasser regime in the hope that the new corporatist arrangements would result in improved wages, job security, and welfare benefits for their members (Bianchi 1989).

Similar efforts were made to mobilize Egypt's peasants by organizing them into state-managed cooperatives, but the peasants were of less concern to Egypt's military leaders than the labor unions (Bianchi 1989). Organized labor was an urban phenomenon that, if left unchecked, could challenge the authority of the regime. Peasants, by contrast, were isolated from the center of power and lacked either the organizational capacity or group consciousness required to pose a sustained threat to the regime (Ayrout 1962).

As Nathan Brown describes the situation during the 1950s, Egypt's peasants were a profoundly negative force in Egyptian politics, and they had to be neutralized if the revolution were to achieve its goals.

> Egyptian peasants devoted much of their political energy to avoiding or evading the state and in the process demonstrated both resourcefulness and tenacity, sometimes even to the point of risking their lives. Yet their aims remained limited. Egyptian peasants never sought to destroy, overthrow, or defeat the state as a whole, instead their efforts generally focused on local officials.... What is striking about the actions of Egyptian peasants is not so much that they tried to evade the state but that they tried for so long. Right up to the end of the period, they persisted in refusing to cooperate with police, in attacking officials acting inimically to peasant livelihood, and in sabotaging railroad lines to ruin the reputation of specific umdas (village mayors). Peasants seemed as irresponsible to their rulers in 1952 as they had in 1882 (Brown 1990, 215–16).

Egypt's professionals were also organized into a variety of government-sponsored syndicates with a view toward better controlling their activities and assuring their subservience to the regime. Of these, the most prominent were the syndicates of journalists, lawyers, teachers, and engineers (Bianchi 1989). Each elected its own leaders, but the victory of government candidates was never in doubt.

Labor, peasant, and most professional associations remain under government control today, but that control has lessened as syndicate elections have become increasingly dominated by opposition parties, including the Fundamentalists. Indeed, by the mid-1990s, the Muslim Brotherhood dominated the largest of Egypt's twenty-two main professional organizations, including the medical, legal, and engineering associations. This clearly demonstrates that the appeal of Fundamentalism is not limited to the lower classes.

Business Associations. Sadat's 1974 infitah, or new economic opening, witnessed a revival of business associations. The influence of these associations, however, has been weakened by their inability to agree on a common strategy for dealing with the Mubarak regime. Some flavor of this debate is provided by Robert Springborg:

> Underlying the conflict are personal and organizational jealousies and the fact that the [Businessmen's] Association is composed principally of a Mubarak generation of businessmen, or, more precisely, those who currently enjoy good access to the elite. The Chamber of Commerce, on the other hand, tends to combine generations of the bourgeoisie that matured in previous eras; hence it includes those with no significant political connections and those who emerged through the public sector, as well as the more traditional, smaller operators. The Chamber of Commerce and its organizational kin, the Federation of Industries, are therefore in many instances closely associated with the state apparatus at lower levels, while the Businessmen's Association and Businessmen's Council are well connected to the political elite. The Chamber of Commerce, representing many who believe their interests are ignored by the political elite, has been willing to coordinate some activities with the political opposition, whereas the Businessmen's Association remains tied to the government's line (Springborg 1989, 70–71).

The Pillars of Power: The Military and Others. While labor, professional, and business associations play an important role in Egyptian politics, the most powerful groups in Egypt continue to be those that are vital to the survival of the system. In this regard, four groups are of paramount importance: the military, the bureaucracy, the NDP, and the religious establishment. All benefit from the status quo and are unlikely to favor a dramatic shift therein. Of the four pillars of the regime, the military is by far the most important (Abdula 1990). Egypt continues to be a predominantly military regime, substantial progress toward democracy notwithstanding. Most of Mubarak's senior advisors are drawn from the military, as are key figures in the Presidential Office, the bureaucracy, the NDP, and the local government apparatus, including governors and district officials. Military officers enjoy subsidized housing and every other perk that a poor society can bestow upon them.

Although it holds a privileged position in Egyptian society, the Egyptian military is not necessarily of one mind. Many officers are loyal to Mubarak, but others incline toward the Nasserites, the New Wafd, and the Islamic Fundamentalists. Indeed, the military leadership has been very restrained in its criticism of the Fundamentalist movement. Government actions against the Fundamentalists, as a result, are generally carried out by special security forces under the control of the Minister of Interior rather than by the army. Information concerning this and most other military issues, unfortunately, remains limited. Suffice it to say that the Mubarak regime works hard to assure the officer corps that its privileged and influential role in Egyptian politics will be retained.

The bureaucracy and NDP were discussed at length earlier in the chapter and require little elaboration other than to say that key officials in both are appointed directly by the president or the Presidential Office. They are the heart of the regime's system of control and patronage. Like the officer corps, they enjoy a privileged position in Egyptian society. To weaken either the bureaucracy or the NDP would be to weaken the regime.

Finally, Egypt's religious establishment has long enjoyed corporate status (Bianchi 1989). Religion, as discussed above, is an essential element in the Egyptian political equation. Mosques are built and maintained by the Ministry of Wafqs (religious endowments). Al-Azhar University, the Islamic university, has been expanded and glorified (Barraclough 1998). Islamic programs abound on Egyptian television, and Egypt maintains a separate Koranic radio station. The Egyptian media also break for prayers five times a day, in line with Islamic traditions, and senior Islamic leaders have free access to Mubarak. It is interesting to note that the influence of mainline religious leaders has increased in response to the Fundamentalist threat as Mubarak desperately attempts to persuade devout Muslims that working within the traditional Islamic institutions is a more effective strategy for achieving Islamic goals than the violence of the extremists.

Social Groups. In addition to the parties and pressure groups described above, Egyptian politics is also influenced by a variety of social groups that have become increasingly politicized in recent years. Some are highly organized, while others lack a well-defined sense of group identity. All, however, are part of the mosaic of Egyptian politics. Particularly important are the Islamic benevolent associations that provide much-needed services to Egypt's poor. Fearing links between these groups and the Fundamentalists, the government has brought all Islamic groups, whatever their nature, under its control (*Associated Press*, May 28, 1999; *Al-Ahram*, Sept. 1, 1999, 12).

Cairo As a Pressure Group. The citizens of Cairo are so vast in number and so fragmented in their interests that it is difficult to think of them as a coherent group. From the perspective of the Government, however, Cairo represents a critical group whose interests must be addressed (Weede 1986). Cairo is the seat of the Egyptian government, industry, commerce, banking, communications, mass media, education, religion, culture, health, and tourism. Little of significance occurs in Egypt that is not controlled in one way or another by Cairo. Fifteen million-plus Cairo residents, for example, constitute more than a fourth of Egypt's population, and a strike in Cairo can cripple the entire country. When people speak of controlling the "streets," moreover, it is the streets of Cairo to which they are referring. To lose control of Cairo is to lose the capacity to rule.

Not surprisingly, the citizens of Cairo receive favored treatment in terms of food, services, education, and housing. Life in many areas of Cairo is difficult, but it is far less difficult than in the countryside. In a cruel irony, the favored position of Cairo has led to the city's inordinate growth. A city of 3,000,000 in 1960 will soon be a city of 20,000,000. Cairo is the heart of Egypt.

University Students. University students also represent a special-interest group that has received the rapt attention of Egypt's leaders (Mubarak 1999). In contrast to the situation in the US, Egyptian students constitute a vibrant political force. They are the most idealistic, the most intellectually aware, and the most articulate segment of Egyptian society. Their awareness of injustice is unfailing. The politicization of

Egyptian students also finds its origins in a profound sense of insecurity and frustration. Many Egyptian students (some place the figure at 25 percent or higher) face the prospect of unemployment. Many of those who do find jobs will find them in the lower rungs of the bureaucracy, a fate that will allow them a marginal existence at best.

Civic disturbances are generally initiated by university students, and if promising, are joined by disgruntled workers, high school students, and other dissidents. Some student disturbances are spontaneous; most have been inspired by external political groups such as the Nasserites or the Muslim Brotherhood. It was the students, for example, who kept the Nasserite movement alive during the purges of the Sadat era.

Mubarak is attempting to strengthen the student wing of the ruling National Democratic Party, but it is the Fundamentalists who are now the dominant force in student politics.

Coptic Christians. Coptic Christians represent approximately 8 percent of the Egyptian population and constitute a far higher percentage of the population in the politically sensitive Cairo region.[12] Historically, as Nadia Farah points out, Copts have been well integrated into the fabric of Egyptian society and have not constituted a cohesive political group.

> In the Egyptian case, while religion is an important descriptive criterion, it does not play a major role in social stratification. The Coptic minority is not isolated either economically, politically, or geographically. The Copts are found in elites, the middle class, the working class and the peasantry. While Copts are not fully represented in the political system...they are not excluded from the political or bureaucratic systems. Moreover, the Copts do not form a political group; they vary in their political ideology and allegiance. Culturally, the Copts are non-distinctive from Muslims.... Both groups share the same Egyptian culture. In this sense, the Copts do not form an ethnic group (Farah 1986, 57).

This picture, however, is changing rapidly. The dramatic rise of the Muslim Fundamentalists and their demands for an Islamic state now threaten to destroy Egypt's long tradition of tolerance and religious harmony. Religious conflicts have become commonplace since the latter days of the Sadat regime, and if present trends toward the Islamization of Egypt continue, yet another key element of Egypt's political stability will come unraveled. The Egyptian Government, for its part, complains that the Western press has blown the problem far out of proportion. Even the Coptic Patriarch has criticized the alarmist nature of the media coverage, saying that inflated reports of communal tension may make the situation worse rather than better (*Al-Waton Al-Arabi,* Nov. 6, 1998, 26).

Women As a Political Force. The political role of women in Egypt is difficult to assess. By Middle Eastern standards, Egyptian women have made dramatic progress toward economic and political equality. By Western standards, they remain an exploited underclass in a male-dominated society (Rugh 1986). Possessing the right to vote, Egyptian women are represented in the People's Assembly and, to a lesser extent, in the Cabinet. The legal status of women, while restricted, has also witnessed improvement in recent years. A 1979 law now requires a man to notify his wife in writing that he has divorced her. The law also states that a wife has the right to divorce her husband if he chooses to take a second wife, a practice limited largely to the rural areas. In such an instance, the ex-wife retains a legal right to the family's lodging until remarriage or until the children are no longer in her custody (twelve

---

[12]Estimates of the size of Egypt's Coptic population vary from 5 to 10 percent.

Cairo schoolgirls attend class, most of them in traditional Islamic dress. Girls in urban areas are more likely to receive an education than those in rural areas; the illiteracy rate for rural females is around 70 percent.

years for girls and ten years for boys). A law passed in 2000 has made it easier for Egyptian women to divorce their husbands, but its effects are regressive in other ways (*NYT,* Jan. 8, 2000, www).

In the economic sphere, the changing role of women has been dramatic. Females now constitute approximately 30 percent of the urban labor force, and the picture is much the same in educational institutions, with females now accounting for approximately one-third of the students attending Egyptian universities. This is in sharp contrast to the 7 percent of the pre-revolutionary era. Progress in the areas of education and employment has been far greater in the urban areas than in the countryside, with illiteracy rates among rural females remaining in the 70 percent range (Sullivan, Leila, and Palmer 1990). It is probable that Egyptian women will continue to gain equality in the economic sphere, inasmuch as the realities of Egyptian economic life increasingly require that families have two incomes. In contrast to an earlier era, holding a good job contributes markedly to the marriageability of an Egyptian female.

Despite having made significant progress in the economic sphere, women do not constitute a major force in Egyptian politics. The surge of Islamic Fundamentalism has also produced a greater conservatism in Egyptian society, and even the prior economic gains of Egyptian women are now being called into question.

Citizens and Politics in Egypt

The dominant position of the president and the power brokers who surround him may tempt us to write off public opinion as a negligible force in Egyptian politics. This would be a mistake. The management of public opinion is a matter of vital concern to Egypt's leaders. This is even more the case today as Egypt inches toward democracy in a politically charged environment that could well spell victory for the Islamic right. The "information" section of the President's Office is charged with both monitoring and shaping public opinion, as are the Ministry of Information and the National Democratic Party. The opinions of Cairo's residents, as might be expected, are of far more importance to Egypt's leaders than the opinions of Egypt's provincial citizens. Cairo is the pulse of Egypt.

The hard core of Egyptian public opinion has traditionally found expression in the sarcastic political humor that fuels the conversation of Cairo's ubiquitous coffee shops. While much of Egypt's political humor loses its bite in translation, suffice it to say that Nasser himself found mass humor to be a subversive force and attempted to suppress it (Hamouda 1990). It is interesting to note, in this regard, that much of the current Egyptian humor portrays Mubarak as a plodding and indecisive bureaucrat.

The Egyptian press now plays an important, if guarded, role in criticizing government policies, and Mubarak prides himself on not having confiscated a single publication during his tenure in office. Egypt's leading literary figures were asked to testify to this fact during the tenth anniversary of Mubarak's rule, with Naguib Mahfouz, Egypt's Nobel Prize–winning author, acknowledging that Egypt enjoyed extensive freedom of the press "within the limits of our traditions" (*Al-Ahram,* Oct. 10, 1991). Self-censorship also assures that few objectionable pieces get published in the first place.

Nevertheless, the views expressed in the mass media are those of journalists, not the public. As such, they provide an imperfect guide to what the public really thinks (Agha 1991). Election results are also an imperfect guide to public opinion inasmuch as the election procedures are not as fair as they might be.

More recently, and for the first time since the 1952 revolution, a genuine public opinion poll was conducted during the fall of 1998 by the Al-Ahram Center for Political and Strategic Studies, a quasi-governmental but outspoken think-tank. Among other results, 59.3 percent of the respondents said that they felt secure about their economic future. Thirty-one percent felt insecure, with the remainder of those surveyed choosing not to respond. Economic satisfaction was lowest in the all-important Cairo region, and residents of Cairo in general were more negative than people living in the countryside (*Al-Ahram Weekly,* Oct. 1–7, 1998, 2). The poll also revealed that voting in the preceding Parliamentary elections was particularly low among the residents of greater Cairo and among youth. Finally, it should be noted that 68.7 percent of the respondents wanted a democratic government as opposed to the 27.9 percent who were content with Egypt's "guided" democracy (*Al-Ahram Weekly,* Oct. 1–7, 1998, 2).

One interpretation of these results is that the Mubarak regime finds most of its support in the countryside. An alternative explanation of the results is that people in the countryside are more cautious than their city counterparts and less willing to express their true opinions.

The least ambiguous expressions of public opinion are the riots that occasionally shake Egyptian society. The bread riots of 1977, among the most severe in Egyptian history, forced Sadat to restore government subsidies on food and other essential items. The Mubarak regime has witnessed a gradual upsurge in political violence, much of it centering on Islamic issues. Particularly serious was the 1986 riot by Egyptian security guards, a special low-level military unit used by the Ministry of the Interior to guard public buildings. Staffed by young recruits, the security guards went on a four-day rampage in which bars, tourist hotels, and other symbols of Westernization offensive to the Fundamentalist right were burned. Order was restored by the army, but the regime was clearly shaken. Since that time, violence between Muslims and Christians has smoldered, as have student protests. Terrorist attacks on foreign tourists and Egyptian government officials have abated but remain a concern of the Government.

One of the most subtle expressions of public opinion to emerge during the latter years of Sadat's rule was the adoption of Islamic dress codes by a sizable portion of

Egypt's younger citizens, especially students. Men began to sport Islamic-style beards, while women wore long robes and Islamic headwraps. Sadat's futile attempt to outlaw beards indicated that the public's message had reached its mark. Islamic dress continues to be popular today, particularly among females. Commentators, however, are not sure whether such dress is an expression of religious piety, a political statement, or merely a convenience. Many Egyptian women simply find Islamic dress to be cheaper and more convenient than upscale Western dress (Rugh 1986). Traditional dress also reduces the risk of being harassed by Egypt's very aggressive male population. Because the significance of religious dress is the subject of some ambiguity, even the Government finds itself confused. As described by Mamoun Fandy,

> Women's dress is not as fixed as many would assume, nor is the state's response to it. One example to illustrate this situationality and contextuality of women's dress is the response of campus police in two different universities requiring different modes of dress. Campus police in front of Al-Azhar University prevent non-veiled women from entering the university because being non-veiled in that context is interpreted as defiance of patriarchal norms of modesty; at the same time the police in front of Cairo University were turning fully veiled (niqab) women away and admitting only non-veiled, because veiling is interpreted as a (sic) Islamic defiance of the state's officially secular policies. This contextuality of dress and what is appropriate in any power-laden context is very obvious here (Fandy 1998).

The Context of Egyptian Politics: Culture, Economics, and International Interdependence

While the actors in Egyptian politics play a vital role in determining who gets what, when, and how, the behavior of those actors is often influenced by the broader environmental context in which Egyptian politics occurs. In this section, we examine three dimensions of that environmental context: political culture, political economy, and international influences.

The Culture of Egyptian Politics

Occasional riots notwithstanding, Egyptian political behavior is seemingly docile. Islamic militancy continues to cast a shadow over Egypt's uncertain march toward democracy, but the much-feared Muslim uprising has yet to materialize. Indeed, by Middle Eastern standards, the Egyptian political system has been remarkably stable. What explains the extreme patience of the Egyptian population?

The most persuasive explanation of the docility of the Egyptian population is cultural in nature. Egyptian political behavior, from this perspective, is the product of centuries of foreign domination that taught the Egyptian people that revolt was largely futile. Over time, this sense of futility or hopelessness became part of the Egyptian cultural map that was passed on from generation to generation.

Centuries of foreign domination, however, produced more than docility. They also created a chasm of distrust between the government and the people. Recoiling from oppressive rulers, Egyptians sought security in the solidarity of their families rather than in the protection of the state. In the case of the Coptic minority, security was also to be found in religious solidarity. Egyptians, accordingly, were slow to develop the sense of political community or civil society that had played such a crucial role in the political development of the West. Rather, Egypt became a society of families and clans, each competing with the others for scarce resources. Egyptians distrusted the government, and they distrusted each other. This situation was painfully alluded to by Abdul Nasser shortly after the Free Officers seized power in 1952.

Every leader we came to wanted to assassinate his rival. Every idea we found aimed at the destruction of another. If we were to carry out all that we heard, then there would not be one leader left alive. Not one idea would remain intact. We would cease to have a mission save to remain among the smashed bodies and the broken debris lamenting our misfortune and reproaching our ill-fate.

Complaints and petitions poured upon us in thousands. If these did refer to cases worthy of justice, or mentioned oppression that might be redressed, they would be understandable and logical. The majority of these were but persistent demands for revenge, as if the revolution were meant to be a weapon for revenge and hatred.

If I were asked then what I required most, my instant answer would be, "To hear but one Egyptian uttering one word of justice about another, to see but one Egyptian not devoting his time to criticize wilfully the ideas of another, to feel that there was but one Egyptian ready to open his heart for forgiveness, indulgence and loving his brother Egyptian." Personal and persistent selfishness was the rule of the day. The word "I" was on every tongue. It was the magic solution of every difficulty and the effective cure for every malady (Nasser 1959).

When Nasser seized power in 1952, then, he was confronted by a population that was both alienated from the political system and divided among itself. These feelings of passivity and alienation helped the military regime to consolidate its power, but Nasser and the revolutionary leadership wanted to do more than simply occupy the throne of power. They wanted to transform Egypt into a modern military and industrial state. They could not do this without the active support of the Egyptian population. That support was not forthcoming.

The Nasser years did much to transform Egyptian political culture. The dazzling foreign policy successes of the early Nasser years fostered a sense of pride and national identity within a population long subject to foreign domination. Indeed, Egypt had become the vanguard of Arab nationalism. Nasser also attempted to build a bond of trust between the government and the masses by forging a "social contract" in which a benevolent dictatorship would use the resources of the state to provide all of its citizens with an acceptable quality of life (Amin 1974). Economic democracy would take precedence over political democracy (Nasser speeches, 1955–1965, published by the Ministry of Information, Government of Egypt, Cairo).

The cultural ramifications of the Nasser era had negative dimensions as well. Nasser attempted to fulfill the social contract by creating a welfare system in which most of the urban population was guaranteed a job by the state. Wages were low, but job security was high. As it was virtually impossible to be fired from a government position once obtained, Egyptians began to look upon a government job as a right rather than as an obligation. Low wages and the absence of merit-based work incentives also led to a pervasive sense of lethargy. Egypt, then, would succumb to the same socialist work ethic that undermined the economy of the Soviet Union. Although increasingly dependent upon the state, Egypt's citizens were unwilling to work hard enough to make the state effective.

The Nasser era was also to unleash a revolution of rising expectations. The masses had expected little from the monarchy. Nasser, by contrast, had promised to transform Egypt into a socialist paradise, a veritable land of plenty. The more difficult things became, the more grandiose were the government's promises. The revolution in rising expectations was also fueled by an explosion in mass education. Educated people demand more of the government than do illiterates.

The cultural obstacles to political and economic development changed little under Sadat and remain very much in evidence today. The Nasser era made some progress in forging a "social contract" between the masses and the people, but attitudes of distrust and suspicion die hard. The Mubarak regime, moreover, is finding it impossible to keep its end of the social contract. A rapidly growing population simply demands more goods and services than either the government or the Egyptian economy can provide. The result is frustration and hostility. The beneficiaries of this situation are the Fundamentalists.

We would be remiss if we did not discuss Islamic culture and its impact on Egyptian culture, political or otherwise. While this is a complex topic that far exceeds the scope of the present text, two points are particularly important. First, as mentioned earlier, Islamic political thought does not draw a distinction between church and state. Indeed, the highest form of political development from an Islamic perspective is a government guided by the Koran. Many Muslim Egyptians, accordingly, do not find the thought of an Islamic state to be alien. To the contrary, adherents of the Islamic right see the struggle for an Islamic state as a holy obligation. Second, Islamic teachings seem to stress fatalism and submission. The fate of everyone and everything is in the hands of God, and what will be will be. Such feelings of fatalism and resignation have probably contributed to the passivity of Egyptian political behavior.

Political Economy and Politics in Egypt

As in most countries, economic considerations are a vital element in Egypt's political equation. The Egyptian monarchy was sustained in power by a landed aristocracy that monopolized much of Egypt's wealth. They were overthrown by a group of lower-middle-class officers intent on redressing the economic balance in the country. Their tool for achieving this end would be a socialist economic system designed to stimulate both economic growth and social justice. While industry was expanded, Egypt's lethargic bureaucracy proved incapable of managing a complex economy, and Egypt's leaders found it increasingly difficult to meet the needs of their population. Sadat responded by allowing a limited return to capitalism, but moved slowly for fear of upsetting a population now dependent upon government jobs, subsidized food, rent controls, and a broad range of health and educational services. As noted above, the capitalist class began to reassert its political influence, money and politics often being difficult to disentangle.

Mubarak and the leadership of the National Democratic Party, from the leftist perspective, now represents little more than a melange of commercial, bureaucratic, and military interests clinging desperately to their privileged positions (Sullivan 1990). The Egyptian Revolution, to use the title of a book on Egyptian politics, is a "stalled revolution" (Ansari 1987). Its leadership has become immobilized, fearing to turn either to the left or to the right (Tuma 1988). The Fundamentalist resurgence, from a leftist perspective, is an economic phenomenon driven by the poverty and despair of the Egyptian masses. The solution of Egypt's problems, in the leftists' view, is a return to true socialism, not the bureaucratic nightmare created by Nasser and his lieutenants.

Neoclassical political economists would not argue with much of the above analysis. They, too, find the Egyptian leadership to be immobilized and incapable of decisive action. They also find the bureaucracy to be a nightmare and the Islamic resurgence to be a largely economic problem caused by decades of unfulfilled promises.

The prescription for Egypt's salvation, from the neoclassical perspective of the International Monetary Fund (IMF) and the United States Agency for International Development (USAID), is breathtakingly simple: get the government out of the economic system and allow the free market to work its magic (Al-Sayid 1990; Weinbaum 1986). As the profit motive rekindles productive skills dulled by four decades of socialism, the economy will flourish and competition between firms will drive up wages by creating a shortage of workers. The only difficulty with this argument is that it assumes that jobs will increase faster than the available supply of workers, thereby producing a scarcity of labor. Unfortunately, this is a flawed assumption (Handoussa 1987; Harik 1997). As noted in the discussion of political culture, the Egyptian birth rate is astronomical, and workers are entering the job market far more rapidly than jobs are being produced. Egypt's capitalists will profit from low labor costs, but the masses will continue to languish in poverty. Unless this situation changes dramatically, the gap between rich and poor will grow larger, as will popular support of the Islamic Fundamentalists and other opposition groups.

If the Mubarak regime is immobilized, it is because it is caught between competing political-economic pressures (Moore 1986). On one side are the IMF and other donors of foreign assistance who are pushing Mubarak to undertake radical economic reforms such as the privatization of public-sector firms and the elimination of subsidies on food. On the other side are fears that these reforms, while they may improve the Egyptian economy in the long run, will trigger mass protests such as the food riots that shook the Sadat regime in 1977. Individuals barely surviving on the basis of subsidized food panic at the thought that those subsidies might be placed in jeopardy. To put the problem in perspective, Egypt's minimum wage is $20 per month for a six-day, forty-eight-hour work week (US Govt., *1998 Country Report on Economic Policy: Egypt,* 1998).

Faced by these competing pressures, Mubarak has responded with economic policies that have vacillated between the two extremes. Bold economic reforms are launched to the applause of the donor community, only to be delayed at the first sign of sustained popular resistance. In an effort to get the best of both worlds, the Egyptian Government now proclaims that its privatization program has achieved spectacular economic growth without causing lay-offs and hardships among the workers. Seeing that private sector firms can only make a profit by eliminating excess workers—a mammoth problem in Egypt—it is difficult to see how this can be the case. In reality, many of Egypt's largest and most effective industries have yet to be privatized, including all of the major utilities and the country's large defense industries. It is this hurdle that efforts at economic reform must cross if Egypt's transition to capitalism is to be successful (*Al-Ahram,* Feb. 15, 1999, 13). The Egyptian economy is growing, but there is little evidence that this has improved the lot of the vast majority of the Egyptian population (interview with leading a Egyptian economist, 1999).

International Interdependence and the Politics of Egypt

Egypt receives approximately two billion dollars in foreign assistance from the United States annually, making it the largest recipient of US aid after Israel and Russia. Egypt also receives substantial foreign assistance from Japan, the states of the European Community, the IMF, the World Bank, and the oil-producing kingdoms of the Middle East. Indeed, the rich states of the world seem to be in heated competition to see who can provide Egypt with the most money.

The race to keep the Mubarak regime afloat is not difficult to understand. The militant Egypt of the Nasser era threatened Western security by opening the Middle East to influence from the Soviet Union (Dawisha 1979). It also threatened the destruction of Israel and came within a hairsbreadth of overthrowing pro-Western regimes in Jordan, Saudi Arabia, and almost every other state in the region. The post-Nasser era, by contrast, has witnessed unparalleled cooperation with the United States. The Soviets were expelled, peace was made with Israel, and the oil kings were left to count their billions. It was also Egyptian participation in the Gulf War that legitimized US actions against Iraq. Neither the United States, Israel, nor Saudi Arabia want to see a radical Egypt.

The Soviet threat to US interests in the Middle East has faded with the collapse of the USSR (Tschirgi 1994). In its place has emerged a resurgent Islam that threatens both Israel and the oil-producing monarchies of the Arabian Peninsula. Islamic Fundamentalism, moreover, cannot be crushed by cruise missiles and superior armaments. It strikes from within. An Egypt ruled by Islamic militants would, in all probability, trigger militant Islamic uprisings throughout the Arab world. It would also threaten a renewal of the Arab-Israeli conflict, a conflict that could involve the use of weapons of mass destruction.

For many years, the United States provided monetary assistance to Egypt with minimal interference in its domestic affairs. If money could buy stability, so be it (Cassen 1986). In the mid-1980s, however, the United States began to demand a price for its aid. Henceforth, it would put immense pressure on Egypt to move from a predominantly state-controlled economic system to a predominantly capitalist economic system. These pressures for economic reform, as noted in the preceding section, have created considerable tension between the United States and a Mubarak regime fearful that the hardships caused by such reforms would fuel popular support for the Fundamentalists.

The United States has also urged Egypt to increase progress toward the democratization of the Egyptian political system. Toward this end, the United States Agency for International Development (USAID) has launched a worldwide "Democratic Initiative" designed to increase democracy in states receiving US assistance. The United States, however, has little desire to push Egypt's democracy to the point of empowering the Muslim Fundamentalists. Too much democracy in Egypt could threaten the interests of the United States throughout the Middle East.

A curious interdependence thus exists between the United States and the Mubarak regime (Walker 1997). The United States could force compliance with its demands by threatening to withdraw its assistance from Egypt, but this would hasten the collapse of the Mubarak regime and threaten U.S. interests in the region. The upshot of this situation is that the United States talks economic and democratic reform while simultaneously subsidizing Egypt's quasi-democratic, quasi-socialist welfare system.

Challenges of the Present and Prospects for the Future

In the introductory chapter we discussed six standards of "good government" established by the UN and its related agencies: democracy, stability, human rights, economic growth, quality of life, and concern for the environment. Over the course of the Mubarak era, Egypt has made substantial progress in each of the above areas. Each, however, remains far below the standard set by the states of the First World, as imperfect as that standard may be.

Democracy

Egyptians are justifiably proud of the progress that has been made toward democracy during the Mubarak era. Members of the People's Assembly are elected in somewhat fair elections, and in most instances, the electorate has a meaningful choice among candidates. Egypt also possesses a number of vocal political parties as well as a reasonably free press.

While progress has been made, much remains to be done. Election procedures are still manipulated to the benefit of the ruling National Democratic Party, and even then, it is not clear that the members of the People's Assembly exercise much real power. They are elected, but they do not rule. President Mubarak not only exercises extraordinary power but was reelected for his third six-year term in the fall of 1993. He was the only candidate in a referendum that Chris Hedges of *The New York Times* described as "a strange, ungainly ballet where choreographed admirers are herded in from the wings to pay homage to a leading man with no rival" (*NYT,* Oct. 4, 1993, A4). The choice before the voters was to accept or reject Mubarak. Mubarak received more than 97 percent of the popular vote, but only 30 percent of the eligible voters had bothered to register (*NYT,* Oct. 4, 1993, A4). Of these, many were illiterate villagers controlled by local political bosses. The process repeated itself in 1999, with Mubarak receiving 93.79 percent of the vote in this one-candidate election.

For the moment, then, Egypt is a partial or guided democracy, a situation that Mubarak justifies as a necessary progression from dictatorship to full democracy. Egyptians, he says, must be educated into democracy. "This country was under pressure for years and years, so when you open the gate for freedom, you will find many terrible things taking place. If you have a dam and keep the water until it begins to overflow, and then you open the gates, it will drown many people. We have to give a gradual dose so people can swallow it and understand it. The Egyptians are not Americans" (*NYT,* Oct. 12, 1993, A3).

Stability

Egypt has traditionally been among the most stable of the Arab states, the Nasser Revolution of 1952 being the only revolution of the modern era. The transfer of power from Nasser to Sadat followed established procedures, as did the transfer of power from Sadat to Mubarak. The stability of the Egyptian political system, however, has now been called into question by the Fundamentalist violence. While Mubarak downplays the terrorist threat as the work of a few gangsters, an official of the Ministry of the Interior (police) candidly declared, "We are at war. People have to die on both sides" (*NYT,* Nov. 28, 1993, A8). By 1999 the Mubarak regime claimed victory in that war, but also found it necessary to deploy new mobile police patrols throughout the country, ostensibly for the purpose of fighting crime (*Al-Ahram,* Aug. 31, 1999).

Few people expect the Muslim extremists to topple the Mubarak regime, but Mubarak remains vulnerable, having survived yet another assassination attempt in 1999. As noted in the discussion of political economy, fear of the Fundamentalists has immobilized the Egyptian government, making it reluctant to proceed with the political and economic reforms essential to its long-term stability (Hafez 1997).

Human Rights

Human rights were a bleak spot of both the Nasser and Sadat regimes. Mubarak attempted to improve Egypt's human rights record, but these efforts were soon sacrificed to the struggle against the Islamic Fundamentalists. New anti-terrorist legislation allows routine searches and seizures, and torture has become commonplace (*CSM,* Feb. 18, 1993, 6).

Far more subtle have been curtailments of human rights resulting from Mubarak's effort to undermine support for the Muslim extremists by portraying himself as the protector of the faith (Kienle 1998; Springborg 1998).

Books and works of art judged offensive by Al-Azhar University, for example, are removed from public forums. As articulated by the president of the religious university: "Al-Azhar does not oppose such freedom of expression as long as it is in conformity with (the teachings of Islam) (sic). These writers against Islamic jurisprudence are destroying the values of society. Al-Azhar can't just stand silently by" (*CSM*, Feb. 18, 1993, 6). More recently, books judged offensive to Al-Azhar have been banned from courses at the American University of Cairo (Soreh 1998).

Civil rights abuses in Egypt are not limited to the struggle against extremism. Peasants continue to be oppressed by landowners and other notables who enjoy the support of the National Democratic Party. Egypt's Coptic Christian minority is increasingly harassed by the growing intolerance of the Muslim majority (*Middle East Times,* 2000, Issue 14, www). The more extreme Fundamentalist groups urge their supporters to avoid any contact with the Christian community. Pressure groups that challenge the government face intimidation, as do opposition political parties (*Middle East Watch,* Sept. 1991). Child labor laws are honored in the breach, for to enforce them with rigor would be to threaten Egypt's precarious economy and to impinge upon traditional social practices that place a strong emphasis on family labor.

Economic Growth and Quality of Life

The Nasser revolution attempted to provide all of Egypt's citizens with a minimally sustainable quality of life. Basic foodstuffs were subsidized by the state, as were fuel and housing. The Government also attempted to provide everyone with a job, and education and health care were free, at least for the poor. The quality of government services was dismal by First World standards, but most people got along. There was also optimism that Egypt was modernizing and that things would get better with time. By the mid-1970s, however, the state was finding it difficult to maintain even a rudimentary level of basic services. The population was growing faster than the economy, and the huge bureaucracy that had been created to manage the welfare system absorbed much of the wealth it was designed to distribute. The situation would improve little during the 1980s and 1990s, and much of the growth that has occurred has been in real estate and banking, areas that create wealth for a narrow elite but produce few jobs.

Today, accordingly, the majority of Egyptians find themselves in a precarious financial position. Most continue to rely on government jobs that pay little more than a subsistence wage. A third of Egyptian workers earn a minimum wage that hovers around the poverty level, and some 20 percent of the population is unemployed, a situation that continues to worsen as some 500,000 new Egyptians enter the job market each year.

Egyptian education, moreover, does little to provide the technical skills needed for economic revival. Almost half of Egypt's engineering graduates are unable to pass standard examinations, and leading educators complain of inadequate equipment as well as poorly motivated teachers who "are always tired because of the long time they spend in tutoring to make up for an inadequate salary" (Professor D. Awatef Ali Shoir, as quoted in *The Egyptian Gazette,* Nov. 29, 1991). Exams at all levels are based heavily on lectures, the copies of which are for sale by the instructor. Not surprisingly, students from affluent backgrounds do far better than their poorer counterparts.

The movement toward Islamic Fundamentalism is not merely a function of the dismal quality of life enjoyed by most Egyptians. It is also a function of the growing gap between rich and poor that now characterizes Egyptian society. The upper classes have the skills and connections required to benefit from the increasing liberalization of the Egyptian economy, but most Egyptians have little chance of improving their station in life. Mass education is poor and imparts few practical skills. It has also ceased to be free. Egyptian students struggle to gain an education, only to find there are few jobs for college graduates. Their hostility toward the

Mubarak regime is understandable. Why should one support a regime that allows the rich to prosper while ignoring the plight of the poor?

The Egyptian government has attempted to bridge the gap between rich and poor by legislating one of the highest tax rates in the world. Indeed, taxes on Egypt's citizens are more than twice the corresponding taxes on citizens of the United States (*NYT,* Feb. 28, 1993, F13). Taxes on the rich, however, are seldom collected, with the International Bank for Reconstruction and Development (World Bank) estimating that "75 percent of persons in high income brackets are not known to the Tax Authority in Egypt" (*Egyptian Gazette,* Nov. 27, 1991). Progress is being made, but tax problems continue (*Al-Ahram,* Sept. 6, 1999, 14; Sept. 13, 1999, 6).

The Environment

Egypt's environment is one of the unhealthiest in the world. As described by Chris Hedges of *The New York Times:* "The air in Cairo, and the industrial belt around the city, is a noxious yellow haze. Plants and factories spew waste directly into the Nile, damaging a river that provides over 90 percent of the country's water needs. Many of Egypt's 60+ million people, especially those in urban areas, are tormented by high lead levels, liver problems and respiratory ailments" (*NYT,* Nov. 26, 1993, A6). The number of cars choking Cairo's streets has increased from some 64,000 in 1970 to more than 400,000 in 1991. The turn of the century would see 1.6 million vehicles in Egypt, most located in the greater Cairo area (Chemonics 1998). Pollution control devices are virtually unheard of.

The Egyptians are painfully aware of their environmental problems. They live with them on a daily basis (Interview, Cairo, 1997). The problem, however, is what to do about them. Egypt has too many people and too many cars squeezed into too little land. It also has too much poverty. Egypt possesses a full slate of environmental legislation but is reluctant to enforce environmental laws for fear of slowing the pace of economic growth or scaring away potential investors. Unfortunately, one of the comparative advantages enjoyed by Egypt in its search for new industries is precisely its lack of environmental regulation. From the perspective of Egypt's embattled government, food and jobs are more important than the environment.

Egypt's environmental crisis poses little direct threat to the stability of the country. Its political impact, however, is profound. Environmental pollution lowers productivity and increases health costs, most of which are subsidized by the government. Tourism, a mainstay of the Egyptian economy, is eroded by the toxicity of the air, and few tourists return for a second visit. Egypt's poor environmental conditions also stand as a daily reminder of the government's inability to cope with a problem that has become a pervasive topic in the Egyptian media.

Prospects for the Future

Egypt currently stands at three different crossroads: between democracy and continued military rule; between Western-style capitalism and the continuation of a predominantly socialist economy that provides at least a basic level of food, shelter, education, and welfare; and between a secular political system and a theocracy based upon the laws of Islam. The three crossroads possess a common denominator: the grinding poverty of the Egyptian people and their desperate search for a better way of life. In years past, the existence of an Islamic regime in Egypt would have been unthinkable. It seems much less so today.

References

Abdel-Fadil, M. 1980. *The Political Economy of Nasserism.* Cambridge, England: Cambridge University Press.

Abdula, Ahmed. 1990. *The Military and Democracy in Egypt.* Cairo: Siani Publishing. (In Arabic.)

Abdul-Hamid, Barlinti. 1992. *The Marshal and I.* Cairo, Egypt: Madbouli. (In Arabic.)

Agha, Olfat Hassan. 1991. "Mass Communicators and Issues of Development: An Empirical Study of a Sample of Mass Communicators in the Egyptian Society." Unpublished Dissertation, Cairo University.

Akhavi, S. 1975. "Egypt: Neo-Patrimonial Elite." In *Political Elites and Political Development in the Middle East,* ed. F. Tachau. Cambridge, England: Schenkman Publishing.

Al-Sayid, Mustafa Kamel. 1990 (Winter). *Privatization: The Egyptian Debate.* Cairo papers in Social Science, vol. 13, monograph 4. Cairo, Egypt: The American University in Cairo Press.

Aly, Abdel Monem Said. 1989 (Oct.). "The Myth and Reality: The Four Faces of the Islamic Investment Companies." Unpublished Paper, Al-Ahram Center for Political and Strategic Studies, Al-Ahram Foundation, Cairo, Egypt.

Amin, Gamal. 1974. *The Modernization of Poverty: A Study in The Political Economy of Growth in Nine Arab Countries, 1945–1970.* Leiden: Brill.

Ansari, Hamied. 1985 (Jan.). "Mubarak's Egypt." *A World Affairs Journal: The Middle East, 1985.* 84(498).

Ansari, Hamied. 1987. *Egypt: The Stalled Society.* Cairo, Egypt: The American University of Cairo Press.

Ayrout, Henry. 1962. *The Egyptian Peasant.* Boston, MA: Beacon Press. Translated by John Williams.

Ayubi, Nazih. 1980. *Bureaucracy and Politics in Contemporary Egypt.* London: Ithaca Press.

Ayubi, Nazih. 1982. "Bureaucratic Inflation and Administrative Inefficiency," *Middle East Studies* 18(3): 286–99.

Ayubi, Nazih. 1983 (Nov.). "The Egyptian 'Brain Drain': A Multidimensional Problem." *International Journal of Middle East Studies* 15(4): 431–50.

Ayubi, Nazih. 1989. "Government and the State of Egypt Today." In *Egypt Under Mubarak,* ed. C. Tripp and R. Owen. London: Routledge.

Bahgat, Gawdat. 1991. "The Impact of External and Internal Forces on Economic Orientation: The Case of Egypt." Ph.D. Dissertation, Florida State University.

Baker, Raymond W. 1978. *Egypt's Uncertain Revolution Under Nasser and Sadat.* Cambridge, MA: Harvard University Press.

Baker, Raymond W. 1990. *Sadat and After.* Cambridge, MA: Harvard University Press.

Barakat, Mohammed and Mahmood Sadiq. 1998 (Nov. 17). "Has the Thought of Religious Violence in Egypt Receded?" *Al-Wanton Al-Arabi* 4–8.

Barraclough, Steven. 1998 (Spring). "Al-Azhar: Between the Government and the Islamists." *The Middle East Journal* 52(2): 236–249.

Beattie, Kirk J. 1994. *Egypt During the Nasser Years: Ideology, Politics, and Civil Society.* Boulder, CO: Westview.

Behrens-Abouseif, Doris. 1990. *Islamic Architecture in Cairo: An Introduction.* Cairo, Egypt: The American University in Cairo Press.

Beinin, J., and Z. Lockman. 1987. *Workers on the Nile: Nationalism, Communism, Islam, and the Egyptian Working Class.* Princeton, NJ: Princeton University Press.

Berque, Jacques. 1967. *Egypt: Imperialism and Revolution.* New York: Praeger.

Bianchi, Robert. 1989. *Unruly Corporatism: Associational Life in Twentieth-Century Egypt.* New York: Oxford University Press.

Binder, Leonard. 1978. *In a Moment of Enthusiasm: Political Power and the Second Stratum in Egypt.* Chicago: University of Chicago Press.

Brands, H. W. 1993. *Into the Labyrinth: The United States and the Middle East: 1945–1993.* New York: McGraw-Hill.

Brown, Nathan J. 1990. *Peasant Politics in Modern Egypt: The Struggle Against the State.* New Haven, CT: Yale University Press.

Carter, B. L. 1986. *The Copts in Egyptian Politics.* London: Croom Helm.

Cassen, R. 1986. *Does Aid Work? Report to an Intergovernmental Task Force.* Oxford: Clarendon Press.

Chemonics International Inc. "Cleaner Air for Better Lives." Adapted from the 1998 *Foreign Exchange,* Chemonics' Annual Newsletter.

Dawisha, K. 1979. *Soviet Foreign Policy Towards Egypt.* New York: Macmillan.

Dekmejian, H. R. 1975. *Egypt Under Nasser: A Study in Political Dynamics.* Albany, NY: State University of New York Press.

Doran, Michael S. 1999. *Pan-Arabism Before Nasser.* New York: Oxford University Press.

El Din, Khaled Mohi. 1995. *Memories of the Revolution.* Cairo: American University of Cairo.

El Gamassy, Marshal Mohaned. 1989. "Memoirs," serialized in *Sharq Al-Ausat,* London, August 18, 1989.

Fahmy, Khaled Mahmoud. 1988 (Fall). *Legislating Infitah: Investment, Currency, and Foreign Trade Laws.* Cairo Papers in Social Science, vol. 11, monograph 3. Cairo, Egypt: American University in Cairo Press.

Fahmy, S. Ninette. 1998 (Autumn). "The Performance of the Muslim Brotherhood in the Egyptian Syndicates: An Alternative Formula for Reform?" *Middle East Journal* 52(4): 551–62.

Fandy, Mamoun. 1998 (Spring). "Political Science Without Clothes: The Politics of Dress, or Contesting the Spatiality of the State of Egypt." *Arab Studies Quarterly* 20(2): 87–104.

Farah, Nadia Ramses. 1986. *Religious Strife in Egypt: Crisis and Ideological Conflicts in the Seventies.* New York: Gordon and Breach.

Farah, T. 1987. *Pan Arabism and Arab Nationalism: The Continuing Debate.* Boulder, CO: Westview Press.

Gershoni, Israel. 1981. *The Emergence of Pan-Arabism.* Tel-Aviv: Shiloah Center for Middle Eastern and African Studies, Tel-Aviv University.

Gillespie, Kate. 1984. *The Tripartite Relationship: Government, Foreign Investors and Local Investors During Egypt's Economic Opening.* New York: Praeger.

Goldschmidt, Arthur, Jr. 1988. *Modern Egypt: The Formation of a Nation State.* Boulder, CO: Westview Press.

Gomaa, Salwa. 1991. "Leadership and Elections in Local Government." *Perspectives in the Center-Local Relations: Political Dynamics in the Middle East,* M.E.S. Series No. 28, 1991, 34–63.

Gorst, Anthony, and Lewis Johnman. 1997. *The Suez Crisis.* London: Routledge.

Hafez, M. H. 1997 (Fall). "Explaining the Origins of Islamic Resurgence: Islamic Revivalism in Egypt and Indonesia." *The Journal of Social, Political and Economic Studies* 22(3): 295–324.

Hamouda, Adel. 1990. *How the Egyptians Mock Their Leaders.* Cairo, Egypt: House of Sphinx Publishers. (In Arabic.)

Handoussa, H. A. 1987 (Sept.). *The Impact of Foreign Aid on Egypt's Economic Development: 1952–1986.* Paper presented to the conference on Aid, Capital Flows and Development, Talloirs, France. Jointly sponsored by the World Bank and International Center for Economic Growth, 13–17.

Harik, Iliya. 1997. *Economic Policy Reform in Egypt.* Gainesville, FL: University Press of Florida.

Heikal, Mohamed. 1975. *The Road to Ramadan.* New York: Ballantine.

Heikal, Mohamed. 1983. *Autumn of Fury: The Assassination of Sadat.* London: Andre Deutsch.

Hosseinzedeh, Esmail. 1989. *Soviet Non-Capitalist Development: The Case of Nasser's Egypt.* New York: Praeger.

Husaini, Ishak Musa. 1956. *The Moslem Brethren.* Beirut: Khayat.

Ibrahim, Saad Eddin. 1980 (Dec.). "Anatomy of Egypt's Militant Islamic Groups: Methodological Note and Preliminary Findings." *International Journal of Middle East Studies* 12(4): 423–53.

Ismail, Salwa. 1998 (May). "Confronting the Other: Identity, Culture, Politics and Conservative Islamism in Egypt." *International Journal of Middle East Studies* 30(2): 199–225.

Kays, D. 1984. *Frogs and Scorpions: Egypt, Sadat, and the Media.* London: Frederick Muller.

Kechichian, Joseph, and Jeanne Nazimek. 1997 (Sept.) "Challenges to the Military in Egypt." *Middle East Policy* 5(3): 125–39.

Khadduri, Majid. 1955. *War and Peace in the Law of Islam.* Baltimore: Johns Hopkins Press.

Kienle, Eberhard. 1998 (Spring). "More than a Response to Islamism: The Political Deliberalization of Egypt in the 1990s." *The Middle East Journal* 52(2): 219–35.

Lane, E. W. 1954. *Manners and Customs of the Modern Egyptians.* London: J. M. Dent & Sons, Ltd.

Lawson, Fred H. 1992. *The Social Origins of Egyptian Expansionism During the Muhammad Ali Period.* New York: Columbia University Press.

Longgood, William F. 1957. *Suez Story: Key to the Middle East.* New York: Greenberg.

Marsot, Afaf Lutfi Al-Sayyid. 1984. *Egypt in the Reign of Muhammad Ali.* Cambridge, England: Cambridge University Press.

McDermott, Anthony. 1975 (Nov.). "Sadat, the Art of Survival." *Middle East International* 53: 13.

McDermott, Anthony. 1988. *Egypt from Nasser to Mubarak: A Flawed Revolution.* London: Croom Helm.

Middle East Watch. 1991 (Sept.). "Egyptian Government to Dissolve Prominent Arab Women's Organization."

Moore, Clement Henry. 1986 (Autumn). "Money and Power: The Dilemma of the Egyptian Infitah." *The Middle East Journal* 40(4): 634–56.

Mubarak, Hosni. 1999 (Jan. 29). "Interview." *Al-Hawadth,* 19–24.

Mustafa, Hala. 1995. *The State and the Opposition Islamic Movements: Between Truce and Confrontation in the Eras of Sadat and Mubarak.* Cairo: Markaz Al-Mahrusa.

Nasser, Gamal Abdel. 1959. *The Philosophy of the Revolution.* Buffalo, NY: Smith, Keynes and Marshall.

Palmer, Monte, Ali Leila, and El Sayed Yassin. 1988. *The Egyptian Bureaucracy.* Syracuse, NY: Syracuse University Press.

Rugh, Andrea B. 1986. *Reveal and Conceal: Dress in Contemporary Egypt.* Cairo, Egypt: American University in Cairo Press.

Soreh, Berween. 1998. "Another AUC Book Slashed by the Censor." *Special to the Middle East Times,* www.

Springborg, Robert. 1989. *Mubarak's Egypt: Fragmentation of the Political Order.* Boulder, CO: Westview Press.

Springborg, Robert. 1998 (Jan.). "Egypt: Repression's Toll." *Current History* 97(615): 32–37.

Sullivan, Denis J. 1990. "The Political Economy of Reform in Egypt." *International Journal of Middle East Studies* 22(3): 317–34.

Sullivan, Earl L., Ali Leila, and Monte Palmer. 1990 (Fall). *Social Background and Bureaucratic Behavior in Egypt*. Cairo Papers in Social Science, vol. 13, monograph 3. Cairo, Egypt: The American University in Cairo Press.

Trimberger, Ellen Kay. 1978. *Revolution from Above: Military Bureaucrats and Development in Japan, Turkey, Egypt, and Peru*. New Brunswick, NJ: Transaction Books.

Tschirgi, Dan, ed. 1994. *The Arab World Today*. Boulder, CO: Lynne Rienner.

Tuma, Eliash. 1988. "Institutionalized Obstacles to Development: The Case of Egypt." *World Development* 16(10): 1185–98.

Walker, Edward S. Jr. 1997 (Winter–Spring). "United States–Egyptian Relations: Strengthening our Partnership." *SAIS Review* 17(1): 147–62.

Waterbury, John. 1978. *Egypt: Burdens of the Past/Options for the Future*. Bloomington, IN: Indiana University Press.

Weber, Max. 1947. *The Theory of Social and Economic Organization*. Glencoe, IL: Free Press. (Translated by A. M. Henderson and Talcott Parsons, 1947, renewed 1975 by Talcott Parsons.)

Weede, Erich. 1986 (Dec.). "Rent-Seeking or Dependency as Explanations of Why Poor People Stay Poor." *International Sociology* I(4): 421–41.

Weinbaum, M. G. 1986. *Egypt and the Politics of U.S. Economic Aid*. Boulder, CO: Westview Press.

Woodward, Peter. 1992. *Nasser.* London: Longman.

Youssef, Hassan Pasha, Head of the Royal Diwan. 1983. Interviews with author in Cairo, Egypt.

Youssef, Samir M. 1983. *System of Management in Egyptian Public Enterprises*. Cairo, Egypt: Center for Middle East Management Studies, The American University in Cairo.

Zaqzug, Hamdi D. 1999 (Jan. 4). "Interview with the Minister of Wafqs." *Al-Wasat* 23–25.

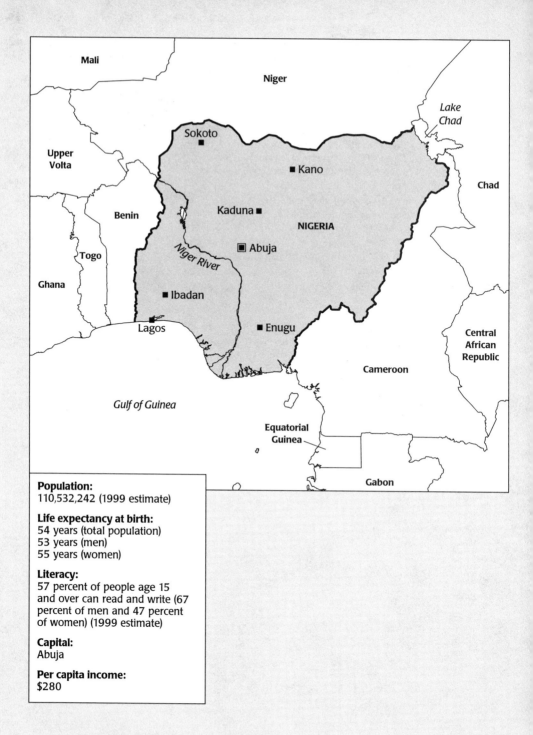

Population:
110,532,242 (1999 estimate)

Life expectancy at birth:
54 years (total population)
53 years (men)
55 years (women)

Literacy:
57 percent of people age 15 and over can read and write (67 percent of men and 47 percent of women) (1999 estimate)

Capital:
Abuja

Per capita income:
$280

11

Nigeria
The Politics of Hope and Despair

The proclamation of Nigerian independence in 1960 was greeted by both the Nigerian population and the world community with a tremendous sense of optimism. It was hoped that Nigeria, being a large and wealthy state, could take the lead in forging a stable, democratic, and economically developed Africa.

There were, of course, problems to be overcome. Nigeria's population was fragmented among diverse ethnic and religious groups. The nation's oil wealth, although substantial, masked a broader economy that was severely underdeveloped. Most of Nigeria's citizens were illiterate and lived in conditions of extreme poverty. Finally, Nigerians lacked political experience. Nigeria had been proclaimed a parliamentary democracy, but neither Nigeria's leaders nor its population had broad experience in democratic procedures.

The optimism that accompanied Nigeria's independence, then, was based upon the hope that democratically elected leaders would be able to set aside their religious and ethnic differences and use the state's abundant oil revenues to build a free and prosperous nation. In retrospect, the optimism of the independence era was misplaced. Democracy gave way to dictatorship, and Nigeria's oil revenues were squandered by corruption and mismanagement. Today, the African state that once had the best opportunity for joining the First World has come to personify the despair of the Fourth World.

In this chapter, we will trace the history of Nigerian politics from its colonial origins to its current struggle to reestablish some form of democratic government. We will see how political, cultural, economic, and international forces have combined to lock the Nigerian population into a seemingly endless cycle of hope and despair. It should also be noted that the problems besetting Nigeria are symptomatic of those facing most of the states of sub-Saharan Africa.

Nigeria in Historical Perspective

Historically, Nigeria was a conglomerate of some 200 diverse ethnic (tribal) groups speaking more than 100 indigenous languages, welded together in 1914 by the force of British arms (Graf 1988). There had been no historic Nigeria, nor was there any sense of Nigerian nationalism. The northern regions were largely Muslim, while the eastern and western regions were either Christian or animistic[1] (Coleman 1965). More than anything else, Nigeria's borders reflected Britain's race with France to colonize the African continent.

The Colonial Era

Deep-seated ethnic, religious, and linguistic conflicts had made it difficult for Nigeria's diverse tribes to resist the British occupation. Such conflict is understandable, for Nigeria's citizens were isolated intellectually by their illiteracy, socially by the prevalence of tribal warfare, and culturally by a profound sense of mutual suspicion. As a result of their intellectual and social isolation, they were unable to envision a world broader than the confines of their tribal boundaries. Tribal life was all they knew (Doob 1964; Lerner 1958).

It was in the interest of the colonial authorities, moreover, to keep Nigeria's citizens as divided and as backward as possible. The pacification of Nigeria had been difficult, and cooperation among the tribes would only impede the economic exploitation of the colony.

British colonial policy in Nigeria was euphemistically referred to as **indirect rule** and centered on three interrelated strategies designed to alter the traditional nature of Nigerian society as little as possible.

First, tribal chiefs were allowed to play their traditional leadership roles, albeit with the assistance of a British advisor. This strategy reinforced traditional cultural arrangements and avoided direct confrontation between the British and the tribal chiefs (Turnbull 1963). Indirect rule was also far cheaper than attempting to maintain a massive colonial bureaucracy in a climatically difficult region.

Second, education and other intrusions of Western culture were kept to a minimum. For the most part, Western education was reserved for the sons of tribal leaders and other influential Nigerians.

Third, the occupation authorities reinforced the fragmentation of Nigerian society by playing upon tribal jealousies, favoring first one group and then another. In one way or another, then, British policy retarded Nigeria's evolution into an integrated country capable of speaking with a single voice (Davidson 1994).

Although British colonial policy stressed indirect rule and ethnic segmentation, it was inevitable that a Westernized elite with nationalistic aspirations would emerge to challenge British authorities for the right to rule. Nigeria's Westernized elite found its origins in the small cadre of Nigerians recruited by the British to assist in the administration of the large and climatically adverse colony. Other members of the Westernized elite included merchants and the sons of tribal leaders educated in British missionary schools (Coleman 1965).

As had happened in India and most other colonies, Westernized Nigerians became restive with a system that precluded them from competing with British nationals for advancement in the bureaucracy, military, and business communities. The few Nigerians to receive advanced positions, moreover, received far lower

---

[1]Local religions.

Art from the pre-colonial era displays the richness of traditional African culture. This plaque shows an entrance to the palace of the Oba of Benin. The turret features a python, messenger of the god Olukun, ruler of the seas. The pillars supporting the turret have representations of the Portuguese, and the door is flanked by four attendants, two on each side.

wages than their British counterparts and supervised only native personnel. As long as Nigeria remained a British colony, Nigerians would remain second-class citizens in their own country.

The tribal chiefs, too, had grown weary of British rule. Much like their Westernized counterparts, they viewed independence as the avenue to enhanced power and prosperity (Coleman 1965). The interwar period would thus find both sets of elites, the traditional and the modern, pressing Britain for a growing voice in the governing of the colony. Cooperation between the modern and traditional elites was facilitated by the overlapping membership of the two elite groups. Indeed, many members of the Westernized elite were the sons and grandsons of tribal leaders.

Faced with growing opposition to its rule, Britain reluctantly began to prepare Nigeria for independence as a democratic state. Shortly before World War II, Nigeria was divided into three administrative districts: a Northern district dominated by the predominately Muslim Hausa and Fulani tribes, a Western district dominated by the Yoruba, and an Eastern district dominated by the Ibo. At the end of World War II, each district was provided with its own regional legislature and allowed to be more or less self-governing. The provincial governments were capped by a federal parliament, the members of which were elected by the regional assemblies. With full independence to be granted in 1960, Nigeria's citizens would have fifteen years in which to resolve their ethnic differences and adapt to a British-style democracy. The task would be a monumental one for a country whose population remained largely rural and illiterate, and in which all areas of life were governed by ethnic considerations. Nigeria, moreover, was to be a federal system in which the state boundaries were drawn along ethnic and religious lines. Each ethnic region, accordingly, would be competing with the others for jobs, development projects, government contracts, and educational opportunities (Miles 1988). Ethnic conflict, already strong, was now interwoven with economic conflict (Diamond 1988).

Other problems also loomed on the horizon. It was not clear, for example, that Nigeria possessed the bureaucratic capacity to administer its own affairs. Nigerians had been excluded from the senior civil service prior to 1946, and by 1954, six years before independence, they constituted less than 20 percent of Nigeria's senior officials (Koehn 1990). Junior officials were promoted to senior ranks shortly after independence but generally lacked the qualifications and experience required to execute their responsibilities in an efficient and impartial manner. Many succumbed to the temptations of tribalism and corruption.

The situation was similar in the Nigerian military, with 90 percent of the officer corps in the Nigerian Army, the former Royal West Africa Frontier Force, remaining in British hands on the eve of independence. Five years later, 90 percent of the officer corps was Nigerian. As a result of the rush to nativize the military, tribal conflicts became deeply embedded within the military structure. In many instances, loyalties to the ethnic group outweighed loyalties to the state.

Independent Nigeria: The First Republic

Nigeria embarked upon independence as a British-style parliamentary democracy. The House of Representatives, the Nigerian counterpart of the British House of Commons, was popularly elected in districts more or less corresponding to Nigeria's main ethnic regions. In classic parliamentary procedure, the members of the House of Representatives elected the prime minister and Cabinet from among their members, the Government serving at the pleasure of the House. The Senate was patterned after the British House of Lords, its role being to provide tribal chiefs and other traditional leaders with a symbolic voice in the political process (Diamond 1988).

Although patterned on the British system, Nigeria's governing structure also borrowed three key elements from the American experience.

■ First, the federal structure established by the colonial administration was retained as a means of coping with Nigeria's regional, ethnic, and religious diversity.

■ Second, Nigeria was provided with a written constitution that defined the role of its political institutions and delineated the rights of its citizens.

■ Third, Nigeria was provided with a Supreme Court empowered to declare acts of the Government unconstitutional.

Whatever the merits of its political structure, Nigeria's first experiment in democracy was a dismal failure. Six years after the celebration of Nigerian independence, democracy gave way to military dictatorship.

What went wrong? Why did Nigeria's first experiment in democracy end in failure? The best answer to this question is that everything went wrong (Graf 1988). Nigeria's citizens remained overwhelmingly traditional in their political outlook, placing loyalty to their ethnic groups above loyalty to the state. Few people beyond the elite actually understood the political system. This was particularly the case among Nigeria's illiterate rural population, which constituted the vast majority of the electorate. The only political system rural Nigerians really knew was the tribal-ethnic system.

The primacy of ethnic attachments was particularly evident in Nigeria's embryonic system of political parties. The Northern region was totally dominated by the Northern People's Congress (NPC), the party of the predominately Muslim Hausa and Fulani tribes. The National Convention of Nigerian Citizens (NCNC) represented the Ibos of the Eastern region, and the Action Group (AG) represented the Yorubas of the West.

The ethnic character of Nigeria's political parties was further intensified by the absence of **cross-cutting cleavages**. Each of Nigeria's three main ethnic groups was concentrated in a specific region of the country and possessed a unique religious character. The contrast between the Muslim North and the predominately Christian regions of the East and West was particularly stark. The three regions were also divided along socioeconomic lines. The North, while having the largest population, was far less developed than either the East or the West, both of which had been influenced more directly by colonialism. The North feared that the greater Westernization of the Ibo and Yoruba would enable them to gain control of the national government. The Ibo and Yoruba, by contrast, feared that the larger population base of the North would give it a commanding position in the Parliament. Ethnic conflict between the three dominant groups, then, was reinforced by religious and economic conflict.

The Government that would lead Nigeria to independence and democracy had been elected in 1959 under the supervision of the British. As expected, the election proved to be a largely tribal affair dominated by the NPC, the party of the Muslim North. The NPC Government allocated most of Nigeria's resources to the North, evoking charges of fraud and corruption from its adversaries.

Nigeria's first election as an independent country was held in 1963 and was supervised by a Government dominated by the Northern People's Congress. The magnitude of the NPC victory surprised even its own leaders. Opposition leaders charged the NPC with fraud, but to no avail. Democracy had merely become a new venue for tribal conflict (Diamond 1988).

The failure of Nigerian democracy must also be attributed to the unwillingness of Nigeria's political elites to put aside personal ambition for the sake of national unity. Rather than urging compromise and tolerance, most sought electoral victory by inflaming hostility toward competing tribes. Instead of building national unity, Nigeria's first experiment in democracy led to a strengthening of ethnic conflict.

Lacking strong leadership from its political elites, Nigeria failed to develop parliamentary and legal institutions worthy of public trust. Legislators raised their own salaries but avoided the difficult issues of nation building (Graf 1988). The courts enforced neither human rights nor fair elections, and corruption became rampant. Not all officials were corrupt, but the prevalence of corruption was staggering (Diamond 1988).

In retrospect, it could also be argued that the failure of Nigeria's first experiment in democracy was the result of an ill-advised attempt to impose British institutions upon a population that had nothing in common with the British. The British "Westminster" model allows a Government unlimited power to do as it pleases as long as it possesses a majority in the popularly elected house of parliament. There are no minority rights, and all restraints on the abuse of power are cultural in nature. In the Nigerian context, this meant that the citizens in the Eastern and Western regions were excluded from the decision-making process. Their leaders could deliver fiery speeches denouncing the predominantly Northern Government, but as long as that Government was supported by a majority in the House of Representatives, however fraudulently elected, there was little they could do to alter its policies. Nigeria's first experiment in democracy, then, exemplified the difficulties inherent in attempting to transplant the political institutions of the West into a region with widely differing sociocultural traditions.

Perhaps Nigeria during the early 1960s was simply the wrong place and the wrong time for an experiment in democracy. Democracy is a "reconciliation" system (Apter 1987). It seeks compromise between the demands of competing groups, assuring that all of the major contenders for power get a fair share of the state's economic resources. As noted above, the demands of Nigeria's major ethnic groups were difficult to reconcile. Each wanted to dominate the system, and each manifested profound distrust of the others. Nigeria needed to build a political community before it could build a democracy.

Whatever the case, the First Republic collapsed with scarcely a whimper. As described by William Graf:

> At first glance, the ease with which the military has been able to assume supreme political power is astounding. Quite literally overnight, this minuscule (10,500 men in 1965), relatively inexperienced (80% of its officers had no more than four years in service), poorly educated (66% of combat and non-combat officers had no more than secondary education before being commissioned) and young (62% were between 20 and 24 years old) entity overthrew the First Republic and eliminated many of its most prominent leaders. In fact the coup itself was engineered by a group of five majors; the military hierarchy merely accepted and took over the fait accompli.
>
> However, a second glance suggests that the army's strength was not the decisive factor, but the weakened and decayed condition of the First Republic (Graf 1988, 41).

The Military As Savior

Nigeria's new military leaders portrayed themselves as the saviors of Nigeria. Continued civilian rule, they said, would have resulted in civil war and the dissolution of the Nigerian state. The military would build the nation and develop its resources. Once the task of nation building had been completed, Nigeria would be returned to civilian rule.

How successful was the military in solving Nigeria's political and economic woes? This is a difficult question to answer, for the early years of military rule saw Nigeria engulfed in an ethnic civil war of unprecedented ferocity. The military coup of 1966 had been executed by predominantly Ibo officers, many of whom were true nationalists distraught by the corruption and general disarray of the First Republic. Nevertheless, some also sought vengeance against the political leaders of the Northern and Western regions. The federal regions were abolished, becoming little more than the administrative provinces of a centralized state. The North erupted in riots, killing scores of Ibos living in the region and looting their property. Northern officers launched their own coup in July of the

Nigeria's military government spent the country's oil revenues constructing modern office buildings, airports, and military facilities. Meanwhile, the agrarian-based economy was all but ignored.

same year, unleashing a series of retributions and counter-retributions that threatened the survival of the Nigerian state. Ibo leaders in Nigeria's Eastern province, the heart of Nigeria's oil industry, seized upon the chaos to secede from the union. The Nigerian army, shorn of its Ibo units, invaded the newly proclaimed Biafran state, igniting a civil war that would endure for two and one-half years. Devastation in the Eastern region bordered on genocide, estimates of the war's casualties reaching the one million mark. The Union was sustained, but bitterness ran deep.

When the war ended, the military, now under Northern leadership, reembarked upon its program of national salvation. The years of military rule were to be boom years as escalating oil revenues made Nigeria the richest country in Africa.[2] Nigeria's new military regime used its unexpected oil revenues to launch a massive program of public works. Seemingly overnight, airports, office buildings, and stadiums transformed the landscape of Nigeria's cities. Such spending generated popular support for the regime by creating the image of development, but it did little to address the inherent weakness of the nonpetroleum sector of the Nigerian economy, most of which was based on agriculture.

The boom economy also saw a coming together of Nigeria's Westernized elite, the members of which had grown wealthy by exploiting the lavish outlay of government revenues. All had a vested interest in assuring that ethnic conflict did not diminish what Nigerians refer to as the "cake." Rather than reducing corruption, military rule merely increased its scope.

[2]Except for the Union of South Africa.

If the military spent lavishly on public works projects, it was to spend more lavishly on itself, buying the latest military hardware and building elegant new facilities. Saving for the future was not part of the military's scheme of things. The gap between rich and poor continued to increase as little effort was made to build an egalitarian society in which all Nigerians had a stake.

Satisfied that the country was well on the path to prosperity and development, Nigeria's military leaders proclaimed that democracy would be restored in 1976, ten years after the original coup. Whether the return to civilian authority would have actually occurred is moot, for 1975 saw Nigeria suffer its third coup d'état in a decade. The new generals, also from the North, said that Nigeria was not ready for democracy. Vowing to end corruption, they pledged that the country's oil revenues would be used to build a sound future for all Nigerians.

The new Nigerian leader, Murtala Mohammed, moved rapidly to put Nigeria's house in order, dismissing more than 10,000 administrative officials, many of senior rank, and establishing special corruption courts throughout the country. All military officers above the rank of Brigadier were retired (with compensation), and plans were made for restructuring the army. A counter-coup in 1976 failed but resulted in the death of Murtala Mohammed. He was replaced by his second in command, who promised an early return to civilian rule. In the view of some observers, the short reign of Murtala Mohammed "had achieved more and greater accomplishments than the three preceding governments" (Graf 1988).

The Second Republic: Structural Solutions to Behavioral Problems

The transition to civilian rule began in 1975 with the creation of a Constitutional Commission charged with drafting a constitution compatible with Nigeria's political and cultural realities. The new constitution was proclaimed in 1979, with national elections occurring shortly thereafter. Nigeria's second experiment in democracy, the Second Republic, would last for approximately four years before giving way to a new round of military coups.

The most interesting feature of the Second Republic was Nigeria's attempt to solve what were essentially behavioral and cultural problems by making mechanical adjustments in the structure of its political institutions. As expressed by General Obasanjo, then-head of Nigeria's military government,

> Political recruitment and subsequent political support which are based on tribal, religious and linguistic sentiments contributed largely to our past misfortune. They must not be allowed to spring up again. Those negative political attitudes like hatred, falsehood, intolerance and acrimony also contributed to our national tragedy in the past: they must not be continued. These negative attitudes must not be allowed to enter into the practice of the new political system (Joseph 1987, 93).

The structural reforms introduced by the 1979 Constitution were threefold. *First, the British "Westminster" system of parliamentary democracy was replaced by a presidential system based upon the American model* (Ayeni, Nassar, and Popoola 1988). The parliamentary system, as noted above, had allowed a single ethnic group to dominate Nigerian politics. Adoption of the American system fragmented power and added the concept of checks and balances to Nigerian politics. Stronger provisions were also made for the protection of minority rights.

Second, the new constitution increased the number of states in Nigeria's federal system from three to nineteen. The purpose of restructuring the federal system was to broaden the base of Nigerian politics by empowering the smaller ethnic groups. Under the old system, a multitude of smaller ethnic groups constituting

Table 11.1
Nigeria: Patterns of Ethnic Distribution

Ethnic Group	Estimated Percentage of Population in 1998
A. Hausa/Fulani	32
B. Yoruba	21
C. Ibo	18
D. Other	29

Source: Data from Internet source detnews.com/1998.

some 29 percent of the Nigerian population (see Table 11.1), were denied an effective political voice. The creation of nineteen states freed many of those groups from domination by their larger neighbors.

Third, the new constitution attempted to assure that the presidents of the Second Republic would be truly national presidents by forcing them to garner both a majority of the popular vote and 25 percent of the vote in at least twelve different states. Under the new rules, the North would no longer be able to dominate national elections simply on the basis of its larger population.

The new constitution was an experiment in social engineering. Its creators attempted to eliminate ethnic politics by forcing Nigeria's politicians to jump through new hoops. The important question was whether structural changes alone could force either the politicians or the electorate to alter deeply entrenched patterns of political behavior.

To what extent, then, did changes in Nigeria's constitutional structure lead to changes in Nigerian political behavior? Very little (Kalu 1987). Merely changing political structures does not solve problems that stem from cultural and economic conditions. The Second Republic collapsed for the same reasons that the First Republic did: ethnic conflict, institutional weakness, elite indifference, administrative ineptness, a lack of democratic experience, mass cynicism, rising expectations, blatant corruption, growing disparities in wealth, and a general inability of the government to meet the needs of its citizens.

The Military Returns

The collapse of Nigeria's second experiment in democracy was not widely mourned (Forrest 1993). The government simply had not worked. The rationale for the military takeover in 1983 was much the same as it had been some two decades earlier. General Buhari, the new Military Head of State, proclaimed that the military's seizure of power was merely corrective and promised a return to civilian rule at the earliest possible moment.

The challenges facing Nigeria's new military regime were the same as those that had faced previous military regimes. Nigeria's political and administrative institutions had to be strengthened, and popular faith in those institutions had to be restored. More fundamentally, Nigeria's diverse ethnic communities had to be welded into a national political community, a goal that could only be achieved by putting Nigeria's economy in order and closing the ever-widening gap between rich and poor.

General Buhari and his successors would not find this an easy task, for a collapse in world oil prices would see Nigeria's per capita income plummet from

$1,000 in the early 1980s to less than $300 by the early 1990s. Nigerians had grown accustomed to the wealth of an oil economy, and the military government would be blamed for its decline.

General Buhari attacked Nigeria's social and political ills with unusual severity. Shop owners were forced to lower prices, and anti-sabotage decrees promised swift penalties for economic and social crimes. The penalties for cheating on school examinations, for example, ran as high as twenty-one years in prison, with death sentences being meted out to women suspected of smuggling cocaine (Graf 1988). The press protested and suffered accordingly. All political parties were abolished, and special "National Consciousness and Enlightenment Committees" were created to lecture the masses in good citizenship. A "War Against Undiscipline" was also launched against a bureaucracy swollen by years of political patronage (Ekwe-Ekwe 1991). Fearing that the severity of his reforms would trigger a counter-coup, Buhari also placed senior military commanders under surveillance (Graf 1988).

While Buhari attacked Nigeria's social and political ills with extraordinary vigor, he did little to restore a sense of ethnic balance to Nigerian politics. If anything, politics became more Northern and more Islamic. As described by Herbert Ekwe-Ekwe,

> Thirteen of the nineteen members of the ruling Supreme Military Council (SMC) were northern Muslims, most of whose families were closely related to powerful local emirs. In an unprecedented move, Buhari breached a crucial long-standing "understanding" in central government (in Lagos) whereby the deputy head of state *always* came from a geographical area in the country different from the head of state's; Buhari, himself a Hausa-Fulani northern Muslim, appointed Tunde Idiagbon, a fellow Hausa-Fulani northern Muslim, as his deputy. Apart from the head of the navy, all service chiefs and commanders of the principal military divisions that Buhari appointed came from the north. Buhari's principal adviser, Mamman Daura, was not only the head of state's uncle, but also the brother of the powerful Emir of Daura in northern Nigeria (Ekwe-Ekwe 1991, 30).

Buhari's reign was to be short-lived. It was not the severity of his reform program that triggered his demise, but the severity of his attacks on his military colleagues. In August 1985, General Babangida, one of those officers placed under surveillance by Buhari, overthrew the Buhari regime and reconstituted the ruling military council. The coup had little to do with either ethnic politics or religion. One Northern general had merely replaced another.

General Babangida promised a quick return to civilian rule and relaxed the more severe measures imposed by his predecessor. In their place, he attempted to stimulate economic growth by stimulating capitalism (Forrest 1993). He also increased the number of states from nineteen to thirty, hoping that the proliferation of state governments would make it difficult for Nigeria's ethnic leaders to consolidate their power (Forrest 1993). Political parties continued to be banned, and all former politicians, a group that included both party leaders and senior government officials, were prohibited from engaging in any form of political activity. Finally, efforts were accelerated to complete the transfer of Nigeria's capital from Lagos to Abuja (Umeh 1993). The new capital in Abuja, an ethnically neutral site in the center of Nigeria, was to symbolize Nigeria's new beginning (Taylor 1993).

In addition to the above reforms, Babangida also restored ethnic balance to the Supreme Military Council, now rechristened the Armed Forces Ruling Council. Many senior positions were allocated to members of minority tribes, and younger officers were brought into the ruling structure (Forrest 1993). It could be argued, of course, that the restoration of ethnic balance was merely illusory. General Babangida made all of the decisions, and the interests of the Muslim North were never in doubt (Ekwe-Ekwe 1991).

In the final analysis, the second round of military rule was not much more effective than the first. The hope that the military's greater efficiency would lead to clean government and economic development was not to be fulfilled.

The Long March Toward New Democracy

In 1986, General Babangida announced that the Government of Nigeria would be returned to civilian rule by the end of 1990. Toward this end, a seventeen-member Political Bureau was appointed by Babangida to stimulate national debate on the future of Nigerian democracy (Graf 1988). The 1990 deadline was not met, but elections for state governors and state assemblies took place toward the end of 1991. Elections for the House of Representatives and Senate took place in July 1992, with the oft-delayed election of a civilian president finally occurring in June 1993.

While the Political Bureau debated the nation's future, it was General Babangida who planned the course of Nigeria's transition to democracy. His concerns were many. Some focused on eliminating the problems that had destroyed the Second Republic. It was essential, for example, that the new government represent the entire nation and that tribalism and ethnic conflict no longer be allowed to destroy the fabric of Nigerian society. Corruption would also have to be eliminated, or at least brought under control. Other concerns were of a more personal nature: the interests of the North required attention, as well as the interests of the military and those of the general himself. As subsequent events would reveal, Babangida was clearly nervous about relinquishing the authority that he had wielded for more than a decade.

Babangida's plan for achieving the above objectives was as complex and potentially contradictory as the objectives themselves. The centerpiece of Babangida's attack on ethnic politics was a forced two-party system. Henceforth, Nigeria would have only two political parties: the National Republic Convention and the Social Democratic Party. The first, according to the General, would be a "little to the right" and the second, "a little to the left" (*CSM,* July 7, 1992).

A two-party system, it was hoped, would force Nigeria's ethnic groups to put aside their differences and forge broad national coalitions for the sake of winning the presidency. It was also hoped that the existence of a party of the left and a party of the right would focus the attention of Nigeria's voters on social and economic issues rather than on issues of ethnicity and religiosity.

The speed with which the new parties were created precluded the establishment of local party organizations other than those financed by the "big men," Nigeria's term for political bosses. General Babangida attempted to compensate for the organizational weaknesses of his new parties by providing them with offices and staff in each of Nigeria's 589 electoral districts. The parties took the support but complained of government interference in their internal affairs (Babatope 1991).

Corruption was attacked by banning all elected officials who had served in the Second Republic from participation in the new elections. Discredited politicians, according to Babangida's plan, would not be able to pick up where they had left off a decade earlier. Eliminating corruption, however, proved to be more difficult than Babangida had hoped. Excluded from the electoral process by military decree, Nigeria's political bosses merely used surrogate candidates to do their bidding. As a result, the candidates of the big men dominated the local elections in 1987 as well as primary elections for the national legislature in 1991.

Babangida countered by annulling the results of the local government elections (1987) and by having the Election Commission cancel the results of 1991 primary

General Olusegun Obasanjo ruled over Nigeria as a military dictator from 1976 to 1979, then was elected president by the Nigerian people twenty years later.

elections in several states (*African Concord,* Oct. 1991, 46). New surrogates were found, only to be disqualified by new exclusionary orders (*Economist,* Dec. 21, 1991, 41). As late as two weeks prior to the 1993 presidential elections, the National Election Commission suggested that one or both of the presidential candidates might have to be disqualified on the basis of alleged fraud.

Particularly interesting were the election procedures devised by the military government to stymie electoral fraud. Rather than secret ballots, Nigerians voted by lining up behind posters of the candidates they wished to support. Election officials then counted the number of individuals in each line and moved on to a new polling place. Having voters stand in line may have prevented the fraudulent stuffing of ballot boxes, but it also added an element of intimidation to the voting process.

For a while, all seemed to go well. Each of the two parties created by General Babangida nominated a candidate for the presidency reputed to be on good terms with the General. Both candidates, accordingly, could be counted on to serve both his interests and those of the military. The candidate of the Social Democratic Party, moreover, was a Yoruba, thereby precluding accusations that the new system was a Northern whitewash. Both candidates were Muslim and, as such, would understand the concerns of the Muslim North.

Democracy, however, would not be achieved. Elections scheduled for early in 1993 were delayed until June. The June elections were held as promised, but the government refused to announce the results, accusing both candidates of electoral violations. The elections were later nullified, with new elections promised in the near future.

Unofficial results published by a Nigerian civil rights group proclaimed Moshood Abiola, the candidate of the Social Democratic Party, to be the clear victor. Mr. Abiola, a Yoruba, reportedly captured 8,341,309 votes, as opposed to the 5,952,047 votes garnered by his Northern opponent. Mr. Abiola's victory, however, was clouded by an incredibly low rate of voter turnout, with only 14 million of the more than 39 million registered voters standing in line behind the portrait of their preferred candidate. This was the lowest rate of voting in Nigerian history (*NYT,* June 19, 1993, 2).

Babangida's reasons for nullifying the elections can only be conjectured. The candidate of the North had lost, thereby threatening both the ethnic dominance of the North and the self-interest of a military establishment controlled by the North. Babangida, moreover, seemed reluctant to relinquish the powers that he had wielded since 1985, despite building a fifty-room retirement mansion in his home village and purchasing a summer home on the French Riviera. In his defense, Babangida could argue that the performance of the state and federal legislatures elected in 1991 and 1992 had demonstrated that Nigeria was not yet ready for a return to democracy. As recounted by Paul Adams in *Africa Report:*

> The National Assembly, which kept two international hotels in Abuja in business but never passed a single law in nearly 18 months, was an expensive irrelevance, while the state assemblies were seen by their electorate as a rabble, shouting, fighting, and sacking their speakers instead of looking after the running of the states (Adams 1994, 49).

Whatever the case, the annulment of elections precipitated mass protests in Nigeria's major cities, many of which turned violent. The military crushed the initial wave of protests, only to confront a new round of protests by business leaders in the Southwest, Abiola's Yoruba power base (Illoegbunam 1994). The Nigerian economy, already a shambles, edged toward total collapse.

With support in the military eroding, Babangida ceded power to an interim civilian regime headed by Chief Shonekan, a Harvard-educated Yoruba businessman. Widely viewed as a Babangida surrogate, Shonekan had a four-month tenure in office that was rocked by both communal violence and a general strike before succumbing to a 1993 military coup led by General Sani Abacha.

In what had now become a tragic ritual, General Abacha proclaimed his seizure of power to be corrective. As if to underscore Abacha's point, General Babangida and his cronies were subsequently charged with having embezzled some $12 billion from various government institutions (Nuanna 1995). A Constitutional Commission, Abacha said, would be established to devise a workable political system for Nigeria. Its proposals, once complete, would then be considered by a full Constitutional Conference (*West Africa,* July 21, 1994, 588). In the meantime, Abiola was charged with twenty-three counts of treason for attempting to establish a democratic government based upon the assumed results of the aborted 1993 elections.

Abacha's Constitutional Conference was eventually convened in June of 1994, but it was stillborn as many major groups refused to participate as a means of protesting Abiola's arrest (*CSM,* June 27, 1994, 2). Indeed, *The African Concord* warned that the Constitutional Conference was "beating the drums of secession" (Ishaka 1994, 14–15). The newsweekly, part of Abiola's media empire, was subsequently banned by the military regime.

Popular apathy toward Abacha's Constitutional Conference gave way to a summer of violence that would see a strike by workers in the petroleum industry, the source of more than 80 percent of Nigeria's revenues, bringing the nation's economy to a halt. Demands for Abiola's release were also underscored by a two-day "general strike" called by Nigeria's major labor federation. The strike was generally effective in the West and East but found little support in the Muslim North (*Economist,* Aug. 13, 1994). For a brief period, it appeared that Abacha would be forced to relinquish power.

Such optimism, however, was misplaced. The strike was broken and its leaders arrested. The opposition press was also shut down, and opponents of the Abacha regime were systematically imprisoned. The democracy movement had made a strong-showing, but it lacked the internal cohesion to challenge a determined general supported by the North.

The Constitutional Conference labored on through the summer and fall of 1994, only to fizzle out in the early months of 1995. The delegates could agree on little and lacked sufficient power to do anything other than make recommendations to Abacha's Provincial Ruling Council. A new constitution was officially proclaimed in 1995, but not released to the public. No mention was made of setting a date for Abacha's departure, but some hinted that he planned to remain in office until 1997.

In the meantime, Abacha abolished the political parties created by Babangida and created five new ones in their stead. This, he proclaimed, was a vital step in Nigeria's return to democracy. With typical Nigerian wit, the five parties were soon labeled "Abacha's Quintuplets" and the "five fingers of a leprous hand" (Onadipe, 1997). All five of the parties named Abacha as their presidential candidate, and he was still deciding which of the five to favor when he died of a heart attack in June 1998 (*Vanguard,* Feb. 12, 1999, www). The Swiss subsequently reported that Abacha and his family had deposited $654 million in Swiss banks (*NYT,* Apr. 5, 2000, www).

Abacha was succeeded by General Abubakr, who lost little time in proclaiming that his sole purpose in office was to lead Nigeria's transition to democracy. Scores of political prisoners were released and elections were scheduled for all levels of government. Abacha's 1995 constitution was also released to the public. It was a ponderous 204-page document, now largely discredited by the brutality of Abacha's rule.

This, however, created a constitutional crisis. How was Nigeria to prepare for the spate of elections scheduled for the end of 1998 and the beginning of 1999 without a constitution?

A Constitutional Review Committee appointed by General Abubakr recommended a return to Nigeria's 1979 constitution, but the Nigerian media later announced that selected clauses would be drawn from the 1979, 1989, and 1995 constitutions. The exact clauses to be used were not revealed (*Vanguard,* Feb. 18, 1999, www). As a result, Nigeria's local government, state, parliamentary, and presidential elections were held without benefit of a constitution. A noted Nigerian jurist warned the population "not to insist on having a real constitution now as this could provide an excuse for the prolongation of military rule" (*Guardian,* Feb. 22, 1999, www).

Among other things, the lack of a formal constitution made it difficult to delineate the respective powers of the Parliament and the president. Nevertheless, 109 senators and 360 members of the House of Representatives were duly elected by Nigeria's citizens, albeit with a low voter turnout.

A multitude of political parties contested the local government elections, with the three dominant vote-getters being allowed to contest the parliamentary and presidential races. The three political parties that established their dominance during the local government elections were the People's Democratic Party, The Alliance for Democracy, and the All People's Party. Each, as might be expected, drew its strength from one of Nigeria's three main ethnic regions (*Vanguard,* Dec. 7, 1998, www). In contrast to the past, however, both presidential candidates emerged from the Yoruba Southeast, guaranteeing the very rare occurrence of rule by a non-northerner.

The Nigerian press offered several interpretations of this remarkable turn of events. In the view of some, the northern population was fed up with the lack of development in the region. Northern politicians and generals had grown rich, but the Northern population had benefited little from its political dominance. In the words of Naajatu Muhammed, "If you go round the north, you see that there is nothing to show for the endless control of a government by northerners except stark poverty" (Muhammed, 1998, 16).

Others pointed to fear of a violent political upheaval if a shift were not made to the South, and especially the Yoruba Southeast. Abiola, a Yoruba, was widely believed

Table 11.2
Summary of Nigeria's Political History

Head of State	Period in Power	Mode of Relinquishing Authority
Alhaji A. T. Balewa	Oct. 1, 1960–Jan. 15, 1966	Killed in coup d'état.
Major Gen. J. T. U. Aguiyi Ironsi	Jan. 16, 1966–July 29, 1966	Killed in coup d'état.
Gen. Yakubu Gowon	Aug. 1, 1966–July 29, 1975	Ousted in a coup d'état.
Major Gen. Murtala Mohammed	July 30, 1975–Feb. 13, 1976	Killed in coup d'état.
Gen. O. Obasanjo	Feb. 13, 1976–Oct. 1, 1979	Handed over the mantle of leadership to Alhaji Shehu Shagari after the 1979 general elections, having survived threats against his government.
Alhaji Shehu Shagari	Oct. 1, 1979–Dec. 31, 1983	Ousted in coup d'état.
Major Gen. M. Buhari	Jan. 1, 1984–Aug. 27, 1985	Ousted in coup d'état.
Gen. I. B. Babangida	Aug. 27, 1985–Aug. 27, 1993	Ousted by a combination of military, civilian, and international pressure following nullification of elections.
Chief Shonekan	Aug. 27, 1993–Nov. 17, 1993	Military coup d'etat.
General Sani Abacha	Nov. 17, 1993–1998	Natural death.
General Abubakr	June 1998–April 1999	Resigned.
General Obasanjo	May 29, 1999–	

Source: Updated from Israel Kelue Okoye, *Soldiers and Politics in Nigeria* (Lagos, Nigeria: New Age, 1991), p. 26.

to have won the 1993 presidential elections annulled by Babangida, a debacle now referred to as the "Third Republic" (Benson, 1999). Cynics also added that the victorious candidate, General Obasanjo, was on very good terms with the Northern elites and that he was widely supported by retired generals anxious to avoid prosecution by a civilian government (*IHT,* Feb. 22, 1999, www; *NYT,* Feb. 22, 1999, www). Whether or not this was the case, two of the first people to congratulate Obasanjo on his victory were former dictators General Gowon (1966–1975) and General Babangida (1985–1993) (*NYT,* Mar. 3, 1999).

On Obasanjo's behalf, it should be noted that he was the only one of Nigeria's military rulers to voluntarily relinquish power to a civilian government. This he did in 1979, having ruled Nigeria from 1976 to 1979, most of the four-plus years in which Nigeria was ruled by non-Northerners. Sixty-one years old at the time of his election and retired from the military, Obasanjo had established himself as an elder statesman of Nigerian politics, a position enhanced by a jail term served for plotting a coup against General Abacha.

Whatever the reasons for his election, Obasanjo and the People's Democratic Party swept to victory in the 1999 elections, claiming both the presidency and clear majorities in the Senate and the House of Representatives. The transition to the Fourth Republic had begun. It was completed in May 1999 when the military formally withdrew to its barracks. A new 1999 Constitution was also promulgated, its main features being similar to the 1979 Constitution.

A brief summary of Nigeria's tumultuous political history is provided in Table 11.2.

The Political Institutions of Nigeria

Political institutions are the arena of politics. It is the executives, legislatures, courts, bureaucracies, and other agencies of government that authoritatively allocate the resources of the state. In this section, we shall examine the political institutions of Nigeria as they are evolving at the onset of the Fourth Republic.

Executive Power in Nigeria

Executive authority in Nigeria has, more often than not, been exercised by a group of senior officers variously labeled the Supreme Military Council or the Armed Forces Ruling Council, depending upon the particular general in power. The military councils have varied in size from nineteen to twenty-nine members and, with brief exception, have been dominated by Northern generals. The Supreme Military Council has generally been paralleled by a largely civilian Council of Ministers charged with supervising the state bureaucracy.

For all of its councils, military rule in Nigeria was one-man rule. Councils existed to build support for the regime by assuring that key military and civilian groups got their share of the "cake." It was the military president and his close advisors within the military council who made the decisions.

By and large, the Nigerian military has been united by a common desire to maintain its privileged position in Nigerian society. This, however, has not always been easy, for the Nigerian military mirrors the same ethnic and religious conflicts that divide Nigerian society as a whole. No institution, military or otherwise, can be fully divorced from the society in which it originates.

Ethnic and religious factors, however, are not the only lines of cleavage within the Nigerian military. Tension between senior officers and their younger counterparts has always been an important feature of military politics in Nigeria. Nigeria's first military coup was instituted by five majors, "the January Boys" (Graf 1988; Diamond 1988). The overthrow of the Second Republic was apparently hastened by General Buhari's fear that younger, more radical officers were plotting their own coup, a coup that in all probability would have retired the senior command structure (Graf 1988). Junior officers were also rumored to be less supportive of Babangida's transition to civilian rule than their senior counterparts (*CSM*, May 28, 1992, 2).

This complex array of ethnic, religious, and related conflicts, in turn, is supported by a vast mosaic of patron-client networks that permeate all dimensions of the Nigerian military. Senior officers attempt to consolidate their authority by assuring that their junior supporters are promoted rapidly, treated generously, and stationed in key positions. The junior officers, in turn, well understand that their fortunes are tied to those of their patron. If he falls, they fall. As a practical matter, patron-client networks tend to form within the broader constellation of ethnic, linguistic, and religious ties, blood being thicker than water. Nowhere is the power of patron-client networks more visible than in the series of coups and counter-coups that have occurred within the ranks of the Northern generals. Buhari, Babangida, and Abacha, all Northern generals, overthrew their predecessors with the support of a personal network of clients reinforced in turn by the clients of their clients.[3]

General Obasanjo, the first elected president of the Fourth Republic, has promised to run an honest if tight ship. Foremost on his "to do" list is a full-scale

---

[3]Abacha was Babangida's chief-of-staff, demonstrating the precarious position of patrons once their power has evaporated.

assault on corruption. This is not an issue of small concern, for according to some sources, Nigeria is the second most corrupt country in the world, being surpassed only by the neighboring Cameroon and beating out such staunch competitors as Mexico, India, and Russia (*Economist,* Oct. 3, 1998). Close behind was a vow to weld Nigeria into a unified nation, a feat that has eluded the country during its tormented history.

Given the ambiguity concerning precisely which of Nigeria's several constitutions was in force at the time of his election, it was impossible to say with certainty what the powers of the president would be. This has been a matter of minimal concern for Abasanjo, for he is a military man armed with a strong popular mandate and the apparent support of the generals. As noted earlier, moreover, Nigeria's presidents have traditionally run roughshod over a divided and confused legislature. If worries exist, their focus is not a lack of presidential power, but its excess. Toward this end, a seventy-person pro-democracy team has been put in place to:

- affirm, assert, activate, and actualize civil rule;
- debunk, countermand, and crush any derailment, manipulation, or coup against the people's rule; and
- generally checkmate military rule (*Guardian,* Mar. 1, 1999, www).

Be this as it may, Nigeria's legislators are openly complaining about President Obasanjo's "dictatorial tendencies and perceived constitutional breaches" (*Guardian,* Feb. 2, 2000, www).

The National Assembly

The National Assembly, Nigeria's Parliament, consists of two houses, a House of Representatives and a Senate. This framework was adopted from the 1979 constitution, Nigeria's last democratic constitution, but the operational details are still being worked out. Indeed, press coverage prior to the legislative elections in February 1999 seemed confused over the precise number of seats in the House of Representatives. Some placed the number at 309, while others suggested 409. It was later clarified that the HR would have 360 seats; the Senate 109 (*Guardian,* Feb. 24, 1999).

According to both the 1979 and the 1995 constitutions, the powers of the National Assembly are similar to those of most democratic legislatures. The National Assembly passes laws, appropriates monies, confirms important officials, and checks the power of the president.

Given the power of the president and the record of past Nigerian Parliaments, many Nigerian view their new legislature with some apprehension. This is particularly the case in regard to the legislature's ability to check the power of the president. These concerns are expressed by John Nwokocha:

> So assessed against the backdrop of past failure of the lawmakers the question, "How far can the national assembly check the president?" becomes pertinent. With the incoming national assembly, keen watchers of previous behaviors of assemblymen have been asking serious questions. One is, "Can they seriously be seen as actualizing the checks and balance function for which they were elected?" Another question is, "Given the nature of present-day politicians who have demonstrated profound love for money, can they dare to scrutinize the president's bills?" (Nwokocha 1999).

Bureaucracy and Politics in Nigeria

Nigeria's crisis of leadership has been paralleled by an equally profound crisis in administration. Decisions are made, but few are implemented in an efficient and

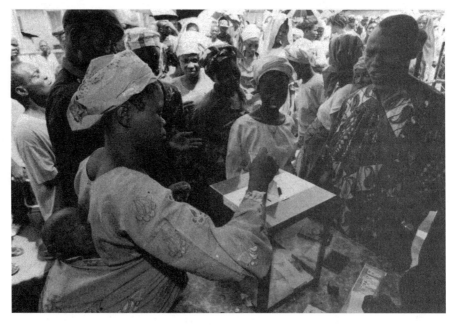

During Nigeria's presidential election in 1999, much of the voting and tallying was done by hand.

impartial manner. This is as true of Nigeria's military regimes as it is of its civilian regimes. A recent study of the Nigerian bureaucracy provides the following assessment:

> Changes in political economy promoted relentless expansion in the size of the public bureaucracy throughout Africa and expanded the privileged economic opportunities available to insiders.... Increases in bureaucratic power and rewards have not been accompanied, however, by noticeable improvements in the performance of public servants or gains in public-sector productivity under civilian or military regimes. A reliable indicator that this is the case in Nigeria is the continued erratic provision of such essential services as water, electrical power, telecommunications, and the maintenance of law and order (Koehn 1990, 46).

According to a report by the head of the Nigerian civil service, the situation had improved little by the turn of the century (*Guardian,* Sept. 14, 1999, www).

The causes of Nigeria's bureaucratic malaise are many. Unlike the Indian experience, Nigeria did not begin independence with a professionalized bureaucracy. Rather, most senior and technical positions remained in the hands of the British until the dawn of independence. The transfer of the bureaucracy into Nigerian hands occurred rapidly following the proclamation of independence, but the new appointees lacked experience. Most were poorly trained (Koehn 1990). Corruption was pervasive, and ethnic loyalties rivaled loyalty to the state. Bureaucratic recruitment hinges as much on ethnic and political considerations as on technical qualifications.

Stark testimony to the continued problems facing the Nigerian bureaucracy can be found in the fact that about 30 percent of all bureaucratic positions remain in the hands of foreigners[4] (Koehn 1990, 20). The continued presence of foreigners reflects the inability of Nigeria's educational system to provide the bureaucracy

---

[4]The figures are higher in the state bureaucracies and lower in the national administration.

with an adequate supply of technically trained officials. It is also an overt manifestation of ethnic distrust. Northern states, in particular, continue to prefer foreign
bureaucrats to bureaucrats recruited from Nigeria's other ethnic communities
(Koehn 1990). Even more damning is the fact that Nigeria is now preparing to turn
over management of its major public corporations to European management firms
(Obadina 1998).

Be this as it may, senior administrators are part and parcel of the ruling elite.
Authority lines in Nigeria are fluid and overlapping, with administrative and military leaders often being linked by ethnic, family, social, and even business connections (Koehn 1990). Nigeria's elites also possess a strong common interest in
strengthening the role of the central government at the expense of the states (Forrest
1993; Imoagene 1989).

The existence of strong links between Nigeria's administrative, political, and
military elites, however, does not necessarily imply a great deal of mutual trust. The
military is particularly suspicious of the administrative elite and has sacked its
members at will. Indeed, the generals have attempted to reduce the influence of the
senior administrators by creating a perpetual game of musical chairs.

It should also be noted that Nigeria's bureaucrats represent a powerful corporate
pressure group that has been very effective in preserving its privileged status in
Nigerian society. A sustained strike by civil servants during the early 1990s, for example, resulted in a 45 percent pay increase. With the advent of democracy, Nigeria's
bureaucrats have again threatened a sustained strike (*Guardian,* Feb. 19, 1999, www).

Law and Politics in Nigeria

The structure of the Nigerian legal system is similar to that of most of the states
reviewed in the preceding chapters, with lower courts giving way to a system of
appeal courts topped by a Supreme Court. The Supreme Court possesses the power
to declare acts of the Government unconstitutional, a power that it used on a limited
basis during the Second Republic. With the return to military rule, the Court's power
of judicial review returned to the realm of theory.

The court system was made the focal point of political conflict during Nigeria's
abortive transition to democracy in 1993, as Chief Abiola, the presumed winner in
the June elections, sued in the Lagos High Court[5] to have the interim government
installed by General Babangida declared illegal. The High Court did so, but the ruling was moot, as General Abacha had seized power before the power of the courts
to dissolve the Government had been tested.

Parallel court systems operate at both the national and state levels, a novel feature of the court system being the practice of Shari'a or religious law in predominantly Muslim areas. The Shari'a courts have jurisdiction over divorce, inheritance,
and related family matters addressed by the Islamic faith. Nigeria thus finds itself in
the difficult position of having two sets of family law: one for Muslims and one for
non-Muslims. Rather than building a unified political community, accordingly, the
legal system consolidates social cleavages. Indeed, Christians now fear that they
may be made subject to Islamic law (*Associated Press,* Feb. 1, 2000, www).

The Nigerian legal system, in sum, continues to fight an uphill battle to retain
its political independence. The intimidation of judges has been commonplace
under both civilian and military regimes and is likely to remain so in the foreseeable future (Ikegwuoha 1987). The courts have been allowed to operate normally

---

[5]Not the Supreme Court.

in the nonpolitical realm, but even here, they are subject to intense ethnic and religious pressures. Whatever the case, the judiciary has promised to play a vigorous role in the Fourth Republic (*Guardian,* Feb. 19, 1999 and Apr. 16, 2000).

Federalism in Nigeria

Nigeria's political system is a federal system, with power being divided between a national government and thirty-one state (provincial) governments[6] (Osuntokum 1979). During periods of civilian rule, the citizens of each state elect both a governor and a state legislature. During periods of military rule, the state legislatures are disbanded and the governors are appointed by the president. Each state also possesses its own bureaucracy and its own legal system (*African Concord,* Oct. 7, 1991, 37).

Center-periphery relations in Nigeria are based upon two fundamentally opposing views of Nigeria's future. The vision of the federal government, as exemplified by Nigeria's ruling elite, is one of a centralized state in which ethnic and religious differences must ultimately give way to national goals and national interests. The states, by contrast, would prefer a Nigeria in which each region is free to manage its affairs in accordance with its ethnic and religious traditions (*Guardian,* Feb. 19, 1999, www).

The differing visions of Nigeria held by the state and federal governments are inherently irreconcilable. Indeed, as Richard Tosanwumi writes:

> In the absence of national consciousness and cohesion, despicable acts of favouritism, nepotism and injustice become the hallmark of ethnic leadership, which leads to agitations crescending in violence and breakdown of law and order. No nation can truly find peace when the component parts are not at ease with one another (*Vanguard,* Feb. 25, 1999).

Military leaders attempted to ease ethnic tensions by fragmenting Nigeria into a multitude of states (provinces), but these efforts have met with minimal success. Declines in ethnic power, moreover, have merely given way to increased religious tensions. Some religious leaders now believe that the only solution to Nigeria's growing religious tension is the creation of two independent states—a Muslim state and a Christian state (*CSM,* July 30, 1992). While such views may be unduly pessimistic, they illustrate the fragility of the Nigerian political system.

The Actors in Nigerian Politics: Elites, Parties, Groups, and Citizens

As noted throughout the text, political institutions are the arena of politics. It is the actors in the political process, however, who give life to those institutions. In this section, we shall examine the four main types of political actors in Nigeria: elites, political parties, groups, and citizens. Of these, elites and groups play a preeminent role in determining who gets what, when, and how in Nigeria.

Elites and Politics in Nigeria

The structure of Nigeria's elite mirrors the broader complexities of Nigerian society (Bienen and van de Walle 1989). As such, it has variously been described as pluralistic, centralized, interconnected, fluid, and self-serving. Each of these adjectives is accurate, and each has had a profound influence on the evolution of Nigerian politics.

---

[6]The Federal Capital District of Abuja is sometimes treated as a separate state (province).

Nigeria's elite structure is **pluralistic** *in the sense that it encompasses a broad array of military, political, administrative, commercial, ethnic, and religious leaders,* each of whom has the power to influence the course of Nigerian politics. No single branch of the elite, moreover, has been able to rule effectively without the support of others. Military leaders, for example, have found it difficult either to build support for their programs or to ease Nigeria's communal tensions without the active support of the country's ethnic and religious elites. Indeed, one of General Abacha's first acts upon seizing power in 1993 was to announce that his administration was "favorably disposed toward traditional rulers because of their nearness to the people" (*West Africa,* Apr. 4, 1994, 595). Ethnic and religious leaders, by contrast, enjoy tremendous influence within their communal enclaves but are dependent upon the support of national leaders to assure that their regions receive a fair share of the nation's wealth. Administrative and commercial elites, in turn, lack the power to rule directly but control the economic resources upon which the success of the political and military elites depends. Unfortunately, Nigeria's elite structure is too pluralistic and too fragmented to chart a coherent course for the country.

As contradictory as it may seem given the above comments, *Nigeria's political elite is also intensely centralized. Until very recently, virtually all political power at the national level was concentrated in the hands of one general or another.* The generals, in turn, were supported by business and administrative elites who shared their belief in a centralized state. Only a centralized state, they argued, could bring order to the confused social mosaic that was Nigeria. As indicated in the introductory chapter, both centralized and pluralistic elites have advantages and disadvantages. Nigeria has managed to get the disadvantages of both.

Total political gridlock in Nigeria has been avoided by the fact that its elite is interconnected and overlapping. Some of its diverse members come from the same "big" families, while others are linked by business and political alliances. All benefit from ready access to the state's resources (Sklar 1967). A self-serving interest in maintaining a corrupt political system, unfortunately, is a poor foundation for nation building.

Finally, it should be noted that *Nigeria's elite system is also very fluid.* Babangida banished all members of the previous political elite from power, yet no sooner had he resigned from office than Chief Shonekan, his hand-picked successor, demoted thirty-six of his chief military aides. The seizure of power by General Abacha was followed by the sacking of an additional seventeen senior pro-Babangida officers, not to mention the supporters of Chief Shonekan. It is now Abacha supporters who are on the losing side. The fluidity of the Nigerian elite system has robbed the country of much-needed political continuity. It has also imbued Nigeria's political leaders with a profound sense of political insecurity, leading many officials to take whatever they can acquire during their short tenure in office. Not all Nigerian leaders are corrupt, but the Nigerian press leaves little doubt that it is a national problem (Williams 1998). It is the elites, moreover, that set the tone for the masses. If the Nigerian public is fragmented and disillusioned, it is not without cause.

Parties and Politics in Nigeria

Nigeria's initial political parties were little more than ethnic associations created to assure that each of the main ethnic groups received its fair share of the "cake." Party leaders were ethnic leaders, party organizations were ethnic organizations, and party campaigns played upon ethnic jealousies. Each party totally dominated the politics of its own region but had little support beyond that region.

Reflecting the logic of their ethnic underpinnings, Nigeria's early political parties used their influence to strengthen the group rather than to strengthen the nation. Parties socialized their followers to support the ethnic group, they mobilized their supporters to harass the candidates of competing ethnic groups, and they defined the issues confronting the new nation in ethnic rather than ideological terms. Fiery slogans proclaimed each party's stance on economic policy, welfare, and human rights, but the underlying message of these slogans was clear to all: the prosperity, welfare benefits, and human rights of our group are totally dependent upon the victory of our group.

Under these circumstances, it was not surprising that Nigeria's first experiment in multiparty democracy would fragment the nation rather than unite it. Indeed, the intensity of ethnic conflict made political compromise all but impossible. The Northern party was dominant, and its opponents had little hope of achieving their fair share of Nigeria's resources by democratic means.

The picture was much the same during the Second Republic. The names of the political parties had been changed to provide broader appeal, but their support still came primarily from a single ethnic region. The Northern party did better at establishing a national constituency than did its counterparts, but it achieved this only by promising the leaders of minority tribes in the East and West enhanced patronage if they supported the North (Joseph 1987).

Being the largest of Nigeria's ethnic regions, the Northern party again dominated Nigerian politics, leaving voters in the East and West with little reason to support a political system that worked to their disadvantage. The East and West could have joined forces against the North, but a long history of ethnic distrust between the two regions precluded this from happening. Once again, then, the Nigerian multiparty system divided the nation rather than uniting it.

The two-party system imposed upon Nigeria by General Babangida forced the creation of two broad multiethnic coalitions, the right-of-center National Republic Convention and the left-of-center Social Democratic Party (SDP). The new party system was tested in the aborted presidential elections of 1993, with Chief Abiola and the SDP being the presumed winners. The SDP's presidential victory was apparently built upon a coalition of Northern Muslims and Western Christians. Being a Western (Yoruba) Muslim, Chief Abiola, the presumed winner, could appeal to both groups (Adams 1993). As the results of the election were impounded, we can only conjecture.

With the advent of the Abacha regime, the two broad coalitions began to disintegrate into their ethnic components (Adams 1993) and eventually disappeared altogether. Be this as it may, Babangida's experiment in two-party democracy did demonstrate that Nigeria's diverse ethnic groups could merge into broad electoral coalitions if they were forced to do so.

The transition to democracy in the fall of 1998 saw the emergence of a wide variety of political parties, the dominant of which were the People's Democratic Party (PDP), the All Peoples Party (APP), and the Alliance for Democracy (AD). The People's Democratic Party is centered in the predominantly Ibo Southeast, but also possesses strong support from the Northern generals, particularly those retired or imprisoned by Abacha. It also has strong support among both businessmen and tribal chiefs, all of which gives it a very conservative orientation (*NYT,* Dec. 6, 1998, www). (Obasanjo, the PDP's successful presidential candidate, reportedly donated $2.5 million to the party, a modest sum for a retired general.) The Alliance for Democracy is a largely Yoruba party of the Southwest, while the All People's Party finds its base of support in the Muslim, Hausa-Fulani North.

Little in the way of ideology separates the three parties, and all are little more than loose coalitions fragmented by personality conflicts and opportunism (Otegbeye 1999). Ethnic consciousness is pervasive and is manipulated by all parties. One official of the PDP states,

We will tell voters if your party wins the presidency, the party will take care of you. You will benefit more from the PDP than from another party. If another party wins they will help their own people before they help people like you, sympathizers, if they remember you at all (*NYT,* Feb. 25, 1999, www).

The PDP swept to victory in the parliamentary and presidential elections because it was more successful than were its opponents in expanding its regional base. A combination of a strong Ibo ethnic base, the tacit support of the Northern generals, and a Yoruba (Southwest) presidential candidate was more than a factious alliance hastily cobbled together by the AD and APP was able to counter (Olawunmi 1999). The PDP was also more successful than its rivals in bidding for the support of Nigeria's smaller ethnic groups. In spite of the broader reach of the PDP, the ethnic foundation of Nigeria's political parties continues to fragment Nigeria's much-conflicted population.

Pressure Groups and Politics in Nigeria

The map of political groups in Nigeria has five basic components: ethnic groups, religious groups, institutional groups, Western-style economic organizations, and social groups. These, in turn, are fragmented into a variety of factions and patron-client linkages (Ayeni, Nassar, and Popoola 1988). Nigeria's two main institutional interests, the military and the bureaucracy, were described previously and will not be included in this stage of our discussion.

Ethnic Groups. More than thirty-five years after the proclamation of Nigeria's independence, ethnic conflict in Nigeria continues to be perpetuated by a lethal combination of fear, uncertainty, suspicion, and envy. Political life in Nigeria is viewed by its citizens as a zero-sum game: what one group gains, the other loses. The creation of a national political community in which all citizens gain through sharing and cooperation remains a distant goal. As lamented by Adebayo Williams:

Nothing better encapsulates Nigeria's endemic crisis of nationhood and the grim reality that it is a nation without nationals. Eighty-four years after amalgamation and thirty-eight years after independence, Nigeria is still searching for authentic Nigerians. At every level there has been a comprehensive failure of leadership...No leader as yet has made it his conscious mission to weld the disparate nationalities of Nigeria into a unified bloc. In a nation containing at least five abridged precolonial empires, no leader has sought to unburden the nationalities boxed into the geocolonial space of the memories of their distinct histories. There is no enduring mythology or grand narrative of the new nation (Williams 1998, 20).

The persistence of ethnic politics is also a function of political failure. The government of Nigeria has proven incapable of providing for the security and the welfare of its citizens. This being the case, people have little option but to seek security in the strength of their ethnic group and to provide for their needs through ethnic connections. As long as it is the ethnic group and not the state that provides, Nigeria's citizens will continue to cling to their ethnic attachments. They have no other choice.

Religious Groups. Ethnic conflict is reinforced by religious conflict (Kastfelt 1993). The Hausa-Fulani of the North are predominantly Muslim, while the Ibo are predominantly Christian. The Yoruba are fragmented between the two religions. Muslims now constitute 50 percent of the Nigerian population, and their numbers are growing. Religious tensions, while never far from the surface, have increased dramatically in recent years as Islamic leaders in the North, perhaps stimulated by the growing wave of Muslim Fundamentalism in the Middle East, are demanding greater sensitivity to Nigeria's Islamic heritage (Forrest 1993). Babangida responded to this pressure by making Nigeria a member of the Organization of Islamic States, an organization dedicated to advancing the status of Islamic populations in multireligious states.

Tensions generated by government efforts to appease Islamic groups have frequently turned violent in areas in which the two faiths co-exist. In 1992, for example, religious riots in Kaduna left more than 400 dead. Christian concerns find expression in the Christian Association of Nigeria, while Muslim concerns are expressed through the Islamic League. Interestingly enough, Nigeria's Christians are also experiencing an explosion of Pentecostalism as they seek new expressions for their despair (Marshall-Fratani 1998).

Western-Style Pressure Groups

Labor. Nigeria possesses most of the economic and social pressure groups found in the West. The Nigerian Labor Congress (NLC) emerged as a powerful force during the First Republic, spearheading a nationwide strike to improve the status of Nigerian workers. Many of the NLC's demands were met, but strikes were subsequently outlawed (Diamond 1988).

A general strike also occurred during the early years of the Second Republic, providing Nigerian workers with a 60 percent increase in pension benefits. It also demonstrated the ability of the unions to intimidate Nigeria's democratic institutions (Otobo 1987). Democracy, however, was short-lived, and the new military regime banned most forms of union activity.

Labor revived during the transition period, orchestrating popular resistance to Babangida's nullification of the 1993 elections. Labor unrest also plagued the reign of General Abacha. In this regard, two strikes were of particular importance. The first, called by the oil workers to demand the release of Abiola, raged for two months before being broken by the arrest of its leaders (*NYT,* July 15, 1994, A5). Although it eventually collapsed, the strike brought the Nigerian economy to a standstill and threatened, however briefly, to topple the Abacha regime.

Far less successful was the general strike called by the National Labor Congress in support of Chief Abiola. The NLC ordered its forty-one member unions to strike in early August 1994, well after the oil workers had brought the Nigerian economy to its knees. A prolonged general strike would, in all probability, have brought down the Abacha regime. Within two days of its initiation, however, the strike was summarily cancelled by Paschal Bafyan, the head of the NLC. The strike was cancelled, he said, in response to a government call for negotiations in "a free and fair atmosphere" (*NYT,* Aug. 5, 1994). *The Economist* would later observe that Mr. Bafyan was subsequently one of a select group of important people allowed to buy prime real estate in Lagos at "knockdown" prices (*Economist,* Aug. 13, 1994, 4). Similar problems continue today (*Guardian,* Feb. 24, 1999, www).

Whatever the reason for its cancellation, the results of the general strike were inconsistent. Support was particularly strong in the Yoruba West, the stronghold of Abiola, but lagged in the predominantly Ibo East. Little support was forthcoming in the predominantly Muslim North, even though Abiola is a Muslim.

Why did the oil workers' strike enjoy success while the general strike elicited little support outside the Yoruba areas? One answer to this question is that the oil workers' strike, whatever its political overtones, had a strong economic foundation. The oil workers were unhappy with government policies that siphoned off most of Nigeria's oil wealth, leaving little for the regions in which it was produced. The general strike, by contrast, was far more political in its motivations and promised little in the way of economic improvements.

The transition to democracy has unleashed a new spate of labor unrest. December 4, 1998, for example, found more than 60,000 people going on what the Nigerian press described as a "rampage" (*Guardian,* Dec. 9, 1998, www). Parallel strikes have spread throughout Nigeria's industrialized areas and oil-producing regions and will clearly pose a challenge to Nigeria's democratic leadership (*Guardian,* Dec. 9, 1998, www; Ihonvbere, 1997).

Despite their successes, Nigeria's unions have been weakened by persistent ethnic and religious tensions as well as by personality conflicts among union leaders. The union movement has also been hampered by a lack of class consciousness among the workers and by the divergent interests of the civil service and blue-collar unions (Cohen 1981). Politicians, moreover, have subverted the effectiveness of the unions by meddling in their elections and by pitting personality against personality and faction against faction (Otobo 1987). Labor suffers from an oversupply of workers as well as from a shortage of cash and an inadequate cadre of trained organizers (Tokunboh 1985).

Business. Business interests in Nigeria are represented by three large peak associations: the Manufacturers' Association of Nigeria; the Nigerian Association of Chambers of Commerce and Industry, Mines, and Agriculture; and the Association of Small-Scale Industries (Ayeni, Nassar, and Popoola 1988). The Manufacturers' Association of Nigeria and the Chambers of Commerce represent Nigeria's larger businesses, a category that includes any firm with ten or more employees.

The business community, being part of Nigeria's Westernized elite, has generally found Nigeria's political and administrative leadership to be responsive to its concerns. This responsiveness, at least in part, is the result of a common interest in perpetuating a system from which all segments of the elite have benefited. It is also the result of blatant corruption, with political leaders receiving a cut of 10 percent or more on lucrative government contracts (Joseph 1987).

In addition to maintaining strong ties with political leaders at the national level, Nigeria's business organizations maintain strong ties with its ethnic leaders. Exemplifying the linkage between business and ethnic interests is the Kaduna Mafia. Kaduna is the business and administrative capital of the Northern region, and its leaders enjoy inordinate power in government circles (Joseph 1987). Indeed, the Kaduna Mafia, in the view of its opponents, "serves as the 'think tank' for the North and maps out the strategy for the North to dominate in all spheres of Nigerian life" (Johnson 1990, 1–8).

Students. Students have spearheaded most of Nigeria's mass protests. This was true of the mass protests that characterized the First and Second Republics, and it continues to be true of Nigeria's tortuous transition to democracy. General Abacha repeatedly appealed for student calm, stating that "the nation could hardly achieve its goals if staff and students of universities...lent themselves to the whims and caprices of politicians..." (*West Africa,* Apr. 18, 1994, 692).

The political activism of Nigerian students is motivated by idealism, by dismay over the ineptitude of Nigeria's politicians, by the miserable conditions prevailing in Nigeria's universities, and by the very real prospect of not finding a job upon graduation. Student protests are also provoked, if not orchestrated, by Nigeria's politicians, all of whom attempt to recruit students allies.

Students have a considerable influence on Nigerian politics, yet they seldom speak with a single voice. As with most other broad-based groups in Nigerian society,

---

Secret Cults on School Campuses

Particularly disconcerting to the military authorities has been the emergence of secret cults on Nigeria's campuses (*Guardian,* Feb. 16, 1999). In addressing the problem of the cults, Dr. Ayu, the Minister of Education, said that "Of late, our collective psyche has been assaulted by the tragic wave of secret cults in our school campuses. Bizarre killings, intimidations, violence, undiscipline precipitated by the activities of secret cults are daily on the rise" (*West Africa,* Mar. 28–Apr. 3, 1994, 349). He went on to say that "the blood-sucking members of these cults have no respect for life or property." He enumerated some of the wilder excesses of the cultists:

They are rude to teachers and intimidate the school authorities to do their bidding. They decide when lectures should start and when examinations should start or end and, in some cases, they infiltrate other campuses to kidnap heads of institutions and force them to sign agreements that violate the rules and regulations of a decent society (*West Africa,* Mar. 28–Apr. 3, 1994, 349).

---

sustained political action is undermined by a mélange of ethnic, religious, political, regional, and personality considerations.

Women. Women's groups have had minimal impact upon Nigerian politics, a fact that reflects the subservient role of women in Nigerian society (Hussaina 1995). Efforts of the United Nations to empower Nigerian women have produced limited results, the most visible of which has been the establishment of an officially sanctioned National Council for Women. The NCW convened a major conference to discuss women's rights in 1993, its opening session being addressed by the wife of General Babangida. Among other things, the conference called upon the government to reserve 25 percent of the positions in the bureaucracy for women and debated whether the role of the First Lady should be formalized. While the conference was an important step in publicizing the plight of Nigerian women, it was but the first step in a process that has a long way to go (*African Concord,* July 5, 1993, 27; *Guardian Online,* Apr. 24, 2000).

Citizens and Politics in Nigeria

Public opinion in Nigeria finds expression in the country's infrequent and irregular elections, in commentary in the Nigerian press, and in strikes, protests, and other forms of direct action. Public opinion polls have been discouraged during the military era. Collectively, the above avenues of public expression portray a population that is both divided among itself and alienated from its political system.

Elections. The elections conducted during the First and Second Republics reflected the pervasiveness of ethnic and religious tensions in Nigeria's political life. This was to be expected, given the recentness of independence and the divisiveness of Nigeria's colonial past.

The results of Babangida's aborted 1993 elections (the Third Republic) were difficult to analyze, as they were flawed by exceptionally low voter turnout and election procedures that forced voters to stand in line rather than cast secret ballots. Nevertheless, the broader context of the elections hinted at some interesting conclusions.

■ First, the presumed results of the annulled presidential election suggest that a sizeable number of Nigerian voters will vote for candidates of a different ethnic or religious group if the elections are structured in a manner that discourages communal (ethnic and religious) voting.

■   Second, Abiola's strong showing in the annulled elections indicates that a non-Northerner can be elected president of Nigeria in popular elections, a fact confirmed by the 1998 elections.

■   Third, the fact that one party dominated the governors' races while the other won a majority of seats in the House of Representatives suggests that Nigeria's traditional ethnic machines may be less monolithic than was formerly the case (*Economist,* Dec. 21, 1991, 41; *CSM,* July 7, 1992, 5).

Collectively, the three sets of results suggest that the influence of communal attachments may be lessening, although the flawed nature of the electoral process makes such conclusions tenuous, at best. The 1998 elections tended to confirm this trend as voters of all regions were clearly fed up with more than three decades of Northern military domination (Ciroma 1998). Nevertheless, ethnicity continues to be the scourge of Nigerian elections.

The Press and Public Opinion.   When allowed, the press has been a vocal, if sometimes intimidated, force in Nigerian politics. Most major groups sponsor their own papers, but the radio and television media are controlled by the Government (Uche 1989; Nwosu 1988). As the following excerpt from a recent issue of African Concord suggests, press coverage during the abortive 1993 transition to democracy was particularly vigorous:

> The President complained during his recent Plateau tour that Nigerians were fastly (sic) becoming cynics. Unfortunately, it is the way and manner the government has been implementing its transition program that is turning Nigerians into cynics. The nation continues to be ruled by surprises.
>
> Why will Nigerians not become cynics in a situation where thirteen political associations were canceled out after some of these associations had received financial assistance from the same government that later turned round to knock them off the stage?
>
> ...I am not afraid to say that if Nigerians are led by the nose through the current transition program...it will be a systematic march to the political slaughter house (Babatope 1991, 46).

Abacha closed all opposition papers during the "long, hot" summer of 1994 and threatened reporters with imprisonment. As one Nigerian reporter lamented, "You never had a time when everybody was locked away. As far as clamp downs go, this had been the most total. It is the infantry man's mentality: just knock down everybody who stands in your way" (E. E. Izeze, cited in *Economist,* Oct. 8, 1994). With the 1998–1999 transition to democracy, the Nigerian press has become even more vocal.

Mass Protest.   Mass protest in Nigeria takes the form of political demonstrations, economic strikes, communal violence, and a lawlessness that has made Nigeria one of the most crime-ridden countries in the world. All are born of frustration with a political system that has been unable to provide its citizens with a sustainable quality of life. Political and economic protest, while harshly suppressed by the Babangida regime, exploded in response to his annulment of the 1993 presidential elections, forcing both his resignation and that of his hand-picked successor. Mass protests have similarly forced General Abacha to promise a new constitution, although the results of this process have yet to be seen. More recent violence has been directed against the Shell Oil Company (*Guardian,* Dec. 1, 1998, www).

While political and economic protests give vent to the frustrations of Nigeria's more modern and urban population, communal tensions continue to flare throughout most areas of Nigeria. Crime, in turn, is the most basic symptom of anomie or institutional collapse. The failure of Nigeria's political institutions has so impoverished the majority of the country's citizens that they have no option but to provide for their personal survival and that of their families by any means at their disposal, legal or otherwise. Indeed, mass frustrations are now so intense that they may defy control by any political regime, whether military or civilian. This situation is unlikely to change rapidly in the near future.

The Context of Nigerian Politics: Culture, Economics, and International Interdependence

The actors in Nigerian politics play a vital role in determining who gets what, when, and how, but the behavior of those actors is often influenced by the broader environmental context in which Nigerian politics occurs. In this section, we shall examine three dimensions of Nigeria's environmental context: political culture, political economy, and the influence of the international arena.

The Culture of Nigerian Politics

The leaders of the First Republic inherited a population that placed loyalty to one's ethnic group above loyalty to the state, that had little understanding of its new and untested political institutions, and that viewed members of other communal groups with profound distrust. From a cultural perspective, Nigeria was not a nation, but a confederation of several nations, each with its own traditions and aspirations.

The colonial experience further fragmented Nigeria's citizens into modern, traditional, and transitional clusters, depending upon their experiences and their aspirations for the future. While the vast majority of Nigerians clung to the ways of their traditional past, a narrow Westernized elite sought the creation of a Westernized and presumably democratic Nigeria. Falling between the two extremes was a large transitional population that aspired to the material benefits of Westernization but lacked either the skills or the opportunities to attain them. For the most part, the transitionals were recent migrants to Nigerian cities and residents of their gruesome slums.

The challenge confronting Nigeria's leaders was to transform Nigeria's essentially tribal political culture into a civic culture in which the majority of its citizens would both identify with their national political institutions and place loyalty to those institutions above loyalties to their ethnic and religious communities.

Toward this end, Nigerian nationalism was taught in the schools and stressed in the mass media. More and more, Nigerians were also welded into a national community via military service or employment in the civil service. Urbanization and education also expanded rapidly.

As a result of these efforts, ethnic loyalties have given way to nationalistic loyalties among many of Nigeria's more educated and urbanized citizens. Some blending of cultures is also occurring in the rural areas as the lines between ethnic and linguistic regions become increasingly blurred (Otite 1976). There also appears to be genuine support for the concept of democracy.

Be this as it may, ethnic and religious loyalties continue to be the dominant features of Nigerian political culture. Three decades of corruption and mismanagement have also created a profound aura of cynicism (Nigerian Economic Society 1986). It is difficult for individuals to develop a deep emotional attachment to political institutions that are corrupt, biased, and ineffective. As expressed by Sam Egwu,

It seems difficult to do away with the negative political culture derived from our historical development.... How, for instance, can we overcome alienation and political apathy and engender people's interest in political participation within the present structure of inequality, injustice and marginalisation of the people? It is not possible for people to have confidence in elections when rigging is rampant and the rules of the game are not observed because political power is a "bread and butter" affair.

...This has dire consequences for our evolving political culture because it plants and waters a culture of silence which in itself is a disincentive to political participation... (Egwu 1990, 200–1).

The ability of General Obasanjo to alter this picture remains to be seen, but the task will be a daunting one.

The Economy of Nigerian Politics

Political economists would suggest great care in attributing Nigeria's political woes to ethnicity and other cultural factors. In their view, tribes, ethnic communities, and other "culturally" defined social organizations are merely the units of political conflict in Nigeria. The source of that conflict, political economists argue, is economic.

Recent patterns of ethnic and religious violence lend strong support to this argument. Increases in communal tensions have paralleled the decline of Nigeria's oil-based economy, a decline that has forced Nigeria's citizens to look to their ethnic groups for economic survival. Indeed, much of Nigeria's recent communal violence has been triggered by economic incidents pitting one group against another.

Ethnic tensions have also been reinforced by the uneven distribution of Nigeria's oil wealth. The Biafran Civil War had its origins in Ibo demands to retain a larger share of their oil wealth than a central government dominated by the North would allow. Parallel tensions are now building between a central government dominated by the North and the minority tribes that currently produce some 70 percent of Nigeria's oil revenues.

Economic scarcity also underlies a crime wave of epidemic proportions. Unemployment has reached record levels, and state welfare agencies lack the funds to ease the plight of the poor and the homeless. For many, and particularly the dwellers of urban shanty towns cut off from their rural support systems, crime is the only means of survival.

Ironically, economic factors have also created much of the precarious unity that Nigeria does enjoy (Ahmad Khan 1994). The Westernized elite has prospered from a unified Nigeria and it is they, buoyed by a lion's share of the nation's wealth, who have kept Nigeria from dissolving into a patchwork of ethnic enclaves. Exact data on this topic are difficult to come by, as are most other politically sensitive data.

How, then, does one sort out the competing economic and cultural explanations of Nigerian politics? The answer is that both economics and culture are essential to understanding Nigerian politics. Ethnic and religious violence in Nigeria is usually precipitated by economic conflict, but the intensity of that violence draws upon culturally transmitted fears and distrust that have accumulated over centuries. The strength of ethnic and cultural ties has also slowed the development of class consciousness in Nigeria, with most Nigerians seeking economic security in the solidarity of their ethnic group rather than in the solidarity of their economic class (Sil 1993).

The importance of ethnic loyalties, moreover, will not decline until the Nigerian state can meet the economic and security needs of its citizens. People must have jobs, and they must be protected from the violence that engulfs them. Ironically, the communal base of Nigerian politics has undermined the capacity of the government to perform either of these tasks. Reflective of this fact has been the flight of an estimated $54.6 billion from Nigeria between 1972 and 1995, much of it to personal bank accounts in the West (*Vanguard,* Feb. 25, 1999).

International Interdependence and the Politics of Nigeria

It would be easy to blame Nigeria's political woes on its lethal mix of ethnic conflict and economic mismanagement. This indictment would not be entirely fair, as many of the problems besetting Nigeria today are of external origin. As noted in the introduction to this chapter, Nigeria did not originate as a coherent geographic or ethnic region. Rather, the concept of a Nigerian state was the outgrowth of a colonial policy that lumped diverse ethnic groups into the confines of a single administrative region for the sake of efficiency. Nigeria entered independence with much of its bureaucracy and most of its military establishment still in the hands of the British. Its economy was also dependent upon that of Britain, and its citizens received little training in self-government. On what basis, then, did Britain and the international community expect Nigeria to blossom suddenly into a prosperous Western-style democracy?

The dramatic rise in world oil prices during the 1970s provided Nigeria with phenomenal wealth, but for reasons discussed throughout this chapter, the young country lacked the political and administrative capacity to manage its oil wealth effectively. Rather, a tremendous opportunity for economic development was squandered through corruption and grandiose spending on flashy public buildings and ill-conceived development projects such as a Soviet-designed steel plant. Much was accomplished, but the return on the investment was low. Agricultural development, the core of the Nigeria's nonpetroleum economy, was largely neglected.

The more oil revenues declined, the more Nigeria was forced to borrow from international banks to keep its financial head above water. By the mid-1980s, its foreign debt was approaching $35 billion, a staggering figure for a country with a per capita income of $300 per year. Faced with the prospect of bankruptcy, Nigeria stopped paying its debts.

Shortly after seizing power in 1985, General Babangida imposed austerity programs designed to bring Nigeria in line with International Monetary Fund guidelines for economic recovery. The economic reforms demanded by the IMF were essentially the same reforms that the donor community has demanded of Russia, India, and Egypt:

- Government-owned firms were to be privatized.
- Tariffs and other obstacles to free trade were to be gradually eliminated.
- Government subsidies on food, fuel, and other basic goods were to be reduced, as were price controls and other regulations obstructing the efficient operation of the free market.
- The bureaucracy was to be downsized and rationalized.
- Nigeria was to reduce its dependence upon oil by stimulating economic diversification.
- The Nigerian government was to reduce spending and use the fiscal measures at its disposal to reduce inflation and promote economic growth (Forrest 1993, 213).

If Nigeria complied with these demands, the IMF said, the loans and grants required to stimulate Nigeria's economic revival would be forthcoming from the donor community. If Nigeria did not "bite the bullet" and accept the IMF recommendations, it would be cut off from the money required for its continued economic survival.

Although the guidelines may have been logical from an economic perspective, compliance promised a sustained period of hardship for most of the Nigerian population. The poor would be deprived of the subsidies upon which their survival depended. Privatization and cutbacks in the size of the bureaucracy would increase an already staggering rate of unemployment, while the opening of Nigeria's markets to foreign goods threatened to destroy much of Nigeria's inefficient industrial base. The Nigerian elite, moreover, offered little support for an economic recovery plan that would reduce its opportunities for corruption and influence peddling.

Faced with intense resistance, Babangida slowed the pace of the IMF reforms (Forrest 1993, 215). General Abacha abandoned them altogether, fearing to further agitate a population that was already on the verge of rebellion. General Obasanjo has promised to reinstate them, adding complications to an already complex transition to democracy (*Guardian,* Feb. 16, 1999, www).

Challenges of the Present and Prospects for the Future

The world community has increasingly defined good government in terms of six goals: democracy, stability, human rights, quality of life, economic growth, and concern for the environment. Most states of the Third World have made substantial progress in achieving one or more of these goals. Some are approaching economic parity with the First World but find democracy and human rights to be elusive. Others have established strong democratic traditions but remain mired in poverty. Nigeria has found all of the goals of good government to be elusive (Olugbade 1992).

Democracy and Stability

Nigeria has witnessed two brief periods of democratic rule. Each was initiated by reasonably fair elections in which voters were offered a meaningful choice of candidates. The victors took office, and they did rule. In neither case, however, was the ruling party willing to relinquish office once its term had expired. New elections were held, but they were neither free nor fair.

The reasons offered for the failure of Nigerian democracy are many.

1. *Nigeria's ruling elites were more concerned with serving themselves and their ethnic communities than with serving Nigeria as a nation.* This is not a value judgment but a statement of the empirical record.
2. *Nigeria's democratic institutions were borrowed from the West and had little grounding in Nigerian culture or experience.* As a result, they performed poorly and failed to gain the confidence of the Nigerian population.
3. *The Nigerian electorate was fragmented by "we/they" ethnic identities that were too ingrained to be reconciled by democratic means.* Being Ibo, Yoruba, or Hausa-Fulani was more important than being Nigerian.
4. *Nigeria's political parties and pressure groups were based on ethnicity.* Rather than building a unified political community, they intensified the fragmentation of the Nigerian state. Pluralism facilitates democracy, but not when loyalties to the group outweigh loyalties to the state.
5. *Abundant economic resources that should have been used to build a political community were not put to that use.* As a result, growing economic scarcity fueled ethnic conflict.
6. *The failure of Nigerian democracy was the product of an adverse international environment.* Colonialism had done little to build an integrated political community, and preparation for democracy had been minimal. The collapse of

world oil prices disrupted Nigeria's development program and caused severe social problems that the Government was ill-equipped to handle. The world community could have forced a return of Nigerian democracy, but was reluctant to impose the same pressures on Nigeria's military leaders that it imposed on the apartheid regime in South Africa.

Nigeria is now embarking upon its third experiment with democracy. The mood is optimistic but all of the old problems remain. General Obasanjo's task will be a difficult one.

Human Rights

Human rights abuses in Nigeria stem from three distinct sources: legal abuses by dictatorial regimes, traditional cultural practices, and ethnic/religious intolerance. Nigeria's military leaders have paid little heed to the constitutional rights of Nigeria's citizens, with most of their critics ending up either in jail or in exile. Political prisoners are now being released, and Nigeria is embarking in a new era of political freedom.

While the abrogation of political rights has received most of the attention in the world press, the violation of property rights has also been widespread. During the development of its oil fields, for example, Shell Oil Company is often "assisted" by the Nigerian army. Shell has responded to local complaints of environment pollution by stating that it paid the government a 3 percent production levy to cover the costs of any personal or property damage and that it was the government's responsibility to see that the money reached the aggrieved parties (*Times of London,* July 9, 1993, 11). Apparently these payments were delayed. Shell has recently announced an $8-billion expansion plan for Nigeria. Ideally, it will reflect concern for Nigeria's citizens and their environment (*Guardian,* Feb. 12, 1999, www).

While many civil rights abuses are politically motivated, others result from a lack of professionalism among the Nigerian police:

> Alhaji Ibrahim Coomassie, the Inspector-General of Police, has said that efforts to bring back the past glory of the police force were being thwarted by what he called the sordid and unprofessional acts of misconduct by some elements. In an address at a graduation at the Police Staff College in Jos, Alhaji Ibrahim also stated that despite efforts to improve the welfare of the force, corruption, arrogant display of power, flouting the rules and regulations guiding detention, collaborating with criminals and general laxity had continued unabated (*West Africa,* Apr. 4–10, 1994, 595).
>
> The group called upon President Olusegun Obasanjo to step up measures for revitalizing the nation's police force (*Guardian,* Feb. 2, 2000, www).

Culturally based human rights abuses, in turn, focus on the exploitation of women and children. Children have historically provided an important segment of the labor force in Nigeria and, while this is less the case today, child labor remains important to the economic survival of the poor (Dennis 1991).

The exploitation of women in Nigeria borders on servitude. As described by Zahra Nwabara:

> The position of women in Nigeria and most parts of Africa is dismal. All over the country women are regarded as the "property" of men, first their fathers and then their husbands. For things that an individual male can get on his own merit, a woman has to first obtain her father's/husband's permission. For example:
> i)   To get a passport or visa
> ii)   To obtain a bank loan
> iii)   To get a scholarship
> iv)   To exercise rights over her own issue (children) (Nwabara 1989, 9).

Nigeria also remains a quasi-polygamous society in which the wives of Nigeria's poor bear most of the responsibility for raising their children. Nigeria's declining economic situation has made this a particularly difficult task (Dennis 1991).

Finally, human rights abuses stem from ethnic intolerance as Nigeria's larger ethnic groups continue to impose their will upon their smaller neighbors. They also practice "ethnic cleansing" by subjecting residents from competing groups to systematic abuse. Religious tensions have similarly led to human rights abuses as the North continues to use its dominant position to impose Muslim religious values upon non-Muslim populations. As noted in earlier sections of the chapter, the causes of ethnic intolerance are both cultural and economic in nature, one feeding upon the other.

The new Nigerian constitution, like the previous one, contains a lengthy enumeration of the rights of Nigerian citizens. The problem, however, is not one of legislation but of enforcement. Legal rights will continue to be abused until a democratic political system demonstrates its ability to perform effectively. Even then, political authorities are unlikely to enforce child labor laws or laws prohibiting the abuse of women, both of which are culturally sanctioned. Ethnic intolerance will also be difficult to alter as long as Nigerian politics is defined in ethnic terms.

Quality of Life and Economic Growth

The quality of life of the average Nigerian is dismal. Life expectancy is 55 years, as compared to 76 years in the United States and 79 years in Japan. The per capita income is below $300 per year and is declining (*CIA Factbook* 1999, www). Half of the population is illiterate, a figure that reaches 62 percent among females. Water and electricity services in Nigeria's major cities are erratic, and schools are falling apart (*West Africa,* Apr. 18, 1994, 692). In the following passage, Anietie Usen compares life in Nigeria to the disrepair of its leading hospital (University College Hospital or UCH):

> UCH is living on past glory: battling with outdated and unserviceable equipment, drug shortages, power outages, the brain drain and even dry taps. Equipment is obsolete; in the haematology laboratory, for instance, doctors count blood cells with their fingers in studied silence, like churchwardens counting churchgoers.
>
> A new multi-million-naira angiographic suite supplied by the government was purchased by an unqualified contractor without even a brochure. It cannot be used. Virtually all of the six elevators that carry patients, doctors, nurses, food, drugs, and oxygen cylinders to the top floors of the five-story hospital ward have broken down (Usen 1998, 10).

More disquieting is a recent United Nations report indicating that one-half of all newborn babies in Africa carry the HIV virus (*IHT,* Sept. 13, 1999, www).

The quality of Nigerian life cannot improve without sustained improvement of the Nigerian economy. Oil revenues must be used more efficiently, and new industries must be developed. Unfortunately, neither goal will be easily achieved and the outlook for the future remains grim (*Vanguard,* Sept. 10, 1999, www).

The Environment

Nigeria is not an environmentally concerned country. Lagos and other major Nigerian cities are so heavily polluted that one of the main justifications for building a new capital city in Abuja was that it would be "healthful." Oil-related pollution in the petroleum regions threatens both the people and the wildlife, while water supplies in some rural states are infested with disease-carrying worms (*West Africa,*

Mar. 28, 1994). The World Health Organization, moreover, estimated that more than 20 percent of the deaths in Nigeria in 1993 could be attributed to faulty drugs (*West Africa,* Mar. 28, 1994). Nor are these problems limited to Nigeria. Some 23 million Africans, for example, have been exposed to the HIV virus (*NYT,* Dec. 27, 1998, 1).

The situation, unfortunately, is not likely to improve in the near future. Nigeria is too poor to pay for sweeping environmental programs, and its public service is too inefficient to implement programs that are already on the books. Strict environmental regulations, moreover, would depress the Nigerian economy, something that no government, civilian or military, is anxious to do.

Prospects for the Future

Nigerian politics was earlier characterized as a struggle between hope and despair. Hope springs from Nigeria's oil wealth as well as from an irrepressible desire for democracy among a large segment of the Nigerian population. Despair is the product of the corruption and mismanagement that have squandered the nation's wealth, leaving much of its population poverty-stricken. Despair also flows from a persistence of ethnic and religious conflict as well as from the fragile nature of Nigeria's fledgling democracy. Finally, despair arises from a sense that the international community seems to be losing interest in Africa and its affairs. This is unfortunate, for Nigeria requires strong international encouragement if it is to achieve the UN's much-vaunted goals of stability, democracy, human rights, economic growth, quality of life, and environmental concern.

References

Adams, Paul. 1993 (July–Aug.). "Babangida's Boondoggle." *Africa Report* 26–28.

Adams, Paul. 1994 (Jan.–Feb.). "The Army Calls the Tune." *Africa Report* 47–49.

Ahmad Khan, Sarah. 1994. *Nigeria: The Political Economy of Oil.* Oxford, England: Oxford University Press. (For the Oxford Institute for Energy Studies.)

Apter, David E. 1987. *Rethinking Development: Modernization, Dependency, and Postmodern Politics.* Beverly Hills, CA: Sage.

Ayeni, Victor, Lanre Nassar, and Dotun Popoola. 1988. "Interest and Pressure Group Activities." In *Nigeria's Second Republic: Presidentialism, Politics and Administration in a Developing State,* (pp. 107–20), ed. Victor Ayeni and Kayode Soremekun. Apapa: Daily Times Publications.

Babatope, Ebenezer. 1991 (Oct. 7). "Notes on the Transition." *African Concord* (Lagos, Nigeria).

Benson, Dayo. 1999 (Feb.). "For Once, the North Bows." *Vanguard* 1–4, www.

Bienen, Henry, and Nicolas van de Walle. 1989 (Mar.). "Time and Power in Africa." *American Political Science Review* 83(1): 19–34.

Ciroma, Adamu. 1998 (Oct.). "Rich but Poor." *Africa Today* 4(10): 10–14.

Cohen, Robin. 1981. *Labour and Politics in Nigeria.* London: Heinemann.

Coleman, James S. 1965. *Nigeria: Background to Nationalism.* Berkeley, CA: University of California Press.

Davidson, Basil. 1994. *Modern Africa: A Social and Political History.* 3rd ed. New York: Longman.

Dennis, Carolyne. 1991. "Constructing a 'Career' Under Conditions of Economic Crisis, and Structural Adjustment: The Survival Strategies of Nigerian Women." In *Women, Development and Survival in the Third World* (pp. 88–106), ed. Haleh Afshar. London: Longman.

Diamond, Larry. 1988. *Class, Ethnicity and Democracy in Nigeria: The Failure of the First Republic.* London: Macmillan.

Doob, Leonard, W. 1964. *Patriotism and Nationalism: Their Psychological Foundations.* New Haven, CT: Yale University Press.

Egwu, Sam. 1990. "Nigeria's Political Culture: Past, Present and Future." In *Nigerian Cultural Heritage* (pp. 189–206), ed. E. Ikenga-Metuh and O. Ojoade. South Onitsha: IMICO.

Ekwe-Ekwe, Herbert. 1991. *Issues in Nigerian Politics Since the Fall of the Second Republic.* Lewiston, NY: Edwin Mellen.

Forrest, Tom. 1993. *Politics and Economic Development in Nigeria.* Boulder, CO: Westview Press.

Graf, William D. 1988. *The Nigerian State: Political Economy, State, Class, and Political*

System in the Post-Colonial Era. London: James Currey.

Hussaina, Abdullah. 1995. "Wifeism and Activism: The Nigerian Women's Movement." In *The Challenge of Local Feminisms*, ed. Amrita Basu. Boulder, CO: Westview.

Ihonvbere, Julius O. 1997 (Dec.). "Organized Labor and the Struggle for Democracy in Nigeria." *African Studies Review* 40(3): 77–110.

Ikegwuoha, Bernard-Thompson. 1987. *Politics and Government of the Nigerian "Second Republic": October 1, 1979–December 31, 1983.* Rome: N. Domenici-Pecheux.

Illoegbunam, Chuks. 1994. *West Africa*, December 27–January 9, 1994, 2339.

Imoagene, Oshomha. 1989. *The Nigerian Class Struggle.* Ibadan, Nigeria: Evans Brothers.

Ishaka, Peter. 1994 (Feb. 14). "Beating the Drums of Secession." *African Concord*, 14–15.

Johnson, Segun. 1990. "Introduction: Nigeria: A Country Conceived in Problems." In *Readings in Selected Nigerian Problems* (pp. 1–8), ed. Segun Johnson. Lagos: Koservices, Ltd.

Joseph, Richard. 1987. *Democracy and Prebendal Politics in Nigeria: The Rise and Fall of the Second Republic.* New York: Cambridge University Press.

Kalu, Vicktor Eke. 1987. *The Nigerian Condition.* Enugu, Nigeria: Fourth Dimension.

Kastfelt, Niels. 1993. *Religion and Politics in Nigeria.* New York: St. Martin's.

Koehn, Peter H. 1990. *Public Policy and Administration in Africa: Lessons from Nigeria.* Boulder, CO: Westview Press.

Lerner, D. 1958. *The Passing of Traditional Society.* Glencoe, IL: Free Press.

Marshall-Fratani, Ruth. 1998. "Mediating the Global and Local in Nigerian Pentecostalism." *Journal of Religion in Africa* 28(3): 278–315.

Miles, William. 1988. *Elections in Nigeria: A Grassroots Perspective.* Boulder, CO: Lynne Rienner.

Muhammed, Naajatu. 1998 (Oct.). "Northerners Have Nothing Concrete to Show for More Than 30 Years in Power. Ask Them." *Africa Today* 4(10): 15–16.

Nigerian Economic Society. 1986. *The Nigerian Economy: A Political Economy Approach.* Essex, England: Longman/Bienen.

Nuanna, Ochereome. 1995 (Jan.). "Corruption Unlimited." *African Business* 195.

Nwabara, Zahra Imam. 1989. "Women in Nigeria—The Way I See It." In *Women and the Family in Nigeria* (pp. 7–16), ed. A. Imam, R. Pittin, and H. Omole. Dakar: Codesria.

Nwokocha, John. 1999 (Feb. 21). "National Assembly: How Far Can it Check?" *Vanguard* 1–3, www.

Nwosu, Ikechukwu E. 1988. "Comparative Analysis of Media–Government Relationship in Nigeria, Britain and the United States of America." In *Contemporary Issues in Mass Media for Development and National Security* (pp. 174–88), ed. Ralph A. Akinfeleye. Lagos: Unimedia.

Obadina, Tunde. 1998 (Sept. 24). "A Dangerous Way to Privatise." *Africa Economic Analysis* 1–2, www.

Okoye, Israel Kelue. 1991. *Soldiers and Politics in Nigeria.* Lagos, Nigeria: New Age.

Olawunmi, Tunji. 1999 (March 2). "Presidency: Why Falae Lost." *Vanguard* 1–4, www.

Olugbade, Kola. 1992. "The Nigerian State and the Quest for a Stable Polity." *Comparative Politics* 4: 293–315.

Onadipe, Abiodun. 1997 (Oct.). "Nigeria's Crucial Month." *Contemporary Review* 271(1581): 169–77.

Osuntokum, Jide. 1979. "The Historical Background of Nigerian Federalism." In *Readings on Federalism* (pp. 91–102), ed. A. B. Akinyemi, P. D. Cole, and Walter Ofonagoro. Ibadan, Nigeria: Nigerian Institute of International Affairs.

Otegbeye, Tunji. 1999 (Feb. 21)."Why Alliances have Failed in Nigeria." *Vanguard* 1–5, www.

Otite, O. 1976. "On the Concept of a Nigerian Society." In *Ethnic Relations in Nigeria* (pp. 3–16), ed. A. O. Sanda. Ibadan, Nigeria: University of Ibadan.

Otobo, D. 1987. "The Nigerian General Strike of 1981." In *Readings in Industrial Relations in Nigeria* (pp. 233–53), ed. Dafe Otobo and Morakinyo Omole. Lagos: Malthouse Press Ltd.

Sil, Narasingha. 1993. "Nigerian Intellectuals and Socialism: Retrospect and Prospect." *The Journal of Modern African Studies* 31(3): 361–85.

Sklar, Richard L. 1967. "Ethnic Relations and Social Class." *Journal of Modern African Studies* 5(1): 1–11.

Taylor, Robert. 1993. "Chapter One." In *Urban Development in Nigeria*, ed. Robert Taylor. Aldershot, England: Avebury.

Tokunboh, M. A. 1985. *Labour Movement in Nigeria: Past and Present.* Lagos: Literamed.

Turnbull, Colin M. 1963. *The Lonely African.* Garden City, NY: Doubleday/Anchor.

Uche, Luke Uka. 1989. *Mass Media, People and Politics in Nigeria.* New Delhi: Concept.

Umeh, Louis C. 1993. "The Building of a New Capital City: The Abuja Experience." In *Urban Development in Nigeria* (pp. 215–28), ed. Robert W. Taylor. Aldershot, England: Avebury.

Usen, Anietie. 1998 (Oct.). "Rich but Poor." *Africa Today* 4(10): 10–11.

Williams, Adebeyo. 1998 (Oct.). "A Nation in Search of Itself." *Africa Today* 4(10): 20–21.

GLOSSARY

amparo A type of legal injunction unique to Mexico that blocks government action because of issues of constitutionality.

anomie A sociological term referring to an absence of social norms caused by the breakdown of social and political institutions.

Arab League Regional organization designed to promote political, military, and economic cooperation among the Arab states.

authoritarian regime Non-democratic political system in which all power is concentrated in the hands of a single individual or small oligarchy (e.g., Saudi Arabia, Iraq).

back benchers British members of Parliament (MPs) who are not in the Government or shadow cabinet. They sit on the back benches of the House of Commons.

baronage Collective term referring to former officers of William the Conqueror's army, who received large grants of land and aristocratic titles such as Duke, Earl, and Viscount after the Norman Conquest of England in 1066. Their heirs inherited their titles.

Basic Law German equivalent of a constitution, which was established shortly after Germany was divided into two countries following World War II.

Berlin Wall A fortified prison wall erected by communist authorities between East and West Berlin in 1961 to prevent East Germans from defecting to the West. In 1989, the citizens of East Berlin tore the wall down.

Bolsheviks Lenin-led faction of the communist movement in tsarist Russia.

bourgeoisie Marx's term for the middle class, particularly industrialists and merchants.

Brahma Hindu god of creation.

Brahman The highest level of the Indian caste system, often referred to as the priestly caste.

British East India Company Private British corporation that established trading posts in India during the 1600s and eventually ruled most of the Indian subcontinent.

Bundesrat The upper house of the German legislature, consisting of delegates selected by the Land (state) governments.

Bundestag The lower house of the German legislature, consisting of delegates elected by the German population.

bureaucrat An administrator who works for a government or large institution. Bureaucrats possess specialized information and are responsible for implementing the political decisions made by the elites. The behavior of bureaucrats directly influences public attitudes toward the government.

by-election An election held to replace a Member of Parliament who has resigned or died.

cadres Dedicated members of a political party or organization who do most of the work that gets done. The original cadres in the Chinese Communist Party were lauded for their idealism and revolutionary zeal, but cadres in later years were criticized for corruption and powermongering. Cadres hold most bureaucratic positions in China and are divided into various ranks and levels.

camarilla In Mexico, a group or network of politicians who rely on one another for advancement.

catch-all party A large, broad-based political party that is more concerned with winning elections than with conforming to a specific ideology (e.g., the Republican and Democratic Parties in the US).

CDU. *See* Christian Democratic Union.

center An ideological classification based on seating arrangements in the parliament of revolutionary France. Traditionally, parties at the "center" of the political spectrum advocate a balance between capitalism and social welfare.

Central European Bank An agency of the EU designed to regulate monetary policy in the European Monetary Union (countries that use the euro as a common currency). Located in Frankfurt, the Bank began operation in 1999.

Chamber of Deputies One house of the Mexican Congress (the other house is the Senate).

chancellor Germany's chief executive, whose role is similar to that of the British prime minister. (Germany's president is the symbolic head of the country.)

charisma In the words of German sociologist Max Weber, *charisma* is "a certain quality of an individual personality by virtue of which he is set apart from ordinary men and treated as endowed with supernatural, superhuman, or at least specifically exceptional powers or qualities." Charismatic individuals have a broad appeal to the masses.

Christian Democratic Union (CDU) Germany's large catch-all party of the center right, which has become identified with business interests and European unification.

civic culture Democratic society whose citizens are committed to democratic values, understand how their political institutions work, and believe in their ability to influence those institutions. In a civic culture, loyalty to the state takes precedence over loyalties to ethnic, religious, and other parochial groups.

coalition government A government in which the legislative seats are fragmented among several political parties, none of which can claim a majority. The prime minister can rule only as long as he or she retains the support of all members of the coalition.

co-determination Policy of involving workers in management decisions.

cohabitation A period during which the French president lacks the support of a majority of the deputies in the Assembly, and therefore the powers of the prime minister equal those of the president.

common law A judicial system based on tradition and custom.

commons In feudal England, the social class comprising knights and merchants. (*See also* House of Commons.)

communism Economic system postulated by Karl Marx (1818–1883) and others, in which everything is owned in common and in which people willingly give according to their abilities and take according to their needs.

communist An advocate or supporter of communism. (*See* communism.)

Communist Party Political party advocating the economic and political system devised by Karl Marx. (*See* communism.)

comparative advantage Doctrine stating that a truly free world market will allow each country to specialize in what it does best. For example, countries with cheap labor will specialize in labor-intensive industries, while those with a highly skilled work force will specialize in high-tech industries.

comparative politics, or **comparative political analysis** A branch of political science that uses comparisons between countries and other political units to make generalized statements about the political process.

conciliation commissions Units of the Japanese legal system that are designed to facilitate out-of-court settlement of disputes.

conflict management Systems and procedures designed to keep political conflict within tolerable limits.

Confucian culture Japanese value system that is based on Confucianism and emphasizes hard work, respect for hierarchical authority, rule by merit, and devotion to the group.

Confucianism A traditional Chinese belief system based on the teachings of Confucius (511–479 BC), who stressed the importance of wise governance, compliance with the laws of the land, family loyalty, responsibility toward others, and self-improvement.

Congress Party Political party that became a symbol of India's independence movement. The Congress Party ruled India for most of its history as an independent country.

Constitutional Council Russia's equivalent of the US Supreme Court.

co-optation Promotional system used within authoritarian political parties, wherein members of higher committees decide which members of lower committees will be elevated to a higher rank.

corporatism A formalized relationship between the state and social organizations, in which organizations exercise control over their particular domains but lose a degree of autonomy. In Mexico, examples include the incorporation of labor unions and peasant organizations into the PRI.

Council of Ministers of the EU Consists of a cabinet-level minister from each EU country assisted by a number of "permanent representatives" depending on the size of the country. Representatives on the Council of Ministers are selected by the national governments of EU countries.

coup d'état Sudden, forceful overthrow of the government.

cross-cutting cleavages Conflicting or competing loyalties felt by group members as a result of their religious, ethnic, economic, political, or other affiliations.

cultural map The framework of values, attitudes, and preconceptions that individuals absorb from their culture and rely on when making choices about politics, economics, and other important issues in their lives.

culture The ideas, values, and expectations shared by a group of people. Culture tells people what they should consider important, defines what is considered right and wrong, and delineates the roles that people are expected to play in life.

daimyo Japanese term for feudal fiefdoms and the leaders of those fiefdoms.

dedazo Literally, the "finger-pointing" process whereby the Mexican president picks his successor.

demands The expectations that citizens, pressure groups, and political parties place upon the government concerning reallocation of scarce resources.

dependency theory A political theory which asserts that First World countries use their dominant economic power to keep Third World countries in a permanent state of dependence and poverty.

development *See* political development.

devotee party A political party whose members are expected to devote their lives to the achievement of the party's well-defined ideological goals (e.g., Communists, Fascists, Hitler's Nazis).

Diet Japan's Parliament, consisting of a House of Representatives (lower house) and a House of Peers (upper house).

dirigisme A mild version of state capitalism in which economic planners establish goals for the French economy and then use the financial resources of the government to encourage private-sector compliance with those goals.

dual society A country in which a sharp division exists between prosperous and educated upper- and middle-class citizens and a minimally skilled and unemployed working class whose members live in poverty.

Duma Lower house of the Russian Parliament (Federal Assembly).

ejido In Mexico, a collective farm that is usually divided into individual plots for peasants.

elite. *See* political elite.

elite analysis A method of political analysis that focuses on the study of elite attitudes and behavior. Elites are assumed to be the most important element in the political process.

enarques Graduates of the Ecole Nationale d'Administration (ENA), who control the bureaucratic apparatus in France.

EU *See* European Union

euro The monetary unit of the Economic Union.

Euro-communism A philosophy based on the idea that one can subscribe to the basic principles of Marxism and still play by democratic rules. If citizens become dissatisfied, they can vote the communists out of office.

European Commission of the EU A branch of European government consisting of twenty members nominated by the member countries of the European Union with the implied accord of the other member countries and the president of the Commission. The commission supervises the European bureaucracy that implements EU policy and may also suggest new legislation to the Council of Ministers. Members of the Commission are expected to act in the best interests of the EU and not to receive instructions from their home countries.

European Council A periodic "summit meeting" of the prime ministers of the fifteen member states in the European Union. All decisions of the European Council must be unanimous if they are to become EU policy.

European Court of Justice of the EU The judicial branch of the EU, which adjudicates disputes related to EU treaties and laws. The court, which is located in Luxembourg, consists of fifteen member judges appointed for six-year terms.

European Parliament A branch of European supranational government consisting of 500 deputies chosen in direct election by the population of the member countries. Seats in the parliament are allocated in proportion to the populations of member states. The European Parliament meets in Strasbourg and Brussels.

European Union (EU) A supranational body composed of fifteen member countries. All have transferred broad areas of economic sovereignty to a supranational government located in Brussels.

external face of culture The national myths, ideologies, religions, and other belief systems that a society uses to socialize or "program" its citizens.

external political culture The political content of a society's ideologies, myths, and religions; the content of political socialization.

EZLN Zapatista Army of National Liberation, a largely indigenous-based Mexican guerilla force that emerged in 1994 in Chiapas.

Fabians A group of British intellectuals who advocated democratic socialism as the means of achieving an equitable society.

fair share Concept based on the myth that Japan is one large family whose members are each entitled to receive a portion of the nation's wealth.

far left An ideological classification based on seating arrangements in the parliament of revolutionary France. Traditionally, the "far left" end of the political spectrum included communists, anarchists, and other parties advocating a mass revolution by violent means.

far right An ideological classification based on seating arrangements in the parliament of revolutionary France. Traditionally, the "far right" end of the political spectrum includes monarchists, supporters of the church, and extreme nationalists.

fascism A right-wing, extremely nationalistic political ideology incorporating a totalitarian and hierarchical power structure.

FDP *See* Free Democratic Party.

Federal Assembly Russian parliament.

Federation Council Upper house of the Federal Assembly (Russian parliament).

feudalism A social, economic, and political system in which members of the landed aristocracy (baronage) maintained order in their domains, provided the king with knights and foot soldiers in times of war, and contributed financially to the royal household. Peasants were relegated to the bottom of the social hierarchy and lived in near-servitude.

First World The advanced industrial societies of the world, which produce most of the world's technology, consume most of the world's resources, and possess most of the world's wealth. The classic countries of the First World are the United States, Japan, Canada, Australia, New Zealand, the United Kingdom, France, Germany, Italy, the Scandinavian states, the Benelux states (Belgium, the Netherlands, Luxembourg), Finland, and Switzerland.

Fourth World Countries that are unable to provide citizens with a minimally acceptable quality of life. Most are dictatorships racked with tribal conflict or open civil war. Human rights are ignored, and inequality reigns in all areas of political, economic, and social life. Environmental protection is minimal or nonexistent.

Fraktionen German parliamentary party comprising all of a party's deputies in the Bundestag. The leader of the majority Fraktionen is the chancellor.

Free Democratic Party (FDP) German political party that plays a pivotal role as a balancer between Germany's two large catch-all parties, the CDU and the SPD.

free-market economy An economic system in which economic decisions are made on the basis of supply and demand, with minimal intervention by the government.

G-7 A group consisting of the world's seven major capitalist powers: the United States, Canada, Japan, the United Kingdom, France, Germany, and Italy. The heads of these countries meet regularly to determine world economic policy. Sometimes Russia participates in these meetings, making the G-8. Russian economic influence, however, is minimal.

governments, Government Political institutions responsible for allocating scarce resources in an authoritative manner. In this text, the word *Government* (capitalized) refers to a country's prime minister, Cabinet, and other relevant positions selected by the prime minister.

grands fonctionnaires A small group of enarques (graduates of the ENA) who are highly influential in French polities.

Greens Political party that began in Germany during the 1970s and spread gradually to other countries. As the name suggests, Green Parties focus mainly on environmental issues.

growth with equity An ideal version of state capitalism in which the government stimulates the development of the economy while ensuring that all members of society share in the benefits of that development.

House of Commons The lower house in the British Parliament, the members of which are elected by universal suffrage for a maximum of five years.

House of Councilors (formerly, **House of Peers**) Upper house of the Japanese Parliament.

House of Lords The upper house in the British Parliament. Members of the House of Lords are referred to as "Peers."

House of Peers *See* **House of Councilors.**

House of Representatives Lower house of the Japanese Parliament.

IFE (Federal Electoral Institute) Agency in charge of organizing and conducting elections in Mexico. It is largely autonomous of other political powers.

IMF *See* International Monetary Fund.

immobilisme (immobilism) French term for a weak Government that is unable to agree on a course of action and move forward with it.

import substitution (*also* **import substitution industrialization**) Strategy of economic development based on promoting and protecting domestic industry. Tariffs are placed on imported goods to encourage consumers to purchase items that are produced domestically.

indirect rule Euphemistic term for British colonial policy in Nigeria and other colonies, which kept tribal chiefs in place, discouraged the creation of a Westernized elite, and reinforced the fragmentation of Nigerian society by playing upon tribal jealousies.

infitah Literally, "economic opening." A partial shift to capitalism initiated by Egyptian president Anwar Sadat in 1974.

institutionalization The process in which organizations and procedures evolve slowly over time, earning a respected place in society.

internal face of culture The cultural beliefs that have been absorbed by the citizens of a society; the predispositions, values, and attitudes that shape their view of their world.

internal political culture People's orientations toward politics: their attitudes and opinions regarding political leaders, political movements, political events, and political institutions.

International Monetary Fund (IMF) Established at the end of World War II to facilitate the reconstruction of a war-torn Europe and to reestablish order in the world economy, the IMF now operates as an international credit union that makes short-term loans to countries. Member states must pay in to the IMF and have the right to borrow up to 20 percent of the contribution without restriction. Larger loans must be approved by the governing board of the IMF.

Japan Inc. Ruling alliance of political, administrative, and business leaders in Japan.

jati Sub-castes within the Indian caste system (there are more than 2,000 jati).

karma An Indian term referring to the soul's predisposition toward good or evil. Karma has been described as everything from a cosmic force to luck or destiny.

KMT *See* Kuomintang.

Kshatriya The second level of the Indian caste system, often referred to as the warrior caste.

Kuomintang (KMT) Chinese nationalist movement initiated by followers of Sun Yat-sen and later led by Chiang Kai-shek. The KMT fought the Communist Party for control of China but eventually had to retreat to the island of Taiwan.

Land The German term for a German state.

Lander Plural form of *Land* (see above).

LDP *See* Liberal Democratic Party.

left *See* political left.

leftist economist An economist who believes that socialism is preferable to capitalism because it is a more equitable system.

legitimacy A government is viewed as *legitimate* if a country's citizens agree that the government's rules are in the best interests of all citizens and should be followed voluntarily.

Liberal Democratic Party (LDP) Political party that dominated Japanese politics from 1955 to 1993. It continues to be Japan's dominant party today.

limited-issue party *See* single-issue party.

linkage function Mechanism for communicating between the elites and the masses. In modern societies, the linkage function is performed by parties, pressure groups, and the mass media.

Lok Sabha Popularly elected lower house of the Indian parliament, also known as the House of the People. The members of the Lok Sabha elect the prime minister.

Maastricht Treaty An agreement that went into effect on January 1, 1993, transforming the European Community into the European Union and providing the framework for the eventual political unification of its member countries. The treaty outlined a method to create (within a ten-year transition period) a single European currency—the euro—and to strengthen the authority of the EU with regard to foreign affairs, trade, and environmental and social policy.

Majlis As-Shab (People's Assembly) Popularly elected body of the Egyptian legislature whose powers are largely theoretical. Ultimately, power rests in the hands of the Egyptian president.

Majlis As-Shoura (Consultive Assembly) Entity within the Egyptian parliament that serves as a debating society designed to air issues of public importance.

maquiladoras Mexican factories located mainly along the US border that assemble imported parts and export finished products.

marginalized group Group whose members exist on the fringes of society and have little influence on politics.

Marxism Economic philosophy developed by Karl Marx (1818–1883), which argues that prosperity and equality are best assured by a socialist economic system in which the government owns factories, farms, and other means of production (e.g., the Soviet Union and China prior to 1990).

masses Citizens, the people, the public, or the population of a state. It is the masses who do most of the work within a society.

mass-membership parties *See* devotee parties.

master race Hitler's theory that Germans were a superior race and therefore historically destined to rule the world.

Member of Parliament (MP) Legislator in the British Parliament.

mestizo Racial designation for the majority of the Mexican population who are of mixed Spanish and indigenous descent.

moderate left An ideological classification based on seating arrangements in the parliament of revolutionary France. Traditionally, the "moderate left" end of the political spectrum includes social liberals and supporters of organized labor.

moderate (or democratic) right An ideological classification based on seating arrangements in the parliament of revolutionary France. Traditionally, the "moderate right" end of the political spectrum includes individuals favoring private property, free enterprise, low taxation, and law and order.

MP *See* Member of Parliament.

multiparty system A political system in which several parties compete for voter support and no party is able to gain a majority of the vote in any election (e.g., Russia, Poland).

Muslim Brotherhood Islamic religious organization dedicated to the creation of an Islamic state in Egypt.

Muslim League Political party that represented the interests of the Muslim segment of the population in pre-independence India.

National Front Political party at the extreme right end of the political spectrum in France. According to the platform of the National Front, immigrants are responsible for France's economic and social problems and thus should be deported from France.

NATO *See* North Atlantic Treaty Organization.

Nazi Party Political party formed by Adolf Hitler in 1919 that rose to prominence as a result of Germany's social disintegration during the 1930s.

neoclassical economists Economic theorists who argue for a world in which monopolistic practices are prohibited and governmental intervention in the economy is limited to facilitating free-market competition.

neocorporatism A technique for managing the influence of pressure groups by allowing them to assist in the drafting of legislation. In return, pressure groups are expected to be moderate in the demands they place upon the government.

new left Political parties with a moderate, slightly left-of-center philosophy, such as the Labour Party in England and the Social Democratic Party in Germany.

New Wafd Pro-business political party in Egypt.

NGO Non-governmental organization—a politically significant group that operates independently from the government. Examples range from small self-help groups in poor countries to large international organizations such as the Red Cross.

nirvana A cosmic soul that embodies the true harmony of the universe. For Hindus, salvation is achieved by attaining nirvana, or merging with the cosmic soul.

no-party system An authoritarian regime in which political parties are not allowed (e.g., Libya, Saudi Arabia).

North Atlantic Treaty Organization (NATO) Military alliance between the United States, Canada, and most countries of Western Europe.

oligarchy A government ruled by a small group of powerful individuals.

PAN (National Action Party) Center-right opposition party to the PRI in Mexico.

pantoflage A process in which senior civil servants in France begin their careers in government service and then jump to the private sector.

parliamentary democracy A democracy in which the population elects the Members of Parliament, who in turn elect the prime minister.

parliamentary party The organization of a political party in the British House of Commons.

party *See* political party.

party families Groups of political parties that share a common orientation and cooperate with each other most of the time. In France, the two major party families are on the political left and the political right.

patron-client network System in which junior members of an organization attach themselves to a powerful leader, hoping to receive promotions and other favors. Similar networks exist between politicians and citizens.

peak association Large pressure group encompassing a variety of smaller organizations that share a common interest, such as the British Trades Unions Congress or the US Chamber of Commerce.

People's Republic of China The name given to mainland China after the Communist Party took over in 1949.

perestroika Structural reform movement initiated by Mikhail Gorbachev in an attempt to break the grip of government and Party bureaucracies on the Soviet economy. Factory managers were given greater flexibility in the management of their plants; elections to government councils featured open discussion, multiple candidates, and secret ballots; and experimentation with small-scale capitalism was encouraged.

petite bourgeoisie A French term referring collectively to small merchants, artisans, farmers, and retirees.

plebiscite An election in which voters indicate their approval or disapproval of a proposal or candidate put forward by the government. There are no other choices.

pluralism Distribution of political power among a broad range of groups and interests.

pluralistic elite Elite structure in which a broad range of individuals and groups share decision-making power (e.g., United States). Systems with pluralistic elites are responsive to diverse interests, but decisive action is impaired by the need to achieve consensus.

plurality The greatest number; for example, the political candidate receiving a *plurality* of votes is the candidate who receives the most votes. A candidate can have a plurality without receiving an actual majority (50 percent or more) of the total number of votes cast in an election.

political actors Individuals and groups that give direction to the political process, such as elites, bureaucrats, citizens, political parties, and pressure groups.

political culture The dimensions of culture that seem to have the greatest influence on people's political behavior.

political development Defined by the United Nations as the achievement of a stable democracy that promotes the economic well-being of citizens in an equitable, humane, and environmentally concerned manner.

political economy approach An approach to comparative political analysis asserting that most areas of political life are shaped by economic factors.

political elites Individuals and groups who dominate the political process, controlling the allocation of scarce resources. Elites often include senior members of the government, wealthy individuals, military leaders, representatives of large groups such as labor unions, and religious leaders.

political institutions Organizational mechanisms for determining how the scarce resources of society will be allocated.

political left An ideological classification based on seating arrangements in the parliament of revolutionary France. Traditionally, leftists included communists, socialists, anarchists, and other diverse groups claiming to be heirs of the Revolution. Today, the left generally inclines toward advocating greater government involvement in the economy and more welfare programs for the public.

political party A group of individuals working together to achieve common goals by controlling all or part of the government.

political right An ideological classification based on seating arrangements in the parliament of revolutionary France. Traditionally, rightists included monarchists, clerics, and supporters of the church. Today, the right generally champions decreased government involvement in the economy and cutbacks in welfare programs.

politics Two widely accepted definitions of *politics* are "the process of deciding who gets what, when, and how" and "the authoritative allocation of scarce values." Politics involves both conflict and cooperation.

Porfiriato Period from 1876 to 1911, when Mexico was under the authoritarian rule of General Porfirio Diaz.

pork barrel Allocation of government funds to public works projects in a certain constituency, which enhances the political fortunes of politicians and their supporters.

PRD (Party of the Democratic Revolution) Center-left opposition party to the PRI in Mexico.

presidentialism Concentration of political power in the hands of the Mexican president.

pressure groups Groups that form for the express purpose of influencing governmental policies (e.g., labor unions or business associations).

PRI (Institutional Revolutionary Party) (*Also PNR, PRM*) Political party that has dominated Mexican politics since its formation in 1929.

proletariat Marx's term for the industrial working class.

quasi-democratic political system A political system that blends democratic and authoritarian tendencies (e.g., Mexico, Egypt).

Question Period (Question Hour) In Britain, the Question Period consists of an hour-long session in which members of the House of Commons are allowed to question members of the Government about issues of concern. In Germany, the Question Hour gives members of the Bundestag a chance to question the Government on issues ranging from matters of national policy to personal grievances of constituents.

Rajya Sabha Upper house of the Indian Parliament, also known as the Council of States.

Rally of the French People (RPF) A movement founded by supporters of Charles de Gaulle, whose platform became the cornerstone of the French right.

Rally for the Republic (RPR) French Gaullist party that advocates law and order, morality, low taxes, and high tariffs and is reluctant to move quickly toward European unity.

Reich A German term meaning *empire*.

Rengo The umbrella or "peak" organization coordinating the Japanese labor movement.

Republic of China The Chinese island of Taiwan, which became the headquarters of Chiang Kaishek's Kuomintang after the KMT's Communist rivals took control of mainland China in 1949.

right *See* political right.

RPF *See* Rally of the French People.

RPR *See* Rally for the Republic.

samurai Warriors in feudal Japan who served their daimyo in exchange for land and money, much as the knights of medieval Europe served their lords.

sati Hindu custom in which a widow committed suicide by throwing herself upon her husband's funeral pyre.

Second World A term that originally referred to countries of the Communist Bloc, such as the Soviet Union and the People's Republic of China. Today, the Second World no longer exists as Russia and most other members of the Communist Bloc are now considered part of the Third World.

shadow cabinet In England, refers to leaders of the opposing party in Parliament.

shogun Military warlord who ruled the central region of Japan during the country's feudal period.

single-issue (limited-issue) party Political party that focuses on a narrow range of issues (e.g., the Green parties of Europe).

single-member, simple-majority voting system An electoral system in which the winning candidate must receive a majority of the popular vote. If no candidate receives a majority of the vote during the first round of elections, a run-off election is held between the two leading candidates.

single-member, simple-plurality voting system An electoral system in which the candidate who receives the greatest number of votes in a given district wins the election, even though the candidate may not receive an actual majority (50 percent or more) of the votes cast in the district.

single-party-authoritarian system A nondemocratic political system in which the ruling party totally controls all political activity (e.g., Nazi Germany, the Soviet Union, Cuba, China).

single-party-dominant system A democracy (or quasi-democracy) that is overwhelmingly dominated by a single party (e.g., Mexico, Egypt).

Siva Hindu god of destruction.

Social Darwinism The belief that "survival of the fittest" applies to groups within society, not just species within the natural world. According to Hitler's version of Social Darwinism, the purity of the "master race" could be preserved by exterminating Jews, disabled people, and others whom Hitler viewed as undesirable.

Social Democratic Party (SPD) A large catchall party in Germany that is now slightly left of the center politically but originated as a Marxist-oriented socialist party. The SPD calls for a balance between economic growth and social welfare.

socialism Economic system based on the collective ownership of the means of production, distribution, and exchange.

Socialist Party Leftist political party advocating the nationalization of industry and social equality for all citizens within a democratic culture.

socialist work culture Work culture that developed under the communist regimes in the Soviet Union and mainland China, in which employment was guaranteed and all workers in the same class received the same wage regardless of how hard they worked. As a result, industries suffered from low productivity and poor quality control.

socialization The process of indoctrinating people into their culture. Parents, peers, schools, religious institutions, and the mass media participate in the socialization process.

social market economy A version of state capitalism practiced in Germany, in which government, business, and labor cooperate to achieve both economic growth and equity.

Soviet Union The former Union of Soviet Socialist Republics, or USSR.

soviets Popular councils that seized control of Russia's local governments during the 1917 revolution.

SPD *See* Social Democratic Party.

standing committee A step in the legislative process. Bills are sent to standing committees for review, modifications are suggested, and then the bills are returned to the legislature.

state A well-defined geographic area in which the population and resources are controlled by a government; the governmental apparatus of a country.

state capitalism An economic system that combines capitalism with government planning (e.g., Japan and the industrial countries of Asia). Under state capitalism, most economic activity is in the hands of individual capitalists, but the government provides extra resources and support to private-sector firms that are involved in high-priority industries.

Sudra Fourth level of the Indian caste system, often referred to as the artisan caste.

supports The actions that people and groups take to strengthen the government (e.g., obeying laws, paying taxes, voting).

supranational government An entity that controls the policies of more than one country (e.g., the European Union).

supranational organization Quasi-governmental organization that attempts to coordinate the activities of its member countries (e.g., United Nations).

systems analysis Analytical scheme designed to provide an integrated picture of the political process in which the various parts are seen as interconnected and interdependent.

technocracy, technocrats Administrative elite whose power is based on the possession of specialized technical knowledge.

theocracy A country ruled by religious leaders (e.g, Iran), in which the full power of the state is used to assure mass compliance with a particular set of religious doctrines.

Third World Countries that have yet to establish a strong position in terms of one or more of the UN indicators of development, such as economic growth, equity, democracy, human rights, and concern for the environment (e.g., Egypt, Mexico). There is wide variation among Third World countries regarding these developmental indicators; some are strong in one area but weak in others. For example, India has the most enduring democracy in the Third World, but most of its citizens live in poverty.

tigers of Asia A term used to describe Taiwan, South Korea, Hong Kong (now part of China), Singapore, and, to a lesser extent, Malaysia. State capitalism is the economic system chosen by each of these countries.

Tories An early British political party, the members of which supported the Crown, the rights of the landed aristocracy, and the dominant position of the Church of England. Today, this term is commonly applied to members of the Conservative Party.

totalitarian society A society in which all political, economic, and cultural activity is under the direct control of the state (e.g., Nazi Germany, the Soviet Union).

transitional society A society in which large numbers of people are trying to adjust to the conflicting demands of tradition and modernity.

two-party system A political system in which the government is always dominated by one of the country's two major parties (e.g., the US, Great Britain, and Germany).

UDF *See* Union for French Democracy.

umbrella association *See* peak association.

Union for French Democracy (UDF) A French Gaullist party of the center right that aspires to unite the interests of big business with those of France's large white-collar class. The UDF advocates free-market capitalism and European unity.

unitary elite A small group of individuals who control decision-making in a broad range of areas (e.g., the British prime minister and Cabinet).

universal manhood suffrage System in which all competent adult males are allowed to vote in elections.

universal suffrage System in which all competent adults (male or female) are allowed to vote in elections.

untouchables The lowest level of the Indian caste system, whose members are expected to perform "impure" tasks such as cleaning sewers.

Vaishya Third level of the Indian caste system, often referred to as the trader caste.

Vishnu Hindu god of preservation.

vote of no confidence Legislative action that can force the resignation of a prime minister and Cabinet, usually by voting down a major piece of legislation.

Wafd Party Political party dedicated to liberating Egypt from British rule. (See New Wafd.)

Westminster model The British pattern of parliamentary democracy characterized by single-member, simple-plurality voting ("winner take all") systems and a lower house of Parliament dominated by one of two major political parties. The Westminster model is far more efficient at making decisions than are most presidential democracies, but it is inclined to ignore the views of minorities.

Whigs An early British political party consisting of prosperous members of the middle class who advocated less restrictive economic laws and a reduced role for the Crown and the Church of England in the affairs of the country. The Whigs later evolved into the Liberal Party. (The term *whig* is an abbreviation of *Wiggamores*, a band of Scottish rebels.)

whips In England, the term *whip* has two meanings: (1) party "policemen" who ensure that the members of a party in the legislature understand the party's position and vote accordingly; (2) written instructions sent to party MPs by the party whips prior to votes in Parliament.

World Bank Established at the end of World War II to facilitate the reconstruction of a war-torn Europe and to reestablish order in the world economy, the World Bank now makes long-term loans to Third World countries and attempts to stimulate democracy in the countries that it assists. The World Bank is controlled by First World member countries, with each member's voting power reflecting the size its financial contribution.

world (capitalist) economic system An informal network of the world's capitalist superpowers, multinational corporations, and international financial institutions such as the World Bank, the International Monetary Fund, and the World Trade Organization.

world (international) political system A concept based on the observation that international relations seem to follow certain regularized patterns. For example, prior to World War II the international system was characterized by a balance of power between nations.

World Trade Organization (WTO) An institution designed to regulate the level of tariffs that countries can place on imported goods.

WTO *See* World Trade Organization.

yakuza Japan's large and quasi-legal crime syndicates.

zaibatsu Large business conglomerates in Japan that are controlled by a single interlocking directorate.

PHOTO CREDITS

NAME INDEX

SUBJECT INDEX

Abortions, in China, 304
Achievement orientation, of German culture, 167
Acid rain, in China, 306
Activism, in Britain, 81
Actors, 12, 18–27. *See also* Actors
  in Britain, 72–81
  bureaucrats as, 19–21
  in China, 291–296
  in Egypt, 416–429
  elites as, 18–19
  in French politics, 115–125
  in German politics, 154–165
  groups, interests, and, 22–23
  in India, 337–348
  in Japanese politics, 195–205
  masses, classes, and, 21
  in Mexico, 376–388
  in Nigeria, 460–468
  in political arena, 18–27
  political parties and, 23–27
  in Russian politics, 248–255
Acts of Parliament. *See also* Parliament (Britain)
  judiciary and, 71
AD. *See* Alliance for Democracy (AD, Nigeria)
Administrators. *See* Bureaucracy
Affirmative action, in France, 131
Africa. *See* Egypt; Nigeria
Air pollution, in Mexico City, 398
Al-Azhar mosque, 403
Al-Azhar University (Egypt), freedom of expression and, 435
Alcohol abuse, in Russia, 256
Algeria, France and, 100
Alienation, in Russia, 256
All-China Federation of Trade Unions, 292
All-China Women's Federation, 292
Alliance for Democracy (AD, Nigeria), 454, 462–463
Allied Powers, after World War I, 139
All People's Party (APP, Nigeria), 454, 462–463
Alsace, 139
American system of government, in Nigeria, 448

Amparo (Mexico), 373
Anarchy, in Russia, 254
Angola, 7
Animal rights groups, in Britain, 80
Anomie, 141
  in Russia, 256
Anti-Re-electionist Party (Mexico), 365
Anti-Semitism, of Hitler, 141, 142
Anti-terrorism, in Egypt, 434
Apathy, in Russia, 255–256
APP. *See* All People's Party (APP, Nigeria)
Arab/Israeli War
  of 1956, 407
  of 1973, 409
Arab nationalism, 407–408
Arab Socialist Union (ASU, Egypt), 407, 417–418
Arab world, 8
  Egypt and, 401–436
Aristocracy
  in Britain, 54
  in Egypt, 404, 431
  in France, 95
  in Germany, 139
  Japanese warriors as, 181
  in Russia, 225
Armed Forces Ruling Council (Nigeria), 450, 456
Art(s), in Mexico, 360–361
Artistic culture, 35
Aryan superiority, Hitler and, 141, 142
Asia, 3. *See also* China; Japan; specific countries
  Japanese impact on, 179
  tigers of, 31
Asian co-prosperity sphere, 184
Assembly (France), 95–96, 97, 102
Associations. *See* Business groups
ASU. *See* Arab Socialist Union (ASU, Egypt)
Aswan Dam, 406
Atomic bombs, Japan and, 185
Attitudes, behavior and, 33n9, 34
Authoritarianism, 14–15
  in China, 303

496

COMPARATIVE POLITICS
Second Edition
Edited by Janet Tilden
Picture research by Cheryl Kucharzak
Production supervision by Kim Vander Steen
Designed by Jeanne Calabrese Design, River Forest, Illinois
Composition by Point West, Inc., Carol Stream, Illinois
Paper, Finch Opaque
Typefaces, Times and Poppl-laudatio
Printed and bound by McNaughton & Gunn, Saline, Michigan